Charles the Bold

Charles the Bold

THE LAST VALOIS DUKE OF BURGUNDY

RICHARD VAUGHAN

LONGMAN

LONGMAN GROUP LIMITED
London

*Associated companies, branches and representatives
throughout the world*

© *Longman Group Limited 1973*

*All rights reserved. No part of this publication
may be reproduced, stored in a retrieval system,
or transmitted in any form or by any means,
electronic, mechanical, photocopying, recording,
or otherwise, without the prior permission of
the Copyright owner.*

First published 1973
ISBN 0 582 50251 9

Set in 11 on 12 point Imprint
and printed by Bell and Bain Ltd, Glasgow

Contents

Maps

Genealogical Tables

Abbreviations

AAAB	*Annales de l'Académie royale d'archéologie de Belgique*
AB	*Annales de Bourgogne*
ABB	*Archives et bibliothèques de Belgique*
ACCAL	*Annuaire de la Commission communale de l'histoire de l'ancien pays de Liège*
ACFF	*Annales du Comité flamand de France*
ACHF	*Archives curieuses de l'histoire de France*
ADN	Archives départementales du Nord, Lille
AE	*Annales de l'Est*
AF	*Annales fribourgeoises*
AGR	Archives générales du royaume, Brussels
AHKB	*Archiv des historischen Vereins des Kantons Bern*
AHS	*Annales d'histoire sociale*
AHVN	*Annalen des historischer Vereins für den Niederrhein*
AJ	*Alemannisches Jahrbuch*
AKV	*Anzeiger für Kunde der deutschen Vorzeit*
AOGV	Archiv des Ordens vom Goldenen Vliesse, Vienna
ASEB	*Annales de la Société d'émulation de Bruges*
AnzSG	*Anzeiger für schweizerische Geschichte*
ASG	*Archiv für schweizerische Geschichte*
ASL	*Archivio storico lombardo*
ASM	Archivio di Stato, Milan
ASMant	Archivio di Stato, Mantua
ASMZ	*Allgemeine schweizerische Militärzeitschrift*
ASN	*Archivio storico per le province napoletane*
ASRAB	*Annuaire de la Société royale d'archéologie de Bruxelles*
BAD	*Bulletin de l'Académie delphinale*
BARB	*Bulletin de l'Académie royale de Belgique*
BARBB	*Bulletin de l'Académie royale de Belgique. Classe des Beaux-Arts*
BARBL	*Bulletin de l'Académie royale de Belgique. Lettres*
BBG	*Blätter für bernische Geschichte, Kunst und Altertumskunde*

BCAA	*Bulletin des Commissions royales d'art et d'archéologie*
BCAM	*Bulletin du Cercle archéologique, littéraire et artistique de Malines*
BCHDN	*Bulletin de la Commission historique du département du Nord*
BCLF	*Bulletin du Comité de la langue, de l'histoire et des arts de la France*
BCRH	*Bulletin de la Commission royale d'histoire*
BEC	*Bibliothèque de l'École des Chartes*
BEP	*Bulletin des études portugaises*
BFPL	*Bibliothèque de la Faculté de Philosophie et Lettres de l'Université de Liège*
BGBH	*Bijdragen voor de geschiedenis van het bisdom van Haarlem*
BGN	*Bijdragen voor de geschiedenis der Nederlanden*
BHPTH	*Bulletin historique et philologique du Comité des travaux historiques,* continued under the title *Bulletin philologique et historique*
BHR	*Bibliothèque d'humanisme et renaissance*
BIAL	*Bulletin de l'Institut archéologique liégeois*
BIHBR	*Bulletin de l'Institut historique belge de Rome*
BIHR	*Bulletin of the Institute of historical research*
BIMGU	Bijdragen van het Instituut voor middeleeuwsche geschiedenis der Rijksuniversiteit te Utrecht
BL	Bodleian Library, Oxford
BLVS	Bibliothek des litterarischen Vereins in Stuttgart
BM	British Museum
BMM	*Bulletin du Musée historique de Mulhouse*
BN	Bibliothèque Nationale, Paris
BNB	*Basler Neujahrsblätter*
BSAB	*Bulletin de la Société royale d'archéologie de Bruxelles*
BSAF	*Bulletin de la Société nationale des antiquaires de France*
BSAMD	*Bulletin de la Société des amis du Musée de Dijon*
BSAN	*Bulletin de la Société archéologique de Nantes*
BSHAG	*Bulletin de la Société d'histoire et d'archéologie de Gand*
BSHF	*Bulletin de la Société de l'histoire de France*
BSSI	*Bolletino storico della Svizzera italiana*
BSSLL	*Bulletin de la Société scientifique et littéraire du Limbourg*
BT	*Berner Taschenbuch*
BVG	*Beiträge zur vaterländischen Geschichte*
BVGO	*Bijdragen voor vaderlandsche geschiedenis en oudheidkunde*
CAPL	*Chronique archéologique du pays de Liège*
CB	*Cahiers bruxellois*
CDIHF	Collection de documents inédits sur l'histoire de France
CDS	*Chroniken der deutschen Städte*
CHF	Les classiques de l'histoire de France au moyen âge

CRH	Commission royale d'histoire
DVF	*De Vrije Fries*
ELJ	*Elsass-lothringische wissenschaftliche Gesellschaft. Jahrbuch*
FACA	Fragments des anciennes chroniques d'Alsace
FG	*Freiburger Geschichtsblätter*
FN	*Flandria nostra,* see under Broeckx, below p. 437
FRADA	Fontes rerum Austriacorum. Diplomataria et acta
GBM	*Gelre. Bijdragen en mededelingen*
GRM	*Germanisch-romanische Monatsschrift*
GWU	*Geschichte in Wissenschaft und Unterricht*
HB	*Haarlemsche bijdragen*
HG	*Hansische Geschichtsblätter*
HKBAW	Historische Kommission bei der bayerischen Akademie der Wissenschaften
HKOM	*Handelingen van de koninklijke Kring voor oudheidkunde, letteren en kunst van Mechelen*
HMS	*Histoire militaire de la Suisse,* see under Feldmann, p. 445 below
HT	*Historisk Tidsskrift*
HZ	*Historische Zeitschrift*
IAB, etc	Printed inventories of archives, see below, pp. 449–50
IG	*L'intermédiaire des généalogistes*
JBHM	*Jahrbuch des bernischen historischen Museums in Bern*
JGKA	*Jahrbuch der Gesellschaft für bildende Kunst und vater-ländische Alterthümer*
JGLG	*Jahrbuch der Gesellschaft für lothringische Geschichte und Altertumskunde*
JSFB	*Jahrbuch der Stadt Freiburg im Breisgau*
JSG	*Jahrbuch für schweizerische Geschichte*
JWI	*Journal of the Warburg Institute*
KHGU	*Kronijk van het historisch Genootschap te Utrecht*
LPL	*Le pays lorrain*
LRA	Landesregierungsarchiv
MA	*Le moyen âge*
MAB	*Mémoires de l'Académie des sciences, belles-lettres et arts de Besançon*
MAD	*Mémoires de l'Académie des sciences, arts et belles-lettres de Dijon*
MAGZ	*Mittheilungen der antiquarischen Gesellschaft in Zürich*
MAMB	*Mededelingen der Akademie van marine de België*
MARB	Mémoires de l'Académie royale de Belgique
MARBL	Mémoires de l'Académie royale de Belgique. Lettres
MCACO	*Mémoires de la Commission des antiquités du département de la Côte-d'Or*

MCMP	*Mémoires de la Commission départementale des monuments historiques du Pas-de-Calais*
MIOG	*Mitteilungen des Instituts für österreichische Geschichtsforschung*
MKVAL	*Mededelingen van de koninklijke Vlaamse Academie voor wetenschappen, letteren en schone kunsten van België. Klasse der Letteren*
MN	*Musée neuchâtelois*
MPSALH	*Mémoires et publications de la Société des sciences, des arts et des lettres de Hainaut*
MSAL	*Mémoires de la Société d'archéologie lorraine*
MSBGH	*Mémoires de la Société bourguignonne de géographie et d'histoire*
MSE	*Mémoires de la Société éduenne*
MSED	*Mémoires de la Société d'émulation du Doubs*
MSHB	*Messager des sciences historiques de Belgique*
MSHDB	*Mémoires de la Société pour l'histoire du droit et des institutions des anciens pays bourguignons, comtois et romands*
MSHP	*Mémoires de la Société de l'histoire de Paris et de l'Île-de-France*
MSHS	*Miscellany of the Scottish historical Society*
MSO	*Mémoires de la Société académique d'archéologie, sciences et arts du département de l'Oise*
MVP	Maetschappy der Vlaemsche bibliophilen te Gent
NBAG	*Notizenblatt. Beilage zum Archiv für Kunde österreichischer Geschichtsquellen*
NDB	*Neue Deutsche Biographie*
NEBN	*Notices et extraits des manuscrits de la Bibliothèque Nationale et autres bibliothèques*
NFZ	*Neujahrsblatt von der Feuerwerkergesellschaft in Zürich*
NH	*Nova historia*
NRS	*Nuova rivista storica*
PCEEBM	*Publications du Centre européen d'études burgundo-médianes*
PJSE	*Politisches Jahrbuch der schweizerischen Eidgenossenschaft*
PSAH	*Publications de la Société archéologique et historique dans le duché de Limbourg*
PSBL	Publications de la Société des bibliophiles liègeois
PSHIL	Publications de la section historique de l'Institut grand-ducal de Luxembourg
PTSEC	*Positions des thèses soutenues à l'École des Chartes*
QBL	Quellensammlung badischen Landesgeschichte
QSG	Quellen zur Schweizer Geschichte
RA	Rijksarchief

RA	*Revue d'Alsace*
RB	*Revue bourguignonne*
RBAHA	*Revue belge d'archéologie et d'histoire de l'art*
RBN	*Revue belge de numismatique*
RCC	*Revue des cours et conférences*
RG	*Rheinische Geschichtsblätter*
RGB	*Revue générale belge*
RGP	Rijks Geschiedkundige Publicatiën
RH	*Revue historique*
RHB	*Rheinische Heimatblätter*
RIHM	*Revue internationale de l'histoire militaire*
RMS	*Revue militaire suisse*
RN	*Revue du Nord*
RS	Rolls Series
RSS	*Revue des Sociétés savantes des départements*
RTA material	Material for publication in the *Deutsche Reichstagsakten* assembled at Göttingen by Dr. H. Grüneisen
RUB	*Revue de l'Université de Bruxelles*
RV	*Rheinische Vierteljahrsblätter*
SA	Stadt-Archiv
SAV	*Schweizerisches Archiv für Volkskunde*
SBAG	*Schweizer Beiträge zur Geschichte allgemeinen*
SG	*Schweizerische Geschichtsforscher*
SHF	Société de l'histoire de France
SMHW	*Schweizerisches Museum für historische Wissenschaften*
SMOW	*Schweizerische Monatsschrift für Offiziere aller Waffen*
SR	*Studies in the Renaissance*
SSG	Schweizer Studien zur Geschichtswissenschaft
StA	Staatsarchiv
TG	*Tijdschrift voor Geschiedenis*
WF	*Westfälische Forschungen*
WG	Werken uitgegeven door Gelre. Vereeniging tot beoefening van geldersche geschiedenis, oudheidkunde en recht
WG	*Die Welt als Geschichte*
WZ	*Westdeutsche Zeitschrift für Geschichte und Kunst*
ZGA	*Zeitschrift für Geschichte und Altertumskunde*
ZGO	*Zeitschrift für die Geschichte des Oberrheins*
ZSG	*Zeitschrift für schweizerische Geschichte (Revue d'histoire suisse)*

Acknowledgements

In the preparation of this account of the Burgundian state under Duke Charles the Bold my debt to others has been greater than ever. In particular I had the singular good fortune, on a visit to Göttingen, to meet and talk extensively with three German-speaking scholars who are maintaining in this century the traditions of exact scholarship which that greatest of all historians of Charles the Bold, Heinrich Witte, laid down in the 1890s. I refer to Professor H. Heimpel, Dr. Karl Bittman and Dr. H. Grüneisen, all of the Max-Planck Institut für Geschichte at Göttingen. I thank Professor Heimpel for his hospitality and help, and acknowledge my debt to the ideas and material brought together by him in a brilliant series of papers on Charles the Bold. I thank Dr. Grüneisen for placing her probably unrivalled knowledge of Charles the Bold at my disposal, and for letting me freely use the invaluable body of material she has brought together for volume xxiii of the *Deutsche Reichstagsakten.* I thank Dr. Bittman for allowing me to pick his brains in conversation, and for enabling me to base at least parts of my narrative on secure foundations, for I owe more than I can say to his masterly and penetrating work on Louis XI and Charles the Bold.

For loans of theses or gifts of material I have to thank Professor A. Abel, Director of the Centre pour l'Étude des Problèmes du Monde Musulman Contemporain in Brussels, Professor John Bartier of the Free University of Brussels, Dr. W. Blockmans of the University of Ghent, Mlle N. Grain of the Centre régional d'études historiques of the University of Lille, Professor Jean Lejeune of the University of Liège, Professor W. Noomen of the University of Groningen, M. Pierre Quarré, Conservateur of the Dijon Museum and Professor Ralph Giesey of the University of Iowa, who generously passed on to me the manuscript Burgundian material of the late Professor Ernst H. Kantorowicz. I wish to thank the authorities of

the Swiss National Library in Bern and Mrs. G. Milis-Proost and
Mrs. G. Schipper-de Nie for bibliographical assistance. I thank Dr.
W. Paravicini for kindly replying to my enquiry. On points of
factual detail I have received important help from Professor E.
Kossman of the University of Groningen and M. J. C. Garreta
of the Dijon Public Library. Several of my colleagues in the University of Hull have devoted time and trouble to helping me translate
the excerpts from source material in the pages that follow. In this
respect my thanks are due to Professor C. E. Pickford, Messrs
Peter Hoare and Derek Attwood, Professor Frank Norman and
Dr. J. R. Woodhouse. Blunders have been removed and this book
considerably improved through the good offices of Professor A. R.
Myers, Dr. Karl Bittmann and Mr. Richard Walsh, all of whom have
kindly read through the typescript. I am glad to thank, too, Miss
Susan Appleton and Mrs. Pat Wilkinson for typing the text from a
nearly undecipherable manuscript.

As I lay down my pen after fifteen years' work on the History of
Valois Burgundy I wish once again to thank the authorities and staffs
of the libraries and archive repositories whose ready assistance has
been so consistently given to me. I wish also to acknowledge the
encouragement I have received from the scholars who have reviewed
the three earlier volumes of this History in many European journals.
I would also like to thank all those colleagues and students, in the
Universities of Cambridge and Hull, and elsewhere, who have so
often put their thoughts and time at my disposal and from whom I
have learned so much. Last, but not least, I here gratefully place on
record my debt to my wife Margaret and my six children, who have
contributed in many ways to the successful completion of this work.

RICHARD VAUGHAN

October 1972

CHAPTER ONE

The Duke and the Towns: Ghent and Liège

For twenty-four hours after his death in the ducal palace at Bruges in the evening of Monday, 15 June 1467, the body of the old duke, Philip the Good, lay on his bed in state for all to see, a black cap placed on the head. On the Tuesday evening the work of embalming was carried out. The body, in a lead coffin, along with the heart and entrails, each in a leaden casket, was taken to the ducal chapel and placed on a six-foot-high bier draped to the ground in black velvet, with four massive candles burning at the four corners. Philip's son, the new Duke Charles, had galloped from Ghent to his father's deathbed as soon as he heard of his illness; and it was he who made the detailed arrangements for Philip the Good's obsequies in the church of St. Donatian on the Sunday and Monday following. He ordered the nave to be hung with black cloth and the choir with black velvet. He had the late duke's coat-of-arms set up everywhere, together with the insignia of his Order of chivalry, the Golden Fleece. All his courtiers and household retainers, as well as those of his father, numbering some 1,200 persons, were issued with eight ells of black cloth each, the quality reflecting the status of the recipient: the chaplains' cost 50 shillings an ell; the *maîtres des requêtes'* cost 40s; the equerries of the four court offices received still cheaper cloth, at 30s an ell; other court officers, at 20s an ell; and servants at 12s.

On Sunday, 21 June, four bishops and twenty-two notable abbots were mustered to accompany Philip the Good's bier in full pontificals from the ducal palace to the church of St. Donatian. Held back on either side by hundreds of torch-bearers clothed in black, a crowd of 20,000 persons lined the streets along which the cortège passed. These people, inhabitants of Bruges and visitors from elsewhere, were expected to turn out in black at their own expense and keep absolutely still while the procession passed. The style of the operation was almost military in its detailed precision. A special marshal was detailed to stand in the courtyard of the ducal palace and call out from a roll the names of those participating in the procession, so as to make sure they stepped forward and joined it in the right order. The clergy and citizens of Bruges and the Franc of Bruges were followed by court servants and officials: equerries, surgeons, doctors, secretaries, councillors, financial officials and chamberlains. After these courtiers came the four bishops, and twenty-four officers and sergeants of arms in black except for their ducal coats of arms, marching two by two. Next came the coffin, carried by some of the late duke's archers and accompanied by the first equerry bearing Philip the Good's sword, and twenty noblemen in long black robes, four of whom supported a magnificent pall, of cloth of gold. The six principal mourners then followed, led by Duke Charles and followed in their turn by two of the late duke's bastard sons and one of his bastard grandsons, and all the personal officers and attendants of the new duke. Inside the church the heat from more than 1,400 candles was such that holes had to be made in the windows to allow it to escape. The celebration of vespers and vigils for the dead occupied some four hours that Sunday evening and the heralds and officers of arms remained through the night. Next day duke and entourage returned to the church at 9.0 a.m., after two early masses had already been celebrated there, for the requiem mass and funeral oration by the bishop of Tournai. Then at last the mortal remains of Philip the Good were interred, the heart and entrails permanently, the body until such time as Duke Charles found it convenient to transfer it to the Charterhouse of Champmol at Dijon, St. Denis of the Burgundian dukes.[1]

---

[1] Lory, *MCACO* vii (1869), 215-46 prints a contemporary account of the funeral which I have for the most part followed here. A different version is shared by the chroniclers: de Haynin, *Mémoires*, i. 206-9, Duclerq, *Mémoires*, 306-8 and de Waurin, *Croniques*, ed. Hardy, v. 356-9. For the next paragraph see Langlois, *Notices et extraits* xxxiii (2) (1889), 284-5, de la Marche, *Mémoires*, iii. 56-7, and Vaughan, *Philip the Good*, 399-400. Among biographies of Charles the Bold, I have found Kirk, *Charles the Bold*, Putnam, *Charles the Bold*, and Bartier, *Charles le Téméraire*, particularly useful in all of what follows, as well as the following essays: Freeman, *Historical essays*, 314-72, Henrard, *Appréciation du règne de Charles le Téméraire*, Heimpel, *GWU* iv (1953), 257-72 and Huizinga, *Verzamelde werken*, ii. 238-65.

In an epitaph, Duke Philip the Good was made to summarize his own achievements in terms of successful territorial expansion, of forcing the king of France to sue for peace, of fighting seven battles and losing none, and of defying both English and French at one and the same time. He was made to boast of being responsible for crowning two kings, Louis XI of France and Edward IV of England, of sending his galleys as far as the Black Sea, and of enabling Pope Eugenius IV to remain pope in spite of the council of Basel. The chronicler-courtier Olivier de la Marche adds that he died the wealthiest prince of his time, leaving a treasure of 400,000 gold crowns, not to mention tapestries, plate, jewels and a magnificent library. But the real significance of Philip the Good's reign lay perhaps less in the personal achievements and conscious policies of the duke, and more in the evolution or emergence of certain specifically Burgundian elements—elements of unity or at least of centralization in the territories he ruled. He inherited from his predecessors the framework of a centralized government: a single all-powerful chancellor, a well-organized court, a *grand conseil* or central council. He created the Order of the Golden Fleece, during his reign a single coinage for the Burgundian Low Countries was established, and the States General were inaugurated: all these promoted unity of a kind. Towards the end of his long reign wars against Ghent and against France fostered a certain Burgundian patriotism. An embryo Burgundian church came into being through ducal manipulation of episcopal appointments, the issue of jubilee indulgences to the duke's subjects, and other developments. Thus were foundations laid on which Duke Charles could hope to build.

Charles's exact status and the extent of his personal authority at the time of his father's death in June 1467 have been debated by historians.[1] In fact, Duke Philip retained power in his own hands till the end, ruling through the *grand conseil*, but Charles had built up a political organization of his own in the last few years of his father's reign. He possessed his own revenues and financial organization. He sought *aides* for himself from the Estates of his father's territories.[2] He had created a veritable system of foreign alliances of his own. He had elbowed his way into power at court and then led his father's armies into battle in France in 1465 and against Dinant

[1] Bonenfant and Stengers, *AB* xxv (1953), 7–29 and 118–33. For what follows see Vaughan, *Philip the Good*, 343, 355–6 and 376–97. For Charles's career before he became duke, see Vaughan, *Philip the Good*, 340–6.
[2] ADN B2064 fos. 91, 118, 137 etc.

and Liège in 1466. Moreover, he had important territories of his own in Holland, notably Gorinchem with its castle on which he had lavished funds, and in Picardy, where he had made extensive acquisitions at the close of the War of the Public Weal. In particular, Louis XI had ceded Péronne, Roye and Montdidier to Charles personally after Charles had conquered them from Jehan, count of Nevers, in 1465: Charles garrisoned them himself thereafter and enjoyed their revenues.[1] The so-called Somme towns, returned by Philip the Good to Louis XI in 1463 were also ceded by Louis in 1465 to Charles, and he retained them thereafter as his personal possession, ruling them through the agency of his first chamberlain Jehan, lord of Auxy, the 'lieutenant-general of his lands and lordships on either side of the River Somme'.

A group of personal adherents, officials, courtiers and councillors of Charles had helped to enhance his power towards the end of his father's reign while he was still only count of Charolais, and these were ready to form the nucleus of a new administrative personnel under the new duke. One of them was Guillaume de Rochefort, already councillor and maître des requêtes of Charles in 1466.[2] A doctor of law of the University of Dole, he came from a noble Franche-Comté family and rose to prominence very rapidly in Charles's service, becoming one of his most trusted and influential diplomats. It was he who was responsible for negotiating the treaty with Bern in 1467. Subsequently he became Charles's regular emissary to Savoy and Venice. The duke's chancellor, Guillaume Hugonet, had also been his councillor and maître des requêtes when he was count of Charolais,[3] and had been sent by Charles on at least two embassies to Louis XI before he became duke. Two other councillors and maîtres des requêtes of Charles before 1467 who remained active throughout his reign were the brothers Ferry and Guillaume de Clugny. The former became bishop of Tournai in 1474; the latter was a papal protonotary. Among noblemen in Charles's service before he became duke his first and second chamber-

---

[1] ADN B2064, fos. 16b, 48b–49, 453b–454, etc. and, for the next sentence, fos. 448, 460b, etc. Compare BN MS. Dupuy 762, fos. 161a–b.
[2] ADN B2064, f. 46, and see Mangin, *PTSEC* (1936), 117–23. For de Rochefort and the Bern treaty, see ADN B2064, fos. 162b and 192b. For all of what follows, see Bonenfant and Stengers, *AB* xxv (1953), 127–31, Bartier, *Légistes et gens de finances*, and Stein, *BEC* xcviii (1937), 283–348.
[3] Paravicini, *Festschrift H. Heimpel*, ii. 449. For Ferry de Clugny in 1466–7, see ADN B2064, fos. 61, 242 and 243.

lains, Jehan, lord of Auxy and Jehan de Rosimbos, lord of Fourmelles were noteworthy and influential,[1] as was the subsequently notorious Peter von Hagenbach. Nor should we forget Charles's close associate Guillaume Bische, said in May 1467 to have had 'my lord of Charolais on a string (gantz yn der hant); he controlled everything'; Charles's ex-tutor Anthoine Haneron, provost of St. Donatian's at Bruges, who became one of the duke's leading financial administrators; the Burgundian Jehan Carondelet, appointed in December 1473 first president of the Parlement of Malines; and the count of Charolais's secretaries Berthelemy Trotin and Jehan Gros the Younger, receiver-general and audiencier respectively. These were among the key men in Charles's service before 1467 who remained prominent in the administration of the Burgundian state after he became duke and, in many cases, throughout his reign. In 1472 these same names crop up again when the Milanese ambassador Petro Aliprandi, who claimed that he 'knew the whole troop from top to bottom', reviewed Duke Charles's leading captains and councillors. Of the latter, he named Guillaume Hugonet, Guillaume de Clugny, Jehan Carondelet, Anthoine Haneron and Guillaume de Rochefort as the most important.[2]

One of the boasts of Philip the Good in the epitaph mentioned above was that he had defeated the rebellious citizens of Liège and those of the Flemish towns, especially Bruges and Ghent. But in fact the urban situation was more complex than this because, inside the town walls, intermittent civil war was being waged between the popular, radical elements and the politically moderate wealthy classes. In this confrontation of merchant against artisan the duke had sided with the merchants. But the radical elements, in Liège and Ghent especially, had by no means been suppressed by Philip the Good. Indeed, if anything, his policies of extending ducal authority at the expense of urban privilege by intervening constantly in urban affairs, had the effect of promoting support for the more revolutionary elements, and these were powerful enough at the end of his reign to cause a series of crises at the start of his successor's. In fact, it was the activities of the towns, in particular those of Ghent and Liège, which dictated the course of events during the first eighteen months of Charles the Bold's reign, rather than the duke

[1] ADN B2064, f. 160b (J. de Rosimbos in 1467). For the quotation which follows, see Bonenfant and Stengers, AB xxv (1953), 129 n. 4.
[2] Cal. state papers. Milan, i. 170.

himself. First, in point of time if not in order of importance, came the crisis provoked at Ghent.

It was on Sunday morning, 28 June 1467, that Duke Charles, accompanied by large numbers of his courtiers, all dressed in black, made his solemn entry into Ghent. At first, all went well. The duke went through the usual inauguration ceremony as count of Flanders in the church of St. John and was formally welcomed by the assembled magistrates and people in the market place. But commotion broke out the following evening. A party of revellers celebrating the annual festival of bringing back the relics of St. Livinus or Lievin, a popular local saint, from the spot where he was thought to have been martyred in the seventh century, demolished a booth which had been erected in the Cornmarket for the collectors of an unpopular local tax or *quellote* (*cueillote*). Thereafter, they assembled in arms in the Fridaymarket yelling 'Down with the quellote!' Chastellain's highly coloured account of what followed has made this episode famous: the duke goes to harangue the mob but then loses his temper and makes things worse by striking one of the agitators. Other things, besides the abolition of the *quellote*, are demanded: punishment of the city authorities for embezzlement, restoration of the craft-gild banners and of Ghent's jurisdiction over the surrounding countryside, opening of the closed gates of the city. Indeed the populace now seeks outright repeal of the harsh settlement of Gavere, imposed by Duke Philip the Good after the great rebellion of Ghent had been put down in 1453, besides measures against the ruling merchant oligarchy of their city. The artisans spend the whole of that night and the next day in angry and defiant mood in the Fridaymarket and Charles only manages to escape from Ghent on 1 July, complete with his daughter Mary and the chests containing the treasure amassed by his father, which he had brought with him from Bruges, by promising concessions.[1]

[1] Chastellain, *Oeuvres*, v. 249–78. The other main chronicle sources for this paragraph and what follows are *Kronyk van Vlaenderen*, ii. 256–63 and *Dagboek van Gent*, ii. 205–25. Less important are de Commynes, *Mémoires*, ed. Calmette and Durville, i. 119–21, de Haynin, *Mémoires*, i. 197–8, and *Cronycke van Hollandt*, f. 314. Documentary material is printed in *Collection de documens inédits*, i. 204–13, de Comines, *Mémoires*, ed. Lenglet du Fresnoy, ii. 628–30 and iii. 85–93, and *Analectes historiques*, v. 109–16; see too *IAG*, 232–4 and ADN B1609, fos. 21–35b. Fris, *Histoire de Gand*, 138–42, and in *BSHAG* xxx (1922), 57–142 is the best modern authority. The accounts show that one of the archers of Charles's bodyguard 'was wounded on the day the men of Ghent were in arms in the market place', ADN B2064, f. 262b.

Writing to Louis XI on 2 July, Charles excused his delays over an affair between himself and the king on the grounds that 'after my entry into Ghent and taking possession of the country, a commotion arose between the commons of the town and those governing it and I had to appease this commotion'.[1] This was putting it mildly. The commons of Ghent certainly were bitterly hostile to their own civic authorities or ruling classes; but the duke was the traditional ally of these merchant patricians, and the riots Charles had just escaped from represented a direct threat to his authority. Naturally, therefore, the story did not end when the duke left Ghent on 1 July. As a matter of fact, the situation remained critical throughout that month. The unpopular ducal bailiff, Clais Triest, had to be dismissed, but his successor, Loys d'Escornaix, managed to restore control. He did this with the help of an execution or two in the last week of July and as a result of important concessions by the duke who, on 28 July, issued documents restoring their banners to the craft gilds, allowing the gates closed by the treaty of Gavere to be reopened, and formally forgiving the citizens for all their misdeeds.

Thereafter negotiations continued, but other pressing affairs, notably the revolt of Liège, intervened, and it was not until the end of 1468 that Charles was finally in a position to impose the full weight of his authority on Ghent. After the city and gild authorities had been persuaded to make a general submission to the duke on 2 January 1469, renouncing in it their banners, the opening of their gates and indeed all their privileges, including that of the annual election of their echevins, Charles received them into his good graces. The histrionics usual on such occasions were laid on in Brussels on 15 January 1469.[2]

First, the said hall was adorned and hung round with very fine tapestries of the great king Alexander, of Hannibal and of other ancient worthies, and on a dais at the head of the hall my lord the duke was seated on a superb throne most nobly decorated and hung round with cloth of gold. Seated similarly, on the lowest of some steps leading up to the throne, was the most high and mighty prince my lord Anthony, bastard of Burgundy, count of la Roche, lord of Beveren and of Beuvry, who, as first chamberlain of my lord the duke, had on this occasion the cognizance of and responsibility for what followed.

---

[1] *Analectes historiques*, iv. 104–5.
[2] *Collection de documens inédits*, i. 204–9, and de Commynes, *Mémoires*, ed. Dupont, iii. 253–60. See too Wielant, *Antiquités de Flandre*, 325–7 and Meyer, *Commentarii sive annales rerum Flandricarum*, 347 for what follows, as well as the sources cited on p. 6 n. 1 above.

Near the said throne of my lord the duke was another very fine and richly decorated bench, on which were seated first, my lord the bishop of Liège, duke of Bouillon and count of Looz; Messire Philip of Savoy, brother of the most noble and excellent lady my lady the queen of France; and the most high and mighty prince my lord Adolf of Cleves, count of la Mark and lord of Ravenstein. After them, in very fine seats, were the most high and mighty lords Messieurs of the noble Golden Fleece and, after them the other nobles. . . . Also present in this enclosure were a number of foreign ambassadors, including those of France, England, Hungary, Bohemia, Naples, Aragon, Sicily, Cyprus, Norway, Poland, Denmark, Russia, Livonia, Prussia, Austria, Milan, Lombardy and others: a wonderful sight indeed.

Next, my lord the duke's lesser court officials took their places on benches erected for them along the hall, each in order according to his status and office. There was a beautifully carpentered passage-way in the hall made like a street for those coming, passing and staying; and the duke's officials made their way along this to their seats, each in order and according to the dignity of his office as has been said. . . .

Monsieur Olivier de la Marche, knight, and Pierre Bladelin, called Leestmakere, *maîtres d'hôtel* of my said lord the duke, deputed for this purpose . . . , went . . . to the square called Coudenberg, in front of the palace, where the Ghenters, that is to say, the magistrates, the fifty-two deans of the craft gilds and the jurors of the town of Ghent, who had come from the town hall of Brussels, were assembled. They led them most graciously from the said square into the courtyard, each dean having before him the banner of his gild unfurled on a lance, where they waited in the snow more than an hour and a half. When they came and entered the hall as a result of the intercession of their guides, each of them knelt down most humbly on the ground three times with his banner before entering the said enclosure, where each placed his banner at the feet of my lord the bastard of Burgundy and they all cried 'Mercy!' together very humbly, which was piteous to see and hear.

Immediately after this the Great Privilege of Ghent was read out in full, particularly the passage concerning the renewal of the magistrature etc. This done, the reading over, Messire Pierre, lord of Goux and of Wedergrate, chancellor of Burgundy, asked my lord the duke what was his pleasure. He replied straight away that the whole of the said privilege should be annulled. Hearing this, Master Jehan le Gros, first secretary and *audiencier*, took a knife or quill-cutter and lacerated the privilege in front of everyone.

This done, my said lord the duke began to speak about the recent wars in Flanders, complaining in detail of the offences and misdeeds [of the Ghenters] and of their behaviour towards the most high and noble person of the late mighty duke Philip his father, whom God pardon. He also explained and demonstrated how he had always supported them to the utmost, even speaking on their behalf to his said most noble father. Among other things, he complained that, when he wanted to have his most noble daughter with him in Brussels they were unwilling to let her leave [Ghent], showing well enough by this that they had offended most against him when he trusted them most. What is more, when he wanted to enter into possession of his land of Flanders and to swear to maintain and respect its privileges etc., they had offended even more vilainously, and vented all their spleen etc. He then outlined how, in reparation, they had agreed first, at his request to close the gates; second, they had brought their banners, as above-mentioned; third, they had very humbly cried mercy for the heinous crime of lese-majesty which they had perpetrated; fourth, they had brought their privileges, also noted above.

'By means of these obeisances, if you keep your promises to be our good people and children as you ought to be you may obtain our grace, and we shall be a good prince and archimandrite'. And he concluded by asking them if entire satisfaction could have been made for their said offence and vilainous disobedience, to which, as might be expected, they did not reply a word.

Thus Ghent was deprived of all semblance of civic autonomy. The hated *quellote* was restored in April 1469 and, in August, the annual renewal of the *loi*, that is, the appointment of new echevins, was carried out without any elective element by ducal commissioners under orders to appoint people favourable to the duke. It seems that Charles even considered building a fortress outside Ghent to ensure his continued dominance over the town.[1]

Flanders was not the only part of Charles the Bold's lands where his inauguration as duke or count was accompanied by dissidence or outbreaks of violence in the towns. In Artois, St. Omer was compelled to pay a fine of £20,000 for certain breaches of the peace in 1467.[2] In Antwerp, there was trouble over a toll before Charles could make his solemn entry on 5 September. Chastellain hints that the Brabant towns hoped to impose conditions on the new duke before they admitted him within their walls; he mentions in particular the hostility of Brussels and suggests that, had it not been for the nobles of Brabant, the three Estates, meeting at Louvain, might have

[1] Duverger, *Miscellanea in honorem A. de Meyer*, ii. 748–51.
[2] Maeght, *Emprunts de Charles le Téméraire*, 20. For the next sentence, see Prims, *Geschiedenis van Antwerpen*, vi (1). 145–7 and, for what follows, Chastellain, *Oeuvres*, v. 278–80, de Barante, *Histoire des ducs*, ii. 280–3 nn., Coninckx, *BCAM* ii (1892), 300–24, *IAM*, i. 149–52, Laenen, *Geschiedenis van Mechelen*, 178–80, and Trouvé, *HKOM* lvi (1952), 65–6. The duke's sentence of 16 October 1467 is printed in *Additions et corrections de Malines*, iii (2). 17–30 and in Coninckx, *BCAM* ii (1892), 317–24.

refused to accept Charles as duke and chosen instead Jehan, count of Nevers, a first cousin of Philip the Good who had fought for Louis XI against Charles in 1465 and who had shadowy claims to Brabant.[1] Be this as it may, it is clear that the trouble at Malines, which broke out some time after Charles's solemn entry there on 3 July had occurred without any untoward incident, was as much a reaction against the ruling classes of that town as a rebellion against the duke. But, since the duke was here, as elsewhere, the traditional ally of the city authorities against the populace or commons, he too was closely involved. Another element in the 'uproar' at Malines was inter-urban rivalry, for the trouble began with the arrest at Heffen of three boats laden with corn for Brussels which, accused of infringing or ignoring the staple rights of Malines, were taken to Malines and there broken up and sent to the bottom of the River Dyle by an angry mob. The duke was involved because some at least of this corn was destined for the provision of his court in Brussels and because the dispute over staple rights between Brussels and Malines was pending before his council.

After the destruction of the boats the riotous people of Malines displayed further animosity, this time against their duke and their own city government, by ransacking the house of the ducal officer in Malines, the *écoutète*, and the houses of two leading burgesses. Then, assembling in traditional fashion in arms on the market place, the commons of Malines dismissed the recently-elected magistrates and appointed new ones. According to the ducal sentence of 16 October, they also 'made several other ordinances, as they pleased, against, and in contempt and to the prejudice of, our dignity and lordship'. Since the duke's *écoutète* had prudently withdrawn or fled for his life they contrived to have another appointed, and they even appropriated the town keys and took control of the gates. But the revolt of Malines was soon quelled. Charles's *procureur général* started criminal proceedings against the conspirators, and the duke himself returned to Malines on 28 August and remained there several days. The sentence against Malines was similar to that imposed on Ghent and marks a similar extention of ducal authority over the towns and a similar erosion of their privileges. In future, the magistrates were to be 'elected', or, better, renewed, annually by the duke or his commissioners; there was to be no banishment without the *écoutète*'s consent; judgements of the *loi* or magistrature of Malines were in future to be subject to the jurisdiction of the duke's

[1] See Vaughan, *Philip the Good*, 378 and below, 14.

great council and reversible by it; and ordinances of the *loi* must be confirmed by the ducal *écoutète*. In addition, a fine of 30,000 Rhenish florins was to be paid by the town, representing 10 per cent of its annual revenue for the next six years, and 160 ringleaders were to be banished.

The sedition at Malines occurred at just the moment, in August 1467, when Charles was preparing to intervene militarily against Liège, a town that was not in his own territories. The situation here, and in the ecclesiastical principality of which it was the natural centre and capital, had become increasingly more complex and more critical after the accession in 1456 as bishop of Charles the Bold's first cousin, Louis de Bourbon.[1] Open revolt against this unpopular prince, led by Raes de Lyntre, lord of Heers, had been combined, in 1465, with a declaration of war against Duke Philip the Good which the Liègeois had been encouraged to make by King Louis XI of France. In the peace of St. Trond, which Philip the Good and his son dictated to Liège on 22 December 1465, and in the similar peace of Oleye, which Liège was persuaded to sign on 10 September 1466 after the count of Charolais had destroyed her sister city of Dinant, the duke of Burgundy was made hereditary guardian or protector of the city and principality of Liège, which was compelled to pay a massive indemnity and to deliver fifty hostages to the duke against payment of the first instalment of it, and a further fifty for each subsequent instalment. But, instead of busying themselves with the publication and implementation of this peace settlement, which included a reconciliation between the city of Liège and the bishop, Louis de Bourbon, the more radical leaders in Liège raised objections, made delays and set about prosecuting, and even executing, those

---

[1] See Vaughan, *Philip the Good*, 391–7. For the whole of what follows, on Liège, see in general Henrard, *AAAB* (2) xiii (1867), 581–678, Daris, *Liège pendant le xvᵉ siècle*, Kurth, *Cité de Liège*, iii, Lallemand, *La lutte des États de Liège contre la maison de Bourgogne*, *Algemene geschiedenis*, iii. 309–12, and Lejeune, *Liège. De la principauté à la métropole* and *Exposition. Liège et Bourgogne*. The main documents are printed or referred to in *Cartulaire de St. Lambert*, v, *Documents relatifs aux troubles du pays de Liège* and *Régestes de Liège*, iv. The principal chroniclers are Basin, *Louis XI*, i, Chastellain, *Oeuvres*, v. 315–58 (1467 only), de Commynes, *Mémoires*, ed. Calmette and Durville, i, *Cronycke van Hollandt*, de Haynin, *Mémoires*, i and ii, de la Marche, *Mémoires*, iii, de Los, *Chronique*, *Magnum chronicon Belgicum*, de Merica, *De cladibus Leodensium*, d'Oudenbosch, *Chronique*, Pauwels, *Historia* and *Alia narratio*, and de Waurin, *Croniques*, ed. Hardy, v.

who had been responsible for negotiating the peace settlement with the duke of Burgundy, while Raes de Lyntre dressed his partisans in red tunics with the words Long Live Liège! embroidered on the sleeves. The rift between bishop and city widened, especially when Louis de Bourbon installed himself in the town of Huy and summoned his clergy, the canons of the cathedral of St. Lambert and the collegiate churches of Liège, to join him there.

When Philip the Good died on 15 June 1467 Liège was thus in a state of partial revolt against the bishop and the duke, and on the verge of serious civil war. A chronicler reports that, when the news of the duke's death reached them, the inhabitants of Beringen 'beat on kitchen utensils by way of mock bells for his obsequies and yelled out insultingly that the old devil had died'. They paid later for this temerity: during the Liège campaign the bastard Anthony was sent with a special force to burn Beringen to the ground.[1] On the day before Duke Philip's death, 14 June, the chancellor and council of Brabant had circulated letters from Charles, count of Charolais, reporting that extremist elements in Liège—members of the so-called Company of the Green Tent—planned to attack and seize the town of Huy, Louis de Bourbon's headquarters.

Early in 1467, King Louis XI of France had sought to effect a settlement between bishop and town which might have served to extend French influence over Liège at the expense of Burgundian. Charles apparently thought Louis's ambassadors were making trouble, for he had some of them arrested at Bouvignes in March 1467, but a royal letter of 24 April shows Louis still trying to mediate, and he consistently rejected the requests from Raes de Lyntre and the Liège extremists for the military assistance against Burgundy, which he had promised (but not sent) in 1465.[2] Again, in July and August 1467, a succession of letters and ambassadors exchanged between Louis XI and Liège prove that the king was still trying to avert war and advising moderation, and Louis's ambassadors to Charles the Bold at this time, and later, urged the same on him.

[1] Petri, *Gesta pontificum Leodiensium*, 167. For the next sentence, see AGR CC2422, fos. 95, 97b, 103 etc.
[2] ADN B2064, fos. 87 and 107a–b (partly printed by La Fons de Mélicocq, *BSHF* (2) i (1857–8), 298–9, who has 'Bonnes' erroneously for Bouvignes) and Bittmann, *SBAG* vii (1949), 140–52. For what follows, see the letters printed in *Analectes historiques*, iv. 99–104, and de Chabannes, *Preuves. Supplément*, iii. 148–51 = de Comines, *Mémoires*, ed. Lenglet du Fresnoy, ii. 631–2, Dabin, *BIAL* xliii (1913), 136–41 and Harsin, *BFPL* cciii (1972), 234–53.

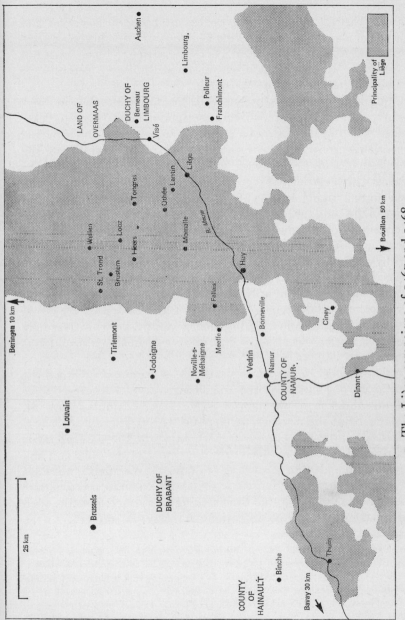

1. The Liège campaigns of 1467 and 1468

Nor is there a shred of evidence to support the contention of some historians that Louis was at this time encouraging Liège to revolt against Charles,[1] even though, earlier in this same year, he had dreamed of a grand alliance against Charles and his father which was to include Liège as well as Bern. As to the antics of Jehan, count of Nevers, they were surely neither encouraged nor even approved of by Louis XI. According to Chastellain, the count of Nevers sent an insulting letter to Duke Charles while he was at Brussels in July-August 1467, and made a direct attempt to incite Liège to rebel against their duke. This move ended in failure when his principal emissary was arrested by the Burgundians after inadvertently entering the village of Ciney, in Namur, which he thought was held by the Liègeois. Other chroniclers mention this incident. Even better attested is the formal taking possession, by a deputation of Liège citizens acting on the count of Nevers' behalf, of certain domains, near Liège, dependencies of the duchy of Brabant. The pseudo-legal comedy was played out on 23 July. Charles retaliated against these provocations by confiscating the hôtel de Nevers at Brussels on 3 August and ceding it on 8 August to his councillor Philippe Pot. It was not these interventions of the count of Nevers, still less those of King Louis XI, which determined the course of events at Liège, but rather the growing aggressiveness of the Liègeois themselves, who were increasingly dominated by Raes de Lyntre and other extremists or revolutionaries.

In the first half of July Raes's military preparations included the manufacture of a huge bombard called Liègeois which he caused to be fired outside each of the churches in Liège, beginning with St. Lambert's. But the next day it blew up. On 25 July the Milanese ambassador at the French court reported that the Liègeois had made difficulties in paying the indemnity they owed to the duke and had even attacked a place in the duchy of Brabant.[2] Whether or not Raes and his colleagues really did write to Ghent, Malines and others of Duke Charles's towns at this time seeking an alliance, remains open to doubt; but a series of executions at Liège, culminating in the

[1] For example, Heuterus, *Rerum burgundicarum*, 159 and Kurth, *Cité de Liège*, iii. 258. For the rest of the sentence, see *Cal. state papers. Venice*, i. 117–18 = *Cal. state papers. Milan*, i. 118–20. For what follows on Jehan, count of Nevers, besides the works mentioned above, p. 10 n. 1 and p. 11 n. 1, see Galesloot, *BCRH* (4) iii (1876), 41–52.

[2] AGR MSS. divers 1173, f. 53b (transcript of despatch of Christoforo de Bollate).

torture and decapitation on 11 August of the ex-burgomaster of
Dinant, Jehan Carpentier, could only be interpreted as acts of
provocation by the extremists against both the bishop and the duke.
On the very same day Charles the Bold found it necessary to pay for
the cost of sending letters from the Liège hostages, who had been
on parole in Brussels since mid-June, to the civic authorities at
Liège, requesting the release of an emissary and secretary of his,
Jehan Stoep, who had been arrested and imprisoned there.[1] This
outrageous act was followed by others. On 18 August the men of
Visé set off to ransack the village of Berneau in Charles the Bold's
duchy of Limbourg. When the Limbourgers retaliated, Raes de
Lyntre led a raiding party of Liègeois into Limbourg and thereafter
acts of violence proliferated until a state of open warfare developed
early in September. Huy, still under the control of Louis de Bourbon
and garrisoned with Burgundian troops, was now threatened and,
in spite of last-minute reinforcements sent there by Charles on 13
September,[2] it was surprised by Raes de Lyntre and his associates
during the night of 16–17 September. While Louis de Bourbon fled
to Namur, Evrard de la Marck, lord of Aremberg, organized a valiant
but fruitless resistance to the assailants. By midday on 17 September
Huy was in the hands of the revolutionaries of Liège.

Charles had been making preparations against Liège months
before the fall of Huy. His justification for involvement in the affair
was threefold. Ever since his father's three deputies took possession
of the *avouerie* or guardianship of Liège on 12 September 1466 the
duke of Burgundy had been associated with the bishop as responsible
for law and order there. Then, on 29 July 1467, Louis de Bourbon
had empowered Duke Charles to arbitrate all the differences between
himself and his subjects, the people of the principality and city of
Liège. Finally, Charles doubtless found it necessary to intervene as
an aggrieved party, because his territory had been attacked by the
Liègeois. His military preparations had begun at least as early as
10–18 July, when couriers had been sent to the grand bailiff of
Hainault, Jehan de Rubempré, lord of Bièvres, to Louis, lord of
Gruuthuse and to other noblemen and captains, ordering them to
muster troops. On 31 July the bailiffs of Flanders were ordered to
have their Flemish forces ready, and Burgundy Herald left Brussels
with orders for the vassals of Luxembourg to be ready to serve their

---

[1] ADN B2064, f. 234b and AGR CC2422, f. 103b.
[2] ADN B2064, fos. 277a–b.

duke in arms.[1] By 12–15 August more definite plans had emerged: the grand bailiff of Hainault and other Hainault nobles were ordered to be at Binche on 20 August ready to serve against the Liègeois. But there were delays. It was only on 21 August that a messenger left Brussels with orders for these troops 'to wear different colours from the others' and they only received orders to move to Huy on 13 September, when it was too late.

Some time before 14 September, that is, before the fall of Huy, the decision had been made by Charles and his council to replace or supplement these piecemeal measures by a mass attack against Liège, to be launched on 8 October. In the second half of September requests or summonses for military assistance went out in all directions. The Flemish towns were asked for pikemen; the vassals of the two Burgundies were called out; the dukes of Guelders and Cleves were invited to come to Brussels and accompany Charles on the campaign; the king of England and the count palatine of the Rhine and other German allies of Burgundy were asked to send what forces they could.[2] The Nürnberg cannoneer, Master Hans, was sent for, and he served Charles from 1 October, when he left home with three varlets, until his return to Nürnberg on 21 November. The duke also paid his wife £50 to help her look after the children in her husband's absence. Thus, the Burgundian military machine rumbled into action and neither the reputed intercession of Charles's mother Isabel, nor the royal ambassador, Louis de Luxembourg, count of St. Pol and constable of France, nor even a cardinal and a papal legate, who arrived in Brussels from France on Louis's behalf as much as on the pope's, with plans of mediation, were able to deter the duke from his projected military solution to the problem of Liège. As the Milanese ambassador at the French court put it, he was 'stubborn, fierce, and only wanted war'.[3]

Duke Charles set out from Louvain to take the field against Liège on 19 October 1467 to a fanfare of twelve trumpets. The size and composition of his army, which, as usual, was said to have been

---

[1] ADN B2064, fos. 187b–189b, 193b and 196; and, for the next sentences, fos. 234b–235, 236b, 237 and 277.
[2] *Collection de documens inédits*, i. 156–162, *Hansisches Urkundenbuch*, ix. 258–9 and ADN B2064, fos. 277b–278, 281b–282, 284, 334 etc., and, for the next sentence, fos. 285b and 417b–418. For the rest of the paragraph, besides the sources cited on p. 11 above, see Petri, *Gesta pontificum Leodiensium*, 166, and *Lettres de Louis XI*, iii. 373 and 377.
[3] *Lettres de Louis XI*, iii. 377.

unequalled in living memory,[1] is difficult to ascertain, but the ducal accounts list the principal noblemen and captains and record payments to them on the basis of 9,830 units or *payes*, while an eyewitness's letter states that Charles had 2,350 lances, not counting archers. The number of combatants represented by these figures has been estimated at 18,000, and the total size of Charles's army at 35–45,000 men; but it was probably a good deal smaller.

The bulk of this Burgundian army of 1476 consisted of the duke's courtiers and their followings and the nobility of the Low Countries and their men. Only a few vassals from Burgundy proper, led by the marshal, Thibaud de Neuchâtel, arrived in time for the campaign: the rest were countermanded in November.[2] It must not be imagined that the entire ducal army was recruited from within the ducal territories. On the contrary, Burgundian vassals arrived from places like Metz, whence a contingent of two vassals and two varlets set out 'in good fettle' on Saturday 3 October, as well as from the bishopric of Liège and elsewhere. By far the largest single contingent was that of Anthony, bastard of Burgundy, with 1,353 *payes*, but five members of the Picardy-based house of Luxembourg contributed over 1,200 *payes* between them, and there were strong contingents from Holland and Flanders. The second largest contingent was led by Adolf of Cleves, lord of Ravenstein, brother of the duke of Cleves, and he commanded one of the three divisions of the ducal army, the other two being placed under the bastard of Burgundy and the duke himself. It is uncertain how successful Duke Charles's officials were in persuading the Flemish towns to muster

---

[1] ASM Pot. est. Borgogna 515/10. All references to Milanese despatches in what follows are to the *busta* followed, after an oblique stroke, by the page number pencilled onto the documents when they were microfilmed. There was a separate pagination for ASM Pot. est. Borgogna 515 (1467–1474), another for 516–17 (1475), and a third for 518–20 (1476). The films used by me are now in the possession of the University Library, Hull. These and other diplomatic documents are in process of publication in *Dispatches with related documents of Milanese ambassadors in France and Burgundy, 1450–1483*, of which the first two volumes only, covering the years 1450–1461, have appeared at the time of writing. For the preceding sentence, see ADN B2064, f. 352b. For this paragraph, besides sources already mentioned on p. 11, see Guillaume, *Organisation militaire*, 184–5, Brusten, *Armée bourguignonne*, 60–70 and *Collection de documens inédits*, i. 156–62.

[2] Plancher, iv. no. 204. For the Metz vassals, see Aubrion, *Journal*, 27; for Ghent, see *Dagboek van Gent*, ii. 208, and for the English, ADN B2064, fos. 334, 337, 355b–356b, 399 etc.

B

the 4,000 pikemen required of them but, after much argument, some of these infantry contingents certainly turned out. At Ghent, in the throes of revolution, the duke's request was flatly refused. Nonetheless, a private contingent was recruited and paid for by 'the good men of the town'. English archers were recruited too, and some arrived at Calais in time to be brought by a ducal guide to Charles's army at the siege of St. Trond; others had to be countermanded later.

It was at Tirlemont in Brabant between 19 and 26 October that Duke Charles made his final dispositions for the campaign. But, before he set out to lay siege to St. Trond, he sent a force in advance to try to recapture Huy by surprise. One of the participants, Jehan lord of Haynin, wrote a graphic account of this operation which perhaps illuminates the nature of contemporary warfare more effectively than descriptions of pitched battles.[1]

And I, Jehan lord of Haynin, and my brother Colart de Vendegies, to obey the command of my lord the duke and at the request and prayer of my most honoured and redoubted lord, the lord of Fiennes, we left my place at Louvignies near Bavay on a Thursday, 8 October, eighteen of us, foot and horse, to go on campaign in the company and under the standard of my lord of Fiennes. We lodged at Mairieux near Maubeuge, and on Saturday 10 October at Bersillies-l'Abbaye, and on Monday 12 October we found the standard and the company of my lord of Fiennes in the fields near Binche. . . . We and the [rest of] my lord of Fiennes's company were reviewed on Friday 16 October and on that day I was 44 years old. On the night of 18 October we lodged at and around Noville-sur-Méhaigne, and on Monday 19th at Moulembais near Jodoigne. While we were there, my lord of Fiennes our chief went to the duke at Tirlemont to get news and to learn what he wanted him to do. This was Tuesday, 20th, and on his return he told me and some others that my lord the duke had charged him and his men with an undertaking he had refused to several others, which, if it pleased God, would be to his profit and advantage. Within an hour everyone was to be fully dressed and armed in his lodgings ready to set out. The time of departure was about 3.0 or 4.0 p.m. Once in the fields, we rode at a fast trot when possible, hoping to get beyond Namur, which was a good five great leagues from our starting-point, that evening. But we had gone only two or three leagues when darkness fell. There was no moonlight . . . and it got so dark that we could neither see the way, nor scarcely pick out one horse from another, unless it was white or grey. People began to get lost; a man-at-arms fell on one side; an archer on the other.

---

[1] De Haynin, *Mémoires*, i. 213–21; compare d'Oudenbosch, *Chronique*, 177–8.

We rode like this for a good two leagues, taking one or two hours in the darkness because we could only go step by step, until most of the company arrived at 9.0 or 10.0 in the evening at a village a league from Namur called Vedrin. One could only find the houses by seeing the lights inside them, and, wherever they could be found, people dismounted without orders and in disarray, taking off and throwing down what they could. We were extremely hungry and continued so, especially as the local people, hearing the disturbance and the noise of men, horses and armour and knowing nothing of our arrival, thought we were from Liège. Several fled and some women were very frightened. We had been told that, as soon as the moon rose, after midnight, we would leave the place, so most of us remained all night in arms with horses saddled, scarcely eating or drinking anything that night except what we had brought with us. But all this trouble and difficulty was to no purpose because we didn't leave early the next morning. It was a wonder that nobody broke a leg or an arm. Some people who went to the church broke down two doors in order to lodge in it; that is to say, the door of the nave and the door of the chancel; but we didn't leave next morning till it was quite late.

That same Tuesday, 20 October, the lord of Bièvres, bailiff of Hainault, and the lord of Aymeries and their company set fire to several houses and villages in the territory of Liège and burnt down a large number.

On the next day, Wednesday 21st, my lord of Fiennes and his company left Vedrin and waited a long time at the gate of La Herbate in Namur for his men to arrive and assemble. And they did this only with difficulty, because it had been such a dark night. When most of them had collected together they passed through Namur and took the direct route towards Huy hoping that there would be no one there, or at most only a few people, and that, when these saw the troops, they would be frightened into abandoning the town. This enterprise had been undertaken partly on the advice of some people of Namur then in the lord of Fiennes's company. That Wednesday they rode all day till evening, when they lodged in a village called Bonneville, in the county of Namur not far from Samson, and around and beyond it. The lord of Fiennes went to see the lord of Boussu at his lodging and he promised that he would accompany him next day, but he sent to excuse himself that night because he had received a letter from my lord the duke summoning him to Tirlemont.

The next day, which was Thursday 22 October, the company left Bonneville at daybreak and went towards Huy, but because of the very bad road through woods, mountains and valleys, where for the most part one could only go in single file and cautiously, though it was only two or three leagues to Huy, it must have been 10.0 or 11.0 a.m., or even later, by the time we arrived outside the town. Some said an undertaking of this kind should be carried out at daybreak; others said no, it could have just as successful an outcome at midday or at 9.0 a.m., as any other time. . . .

When we were half a league away [from Huy] it began to rain hard, which continued most of the day. The infantry, numbering about three or four hundred, were ordered to advance. Some of them were from the town of Huy, having left it when it was taken [by the men of Liège]. These infantrymen were led to the summit of the highest hill overlooking the town and castle towards the paper-mill, from which [the enemy] could soon be seen and discovered. After the infantry went the mounted archers, four or five hundred strong. When they reached the top of the hill these troops, with the men-at-arms after them, numbering about sixty, their swordsmen with them, might altogether have numbered at most 900 combatants, not more. The archers dismounted, took off their spurs, and with the infantrymen, who were all from Namur, as well as my lord Anthoine de Halewin, Baudoin de Lannoy, Hue de Humières the bailiff of Namur and the bailiff of Messines in Flanders, Hollebeque by name, they descended the hill, crossed the stream called Le Hoyoux and approached the walls to shoot at the town gate, which they found closed. They set fire to it. On the way they found a single man outside the town, whom they killed. My lord of Fiennes and his men-at-arms had stayed in order of battle on the top of the hill, out in the open and within cannon-shot of the castle, to cover and support the archers and infantry if they had to retreat. Some of the infantrymen, especially some twelve, sixteen or twenty who lived at Huy, left the rest without giving word, and worked round to the left to try to enter the town by a hidden postern they knew of. Most of them were taken or killed but the rest escaped. When the people in the town, and the lady of Lyntre and Collart delle Porte who were in the castle, realised that they were under attack, they summoned all their people to arms as fast as possible, rang their bell and sounded a bugle in the castle and began to fire at the infantry with cross-bows, culverins and serpentines. One of Lois de Bournonville's archers was hit through the thigh by a culverin, the bullet from which remained in the other thigh; he had to be taken to a doctor at Binche, where he recovered. One man, named Henry de Bournonville, was killed by a cross-bow bolt, as well as two of Hustin de Lannoy's archers . . . and several others, some ten or twelve in all, at most. When [the defenders] saw that the skirmishing was continuing so long, they lit a fire high up in the castle as if signalling for help. From the castle they fired three or four serpentine shots right among the men-at-arms drawn up on the hill. It was amazing that several weren't killed or wounded for there is no sense in remaining drawn up in battle order within cannon-shot except when marching against the enemy. . . . The men who had gone down [to the walls] attacked them and skirmished for at least an hour or thereabouts and clearly saw that they were labouring in vain, for they had neither a single ladder to scale the walls, nor a pick-axe nor a hook to remove stones, nor any device for cutting or breaking down the gate, nor any artillery and, though some of the men from Namur said: 'They are fleeing and we'll dine and drink good wine again at night inside the town', the contrary was the truth, because they weren't fleeing at all. . . . So everybody climbed back up the hill and got back to their horses as fast as they could, and so returned without having achieved anything else. . . . If those in the town had been powerful enough to sally out in force our company would have been in great danger unless God had come to their aid. For they numbered only a few and were a good ten leagues in advance of any men-at-arms who might have been able to help them. Moreover they could only retreat or depart in single file from the said hill.

At Liège, the influence of the extremists and their popular leader Raes de Lyntre, whose wife had helped to defend Huy on 22 October, had become gradually more assured and aggressive ever since their successful capture and thorough looting of that place more than a month before. Although their hated bishop had contrived to escape from Huy, the Liègeois had appropriated his standard, his vestments and his herald's tunic, and even placed them on public exhibition in Liège. Rejecting the advice of a French royal emissary, François Royer, that they should proceed with extreme caution, and relying on the help of our Lady of Montenaken and the patron saint of Liège, St. Lambert, they reacted to the Burgundian raids of 20 October, mentioned by Jehan de Haynin, by preparing on the next day to march out in arms against the duke. But the downpour on 22 October, as well as the killing of one of their leader's horses, put off their departure. Eventually, in the afternoon of 23 October, the citizen army of Liège, accompanied by a veritable procession of clergy who were forcibly persuaded to accompany it with the banner of St. Lambert and a statue of our Lady, left the town after the traditional peals had been rung on all the church bells. What happened next is a mystery which puzzled at least one contemporary chronicler, [1] for the Burgundians who arrived at St. Trond to begin the siege on

---

[1] De Haynin, *Mémoires*, i. 224; compare d'Oudenbosch, *Chronique*, 177–8. These are the two main authorities for what follows on the Brustem campaign. De la Marche, *Mémoires*, iii. 63–8 and de Commynes, *Mémoires*, ed. Calmette and Durville, i. 105–10 are important too, though de Commynes is here as mendacious as ever. For other sources, see p. 11 n. 1 above. The documents printed by Diegerick, in *BSSLL* v (1861), 357–71 are reprinted in *Régestes de Liège*, iv. 233–50. Brusten, *L'armée bourguignonne*, 162–3 has a map.

the evening of Tuesday, 27 October, and spent the night in arms there, discovered next day that the Liègeois were advancing only distantly towards them. What had they been doing since their departure from Liège the previous Friday? Why was it only on Wednesday, 28 October that their van, comprising the men of Looz and Tongres, began to take up defensive positions in and around the village of Brustem, which was a mere 35 km from Liège?

Duke Charles lost no time in arranging his men in order of battle outside Brustem on the afternoon of 28 October. He had drawn up battle orders in writing the night before and now personally rode round the various companies carrying these instructions with him. Battle was joined in the first place by the artillery, with which each side was well supplied, but to little effect. The fire from the army of Liège mostly went harmlessly over the Burgundians' heads, while the Burgundian artillery seems to have done the same over the Liègeois, though it inconvenienced them by bringing down branches of trees as thick as legs and arms onto their heads. The Liègeois enjoyed the better defensive position, protected as they were by trees and thick hedges, with marshes covering their flanks, and Duke Charles, fearful of a surprise attack by the enemy during the coming night, resolved to try to dislodge them by sending his archers against them. These archers were ordered to dismount, leaving their horses to be looked after by some of their companions, a single man holding up to ten or twelve horses. Even then, many of them were stolen during the battle.[1] With some difficulty the archers successfully fought their way through hedges and ditches into the village of Brustem, the mounted men-at-arms following where they had cleared the way. A mounted attack down the main road from St. Trond to Brustem by Philip the Good's bastard son Baudouin was beaten off by the defenders and, indeed, de Haynin tells us that there was no way in which the Burgundian cavalry could successfully attack the enemy: the infantry, apparently consisting of two or three thousand archers only, won the day for Duke Charles. The battle had not begun until the afternoon, and nightfall saved the lives of many of the Liègeois, though their tents and pavilions, their carts and baggage, and their artillery, all fell into the hands of the Burgundians. Many of their leaders remained dead on the field of battle, together with three canons of St. Lambert's. But the seneschal of Lyons, François Royer, and

[1] Compare de Haynin, *Mémoires*, i. 225 and 230 with ADN B2064, f. 333a-b.

Raes de Lyntre, the most prominent of all the Liège revolutionaries, escaped.

Brustem was a brilliant victory for Duke Charles, but the success was by no means effectively exploited. His soldiers now dallied at Brustem viewing and robbing the corpses and amassing loot.[1]

> We found provisions in their carts which came in most handy to some of the troops. Among others, some of my, Jehan de Haynin's, archers brought in a cart with a barrel of wine which lasted us, nineteen in number, two days, together with bread, salt meat and cheese in another cart, which lasted fourteen days. . . . Several people thought that if the van or another large body of troops had advanced into enemy territory the day after the battle, they would have done very well and freely and easily got as far as Looz, or Tongres or even the city of Liège. But nothing was done.

It was only on 1 November that troops of the Burgundian van left the siege of St. Trond to advance towards Liège. They returned, on finding the route blocked and defended, but advanced the next day along another road, burnt down the castle and town of Heers, belonging to Raes de Lyntre, and took Looz without opposition. On the same day, 2 November, St. Trond surrendered. Meanwhile the Liègeois were in disarray though their leader Raes, aided by the French seneschal, did his best to restore morale. It was the clerics who took the initiative in treating for peace and, as place after place in the territory of Liège fell to, or was ransacked by, the Burgundians so, inside the walls of Liège the will to fight on ebbed away. Wellen was burnt; Tongres surrendered on 6 November; and by the time Charles was lodging on 9 and 10 November at Othée, scene of his grandfather's victory against Liège in 1408, negotiations were in full swing. On 11–12 November, as the Burgundians took up quarters in the outskirts of the city, Liège was convulsed by an internal crisis which led to the precipitate flight of the extremists and their leader Raes de Lyntre, as well as of the French seneschal François Royer, who departed so hurriedly that he left behind his superbly ornamented sallet. On 12 November ducal banners were symbolically raised above the gates of the conquered city; on 13 November the destruction of gates and walls began, and the duke and his army made their triumphal entry on 17 November, after a civic deputation numbering 340 persons had been forced to grovel before him in their shirts and socks.

[1] De Haynin, *Mémoires*, i. 230–1.

The peace settlement, or judicial sentence, dictated by Charles to Liège on 28 November 1467 was absolutist in character and more extreme, in its severity, than the similar settlement imposed by Duke John the Fearless in 1408 after the battle of Othée.[1] Then, the town's charters of privileges were confiscated, the craft gilds of Liège were suppressed, the currencies of Flanders and Brabant were made legal tender in the bishopric, and the duke of Burgundy was given free passage through Liège for himself and his troops. That ducal sentence against Liège was revoked in 1417 by the Emperor-elect; now all these measures were repeated. But now, even more than in 1408, the rights and interests of the Empire, and of the Church, were totally disregarded. For Duke Charles's sentence abolished the laws and customs, the lawcourts, indeed the entire civic constitution, of Liège. The *perron*, a bronze column in the market place, symbol of the civic dignity and jurisdiction of Liège, was removed to Bruges. Instead of the many existing lawcourts and jurisdictions all justice was in future to be administered by fourteen echevins appointed annually by the bishop, and they were to judge cases 'according to reason and written law, without regard to the bad styles, usages and customs' formerly in use. Liège itself was declared no longer fit to be the seat of a bishop and its spiritual court was to be removed and divided between Louvain, Maastricht and Namur. An attempt was made utterly to demilitarize the city: her citizens were forbidden to carry arms, her artillery was confiscated, her walls and gates were demolished, her alliances were abrogated. Finally, as in 1408, a large sum of money, in addition to what was already owing under the terms of the 1466 treaties, was to be paid to the duke, who was to be recognized once again as hereditary guardian or *advocatus* of the city and territories of Liège.

Other ducal documents of the same date, 28 November, were concerned with the implementation of this judgement. A special financial official, to act under the supervision of the *chambre des comptes* at Brussels, was appointed to receive and administer the money owing from Liège, and Guy de Brimeu, lord of Humbercourt, was confirmed in his office of ducal representative at Liège, with his title altered from governor to lieutenant-general. But Liège, though conquered, penalized and temporarily occupied by the duke of

---

[1] Vaughan, *John the Fearless*, 63–5. The text of the 1467 treaty is in *Collection de documens inédits*, ii. 437–73, and *Recueil des ordonnances de Liège*, 615–28 (see too the conditions imposed on St. Trond and Franchimont on pp. 608–11 and 629–31). See too Gorissen, *BFPL* cciii (1972), 129–35.

Burgundy, could not be incorporated into the Burgundian state. It was part of the Empire; it belonged to the Church; its ruler was Charles's cousin and ally, the prince-bishop Louis de Bourbon. All Charles contrived in the direction of actual ownership was the confiscation of the lands and rents in Brabant and Hainault belonging to Liègeois and their application to his domains there, and the purchase of the mortgaged provostship of Bouillon from the person to whom the impecunious bishop had sold it. [1] Needless to say, there is no truth in the Augsburg chronicler's assertion that Duke Charles, already part-owner of Maastricht, now took over the whole of it. In fact, he continued, as before, to share power there with the bishop and chapter of Liège though he certainly issued letters 'given in *our* town of Maastricht'.

Through the winter of 1467–8 the unhappy city of Liège was administered jointly by Louis de Bourbon and Guy de Brimeu, while her clergy and citizens argued about the best means of raising the money to pay the duke and watched his commissioners dismantling their walls and gates. Though the extremists among the artisan elements of her population, together with the anti-Burgundian burgesses and nobles numbering several hundreds at least and including such leaders as Raes de Lyntre, had fled or been exiled after the battle of Brustem, the moderate leaders and the rest of the populace bitterly resented the harsh treaties imposed on them in 1466 and 1467. Indeed the clergy had drawn up a formal but secret protest against the treaty of Brustem immediately after its publication. Now, in the spring of 1468, powerful support for their cause appeared in the shape of a papal legate. Originally appointed in August 1467 as a result of Duke Philip's request for papal ratification of the treaty of St. Trond and formal raising of the interdict over Liège, Onofrio de Santa Croce, bishop of Tricarico, had received further instructions from the pope at the time of his departure from Rome in February 1468. He was sent as a mediator between the bishop and his discontented flock, and in order to persuade Duke Charles to modify the treaties of St. Trond and Brustem so that they no longer infringed the rights of the Church. No wonder his arrival on 30 April at Liège was greeted with popular rejoicing. He raised the interdict, enabling the bishop to celebrate his first mass in St. Lambert's cathedral, and on 8 June 1468 he set out to see Duke Charles at Bruges.

[1] AGR CC134, fos. 29–30 and *IAGR CC*, iv. 129. For the next sentence, see *CDS*, xxii. *Augsburg*, iii. 217 and de Dadizeele, *Mémoires*, 45.

B*

The negotiations which followed, between legate and duke, were protracted and interrupted but not unfriendly. Though Charles kept insisting that the legate should confirm the treaties as they stood, he could not afford an open break with the pope at a time when his relations with Louis XI were verging towards open warfare. The legate, on his side, was adamant in his defence of Church rights and even had the courage to remind Charles that he had openly proclaimed in all the churches in Brabant that he was taking arms against Liège to 'protect' the Church. He did however promise apostolic approval to any settlement which had been fully accepted by the bishop and clergy of Liège. Negotiations were delayed through the summer months while the duke was married and visited Holland, but they came to a head on 10 August when Charles, about to set out with his army to make war against the French on the Somme, gave audience in the chapel of his palace at Brussels to both Louis de Bourbon and Onofrio, in the presence of Louis's brother Charles de Bourbon, archbishop of Lyons. Evidently he hoped to achieve a rapid settlement of his difficulties over Liège. Onofrio, a most careful and accurate recorder of events, describes the conference thus.[1]

> The duke first turned to the legate and asked him if he still held to what he had said before, that is, that he would confirm with his and indeed the pope's authority whatever was agreed to by the duke himself, the bishop and the people of Liège. He again replied in the affirmative and the duke asked the bishop what he had to say, and whether he wanted the treaties to be confirmed, or had anything to say against them. To this the bishop replied in some trepidation that he would like to do whatever was advised by the senior clerics and Estates of Liège. Somewhat aroused, the duke turned to the bishop:
> 'I am amazed that you and the elders of your church think you might be wiser now than you were when these treaties were agreed to at Liège, especially as the crisis ought at that time to have sharpened your minds. You should remember that everything I did then at Liège to subdue the discontented populace was done at your request and in the interests of your country and church. I cannot understand what this ambiguity and anxiety means nor what causes it.'
> The bishop replied to the duke:
> 'As I understand it, most noble prince, the legate wants to ascertain

---

[1] Onofrio, *Mémoire*, ed. Bormans, 41–4. This edition superseded Bormans, *Liègeois et Bourguignons en 1468*. Besides Onofrio, who is the major source for all of what follows, and works already referred to on p. 11 above, I have used Angelo de Curribis Sabinis, *De excidio civitatis Leodiensis*. Bittmann, *Ludwig XI und Karl der Kühne*, i (1). 217–38, is of prime importance henceforth.

from us on oath whether we entirely agree to all these clauses, and if they all promote the honour, liberty and utility of the Church. Since we shall be on oath concerning this matter, we are bound to speak the truth.'

The duke was extremely annoyed on hearing this and, speaking rapidly in French, almost in a stammer, said:

'Now I recognize the tricks and deceipts of the French king Louis, who habitually rescinds afterwards with a protest what was before promised and agreed to in writing and on oath. Now Louis de Bourbon, you're trying to follow in his footsteps, but I don't care whether or not these articles are ratified. I shall put to the sword anyone who infringes my sentence, duly promulgated and accepted.' With these words, putting his hand on the hilt of his sword, he called for his horses in order to set out with his army against the king. The two brothers, the prelates of Lyons and Liège, stood there astonished, but when the legate explained that he hadn't understood what the duke had said, so rapidly and in French, first the archbishop of Lyons, then indeed the duke himself, translated it for his benefit into Latin. Having understood what he had said, the legate now turned to the duke:

'The bishop, glorious prince, did not speak so badly. You must allow the bishop, the elders of the church and the leading men of the country to offer their opinions freely on this matter. He and I will take on this business and ascertain these things from them separately. I feel sure we can deal with the matter in such a way as to preserve the honour of God and of the Church and yet not inconvenience you. . . . After all, only ten or twelve out of almost fifty articles in that peace treaty need to be altered or improved in some way because they seem to be damaging to the Church. . . . And in order that this can be achieved more solemnly and expeditiously, may it please your highness to send two of your councillors to Liège with me and the bishop to deal with the matter with us.'

The duke thought a little on hearing this, then called the legate aside and replied briefly that it did not seem to him that it would help matters for his councillors to go with them to Liège, for if this were done people might well think that he wanted to abandon his earlier treaties. Rather he alone, as legate, could ascertain from the bishop and clergy whatever in these articles they thought needed correcting or altering and he could notify the duke. But nothing must be changed without his being consulted. The legate accepted the duke's wishes. . . .

It was at this moment when a negotiated settlement seemed in sight, that the affairs of Liège took a turn for the worse. The departure of Guy de Brimeu, the duke's lieutenant-general, early in August, emboldened the exiles and fugitives from the city to begin operations with a view to returning to their homes and seizing power at Liège. They were convinced that Duke Charles would shortly be at war with France. After all, he had set out from Brussels on 10 August fully determined to attack the French, and he had ordered the general mobilization of all his vassals for 8 August. Moreover the outlaws from Liège were convinced that Charles would be defeated. Several hundred of them tried, but failed, to seize Bouillon on 4 August and, after other escapades, successful and unsuccessful, they eventually succeeded in their ambitions on 9 September. The bishop had left Liège some time before, but the legate was there, and gives a graphic description of the commotion and slaughter on that eventful day. The exiles returned with shouts of 'Long live the king and a free Liège!' and massacred those of their opponents who failed to escape in time. The legate stayed a few days to try to negotiate, then took ship down the Meuse to Maastricht, halting to bury the bodies he found floating in the river, mangled by dogs and birds. Most of those in civic office in Liège had fled or been killed, and power was assumed by the newcomers, who enjoyed considerable support among the artisans and peasants though it has yet to be demonstrated that they had been encouraged by Louis XI.

The new revolutionary leaders at Liège, like their predecessor Raes de Lyntre, belonged to the lesser nobility of the local country-side. The most prominent were Gossuin de Streel, whose father had been killed at Brustem, Jehan de Hornes, called de Wilde, and Vincent de Buren. Raising, as they openly and immediately did, the standard of revolt against Duke Charles the Bold, they snuffed out at once the flickering flame of negotiation which Onofrio had patiently lit. For, while the legate, courageously and persistently, during the next few weeks, tried and tried again to encourage the new leaders of Liège to be reasonable and moderate; to persuade the bishop to come to terms with them while taking a stronger line with the duke; and, finally, to avert the hostility of Charles and his leading men; while the legate bustled to and fro on these pacificatory missions, Charles was organizing a punitive expedition to destroy the city which had so repeatedly defied him. On 17 September he appointed Guy de Brimeu to a new office: that of lieutenant and captain-general with orders to assemble forces in Brabant, Limbourg, Luxembourg, Hainault, Namur and elsewhere and march against Liège. From 9 September onwards the fate of Liège was sealed. Its fortifications had been thoroughly and systematically demolished during the previous winter. It was an open city. Moreover, as the events of the next few weeks were to show, the presence, and the activities, of the legate Onofrio, well-meaning and courageous as he was, and immensely loyal and sympathetic to the citizens of Liège, served only to hamper, even at times to paralyse, the frantic efforts of the stricken city to offer effective military resistance to the duke.

While the legate strove for peace, the revolutionary government at Liège prepared for war. Cannon were borrowed from Aachen. A high earth wall was hastily thrown up all round; stones were piled in front of what was left of the gates; wooden blockhouses were erected. Guy de Brimeu for his part lost no time in gathering forces and moving in to attack. On 1 October he was reported on the borders of the principality, at Meeffe, and at midday on 9 October he had reached Tongres with his men. There he was confronted, not by military resistance, but by Onofrio the apostolic legate, with whom however he flatly refused to treat, alleging that he was under firm orders from the duke to negotiate with no one and to kill anyone from Liège he came across. Joining forces with those of the bishop, he fully intended to attack Liège itself the very next day. He pressed the legate to accompany their expedition, as his presence would help to intimidate the Liègeois and, after all, they were fighting these rebels on behalf of the Church. Onofrio was livid. He told Guy de Brimeu bluntly that, far from fighting for the Church, his war against Liège was being fought for booty, vengeance and blood. His warning to Guy that he would find plenty of people in Liège contemptuous of death and fully prepared to fight was justified that very night, when Jehan de Wilde and Gossuin de Streel led a picked band of men into Tongres, the fortifications of which, like those of Liège, had been demolished by the Burgundians. Not only did Tongres fall into their hands, but they held Guy de Brimeu himself prisoner for a time, and the next day they returned in triumph to Liège, taking their bishop and the legate with them.

Charles's initial attack against Liège had foundered, but his whole military situation was rapidly changing for the better. His war against France, which in August and early September had seemed so inevitable to the rebels of Liège, and to many others, had been post-poned: on 1 October the conference of Ham at last resulted in a truce and on 6 October Cardinal Balue arrived at Péronne with offers from Louis XI of a firm alliance between Burgundy and the French crown. On 9 October King Louis himself went to see Charles there in the hopes of a permanent settlement. From Péronne, on 6 October, three days before the events at Tongres related above, Charles sent a messenger to 'the army of Burgundy' ordering it to proceed at once to attack Liège.[1] These were the forces from Burgundy and Savoy, commanded by the marshal of Burgundy, Thibaud de Neuchâtel, and Philip of Savoy, count of Bresse, which were then at Namur and in Hainault on their way to join the duke. They recaptured Tongres without difficulty on 12 or 13 October. During the next ten days or so, while Onofrio did his best to induce the Burgundian captains to accept a truce and to persuade the Liègeois not to fight but to rely instead on the pacific assistance of God and St. Lambert, Charles prepared to march against them in person, with his main army. He even persuaded the king of France to accompany him, though against the wishes of the royal captains and councillors.[2]

Louis's role in the affairs of Liège in 1468 had so far been virtually limited to the despatch of a messenger or two early in October offering to help the legate in his efforts to stave off a disastrous war. He may now have been persuaded to take an active part, hostile to the city which had persistently counted him among its allies, by Duke Charles himself, who perhaps feared a French attack in his rear if he advanced to Liège without the king. But Louis's Liège policy was more probably dictated by his political situation in France, where his power was coming increasingly to rest on his alliance with the house of Bourbon, and it may have been the influence of the three brothers of Louis de Bourbon which decided King Louis's actions at this time. After all, the bishop's whole political future was at stake, and his life remained in danger throughout these critical weeks. Indeed, some chroniclers allege that he was reported killed to the king and duke at Péronne after the Liègeois raid on Tongres and that this news was only corrected a day later. Thus, from the point of view of Louis de Bourbon's three brothers, which may have been shared by the king, the Liège campaign was an expedition to rescue their brother and restore him to power at Liège. They all accompanied the king and the duke in the field: at the castle of Fallais, on 25

[1] ADN B2068, f. 285b, cited by Bittmann, *Ludwig XI und Karl der Kühne*, i (1). 257. On this and the next sentence, besides de Haynin, *Mémoires*, ii. 70–1 and Onofrio, *Mémoire*, 108–9 (who wrongly makes the diversion of troops a result of the Tongres news but admits he does not know whether or not they received orders from the duke) see especially the full version of Anthoine de Loisey's letter in de Commynes, *Mémoires*, ed. Dupont, iii. 238–42 (see below p. 23 n. 1).
[2] De Chabannes, *Preuves*, ii. 261–3. For what follows see Michelet, *Histoire de France*, viii. 59–62, Pauwels, *Historia*, 215–16, de Roye, *Chronique scandaleuse*, i. 215–16, and d'Oudenbosch, *Chronique*, 211. See too below, pp. 53–6.

October, as Guy de Brimeu, lord of Humbercourt afterwards related to the chronicler Adrian d'Oudenbosch, the king ate at one table, the duke of Burgundy sat at another, and the bishop of Liège, who had only that day finally escaped from danger, ate at a third with his three brothers the archbishop of Lyons, Charles de Bourbon, the duke of Bourbon, John II, and Pierre, lord of Beaujeu. Nor should it be forgotten that one of Charles's principal captains at this time, Jehan de Chalon, lord of Arguel, had been married the year before to Jeanne de Bourbon, sister of the above-mentioned brothers. She too was present at Fallais on 25 October.

The war which now began was brief but bitterly contested. It was characterized by a series of desperate but unsuccessful counter-attacks by the Liègeois against the advancing ducal contingents. The first such engagement was fought at Lantin on 22 October while Charles was still at Namur. According to Onofrio, who was in Liège at this critical moment, the Liègeois, though unused to fighting on horseback, insisted on riding into battle on the many superb Burgundian horses they had captured at Tongres. They were easily defeated, though a detachment fought bravely on in the village of Lantin till it was surrounded and wiped out. Near panic followed this defeat in Liège: the legate, the bishop, and many of the clergy judiciously withdrew with two days' food supply into the great tower of St. Lambert's cathedral. But the expected Burgundian assault on the city was delayed, and it was not until 26 October that the duke's army took up quarters in the suburbs, while Charles and the king were only at Momalle, 17 km away. Late that evening the Liègeois sallied forth and captured two Burgundian banners during a three-hour skirmish. Later still, at 4.0 a.m. on 27 October, Jehan de Wilde and his men delivered another fierce attack on the Burgundians lodged outside the city. The chronicler Jehan de Haynin had a narrow escape, and his half-brother, Colart de Vendegies, who was with him, was never seen again after this nocturnal affray, though it was not till 1475 that a court finally pronounced his demise.[1] In the event, though Guy de Brimeu and others were wounded, the Liègeois were driven off with heavy casualties. Their leader, Jehan de Wilde, crawled back into the city mortally wounded.

King Louis and Duke Charles arrived at the scene on 27 October, but bad weather on Saturday, 29 October, caused the planned general assault on Liège to be deferred. That night, 29–30 October,

[1] Poncelet, *ACCAL* viii (1940), 268–95.

Gossuin de Streel led out a body of picked men, whom de Commynes, probably erroneously, described as Franchimontois, that is, from the district of Franchimont,[1] to make a last desperate attack on the Burgundians. Their aim was apparently to penetrate silently and undetected to the lodgings of the king and duke and kill or capture them both. But the alarm was given as the attackers entered the kitchen of the house where Duke Charles was quartered by a group of women camp-followers who recognized the Liège accent of one of their number, and a confused struggle ensued in which the majority, including their leader, were killed. With Louis XI on this occasion was the sixteen-year-old Bernese nobleman, Ludwig von Diesbach. He records that the king's life was only just saved, and that his tent was set on fire. As to Duke Charles, he was saved by the archers of his bodyguard, 'unfortunately', says Ludwig, 'for it would have been a good thing' if he had been killed there and then, 'so as to save the life of many a fine knight and soldier whom he subsequently killed'.[2]

The assault on Liège took place on the morning of Sunday, 30 October 1468. According to Diederik Pauwels, a canon of Gorinchem who obtained much information from one of Charles's bodyguards, the duke swore by St. George that, as the Liègeois had visited him that night, he would now pay them a visit, even if he lost half his army doing it. He then issued free wine at his lodgings to all his men. Jehan de Haynin claims that the signal for the assault was to be the firing of a great bombard, but many of Charles's men did not even wait for it. There was little or no organized resistance. The wretched city was overrun by an army which was almost international in character. Amongst its leaders and captains, besides Duke Charles himself and King Louis, were Louis de Luxembourg, count of St. Pol and constable of France; Duke John II of Bourbon and his brothers the archbishop of Lyons and the bishop of Liège; Philip of Savoy, count of Bresse with his brothers the count of Romont and the bishop of Geneva; Thibaud de Neuchâtel the marshal of Bur-

---

[1] No doubt some were from Franchimont, but others must surely have been from Liège and perhaps elsewhere in the principality. The controversy about their number and identity has been recently reviewed, with references, by Legros, *La vie wallonne* xliii (1969), 113–21, but few have dared to question the authority of de Commynes, supported as it has been by the historian of Liège, G. Kurth, as well as by two famous Franchimontois, Pirenne and Fairon (the latter in *Wallonia* xxii (1914), 136–55).

[2] Von Diesbach, *Chronik*, 173.

gundy; Anthony, bastard of Burgundy; Adolf of Cleves, lord of
Ravenstein and brother of the duke of Cleves. No doubt the near
unanimous report of the chroniclers, that Louis XI wore a cross of
St. Andrew, the Burgundian insignia, as he entered Liège, is accurate;
but they and other contemporaries are less likely to be right in stating
that he too cried out 'Long live Burgundy!' According to Diederik
Pauwels what he did was to reprimand those of his people who cried
'Long live the king!', telling them that they ought to be shouting
'Long live Burgundy!', and this is borne out by de Haynin's version:
'Avant, enfans! cryes Bourgogne.'[1]

Three contemporary letters, written by soldiers in Duke Charles's
army, provide information about the conquest of Liège. One of them,
who was in the company of Count Engelbert II of Nassau, wrote to
Engelbert's father Count John that very night, finishing a long and
interesting letter with the remark that he was very tired because it
was around midnight, and he had run out of paper. Another, the
Burgundian Anthoine de Loisey, writing a few days later, grumbles
that the town had by then been so thoroughly sacked that he could
not even find a piece of paper, until he discovered some in an old
book. He complained that, though the Burgundian contingent had
the honour, on 30 October, of leading the attack on Liège, they had
been ordered thereafter to remain in arms and in battle order in the
market place during the whole of the rest of that day in case of trouble.
Thus, while they did their duty, the Picards and others enjoyed the
best of the looting. His countryman, Jehan de Mazille, the third
correspondent, bears this out, alleging that while they were stationed
in the market place, 'the other men-at-arms and archers ransacked
all our lodgings and broke all the duke's orders'.

Before he embarked on the organized destruction of the conquered
city, Charles permitted his soldiers several days of systematic looting.
Though he ordered the churches to be spared, they were not: indeed
in some cases people were actually killed inside them. One chronicler
says that not a single book, or chalice, or cassock was left in them:
Charles's troops removed the clocks, they put on the vestments and

---

[1] Pauwels, *Historia*, 223 and de Haynin, *Mémoires*, ii. 80. For the next paragraph, see the letters of Anthoine de Loisey and Jehan de Mazille, of 3 and
8 November, partly printed in Gachard, *BCRH* iii (1840), 29–34 and *Régestes
de Liège*, iv. 302–7, and in full in de Commynes, *Mémoires*, ed. Dupont, iii.
238–49. De Loisey's letter is also printed in de Comines, *Mémoires*, ed.
Lenglet du Fresnoy, iii. 82–4. The letter sent to Count John of Nassau is
printed under the year 1467 in *Speierische Chronik*, 497–9.

danced in them, behaving like Turks or heathens, and everyone they could lay their hands on was thrown into the Meuse.[1] The sources which report thirty or even forty thousand people killed are certainly wide of the mark: many had fled, and there seems to have been little large-scale massacring. For looting purposes the different quarters of the town had been allotted to different divisions of the army, and the main business in the next few days was the search for and removal of valuables. One person who did particularly well was the bishop of Geneva, Jehan Louis de Savoie. His return through Lyons with several cartloads of loot from Liège was noted by an Italian observer there in January 1469. Many of the precious possessions of the Liège churches found their way by gift or purchase into other churches, but Duke Charles expressly ordered all the ecclesiastical loot to be returned whence it came, or reparation made. This no doubt explains the existence of a curious document in which these objects are listed in detail: relics, books, bells, missals, ornaments, chalices and so on are reported in the churches of Picardy, Hainault, and Flanders as well as in private hands. A cope from the church of St. Denis at Liège found its way into the abbey of St. Denis at Rheims; some of the church of St. Denis's books were bought by a canon of Tournai; a silver cup of theirs was in the bailiff of Hainault's possession. On 10 November a Dominican staying at the hôtel du Vent in Diest 'had with him a box full of service books given him by Oste Gosson'. From another source, we learn that efforts were made, in spite of the duke's decree, to obtain some of the stalls and stained glass from the Liège churches for the church of Notre-Dame at Namur! Every chronicler, however distant or ill-informed, has some account of the sack of Liège, using imagination where information lacks. The Austrian parson, Jacob Unrest, has the burnt ruins of Liège dismantled and buried, and even contrives a fall of red snow, soon afterwards, in Carinthia.

The burning and demolition of Liège, like the looting, was organized and systematic, but recent scholarship has shown that it

---

[1] *Chronijk van Overmaas*, 28–9; compare *Chronijk van Maastricht*, 75. For the next sentence, see, for example, Maupoint, *Journal*, 111 and *CDS*, xxii. *Augsburg*, iii. 217. Apart from the sources already cited (especially p. 11 n. 1 above), I have used for this paragraph, AGR MSS. divers 1173, f. 122 (transcript of Janono Choyro's despatch to Milan of 12 January 1469), Bormans, *BIAL* viii (1866), 181–207, Zumthor and Noomen, *Un prêtre montheysan et le sac de Liège en 1468*, and Unrest, *Österreichische Chronik*, 22–3.

was only partial.[1] Besides the churches, many houses were left intact, though the city centre was effectively gutted. An entry in the ducal accounts records that, on 3 November, a messenger was sent to Tirlemont and Maastricht asking for all available carpenters and workmen to be sent to demolish the houses nearest the churches of Liège to stop the churches from being burnt when the duke set fire to the city. The work of destruction was carried out by Frederic de Wittem, the castellan and *drossart* of Limbourg, and a team of men from that duchy, traditional victim of Liègeois raids. They are said to have lit a new fire in a different place in the city every morning for seven weeks. Long after Charles himself left the city the demolition and repression continued. Special commissioners inventoried, sought out and confiscated the belongings of those hostile to the duke; the Pont des Arches, the only bridge across the Meuse in Liège at that time, was partly demolished by labourers from Liège's rival Maastricht; new law courts were set up as laid down in the 1467 treaty, and efforts were made to remove the Church courts to Maastricht, Namur and Louvain; the duke's financial officers continued to collect the moneys owing by way of fines and reparations until eventually some three-quarters of a million pounds had been paid over; and a ducal garrison was installed and a fortress built on the so-called Isle de la Cité, a quarter of the city cut off from the rest by a branch of the Meuse, which Charles persuaded Louis de Bourbon to make over to him. This was to be repopulated by ducal subjects from Brabant and to be given the name of Brabant. Instead, it became known as the Isle le Duc. All this was presided over by Duke Charles's lieutenant-general at Liège, Guy de Brimeu, lord of Humbercourt, whose close and continuous supervision of the bishop ensured that the status of that prelate, as a Burgundian puppet, remained unchanged. Henceforth Liège was, as near as could be, Burgundian. Political and military control was exercised through the Isle le Duc; judicial influence was wielded through the new courts of law; financial pressure was kept up by the ducal receivers; and

---

[1] Vrancken-Pirson, *CAPL* xxxix (1948), 35–6. I have not been able to consult her 1947 thesis, *Contribution à l'étude critique de la destruction de Liège*. For what follows, see ADN B2068, fos. 306a–b, Fairon, *BIAL* xlii (1912), 1–89, *IAGR CC* iv. 129–32, and de Barante, *Histoire des ducs*, ii. 325–6nn. as well as sources already cited. The documents in *Recueil de documents relatifs aux conflits soutenus par les Liégeois*, 314–18 and *Analectes historiques*, ix. 345–6 are re-edited in *Régestes de Liège*, iv. nos. 1068, 1093 and 1084 respectively.

there was even a Burgundian commercial infiltration in the shape of a toll on all merchandise passing through the city on the Meuse, which Louis de Bourbon allowed the duke of Burgundy to levy for thirty years.

It used to be thought that the magnificent gold and enamel reliquary, surmounted by statuettes of Duke Charles the Bold and St. George, which the duke gave to the cathedral of St. Lambert in 1471, represented an attempt at expiation or atonement for damages he had caused at Liège. But it is now accepted that Charles had ordered it from his goldsmith, Gerard Loyet, as long ago as 1467.[1] No doubt he left Liège for Maastricht on 9 November with a clear conscience, but he had by no means completed his planned military operations in the principality of Liège. In spite of the lateness of the season and the inclemency of the weather he was determined to invade and lay waste the land of Franchimont, where the refugees from Liège had fled and where they were said to be preparing to defend themselves. Indeed the chronicler Pauwels reports that they raided Liège one night soon after the sack in order to recover some of their valuables left hidden there, and returned to Franchimont. De Haynin describes the savage but brief campaign which followed, in mid-November, 1468; and throws light, too, on the attitudes and personality of Duke Charles.[2]

> While [the duke] was in Liège he was told that several refugees from Liège and others had withdrawn to and established themselves with their belongings in Franchimont and the surrounding woods. Since the way there, and the country, was difficult and dangerous because of the great many woods, rocks, rivers, narrow paths, mountains and valleys in the area, and since also the weather was then wintry, with rain one day and snow, hail and ice the next, most of the captains feared to go there. They also feared they might not find lodgings under cover and would have to camp in the open, which is extremely hazardous and unpleasant in the long and cold nights; though nobody can appreciate this save those who have experienced it. Moreover, for fear that provisions would neither be available for themselves nor for their horses they had little inclination to go or to undertake this [campaign], especially as some of the captains had already returned home and likewise almost all the archers, with their loot.

---

[1] Coremans, *Flanders in the fifteenth century*, 298–300, and compare de Los, *Chronique*, 66.

[2] De Haynin, *Mémoires*, ii. 84–5. Pauwels, *Historia*, 225 and 228, and de la Marche, *Mémoires*, iii. 212–13 are the other important sources for the Franchimont campaign.

When the duke had examined and considered these things, being a man of assurance and courage, who feared nothing save God, he proclaimed that everyone was to obtain three days' supply of food. He proposed to go in person and anyone who wished could follow him. And, though it was freezing very hard so that many a horse fell on the road because of the ice and there was a great deal of snow . . . nevertheless he set out and arrived at the castle and town of Franchimont. They met little or no resistance there . . . and [the duke] himself went in person through the woods on foot and on horseback after other [fugitives] who had made lodgings and huts to take refuge in. Some were killed, some taken, others fled, but all their refuges and huts were burnt down and all their belongings taken or burnt so that they lost them. Likewise the town of Franchimont was burnt and the villages around it. The provisions [our men] had taken with them came in very useful, for they found little or nothing else there. Some had their feet so badly frozen that their toe nails came out, and they suffered much from hunger, thirst and cold.

Some time later, in January 1469, news was sent from Lyons to the duke of Milan of some refugees from Liège taken prisoner on the Franchimont campaign. At Brussels Charles offered them their lives and freedom if they would swear fidelity to him. They refused, 'saying that they would rather die Liègeois than live Burgundians'.[1]

The sack of Liège sent a chill of fear through the towns of Europe. On 5 November the secretary of the Hansards at Bruges wrote to the burgomaster of Lübeck describing the Burgundian atrocities in Liège and urging solidarity among all towns. The civic authorities of Frankfurt wrote to Cologne and Aachen seeking information about the fate of Liège and received detailed replies from both cities, and Nürnberg wrote similarly to Frankfurt and Cologne. Cologne had already been accused by Duke Charles, in December 1467, of harbouring refugees from Liège. Indeed he asked the provost of St. Andrew's, Cologne, when he met him at Brussels at that time, if Raes de Lyntre was there. Again, in the winter of 1468–9, Cologne was under suspicion and sent a grovelling letter to Charles in April 1469 apologizing for harbouring refugees and promising to see that this did not happen again.

Cologne was powerful and relatively distant from the Burgundian Low Countries. Nearer, smaller, and much more at risk, was the

---

[1] AGR MSS. divers 1173, fos. 119a–b (transcript of Janono Choyro's despatch of 8 January 1469). For the next paragraph see *Hanserecesse*, vi. 87–9, Kurth, *Cité de Liège*, iii. 360–4 = *Régestes de Liège*, iv. 307–12 and 324–5, and *Hansisches Urkundenbuch*, ix. 273.

neighbour of Maastricht and Liège, the imperial city of Aachen, only some 35 km from Liège as the crow flies and actually forming part of its diocese. It seems that Charles, angered by the assistance afforded to Liège by Aachen, which is said to have included the despatch of some cannon, and prompted perhaps by his imperial ambitions, considered seriously the possibility of an attack on Aachen immediately after the sack of Liège. He certainly threatened such an action, and the terrified civic authorities brought him the keys of their city and abject apologies while he was at Maastricht on 10–12 November. Moreover there is every reason to believe de la Marche's story that, while Charles was at Polleur on 14 to 17 November, ravaging the land of Franchimont, he and his men received a welcome gift of four queues of wine from Aachen. By that time the Aachen authorities had settled with Charles for his pardon in return for 80,000 Rhenish florins, after some initial haggling in which he asked for 100,000 and they offered 60,000; but they had also to permit him and his men free entry into the town. More negotiations followed, and on 20 June 1469 a treaty between the duke and Aachen was signed in which the city placed itself under Charles's special protection and safeguard and agreed to pay him 200 Rhenish florins per annum in lieu of its obligation under an old treaty to provide archers for certain Limbourg garrisons. Charles visited Aachen in person only once: from 22 to 26 August 1473. The citizens' attitude to him on that occasion is illustrated by the fact that as soon as he had departed the town authorities, in the presence of an imperial herald, solemnly removed his 'Privy chamber' and a tent with his arms on it, which he had left standing in the market place. [1]

A few days after his visit to Aachen Duke Charles's movement south through the duchy of Luxembourg struck fear into the hearts of the town councillors of Metz. In the hope of winning his good graces they sent a deputation, on 2 September 1473, to make abject speeches to him and to present him with a gift of 100 queues of wine. These ambassadors were well received and entertained by the duke, but they were delayed, and when eventually they returned to Metz they found that their colleagues, thinking Charles must have had them killed, had busied themselves fortifying the town against the expected

[1] On Aachen see *Cronycke van Hollandt*, fos. 319 and 321b, Pauwels, *Historia*, 226–7, de la Marche, *Mémoires*, iii. 212–13, *Aachener Chronik*, 14–15 (describing Charles's 1473 visit but dating it wrongly) and Brüning, *Aus Aachens Vorzeit*, xiii (1900), 34–52. For what follows on Metz, see Aubrion, *Journal*, 54–5.

Burgundian siege and had even given shelter to numerous people who had flocked in from the countryside.

It is unnecessary to prolong here this catalogue of urban suspicion and hostility towards Charles the Bold: there will be numerous other examples in the pages that follow. The same is true of Charles the Bold's attitude to towns, already amply demonstrated in the case of Ghent and Liège. But in those places repression by force of arms was the outcome. Elsewhere, Charles's attitudes were implemented in a more subtle way. For example, on 22 August 1468 he wrote to the authorities at Abbeville forbidding them to proceed with the annual renewal of their *loi* on St. Bartholomew's Day. When they sent to enquire the reason for this prohibition, they were informed by Duke Charles that 'he had heard that those who had had the policing and government of the town during the past year were persons of good will who had governed well, with public spirit, and in the interests of the people, and this was why he had written those letters'.[1]

Charles's constant attempts to appoint to civic offices are another significant measure of his attitude to urban privileges. What right had he to ask the authorities at Courtrai to appoint his nominee as concierge of the town hall or dean of the gild of fullers? In 1469 the Four Members of Flanders received complaints that he had been intervening in appointments to offices, such as those of receiver, clerk, secretary and so on, in Ghent, Oudenaarde, Aalst and elsewhere in Flanders as well as in Courtrai, none of which were in his gift. The duke tried to do exactly the same thing in Holland and, at Dijon in 1472, the duchess Margaret of York tried but failed to intervene in the appointment of the town *procureur*. One town of importance, because of its strength and because of the protection of the king of France, to whom it belonged, was troubled very little by Charles the Bold. This was Tournai, an enclave in his territories, which he would certainly have liked to conquer or obtain. But he had to rest content with a treaty similar to that negotiated by his father Philip the Good: Tournai agreed to pay Charles the Bold 10,000 francs per annum in return for being left in peace and quiet.

At the start of Duke Charles's reign towns had taken significant initiatives which had to some extent dictated the course of events.

---

[1] Prarond, *Abbeville au temps des ducs de Bourgogne*, 195–9. For what follows, see Paris, BN MS. 5044, nos. 53, 55 and 56 (Courtrai), *Dagboek van Gent*, ii. 225–6, Blok, *BVGO* (3) iii (1886), 43, and *Correspondance de la mairie de Dijon*, i. 124–5. For Tournai, see *Extraits analytiques de Tournai, 1431–1476*.

Popular elements in the duke's own towns of Ghent and Malines had temporarily seized control and defied his authority. The commons of Liège had dared to ravage his lands and offer him armed resistance instead of dutiful submission. If the names of these three, Ghent, Malines and Liège, point to the most significant events of 1467–68, so the names of Cologne, Strasbourg, Mulhouse, Neuss, Basel, Nancy and, above all, Bern, underlie the course of events during the rest of Charles's reign; for much of the narrative that follows inevitably revolves round the policies and the attitudes of these and other towns. The real enemy of Duke Charles the Bold, opposing him with a bitter and consistent hatred, was urban. It was not, as the chroniclers and many modern historians would have us believe, King Louis XI of France; it was the towns. In particular, it was that mosaic of city-states which had been brought into existence by the avaricious, grasping and dynamic merchant communities of the great borderland of the Europe of those days, where the French and German speaking worlds met and merged. It would be going too far to see Duke Charles as the first of a new generation of European rulers, intent on smashing the power and demolishing the privileges of the medieval cities, but it is nonetheless true that his sweeping ambitions and radical policies were stubbornly opposed by these communities or elements in them. It is high time that the history of Charles the Bold, which was created in the first place by Chastellain and de Commynes in terms of a violent and dramatic clash between two opposing personalities, each full of scorn and hate for the other, that is, the king of France and the duke of Burgundy, was rewritten in more realistic and more accurate terms. Of course, relations with France take their place in any history of Burgundy, but it is as well to remember that the prince who tore up the privileges of Ghent, sacked Dinant and demolished Liège was later successfully defied by Cologne and Neuss and finally destroyed by the citizen militias of Bern, of Zürich, of Basel and of Strasbourg.

CHAPTER TWO

Burgundy, France and England, 1467-1472

Thanks to the imaginative genius and gross inexactitude of a handful of contemporary chroniclers and generations of historians, the relations of France, Burgundy and England at about the time of Charles the Bold's accession as duke have been systematically falsified and dramatically simplified into a clash of personalities: Louis against Charles. 'There always had been rancour between these two princes', wrote Chastellain; 'there could never be true friendship between them, for their personalities and habits of mind were incompatible, and they invariably disagreed.'[1] No doubt each disliked and feared the other, but the situation between them was far too complex to be envisaged as a sort of duel, or single combat, on however grand a scale. After all, Louis was faced with at least three traditional enemies, each as deadly and powerful as Burgundy: the dissident elements among the French princes and aristocracy, including his own brother Charles of France and the duke of Brittany, Francis II; King Edward IV of England and, as he claimed, of France,

---

[1] Chastellain, *Oeuvres*, v. 455–6. For this chapter as a whole, Bittmann, *Ludwig XI und Karl der Kühne*, i. overshadows and partly supersedes earlier narratives, the most valuable of which are *Algemene geschiedenis der Nederlanden*, iii. 274–82 (J. Bartier), Calmette, *Louis XI, Jean II et la révolution catalane*, Calmette and Déprez, *Les premières grandes puissances*, 39–75, Calmette and Périnelle, *Louis XI et l'Angleterre*, Petit-Dutaillis, *Charles VII, Louis XI et les premières années de Charles VIII*, 341–68, Stein, *Charles de France*, Dupuy, *Histoire de la réunion*, Pocquet du Haut Jussé, *François II et l'Angleterre* and in *RCC* xxxvi (2) (1934–5), 177–86 and 363–75, Scofield, *Edward IV*, and Jacob, *The fifteenth century*. The main chroniclers, used throughout, are Basin, *Louis XI*, i and ii, de Commynes, *Mémoires*, ed. Calmette and Durville, i, de la Marche, *Mémoires*, iii, de Roye, *Chronique scandaleuse*, i, and de Waurin, *Croniques*, ed. Hardy, v and vi.

who regarded Louis as a usurper, 'falsely asserting that he is king of France';[1] and, perhaps the most profoundly hostile and potentially dangerous of them all, John II, king of Aragon. It was thus quite impossible for Louis to concentrate his attention exclusively on Burgundy.

As for Charles, he had obtained everything he so desperately needed from France in 1465, as a result of the War of the Public Weal. That is, he had regained possession, lost by his father, of those vital strategic bastions against French military power, the so-called Somme towns—St. Quentin, Corbie, Amiens, Abbeville, Doullens, St. Riquier, Crèvecoeur, Arleux and Mortagne—as well as Péronne, Roye and Montdidier.[2] Thereafter, his policy towards France was more or less defensive, at least until, in January–February 1471, Louis recaptured St. Quentin and Amiens and Charles became willing or perhaps eager to fight to regain them. But in the early years of his reign, as later, although the fantasy of the destruction of French royal power kept recurring in his mind, his ambitions, his field of action, his dreams of conquest, all were towards the Empire. Even before he became duke, in May 1467, Charles was reported to be 'trying, with the help of the count palatine of the Rhine and other German prices . . . to become vicar of the Empire'.[3] All this is not to deny the mutually hostile posture of France and Burgundy. The confrontation was a very real one, but the policies of the two rulers by no means derived merely from hatred or incompatibility, nor was the course of events after 1467 dictated by this antipathy.

Charles the Bold became duke of Burgundy in June 1467 at a time when his relations with Louis were strained almost to breaking point. From June onwards he received a constant stream of complaints against the activities of French royal officials in the duchy and county of Burgundy. In May the royal lieutenant in Champagne had put pressure on certain Franche-Comté vassals who also possessed lands in French territory to agree to serve the king in arms against anyone, even including the duke their sovereign lord. In June 1467, the very month of Duke Charles's accession, his officials at Dijon found it necessary to send to Auxerre to urge that town to remain loyal to Burgundy and to assemble the three Estates of the duchy of Burgundy to discuss defence. On 24 June a mounted messenger was sent

---

[1] *Foedera*, xi. 810.
[2] Vaughan, *Philip the Good*, 355–6 and 390.
[3] AGR MSS. divers 1173, f. 53 (copy of Panigarola's and de Jacopo's despatch to the duke of Milan, 9 May 1467).

to inform the new duke that French troops were gathering in various places, apparently with a view to invading 'the land of Burgundy'. By autumn, the situation had deteriorated still further. Royal troops were said to have tried to take Cusey by force of arms, and to have forcibly harvested grapes at Montsaugeon on the lands of a Burgundian vassal. Both places were on the borders of the duchy towards Langres. The Paris *Parlement* was accused of dealing with duchy cases to the detriment of ducal rights. The chancellor of France responded to complaints by pointing out that this sort of thing would continue until Duke Charles did homage to the king for all his lands, and grumbled that the duke had not even troubled to address the king as his sovereign when letting him know of his father's death.[1] These royal provocations constituted a veritable crisis for the ducal authorities at Dijon, which came to a head in September, at just the time when the duke was becoming increasingly preoccupied with the affairs of Liège.

Similar incidents and provocations were reported to Charles in 1467 from the area of the Somme towns, which King Louis was as determined to regain for France as Charles was to retain for Burgundy. Amiens, coveted above all by Louis, was a special bone of contention: in April and May 1467 her citizens had received letters from both king and duke, each assuring them of his pacific intentions and accusing the other of preparing armed aggression. While Louis complained at this time that Charles was assembling vassals in Picardy, that he had garrisoned Amiens, that in the area of the Somme towns he had usurped royal judicial and other rights and that he had unjustly retained possession of the lordship of Nesle and garrisoned Beaulieu, Charles replied with complaints that Louis had been recruiting archers from among his Picard subjects and had not allowed him to take possession of certain lands ceded by treaty.

While these local disputes and minor dissensions rumbled on through 1466–7, French royal diplomacy had been active in seeking allies against Burgundy. Anthoine, lord of Croy, was later accused by Charles of joining with Louis XI at this time in an elaborate plot designed to destroy Burgundian power on the death of Duke Philip. With the help of various Picards and Germans, besides that of the

[1] BN Coll. de Bourg. 29, pp. 100 and 106 and BN MS. fr. 5041, f. 37, referred to and summarized in Plancher, iv. 358–9 and no. 201. For the next paragraph, see *Analectes historiques*, xi. 21–3, Reilhac, *Jean de Reilhac*, i. 247–50, and BN MS. Dupuy 762, fos. 161–6.

kings of France and England and the city of Liège, the lord of Croy was to take possession of Boulogne, Namur and Luxembourg while Jehan de Bourgogne, count of Étampes and Nevers, was to be assisted in obtaining Brabant. In February 1467 Louis protested against Charles's ambassador's assertion that he, Louis, was planning a combined Anglo-French move against Burgundy, yet on 18 April the Milanese ambassadors at Blois were able to report in detail on a project for the partition of Burgundy which Louis hoped he was in the process of arranging with King Edward IV through the good offices of Richard Neville, earl of Warwick, who was to meet Louis at Rouen before 8 May next to determine the details. As outlined to Panigarola and de Jacopo by Louis, the scheme entailed Edward IV's renunciation of his claims to the throne of France and a joint Franco-Burgundian invasion of the Burgundian Low Countries. King Edward's brother, George, duke of Clarence, was to have Holland, Zeeland and Brabant, while Flanders and the rest would fall to Louis. To foil Charles's attempts to marry King Edward's sister Margaret, she was to be married instead to Philip of Savoy, count of Bresse. Thus it happened that, at the very moment when the old Duke Philip was dying at Bruges, the king of France was plotting the downfall of the new duke with the earl of Warwick at Rouen.[1]

Long before he became duke of Burgundy on 15 June 1467 Charles, then count of Charolais, had taken important diplomatic initiatives to protect himself, specifically, from possible French aggression. Now, in 1467, he set about consolidating and extending the system of alliances which already included Cleves, the elector palatine, the duke of Bavaria, Edward IV of England and Francis II, duke of Brittany. In February 1467 Charles entertained the elector palatine at an elaborate state banquet at Ghent and took him on a tour of Flanders. In March 1467 his ambassadors went to Utrecht and negotiated a treaty of alliance with King Christian I of Denmark which included also Louis's brother Charles of France and the duke of Brittany. Indeed, throughout 1467 Charles hovered on the fringe of what looked like becoming a powerful coalition of princes aimed against Louis, to include the king's brother, Charles, who had just

[1] For this paragraph, see AOGV Reg. 2, f. 7b and *Cal. state papers. Milan*, i. 118–20. For the next paragraph, see Vaughan, *Philip the Good*, 377; ADN B2064, fos. 77 and 78b; Johnsen, *HT* (2) ii (1947), 111–31; Perret, *France et Venise*, i. 474–80, Durr, *ZGA* xiv (1915), 255–73, and Guichenon, *Histoire de Savoie*, iv. 406–8; Vicens Vives, *Juan II*, 303–4; *Cal. state papers. Milan*, i. 121, and Samaran, *La maison d'Armagnac*, 157–8 and 405–6.

had the duchy of Normandy wrested from him by the king, Yolande of France, duchess of Savoy, Louis's sister, the kings of England, Denmark, Aragon and possibly Castile, as well as the dukes of Savoy and Calabria. On 1 October 1467 John, duke of Alençon, signed treaties with Charles of France and the duke of Brittany, as well as with Charles the Bold, 'to enable him to obviate and resist more effectively the sudden, swift, and devious enterprises which my lord the king may contrive'.[1] With that powerful and important figure, Philip of Savoy, former enemy of Louis XI, Charles signed a treaty on 20 July; already, in April, Bern and other Swiss communities had made an alliance with Burgundy.

Against all these Louis had little to show. True, he had at this time temporarily won over the shifty and self-interested count of St. Pol, Louis de Luxembourg who, after leading the duke of Burgundy's forces against the king in 1465, was now constable of France. Moreover the unreliable and indeed infamous count of Armagnac, John V, who had been condemned by the Paris *Parlement* in 1460 for lesemajeste, rebellion, and incest with his younger sister Isabel, was in autumn 1467 prepared to render military assistance to the king. But these did not count for much; nor did the Bourbon and Angevin connections give Louis anything like an aggressive stance vis-à-vis Burgundy. Worse still, in 1467–8 the king's English policies failed utterly.

Though some of the chroniclers pretended that Charles the Bold, a Lancastrian at heart, was only persuaded to ask for Edward IV's sister in marriage because Louis XI's aggressive intrigues gave him no alternative,[2] in fact he despatched Guillaume de Clugny to England to request her hand within a few months of the death, on 25 September 1465, of his second wife, Isabel of Bourbon. Edward responded in March 1466 by sending the earl of Warwick to Charles to negotiate two marriages: that of Margaret of York to Charles himself and that of George, duke of Clarence, Edward's brother, to Charles's daughter, Mary of Burgundy. No more is heard of this second marriage, and even the first seems to have been lost sight of for a time. In October 1466 Edward issued a safe-conduct to Anthony, bastard of Burgundy, to visit England, but for the purpose of accepting a

---

[1] Plancher, iv. 359 and no. 202.
[2] For example Chastellain, *Oeuvres*, v. 310–12 and vii. 232–3 and Basin, *Louis XI*, i. 292–4. For what follows, besides the works cited on p. 41 above, see *Foedera*, xi. 563–99, Hommel, *Marguerite d' York*, 27–34, and especially Armstrong, *AB* xl (1968), 44–7.

challenge to joust with Anthony Woodville, Lord Scales, the queen's brother. It was at this time, October 1466, that the king of England signed a treaty of friendship with Charles, count of Charolais as he then was, but the proposed marriage alliance was not mentioned. In the early months of 1467, while Louis did his best to offer an alternative, French, spouse to Edward for his sister to wed, embassies passed to and fro between England and Burgundy.[1] Edward was happy to negotiate with both Charles and Louis, but his own inclination, encouraged by commercial considerations as well as political need, was towards Burgundy, not France. In May 1467 Sir John Paston made his famous wager with a London mercer: he would pay 80 shillings for the horse he was buying if Margaret of York married Duke Charles within two years, but only 40 shillings if not.[2] The marriage, doubtless, was still under discussion at the English court when the jousts between the two Anthonies were interrupted by the news of Duke Philip's death, at the very time when the earl of Warwick, conferring with Louis in Rouen, still hoped to arrange an Anglo-French alliance instead.

After Duke Charles's accession on 15 June the negotiations moved faster. In July-August he and Edward exchanged promises of friendship,[3] and by the early autumn the marriage was in principle agreed. Edward appointed the bishop of Salisbury and other ambassadors to negotiate the details on 20 September; Margaret's public consent was obtained on 1 October at a meeting of the royal council; and, later that month, Charles sent off to Rome for a dispensation[4] and empowered his mother, Duchess Isabel, to undertake the detailed negotiations with Edward's ambassadors. Parallel with the marriage treaty, a commercial treaty was to be negotiated, and Edward demonstrated his good faith in this respect by annulling, at the end of September, the statutes of 1463 and 1464 prohibiting the import into England from the duke of Burgundy's lands in the Low Countries of all manufactured products.

Throughout 1467, while Charles the Bold was competing with Louis XI for the friendship of Edward IV, he was eyeing the French

[1] See, for example, ADN B2064, fos. 64a–b, 107, 115b, 118, 143b–144, etc.
[2] *Paston letters*, i. 397–8. For the jousts in June 1467, see *Excerpta historica*, 171–212.
[3] Edward's document is printed in *Documents pour servir à l'histoire des relations entre l'Angleterre et la Flandre*, 460–2 and in *Actes concernant les rapports entre les Pays Bas et la Grande Bretagne*, no. 10; Charles's is in *Foedera*, xi. 580–1.
[4] ADN B2064, f. 334.

king with fear and suspicion. But he made no effort to organize a
concerted attack on Louis. If the grand alliance which appeared to be
mustering against France in 1467 had any guiding hand, it certainly
was not his. When, in October, the duke of Brittany launched his
campaign against Louis with the aim of reconquering Normandy for
Charles of France, Charles of Burgundy was preoccupied with Liège.
Indeed, in the very same month, when Louis asked him for a truce
he agreed to sign one for six months, beginning on 1 November 1467. [1]
A bold fighting posture, but no war, was the Burgundian response to
Louis at this time. Thus, in spite of the winter truce, there was talk
in Charles's army at Liège early in November of marching thence
against France. [2] On 25 November Charles actually ordered the
mobilization of troops at St. Quentin on 16 December and this
general military summons was subsequently deferred till 16 January
1468. His attitude is typified in the report sent to Cologne from
Brussels by the provost of St. Andrew's, Cologne, on 4 January
1468: Duke Charles was resolutely determined to respond to the call
for assistance he had received from the dukes of Berry and Brittany
by taking the field against King Louis in person. But time passed and
Charles continued militarily inactive. There was an abortive peace
conference at Cambrai in April and embassies continued to and fro,
but when war again broke out, in the summer, between the dukes of
Berry and Brittany on the one side and King Louis on the other,
Charles contented himself with the despatch of the bailiff of St.
Omer to Caen with thirty or forty men-at-arms and 500 Picard
archers. [3] Even in July 1468, when the French and Burgundian
armies were mustering against one another along the frontier in
Picardy, Charles showed no enthusiasm to take the field in person.
But by this time he had a new ally against Louis XI: on 17 May
King Edward's chancellor had announced to the English Parliament
not only the imminent marriage of the king's sister Margaret to the
duke of Burgundy, 'oon of the myghtyest Princez of the world that

---

[1] ASM Pot. est. Borgogna 515/10, letter of T. Portinari of 28 October 1467.
[2] *Collection de documens inédits*, i. 180–1 and, for the next sentence, the same,
183–4, and ADN B2064, fos. 397, 412b, 413b, 414a–b, etc. For what follows,
see *Hansisches Urkundenbuch*, ix. 278.
[3] De Waurin, *Croniques*, ed. Dupont, iii. 267–70. For the Cambrai conference
in April 1468, see ADN B2068, fos. 71 and 73, de Comines, *Mémoires*, ed.
Lenglet du Fresnoy, iii. 6–8, AGR MSS. divers 1173. fos. 91–94b (copies of
Panigarola's despatches of 12 and 16 June 1468), and Bittmann, *Ludwig XI
und Karl der Kühne*, i (1). 307.

bereth no crowne', but also the royal plan for an invasion of France to recover the duchies of Normandy and Gascony from the 'usurpaunt kyng' of France, the king of England's great rebel and adversary.[1]

Naturally Louis XI had done his utmost to prevent Charles the Bold's marriage to Margaret of York. Ambassadors were sent to Charles and to Edward to try to dissuade them, and to Rome in the hope of persuading the pope not to issue the necessary dispensation.[2] Rumours were even spread abroad to the effect that the twenty-two year-old Margaret was not everything that a bride ought to be; indeed, some went so far as to say that she had had a son. According to the Milanese ambassador at the French court, Charles scotched these rumours by ordering that anybody heard repeating them was to be thrown forthwith into the nearest river.

[The wedding was delayed, much to Charles's annoyance, for he had hoped to make it coincide with the chapter and festivities of the Golden Fleece in early May.] The trouble was due, in the first place, to difficulties connected with the issuing of the dispensation, and, secondly, to Edward's financial situation:[3] according to the marriage contract, he had to pay the first instalment of Margaret's dowry, which was 50,000 crowns, at Bruges, fifteen days before the wedding. It was eventually celebrated on Sunday, 3 July 1468, in the church of Notre-Dame at Damme, near Bruges, accompanied by the most splendid and extravagant festivities ever contrived in the entire annals of Burgundy, and followed by an elaborate tournament only marred by an unfortunate accident to the principal challenger, Anthony, bastard of Burgundy, whose leg was kicked and broken: he was still being attended by the ducal doctors more than two months later.[4]

[1] *Rotuli Parliamentorum*, v. 622–3.

[2] For this and the next sentence see de Waurin, *Croniques*, ed. Hardy, v. 552 and *Cal. state papers. Milan*, i. 121–2, 123 and 95–6. For what follows on Charles's wedding, see Calmette, *AB* i (1929), 193–214, Cartellieri, *GRM* ix (1921), 168–79 and *TG* xxxvi (1921), 14–30 (compare the same author, *The court of Burgundy*, 124–34 and 157–63), Hommel, *Marguerite d'York*, 25–52, and Armstrong, *AB* xl (1968), 46–50. Zuylen van Nyevelt makes use of Fastre Hollet's account, printed in de Laborde, *Ducs de Bourgogne*, ii. 293–381, in his *Épisodes de la vie des ducs de Bourgogne à Bruges*, 287–94.

[3] ASM Pot. est. Borgogna 515/12–13, letter of T. Portinari of 8 April 1468 = *Cal. state papers. Milan*, i. 122–3 (no. 158, wrongly dated 18 April and ascribed to 'T. Portt'), and AGR MSS. divers 1173, fos. 93–94b (copy of Panigarola's despatch of 16 June 1468).

[4] ADN B2068, f. 223, 'sa jambe rompue aux joustes'; compare Stuart, *History Today*, viii (1958), 256: 'Many lances were splintered but no bones were broken.'

To record some of the expenditure a special account was opened, and entrusted to Fastre Hollet, of 'the works and also the entremets and decoration carried out at Bruges for the wedding of my lord the Duke Charles'. A lengthy report on the proceedings was written in Flemish by Anton de Rovere, a local writer and poet, and it was probably this which the secretary of the Hansards at Bruges sent later that year to the burgomaster of Lübeck. He took care to ask for it back, as he did not have a copy.[1] A Latin account, apparently by an eyewitness, was circulated, and another description of the ceremonies found its way into the German town chronicle of Strasbourg complete with detailed figures of the average daily consumption of different animals and birds which appear at least to be of the right order of magnitude, unlike the ridiculously exaggerated figures given by the dean of Heinsberg, Symon Mulart, in his eulogy of Charles. An English report of considerable interest has found its way into print three times. John Paston was there, and sent his mother an account of what happened. Naturally, the chronicler-courtier Olivier de la Marche has inserted a detailed report into his memoirs, and another very full description in French has been printed under his name and attributed to him. He had a special interest in the matter since he and the equerry Jaques de Villers, with advice from Jehan Hennecart, Pierre Coustain and other artists and craftsmen, had been put in charge of the entremets.[2]

Among all the eyewitness accounts perhaps the most lively and charming is that of the chronicler Jehan de Haynin, who is particularly careful to define the limits of his information.

I, Jehan, lord of Haynin and of Louvignies, knight, intend to pass the time by writing down here what I have seen and discovered of the departure, welcome, entry, wedding, festivity, jousts, tournament and banquets which occurred in the town of Bruges because of the alliance

---

[1] Enschedé, *KHGU* xxii (1866), 17–71 and *Hanserecesse*, vi. 87–9. For what follows, see de Ram, *BCRH* (1) v (1842), 168–74, *Straszburgische Archiv-Chronik*, 189–92, *Excerpta historica*, 223–39 Phillipps, *Archaeologia* xxxi (1846), 326–38 and Kervyn de Lettenhove, *BCRH* (3) x (1869), 245–66, *Paston letters*, i. 538–40, de la Marche, *Mémoires*, iii. 101–201 and iv. 95–144. See, too, on the wedding, Angelo de Curribis Sabinis, *De excidio civitatis Leodiensis*, 1420–9, Boeren, *Twee Maaslandse dichters*, 91–4 and 235–9 (Symon Mulart), de Waurin, *Croniques*, ed. Hardy, v. 559–62, and de But, *Chronique*, 489–90.

[2] De Laborde, *Ducs de Bourgogne*, ii. 322. What follows is from de Haynin, *Mémoires*, ii. 17–62.

C

and marriage of the most excellent, high and mighty prince, my most redoubted lord Charles, by the grace of God duke of Burgundy . . . and the most high and mighty princess Madame Margaret of York . . . subject to the correction of those who were present and who saw and found out about them better or more certainly than I. I hope I may be forgiven if I write anything false for I certainly do not wish to include anything except pure and certain truth. Indeed I would not take the trouble nor waste the time to record lies or anything controversial, which would give me no pleasure. I began to write this present chapter on a Monday, 18 July 1468, in my house at Louvignies near Bavay, at the age of forty-four years and nine months, or thereabouts, after my return from the said festivities, about which, being present myself, I have recorded most of what I saw or could discover from various worthy people. Moreover, these things are still to some extent in my memory, though I would not at all want to boast of having seen and found out everything.

In fact, Jehan de Haynin took the trouble to visit the English at Sluis and inspect there a blue and red silk standard with a white cross on it which had come from a French ship they had captured after a skirmish on their way over from Margate with the princess. They also told him that, as soon as they could see the church towers of Sluis and Aardenburg, Margaret knelt and prayed. On her arrival, on Saturday 25 June, she stayed at Sluis in the town hall, Charles visiting her for the first time on the Monday. Every night she was there, there were fireworks in Sluis, and on two evenings the duke and his courtiers attended a special firework display in the market place of Bruges. It was in Bruges, in the courtyard of the duke's palace, normally used for tennis, that the wedding feast and other festivities were to take place, and de Haynin gives an enthusiastic description of the elaborate wooden banqueting hall which had been erected there two months before for the chapter of the Golden Fleece. This was now fitted out with all the elaborate paraphernalia proper to such an occasion, including two superb candelabras and two galleries, one for 'trumpets, clarions and minstrels'; the other for those ladies whom space would not permit to sit at table. De Haynin took particular note of the tapestries:

The ceiling of the great hall was lined with white and blue silk or cloth, and the walls were hung with fine and rich tapestries of embroidered serge, depicting the story and mystery of Gideon and the Fleece. Behind and above the high table was, in the centre, a very rich piece of grey cloth of gold with the duke's arms embroidered on it and, on either side, several pieces of crimson, blue and green cloth of gold.

In the hall where the sideboard was situated were hung the tapestries of the great battle of Liège, where Duke John of Burgundy and Duke William of Bavaria, count of Hainault, defeated the Liègeois near Othée in the year 1408, on a Sunday, 23 September.[1] The hall ... of the chamberlains was hung with a superb tapestry showing the coronation of King Clovis, called Lois, the first Christian king of France; the renewal of the alliance between him and King Gundobad of Burgundy; the wedding of King Clovis to Gundobad's niece; his baptism with the Holy Ampulla; his conquest of Soissons; how the stag showed him the way across a river which he had not dared to cross; and how the angel gave an azure cloth with three fleurs-de-lys in gold to a hermit, who gave it to the queen, who passed it on to the said King Clovis to bear for his coat of arms. . . .

Before the festivities the hall in front of the chapel was hung with haute-lice tapestries of the history of Duke Begues of Belin, brother of Garin le Loherant; how he set off from his house and his lands to go hunting the great boar and was killed as he stood by the animal he had killed, by one of the foresters of Fromont of Lens, who shot him with an arrow because he feared to fight him hand to hand. . . .

Soon afterwards, just before the wedding day, another tapestry was hung in this place, of King Ahasuerus, who governed 127 provinces. . . . The chapel was hung with a fine embroidered tapestry of the Passion; before then it had been of the human pilgrimage. In the duke's oratory, the altar cloth showed the seven sacraments. . . . In Madame's dressing-room, which was chequered throughout with white, red and green squares, the colours of the marguerite, was the history of the good Lucretia. . . . In Mademoiselle of Burgundy's room, a haute-lice of trees and personages in antique fashion. In my lord the bastard's room, a haute-lice with his arms and, in his dressing-room, very richly embroidered ancient histories. And that is all I saw and can remember about the tapestries.

Early on Sunday morning, 3 July, Charles went to Damme to marry 'Madame Margaret, waiting to be duchess of Burgundy' and the couple made their processional entry into Bruges that morning, proceeding through crowded and richly decorated streets to the specially ornamented ducal palace. The bride was welcomed by the foreign merchants resident in Bruges. De Haynin correctly names them as Easterlings or Hansards, Genoese, Catalans, Florentines and

---

[1] See Vaughan, *John the Fearless*, 59–62, and *Philip the Good*, 152.

Venetians; but he explains that he was unsure of the identity of the
Genoese, who were led by a mounted man-at-arms representing St.
George. At the time he could find no one near him from Bruges who
knew who they were. Later, he was told that it was the English
deputation which had the representation of St. George, 'but others
said it was the Genoese; however I leave this to be decided by those
who will know, or who can ascertain, the truth'.

The foreign merchants were joined, in the procession, by the
local clergy supported by the papal legate Onofrio, whom Charles
had invited to his wedding from Liège, and a group of bishops among
whom de Haynin identified those of Cambrai and Utrecht, both of
them bastards of the house of Burgundy, and those of Salisbury,
Tournai, Metz and Verdun. He interrupts his description of the
procession to explain that windows mostly cost a *maille* of the Rhine,
or a crown, to rent, then continues with a lively account of the jousts
in the market place and of the banquet which was held that evening
at the ducal palace.

> Here is part of the seating arrangement of the high table at the said
> banquet. First, the bride, in the middle of the table and, on her right,
> first, the legate of our holy father the pope, then Madame the dowager
> duchess [of Burgundy, Isabel], my lord of Cambrai, Mademoiselle
> [Mary] of Burgundy and others I have forgotten. And on the left of the
> said bride, my lord the bishop of Metz, the duchess of Norfolk, my lord
> the duke, Mademoiselle of Arguel and others; the others, I have for-
> gotten them.

De Haynin's memory served him better when describing the banquet itself: the roast was brought in on thirty superbly made wooden
ships, painted and gilded, 'complete with cords, masts, anchors and
sails of grey taffeta', each bearing the name and coat of arms of one
of the duke's lands. The entremets included a leopard with the arms
of England and Mary of Burgundy's dwarf riding on a lion and, inevitably, holding the duke's coat of arms. Then, when they had been at
table for some three or four hours, 'that is, from ten in the evening
till one hour after midnight, or thereabouts', the tables were cleared
and there was dancing. This pattern of joust and banquet was followed
every day for more than a week. After the first day, when the centre
of the banqueting hall was occupied by an exhibition of the ducal
plate, this was removed and, in its place, was set up the famous model
of the castle Duke Charles had begun to have made at Gorinchem in
Holland. Here, as elsewhere, the descriptions of participants like de

Haynin can be supplemented from the ducal accounts, where we learn that this 'great tower' consisted of a wooden framework covered with painted cloth. It had four windows which opened to reveal successively four wolves which sang a ballad about the festivities; four hares playing on flutes; four boars blowing trumpets and four reed-playing donkeys. [1]

The wedding of Charles the Bold and Margaret of York, and the close alliance between England and Burgundy that went with it, was of considerable significance for the duke. It was infinitely more important than that allegedly momentous event of 1468, which occurred just three months later: his meeting with King Louis XI of France at Péronne. As a matter of fact, at the time of his wedding and afterwards, Charles showed little sign of an obsession with France, nor of that fanatical hatred of Louis XI which has often been attributed to him. Instead of riding forward after his wedding on Tuesday next to do battle against the king, as John Paston informed his mother on Friday 8 July, the duke embarked from Sluis for Zeeland and Holland, to make his solemn entry into Middelburg, The Hague and elsewhere, and he spent a fortnight there before returning to Brussels. [2] It was only on 10 August that he set out ostentatiously on campaign against the French, not before convincing a number of contemporary observers that he was only doing this for the sake of his allies, the dukes of Berry and Brittany, who had asked for his help against the king of France.

The military events of August-September 1468 showed conclusively that Charles only meant to keep up appearances and had no intention of fighting a serious war with Louis. Still less did Louis plan an attack on Charles. Throughout August the French army and king remained at Compiègne on the Oise, while the Burgundian army was stationed on the Burgundian side of the Somme. In September the duke camped with his men at Moyencourt but was flooded out thence and consequently withdrew to Lihons-en-Santerre. [3] Mean-

---

[1] De Laborde, *Ducs de Bourgogne*, ii. 326–7.
[2] *Paston letters*, i. 539, and *Cronycke van Hollandt*, 318a–b. For the next sentence, see above, p. 26 and, for example, de Merica, *De cladibus Leodensium*, 285–6 and *Magnum chronicon Belgicum*, 430–1.
[3] For these places, see the map on p. 78 below. Besides the sources cited on p. 41 n. 1 above, see on this Chastellain, *Oeuvres*, v. 423–32 and the despatches of Panigarola and Magalotti, copied in AGR MSS. divers 1173, fos. 54b–56 and 100–8. For the next sentence see Wielant, *Antiquités de Flandre*, 53, de But, *Chronique*, 495, and Bittmann, *Ludwig XI und Karl der Kühne*, i (1). 335–6.

while the constable of France, Louis, count of St. Pol, acted as mediator and, from 21 September, as president of a peace conference at Ham which ran into difficulties because of a Burgundian complaint that the French ambassadors' benches were six inches higher than the Burgundians', but nevertheless ended in the promulgation of the Franco-Burgundian truce for a further six months from 1 October. Since Louis had already defeated Duke Francis II of Brittany and imposed the peace of Ancenis on him on 10 September, there were hopes that this truce might be converted into a firm peace, but at first Charles's conditions were quite unacceptable to the king. At Ham, he asked Louis to exempt him and his subjects from all French jurisdiction by abolishing every vestige of royal authority in the Burgundian territories; to guarantee that he would never try to regain the Somme towns; to absolve Charles from doing homage for his French lands; and to pay him 100,000 crowns in reparation for his current military expenses against France.[1] But now a more skilful negotiator intervened on Louis's behalf in the shape of Cardinal Jehan Balue, bishop of Angers, and it was he who arranged the personal meeting of Charles and Louis which took place at Péronne between 9 and 14 October, rather than Louis, count of St. Pol, as Diederik Pauwels would have us believe. It is, however, only with reluctance that history must reject the canon of Gorinchem's charming account of how Louis XI, incognito, was secretly taken by his constable to inspect the Burgundian army. But the constable had warned Charles in advance of this unofficial royal visit, so that the duke was able to have all his men impeccably turned out, and to make suitable protestations of loyalty to the king in the king's hearing. Louis, overjoyed and convinced of Charles's good will, set out forthwith to meet him at Péronne.[2]

---

[1] Bittmann, *Ludwig XI und Karl der Kühne*, i (1). 335 and n. 68.
[2] Pauwels, *Historia*, 214. The most important chronicle accounts of the Péronne meeting are Basin, *Louis XI*, i. 300–4, de But, *Chronique*, 495–7, de Commynes, *Mémoires*, ed. Calmette and Durville, i. 125–45, von Diesbach, *Chronik*, 172–3, de Haynin, *Mémoires*, ii. 69–70, de la Marche, *Mémoires*, iii. 82–4, Maupoint, *Journal*, 107–10, Pauwels, *Historia*, 214–17, and de Roye, *Chronique scandaleuse*, i. 213–14. Other important sources are in Chastellain, *Oeuvres*, vii. 342 n. 1, 342–4, *Eidgenössischen Abschiede*, 400–2 (von Diesbach), Buser, *Beziehungen der Mediceer zu Frankreich*, 438–9 (Panigarola's despatch of 17 October 1468) and Bricard, *Jean Bourré*, 108. Documents are printed in *Collection de documens inédits*, i. 196–200, de Comines, *Mémoires*, ed. Lenglet du Fresnoy, iii. 18–20 and 81–2, de Commynes, *Mémoires*, ed. Dupont, iii. 228–36 and 250–1, Delisle, *BEC* xlv (1884), 196–202, *Lettres de*

The real reason for Louis's departure for Péronne, which 'caused everyone as much astonishment as a stag flying through the air would have done'[1] was his desire and hope for a firm and lasting peace settlement with Charles. At first, all went well between king and duke. No hard feelings were caused by the incidental presence in Péronne of some noted enemies of the king, in particular Philip of Savoy, lord of Bresse and, in any case, they soon left. Nor did the news on 10 October of the capture of Tongres by the Liègeois damage Charles's relations with Louis, as de Commynes claims, though it did make him more determined than ever on the destruction of Liège and it did cause Louis, very much on the spur of the moment, to offer to accompany and help the duke on a punitive expedition against the rebel city. Louis, however, hesitated and went back on his word, trying to excuse himself, and it was this which really interfered with the progress of the negotiations. This, coupled with Charles's deep-seated fear and distrust of Louis: he probably sincerely believed that Louis might attack him in the rear if he did not go with him to Liège. At one time, it seems, the king was actually in danger of arrest but, in the event, he bowed to the force of circumstances and conceded almost everything Charles demanded, including the joint campaign against Liège. The two swore solemnly on 14 October to be good friends, and Charles agreed to do homage for his French lands. Louis promised him the 100,000 crowns in reparation he had demanded at Ham, and paid over half of it on the spot. When at last, after the conquest of Liège on 30 October, Charles allowed the king to leave, he insisted on retaining a royal seal and a royal secretary and, with the help of these, forty-two royal letters were concocted at Brussels in November and issued under the date of 14 October and the place, Péronne. The contents of thirty-six had been agreed at Ham; Louis had conceded the substance of the

---

Louis XI, iii. 286–302, *Lettres missives de Thouars*, 52–5, and Vayssière, *RSS* (6) vii (1878) 363–7. The actual treaty documents are printed in de Comines, *Mémoires*, ed. Lenglet du Fresnoy, iii. 22–64 and 72–81 (especially 74–6), and *Ordonnances des rois*, xvii. 126–59; see too *IAEG*, 186–90. They are discussed in Bittmann, *Ludwig XI und Karl der Kühne*, i (1). 289–301, Lameere, *Grand conseil*, 181–2, and Gandilhon, *Politique économique de Louis XI*, 371. The only detailed and critical account of Péronne is by Bittmann, *Ludwig XI und Karl der Kühne*, i (1). 193–367, which supersedes the same author's papers in *WG* xvi (1956), 98–123, and *HZ* clxxxiv (1957), 19–64.

[1] AGR MSS. divers 1173, f. 62b (copy of A. Magalotti's letter to the duke of Milan of 13 October 1468).

remaining six at Péronne. Such was the much-famed 'treaty of Péronne'. Small wonder that Louis and his councillors resented it. Moreover, the king's subsequent actions and negotiations showed that he never had the smallest intention of abiding by its terms.

In essence, the meeting at Péronne was a trivial incident without serious impact on the course of events. Its significance has been much exaggerated by historians. Their research on the subject, until Karl Bittmann's work was published, consisted of blindly following de Commynes, whose famous account of the Péronne meeting, though vivacious and dramatic, has the disadvantage, as Dr. Bittmann has shown, of being largely fictitious. The treaty of Péronne, too, was politically insignificant, mainly because of its unilateral nature. Its terms, however, as embodied in the above-mentioned documents, are not without interest as representing, to some extent, the aspirations of Charles the Bold. This is particularly true of the six concessions, or points, the actual texts of which have not come down to us:

1. The king promised to abide by the treaties of Arras (1435) and Conflans (1465).
2. He permitted the duke to make alliances with England provided they were not aimed against France.
3. A general amnesty was conceded for all Burgundian supporters living in France, and their possessions were to be returned.
4. The king promised to give to his brother Charles the counties of Champagne and Brie for an appanage.
5. Full satisfaction, including restitution of conquered territory in Bresse and reparations, was promised by Louis to Philip of Savoy, who was to be included in the peace.
6. The king agreed that, if he infringed any of the treaties of Arras, Conflans or Péronne, then the Burgundian territories normally dependent on the French crown would automatically be freed from all French jurisdiction.

These clauses were evidently designed to guarantee to Charles the Bold those grants of territory which had been made originally in 1435 by King Charles VII to Duke Philip the Good and made again, or confirmed, by King Louis to Charles the Bold while he was still only count of Charolais, in 1465: in particular, the Somme towns and Péronne, Roye and Montdidier. Furthermore, in these clauses Charles was particularly concerned to reinforce his relationship with two influential allies and partisans, Philip of Savoy and Charles of France. Philip had already in May 1468 been offered the Golden Fleece; now Charles secured for him what he hoped was an advantageous reconciliation with the king. As to the weak but disloyal brother of the king, Charles the Bold doubtless hoped to be able to treat Champagne, once it became Charles of France's appanage, as if it were an extension of Burgundian territory, while its ruler would become a Burgundian puppet. Actually, at the very moment when Louis was swearing on 'the cross of St. Charlemagne' at Péronne, to abide by this and the other above-mentioned articles, he was making arrangements for his brother to have the duchy of Guienne, on the other side of France, far removed from Burgundian influence. The last of these clauses probably conceals Charles's most profound aspiration of all: the severance of all connections between France and Burgundy which in any sense reflected or maintained the subordinacy of the duke to the king. This hope runs through many of the other concessions, set out in surviving letters-patent. For example, the king is made to concede that the Four Members of Flanders, Ghent, Bruges, Ypres and the Franc of Bruges, are to be 'free, quit and exempt from us, from our said court of *Parlement* and from all our officers whomsoever' because 'the said land is of a language other than French and its inhabitants are particular in their way of life, their police, administration and justice, and they are different from the people of the other lands, provinces and countries of our kingdom'. Again, appeals in the castellanies of Lille, Douai and Orchies are no longer to go direct to the Paris *Parlement* but, in future, first to the governor of Lille, Douai and Orchies, then to the duke's council in Flanders, and only thereafter to the French royal *Parlement*. Similarly, appeals against judgements of ducal officers are no longer to be made to the bailiff of Sens; only to the Paris *Parlement*, and the king is made to explain that he wishes thereby 'to keep and maintain the rights, prerogatives, pre-eminences and noblesses of our said brother and cousin and of his said duchy of Burgundy without any diminution, or even to increase and augment them'.

While this underlying theme, of diminishing wherever possible the crown's powers over the Burgundian territories, runs through the entire Péronne treaty, it is also true that every dispute between France and Burgundy, however trivial, is settled here firmly in Burgundy's favour. Moreover the opportunity was grasped to reiterate many concessions already made by the crown but not implemented: for example, the cession of the land and lordship of Mortagne, one of the

C*

'Somme towns' of the 1435 and 1465 treaties. The crown, however, had no intention of implementing the terms of the treaty of Péronne, nor would Charles rest content with the measure of royal jurisdiction over his territories that they still permitted the king to retain. Furthermore, Louis remained just as determined on the recovery of the Somme towns as Charles was on their retention.

In view of all this, it is hardly surprising that Franco-Burgundian relations remained much the same after Péronne, as before. At first the emphasis was on friendship between Louis and Charles: on 19 November the treaty of Péronne was publicly proclaimed in Paris and every manner of insult against Charles the Bold, whether 'verbal, in writing, gestures, paintings, rondeaux, ballads, virelays, defamatory libels, *chansons de geste* or otherwise' was prohibited.[1] Burgundian embassies were well received at the French court in February and March 1469, and as late as 30 May the Milanese ambassador at Tours reported, though perhaps with a touch of hyperbole or irony, that the king and Duke Charles were on better terms than ever. A very different impression was made on the ambassadors of Bern, Wilhelm and Niclaus von Diesbach. Visiting Louis in July, they heard the French version of events at Péronne and were told that the king had had the treaty forced on him and would not rest until he had revenged himself on the duke of Burgundy. Charles himself at this time was not without his habitual suspicion and distrust of Louis: he informed the king's ally, Duke Galeazzo Maria Sforza of Milan, that he for his part fully intended to keep the peace with France, providing that the king similarly observed it, and remained content with his 'extensive kingdom, just as he (Charles) is content with his state and principality'[2]. By the autumn of 1469 the Milanese ambassadors at the French court were fully convinced of Louis's aggressive and indeed belligerent intentions towards the duke of Burgundy. Panigarola, for example, reported on 8 October that Louis planned to make war against Duke Charles in the following year. It was said, however, that the king would not take the field in person, since he had sworn on a relic of the Cross not to do so. Instead, the French

---

[1] De Roye, *Chronique scandaleuse*, i. 219–23. For the next sentence, see the same, i. 224 and AGR MSS. divers 1173, fos. 136–8 (copy of Sforza de Bettini's despatch of 21 March 1469 from Amboise). For what follows, see Bittmann, *Ludwig XI und Karl der Kühne*, i (2). 400 n. 1 (*Cal. state papers. Milan*, i. 129–30), and *Eidgenössischen Abschiede*, 400–2.

[2] ASM Pot. est. Borgogna 515/27–9. For what follows, see Combet, *Louis XI et le Saint-Siège*, 235–7 (despatch of Panigarola of 8 October 1469).

forces would be led by his brother Charles. This weak-minded and vacillating prince had accepted the duchy of Guienne from Louis as an appanage after Charles had failed, at Péronne, to ensure that he was given Champagne. In the autumn of 1469 the duke of Burgundy made another bid to retain him as an ally, by offering him the Golden Fleece and, if he accepted, his only child, Mary of Burgundy, in marriage. But Charles of France, firmly reconciled to, or under the control of, Louis, refused these blandishments. He even promised the king that he would never try to marry Mary of Burgundy.

We are well informed of Charles the Bold's fears of a war with France, and of his military preparations in autumn 1469, because of the survival, in the archives of Mantua, of a series of letters sent from the Burgundian court at this time by Rodolfo Gonzaga and a compatriot of his to his mother the marchioness of Mantua. On 4 October, from The Hague, he hinted at his hopes of being given one of Duke Charles's new Venetian-type companies of mercenaries to command. By 27 November there was nothing but talk of war at Brussels. Louis 'has sworn and protested that the duke of Burgundy is his worst enemy' and his men have seized a castle 'called Beaulieu on the River Somme'. On 26 December Rodolfo informed his mother that Charles was having troops mustered and reviewed in every province. Early in the New Year the duke spoke of his own and his father's wars in France and of his grandfather's death there, and added that, before the year was out, there might well be further, and greater, wars in France. On 10 March 1470 the ducal forces were reported to be under instruction to stand by to enter on campaign, but the duke was unlikely to attack the king unless Louis attacked him or the duke of Brittany first.[1]

The truth was that Louis feared to attack Charles the Bold without first neutralizing Brittany. He offered Duke Francis II membership of the Order of St. Michael, the royal counter-attraction to the Golden Fleece, but Francis refused, explaining his grounds in interesting and somewhat provocative detail. At Angers, in February 1470, the royal ambassadors to Francis II claimed that Charles the Bold had 'declared himself the mortal and long-standing enemy of the realm, in taking the Order of the Garter of England'. They presented

[1] ASMant Archivio Gonzaga 2100, letters of 4 October, 27 November and 26 December 1469, and 10 March 1470, and 567, letter of Suardo of 21 January 1470. For the next paragraph, see Dupuy, *Histoire de la réunion*, i. 239–44 and 419–20, and de Comines, *Mémoires*, ed. Lenglet du Fresnoy, iii. 118–20 (letters patent of Duke Charles of 19 April 1470).

Francis with an ultimatum: either he must help Louis against Charles or be himself attacked. Charles intervened and in his turn presented an ultimatum to the king: if Louis attacked Brittany he would serve its duke against him 'in his person and with all his power'. This was followed, in April 1470, by a renewal of the ancient alliance between Brittany and Burgundy. But more important even than the attitude of Brittany, in determining the moment when Louis could open his war of revenge against Charles, was the situation in England. Indeed the course of events there was now, in 1469–71, of special significance in Franco-Burgundian relations.

The friendship between Edward IV and Charles the Bold had been further cemented, at about the time of Charles's marriage, by an exchange of their insignia of chivalry; though this entailed the prior settlement of several knotty questions of protocol. Edward was elected a Knight of the Golden Fleece on 14 May 1468; Charles was made a Knight of the Garter on 13 May 1469 and received this adornment ceremoniously on 4 January 1470 at Ghent.[1] The Feast of the Garter was celebrated at the Burgundian court on St. George's Day in 1471 and 1472 and probably annually. While he was at the siege of Neuss, in 1475, Charles publicly wore the Garter on the eve of St. George's Day and on 23 April he attended mass wearing the sky blue robes of the Order, powdered with Garters. At Trier, too, in autumn 1473, the duke wore the Garter on at least one ceremonial occasion, though it was misleadingly described by one observer as 'the garter of the companionship of the ladies of England'. He was evidently proud of it. After all, he was in good company. The king of Portugal went through the same rigmarole on St. George's Day, though the Garter itself and the costumes struck the Milanese ambassador at his court as being 'ridiculous enough' (assay inepta). Charles the Bold lost a superbly jewelled Garter in the débacle after the battle of Grandson. Could this have been the actual Garter sent him by Edward which, made by John Brown of London, cost £8. 6s. 8d?

---

[1] On this and what follows see de Comines, Mémoires, ed. Lenglet du Fresnoy, iii. 99–103 and ii. 195, 198, 201 and 213 (= Vander Linden, Itinéraires, 21, 22, 30, 39 and 61); AOVG Reg. 2, fos. 71b–76b, partly summarized in de Reiffenberg, Toison d'Or, 61–2; Lists and indexes, xlix. 54; Molinet, Chroniques, i. 172; ASM Pot. est. Borgogna 516/31–4 (Panigarola's despatch of 24 April 1475); Baader, AKV (N.F.) xi (1864), col. 239, compare p. 146 below; Cal. state papers. Milan, i. 174; Evans, The Antiquaries Journal xxxii (1952), 70–1 and Deuchler, Burgunderbeute, 122–3.

By wedding his sister and donning his Garter Charles had made
King Edward of England into a close and intimate ally. But how
secure was that ruler's throne? He had won it by force of arms in 1461
with the indispensable assistance of Richard Neville, earl of Warwick.
But Edward's Burgundian alliance, as well as his marriage into and
promotion of the Woodville family, had driven Warwick into
opposition and eventually provoked him into organised rebellion.
Indeed by 1469 he was seriously considering replacing Edward IV
on the throne of England, perhaps by the king's younger brother
George, duke of Clarence. Charles the Bold's response to
these internal disputes was one of cautious neutrality. He was neither
Yorkist nor Lancastrian; his attitude towards English affairs was
conditioned less by sentiment, and more by his relations with the
other north-west European maritime powers: France especially, but
also the Hanse and Denmark. Thus, though he had married Margaret
of York, Charles still maintained two notable Lancastrian exiles at
his court, who were however sent away temporarily for the wedding
itself:[1] Edmund Beaufort, earl and duke of Somerset, and Henry
Holland, duke of Exeter or *comte d'Yvenchier* as he is described in the
accounts of the duke's household. And though both of these were
personal enemies of the earl of Warwick, Charles received Warwick at
St. Omer in April and May 1469 with the utmost ceremony and
civility. Later still, he seems to have tried hard, and perhaps nearly
succeeded, in mediating between the earl and the king.[2]

For a time, in the late summer of 1469, Warwick and Clarence had
King Edward in their power, but he contrived to extricate himself
with the help of his supporters, and Warwick was proclaimed a rebel.
By April 1470 he had been forced to escape by sea and, after Sir
John Wenlock had refused or found it inadvisable to admit him to
Calais, he sailed for the coast of Normandy. In the course of these
manoeuvres the earl of Warwick made a piratical attack on Burgundian
shipping which drew forth an immediate reaction from Charles. On
24 April 1470 the duke ordered his officials to start manning warships
to sail against Warwick, who was accused of seizing some sixty to
sixty-four ships belonging to Charles the Bold's subjects in Flanders,

---

[1] *Paston letters*, i. 539. For the count *d'Yvenchier* = Devonshire, see for
example, Brun-Lavainne, *BCHDN* viii (1865), 203.
[2] AGR MSS. divers 1173, f. 161a–b (despatch of de Jacopo and de Bettini
from Amboise, 13 February 1470). On Warwick, see Kendall, *Warwick the
kingmaker*.

Zeeland and Holland.[1] Burgundian naval preparations had actually begun the summer before; now, Duke Charles moved to Sluis to supervise the mobilization of his fleet and soon the earl was being harried and pursued along the north coast of France by Burgundian, as well as English, naval squadrons. Further events, which involved Duke Charles in a confrontation with King Louis of France, are described in ducal letters sent, by way of propaganda, to Ypres and no doubt other towns, on 10 June 1470 from Middelburg in Zeeland.

Dearest and well beloved, you may have already learnt how, after the duke of Clarence and the earl of Warwick were expelled from the kingdom of England for their seditions and mischiefs, of their own accord and without any rational cause they have constituted, declared and proved themselves to be our enemies by words, deeds and exploits of war. On 20 April, in putting into execution their said declared enmity and hostility against us our lands and subjects, they seized by trickery and fraud a large number of ships and goods belonging to our subjects; inflicting more damage and taking a larger number of ships than had ever been done before at a single stroke, and continuing since then whenever they had an opportunity.

To obviate this, we thereupon gave orders for the mobilization of our navy. Moreover, at the same time, we were informed that Clarence and Warwick and their people, after the defeat inflicted on them at sea by the men of the most high and mighty prince and most honourable lord, our brother the king of England, had withdrawn to the coast of Normandy and, on orders from the king of France, had been received and welcomed at Honfleur by the admiral of France and other officers, together with everything that they still retained, after the said defeat, of the booty taken from our subjects. Since they had openly declared themselves our enemies, this constituted a direct infringement of the treaties of peace made and agreed between my lord the king and ourselves, and so we wrote at once to the king, asking him not to aid, help, welcome, sustain or favour the said Clarence and Warwick in his land of Normandy nor elsewhere in his realm, nor to permit them to sell and distribute the

---

[1] *IADNB* i (2). 65. The letter extracted below is printed in *Collection de documens inédits*, i. 226–31, compare Plancher, iv. no. 218 = *Dagboek van Gent*, ii. 230–3. For what follows on the events of 1470, besides the works cited above, p. 41 n. 1, see de la Roncière, *Histoire de la marine française*, ii. 339–47, Gandilhon, *Politique économique de Louis XI*, 372–3, and Degryse, *MAMB* xvii (1965), 166–9. Documents are printed in de Comines, *Mémoires*, ed. Lenglet du Fresnoy, iii. 122–5, 120–1 and 145–7, Plancher, iv. nos. 210–29, and *Lettres de Louis XI*, iv. 110–14, 121–6, 140–4, 146–8 etc.

belongings of our subjects, and [we asked him] to make his wishes plain by causing this to be proclaimed and published throughout Normandy and elsewhere as necessary. We wrote similarly to the court of *Parlement* at Paris and to the councillors of my lord the king at Rouen.

Although my lord the king, the said court of *Parlement*, and the Rouen councillors have written and signified to us that it is the king's wish and pleasure to respect and maintain the said treaties made between him and us . . . and he has prohibited all his subjects in Normandy from keeping any goods belonging to our said subjects . . . , yet nevertheless we were then, and have been since, reliably informed that, among the ships taken to Honfleur by Clarence and Warwick, there were three bearing our coat of arms as well as ensigns of our subjects, which were removed along with the other ships belonging to our subjects; and that the possessions of our subjects were sold, distributed and dissipated . . . , some being held in custody and ransomed with the approval, and the seal, of the admiral of France and other officers there. . . .

Since our said letters were written, the above-mentioned have re-freshed and reinforced themselves with provisions and men at Honfleur and elsewhere in Normandy and put to sea with their ships as well as those taken from our subjects and, continuing the said hostility against our subjects, . . . have attacked a number of ships from our lands of Holland and Zeeland and have captured, pillaged or destroyed fifteen or sixteen, which they have taken to the said River Seine and elsewhere in Normandy. . . . This they could not have done without help, favour, support, provisioning and reinforcement . . . from Honfleur and other places in Normandy. Besides this a certain caravel belonging to the said admiral has recently appeared off our harbour of Sluis, planning to surprise and destroy or capture, by setting fire, cutting cables or other-wise, several of our ships fitted out for our navy, and take them away, and us with them, or some of our captains if they could find opportunity, to Honfleur or elsewhere in Normandy. But, finding they could achieve nothing, on their return they attacked and pillaged a Zeeland boat with cries of 'Warwick!'

On the whole, Duke Charles's navy, which was under the overall command of a Dutch captain, Henrik van Borselen, lord of Veere and most of the island of Walcheren, was singularly unsuccessful, though this was not necessarily due, as some afterwards supposed, either to treachery or incompetence. Quite apart from failing to stop Warwick and his men from taking upwards of a hundred Burgundian ships, Charles's fleet contrived to be nowhere in evidence on that fateful day, 9 September 1470, when Warwick and his followers, escorted by French warships, sailed out of La Hogue and crossed successfully to England.[1] This failure of the Burgundian fleet to blockade Warwick in Normandy and prevent his return to England has charitably been put down to a storm. The only notable success of the Burgundian navy was apparently at Southampton, where some of Charles's sailors under Floris, bastard son of Frank van Borselen, count of Ostrevant, had landed for purposes of recreation when they were attacked by the local inhabitants, partisans of Warwick. A struggle ensued in which cries of 'Warwick!' and counter-cries of 'Burgundy!' resounded through the streets of Southampton and, subsequently, a detachment of the Burgundian fleet helped King Edward to capture this place after a short siege.[2]

The nonchalant Edward seems to have been sublimely unaware of the trouble Louis and Warwick had concocted for him in the late summer of 1470. Within a month of his return to England, Warwick, who had been reconciled to Margaret of Anjou under the auspices of the king of France, had extricated her unfortunate and lunatic husband Henry VI of Lancaster from the Tower, where he had been King Edward's prisoner ever since 1465, and set him once more on the throne of England. On 14 October two of Edward IV's gentlemen arrived at Charles's castle at Hesdin, in Artois, to report that their king was at The Hague with Lord Scales, the queen's brother, and about 2,000 other fugitives.[3] He had narrowly escaped capture in the Marsdiep off Texel by some ships of the Hanseatic League, then at war with England. Charles, who had no wish to endanger his relations with the new regime in England, was extremely cautious in his attitude to the royal refugee seeking asylum in his territories. All he would do for Edward at first was to pay his and his retinue's expenses in Holland.[4]

In the months before Edward's flight from his kingdom Franco-Burgundian relations had been slowly deteriorating even though Louis was careful, during the summer, not to provoke Charles the Bold into a declaration of war. Louis's attitude to Warwick's and Clarence's depredations, and their presence on French soil, was non-committal but consistent. He hoped and planned to send them back

---

[1] AGR MSS. divers 1173, fos. 163 and 169 (letter of J. Spinola to the duke of Milan dated 21 May 1470, and despatch of de Bettini of 9 September 1470).
[2] *Cronycke van Hollandt*, f. 127a–b.
[3] BN MS. fr. 3887, account of the treason perpetrated in England as related on 26 October 1470 by the bailiff of Dijon, then on a visit to Flanders.
[4] *IADNB* i (2). 65.

to England as soon as possible in order that they might cause trouble there for Edward, while at the same time, fearing an alliance of Edward and Charles against him, he adopted a more or less conciliatory attitude towards Charles, who protested vociferously and repeatedly both in letters and embassies at Louis's alleged connivance in Warwick's piratical escapades. In one of his letters of protest, sent to the royal councillors at Rouen on 29 May, the duke added in a personal and somewhat undiplomatic postscript:

> Archbishop, and you admiral, the ships which you say were sent by the king against the English have now attacked my subjects' ships on their return to my territories; but, by St. George, if anything can be done, with the help of God, I shall do it, without waiting for your leave, nor your explanations or judicial decision.[1]

Diplomatic relations between France and Burgundy became just as heated as these epistolary exchanges. They culminated in the confrontation at St. Omer on 15 July 1470 when Chastellain, in a speech which has become famous, made Duke Charles tell the French ambassadors with reference to Louis's attitude to Warwick: 'Among us Portuguese there is a custom that, when anyone we have reckoned among our friends makes friends with our enemies, we commend them to all the hundred thousand devils in Hell.' According to the Italian prince Rodolfo Gonzaga, who was among the courtiers grouped on that occasion round Charles's ornate throne and who wrote dutifully home to his mother later that very day, Charles actually complained 'that the king was proving himself in every way to be his greatest enemy in the world' and went on to refer to

> a proverb or saying which is used in Portugal, whence he came on his mother's side, that those who are friendly with one's enemies are condemned to the devil in perpetuity; affirming on his honour that he knew of no enemy of his with whom the king, because of him, was not friendly, nor any friend of his who was not the king's enemy, and that no lord nor city nor castle nor commune had ever insulted or disputed with him except at the instigation and suggestion of the king.

---

[1] Plancher, iv. no. 215. For what follows, see the chancellor's and the duke's speeches in Plancher, iv. no. 219 (the chancellor's is also partly printed in Dupuy, *Histoire de la réunion*, 423–8) and see too Chastellain, *Oeuvres*, v. 450–3, and ASMant Archivio Gonzaga 2100, letter of Rodolfo Gonzaga of 15 July 1470.

This version of the duke's speech is a good deal nearer the text printed by Plancher, which may have been the official one, than Chastellain's colourful fabrications.

It was not, however, until the autumn of 1470 that the royal hostility, which Charles had so accurately perceived and passionately denounced to Louis's ambassadors, became fully apparent. Only on 8 October did Louis eventually retaliate against Duke Charles's letters of 12 June confiscating the belongings of all French merchants in Burgundian territories, by prohibiting the export of French goods to the duke of Burgundy's lands. Two things had moderated Louis's anti-Burgundian policies in the summer of 1470: firstly, the hostile attitude towards France of Duke Francis II of Brittany, Duke Charles's ally, and secondly, the uncertain situation in England.[1] But in July, just at the time of Charles's speech at St. Omer, Louis's diplomats at last succeeded in persuading Duke Francis to sign a neutrality treaty with France: he swore in part the very oath Louis had made his brother swear the year before, promising never to attempt to capture or kill the king but to do all in his power to defend him. Then, in September, the earl of Warwick not only returned to England, but very soon drove King Edward off his throne and into exile in Holland.

Louis's hostility towards Burgundy matured rapidly in the ensuing months. On 13 November 1470 the king instructed his ambassadors to negotiate a treaty with Warwick in which the scheme of 1467 was revived: the earl was to have Holland and Zeeland in return for an English attack on Burgundy timed to coincide with the French assault. They were also to ask Warwick to search the English governmental papers on Louis's behalf for any evidence that Charles had broken the terms of his treaties with Louis by planning an anti-French alliance with Edward.[2] On 3 December, at Amboise, Louis published what amounted to a declaration of war against Burgundy in which Charles was denounced in general for breaking his treaty terms with France and in particular for confiscating the belongings of French merchants going to the Antwerp fairs and sending forces to Normandy which, 'landing with banners raised and deployed and with great hostility, armed and accoutred, attacked our people and

[1] *Cal. state papers. Milan*, i. 136–7.
[2] De Waurin, *Croniques*, ed. Dupont, iii. 196–204. For the next sentence, see *Ordonnances des rois*, xvii. 353–6; also printed in de Comines, *Mémoires*, ed. Lenglet du Fresnoy, iii. 68–72, and de Chabannes, *Preuves*, ii. 247–52.

subjects, setting fire to houses and ships, killing and murdering some and taking others prisoner, with the intention of acquiring and usurping for themselves the government and all the country'. The king went on to declare the dukes of Guienne and Brittany 'quit, free, released, delivered and discharged' from all their treaty obligations towards the duke of Burgundy. As to his own treaty obligations, Louis simply stated: 'We have been and are quit and discharged of all promises and of anything else which the said duke of Burgundy can say, pretend or maintain that we are bound or obliged to do because of the treaty of Péronne or otherwise.' Finally, all the duke's lands and lordships were declared forfeit to the crown.

This provocative declaration is accompanied in the printed version by a more detailed accusation against Charles the Bold which, however, scarcely contained material sufficient to serve as a serious pretext for war.[1] Dutch subjects of the duke were said to have captured French ships from Dieppe, and Burgundian troops, committing ravages along the Norman coast during operations against Warwick and Clarence, had joined forces with the English with cries of 'Burgundy!' and 'King Edward!', and even raised 'the ensign of the red cross ... the ancient ensign of England and the English' on French soil. The document also alleged that when Galerant Denys, mounted sergeant of the Châtelet at Paris, was sent to Bruges to carry out a sentence of the Paris *Parlement*, he was arrested and held in prison for four months, and a similar fate overtook Guillaume de la Haye, *président des requêtes* of the Palais, who was sent to extricate him. On 4 January 1471 Louis ordered the halving of wages and salaries to pay for the war against 'Charles, soi-disant duke of Burgundy' and accused him of allying with 'Edouard de la Marche, soi-disant king of England', of wearing the Garter, and of refusing to do homage to the crown. Although these things may have rankled with Louis, his real motive in accepting the policy apparently urged on him by his constable, Louis de Luxembourg, count of St. Pol, of launching a campaign against Charles, seems to have been the total destruction of Burgundian power by the conquest of all Charles's lands.[2] But if this aim, the success of which depended on the materialization of English military aid from the earl of Warwick, proved

[1] For this and what follows, see de Comines, *Mémoires*, ed. Lenglet du Fresnoy, iii. 72–81 and 154–5 (royal letters of 4 January 1471, summarized in Tardif, *Monuments historiques*, 489; compare de Chabannes, *Preuves*, i. 282–4).
[2] Plancher, iv. no. 230, p. 301.

unattainable, then Louis probably hoped for the return to the French crown of the Somme towns which, though they were only mortgaged to Charles, were being treated by him, much to the king's annoyance, as if they were Burgundian possessions.

At first, in the winter of 1470–1, Franco-Burgundian hostilities were limited to confiscations, conspiracies and angry exchanges. Louis's officials seized the disputed Somme provostships of Vimeu, Foulloy and Beauvaisis. French emissaries or conspirators turned up at Auxerre, probably in December, but were rebuffed. At Amiens French troops brought royal letters with them in January, but both troops and letters were rejected. On 6 January, however, the citizens of St. Quentin were persuaded by the count of St. Pol to declare for Louis and to accept both the constable himself and a substantial French garrison.[1] On 12 January Charles the Bold prohibited his subjects from receiving letters from the king, and on 16 January he protested vigorously in writing against King Louis's aggressive activities in a letter to Anthoine de Chabannes, count of Dammartin, the French commander-in-chief, receiving a highly acrimonious reply.[2] But Louis meant business. On 6 February he issued a general proclamation, promising to treat as his own subject anyone who went over to him from the duke of Burgundy within a month, and to maintain him in all his lands, lordships and revenues. The privileges of any town doing likewise would be guaranteed in like manner. France and Burgundy were now on the verge of war: Amiens, queen of the Somme towns, confronted with a body of French troops and a royal ultimatum on 31 January, this time opened her gates to them, and went over to Louis on 2 February.

St. Quentin and Amiens were notable gains for Louis: two of the much-prized Somme towns had been gained without a blow. But a third, Abbeville, had been taken in hand by the Burgundian officer Philippe de Crèvecoeur, lord of Esquerdes, on 13 or 14 January. He made every burgess over eighteen years of age swear loyalty to the duke of Burgundy and confiscated all their weapons, so that there was

---

[1] De Waurin, *Croniques*, ed. Hardy, v. 613–14. This chronicler (v. 620–30), and de Haynin, *Mémoires*, ii. 95–124 are the most important chronicle sources for the 1471 campaign. For the next sentence, see Plancher, iv. no. 229.
[2] Printed in *Cabinet du roy*, 29–35, de Comines, *Mémoires*, ed. Lenglet du Fresnoy, ii. 237–41, and de Chabannes, *Preuves*, ii. 259–63. For what follows, see Plancher, iv. no. 230, and, for the surrender of Amiens, de Commynes, *Mémoires*, ed. Dupont, iii. 272–5.

hardly a knife left to cut bread.[1] At Roye and Montdidier the royal forces enjoyed easy victories. Montdidier was Burgundian in sympathy, but in spite of his long-standing preparations for the war he had long expected, the duke of Burgundy had been off his guard. His army was by no means ready to take the field and the citizens, deprived of any possibility of help in the immediate future, decided to surrender. At Paris, on 4 February, solemn processions of thanksgiving were held for these royal successes at Amiens, Roye and Montdidier; and Abbeville was erroneously added. Soon workmen recruited in Paris were on their way to fortify these places for the king, though in fact Louis ceded Roye and Montdidier, as well as Péronne if it could be conquered from Charles, to Louis de Luxembourg, count of St. Pol.

The campaign which now ensued was a war of raids and skirmishes fought in late February and March, for the most part in brilliant sunny weather, though the nights were sometimes bitterly cold. That faithful Burgundian vassal, Jehan, lord of Haynin, wrote a vivid first-hand account of it in his memoirs. He left home on Saturday 19 January with his twelve men, whom he names: three mounted swordsmen or *coustilliers*, seven archers, a page and a wagon-driver. Advancing slowly towards Amiens, Jehan de Haynin and other ducal vassals drew up in order of battle after dinner on 22 February at the gibbets outside that town. But they were only forty-four or forty-six lances strong, with no archers, and soon found themselves threatened by three separate enemy contingents which had sallied forth to attack them from Amiens, from the cathedral of which their movements had been closely observed. The only way they could extricate themselves was by making their horses step backwards, for they were sure the enemy would have charged them if they had turned their backs. On 24 February occurred the only significant military success achieved by either side during the entire campaign: the Burgundians seized Picquigny, town, castle and bridge over the Somme. De Haynin and his men were glad to find there bread, pastries, meat in great plenty and a large quantity of wine, 'which came in very useful to those who had breakfasted badly'. In spite of this success, Charles the Bold's attempt to reconquer Amiens was not seriously pressed home, though that town was more or less

---

[1] Renet, *Beauvais et le Beauvaisis*, 137. For what follows, see Beauvillé, *Montdidier*, i. 169–70.

besieged by his men during most of March.[1] Nor did Louis press home his attack on Charles, being probably deterred by his brother's failure to join the campaign, by his suspicions of the duke of Brittany and, perhaps, of the count of St. Pol, and above all by the effectiveness of the Burgundian military presence on the Somme.

There were other theatres of war in the early months of 1471, besides Picardy. Hainault was invaded in March by a combined force of French and exiled Liègeois. Among the latter, Raes de Lyntre was prominent.[2] From Calais, the English pillaged Burgundian territory on Warwick's orders. They even claimed to have killed two members of the ducal garrison of Gravelines. But Warwick never provided the comprehensive military aid Louis had hoped for from England. Instead, he wrote on 12 February to assure Louis that he would be with him in person, without fail, to serve him 'against this cursed Burgundy', as soon as possible. In the south French troops raided the county of Burgundy, and on 26 February, two days after the formal confiscation of the duchy to the crown on the grounds of its duke's failure to perform the homage promised at Péronne but never done, a substantial royal army invaded the Mâconnais. Occupying Cluny, it penetrated northwards in early March past St. Gengoux-le-Royal to Buxy, 15 km south-west of Chalon. Here, on 14 March 1471, a hard-fought engagement took place which both sides claimed as a victory. The lawyer Jehan de Ventes, who accompanied the French army on this campaign, claimed that over 1,500 Burgundian traitors, 'enemies of the king and of France', were killed in the battle which, he hoped, would put an end to the war by leading shortly to the conquest of Burgundy for the king.[3] But the Burgundian commander, Jehan de Neuchâtel,

---

[1] Janvier, *Les Clabault*, 286–303, Roux, *Histoire de l'abbaye de Saint-Acheul-lez-Amiens*, 61–77, letter of Jehan de Molesmes of 25 March 1471, printed in de Commynes, *Mémoires*, ed. Dupont, iii. 278–81, and Gachard, *Rapport sur les archives de Dijon*, 159–61, letter of 24 March 1471, excerpted in de Barante, *Histoire des ducs*, ii. 371 n. 2, and Plancher, iv. no. 233 (letter of 19 April 1471).
[2] De Barante, *Histoire des ducs*, ii. 367 n. 4 and AGR CC4181, f. 149. For the next sentences, see de Haynin, *Mémoires*, ii. 117 and Myers, *BIHR* xxxiii (1960), 114–15. For what follows on the war in the two Burgundies, see de Chevanne, *Les guerres en Bourgogne*, 37–108.
[3] His letter, and another written on the same day by the French marshal, are printed by Prunelle, *BAD* ii (1849), 641–6 and de Chevanne, *Les guerres en Bourgogne*, 219–23. Jehan de Neuchâtel's letter is printed in *Correspondance de la mairie de Dijon*, i. 117–19 and de Chevanne, *Les guerres en Bourgogne*, 229–30. See too, on the battle of Buxy, Lot, *L'art militaire*, ii. 103–4; AGR MSS. divers 1173, f. 181a–b (despatch of Sforza de Bettini of 28 March 1471), and AOGV Reg. 3, fos. 17b–19b.

lord of Montagu, thought differently. The day after the battle he wrote to the inhabitants of Dijon explaining that it was not the enemy, but the onset of darkness, which caused him to withdraw, and admitting losses of only ten or twelve men-at-arms dead, and eighteen or twenty others. The outcome of the battle of Buxy was, in fact, a gradual withdrawal of royal troops from the duchy, though sporadic skirmishes and sieges continued into April.

The Franco-Burgundian truces which became operative on 4 April, applicable both to Picardy and Burgundy, had been negotiated at Amiens from 19 March onwards by the count of St. Pol. Charles explained that he had waited at Amiens for some time in the hopes of a battle and only accepted the proffered three-month truce when he realized that the king had no intention of fighting. Louis claimed that 'Charles of Burgundy sent to us protesting that he . . . desired above everything to pacify and appease the war and dispute . . . , entreating us to give him truces for three months'.[1]

At the time of the truce of Amiens the affairs of England were once again in the balance. In January 1471 Charles the Bold received the royal refugee, Edward IV, at his court. In addition to the modest monthly allowance he had been receiving from the duke of Burgundy during his exile he was now granted by Charles, on 31 December 1470, the sum of £20,000 'for his and his brother the duke of Gloucester's expenses . . . and for their departure from my lord the duke's lands to return to England'.[2] With the help of these substantial funds the king hired a few Hansard and other ships to take him and his 'ij thousand Englysh men, well chosen' back to England. Sailing from Flushing in the Antonie of Veere on 11 March and landing on 13 March at the mouth of the Humber, he reached London on 11 April. Two days later Warwick was defeated and killed at Barnet. With this decisive royalist victory, followed a few weeks later by another at Tewkesbury, King Louis's dreams of the conquest and partition of Burgundy were shattered. By early June, when negotiations for a prolongation of the Franco-Burgundian truce were in progress, Anglo-Burgundian relations were more or less restored to their former state. Edward wrote on 28 May thanking Charles for his help, not forgetting to enclose an account of his successful regaining of the throne, and assuring him of his continued

[1] Plancher, iv. no. 234, and *Lettres de Louis XI*, iv. 212.
[2] Henrard, *Appréciation du règne de Charles le Téméraire*, 46 n. 1; see too Huizinga, *Verzamelde werken* iv. 183–94. For what follows, see *Historie of the Arrivall* and Thomson, *Speculum* xlvi (1971), 84–93, with references.

friendship and alliance. A slight coolness between the two perhaps existed that summer and autumn and would no doubt have evolved further had Edward known of Duke Charles's notarial instrument, drawn up on 11 November 1471, in which he set out his claims to the English throne and promised to take them up when a suitable opportunity occurred. These claims had been ceded to him on 16 June 1471 by his mother, Isabel of Portugal, who, as the grand-daughter of John of Gaunt, considered herself, after the murder of Henry VI on 21 May and the death of his son Edward prince of Wales at Tewkesbury on 4 May, the senior surviving representative of the house of Lancaster.[1]

Between 4 April 1471 and the first week of June 1472 a state of armed peace and almost continuous negotiation existed between Charles the Bold, determined to recover both St. Quentin and Amiens, and Louis, forced somewhat on the defensive by the turn of affairs in England. Moreover, during 1471, while the Burgundian position was sedulously strengthened in all directions by Charles's diplomats, Louis's was weakened and eroded. Thus, within the boundaries of his kingdom, Louis found himself confronted by an increasingly hostile duke of Brittany and a brother who, dissatisfied and disloyal, began in the summer months to entertain seriously the possibility of breaking his promise to Louis and marrying Mary of Burgundy. In August Louis tried to deter him by sending ambassadors who hinted darkly that the daughters of the house of Burgundy suffered from hereditary disease and were hence incapable of bearing sound, healthy children.[2] If at this time Louis gained an ally in the shape of Philip of Savoy, lord of Bresse, who abandoned Charles in 1471, he lost one in Nicolas of Anjou, duke of Calabria and Lorraine, who, succeeding his father Duke John in December 1470, was a Burgundian sympathizer by May 1471 and finally became a firm ally of Charles a year later. Louis's new-found friendship with his old enemy Philip of Savoy caused, in the summer of 1471, a growing estrangement between him and his sister Yolande, duchess of Savoy, and this in its turn led to a closer alliance between the king's brother and sister, Charles and Yolande. Faced with this partial re-emergence of a coalition of princes against him, Louis sought more and more, in late 1471 and early 1472, to make a separate peace with the duke of

[1] The text of Charles's 3 November 1471 declaration is printed by Gachard in *Trésor national*, ii. 122–7, and *Études et notices historiques*, ii. 345–52. Isabel's declaration of 17 June 1471 is BM Add. charters 8043.

[2] De Comines, *Mémoires*, ed. Lenglet du Fresnoy, iii. 162.

Burgundy which would exclude the other princes. But Charles, even when offered the return of St. Quentin and Amiens, was unwilling to stand by while Louis crushed his allies. Moreover, as his *mandemant* of 12 November 1471 declaring the duchy of Burgundy and dependent territories completely exempt from the jurisdiction of the French crown and *Parlement* abundantly demonstrates,[1] Charles could never bring himself to accept the recognition of French royal suzerainty which Louis insisted on as part of the peace settlement. Nonetheless, in spite of this unilateral Burgundian declaration, justified by the duke on the grounds that Louis had infringed the terms of the treaty of Péronne, negotiations continued through the spring of 1472. At one point a peace settlement was on the verge of mutual acceptance, but in April 1472 both sides began serious military preparations and, in the middle of May, Louis at last launched his long-expected campaign against his faithless brother Charles, duke of Guienne. Charles the Bold's counter-attack was not long delayed: it had been carefully prepared. Early in June, Burgundian forces were thrown across the Somme in a war of pillage and conquest while at the same time Charles's ally, Duke Francis II of Brittany, also advanced his forces against France.

Even the stars were on Charles the Bold's side in 1472 for, according to a noted astrologer, the town doctor of Brussels, Jehan de Wesalia, the comet which appeared in January 1472 presaged victory for Burgundy and disaster for Louis XI.[2] Moreover, in the search for allies that inevitably preceded every war, Charles had this time succeeded where Louis had failed. If his relations with Scotland were mainly commercial, and somewhat distant,[3] he had the assurance of English friendship, even though Edward was not to be persuaded at this juncture into a war against France. In Italy, Burgundian diplomats had by no means been idle, while Charles the Bold's influence and fame there were increased by the princes of the houses of Este and Gonzaga whom he maintained for long periods at his court. It is not clear why Antonio Dandolo's embassy to Brussels in December 1467 did not result in the treaty of alliance both sides apparently wanted, but the privileges of Venetian merchants in Bur-

---

[1] *Ordonnances des ducs*, 194–6.
[2] See Abel and Martens, *CB* i (1956), 41–86.
[3] *Cartulaire de l'ancienne Estaple de Bruges*, ii. 197–200 and 215–16, *IAB* vi. 32–3 and 36–43, Varenbergh, *Relations diplomatiques entre le comté de Flandre et l'Angleterre*, 589–90, and Armstrong, MSMS viii (1951), 19–32.

gundian territory were soon afterwards confirmed,[1] and friendly relations maintained in spite of one or two minor disagreements. Dandolo was back again in May 1469 and there was more talk of an alliance. It was said in November that year that the Venetians had Duke Charles's ear all the time,[2] and this was even truer after Dandolo has been replaced, in 1471, by Bernardo Bembo, whose first despatch from the Burgundian court was sent on 16 September. Finally, on 15 June 1472 Charles signed a treaty of alliance with Venice which, however, was aimed more against the Turks than the king of France.

In spite of the long-standing alliance of King Louis of France and Duke Galeazzo Maria Sforza, Charles the Bold was never wholly out of touch with Milan. Indeed, in May 1469 a full scale Milanese embassy was sent to him, under instructions to seek an alliance and, if possible, to obtain, or allow Galeazzo to obtain, some gyrfalcons:[3]

> On Wednesday afternoon, 13 June 1469, ten ambassadors of the duke of Milan, the two principal ones clad down to the ground in cloth of gold, the others also magnificently dressed in velvet and other cloth, with thirty-six attendants, were received in Ghent in the hall of the [duke's castle, the] Gravenstein, which was exquisitely decorated. The duke sat there in splendid majesty with the duke of Cleves on his left and the chancellor on his right, and all his noble officers and attendants stood in order along both sides of the hall. The ambassadors brought their credentials there and were given audience. They said that the duke of Milan was willing to serve my lord [the duke of Burgundy] and wanted to be on friendly terms with him, as their predecessors had always been.

Nothing came of this proposal and by January 1470 Milanese-Burgundian relations were decidedly strained. According to Rodolfo Gonzaga, the duke of Milan was one of Duke Charles's two great hatreds; the other, predictably, being Louis XI. He explained in a letter to his mother that Charles was so angry when he was told that one of his people, sent to Rome on ducal business, had been arrested on Milanese territory and his letters opened and read by Galeazzo, that he ordered his messengers to Rome to travel in future through

---

[1] *Hansisches Urkundenbuch*, ix. 274 and *IAB* v. 559–64. On this and what follows, see Perret, *France et Venise*, i. 480–570.
[2] ASM Pot. est. Borgogna 515/40–41. For the 1472 treaty see Sanuto, *Vitae ducum Venetorum*, cols. 1196–7.
[3] Their instructions are copied into AGR MSS. divers 1173, fos. 143–146b; the extract that follows is from *Dagboek van Gent*, ii. 223.

Germany rather than through the territories of Milan.[1] [In spite of this incident Duke Charles was reported in August 1470 to have sent Galeazzo an offer of alliance and of the Golden Fleece. But in fact it was only later that the duke of Milan was persuaded to abandon his traditional alliance with France in favour of Burgundy.]

While Florence, like Milan, was a French ally at this time, the pope could be counted in Charles's political system and, beyond Rome, Naples under King Ferrante was brought into the Burgundian orbit in 1471. De Haynin describes the departure of Philippe de Croy, lord of Quiévrain, from Valenciennes in September 1471 on embassy to Rome and Naples, complete with jewels, plate and a hundred horse. The treaty of alliance between Charles and Ferrante, which had partly been negotiated the previous spring, was solemnly announced on 1 November at St. Omer and published elsewhere later that month.[2]

Thus in Italy Charles the Bold more than held his own, diplomatically, against Louis XI. In the Spanish peninsula, quite apart from his family connection with Portugal, he was able to exploit to the full the enmity between France and Aragon. Only Castile stood firm in its French alliance if, as seems probable, we may discount Chastellain's assertion, with reference apparently to 1468, that King Henry IV of Castile offered Charles military assistance against Louis. As to Aragon, the alliance with Burgundy was of long standing. [John II had been a member of the Order of the Golden Fleece since 1461 and he sent his envoy to the chapter of the Order held at Bruges in May 1468.] On 1 November 1471, in the church of St. Bertin at St. Omer, Charles ceremonially received the royal Aragonese Order of chivalry and the Burgundian chancellor Guillaume Hugonet made a more than usually pompous and tedious speech, bristling with his

---

[1] ASMant Archivio Gonzaga 2100, letter of 23 January 1470 and, for the next sentence, AGR MSS. divers 1173, f. 167 (copy of Sforza de Bettini's despatch of 23 August 1470).

[2] For this and what follows on Naples and Aragon, see *IADNB* i (1). 240, Bartier, *Légistes et gens de finances*, 442–7, ADN B10437, f. 18, AOGV Reg. 2. f. 56, Vander Linden, *Itinéraires*, 35, Perret, *France et Venise*, i. 577–8, Calmette, *Louis XI, Jean II et la révolution catalane*, 319 and n. 1, and Dürr, *MIOG* xxxv (1913), 327 and n. 2. Vicens Vives, *Juan II*, 328–9, errs in excluding Naples from the alliance owing to confusion between King Ferrante of Naples and Ferdinand of Aragon, both of whom are often referred to in the sources as 'Fernando, king of Sicily'. For Castile, see Daumet, *Étude sur l'alliance de la France et de la Castile*, 109–10.

customary allusions to Cicero, Lactantius and even Pythagoras and the Bible. He was followed by the *audiencier*, Maître Jehan Gros, who announced the conclusion of the new treaty between Charles and Ferrante and proudly, though perhaps rather optimistically, numbered among the duke of Burgundy's allies

> the pope, the Emperor, the king of England, the king of Aragon, the king of Scotland, the king of Denmark, the king of Portugal, the dukes of Brittany and Austria, the house of Savoy, the doge and signory of Venice, the count palatine of the Rhine, elector of the Empire, the dukes of Bavaria, of Cleves and of Guelders, and my lords the archbishops of Mainz, Trier and Cologne, imperial electors.

On the very same day, Charles empowered his ambassadors to consolidate his existing alliances with John II and Ferrante into a defensive and offensive league, which was also subscribed to by Ferdinand of Aragon and Isabel of Castile, married in 1469 and heirs to a united Spain.

Long as it is, this list of Burgundian allies was lengthened still further by the time Charles declared war on Louis on 6 June 1472. The most significant additions were Nicolas of Anjou, duke of Lorraine, Count John V of Armagnac and Charles of France, duke of Guienne. Duke Nicolas brought a substantial body of troops to augment Charles's army and commanded them in person throughout the campaign. This military service was performed in return for a promise of Mary of Burgundy in marriage; but Nicolas was not permitted to leave Charles the Bold's court after the campaign until he had renounced this marriage in writing.[1] The count of Armagnac pinned down a royal force besieging his capital of Lectoure until he was forced to surrender on 16 June. Charles of France was, however, the crucial element in the Burgundian system of alliances, and the king's situation was greatly strengthened on 24 May, ten days after his invasion of Guienne, by the sudden death of his brother. Charles the Bold made it quite clear on 7 June, to the papal envoy at his court, Luca de' Tolenti, bishop of Šibenik, that he believed, or wanted the pope to think he believed, that Charles of

---

[1] *Chronique de Lorraine*, ed. Marchal, 107–23, de la Marche, *Mémoires*, iii. 79–80 and de Comines, *Mémoires*, ed. Lenglet du Fresnoy, iii. 189–195. For the next sentence, see Samaran, *La maison d'Armagnac*, 181–2. For what follows, on Charles's death, see Paquet, *BIHBR* xxv (1949), 77–80, and de Comines, *Mémoires*, ed. Lenglet du Fresnoy, iii. 198–201 (manifesto of 19 July 1472).

France had been murdered by a combination of poison and magic. Indeed the allegation that Louis had murdered his brother was seized on by Charles as a *casus belli*, and in a manifesto dated 16 July he announced to all the world his intention of avenging his late ally's death, occasioned by 'poisons, malefices, sortileges and diabolical invocations'. Most recent historians have suggested instead a death by natural causes, but one has retained the multiple element in the explanation by asserting that the unfortunate Charles died of 'tuberculosis probably aggravated by venereal disease'.[1] The exact truth will never be known, but he was certainly killed by disease rather than by poison.

Duke Charles kept up his verbal warfare against the king through the summer of 1472. Reviving the accusation first made in a broadside of 13 December 1470, that Louis had plotted his assassination, he now accused the king of homicide and murder, attempted murder, treason against 'the crown, the princes and the public welfare', perjury, violation of peace treaties and truces, heresy and idolatry, parricide, conjuration or conspiracy and sedition.[2]

The animosity apparent in these and other ducal documents was dramatically evident in the campaign itself, which opened with a display of ferocity. It seems that a body of Charles's cavalry, accompanied by a herald, reached Nesle in the evening of 12 June and a parley ensued, during which the herald was killed by arrows fired from the town. The Burgundian men-at-arms responded by a sudden

---

[1] Kendall, *Louis XI*, 247.
[2] Plancher, iv. no. 245; the 13 December 1470 manifesto is no. 228. For the next paragraph, see Paquet, *BIHBR* xxv (1949), 86, de Roye, *Chronique scandaleuse*, i. 268–70, and the *Procès-verbal de Nesle* in *BSHF* i (2) (1834), 11–17 and *BCLF* ii (1853–5), 231–5. The main chronicle sources for the 1472 campaign are Basin, *Louis XI*, ii. 124–38, *Chronique de Lorraine*, ed. Marchal, 110–23, de Commynes, *Mémoires*, ed. Calmette and Durville, i. 227–39, de Haynin, *Mémoires*, ii. 134–48, *Histoire de Charles, duc de Bourgogne*, 293–301, de la Marche, *Mémoires*, iii. 76–81, and de Roye, *Chronique scandaleuse*, i. 268–85. Documents are printed in *Lettres de Louis XI*, v. and de Chabannes, *Preuves*, ii. 330–69. Also important are the letter of 28 September 1472 in de Comines, *Mémoires*, ed. Lenglet du Fresnoy, iii. 225–7 and ed. Dupont, iii. 293–6; the ducal letter of 4 October 1472 in *Correspondance de la mairie de Dijon*, i. 127–8; the burgess of Nürnberg's letter in *Urkundliche Nachträge zur österreichisch-deutschen Geschichte*, 183–5, and the letters of Bernhart von Ramstein in Innsbruck, LRA Urk. I. 8208 and Sigmundiana IVa no. 182 (RTA material). The most recent detailed narratives of the campaign are von Rodt, *Feldzüge Karls des Kühnen*, i. 129–57 and Kirk, *Charles the Bold*, ii. 120–36!

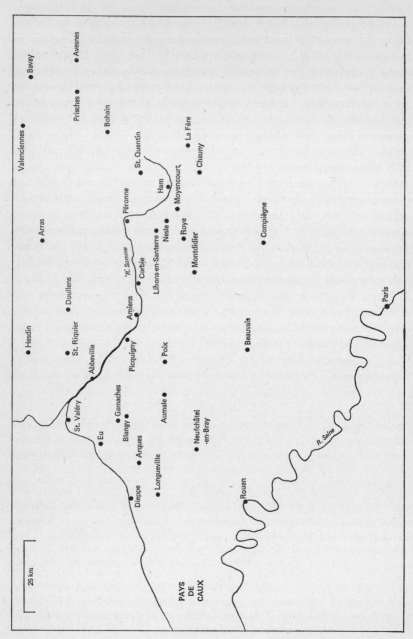

2. The campaigns of 1472 and 1475

and determined assault, and the citizens and garrison of Nesle were overrun. Before the duke and the rest of the army arrived on the scene the town had been sacked and everyone found bearing arms, including the royal archers and others who had taken refuge in the church, had been put to death. Long afterwards, in 1522, when an enquiry was held into these events, a group of old people, including an eighty-year-old publican and a weaver of 'about seventy-four', testified jointly to the atrocities of the Burgundians, perhaps not without a touch of exaggeration; certainly with a degree of agreement among themselves which can only rouset he historian's doubts. Into their mouths was put the story, found also in the pages of the chronicler Jehan de Roye, of Duke Charles riding his horse into the church amid the blood and corpses of the dead franc-archers and exclaiming 'By St. George! This is a fine butchery! I've some excellent cut-throats!' It is quite certain that the duke did order the drowning, or mutilation, of a number of prisoners and that the town was burnt and devastated before the Burgundian army continued its advance. At Roye, where the garrison put up some resistance before surrendering, there was no repetition of the atrocities of Nesle, and at Montdidier a civic deputation came out with the keys to meet the duke. These two places had, of course, been Burgundian until King Louis seized them in January 1471.

Advancing now beyond the disputed frontier area of the Somme, Charles struck deep into French territory. Heading towards Normandy, where he might hope to join forces with his ally Duke Francis II of Brittany, against whom King Louis was about to take the field in person, he halted en route to lay siege to Beauvais. It was about 7.0 a.m. on Saturday, 27 June, that Charles's advance forces arrived outside the town. An hour later trumpets announced the first assault but, in spite of a series of attacks that day, Charles's men got no further than the faubourgs and inflicted no worse casualties than one citizen killed by an arrow in the neck. That evening, and subsequently, substantial reinforcements reached the beleaguered town, which was by no means fully invested, especially on the side facing Paris. This military error proved fatal to Charles's hopes of success. Throughout the siege, it seems, the defenders had little difficulty in obtaining provisions, ammunition and reinforcements: the civic authorities of Orleans, in a generous display of urban solidarity, sent them 100 barrels of the finest wine. Charles found it necessary to withdraw his army, by then extremely short of food, after a siege of twenty-five days. During it, a succession of assaults and artillery bombardments had alike proved of no avail, even though about a quarter of the walls was demolished. Beauvais had been well defended by over a thousand men-at-arms and some 4,000 archers, not to mention her heroic women-folk, who were afterwards granted by a grateful crown the privileges of wearing whatever clothes they pleased and of preceding the men-folk in civic processions.[1]

Louis XI, though personally engaged in the field against the duke of Brittany, did his best to organize countermeasures against the invader. Repeatedly, he urged the grand master of his household, Anthoine de Chabannes, to 'strike some good blow against the duke of Burgundy', or to do what Charles did to Nesle 'in his territories, wherever you can, without sparing anything'.[2] On 14 July some 3,000 French troops, with four cartloads of scaling-ladders and other siege equipment, invaded Hainault and did just this, burning down the church at Prisches with the men, women and children who had taken refuge in it. Meanwhile Charles, withdrawing north-westwards from Beauvais past Poix towards the coast, burning everything he could lay his hands on, made slowly for Rouen. A Burgundian correspondent reported on 1 August from conquered Eu that all was going well with the campaign after a carefully executed withdrawal from Beauvais during which only one contingent of the army marched at once, the other two remaining drawn up facing the town to repel sorties. Since then Aumale and Poix had been demolished, while St. Valéry had already surrendered to the Burgundian garrison of Abbeville, which had also destroyed Gamaches. But Dieppe, outside which Charles waited hopefully in the third week of August, refused to follow the example of the smaller coastal towns and remained firm, feeling safe perhaps in the knowledge that, this year, Charles had not commissioned a fleet. Meanwhile the French struck back again. The garrisons of Amiens and St. Quentin raided Artois, and on 18 August royal troops hurled themselves at Montdidier. The *drossart* of Valkenburg, Diederik van Palant, and his men, who had been placed in garrison there by the duke, suddenly found them-

---

[1] On the siege of Beauvais, besides the works cited in the preceding note, see the *Discours du siège de Beauvais* in de Comines, *Mémoires*, ed. Lenglet du Fresnoy, iii. 203–18, *ACHF* i. 111–35 and *Album historique et paléographique beauvaisien*; and Renet, *Beauvais et le Beauvaisis*, 124–223. See too Sforza de Bettini's despatch of 22 July 1472 in AGR MSS. divers 1173, f. 60; de Comines, *Mémoires*, ed. Lenglet du Fresnoy, iii. 218–25; and Leblond, *MSO* xxiii (1922), 385–422.

[2] *Lettres de Louis XI*, v. 5 and 20.

selves in the front line.[1] Diederik himself was wounded; his chaplain and secretary were killed with a dozen others. In a series of assaults the enemy penetrated within the walls but were eventually repulsed, thanks in part to the heroic efforts of the inhabitants who were firmly Burgundian in sympathy.

During August, Charles's men had ravaged and devastated the land of Caux, but his way across the Seine was firmly barred by royal forces posted at Rouen. On 4 September he sent the following letter to his ally the duke of Brittany:

My good brother, I heartily recommend myself to you. I had some expectation, having marched as far as Rouen, of a success there, at least so that I could get over the Seine. But the enemy's full power is on that frontier, together with [Anthoine de Chabannes] the grand master, about whose loyalty I have no doubts. So far matters are still in the balance and I do not know what will happen. Realizing this, I have given them something to think about elsewhere and I have pitched camp here between Rouen and Neufchâtel with the intention, still, of returning towards Rouen, unless I pursue the war somewhere else more damaging to the enemy. I shall do everything in my power to compel them to retreat from your frontiers.

My men-at-arms from Burgundy and Luxembourg are doing good work in Champagne and I am glad to hear that you are doing likewise in your area. I have burnt and ravaged the whole land of Caux so that it won't cause any trouble either to you or to us for a long time. I shall not lay down arms without you, just as I am sure you will not do so without me, but I shall continue what was begun according to your advice and remonstrances to the pleasure of our Lord. May he give you a good life and a long one and a fruitful victory.

Written in my camp, near Boissay, the fourth of September.

Your loyal brother Charles.[2]

A week after this the duke began a slow retreat towards his own territories. Again, the troops were short of provisions, though a Lille merchant helped matters by sending them several cartloads of biscuits as a personal gift. At Blangy on 11 September Charles received an English embassy accompanied by a herald, Bluemantle Pursuivant, who wrote this account of his errand to the duke:[3]

[1] For this and the next sentence, see *Chronijk van Overmaas*, 35–6.
[2] Printed de Comines, *Mémoires*, ed. Lenglet du Fresnoy, ii. 258, and de Chabannes, *Preuves*, ii. 346–7.
[3] Kingsford, *English historical literature*, 381–2 with modernized place names.

D

I rode as far as a vyllage called St. Quentin a lege fro Péronne, where I met w^t the capytayne of the forward called my lord Phelippe of Creuecure, the wch for the Kinges sake made me right grete chere and caunsled me to abyde in his company tyll I shoulde goo thense to the Duc. And on the morne he reine to Blangy, where he bode tyll the Duke come. Also he had under hym CCCC. speres, wch were loged in vylages all about hym, ridying all wey in batell thus: euery C. speres had a standart and ij penons, j penon for the custerelles, and ye bowes on horsebake, wch went before, anoder for the fotemen, and the standart for ye speres; vnder or fast by the standart rode the capytene of ye C. speres; and lyke order kepte euery C. speres. These were the capitaynes: Syr Phelippe Creuecure, capitayne of all ye forward; Syr Oliuer de la Marche, capytayne de C. l.; Syr Baudwyn de Lanoy, capy^t de C. lance; Mounser Mount taverne, capt. de C. lance; the baylie of St. Quentin, capt. de C. lance; Mounsyr de Boi esser, capt. de C. lance. And on the fryday about ix of the cloke I had word ye Duc was but iij leges thens comyng thedder ward. I rode agenst hym and saw his holle host in Remeving; to my Jugement there was mor then a M. cartes charged w^t gonnes, tentes, vyttalles, mylles, pauys, gunstones and innumerable necessaryes, the Duc hym[self] being in his rereward, wher I present hym my letter.

The 1472 campaign, which was the last fought on French soil by Charles the Bold in person, ended in anticlimax, even failure. According to Bernhart von Ramstein, when the duke demonstrated outside Amiens in the third week of September, his army was still 'a wonder to see, and there were enough there to fight two kings with all their power'. Yet the same soldier admits that, on the whole, the war went badly for the Burgundians. If they burnt French territory, the French burnt theirs, and he complains that the Burgundian garrisons in newly won St. Valéry and Eu surrendered those places back to the French without serious resistance. An Italian report in early October stated that the duke's men were living on fruit and suffering a great deal from dysentery.[1] At sea, no effective Burgundian response had been made to the depredations of French pirates or warships against the Dutch herring fleet and other shipping. Only in the two Burgundies were there any military gains to be recorded against the French in the autumn of 1472. While the Auxerrois was

---

[1] *Cal. state papers. Milan*, i. 162–3, excerpted from ASM Pot. est. Borgogna 515/79. For what follows, see for example de la Roncière, *Histoire de la marine française*, ii. 353–4, Daenell, *Blütezeit der Hanse*, ii. 115–16, and *Hanserecesse*, vi. 517–20. On the war in the two Burgundies, see de Chevanne, *Les guerres en Bourgogne*, 111–50.

cleared of enemy troops, Anthoine de Luxembourg, count of Roussy and marshal of Burgundy, marched northwards between 30 September and 13 November far into Champagne, conquering a score of places around Bar-sur-Seine, Châtillon and Langres. It was perhaps these Burgundian successes which persuaded Louis to sign a five-month truce with Charles on 3 November; a Franco-Breton truce had already been in force since mid-October.[1]

The general relationship of Burgundy, France and England, as described in this chapter, continued without significant change in the years after 1472. In that year, wrote Bernhart von Ramstein, Duke Charles 'had the finest and largest army that ever entered France, though it is nothing to what he intends to have next season'. But, in the event, other things intervened, and the regime of truces persisted unbroken till 1475. Nor was it till then that Edward IV's necessarily intermittent preparations for an invasion of France bore fruit. There is some doubt about his contribution, if any, to Duke Charles's campaign in 1472. Did the archers and warships he is said to have promised actually arrive? Petro Aliprandi, writing on 25 November from Gravelines, reported that those 'wicked islanders,who are born with tails', the English, who are like angels in the morning and devils after dinner and who spend all their time eating, had cheated the duke of Burgundy by receiving his money for the promised troops, but not sending them.[2] Be this as it may, after 1472 as before, Charles had to be content with the assistance of contingents of English mercenaries rather than of an English army in his campaigns which, except in 1471–2, were not directed against King Louis XI. His immediate interests and his most cherished ambitions lay elsewhere, in spite of his recurrent dream of the destruction of French power and his almost paranoiac suspicion of the king of France.

[1] De Comines, *Mémoires*, ed. Lenglet du Fresnoy, iii. 228–33.
[2] *Cal. state papers. Milan*, i. 164–70.

CHAPTER THREE

Territorial Aggrandizement, 1469-1473: Alsace, Lorraine, Frisia and Guelders

No European ruler in the late middle ages could afford to neglect opportunities for territorial expansion, and many concentrated all their political energies and financial resources on this task. But, in spite of his undoubted ambitions and military zeal, Charles the Bold cannot compare, in this respect, with either his father Philip the Good, in his early years as duke, or with his great-grandfather, Philip the Bold, who put together the Burgundian state in the first place. Nor was this merely a matter of opportunity. Charles, for example, made no vigorous efforts to follow up or support his instructions, issued on 14 January 1472, to Jehan de Jaucourt, lord of Villarnoul, to seize possession of 'the county of Nevers and the land of Nivernais'.[1] It is remarkable too that, in spite of opportunities, he made no serious attempt on the duchy of Lorraine until 1475, though at least one observer thought that he had gained possession of it in 1472. Perhaps the mere acquisition of territory was too mundane a task to focus Duke Charles's interests. Certainly he seldom pursued this activity for its own sake. After all, there was an ultimate aim behind his purchase of Alsace, his attempt on Frisia and his conquest of Guelders: the acquisition of the imperial throne.

Though historians almost unanimously attribute to Charles the Bold a conscious desire, or ambition, to gain control of Alsace, the evidence for this is scanty, and it is geographically ridiculous to suppose, as some writers have, that Alsace could possibly have constituted a link between his northern and southern territories.

---

[1] De Chevanne, *Les guerres en Bourgogne*, 114–15 and nn. For the next sentence, see Paquet, *BIHBR* xxv (1949), 76.

Moreover, even if it was true that Charles wanted Alsace, there was little that was new, or specifically personal, about such a desire. Ever since 1377, when negotiations for an Austro-Burgundian marriage alliance were taken up by Philip the Bold, the duke of Burgundy had had a close interest in this fertile and economically important region which abutted on the Franche-Comté. John the Fearless and Philip the Good had both tried to maintain, if they could not extend, Burgundian influence in Alsace, which was at its height in the years 1406–11 when Catherine of Burgundy held court at Ensisheim during the last few years of the life of her husband Leopold of Austria. The abundant documentation at Dijon shows that Alsace had not been forgotten since then, and underlines the fact that the treaty of St. Omer of 1469 came at the end of a long process of Burgundian penetration into this area.[1]

Since the end of the fourteenth century the lands of the house of Habsburg, which stretched discontinuously across Europe from Vienna to Basel, had been divided between two, or even three, princes who described themselves as 'duke of Austria'. In the late 1460s, while the Emperor Frederick III ruled the eastern territories, centred on the duchy of Austria itself, his cousin Sigmund ruled Tirol and the so-called Vorlande, a group of territories and rights scattered along both banks of the Upper Rhine. These outlying Habsburg territories were subject, from early on, to Swiss aggression. In 1415 the *Eidgenossen* had conquered the Aargau; in 1460–1 they forcibly annexed the Thurgau; and in 1468 they invaded the Sundgau to aid their ally Mulhouse against the local nobility, and they laid siege to Waldshut. The most dynamic and powerful of their members, Bern, certainly hoped for a decisive battle against Sigmund, and she hoped, too, to acquire Waldshut itself and perhaps make other conquests in the Vorlande. Sigmund did his best to obtain allies against these formidable enemies, but his cousin Frederick was more concerned to resist the Turks; the princes of south-west Germany preferred to remain on friendly terms with the Swiss; and Basel and other towns preferred peace to war. The treaty of Waldshut, of 27 August 1468, was accepted unwillingly on the one side by Sigmund, on the other by Bern. Sigmund had to

---

[1] Stouff, *Catherine de Bourgogne*. For the next two paragraphs, see especially Witte, *JSG* xi (1886), 261–332, Meier, *Waldshuterkrieg*, the same in *ZGO* (N.F.) li (1937–8), 321–84, Krebs, *Die Politik von Bern, Solothurn und Basel*, and Grüneisen, *Aus Reichstagen des 15. und 16. Jahrhunderts*, 154–212, all with references.

guarantee the future safety, against the depredations of the local 'Austrian' nobility, of Schaffhausen and Mulhouse, and to pay 10,000 Rhenish florins before 24 June 1469 in reparations to the *Eidgenossen*. Bern would have preferred conquests to cash and probably hoped for a further opportunity of military expansion when, as seemed likely, the impecunious Sigmund failed to pay the promised reparations.

Duke Sigmund is said to have been the proud owner of six castles all bearing his own name; Sigmundsburg, Sigmundseck, Sigmundsfreud, Sigmundskron, Sigmundslust and Sigmundsfried. But, as a statesman, he was indolent and unrealistic, and much more interested in his home country of Tirol than in Alsace and the Black Forest. He was quite used to pawning his domains in order to raise money, and in February 1469 he decided to seek finance in France or Burgundy by offering part of the Vorlande to Louis XI or Charles the Bold. Rebuffed by Louis, Sigmund arrived at Arras to confer there with Charles the Bold on 21 March 1469. It was only on 9 May, however, after some weeks of hard bargaining, that Charles agreed, in the treaty of St. Omer, to accept the Upper Rhine Vorlande in mortgage for 50,000 Rhenish florins. Even then Sigmund must have left the Burgundian court a disappointed man for, instead of the anticipated treaty of alliance with Charles, instead of the contemplated Burgundian promise of military assistance against the *Eidgenossen*, all he obtained, apart from vague verbal assurances, was a document taking him formally into Burgundian protection.[1]

Even though, at St. Omer and in subsidiary negotiations afterwards, Charles drove the hardest possible bargain with Sigmund, what he obtained never remotely resembled an outright sale, still less grant, of territory. The references in a document of Duke Sigmund to 'our landgraviate of Alsace, our county of Pfirt and our towns on the Upper Rhine including the Black Forest', and in a Burgundian financial record to 'the landgraviate of Alsace, the county of Ferrette and the four Rhine towns with their appurtenances' were

---

[1] The treaty of St. Omer and related documents are printed in *Urkundliche Beleuchtung*, 116–23 and 299–301, *Urkunden, Briefe und Actenstücke*, 223–36, and Stouff, *Origines de l'annexion de la Haute-Alsace*, ii. 99–109. See too Krause, *Beziehungen zwischen Habsburg und Burgund*, 69–73 and the recent discussions, with references, of Cartellieri, *ZGO* xlii (1928), 629–36, Matzenauer, *Studien zur Politik Karls des Kühnen*, 110–18, Brauer-Gramm, *Peter von Hagenbach*, 58–62, and Bittmann, *Ludwig XI. und Karl der Kühne*, ii (1). 304–10.

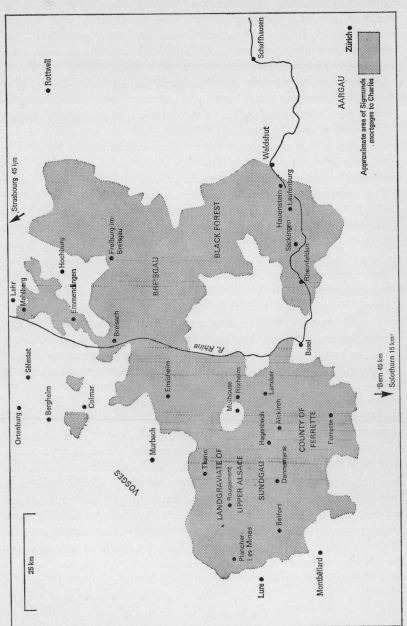

3. The Sundgau and the Breisgau

crude simplifications.[1] In actual fact, what Charles now acquired in mortage was a miscellaneous collection of rights rather than a group of territories. Moreover, Sigmund had the right to redeem this mortgage at any time, though Charles made it as difficult as possible for him to do this by insisting on adding all his administrative expenses in the meanwhile to the original loan. He also laid it down that if Sigmund wanted to repay the loan and redeem the mortgage the entire sum must be handed over in a single payment at Besançon: repayment by instalments was disallowed.

The landgraviate of Upper Alsace and the county of Ferrette or Pfirt, which were more or less distinct, extended across the flat lands of the Rhine plain and the lower foothills of the Vosges between the wooded heights of that range in the west to the Rhine itself on the east, and southwards towards the Jura and the frontier of modern Switzerland. The county of Ferrette, which was nearly identical in extent with the Sundgau, comprised comital rights over the lordships of Ferrette or Pfirt itself, Altkirch, Thann, Belfort, Rougemont and others. The system of rights which comprised the landgraviate of Upper Alsace lay mostly to the north of the county of Ferrette and centred round Ensisheim and Landser. In both landgraviate and county Charles the Bold's rights were severely limited by the fact that a large number of them had been mortgaged to the local nobles or towns. Thus Christoph von Rechberg held the lordship of Pfirt in pawn for 7,000 florins and Landser was mortgaged to Thüring von Hallwil. Besides the rights of these mortgagees, the part of Alsace now to become Burgundian was riddled with rights belonging to others; so much so that a more accurate way of putting it would be to suggest that Upper Alsace was partitioned jig-saw puzzle fashion between six or more powers. In the north, the bishop of Strasbourg, who was landgrave of Lower Alsace, ruled extensive lands in the sphere of influence of the town of Strasbourg, itself a power to be reckoned with. In the south, a similar situation existed around Basel, for here too, town and bishop were rivals in the extent of their lands and their jurisdiction. Of course the whole of Alsace was part of the Empire, and ten of its principal towns, all of them imperial and therefore in no sense subject to the landgrave of Alsace, had long ago formed themselves into a league, the famous Alsatian Decapolis. The most important of them were Haguenau, Sélestat, Colmar and Mulhouse. They were under the jurisdiction of an imperial official,

[1] *Urkundenbuch der Stadt Basel*, viii. 271, and ADN B2079, f. 7b.

the bailiff or *Landvogt* of Alsace.[1] This office was currently mortgaged to Frederick I, the elector palatine of the Rhine, a ruler with territorial ambitions in Alsace as well as elsewhere. Careful distinction needs to be made between his office, which was imperial, and the bailiwick or *Landvogtei* of Upper Alsace, which belonged to the dukes of Austria. Attached to no exactly defined territory, its seat was at Ensisheim and it was filled by Charles the Bold on 20 September 1469 with the subsequently notorious Peter von Hagenbach, who was described thereafter in ducal letters as 'bailiff' or even sometimes as 'grand bailiff of Ferrette and Alsace'.[2]

Other important cessions, outside the landgraviate of Alsace and the county of Ferrette, were also made to Charles the Bold in the treaty of St. Omer: the lands and lordship of mortgaged Ortenberg in the north; Breisach, with the only Rhine bridge between Basel and Strasbourg; the county of Hauenstein with a large part of the Black Forest; and the four so-called Forest towns on the Upper Rhine: Rheinfelden, with the lordship of the same name which was mortgaged to Basel, Säckingen, Laufenburg and Waldshut. All of these were included in the jurisdiction, or bailiwick, of Peter von Hagenbach.

Weeks before von Hagenbach's appointment as bailiff, Duke Charles had sent commissioners to take over the new territory by accepting oaths of allegiance from the inhabitants and setting up the ducal arms on public buildings. These *commis*, who included in their number Peter von Hagenbach, Rudolf, margrave of Hochberg, and two Franche-Comté officials, Jehan Carondelet and Jehan Poinsot, began their tour at Rheinfelden on 28 June and completed it at Ensisheim on 7 July 1469 with a grand assembly of the Estates of all the lands mortgaged to Charles the Bold. It was only on 17 July, however, that Sigmund finally resigned himself to handing Breisach over to the Burgundian commissioners. They had been entertained to supper at Thann castle on 21 June by Sigmund but,

---

[1] See Sittler, *La Decapole alsacienne* and, for the next sentence, Cohn, *The government of the Rhine Palatinate*, 60–1 and 182–3, with references. On this and what follows on Alsace in general, see especially Witte, *ZGO* (N.F.) i (1886), 129–69, Nerlinger, *Pierre de Hagenbach*, Bernoulli, *BVG* xiii (1893), 313–80, Stenzel, *RHB* iv (1927), 50–7, Heimpel, *JSFB* v (1942), 139–54 and *Genius* ii (1948), 19–44, and, above all, Brauer-Gramm, *Peter von Hagenbach*, with full references, and RTA material.
[2] Griveaud, *BHPTH* (1932–3), 155 and 159.

D*

if one can judge from the rather disparaging account of it which follows, the meal was not quite up to Burgundian standards.[1]

News sent from the county of Ferrette by those who went there to take possession for my lord of Burgundy.

Details of the supper at Thann, given at four p.m. on 21 June 1469.

The seating arrangements at the supper

First, my lord the marquis of Baulde.

My lord of Baudeville.

My lord the *maître d'hôtel*.

My lord the marquis of Rothelin.

My lord the judge of Besançon, Maître Jehan Carondelet.

My lord the *procureur* of Amont, Maître Jehan Poinsot.

After the above-mentioned had taken their places my lord the duke of Austria came and sat down next to the marquis of Baulde. On the table at which the said duke and marquis were seated was placed, near the duke, a small table-cloth on which were two large covered silver-gilt cups full of wine, weighing eight or ten marks.

The dishes at the supper

First a dish full of poached and boiled eggs placed in the middle of the table, which was square.

Next, a dish of boiled minnows.

Next, fried chub, which my lord of Austria spread out on the table.

Next, a large dish of boiled turnips cut into small pieces.

Next, a dish of small trouts, cut in half, and boiled in water, and two bowls full of vinegar for the whole company.

Next, a dish of soup and some cherries.

Next, trout in yellow sauce.

Next, peas in the pod.

Next, roast trout and similarly, fritters with pear stuffing.

Afterwards, water for washing was brought to the duke of Austria only; then to my lords the marquises of Baulde and Rothelin.

As regards the waiters, there was a squire with a large knife who sliced the bread as each dish was served and presented a slice to each person.

---

[1] BN MS. fr. 3887, fos. 185–6; compare Nerlinger, *AE* vi (1892), 605–6, and Gasser, *RB* vi (1916–17), 328–9. The first four persons mentioned here are, respectively, Karl, margrave of Baden, the out-going bailiff; Philipp von Hochberg, lord of Baudeville or Badenweiler; Peter von Hagenbach; and Philipp's father Rudolf, margrave of Hochberg.

[Afterwards] . . . he threw them into a grape-basket in the middle of the room. Then he cut new slices with his knife and took them round on it.

When my lord of Austria wanted to drink, the said squire served him unhesitatingly with one of the above-mentioned cups, but, while he drank, he held the lid of the said cup underneath [the duke's chin]. . . . As to my lord the marquis of Baulde, when he wanted to drink another squire served him with the other cup in just the same way except that he did not hold the lid underneath, but held it carefully in his hand just as the cover of the chalice is held, from the Corpus domini prayer to the Pater noster, at some high masses.

It should be known that the cloth covering the said square table, and the napkins, were of plain material, without embroidery. There were two other tables in the room, at one of which sat knights and gentlemen and, at the other, people of lower estate. All the courses were liberally served with powder[ed spices sprinkled] round the edges of the dishes. It is noteworthy that, as soon as a dish was placed on the table, everyone grabbed with their hands, and sometimes the least important person was first. It should also be recorded that my lord of Austria, without hose, was wearing a pourpoint with a cloth of silver collar and a long gown reaching to his feet. Over this was the robe of scarlet which he had worn at Arras. And my lord the marquis of Baulde was wearing a red mantle, with a small hood with a jagged edge and no coronet.

The principal task of Rudolf of Hochberg and his companions was to take formal possession of Burgundian Alsace. They did, however, make certain recommendations to Charles the Bold about its administration, some of which were implemented. For example the appointment of Hagenbach as bailiff must have been in response to their recommendation that someone 'of estate and authority' be chosen to govern the country, and their suggestion, that the existing Ensisheim councillors be retained to serve the new ruler and advise his bailiff, was carried out.[1] At least three more commissions were sent into Alsace by Charles the Bold during the ensuing years. They were fact-finding missions, but their investigations were usually cursory and their recommendations ignored. They can hardly be seen as evidence, on the part of the duke, of any sort of policy for the new territories. Rather, their existence and activities served as a

---

[1] Their report is printed in Stouff, *Possessions bourguignonnes*, 68–86. For what follows, see the same work, pp. 30–68, where Poinsot and Pillet's report is printed, and Stouff, *Déscription de plusieurs forteresses par Maître Mongin Contault, 1473*. See too Nerlinger's articles in *RA* (1896), 87–101 and *BEC* lix (1898), 304–21, and Stintzi, *AJ* vii (1959), 147–58.

kind of administrative camouflage to conceal the absence of ducal policy in the region of the Upper Rhine.

The instructions for Jehan Poinsot and Jehan Pillet, whose hurried tour through Alsace took place in the second half of September 1471, were issued by Charles the Bold on 13 June 1471. They show that the aim of this mission of enquiry was a routine one of setting down in writing full details of the duke's rights and revenues in Alsace, scattered and exiguous though these were. To save themselves the trouble of travelling to distant Waldshut, the ducal commissioners managed to interview the relevant local officials at Basel. At Säckingen, typically, they found that their duke was sharing power with the citizen mortgagees and a local abbess. They disapproved of a number of Peter von Hagenbach's activities, hinting that the fifty mercenary soldiers he had at Ensisheim, one of whom came from Constantinople, were quite unnecessary, and that he might be made to exercise his office in a less dictatorial manner if the duke appointed some other officers alongside him. They concluded:

> And with regard to their government, we have ascertained that the said lands are in excellent obedience to you and that, to maintain your subjects in better justice, it would be expedient and appropriate for you to appoint and establish there a notable councillor and *avocat fiscal*, a sufficient treasurer, and a loyal and knowledgeable *procureur général*; men such as you would be pleased to choose and appoint in your other territories, speaking and understanding the language of the said land of Germany. This would be most agreeable to your said subjects in Germany.[1]

Although Poinsot and Pillet had made it abundantly clear in their report that the chaotic and utterly inadequate administration of Upper Alsace was not even effectively based on the use of written records, nothing seems to have been done to ameliorate this situation until, on Hagenbach's advice, the Dijon *maître des comptes* Mongin Contault was commissioned in May 1472 to make yet another investigation into the duke's revenues there. He was also empowered to see to the repair of ducal castles, to pay arrears in wages, and to audit accounts. Working hand in glove with Hagenbach, this elderly financial official, who knew no German, spent most of January 1473 carrying out his investigations. These were hampered by the severe weather, especially in the Black Forest, where the snow was up to

---

[1] Stouff, *Possessions bourguignonnes*, 65–6.

half-a-lance deep and people had not been able to leave home for a month. At Thann Mongin inspected the castle with Hagenbach and some masons and carpenters. He found the ascent long and difficult. It was pouring with rain, and he noticed places where gutters were leaking and water was dripping on to the masonry. There was some artillery in the castle, but it belonged to Hagenbach. He was told that the 'Austrians', before they left, had removed all the doors, windows, locks and stoves and sold them. In general, Mongin found things just as his predecessors had found them: receivers on the point of resignation, accounts in deficit, wages not paid, ducal rights mortgaged or eroded in some other way. He submitted a detailed report which demonstrates a certain gift of style and considerable powers of observation, but nothing was done. Charles the Bold went no further than investigation: he introduced no radical reforms in the administration of Alsace.

If these successive commissions of enquiry ordered by Duke Charles in his new Alsatian lordships demonstrate no very clear or forceful policy, the same is true of his other activities there. The only matter that seems to have been dealt with with reasonable efficiency and expedition was the implementation of the financial clauses of the treaty of St. Omer, for the 10,000 florins which Sigmund had to pay to the Swiss by 24 June 1469, according to the terms of the treaty of Waldshut, were duly paid over by Charles's emissaries, albeit at the last moment. As to the remaining 40,000, of the 50,000 florins Charles was to lend Sigmund in return for his mortgaged rights in Alsace, they were paid over in February 1470, only a few months late.[1] After this, the flow of Burgundian finance dwindled at best to an intermittent trickle. This absence of financial support, already underlined by Mongin's picturesque account of the castle of Thann, is strikingly apparent in the policy of the new administration towards the numerous unredeemed mortgages in Alsace.

It has been pointed out above that a quite high proportion of Duke Charles's newly acquired lordships and other rights were already mortgaged to local nobles or towns, and most historians have assumed that Charles had caused the right to redeem these mortgages to be granted him in the treaty of St. Omer with a view to their large-scale repurchase as soon as this became practicable. Certainly the commissioners he sent to take possession of Upper Alsace in June 1469 had done their best to obtain from every mortgagee a written promise

[1] ADN B2079, f. 7b.

to renounce his mortgage as soon as his capital outlay had been repaid. Certainly these and subsequent ducal commissioners in Alsace, not to mention Hagenbach himself, recommended the redemption of the outstanding mortgages. But, in the counsels of the duke, in his inmost attitudes and motivations, Alsace evidently enjoyed the lowest possible priority. The money for redeeming the mortgages either was not forthcoming at all or else it came only slowly and fitfully. Breisach itself, later described as 'the strongest and most handsome town in all the Vorlande', a place of the utmost strategic significance, was only finally redeemed at the end of 1473, while Bergheim, Ensisheim, Pfirt, Belfort and numerous other lordships, places and rights held in mortgage never were redeemed. All that Peter von Hagenbach contrived to do was to confiscate Landser after the principal mortgagee's death; conquer Ortenberg by force of arms;[1] and redeem Thann in 1470 and the lordship of Rheinfelden in 1472. The only legitimate judgement on this situation is that Charles the Bold had no primary interest in developing his power in Alsace by means of a systematic mortgage redemption. He contented himself instead with encouraging Hagenbach to obtain control of a mere handful of strategically important places.

An equally effective means of extending Burgundian power would have been a thoroughgoing distribution of annual grants or pensions in return for the acceptance of Burgundian protection. But nothing of the sort occurred. Instead, there were only isolated cases of this as when, for example, on 13 June 1471, Charles took Ludwig von Landeck into his protection and gave him an annual pension of 200 florins in return for the use of his castles of Landeck and Keppenbach near Emmendingen in the Breisgau. It seems that the duke did not take up his bailiff's advice that the count of Saarwerden's offer be accepted, of his places of Lahr and Mahlberg on similar terms. Moreover, it was apparently left to Peter von Hagenbach, acting on his own initiative, to extend to Count Rudolf of Werdenberg, Bernhart von Eptingen and probably others, the protection of the duke of Burgundy.

The relationship of the Burgundian administration in Alsace to the towns reveals a similar absence of systematic policy though here, especially, a certain radical attitude, an extremist posture, is manifested time and again. Just as Charles the Bold at any rate gave the

[1] See Nerlinger, *AE* viii (1894), 32–65 and Pons, *Annuaire de Sélestat* (1967), 94–7.

impression, with his commissions of enquiry, that he was planning serious administrative reforms in Alsace; just as the extraction of written promises from the mortgagees made it look as though he planned a large-scale mortgage redemption; so, in his relations with the towns, the activities especially of von Hagenbach, gave rise to a near-universal belief that Duke Charles intended to engulf them and to incorporate them into the Burgundian state. But, here again, the means to achieve such a scheme were by no means forthcoming.

This antithesis, between attitude and actuality, is nowhere better demonstrated than in the case of the imperial town of Mulhouse, which had for years been a thorn in the flesh of the previous, Austrian, administration in Alsace.[1] Time-honoured disputes divided her citizens from the local nobility, while the situation was aggravated by the fact that many of them were Mulhouse's creditors. Moreover in 1466 Mulhouse had sought to obtain powerful assistance against her 'Austrian' persecutors by means of an alliance with Bern and Solothurn. Even before Charles the Bold's commissioners had had time to take formal possession of the new lands, this alliance was invoked against them. On 25 June 1469 the civic authorities at Bern sent a letter to Rudolf of Hochberg on Mulhouse's behalf, complaining in the strongest possible terms of the provocations and deeds of violence of the local nobles, lately Austrian, but now Burgundian, vassals. Mulhouse people had been attacked and robbed, their commercial activities had been disrupted; five Mulhouse women had been stripped and suffered other indignities; an old man of eighty had been hurt. Indeed, it was scarcely safe for them to leave the town at all, still less to work in the neighbouring fields. These incidents continued during the Burgundian administration, against a background of constant negotiation in which Frederick I, count palatine of the Rhine, was involved as imperial bailiff of Mulhouse and the other towns of the Decapolis; Bern and Solothurn were involved; Peter von Hagenbach and his lieutenant Bernhart von Ramstein were involved. At the end of May 1470 Hagenbach made a series of propositions to Mulhouse which were rejected out of hand. It seems probable that he had ducal backing in principle for these proposals, which were however submitted and phrased in Hagenbach's typically forthright manner. He demanded that Mulhouse

---

[1] For what follows, see *Cartulaire de Mulhouse*, iii. 343–iv. 99, Rettig, *AHKB* xii (1887–9), 163–215 and now Mieg, *BMM* lxxiii (1965), 31–84, lxxiv (1966), 5–109, lxxv (1967), 39–118 and lxxvi (1968), 47–154, with numerous *pièces justificatives*.

should accept in perpetuity the protection of the duke of Burgundy and his successors, and that she should open her gates to Charles and his men. In return, Charles would protect Mulhouse just as he protected the towns in his own lands; he would settle Mulhouse's debts to his vassals at his own expense; he would arbitrate all outstanding disputes involving Mulhouse. Mulhouse citizens would be free to travel on Burgundian territory and no Burgundian garrison would be introduced into Mulhouse without her consent. This plan naturally aroused the instant opposition not only of Mulhouse herself but also of the count palatine of the Rhine.

A year later, the situation was still much the same, with Mulhouse still complaining of endless minor provocations: a stone had been thrown at one of her burgesses; a Mulhouse butcher had been menaced; on Wednesday 17 April 1471 some people from Rixheim spat on the bread which Conrad Veiler was hoping to sell there; and so on. Later still, in January 1473, we find Hagenbach making what some contemporaries interpreted as another attempt to gain possession of Mulhouse for the duke of Burgundy, though in fact he may have been more concerned with persuading Mulhouse's allies Bern and Solothurn and their friends to come to her financial assistance. On this occasion, he uttered a series of crude threats and inducements: the duke of Burgundy would treat Mulhouse as he had Liège; 'there was no jollier rose-garden than the Sundgau, Alsace and the Breisgau', but Mulhouse might be regarded as a weed in this garden which needed uprooting; Duke Charles would like nowhere better to live than Mulhouse; it was not true that there was a possibility of Sigmund redeeming his mortgaged lands from Charles, on the contrary, he was planning further grants to the duke of Burgundy, and so on. But, though the Burgundian bailiff stormed, threatened, and coaxed Mulhouse in this way, she remained resolute in her opposition to any sort of Burgundian penetration.

Mulhouse was successful in resisting Burgundian encroachments because she had powerful allies, because she was an imperial town, and because the count palatine of the Rhine was a firm friend of Charles the Bold. For these reasons, quite apart from general considerations, ducal Burgundian policy did not in this instance permit things to be taken to extremes. What those extremes were was demonstrated, somewhat later, at Breisach, which was compelled to accept a Burgundian garrison and a burgomaster and councillors appointed by the Burgundian administration, and suffered too the abrogation of its privileges and the abolition of its gilds. But Breisach was small and relatively isolated, and in any event Burgundian rule there was shortlived. By and large ducal policy towards the towns was limited to verbal threats, to hostility, to an anti-urban attitude. For all their understandable fear of Burgundian ambitions, Mulhouse, Strasbourg and Basel were safe simply because Charles the Bold was not prepared to give priority, in men and money, to their reduction. His immediate political ambitions lay elsewhere.

The same sweeping or almost revolutionary attitude, coupled with a quite restrained policy, is apparent in the Burgundian treatment of other, non-urban, privileges, jurisdictions and communities in Alsace. In a set of instructions issued on 13 June 1471 the duke ordered his bailiff to 'protect' his Alsace subjects from the imperial court at Rottweil, to prevent them from appealing to imperial courts, and to bring to an end the abusive issue of safe-conducts by the bishop of Strasbourg.[1] All this was apparently part of an intended judicial reform which would have made the ducal council at Ensisheim the supreme court of Upper Alsace, with appeals going thence not to the Emperor, but to the duke; an intended reform which, like the modernisation of the administration, the redemption of the mortgages and the suppression of urban independence, was never carried through. Thus the conversion of the bundle of rights in Alsace mortgaged to Charles by Sigmund in 1469 into a genuine territory and its incorporation into the other Burgundian lands remained a mere aspiration, nor were the possibilities opened to Charles the Bold by the treaty of St. Omer ever effectively exploited.

A further important question about the acquisition of Alsace is the exact nature of the relationship between the duke and his bailiff. The affair of the abbot of Lure's silver mines in the southern Vosges throws some light on this problem, as well as on Duke Charles's attitude to local privileges.[2] The powerful abbey of Lure, in the county of Burgundy, had contrived to maintain possession of its mines of silver and other metals at Plancher-les-Mines partly because they lay on the frontier between the counties of Burgundy and Ferrette. Before 1469 claims by the duke of Burgundy were met, and, in a sense, cancelled out, by the counterclaims of the duke of Austria. After the treaty of St. Omer, the ruler of both counties was the duke of Burgundy and, on 4 September 1470, Charles the Bold ordered his officers to take possession of the mines on the sweeping but quite

---

[1] Innsbruck LRA, Sigmundiana I 80.
[2] Griveaud, *BHPTH* (1932–3), 143–65; the excerpt is from pp. 161–2.

unjustified grounds that 'the said mines are regalian rights belonging to the princes of the land' and that 'all mines, wherever they may be found or situated belong by common law, and because they are regalian, to the princes of the lands in which they are situated'. Naturally this juridical nonsense was rejected by the abbot out of hand. Duke Charles accepted his plea to be heard by a court of law, and ordered his council at Dijon to take the matter up and send the result of its investigations to his great council. Peter von Hagenbach, who had a private grudge against the abbot of Lure, went much further in this affair than his duke, who was persuaded in letters of 17 January 1472 to dissociate himself with his bailiff's behaviour:

And what is more, and worse, our said bailiff of Ferrette went one day to the said abbey and spoke threateningly to the said petitioner [the abbot of Lure], hoping to constrain him to swear in his hands more than the customary oath which he had already sworn to us as his guardian in the hands of certain commissioners of ours who had been sent there to take possession of our said lands of Ferrette and Alsace. On this a dispute arose between the parties, in order to appease which a day was agreed on for them to appear before the councillors resident in our town of Ensisheim. The said parties appeared at the appointed time and place and there, after the said petitioner had submitted himself, concerning the dispute in question, to the judgement of us or of our councillors, our said bailiff, as if angry, replied that this had nothing to do with our councillors but concerned him alone, and, again using menacing words, he arrested the said petitioner and took him prisoner, together with some knights and squires who were in his company, including a person called Messire Jehan Gros, provost of the church of Notre-Dame at Murbach, an imperial notary, whom the said petitioner had asked to make a written record of his evidence and declarations. He took the said provost to the prison of Ensisheim castle, from which none of the above-mentioned could obtain release and deliverance until the said petitioner had agreed to swear the oath in [the bailiff's] hands as he commanded; all of which is to the great contempt and scorn of certain appeals made to us concerning this matter by the said petitioner . . . and to the very great grief, prejudice and damage of the said abbey, as the said petitioner alleges. He asks us to annul and repeal the oath made by him as described, as not being customary and as being an infringement of the franchises, liberties and powers of his said church, and [he asks] that condign and sufficient reparation be made to him for the shame, injuries, violences and arrest inflicted on him and the others above-mentioned by our said bailiff and that, above all, it may please us to administer brisk and fair satisfaction and justice.

In his treatment of the abbot of Lure as well as, for example, in his behaviour towards Mulhouse, Peter von Hagenbach displayed a certain tactlessness, even acrimony which, in the case of the abbot of Lure at least, certainly overstepped the bounds of ducal policy. Undoubtedly, Hagenbach's strongly developed streak of crudity or brutality made him too forthright and insolent to be an accurate mirror of his duke's rather more sophisticated and diplomatic attitudes. Moreover, Hagenbach had ideas of his own. Along with some of his colleagues and friends from the Sundgau he loathed and despised the Swiss and maintained a quite definite loyalty to their hereditary enemy the house of Habsburg. His intense disdain for the towns was made clear by his insulting remarks to the citizens of Basel, Strasbourg and elsewhere. Hagenbach was a practical man, a soldier at heart, who enjoyed power and found the limitations and restrictions on his bailival authority extremely irksome. But this frustration was certainly shared by Charles, and the sources demonstrate time and again his support for and trust in his bailiff. Many of Hagenbach's activities were undertaken at his express command, though often as a result of representations made to him by Hagenbach in the first place. It is possible, for example, that Charles only agreed to sign the treaty of St. Omer on Hagenbach's persuasion. In the duke's letters to Hagenbach of 28 August 1470 he orders him to undertake the siege and conquest of Ortenberg castle, 'in accordance with your memorandum (*advertissement*)', which seems to imply that Charles was here acting on detailed advice to take Ortenberg sent him by Hagenbach[1]. As to other mortgaged places, the bailiff wrote to Charles describing how he had seized possession of Landser and seeking the duke's approval, which was given on 6 January 1474. On the other hand it was Charles who took the initiative over Bergheim, which did not in the event fall into Burgundian hands. On 26 December 1470 he wrote congratulating Hagenbach on taking Ortenberg and ordered him with reference to Bergheim, 'if he could, to try some undertaking against the said town, to place it in our hands'. The closeness of Duke Charles and Hagenbach, which dates from well before Charles became duke, is well attested. In a letter to Hagenbach from his lieutenant, Bernhart von Ramstein, written on 2 October 1472 from Picardy, where he had been sent by Hagenbach on a mission

---

[1] Transcript in RTA material of Innsbruck LRA Schatz-A, Urk. I, 7468. For what follows, I have used copies of the following Innsbruck LRA documents in RTA material: Sigmundiana XIII 110; Schatz-A, Urk. I. 7471; Schatz-A, Urk. I. 8208; and Sigmundiana IV 9.

to the duke, Bernhart says that Hagenbach is very much in Charles's favour and continues: 'you have the master eating out of your hand (*a vostre main*)'. Hagenbach himself assured the duke on 18 September 1471 that he would 'work to maintain your dignity and lordship and your rights' adding, almost prophetically as it afterwards turned out, that he would serve the duke's pleasure 'loyally until his dying day'. The sombre tale of Peter von Hagenbach's further activities in Alsace will occupy our attention later in this book.

Much more significant than Alsace, as a possible link between Charles the Bold's northern or Netherlandish and southern or Burgundian territories was the imperial, but for the most part French-speaking, duchy of Lorraine. Since this was not annexed by Charles until 1475, the history of its temporary incorporation in the Burgundian state must be left to a later chapter but, a brief account of Burgundian territorial policies and activities in this area in the early part of Duke Charles's reign, even though they did not result at this time in the acquisition of new territory, may not be out of place. Throughout most of the fifteenth century the dukes of Lorraine of the house of Anjou lived in the political shadow of their powerful neighbours the kings of France and the dukes of Burgundy, while their activities in Lorraine and the surrounding territories were hampered by their intermittent absences in Italy or Spain and limited, especially after about 1425, by the growing power of the Estates of their duchy. Charles II had been a Burgundian partisan whose anti-French sentiments were reflected in his first will, in which he prohibited his daughter from marrying a subject of the king of France. Later, he relented, but his son-in-law King René disregarded his advice to maintain the Burgundian alliance and was defeated in 1431 by a Burgundian force sent to help his rival Anthony, count of Vaudémont. He found himself a prisoner of war at Dijon. At first Duke Philip the Good demanded the duchy of Bar in return for his release, but later he contented himself with the temporary cession of a group of places in Lorraine; a Burgundian foothold there which was relaxed after their return in 1445. When his wife died in 1453 René transferred the duchy of Lorraine to his son John, duke of Calabria, who was one of the staunchest Burgundian allies in the war of the League of the Public Weal. After the war, however, Duke John succumbed to the blandishments of Louis XI, who offered his eldest daughter, Anne of France, in marriage to John's son Nicolas and ceded to him the strategically important town and castle of

Épinal on the upper Moselle. Although in fact Louis never permitted the relationship of Nicolas and Anne to develop beyond an engagement, and though he had already given Épinal to Thibaud de Neuchâtel, marshal of Burgundy, nevertheless Duke John of Lorraine seems to have remained loyal to the king at least until shortly before his death at the end of 1470.[1]

Meanwhile, Burgundian penetration in Lorraine had been continued, informally or privately as it were, by members of the noble Burgundian family of Neuchâtel, which had acquired certain fiefs in Lorraine by marriage, notably Châtel-sur-Moselle. In 1451 Thibaud IX de Neuchâtel, marshal of Burgundy, tried to seize the town of Lunéville by smuggling into it some troops disguised as pilgrims. In 1460, with Philip the Good's assistance, Thibaud's twelve-year-old son Anthoine was promoted to the espiscopal throne of Toul, while his father was appointed administrator of the bishopric. Thus the lands of the bishopric, which lay between the duchies of Bar and Lorraine and included some important castles, fell into the hands of the Neuchâtel family and their partisans. The gift of Épinal by Louis XI in 1463 did not add significantly to their possessions in Lorraine, for ownership of it was disputed by the bishop of Metz and, in any event, its inhabitants refused to accept Thibaud de Neuchâtel as their lord and placed themselves instead under the protection of the duke of Lorraine. Thibaud, however, was determined to make good his rights and in 1467 he attacked Épinal. Soon a state of war existed between the houses of Neuchâtel and Anjou, and when Charles the Bold became duke of Burgundy in June 1467 he was faced with a request from his marshal for the loan of some men-at-arms to help him in his private war in Lorraine, just when he himself was ordering his marshal to muster troops for his war against Liège. Apparently, Thibaud found it possible to make use of these ducal forces to his personal advantage in Lorraine, while he was on his way with them to Liège.

[1] For this and what follows on Lorraine, see especially *Chronique de Lorraine*, ed. Marchal, 69–138, Lud, *Dialogue*, ed. Lepage, 149–61, Calmet, *Histoire de Lorraine*, v and vi, Witte, *JGLGA* ii (1890), 1–31, Berlet, *MSBGH* viii (1892), 297–311, Goechner, *AE* xii (1898), 412–20, Gain and others, *Histoire de Lorraine*, and, with references, Bittmann, *Ludwig XI. und Karl der Kühne*, ii (1). 122–56, and Grüneisen, *RV* xxvi (1961), 44–6, 58, 59 and 70–1. For the Neuchâtel family in Lorraine, see too Bernoulli, *BVG* xiii (1893), 366–8, Brauer-Gramm, *Peter von Hagenbach*, 37–9 and 162–4, and Marot, *AE* xliv (1930), 21–36; I have also used transcripts from BN Coll. de Lorraine 386, in RTA material.

THE DUKES OF LORRAINE IN THE FIFTEENTH CENTURY

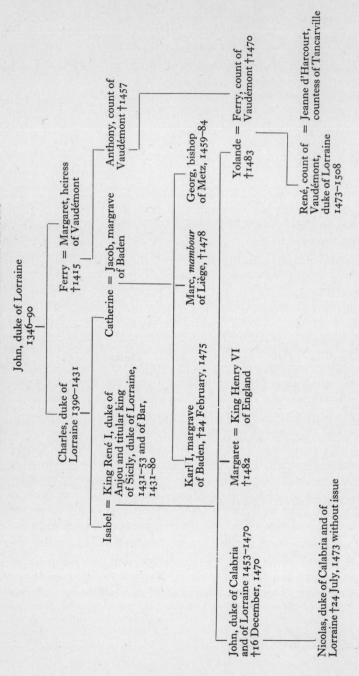

John, duke of Lorraine
1346–90

Charles, duke of
Lorraine 1390–1431

Ferry = Margaret, heiress
†1415   of Vaudémont

Anthony, count of
Vaudémont †1457

Isabel = King René I, duke of
Anjou and titular king
of Sicily, duke of Lorraine,
1431–53 and of Bar,
1431–80

Catherine = Jacob, margrave
of Baden

Karl I, margrave
of Baden, †24 February, 1475

Marc, *mambour*
of Liège, †1478

Georg, bishop
of Metz, 1459–84

Yolande = Ferry, count of
†1483   Vaudémont †1470

René, count of = Jeanne d'Harcourt,
Vaudémont,   countess of Tancarville
duke of Lorraine
1473–1508

Margaret = King Henry VI
†1482   of England

John, duke of Calabria
and of Lorraine 1453–1470
†16 December, 1470

Nicolas, duke of Calabria and of
Lorraine †24 July, 1473 without issue

What was Charles the Bold's attitude to his marshal's activities in Lorraine? To all intents and purposes, he posed and perhaps even acted, in 1467–9, as a mediator between the marshal on the one hand, and Duke John of Calabria and Lorraine, who was away campaigning in Catalonia at the time, and his councillors and son Nicolas in Lorraine, on the other. He proposed a cease-fire and truce, and offered to garrison some of the disputed places with his own men. In particular, he suggested the withdrawal of all Thibaud's people from Châtel-sur-Moselle and their replacement by a Burgundian captain and garrison. In May 1468, when the confrères of the Golden Fleece held their chapter at Bruges and indulged in their customary criticism of each other, Thibaud IX was accused of 'having undertaken a war against my lord of Calabria and the Lorrainers without the leave and agreement of my lord the duke, sovereign [of the Order], and without informing Messieurs of the Order'.[1] But he was readily excused and if, in 1469, Charles was still maintaining official neutrality, for example at the protracted but abortive peace conference in Ghent in June, he saw to it in March 1471 that a Burgundian force was sent to relieve Châtel-sur-Moselle when it was besieged by the Lorrainers. He also lent his firm support to Anthoine de Neuchâtel when the canons of Toul endeavoured to replace him, as their bishop, by a secretary of the duke of Lorraine, writing in the strongest possible terms on 18 April 1470 to the 'governors, magistrates and inhabitants of the city of Toul', 'requesting and requiring' them 'for honour and love of us, to obey our said cousin as your bishop . . . and to help him to resist all difficulties and impediments wrongfully contrived against him'.[2]

The situation in Lorraine changed considerably after the deaths of Thibaud IX and Duke John in 1469–70. The new duke, Nicolas, was as easily (and as fraudulently) enticed into a close alliance with Charles the Bold by the offer of Mary of Burgundy in marriage as he had been into Louis XI's friendship by the offer of Anne of France. In May 1472 he signed a treaty of alliance with Charles which gave the duke of Burgundy and his troops transit rights in the duchy and the right of entry into its towns and fortified places. The new lord of Neuchâtel, Henry, by gladly doing what his father Thibaud had refused to do, that is, rendering homage to the duke of Lorraine for his possessions in that duchy, aroused Charles the Bold's suspicions

[1] AOGV Reg. 2, f. 44b.
[2] Marot, *AE* xliv (1930), 32.

that he was more of a Lorrainer than a Burgundian. When he was proposed in May 1473 for election to the Golden Fleece, the duke successfully opposed his candidature on those grounds.[1] Thus Burgundian pressure on Lorraine was modified in 1472–3 because the duke of Lorraine had become an ally, or protégé, of Charles the Bold and the Neuchâtels had made their peace with him.

The unexpected death of Duke Nicolas of Lorraine on 24 July 1473, when Charles the Bold was in the midst of his triumphant conquest of Guelders, threw open the future succession of the duchy of Lorraine but did not initiate a new chapter in the story of Charles the Bold's relations with it. There were two claimants to the duchy, and two rulers closely concerned with its fate. The claimants, both of them descended from daughters of Duke Charles II of Lorraine, were Yolande of Anjou and Karl I, margrave of Baden. The interested rulers were Louis XI of France and Charles the Bold. These two had already been confronted in battle in 1471 and 1472; naturally they were now rivals for influence in Lorraine. Nor was it merely Lorraine that was at stake, for King René of Sicily, having lived to see the death of his son and grandson, now had no male heir. Thus, with Nicolas's death the succession to Anjou, Provence, Maine, Bar and other lands was also thrown open. Charles the Bold had his eye on Provence, but King Louis XI desperately hoped to acquire all these territories for the French crown.

Events in Lorraine moved with unusual rapidity in the late summer of 1473. Nicolas had died in Nancy, the capital, on 24 July. The Estates, dominated by the nobles of Lorraine, assembled there on 1 August. The envoys of Baden were unceremoniously rebuffed, and Lorraine was offered on 2 August to Yolande, who was at Joinville not far from the borders of the duchy. She promptly abdicated in favour of her twenty-three-year-old son René, count of Vaudémont, who made his solemn entry into Nancy on 4 August. René had visited Charles the Bold in Brussels at the end of November, 1469, and there is no evidence that he and his mother were hostile to Burgundy at this time. Charles's despatch of Guy de Brimeu, lord of Humbercourt, to Luxembourg, on 2 August, with instructions to prepare for a possible attack on Lorraine and to take possession of any places there which were willing to submit to him,[2] was probably more a move against Louis XI than a step towards the Burgundian conquest of Lorraine. In spite of his march from Guelders to Luxembourg,

[1] AOGV Reg. 3, f. 34.
[2] Printed in Gorissen, *De Raadkamer te Maastricht*, 293–6.

where he arrived at the beginning of September with a large part of his army, Charles seems to have had no intention even then of invading Lorraine. After all he could hardly entertain serious hopes of success in this direction when faced, as he was, with a hostile Louis XI, whose troops were assembled in Champagne. Indeed all the evidence points to the probability that Charles the Bold, in spite of his imperial ambitions, which took him to Trier at the end of September to confer with the Emperor Frederick III, was now revolving in his mind the possibility of taking up arms with his allies in England and Spain, against France, in order to crush Louis XI once and for all. But, though he was not therefore immediately interested in the conquest of Lorraine, Charles still needed, as several contemporary observers noted, to keep open his lines of communication between the northern territories and both Burgundy and Upper Alsace. For example, the Neapolitan ambassador reported from Luxembourg on 12 September that the duke hoped to gain possession of the principal fortresses in Lorraine because that 'duchy was like a barrier between here and Burgundy'.[1]

In the event Charles the Bold was able to obtain more or less what he wanted in Lorraine in the autumn of 1473 by diplomacy rather than force of arms. First he consolidated his connections with an old ally, Bishop Georg von Baden of Metz, who had been given a horse by Charles when he visited him in Brussels in February 1467 and who was thereafter paid or promised an annual pension of £1,200 and made a 'domestic' councillor of the duke of Burgundy.[2] Now, at the end of September 1473, a treaty was signed by Charles and Georg which made them allies in what could easily have become a war against the duke of Lorraine. In return for a promise to cede Épinal to the bishop and help him recover Sarrebourg and other places from the duke of Lorraine, Charles obtained the right of free passage for his troops through the lands of the bishopric of Metz as well as permission to redeem several places which the bishops of Metz had in the past mortgaged to the dukes of Lorraine. Free passage of troops was of some importance, for the lands of the bishopric of Metz extended south-eastwards from the southern tip of the duchy of Luxembourg almost as far as the ill-defined borders of Upper Alsace.

[1] Lud, *Dialogue*, 161 and ASM Pot. est. Borgogna 515/147.
[2] ADN B2064, f. 71 and B2068, fos. 18b–19a.

Meanwhile René had been negotiating with Louis XI, but the king found it impossible to accept the new duke's extravagant conditions.[1] René turned instead to Charles the Bold and the treaty of Nancy between them was signed on 15 October. A number of clauses were aimed specifically against Louis, and each signatory promised to help the other against a French attack. Moreover, the two princes permitted the free passage of their troops through each other's territories, and each was for this purpose to be prepared to open his castles to the other. Further detailed arrangements were distinctly one-sided: the nobles of Lorraine were to be guarantors of the treaty on René's side, and René was to place the castles or towns in Lorraine which were deemed important for the passage of Charles's troops in the hands of captains agreeable to Charles. Although in the treaty the right of free passage of Burgundian troops through Lorraine was granted only 'during the time or on any occasion when a state of war exists between the king and the duke' of Burgundy nonetheless Charles had effectively regained the right to move troops through Lorraine whenever he wanted: a right which he had certainly exercised on previous occasions, for example in transferring forces from Burgundy for the Liège campaigns of 1467 and 1468, and which, as we have seen, had been granted or confirmed to him by Duke Nicolas in 1472.

Which were the fortified places in Lorraine of strategic importance referred to in the treaty of 15 October 1473? Later documents show that, in the first place, five places were involved, one, Amance, about 12 km north-east of Nancy; the other four, Épinal, Darney, Charmes and Dompaire, in or near the valley of the upper Moselle. The documents also show that no Burgundian captains were appointed in these places, but the two Burgundian commissioners simply took the oaths of the captains already installed or appointed by René, who were all of them local people, some being the duke of Lorraine's officials.[2] The oaths they swore were not oaths of loyalty to Charles, but promises to keep the terms of the treaty. Moreover, no evidence has yet been unearthed to show that these five places received Burgundian garrisons at this time. They were not, in fact, handed over in any real sense to Charles; nor was anything approaching a

---

[1] See below p. 307. For what follows, see the text of the treaty in Toutey, *Charles le Téméraire et la Ligue de Constance*, 433–7.
[2] The documents are analysed by Gachard in de Barante, *Histoire des ducs*, ii. 708–9.

Burgundian protectorate over Lorraine set up in 1473. Relations between René and Charles remained good, and Charles paid a friendly visit to René in Nancy on 16–18 December 1473. Thus the situation in Lorraine, and the relations of Burgundy and Lorraine, were by no means significantly altered at the time of René's accession. It was only later that René's policies provoked Charles into that massive armed intervention from which he had so conspicuously refrained in 1473.

As with Alsace and Lorraine, so with Frisia or Friesland, there was nothing novel about Charles the Bold's pretensions or ambitions. Counts of Holland from time immemorial had described themselves as lords of Frisia and entertained serious claims over that territory or a good part of it. Friesland, in fact, comprised in those days three separate territories. West Friesland was the extreme north-eastern part of the county of Holland, including the towns of Enkhuizen and Hoorn. Friesland proper, corresponding to the present day provinces of Friesland and Groningen, occupied the area between the Zuiderzee or, as it now is, the Ijsselmeer and the Lauwerszee; while East Friesland extended from the Lauwers to the Weser. Groningen and the surrounding territory was somewhat aloof, being a separate political entity, or belonging to the ecclesiastical principality of Utrecht, rather than a part of Friesland. An important change took place in 1464, shortly before Charles became duke of Burgundy: most of East Friesland became an imperial county, under Ulrich I and his wife Theda, and was ruled for 300 years thereafter by the house of Cirksena.

Philip the Good had almost certainly cherished the ambition of conquering Frisia, and probably planned to undertake this in 1456 when he besieged Deventer and placed his bastard son forcibly on the episcopal throne of Utrecht. Nor were Charles the Bold's designs on Friesland purely pacific: in 1467 or 1468 he was considering the possibility of a military expedition and sent a spy to report in detail on the topography and general situation there.[1] In 1469 he

---

[1] Algra, *Een spionagerapport van omstreeks 1468*, and Stracke, *JGKA* xlviii (1968), 25–33. For this and what follows see *Groot Placcaet en Charter-Boek van Vriesland*, i. 626–43 (the quotation is from pp. 626–7), *Cronycke van Hollandt*, fos. 322–3 and 328, Ankringa, *DVF* vi (1852), 186–94, Zilverberg, *David van Bourgondie*, 31–2, Jongkees, *DVF* xli (1953), 63–78, and Grüneisen, *RV* xxvi (1961), 61–2, the last three with references. See too ASMant Archivio Gonzaga 2100, letters of Rodolfo Gonzaga of 29 August 1469 and 4 October 1469.

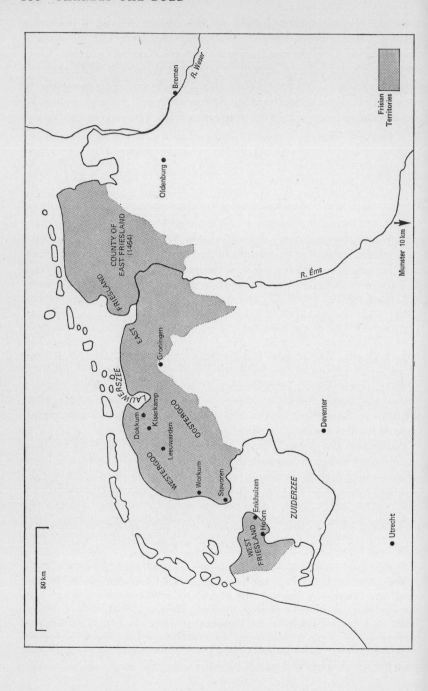

tried to persuade the Frisians of the advantages of Burgundian rule:

Today, 2 October 1469, the reverend fathers in God Messire Thierry, abbot of Stavoren, Messire Bernard, abbot of Klaarkamp, Master Mamo de Fraenker, and Master Wabbo Junois burgomaster of Workum, appeared before my most redoubted lord Monsieur the duke as deputies of the three Estates of the lands of Frisia, [that is] of Oostergoo and of Westergoo, summoned by my lord to appear before him to hear what he had to say and expound to them, and afterwards to report it to the members of the said three Estates. It was explained to the deputies on behalf of my lord that his predecessors, counts of Holland, had been true and rightful lords of Frisia; that some of them had been peaceably received there and had ruled there as legitimate lords by right of birth, doing everything to their subjects that lords are accustomed to do; that this is altogether notorious, and that even today there were in the said land enough people alive who knew and had seen that it had been subject to the said counts of Holland, even though the said Frisians of Oostergoo and Westergoo had at certain periods taken over their government themselves, without obeying my lord [the duke]'s predecessors, nor recognising them as their legitimate lords, as they should have done. Nevertheless, my most redoubted lord was a merciful and good-natured prince, and therefore more inclined to forgiving and mercy than to rigour. Moreover, since he holds the said peoples of Oostergoo and Westergoo to be his true subjects, with whom he wishes and desires to treat amicably to the end that they may willingly receive him and render to him those rights which they are in duty bound to render to their rightful lord, he would be happy to forget and forgive their said disobedience and conspiracy, provided they rendered the obedience which they owe and are bound to make to my said lord.

After these things had been thus expounded to the deputies and it had been added that all the lands, countries and lordships of Monsieur the duke his father and his other deceased predecessors, of noble memory, may God pardon them, had succeeded and fallen to him by direct and lawful line and succession, and that he neither wanted nor intended in any way to forgo recovering all these lands and patrimonies which belonged to him by right, it was finally requested on my lord duke's behalf of the said people of Oostergoo and Westergoo, who belong to his true patrimony, in the persons of their deputies, that they receive and accept him as their rightful lord, as they are bound to do by law.

In the event of their generously doing this, as in reason they should, my said lord would be inclined to accept them gladly and to maintain them in good peace and unity and favourable commerce; he would defend and support them against all those attempting to damage them as [he did] his other lands and subjects; and he would maintain their good customs and usages, as well as their rights, franchises, liberties and privileges, and would deliver them the necessary documents. . . . This would be extremely profitable and very useful for the said people of Oostergoo and Westergoo, as they can clearly see by experience in the other lands and lordships of my said lord, especially in Holland, Zeeland and West Frisia, which have all been enriched, more than they had been before, since the time they came into the hands of the said deceased duke his father. This came about by the grace of God and because of the good and praiseworthy government of the said duke his father, who had maintained them in peace and unity and conserved their commerce. My said most redoubted lord is firmly and fully decided to follow this example, with God's grace, and he has as much power to do it as any of his said predecessors, or more.

Instead of joyfully submitting to Charles the Bold, the Frisians contrived excuses for delaying further negotiations until the following May. Meanwhile, the civic authorities of Groningen had applied to David of Burgundy, bishop of Utrecht, for help and support, and he, jealous of his rights over the town, insisted that it formed part, not of Friesland, but of the *sticht* of Utrecht. Thereafter, ownership of Groningen was debated in the great council of the duke of Burgundy and naturally decided in his favour, and also at the imperial High Court. The affair dragged on indecisively but, as with Mulhouse, so with Groningen, the Burgundian claims were never successfully pressed home.

Negotiations with the two main territories of Friesland, Oostergoo and Westergoo, were taken up again at the end of May 1470, at Enkhuizen. The Burgundian deputies again tried to persuade the Frisians to accept Charles as the lord of Friesland and their 'legitimate and natural prince and true ruler'. They must agree to pay taxes but would not be bound to do military service. Civil and criminal law would continue as before 'according to the ancient Frisian rights and good old customs in force there from ancient times', except when the prince's prerogatives were involved. The inhabitants would be permitted to choose annually a notable person to be called *potestaet* or *potestas*, who would be appointed by the duke and be answerable to him. With the exception of the town of Dokkum, which swore allegiance to Charles at St. Omer on 8 July 1470, the Frisians flatly refused to accept these arrangements. Typically, Charles the Bold drew up all the rejected terms in a formal Latin document and issued it on 9 July as if the Frisians had approved it. Then, he prepared for a war against Frisia which was formally declared on 5 November

1470 but never actually waged. The Frisians were saved, if Charles was indeed serious, by a French offensive against Burgundy which claimed the duke's attention and all his available military forces during the winter of 1470–1.

In 1473 an opportunity to seize Friesland by force of arms was presented to Charles by the campaign in Guelders, and two people with him on that campaign, Olivier de la Marche and an unknown Nürnberg burgess reported his intention of doing just this.[1] Indeed, rumours circulated in Germany in September 1473 to the effect that Duke Charles had 'conquered Friesland'. But in fact Burgundian military operations in the Low Countries in 1473 had ended with the submission of Zutphen early in August. Once more Friesland was saved from foreign invasion. This time there were at least three possible explanations. Firstly, Charles's enthusiasm for a personal meeting with the Emperor, whose crown he hoped to obtain or inherit; secondly, the death of the duke of Lorraine on 24 July, which demanded Charles's attention there; and thirdly, the arrival in the Burgundian camp at Zutphen of Archbishop Ruprecht of Cologne, seeking Charles's help against his rebellious subjects.

In spite of these and other diversions in August 1473, Friesland was by no means forgotten or ignored by Charles. At the very moment when, at Trier, a deputation from Countess Theda of East Friesland arrived to complain to the Emperor that Charles was about to invade those Frisian territories immediately bordering her own lands, the duke of Burgundy was discussing with Frederick III the possibility of his coronation as, among other things, king of Frisia. Obtaining no help from Frederick, Theda set about organizing her fellow-countrymen throughout non-Burgundian Friesland into a defensive league against Charles the Bold, which also embraced Groningen. It was agreed that in the event of a Burgundian attack on either Groningen or any one of the Frisian lands the others would field a thousand men against Charles within eight days. Undeterred, Charles pursued further plans against Friesland. Having failed, both in 1471 and again in August 1473, to enlist the military assistance of Bishop

---

[1] De la Marche, *Mémoires*, i. 135 and *Politische Correspondenz*, i. 563. For the next sentence, see *Frankfurts Reichscorrespondenz*, ii. 302, and, for what follows, Bittmann, *Ludwig XI. und Karl der Kühne*, ii (1). 118 and 120–2; *Ostfriesisches Urkundenbuch*, ii. nos. 919, 924 and 941, and *CDS*, xxxi. *Lübeck*, v. 122–3 and 135–6. See too, with important references, Petri, *Gemeinsame Probleme*, 120–3, and Pfeiffer, *Der Raum Westfalen*, ii (1). 123–8.

Heinrich von Schwarzburg of Münster for his projected invasion of Friesland, he turned instead to that bishop's territorial rival and enemy. On 29 November 1474 he signed a treaty with Count Gerd of Oldenburg, the brother of King Christian I of Denmark. Gerd promised to help Charles conquer both East and 'central' Friesland in return for an annual pension of 2,000 Rhenish florins and his appointment as governor or stadholder of Frisia for life. But this scheme came to nothing. Frisia never was engulfed by Burgundy. Instead, other projects, notably the intervention in Cologne, were taken up by Charles the Bold, who did, however, maintain an interest in Frisia to the extent, for example, of trying to negotiate a truce or peace between Count Gerd and his enemies in 1475–6.[1]

It is almost axiomatic that Charles the Bold made no serious attempt on any territory which had not already aroused the expansionist appetites of his father Philip the Good. The duchy of Guelders, with its dependent county of Zutphen and the four principal towns of Arnhem, Nijmegen, Roermond and Zutphen, was no exception to this rule. Philip the Good actually marched across part of the country in 1456 on his way to Utrecht and, throughout his long reign, he was closely involved with the internal affairs of Guelders. In the bitter series of quarrels between the reigning Duke Arnold of Egmond and his son Adolf, which dominated the history of Guelders throughout the 1450s and 1460s, Philip the Good favoured the young Adolf, who drew much of his support from the towns, but who was encouraged also by his mother Catherine of Cleves. In 1459 a flimsy settlement was made, whereby Adolf was to rule as duke of Guelders in Nijmegen and certain other parts of the duchy. But the quarrel had broken out again by 1461, and by 1463 a state of near civil war existed between Adolf and the towns on the one side and Arnold on the other. Meanwhile Philip the Good

---

[1] *Hanserecesse* vii. 496, n. 1. For what follows on Guelders, see the documents in *Urkundenbuch für die Geschichte des Niederrheins*, iv. 415–19 and 440–7 and *Gedenkwaardigheden*, iv. 386–487 and v. 3–71. The main chronicler is van Berchen, *Gelderse kroniek*, 98–138 but see too Basin, *Louis XI*, ii. 160–72, *Chronijk van Overmaas*, 26–44, and *Cronycke van Hollandt*, fos. 322, 328b–9 and 334–336b. Among modern authorities I have relied chiefly on Alberts, *De eerste Bourgondische bezetting* and *De Staten van Gelre en Zutphen*, ii. 1–106, *Algemene geschiedenis der Nederlanden*, iii. 361–9, Bittmann, *Ludwig XI. und Karl der Kühne*, ii (1). 86–118, Grüneisen, *RV* xxvi (1961), 47–66, and RTA material, Niessen, *RHB* iv (1927), 80–3, and van Veen, *GBM* xxxii (1929), 45–127.

was happy to extend Burgundian influence over Guelders in these
years by arranging for Adolf of Egmond's election to the Golden
Fleece in 1461 and for his marriage in 1463 to Catherine of Bourbon,
whose sister Isabel was married to Charles the Bold, then count of
Charolais.

On 10 January 1465, in the dead of night, Adolf carried out a
treacherous and violent *coup de main* against his father, which some
claimed to have been planned at the Burgundian court. Duke Arnold,
who had retired early after a dinner to celebrate the reconciliation
of himself and his son, was called out of his bed in the castle at Grave,
arrested, and taken off across the frozen River Maas 'in the fearful
cold of the night dressed only in a fur-lined tunic and a tabard,
without stockings, and with a wimple and nightcap on his head just as
he had on in bed, as far as the castle of Lobith'. Soon afterwards
he was obliged to abdicate formally, and Adolf became duke in his
place. But, though Arnold languished for five years in the castle of
Buren, the internal strife in Guelders continued unabated. The
imprisoned ex-duke had powerful friends in his own family, notably
his brother Willem van Egmond, and his cause was championed by his
brother-in-law John, duke of Cleves, whose intervention in the years
1466–9 turned a civil war into a war between Guelders and Cleves.
Adolf, on the other hand, found an ally in the shape of Ruprecht,
archbishop of Cologne, and he also enjoyed the support of Vincenz,
count of Moers.

Burgundian mediation attempts in Guelders, which had occupied
Philip the Good in the last year of his life, were continued in the
early years of Charles the Bold's reign. Their aim was still the maintenance and extension of Burgundian influence in the duchy. Their
justification was by no means difficult. After all, Duke John of
Cleves and 'my lord Adolf, the young duke of Guelders' were both
members of the Burgundian Order of Chivalry, the Golden Fleece,
of which Charles the Bold was sovereign. But, while Burgundian
policy had in the past consistently supported Adolf, that prince's
savage treatment of his father evidently lost him some Burgundian
sympathy. In May 1468 the situation was discussed at length at the
chapter of the Order of the Golden Fleece held at Bruges. Adolf was
criticized for his disgraceful treatment of his father, whom he had
kept in prison even though an agreement had been made for his
release; he had also infringed the ordinances of the Order by making
war on a fellow member. Duke John of Cleves was accused of a
variety of faults: he had occupied Soest, which belonged to the church

E

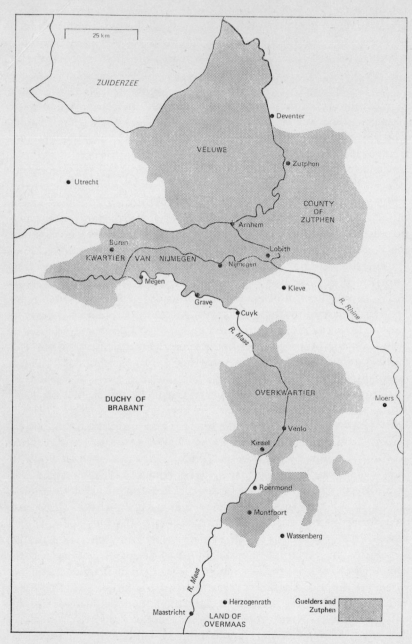

5. Guelders and Zutphen

of Cologne: he had made war on his confrère and nephew Adolf; he had infringed the fifth ordinance by withholding from Charles the military assistance against Liège which he had requested; and he had wrongfully caused a village in Brabant, belonging to his brother Adolf, lord of Ravenstein, likewise a member of the Order, to be burnt down in a nocturnal raid. It was resolved to send forthwith the registrar of the Order, together with one of its knights, to order the two contestants to make an immediate truce and to appear in person before their sovereign. Failing this, they were to be summoned to appear before the next chapter of the Order.[1]

For a time, Duke Charles the Bold maintained his arbitral status in this dispute. At Ghent, on 11 July 1469 in the presence of both dukes, he issued a formal mediatory judgement, reserving to himself all future arbitration between the parties and threatening either of them who attacked the other with military intervention. But within a few months of this settlement he had abandoned Adolf and his allies the Guelders towns and taken sides firmly with Cleves and Egmond. On 20 July he granted to John, duke of Cleves, an annual pension of 6,000 francs; on 29 September 1469 he took Willem van Egmond and all his possessions under his protection and a Burgundian herald appeared in Arnhem on 12 October to fix the ducal arms over the gates of the palace of Egmond there. But it would be going too far to say that this event marked the start of Burgundian penetration in Guelders, for Charles the Bold had as yet no firm plans of annexation or conquest. His aim in 1470 and early 1471 seems still to have been limited to the settlement of the dispute between father and son and, above all, the release of Arnold, which in September 1470 was urged on both Adolf and Charles by Pope Paul II. Throughout November and December 1470 Adolf was with Charles at Hesdin in Artois. Whether or not he agreed to his father's release is uncertain, but at the end of the year a body of Burgundian troops under Henric van Horne, lord of Perwez, was sent to Guelders to effect this, and Arnold was brought to Hesdin early in January 1471.[2]

Even with both dukes of Guelders safely under his control, Charles found it impossible to achieve a settlement. Adolf was adamant: he told Charles 'that he was answerable to no prince in the world other than the Emperor' and flatly rejected any agreement which entailed

---

[1] AOGV Reg. 2, fos. 43b–44 and 45b–47; compare ADN B2068, f. 369b.
[2] AGR CC 1925, fos. 319b and 321.

his sharing power with, still less transferring it to, his father.[1]
Meanwhile the citizens of Nijmegen and other supporters of Adolf in
Guelders feared for his safety. On 28 December 1470 Charles found
it necessary to wrote to Nijmegen denying that he was holding Adolf
prisoner; on the contrary, he was merely trying, out of love for the
house of Guelders, to persuade him to set his father free. But the
suspicions of Adolf's supporters soon proved to be well founded.
When, on 10 February 1471, Adolf 'secretly and disloyally' left the
Burgundian court and was arrested while trying to escape by boat
from Namur, he was indeed held prisoner, first at Vilvorde and
subsequently at Courtrai, and he remained a Burgundian prisoner
during the rest of Charles the Bold's lifetime.[2]

Just as Adolf had not found it possible, even when his father was
in prison, to obtain full control of Guelders, so now Duke Arnold,
though his son and rival was in prison, failed to master the duchy.
Indeed he only contrived to be accepted as ruler in a single town,
Grave, and in a limited area, while in the summer of 1471, Nijmegen,
Arnhem and Zutphen allied against him, appointing first Willem
van Zommeren and then, in 1472, Vincenz, count of Moers, as
Adolf's lieutenant and governor, and their leader and protector
against Burgundian intervention. Others were interested in the fate of
Guelders and took initiatives on Adolf's behalf, notably King Louis
XI of France, to whom Adolf had turned for help and who was
campaigning in Picardy against the duke of Burgundy at the very
moment of Adolf's escape from court. In mid-February 1471 royal
ambassadors were instructed as follows:[3]

1. They are to congratulate Adolf on his escape.
2. They are to tell him that the king is 'very sorry about the great out-
   rage and injury inflicted on him by Charles, soi-disant duke of
   Burgundy,[4] in holding him prisoner and in captivity for such a long
   time, though the said [duke] of Burgundy does habitually commit
   outrages and injustices because of his fury and tyranny . . .', and they

---

[1] AOGV Reg. 3, f. 4, and de Commynes, *Mémoires*, ed. Calmette and
Durville, ii. 2–3.
[2] AOGV Reg. 3, f. 4, transcript from Arnhem RA, Archief van Hertog
Karel vl. no. 8, in RTA material, and de Commynes, *Mémoires*, ed. Dupont,
iii. 277 and ed. Calmette and Durville, ii. 3–4.
[3] Transcript of BN MS. fr. 3884, fos. 270–2, in RTA material.
[4] The epithet soi-disant was no doubt used by Louis on the grounds that
all Charles's French possessions had been declared forfeit to the crown in
the declaration of Amboise of 3 December 1470, see above, p. 67.

are to offer him an alliance with the king if possible 'expressly against the said Charles' and to do their utmost to persuade him to make war on Charles.

3. 'Item, if they see that the said [duke] of Guelders is well-disposed towards the king and prepared to take action against the duke of Burgundy, speaking as if on their own initiative, they are to tell him of the great prosperity which, thanks be to God, the king enjoys at present and of the large number of lords, knights and squires whom he has recently recruited in honour of God, of the glorious Virgin Mary and of the glorious archangel Monseigneur St. Michael, prince of the chivalry of Paradise, whose insignia the kings of France have always been accustomed to bear. They are to tell him also how several great princes and lords have taken and accepted the said Order, which is today the most noble and worthy among Christians and, speaking on their own part, they can add that the said Order would be most fitting for so notable, virtuous and valiant a prince as my said lord Adolf of Guelders.' If he enquires further on this matter, they are to tell him that he will have to ask the king.

Far from helping Adolf, Louis's unfortunately timed intervention seems only to have served to give credence to rumours of his treacherous dealings with the king of France.[1] A year later, in March 1472, five German princes wrote to Charles the Bold on behalf of the Estates of Guelders, asking him to set Adolf free. But none of these efforts succeeded and throughout 1471 and 1472 the originally tenuous Burgundian threat to Guelders gradually took firmer shape. At the end of 1471 Duke Arnold, in an effort to obtain Burgundian assistance, offered to Charles the guardianship (*advocaciam et protectionem*) of Guelders, which he accepted. But the towns of Guelders, supported by a fair proportion of the nobles and led, from September 1472 onwards, by Count Vincenz of Moers, remained firm in their loyalty to Adolf. At last, on 7 December 1472, the sixty-two-year-old Arnold mortgaged Guelders and Zutphen to Charles the Bold for 300,000 Rhenish florins. Although Arnold was to enjoy possession, if he could obtain it, during his lifetime, and Charles only insisted on the immediate transference to himself of certain strategic points, the complete Burgundian conquest of the duchy seems henceforth to have been given the first priority in Charles the Bold's immediate plans. That he did not intend to wait until Duke Arnold's death, which intervened conveniently enough on 23 February 1473, three days after he had left the duchy of Guelders

[1] See for example Pauwels, *Alia narratio*, 295.

to Charles in his will, is shown by the reports of troop movements and of Charles's firm intention to seize Guelders, in January and early February 1473.[1]

Although nothing was said at the chapter of the Golden Fleece in May of the duke's plans to invade Guelders, Charles did announce that he proposed to continue to hold Adolf prisoner in Courtrai castle. On the eve of the attack, in which Burgundy was to have the military assistance of the duke of Cleves, a treaty was signed between Charles and Duke Gerhard of Jülich-Berg in which Gerhard sold to Charles his rights over Guelders for 80,000 Rhenish florins. The way was now clear for the conquest of Guelders by Charles even though the Estates of Guelders and, above all, the towns of Nijmegen, Arnhem and Zutphen, denied the legality of Arnold's will and of his other transactions with Charles the Bold, and even though Duke Adolf was alive and well though held in custody against his will. Louis XI's last-minute attempt, on 11 June 1473, to persuade the Emperor Frederick III to take Guelders into his protection was a futile one:[2] Charles was in close diplomatic contact with the Emperor at this time, and Frederick evidently had no objection to the Burgundian seizure of Guelders. One other interested party was the king of Scotland, who had sent an embassy to Charles to expound his claim to Guelders.[3] It was ignored.

Historical scholarship has so far assembled only scanty information about the army which gathered at Maastricht at the end of May and early in June 1473. Though Charles himself pretended he only had with him 'the troops of my ordinance', his forces certainly included supplementary infantry contingents.[4] For example his officers in Hainault had been ordered on 30 April to recruit 300 or at least 200 'of the finest and boldest fellows, expert at warfare', to be ready fully equipped with a long sword and a long pike each, by 31 May. His army included, too, the usual contingent of English archers:

[1] For example Cal. state papers. Milan, i. 172, and see Bittmann, Ludwig XI. und Karl der Kühne, ii (1). 88. For the next sentence, see AOGV Reg. 3, fos. 3b–4b.
[2] Lettres de Louis XI, v. 143–5.
[3] IADNB i (2). 372. For the conquest of Guelders, besides the works mentioned on p. 112 above, I have used Geldersche kronieken, ix. 182, de la Marche, Mémoires, iii. 205–6, Politische Correspondenz, i. 561–2, Frederiks, De intocht van Hertog Karel de Stoute te Zutfen, and Maris, BMVG lvi (1957), 47–9 and 121–3.
[4] ASM Pot. est. Borgogna 515/145 (letter of Charles to Yolande, duchess of Savoy, of 2 August 1473). For the next sentence, see ADN B10438, f. 31b.

500 of them, according to the chroniclers who recorded their deeds of valour at the siege of Nijmegen. The campaign which followed was carefully planned, well executed, and brilliantly successful. But the opposition was inherently weak, comprising a section of the nobles only and some of the towns. There was nobody to field an army against the duke of Burgundy; he merely had to mop up the few defended places.

Charles left Maastricht on 9 June and advanced northwards into the south of Guelders along the Maas. Already on 5 June a deputation from one of the four principal towns of the duchy, Roermond, had presented their keys, and their formal submission, to Charles, in the church of Our Lady at Maastricht. Other towns surrendered to the advancing Burgundians after little or no resistance. Even Venlo, 'a large and strong town on the Maas, well garrisoned with men-at-arms', with its well fortified gates, walls and towers,[1] held out for only a few days against Charles the Bold's artillery. The duke entered it on 21 June. It was lucky to escape with a long lecture from Charles, delivered in front of the town hall to the assembled citizens, and a few executions. The last substantial place in the Overkwartier, as this part of Guelders was called, was Goch, which had successfully resisted an attack by the duke of Cleves while Charles was besieging Venlo; but it was now glad to surrender to Charles and recognise him as duke of Guelders. The conquest of the Overkwartier was completed, or supplemented, by the conquest of Moers, whose count was the champion and leader of the resistance to Charles in Guelders, though his county, lying along the left bank of the Rhine opposite Duisburg, was not actually part of Guelders.

The heart and soul of the opposition to Charles the Bold was the town of Nijmegen, to which his men laid siege on 28 June while he paid a fleeting visit to Kleve. Here, for three weeks, the fate of Guelders hung in the balance, for the other towns had by now either already surrendered conditionally on Nijmegen also submitting, or were preparing to follow their example. Though a chronicler boasted that Nijmegen had originally been fortified by Julius Caesar, it was really only a matter of time before she succumbed to the combined armies of Cleves and Burgundy. She was small enough to be completely invested from the start of the siege, and she could expect help from no one, for even her allies Arnhem and Zutphen were powerless, or unwilling, to send her provisions. She capitulated on 17 July,

[1] *Cronycke van Hollandt*, f. 336.

not before she had inflicted considerable casualties on Charles's
army and suffered important damage to her walls and gates. After
the fall of Nijmegen there was no further resistance to Charles in
Guelders. On 31 July he crossed the Rhine to receive the surrender
first, of Zutphen, where he stayed from 4 to 10 August, and then,
of the capital of Guelders, Arnhem, and of the Veluwe. His men had
plundered and raided far and wide, making the Burgundian presence
felt on both banks of the lower Rhine. In Zutphen he had received
the archbishop of Cologne and the bishop of Utrecht while his men
went off to visit the ladies of Deventer who, according to the Burgundian courtier de la Marche, 'are extremely gracious, taking
pleasure in entertaining strangers'.[1]

The interest, for the historian of Charles the Bold, in the Burgundian conquest of Guelders, lies not so much in the campaign
itself but rather in the treatment of the conquered towns and territories and the arrangements which were made for their administration. For here indeed was a land which Charles, in his own phrase,
had 'reduced completely to my obedience'.[2] First, it was made to
meet the cost of its own conquest: a total of some 250,000 Rhenish
florins was levied in reparations. As to the towns, though their
walls were left intact and there was no organized looting, Jobst
Tetzel, the German mercenary serving with Charles, reported from
Zutphen on 14 August that 'my lord [the duke] had given to his own
officials every suitable office in the conquered towns, and in every
town he has appointed an official (*Schultheiss*) who is in charge of the
town and sits on the council, without whom the burgesses can do
nothing'.[3] Modern historical scholarship has at least partly confirmed this: an entirely new town council was appointed at Venlo
in August 1473 by the Burgundian administration; certain magistrates and councillors were excluded from continuing to serve at
Arnhem; and town privileges were surrendered. Moreover a permanent and substantial Burgundian garrison under a captain, or
military governor, was established in each of the chief towns, or

---

[1] De la Marche, *Mémoires*, iii. 205–6.
[2] ASM Pot. est. Borgogna 515/145 (compare van Hasselt, *Oorsprong van
het Hof van Gelderland*, 80). For what follows, besides works already mentioned on p. 112 n. 1, see van Hasselt, *Oorsprong van het Hof van Gelderland*,
van Veen and van Schilfgaarde, *GBM* xxxvi (1933), 23–36, van de Ven,
GBM xlvi (1943), 46–8, Maris, *GBM* lvi (1957), 45–123, and Maris, *GBM*
lx (1961), 157–62.
[3] *Politische Correspondenz*, i. 562.

administrative capitals, of the three quarters of Guelders: Arnhem, Nijmegen and Roermond, as well as in the county, or quarter, of Zutphen. Thus across the Rhine, at Zutphen, was posted Baudouin de Lannoy, lord of Solre and Molenbaix; and in the capital of Guelders, Arnhem, the captain was Hagenbach's associate, Bernhart von Ramstein, lord of Gilgenberg. Later, some at least of these garrisons were composed of Italian mercenaries: in April 1476 two companies of Italians found themselves without orders at Maastricht; they were sent on to Venlo and Zutphen.[1] Throughout the rest of Duke Charles's reign, indeed, Guelders was held in the forceful grip of an organized military occupation.

What were the administrative measures applied by Charles in Guelders? Contemporaries were universally impressed by these reforms even though their accounts of them are either partisan or misinformed. On 16 July 1473 Charles appointed Duke Arnold's brother, Willem van Egmond, stadholder general of Guelders and Zutphen and he remained in office until replaced eventually in January 1476 by Philippe de Croy, count of Chimay, who had originally been appointed in November 1474. Thus at first the house of Egmond continued, in a sense, to rule Guelders. The Burgundian stadholder governed with the help of a council at Arnhem which had its own president and whose jurisdiction, like the stadholder's, extended over the whole of Guelders and Zutphen. Subsidiary councils were established under the presidency in each case of the captain of the garrison, whose title included that of governor and whose duties were both civil and military, at Zutphen, at Nijmegen and at Roermond. These, like the other Burgundian councils, were political and administrative, as well as judicial in function, and appeals lay from them to the *Parlement* of Malines. While the office of receiver-general, or *rentmeester*, of Guelders was allowed to lapse under the Burgundian administration, local receivers of the duke's revenues were installed in the three quarters of Guelders and in Zutphen. In sum, a new administrative system was established in Guelders which brought that territory almost overnight into line with Duke Charles's other lands, while at the same time placing it firmly in the control, or jurisdiction, of the central institutions which Charles set up soon afterwards at Malines: the *Parlement* and the *chambre des comptes*. The finishing touches, as it were, were put to this administrative edifice by two important ducal ordinances of April

---

[1] Gorissen, *De Raadkamer te Maastricht*, 212–13.

E*

1474. One of these comprised a series of instructions in twenty-three separate articles for the duke's judicial officers in Guelders; the other, which incorporated the recommendations of two commissioners sent by Charles into Guelders, dealt in similar comprehensive detail with the administration of the domain and the duties of the four local receivers. The general effect of all this administrative activity was a radical enhancement of the power of the ruler at the expense of the Estates and, above all, of their most important constituent element in Guelders, the towns. Once more, in Guelders as in Alsace, urban privilege and power is seen to be confronted and at times overwhelmed by the growing forces of central princely authority.

To what conclusions then do the events briefly outlined in this chapter point? We see Charles the Bold take up radical attitudes in Alsace, but withhold the funds and other means necessary for the further development of Burgundian power there. In Lorraine and Frisia he applies pressure but draws back from outright conquest in this period. Here, golden opportunities for territorial aggrandizement seem to be missed. Only in Guelders does Duke Charles appear in the traditional guise of iron-fisted conqueror intent on the outright incorporation of new territory into the political and administrative framework of his own lands. Even here, we note that the conquest did not take place until years after the first pretext for intervention had presented itself. In all this, Charles the Bold seems to have been by no means an over-ambitious, still less rash, conqueror. His plans were carefully laid, his interventions judiciously timed and limited in extent. However, his aspirations and activities in these four territories, which were all of them imperial, must be considered against the background of his diplomatic relations with the Emperor and the imperial princes in the years before 1473, for his royal or rather imperial ambitions certainly took precedence over mere territorial conquests.

CHAPTER FOUR

The Duke and the Empire: 1467-1473

The federation of polities that went under the name of Holy Roman Empire was sometimes misleadingly qualified by contemporaries as being 'of the German nation'. In fact, it comprised populations speaking Italian, French, Dutch and Danish as well as several east European languages. But its ruler, its government, its centre of gravity, were all of them German. Its Emperor, at least from his coronation in Rome in 1452, was Frederick III, head of the house of Habsburg, duke of Austria, Styria, Carinthia and Carniola. He had ascended the German throne in 1440 and ruled, in the event, for fifty-three years, as has been said, without help, without advice and without power.[1] His grandiose motto, AEIOU, which could have stood either for *Austriae est imperare orbis universo* or *Alles Erdreich ist Österreich untertan*, underlines the fact that his energies, which were displayed only fitfully, and his interests, were dynastic, not imperial.

Besides his cousin Duke Sigmund, who employed exactly the same Austrian titles as he did, though he could have more modestly and accurately described himself as count of Tirol, Frederick could usually rely, in the 1460s, on a handful of imperial princes as his staunch allies and friends. Notable among these were the two brothers of Saxony, the elector Frederick II and Duke William, and the active and ambitious margrave of Brandenburg, Albert, later surnamed Achilles. But these were lesser powers. The princes who were really influential in the Empire at this time were King Christian I of Denmark, Norway and, in 1457-71, Sweden; King George Podiebrad of Bohemia; King Matthias Hunyadi, called Corvinus, of Hungary; and Charles the Bold. The lands of one of these four rulers, Matthias

---

[1] Vernunft, *JSFB* v (1942), 123.

Corvinus, lay wholly outside the borders of the Empire; the lands of
another of them, George Podiebrad, lay wholly within it. King
Christian was an imperial vassal for a small fraction of his extensive
territories, Holstein; he was the only one of the four who could with
accuracy be described as a German. As to Duke Charles, some two-
thirds of his territories lay within the Empire but the county of
Flanders and the duchy of Burgundy lay outside it, in France.

One other imperial prince, who could almost compare in power and
influence with the four just mentioned, was Frederick I the Victorious,
elector palatine of the Rhine, who was engaged from 1464 onwards
in a series of bitter quarrels with the Emperor, supported by his
brother Ruprecht, archbishop of Cologne. They belonged to the house
of Wittelsbach, which was represented at this time in its Bavarian
homeland by the influential Ludwig the Rich, duke of Bavaria-
Landshut, among others. Princes like Counts Ulrich and Eberhard
of Württemberg, and Landgrave Henry III of Hesse, and prelates
like Heinrich von Schwarzburg, bishop of Münster and archbishop
of Bremen were likewise influential, though less so. Nor, in considering the state of affairs in the Empire in the late 1460s, must one fail to
mention the powerful imperial towns, suspicious of and hostile to
Charles the Bold, like Cologne, Strasbourg and Basel. The south
German communes and communities of what is now Switzerland,
the so-called *Eidgenossen*, will find their place in later chapters.

As imperial princes, the Valois dukes of Burgundy had always taken
part in imperial affairs, sending their deputies to meetings of the
imperial diet or *Reichstag* and maintaining a network of alliances and
connections on imperial territory. Furthermore, circumstances had
for the most part dictated that, right from the start, their territorial
expansion had to take place in the Empire. Thus all their conquests
and annexations, apart from a few towns and places, notably the
Somme towns, were of imperial territory. Philip the Good had added
Brabant, Holland and Luxembourg to the Burgundian lands, all of
them imperial, and, as we have seen in the previous chapter, Charles
the Bold's territorial policies involved intervention in imperial
affairs, if not annexation of territory, in Alsace, Lorraine, Guelders
and Frisia. This territorial activity of Charles the Bold within the
Empire reached a peak in the summer and autumn of 1469, when he
acquired Upper Alsace in mortgage from Duke Sigmund, presided
over a conference of the rival claimants to the duchy of Guelders at
Ghent and passed sentence between them, and made his bid to
annexe Friesland.

In economic affairs, too, the duke of Burgundy took important initiatives within the Empire. He was particularly interested, for example, in the movement of wine along the Rhine, for nearly all the wine consumed in the Low Countries seems to have come, from Burgundy or elsewhere, down that river. Almost every autumn in the early part of his reign, Charles the Bold's letters on the subject of the general security of the river, or on the tolls levied on wine shipped along it, were sent out to interested parties. On 24 November 1467 the dukes of Guelders and Cleves and the archbishop of Cologne were asked to protect trade on the river.[1] On 26 October 1469 Charles the Bold wrote to the rulers of Guelders, Cleves and Jülich and the civic authorities of Cologne complaining of the exorbitant tolls being levied on wine shipments, which had caused the merchants to transfer the wine to wagons and transport it by land instead. The duke asked for a general lowering of tariffs and the prohibition of landings of wine for transferral to wagons. In the autumn of 1470 the scope of this Burgundian intervention was widened. Letters complaining about the tolls were sent to the archbishops of Cologne and Mainz, the bishop of Utrecht, the city of Cologne, the duke of Jülich and to the elector palatine of the Rhine; and a conference was summoned by Charles to meet in Cologne on 20 February 1471 so that his deputies could discuss the lowering of the tariffs, especially 'those that people are levying on wines coming from Burgundy', with 'those rulers and princes who possess tolls on the River Rhine'. Later, it was a tariff on Rhenish wines levied by the city of Cologne and at Bonn which gave offence, and early in 1476 the duke of Burgundy ordered a boycott of all wines on which this excessive duty had been paid. Anyone caught importing such wine into the duke's lands was to be punished 'in body and goods' and their wine was to be confiscated, one-third of it going to their accusers.

In part because of these territorial and economic activities within the Empire, the dukes of Burgundy naturally entertained ambitions there. Charles the Bold's father, Philip the Good, had made a sort of triumphal progress through the Empire in 1454, when he attended the diet of Regensburg. In 1447 and again in 1459–60 the possible creation of an imperial vicariate for Philip the Good was under serious

[1] ADNB 2064, f. 412. For the next sentence, see *Hansisches Urkundenbuch* ix. 611, and, for what follows, the same, ix. 693, AGR CC4181, fos. 163b, 164 (whence the quotation) and 187b, transcript from Köln, Hist. Arch. K. u. R. no. 3 (Burg. Kopialbuch), fos. 61b–63b, in RTA material, Gorissen, *De Raadkamer te Maastricht*, 268–9 and ADN B10440, f. 26.

discussion, and in 1463 Frederick disclosed that he would not be averse to a marriage alliance between Charles the Bold's only child Mary and his son Maximilian, and to the promotion at the same time of the duke of Burgundy to the royal dignity. This scheme was linked to the proposed appointment of Philip the Good as vicar of the imperial territories on the left bank of the lower Rhine. On 9 May 1467, a month before he became duke of Burgundy, Charles the Bold was said by Louis XI to be trying, with the help of Frederick the Victorious, to become vicar of the Empire,[1] and it was at just this time that the projected marriage of Maximilian and Mary was again under negotiation. In these circumstances it is hardly surprising that this project became, in one form or another, the dominant theme of Charles's diplomatic relations with the Empire. Like all his other ambitions, or policies, it had been taken over from his father. But before examining the further evolution of these imperial aspirations under Duke Charles, we must look briefly at the situation and prospects of his daughter Mary.[2]

Charles the Bold's only child and heiress, Mary of Burgundy, was born on 13 February 1457. She was the bait used to tempt the rulers of the house of Habsburg, who might be expected to sacrifice their imperial power by ceding some or even all of it to Charles in return for the eventual acquisition by Maximilian of Austria of the entire complex of Burgundian territories. But Mary of Burgundy was not only significant in Burgundian relations with the Emperor; she was a diplomatic weapon of universal value, which could be, and was, used by her father on numerous occasions and with many different rulers. Indeed, at one time or another, almost everybody was offered the

---

[1] See above, p. 42.

[2] For this paragraph and the rest of this chapter the main collections of sources are *Aktenstücke und Briefe zur Geschichte des Hauses Habsburg*, i and *Reichstags-Theatrum unter K. Friedrichs V*, ii. I am fortunate in having been able to use also the material assembled by Dr Grüneisen at Göttingen for vol. xxiii of the new edition of the *Deutsche Reichstagsakten* (RTA material). Among modern authorities, I have leaned heavily throughout this chapter on Müller, *Die deutschfeindliche Politik Karls des Kühnen*, Krause, *Beziehungen zwischen Habsburg und Burgund*, Rausch, *Die burgundische Heirat*, Bachmann, *Deutsche Reichsgeschichte*, von Kraus, *Deutsche Geschichte zur Zeit Albrechts II und Friedrichs III*, Matzenauer, *Studien zur Politik Karls des Kühnen*, Janeschitz-Kriegl, *ZGO* cv (1957), 150–224 and 409–13, Bittmann, *Ludwig XI. und Karl der Kühne* i (2) and ii (1), and, above all, Heimpel, *ELJ* xxi (1943), 1–54, and Grüneisen, *RV* xxvi (1961), 35–77 with references. On Mary of Burgundy, see van Ussel, *Maria van Bourgondië* and Cazaux, *Marie de Bourgogne*.

hand, and the lands, of Mary of Burgundy, in return for an alliance, or some, usually military, favour. These offers were all of them insincere: history showed that Charles could not bear to part with his daughter while he lived. He could not bring himself to watch with his own eyes while some non-Burgundian prince prepared to take over his territories: unless perhaps his own personal power was thereby immeasurably increased. But if Duke Charles's matrimonial diplomacy was limited in scope and for the most part insincere, this was evidently because of the almost complete absence, in his case, of suitable matrimonial material other than his daughter Mary. His great-grandfather Philip the Bold had had numerous sons and daughters for matrimonial manipulation, and Philip the Good's sisters provided him with nephews and nieces for this purpose in the houses of Cleves and Bourbon. But Charles the Bold had no brothers or sisters save for his father's immense brood of bastards, who possessed no value or status in the European marriage market; nor had he any sons, no daughters other than Mary, no nephews and no nieces except by marriage. However, no one has ever denied that he made the best possible use of the material available to him in the shape of Mary of Burgundy.

In spite of the adverse rumours circulated about her health and physique by the enemies of Burgundy, Mary was a most attractive proposition; a standing temptation to any prince looking for a wife and hoping for territorial advancement. Some of the earliest negotiations for her marriage seem to have been in response to advances of this kind: in 1461–2 King John II of Aragon offered his son and sole heir Ferdinand as a prospective husband for her, and in 1464 King René of Sicily put forward his grandson Nicolas.[1] In March 1466, when King Edward IV of England empowered ambassadors to negotiate the marriage of his sister Margaret to Charles the Bold, they were also instructed to try to arrange the marriage of his brother George, duke of Clarence, to Mary of Burgundy. A year later, rumour had it that Mary was to wed the elector palatine's nephew and eventual successor, Philip; and this rumour was current again in

---

[1] Calmette, *Études médiévales*, 221 and Durr, *HZ* cxiii (1914), 39, and *Dépêches des ambassadeurs milanais en France*, ii. 229. For the next sentence see *Foedera*, xi. 565 and, for the rest of the paragraph, *Urkundliche Nachträge zur österreichisch-deutschen Geschichte*, 45 and 110, AGR MSS. divers 1173, f. 153a–b (despatch of 17 October 1469), and Plancher, iv. no. 239, and de Comines, *Mémoires*, ed. Lenglet du Fresnoy, iii. 300–01. See too, in general, Hommel, *Grand héritage*, 183–98 and Armstrong, *AB* xl (1968), 29–33.

October 1469, at the very moment when Sforza de' Bettini reported from the French court to the duke of Milan that Charles had offered Mary in marriage to Duke Francis II of Brittany, whose wife had died a few months before. If this is true, we can be sure that the initiative was Charles's and the motive was his hope of a military alliance. Two years later, in November 1471, Mary's future was involved in a projected Franco-Burgundian peace settlement: she was to marry the one-year-old dauphin of France, Charles, later King Charles VIII. It was in 1471, too, that Louis XI's brother Charles approached the duke of Burgundy with a view to his marriage to Mary, even though he had earlier sworn not to do so. Negotiations for this alliance, which was opposed at the Burgundian and papal courts by Louis XI, continued nearly until Charles's death on 24 May 1472. It was perhaps in 1472 that Duchess Yolande of Savoy's son Philibert was suggested as a possible husband for Mary of Burgundy, but Charles the Bold needed her at this juncture, as we have seen in an earlier chapter, to tempt Nicolas of Anjou, who had become duke of Lorraine since his first candidature for her hand in 1464, into a military alliance with him in May 1472. This affair was provisionally clinched by a curious letter which the fifteen-year-old princess was made to send Nicolas from Mons on 13 June 1472.[1]

Since, my cousin, it is my most redoubted lord and father's pleasure, according to the treaties drawn up and sealed between my said lord and you, which you shall observe and accomplish in their entirety, that you shall return in person to my most redoubted lord and father and stay with him without leaving him or his lands for whatever reason except with his knowledge, consent and agreement; you shall not for whatever reason or on whatever occasion make any abstinence from war, truce or agreement or make peace for your person, lands, subjects and lordships . . . otherwise than with the knowledge, leave, good pleasure and express consent of my said lord and father . . . ; you, your said lands, subjects and lordships, shall, according to the above-mentioned conditions, make and continue making war [against France] with good will and with all your power, without any fraud, deceit or trickery . . . ; and you shall for ever be well-disposed, true, loyal and obedient to my most redoubted lord and father, neither procuring nor permitting nor agreeing to any displeasure, hindrance, evil or damage to him or any of his possessions, but informing him or causing him to be informed, straight away

---

[1] De Comines, *Mémoires*, ed. Lenglet du Fresnoy, iii. 192–3. For what precedes, see Stein, *Charles de France*, 399–409, and Colombo, *Iolanda, duchessa di Savoia*, 84, and Perret, *France et Venise*, i. 591–2.

and with all possible diligence, according to the above-mentioned written conditions, of any evil, displeasure, hindrance or damage which might happen to my said lord and father; my cousin, since it is my most redoubted lord and father's pleasure, I promise you that, while you are alive, I will never have any other husband but you and, for the present, I take and promise to take you in so far as I am able with God's pleasure.

Marie de Bourgoigne

Nicolas, of course, subsequently joined the ranks of Mary's disappointed suitors. But, though he and all the others sooner or later made way for the ultimately triumphant Maximilian of Austria, son of the Emperor Frederick III, nevertheless in Charles the Bold's lifetime the negotiations for this alliance moved only slowly and fitfully. For Charles the Bold, Mary's marriage to Maximilian was not an aim or an end in itself, it was a means; a means to imperial power. Enlarging the scope of his father's imperial dreams, he conceived the idea of obtaining for himself first the crown of the Romans, and then succession to the imperial throne on Frederick's death or abdication. At Hesdin in May 1469, when Duke Sigmund of Austria came to obtain his help against the Swiss and a loan of 50,000 Rhenish florins in return for mortgaging to Charles his rights and lordships in Upper Alsace, Charles perhaps drove a harder bargain than Sigmund had intended: in return for a promise of help against the Swiss which was never fulfilled and probably never was intended to be fulfilled, he insisted that Sigmund raise with Frederick III the possibility of his election as king of the Romans, offering as an inducement the marriage of Mary to Maximilian.

A further opportunity for intervention in the Empire presented itself to Charles later that summer for on 2 July 1469 King George Podiebrad of Bohemia, who was fighting for his throne, his Hussite faith and even his life against the king of Hungary, the Emperor, the pope, and almost everyone else, sent an embassy to Charles the Bold seeking an alliance and Burgundian diplomatic aid. The existence of a treaty drawn up in draft shows that Charles was interested: in return for his election as king of the Romans, which King George thought could be contrived without difficulty by bribing some of his fellow-electors and persuading others that a strong king was essential to defend the Empire against the Turks, Charles would reconcile George with the pope and pay him 200,000 Rhenish florins.[1] Yet

---

[1] De Comines, *Mémoires*, ed. Lenglet du Fresnoy, iii. 116–18; and see Odlozilik, *The Hussite king*, 239–40, and Boeren, *Twee Maaslandse dichters in dienst van Karel de Stoute*, 94–7.

another diplomatic move favouring Duke Charles's imperial ambitions was made in the autumn of 1469, this time by Archbishop Adolf of Mainz, encouraged on the Burgundian side by his relative, the seneschal or stadholder of Brabant, Count John IV of Nassau-Dillenburg. In return for a treaty of alliance and other favours the archbishop promised to visit the Emperor on Charles the Bold's behalf and try to obtain for him a general imperial vicariate as a preliminary to his election as king of the Romans and his eventual succession to the Empire. The marriage of Mary to Maximilian was again proposed as an inducement.

These diplomatic initiatives of 1469 were not just isolated or spontaneous moves by different princes. They all stemmed, directly or indirectly, from the Burgundian court, if not from Charles himself, and they reflect an almost universal belief, in the summer of 1469, that some move in the direction of placing Duke Charles at the head of the Empire's, and Christendom's, defences against the Turks, which would also have the effect of restoring that institution's unity and political strength, was desirable, possible and even imminent. The pope supported this idea, and favoured the Habsburg-Burgundian marriage alliance. He even hoped to persuade Charles to intervene in Italy, to promote the interests of the Holy See there. The Milanese too, were well aware of Charles's ambitions, though they preferred to see him as the instrument of a diabolical Venetian plot to assume world power for themselves. On 22 August 1469 Johanne Ludovico, marquis of Palavicini, informed the duke of Milan that the Venetians were hoping that the imperial princes and powers would elect Charles 'vice-Emperor, vicar or coadjutor' and would encourage him to organize an expedition into Italy; he advised Galeazzo to make an alliance with the duke of Burgundy. [1]

It was almost certainly in 1469 that one of Charles the Bold's personal doctors wrote and dedicated to the duke his *De custodia principum, On the government of princes*. In this otherwise somewhat insipid work is a lively description of a dinner-time discussion on the subject: which princes are most suitable for election to the imperial dignity? It developed into a sort of miniature imperial election and the choice of the assembled company unanimously fell on Charles the Bold. A burly German who spoke with his mouth

---

[1] ASM Pot. est. Borgogna 515/37–8, and see *Urkunden und Actenstücke*, 486. For what follows, see Wickersheimer, *RN* xxiv (1938), 46–9, and Boeren, *Twee Maaslandse dichters in dienst van Karel de Stoute*, 71–107 and 198–267.

full assured the other diners that 'throughout Germany people agreed in thinking that, on the death of Caesar (i.e. Frederick III), the duke of Burgundy would become Emperor of the Romans', and the Flemish host raised his cup to Charles's health with the words: 'Oh happy country whose defender is Charles, most illustrious prince.' More significant, more explicit and more relevant than the *De custodia principum* is another Latin work of the same year, 1469, by the dean of Heinsberg, Symon Mulart, entitled *De ortu victoria et triumpho domini Karoli ducis Burgundie moderni*: *On the origin, victory and triumph of the lord Charles, present duke of Burgundy*. This part-prose part-verse treatise, abounding in almost ridiculously fulsome praise of Charles the Bold, who is represented as a new Alexander the Great and compared repeatedly to Charlemagne, was formally presented by the author on 15 March 1470 to the city council of Cologne. It is, in effect, quasi-official Burgundian propaganda, in which the princes of the Empire are urged to promote Charles to the imperial dignity or, at the least, to elect him king of the Romans, and his qualifications for this are set out at length.

Negotiations for Charles the Bold's elevation, with Sigmund of Tirol acting as an intermediary between Charles and the Emperor Frederick III and with the marriage alliance figuring as an essential part of the arrangements, continued intermittently through 1470. They may have been restrained by the fact that, at just the same time, King Matthias Corvinus of Hungary was negotiating with Frederick for the crown of the Romans as well as for Frederick's daughter Kunigunde in marriage. They may have been hampered by Charles's repeated refusal to accede to Sigmund's requests for military aid against the Swiss. But Charles's hopes of a successful outcome were certainly not extinguished by these falterings, nor by Frederick's refusal to permit his coronation as king of the Romans, though he was prepared to make him king of any one of his lands. Charles was by no means wholly sincere in the letter he sent to Sigmund at the beginning of 1471.

> To the illustrious and powerful prince Lord Sigmund, duke of Austria, Styria, etc. and count in Tirol, our dearest relative.
> Illustrious and powerful prince and kinsman, your letters were most agreeable to us and we have gladly listened to your communications. What has pleased us most is that you have gone to his imperial highness in order to persuade his majesty of what seemed advantageous [to us] concerning the kingdom of the Romans. For this, we owe you and we wish to express to you as much gratitude as we can. Concerning that

kingdom, however, nothing was initiated by ourselves, nor at first did we think of wanting it until we were solicited by many people and even persuaded by the most serene Lord Emperor. Indeed, in this affair we have no consideration of personal interest, nor were we easily brought to accept the opinion of those persuading us, as we think you will have understood from our ambassadors. We are not therefore vexed by the response of the most serene Lord Emperor which, if he perseveres in it, will relieve us of no little trouble and solicitude. Nonetheless, lest we seem to have failed Christianity, the Empire and your exalted house, we are handing over the whole of this affair to you; but we can only accept as our son-in-law the person you refer to if we are permitted to arrange for the continuation of the Empire in his person.[1] Nor is this unknown to you, for it has been fully expounded by our ambassadors. For the rest, we do not wish our dominions to be elevated into a kingdom, nor [do we wish] to be crowned as the result of any treaty, unless this is for the public welfare and the common advantage. . . .

Illustrious and powerful prince and dearest kinsman, may the all highest keep you.

At Hesdin, 15 January 1470/71

Frederick III's lack of enthusiasm for Charles's coronation as king of the Romans is in itself readily understandable; it would inevitably have entailed the partial, or even complete, abdication of his own imperial authority. But there were other reasons for the distinct cooling of his relations with Charles the Bold which was a feature of the year 1471. In particular, Charles the Bold was the principal ally of Frederick's enemy and namesake, the elector palatine of the Rhine. This prince had earned his surname Victorious in 1463, when he contrived to capture three of his rivals all at once on the field of battle: Ulrich of Württemberg, Karl of Baden and Bishop Georg of Metz. He was the most successful, and the most powerful, prince in the whole of western Germany and his councillors and officials were active and influential in Alsace, where he was imperial *Landvogt*, and in Cologne where his younger brother was archbishop. Even before Frederick the Victorious and Charles the Bold had signed their treaty of 29 December 1465 the former had sent important military aid to the latter, for a contingent of mounted Rhinelanders served with the Burgundians in the war of the Public Weal and

---

[1] See p. 136 below. This letter is printed in *Aktenstücke und Briefe zur Geschichte des Hauses Habsburg*, i. 13–4, and partly translated by de Mandrot, *JSG* v (1880), 150–1. For what follows, besides the works cited on p. 126 above, see Grüneisen, *NDB* v (1961), 526–8, Kremer, *Geschichte des Kurfürsten Friedrichs des Ersten* and Stenzel, *Politik der Stadt Strassburg*, 49–55.

distinguished and amused themselves by breaking into the royal
park at Vincennes and hunting the animals there. Frederick's personal
visit to Charles in the Low Countries, just before he became duke
in 1467, may have strengthened the alliance, but it is uncertain how
he responded to Charles's request for troops to fight Liège later that
year, nor is it likely that the report, attributed to early 1469, that
Frederick had sent Charles 300 horse, was more than an empty
rumour.[1] But the two rulers remained staunch allies. When, in
1469–70, Mulhouse complained to Frederick, as *Landvogt*, of Peter
von Hagenbach's oppressions and threats, Frederick pretended
that he thought Charles the Bold must have been unaware of
what was happening and, though he did encourage and help co-
ordinate the anti-Burgundian opposition in Alsace, he took care that
this did not put his alliance with Charles at risk. In 1470 Frederick's
quarrel with the Emperor flared up into open war. Not only did he
suffer the confiscation of his office of imperial *Landvogt* in Alsace,
which he stoutly refused to hand over, but he found his cousin and
rival, Ludwig von Zweibrücken, count of Veldenz, who also used
the titles 'count palatine of the Rhine and duke in Bavaria', invading
and ravaging his territories with an imperial army and an imperial
banner: he had been appointed captain of the *Reichskrieg* against
him. In January 1471 Charles the Bold was invited by the Emperor to
desert his ally the elector palatine and join this feud against him
with a thousand horse,[2] but in February he ordered Peter von
Hagenbach to stop Burgundian subjects from joining the count of
Veldenz's forces. Although in March 1471 he sent the president of
the council of Luxembourg, Girard Vurry, to try to mediate between
the two cousins, and in May he even went so far as to arrange a
conference between his deputies and those of the count of Veldenz
with a view to a treaty of alliance, in the event he remained loyal
to his ally, whose support was indeed an unchanging and essential
part of the Burgundian political system in Europe throughout
Charles the Bold's reign. Needless to say, Frederick the Victorious
won his war against Ludwig, count of Veldenz. He died only a few
weeks before Charles himself, on 12 December 1476.

---

[1] Above, pp. 44 and 16, and *Urkundliche Nachträge zur österreichisch-
deutschen Geschichte*, 80. For what follows, see *Cartulaire de Mulhouse*, iii.
426–iv. 42, Bittmann, *Ludwig XI. und Karl der Kühne* ii (1). 352–62, and
Grüneisen, *RV* xxvi (1961), 58–9 and nn.
[2] *Briefe und Acten zur österreichisch-deutschen Geschichte*, 673 = *Politische
Correspondenz*, i. 197–8.

The Emperor Frederick's discontent with Charles the Bold over his failure to move against the elector palatine coincided with a meeting of the *Reichstag* or imperial diet which was opened by Frederick in person at Regensburg on 24 June 1471 and afforded ample opportunity for Charles the Bold, through his deputies, to demonstrate his dissatisfaction with the Emperor. 'The councillors of Burgundy, with twenty horse', must have cut a poor figure beside the Emperor with his 1,800 horse, Duke Ludwig the Rich of Bavaria-Landshut with 1,300, or the archbishop of Trier with 360. Even such minor princes as Count Eberhard of Württemberg or the landgrave of Hesse arrived in person with 265 and 400 horse respectively. But the Burgundian deputies endeavoured to compensate for the small size of their retinue by the extravagance of their claims. The bishop of Basel's chancellor, Wunnebald Heidelbeck, described the proceedings in a report which the chronicler of Bern, Diebold Schilling, found 'charming and droll' enough to copy out into his chronicle.

> The duke of Burgundy has here a doctor and two nobles with a small company who maintain that they should be seated in an honourable place over and above all the electors and princes. So far this matter has been debated and is still unsettled and it is to be feared that, because of it, we shall be admiring the fine decorated houses of Regensburg thoroughly and at length. . . .
>
> Item, after mass the Emperor together with the cardinal and all the princes and ambassadors went to a large room in the town hall where one of the Emperor's attendants, called Tredentinus,[1] explained publicly on the Emperor's behalf why he had convoked this assembly. . . . Then he spoke of another matter which nobody could follow or understand, for Tredentinus is a little man and not well spoken, so that even those standing right by him could not well understand what he said. He had a voice which resounded like the chime of the clock at Olten; a voice which rang like an old kettle. Everyone left the room, except for those princes, lords and ambassadors who were in honour bound to stay. Thus Tredentinus stood before the Emperor, but nobody could see or hear him. It would have been better to have had a gallant eloquent man on a high seat with an intelligible, loud voice who could have been seen, but things were arranged otherwise.
>
> All the princes, lords and ambassadors were seated according to rank, but the Burgundians remained standing and refused to sit down. They

---

[1] Johann Hinderbach, bishop of Trent. This passage is from Schilling, *Die Berner-Chronik*, i. 75–87. Other material on the *Sitzstreit* at Regensburg has been kindly communicated to me by Frau Dr I. Most, who will be editing it in volume xxii of the *Deutsche Reichstagsakten*.

maintained that their lord the duke was also an electoral prince and that therefore they should be seated above all other princes, but the Emperor would not accept this. Moreover, according to the electors, the duke of Burgundy belonged to the Empire neither as an Emperor, nor as an elector, nor as a prince, but they insisted that he belonged only as a count of the county of Burgundy. Thus things were left in dispute.

Although Tredentinus was unintelligible, yet the gist of his speech was that the Turks ruled with great power, putting to death all Christians they met with, both young and old. . . . They had conquered as much Christian land up till Gratz, as there was far and wide between Gratz and Cologne, which was a disgraceful thing. . . .

Item, on Wednesday 26 June, Duke George, son of [Ludwig] the Rich, duke [of Bavaria], arrived with a few people belonging to him; some 400 of his father's and other princes' attendants rode to meet him. On the same day the Emperor, princes and lords conferred together and eventually after a discussion lasting three hours the duke of Burgundy's ambassadors were seated. They were placed like this. A bench was set beside us on which Count Frederick of Helfenstein, the king of Denmark's ambassador, and likewise the duke of Burgundy's ambassadors both sat; in this way they were seated next to a royal embassy.

The coolness between Frederick and Charles in 1471 was followed, in 1472–3, by a rapprochement. The initiative came from Burgundy, and again it was a three-sided affair: Charles the Bold wanted the imperial crown for himself; Frederick hoped for a marriage alliance which would bring the Burgundian lands into the hereditary Habsburg possessions; Duke Sigmund still needed Burgundian military assistance against the Swiss. The trouble was that Charles the Bold had no intention of fighting the Swiss, and Frederick had no intention of abdicating his imperial authority to Charles. The diplomat chosen on the Burgundian side to conduct these delicate negotiations was no subtle or experienced ambassador but the forthright bailiff of Alsace, Peter von Hagenbach, whose principal qualification perhaps was that he spoke German. He and his associate Bernhart von Ramstein, lord of Gilgenberg, had raised the matter unofficially in the late summer of 1472 with an imperial councillor, Alwin, count of Sulz, and Charles the Bold had been pleased and encouraged by Bernhart's subsequent verbal report of these discussions. Early in 1473 he sent Peter von Hagenbach on embassy both to the count of Sulz and to the Emperor. With the count it was a simple question of bribery: when the duke of Burgundy became king of the Romans he would receive 10,000 Rhenish florins, a place at the duke's court, and an office of his choice in Austria or the Empire. Moreover, the duke of Burgundy would meet the cost of any bribes Alwin found it necessary to make to achieve his coronation as king of the Romans. With the Emperor, to whom Charles had already sent Augosto de Lignana, abbot of Casanova, in December 1472, it was a case of careful exposition and persuasion. Hagenbach's instructions define Charles the Bold's imperial ambitions more or less exactly. They also include a proposal for a conference between deputies of Charles and Frederick, to be held at Aachen.[1]

Instructions for Messire Pierre de Haguembac, knight, councillor and *maître d'hôtel* of my lord the duke and his bailiff of Ferrette, concerning what he has to negotiate with the Emperor, to whom my said lord the duke is now sending him.

And firstly the said Messire Pierre will present his credentials, which my lord [the duke] is sending him, to the Emperor, and will convey the said lord [duke]'s humble recommendations as is proper and usual on such occasions.

As to his message, he will explain to [the Emperor] how [the duke] recently sent the abbot of Casanova to him concerning the conversations about the marriage between the high and puissant prince my lord Maximilian, duke of Austria, his son, and Mademoiselle the daughter of the said lord duke. And because [the duke] understood that the Emperor had been told that my lord [the duke] would on no account agree to the said marriage unless the Emperor in every way abdicated the imperial dignity, the said Messire Pierre is to explain that this is not true; but the intention of my lord [the duke] was and is altogether the contrary, for he has always desired and [still] desires the Emperor to remain in that dignity even if the marriage comes about. What he wanted was to be made king of the Romans during the life of the said Emperor so that after the Emperor's death he could have the said lord Maximilian, who, in undertaking the said marriage will become his son, created and made king of the Romans. From this both the Emperor and my lord Maximilian would derive notable advantages. In particular, my lord the duke, being thus king of the Romans, will be able to continue the imperial dignity in the person of my lord Maximilian: a thing which could not be done in any other way or, at least, not so easily, because, immediately after the Emperor's death my lord [the duke], being designated to succeed him, will create and institute [the said lord Maximilian] king of the Romans, and thus future Emperor.

[Messire Pierre will add] that the said lord Maximilian, by means of this marriage, will become heir apparent to the largest and finest lordships in Christendom and will also succeed without difficulty to the lordships of

---

[1] *Aktenstücke und Briefe zur Geschichte des Hauses Habsburg*, i. 32–4.

the Emperor's patrimony, both those of which he is the peaceable possessor and those disobedient to him. These lordships, taken together, will be larger than those of any living prince and the house of Austria will be the greatest and most powerful in the whole world. The Emperor will be unburdened of many of his responsibilities, labours and expenses and, with the help of my lord the duke, he will be obeyed and esteemed in his estate more than any other Emperor in the last three hundred years. Also in this way Christianity will be supported and helped and the Turks will be driven back. There will be no prince in the world powerful enough to dare offend the imperial majesty nor the lord Maximilian, and those imperial princes and cities who are rebels will submit to him in full obedience.

By these and other means the said Messire Pierre will [try to] persuade the Emperor to accept what he wants, and he may persist for as long as he judges necessary. He may also point out that this is not the first time the Emperors have done something of this sort. And if he finds the Emperor inclined to this in whatever manner and on whatever terms, the said Messire Pierre may propose the holding of a conference in the town of Aix, the Emperor to send there anyone he pleases at a time convenient to him, and my lord [the duke] to send similarly some of his people, honourably, as is proper in such cases.

And if after several discussions this business of the king of the Romans is in every respect rejected, in this case and not otherwise the said Messire Pierre may suggest that, if it please the Emperor to make my lord [the duke] his irrevocable vicar-general in the whole Empire with a guarantee from the electors that, if the Emperor dies before my lord, he will be chosen Emperor, then my lord will also in this case be content to give effect to the said marriage, provided [he] has been fully assured by the Electors and authorised and confirmed by the pope. If any difficulties arise over this the said Messire Pierre may likewise arrange a conference at Aix, as mentioned above.

If the said Messire Pierre finds the above-mentioned matters progressing well towards one conclusion or the other, he is to visit the said lord Maximilian in person and examine his stature and physical appearance, his habits and health, in order to report on them to my lord [the duke]. He shall communicate all these things to the said abbot of Casanova and expound them, in his presence, to the Emperor, being careful to keep my lord [the duke] informed of the progress of the negotiations by some of the mounted messengers he took with him.

Charles

The details of the negotiations which followed in the first half of 1473 are unknown to us. At this time Charles the Bold's prestige in the Empire was increasing and his connections with King Matthias Corvinus of Hungary and the elector palatine of the Rhine allowed him to take on the semblance of a potential opposition leader to Frederick, the role formerly played by King George of Bohemia. On 24 April 1473 he was appointed one of the arbitrators in the struggle between the kings of Hungary and Poland for the succession to Bohemia and in May he received at Valenciennes a stately embassy from Hungary.[1] By many, he was thought of as a mediator in the disputes which disturbed the west, as well as the east, of the Empire. Might he not arbitrate the prolonged and bitter quarrels between Frederick the Victorious and the Emperor? Also, perhaps, those between Archbishop Ruprecht and the Estates of Cologne? In any event he could have been an invaluable ally to the Emperor in 1473 and it was probably Frederick who took the initiative in writing to Charles, in June of that year, soon after the close of the diet of Augsburg, to offer him, not a conference of deputies, but a personal meeting of the two rulers, to take place at Trier on 1 August. Charles's ambassadors had already accepted this arrangement before 24 June, though some time before 9 July the meeting had been deferred until 12 August. At first the delays were not due to the habitual lethargy and procrastination of the Emperor, but to Duke Charles's military commitments in Guelders. He laid siege to the capital, Nijmegen, on 28 June, but it did not capitulate until 17 July, and he found it necessary to send Peter von Hagenbach to Frederick at the end of the month to assure him that although he was planning to be at Trier on 12 August next and 'he hoped definitely to be there without fail,

---

[1] *IAEG* 196 and *IADNB* iv. 242. For what follows, on the Trier conference, besides the works mentioned on p. 126 n. 2 above, I have used the documents in Baader, *AKV* (N.F.) xi (1864), cols. 201–7 and 232–42, Bertalot, *WZ* xxx (1911), 419–30 (letters of 7 October and 2 November 1473), Colombo, *Iolanda, duchessa di Savoia,* 283 (letter of 14 January 1474), Cusin, *NRS* xx (1936), 34–57, *Eidgenössischen Abschiede,* 459–62, Heimpel, *ELJ* xxi (1943), 50–4, Paquet, *BIHBR* xxv (1949), 118–28 (despatches of 13 and 17 October 1473), *Politische Correspondenz,* i. 513–601, and *Urkundliche Nachträge zur österreichisch-deutschen Geschichte,* 221–39. The most important chronicles and other contemporary accounts are Basin, *Louis XI,* ii. 172–82; Knebel, *Diarium,* ii. 20–36; de Lalaing, *De congressu Friderici III imp. et Caroli ducis Burgundiorum,* printed in *Reichstags-Theatrum unter K. Friedrichs V,* ii. 561–2, *Rerum germanicarum scriptores,* ii. 302–5 and de Comines, *Mémoires,* ed. Lenglet du Fresnoy, iii. 258–62; *Libellus de magnificentia ducis Burgundiae* in *Basler Chroniken,* iii. 332–64; Moltzer, *Frederick III en Karel de Stoute te Trier, 1473*; von Schaumburg, *Die Geschichten und Taten,* 14–17, and *Speierische Chronik,* 508–10. To the modern works cited above, p. 126 n. 2, should be added Lindner, *Die Zusammenkunft Kaisers Friedrich III mit Karl dem Kühnen,* and Cusin, *NRS* xix (1935), 137–72.

yet if nonetheless it happens that the said lord [duke], because of his considerable military preoccupations . . . cannot be there for the conference precisely on the twelfth, he will by no means be later than nine or ten days'.[1] While Charles the Bold postponed the meeting, rumours of it flew fast across Europe. As early as 2 July the authorities at Bern wrote informing Strasbourg that they had heard that the marriage of Maximilian and Mary had already been agreed on; Peter von Hagenbach had been given 1,000 gulden by the Emperor for his part in the negotiations, and the personal meeting was to be at Breisach or Cologne or elsewhere.

Charles the Bold's military problems in Guelders were rapidly solved but, as he moved southwards in August through the scorched landscape in the sultry and feverish heat of the warmest summer in living memory, accompanied by the imperial ambassadors, other preoccupations engaged his attention, notably the question of his relations with the new duke of Lorraine, René of Vaudémont. At Luxembourg, where he arrived on 6 September, he was well placed to intervene in Lorraine and only 45 km. from the proposed meeting-place with the Emperor at Trier. But Frederick was now dawdling. True, he set out from Baden-Baden at last in the middle of August, but at the very time when Charles was moving south towards him, he moved south away from Charles, to Strasbourg first and then, just as Charles reached Luxembourg, he entered Basel, after dallying a week in Freiburg im Breisgau. It was at Basel on 9 September that his ambassadors to Charles the Bold, Count Rudolf of Sulz and Master Hans Keller, returned, accompanied by the Burgundian ambassadors Peter von Hagenbach and Anthoine Haneron. They urged Frederick to hurry: if their duke could not meet him soon urgent affairs would deflect him elsewhere, probably to the duchy of Burgundy. Even then, Frederick contrived not to reach Trier until 28 September.

Some time in August, apparently, Frederick had suggested that Metz would be a more suitable place for a meeting than Trier: among other things, it was considerably larger. On Saturday 18 September 1473 Burgundian ambassadors arrived in Metz and requested permission for their duke to enter the town with 10,000 horse. The civic authorities, already faced with the prospect of putting up the Emperor's people with 1,800 horse, refused, offering instead to allow Charles into their city with 500 horse only. They also turned

---

[1] *Aktenstücke und Briefe zur Geschichte des Hauses Habsburg*, i. 37.

down his ambassadors' request for one of the city's gates to be handed over entirely to the duke of Burgundy.[1] It may have been this refusal, rather than the plague, which caused Charles to request that, after all, the meeting should be at Trier, but his demands to the authorities there were even more excessive: he asked to be permitted entry with 6–7,000 horse and he wanted also 'half the town with its hotels and streets, and two gates opened to him, one over the Moselle, the other in the parish of St. Simon, and no Germans to be allowed to enter this quarter'. When Trier made excuses, Charles's emissaries explained that he did not mind in the least and would be very happy to camp with his people outside the town walls. One should not mistake these bombastic Burgundian requests for crude efforts at urban conquest or appropriation. Much as he disliked the towns, Charles knew perfectly well that a major military expedition, such as he had recently mounted in Guelders, would be necessary before any of them would succumb to Burgundian rule. Even at Aachen, where he had stayed for a few days in August with his army camped outside the walls, he had made no aggressive moves, apart from the traditional formal receipt of the town keys and the setting-up in the market-place of a tent with his arms on it.[2]

It was on 30 September that the long-expected meeting of duke and Emperor at last took place, outside Trier. Charles the Bold evidently regarded the conference in part as a kind of gigantic public exhibition of Burgundian wealth and splendour, and the magnificence of the clothes and accoutrements of himself and his retinue was commented on and subsequently grossly exaggerated by numerous chroniclers. A more exact notion of the appearance and number of the Burgundian courtiers and attendants who accompanied their duke to Trier that day is probably afforded by an elaborate entry made by the duke's *argentier* or treasurer, Nicolas de Gondeval, acting on Charles's instructions of 24 October 1473, in his account of the special issue of materials for robes, which cost the duke a grand total of £38,830.

---

[1] Aubrion, *Journal*, 59 and 61–2. For what follows, see Baader, *AKV* (N.F.) xi (1864), col. 203.
[2] *Cronycke van Hollandt*, f. 337 and above, p. 38. What follows on the Burgundian courtiers' robes is from ADN B2098. The persons enumerated only here are all named in full in the account.

Colour and type of material or its product	Persons	Number of persons
Cloth of gold	John, duke of Cleves, and 24 other leading courtiers	25
Short crimson robes and black satin pourpoints	Golden Fleece herald, the mayor of Namur, and 51 others	53
Long robes of crimson velvet	The lord of Baudeville, Angelo and Jehan de Monfort, and 12 others	15
Short robes of black damask and crimson satin pourpoints	Gilles d'Oignies and 64 others	65
Long robes of black velvet and crimson satin pourpoints	Four persons only	4
Long robes of crimson velvet and crimson satin pourpoints	Messire Olivier de la Marche and 3 others	4
Short robes of velvet on tawny velvet	The lord of Harchies, Messire Bernard de Ramstein and 11 others	13
Short robes of black damask and crimson satin pourpoints	Simon Damas and 91 others	92
Short robes of crimson velvet and black satin pourpoints	Charles de la Viefville and 15 others	16
Long robes of tawny velvet	Jehan le Tourneur the elder and 17 others	18
Long robes of black figured satin	Seven persons	7
Mid-length robes of black figured satin	The provost of the marshals, the burgomaster of Nijmegen, and 7 others	9

Gold brocade	My lord the chancellor	1
Velvet on crimson velvet	The provost of St. Donatian's, Bruges, Messire Ferry de Clugny and another	3
Crimson-violet figured satin and pourpoints of crimson satin	Messire Jehan Carondelet, Maître Vas de Lucene, Thomas Portinari and 6 others	9
Long robes of black velvet	Messire Girard Vurry and 7 others	8
Long robes of crimson-violet damask and black satin pourpoints	Maître Jehan Candida, Maître Nicolas Bouesseau and 5 other *maîtres*	7
Long robes of black damask and pourpoints of violet-crimson satin	The *greffier* of Luxembourg, Gerard Loyet and 31 others	33
Half-length robes of black damask and pourpoints of violet-crimson satin	The controller of the artillery and 19 others	20
Short robes of white damask and pourpoints of black satin	Two persons only	2
Yellow velvet robe, olive-green satin for his pourpoint and blue velvet for his hood	Le Philosophe	1
Green satin for his robe, crimson velvet for his pourpoint, etc.	Monsieur le Glorieux (the duke's fool)	1
Short robes of black damask and pourpoints of violet-crimson satin	Jehan de Longchamp and 28 others	29
Robes of blue and white damask and pourpoints of black satin	Seven persons	7
Short robes of violet-crimson satin and pourpoints of black satin	Twenty persons	20

Robes of crimson damask and pourpoints of violet satin	Le roy des royers and Kings-of-Arms of Brabant, Artois and Flanders	4
Short robes of damask and pourpoints of black satin	Burgundy Limbourg, Lotharingie, the old herald of Guelders, Je l'ay emprins, Ferrette, le roy des menestriers, Rousset the new trumpet and 25 others	33
Robes of camlet and pourpoints of black satin	Two trumpets of the guard and 36 others	38
Blue velvet for his *jacquecte*, and a white damask pourpoint	The captain of the archers	1
Paletots of black and violet camlet and pourpoints of black satin	Court servants etc.	60
Pourpoints of camlet	Big John and 44 other menials	45
Taffeta of various colours for horses' trappings	Twenty-eight knights and squires who took part in a tournament at Trier in front of the Emperor	28
Paletots and mantles of cloth of gold, cloth of silver and of silk, and blue velvet; and pourpoints of crimson satin	My lord's guard of men-at-arms	110
Very rich silver brocade for robes, and crimson velvet pourpoints	The 12 *diseniers* of the guard	12
Crimson cloth of gold for his robe, lined with taffeta, and crimson velvet for his pourpoint	Olivier de la Marche, captain of the guard	1
Blue and crimson velvet and white taffeta for a robe with lining and pourpoint	Julian de Padua, Venetian, who brought news of the new doge of Venice	1

Woollen cloths of different qualities	Johannes, clerk of St. Maximin's, the porters of Luxembourg castle and of St. Maximin's, and 205 other persons	208
TOTAL NUMBER OF PERSONS		1003

Not all Charles the Bold's company on 30 September as he rode to meet the Emperor at Trier is mentioned in this treasurer's account. He also had with him the bishop of Liège, Louis de Bourbon, and his bastard half-brother David, bishop of Utrecht. Even with them, his entourage could not compare with the galaxy of worthies which rode out of Trier with the Emperor to meet him, among them the archiepiscopal electors of Mainz and Trier, at least three dukes of Bavaria, a captive Ottoman prince, Karl, margrave of Baden and his brother Georg, bishop of Metz, Count Eberhard of Württemberg and Maximilian of Austria. Outside Trier difficulties arose because the imperial party had halted on the far side of a moat. An eye-witness on the imperial side reported in a letter to his home town of Strasbourg that at this juncture 'Herr Peter von Hagenbach rode up to Count Adolf of Nassau and we distinctly heard him say: "Tell the Emperor to ride out from behind the moat or else my lord of Burgundy will have to change his dispositions completely." '[1] This typical piece of tactlessness on the part of the bailiff of Alsace fortunately did not affect the issue. The Emperor did move forwards as requested and the meeting of the two princes was so friendly that it looked as if they were going to kiss. After a lengthy but honourable altercation concerning whether they should ride side by side or one behind the other, Emperor and duke reorganized their retinues in a single cortège and rode into Trier in a downpour of rain. In the market place, further difficulties of etiquette arose: Charles the Bold 'wanted to accompany the Emperor as far as his lodgings, and likewise the Emperor wanted to accompany the duke to his lodgings, and they were a good half-hour in this dispute, each with his hat in his hand'. In the end, Frederick went off to his quarters in the archiepiscopal palace, and Charles went to take up residence in

[1] Transcript of a letter of 4 October 1473 from Philip von Mulenheim and Peter Schott to Strasbourg, in RTA material. The quotation that follows is from *Aktenstücke und Briefe zur Geschichte des Hauses Habsburg*, i. 59–60 = *Collection de documens inédits*, i. 232–3.

and around the famous monastery of St. Maximin just outside the town, of which as duke of Luxembourg he was official guardian.

At Trier the emphasis at first was on formal public harangues, honorific ceremonies, feasts and tournaments, while ambassadors, spies, place-hunters and mere curious observers gathered round like a swarm of flies. The duke of Burgundy's sartorial extravagances and lavish display of jewellery aroused astonishment. He visited the Emperor more than once in an ermine-lined open-fronted cloth of gold mantle reaching to the ground, with a collar or cape which reached half-way down his back, longer than the capes of the electors. Underneath his mantle, which was entirely open down the front, his black cloth of gold coat was thickly bordered with pearls and studded with diamonds, sapphires, rubies and balas-rubies. In his hat on one occasion he wore a large balas-ruby with a massive diamond below it, to which were attached three superb pearls. On another occasion his hat sported a jewelled ostrich-feather.

The climax of the first few days was a banquet given by Charles the Bold at St. Maximin's on 7 October for the Emperor and his retinue. A description of it was circulated far and wide in Latin, German, and Dutch and copied by numerous chroniclers, under the title *Libellus de magnificentia ducis Burgundiae*. A member of the archbishop of Mainz's entourage claimed in a private letter that the very memory of this feast made his mouth water, and one German captain, the chronicler Wilwolt von Schaumburg, was apparently so impressed by Burgundian hospitality on this occasion that, with the Emperor's express permission, he took service thereafter with Charles the Bold. The author of the *Libellus* describes the events of 7 October 1473 as follows:[1]

On 7 October the duke of Burgundy invited his imperial majesty and all his great lords and princes to come and dine with him. The abbey church of St. Maximin and the great hall, where they were going to eat, were made ready and decorated with cloths and tapestries at indescribable cost. And so the Emperor came with all his lords and princes in great pomp and magnificence to St. Maximin's with some fine good fellows preceding him, well-skilled and armed according to knightly custom and exercises. The Emperor was dressed in an extremely costly cloth of gold robe, with a very fine and precious cross on his breast. The duke went out to the abbey gates to meet him wearing an exceptionally fine tabard of cloth of gold and silver. He also wore many fine precious

---

[1] *Libellus de magnificentia ducis Burgundiae*, 361–4.

stones that stood out and twinkled like stars, valued at 100,000 ducats. His tabard was open on either side to show off the beauty and richness of his hose, on which he was wearing the [Garter of the] Order of King Edward of England. . . .

After this they went into the church to hear mass. There stood all the lords of the [two] princes, each in his correct place, dressed in new clothes. The knights wore red, black and sanguine velvet, but the principal lords of the chamber were dressed in blue robes of cloth of gold. The lords of the Order of the Golden Fleece wore costly sanguine. There were eight of the princes' heralds and six Kings-of-Arms clothed in damask down to their feet. Accompanied by all these lords, the duke led the Emperor into the church with wonderful pomp and splendour. One side of the church was hung with rich gold and silver tapestries embroidered with the Passion of our Lord Christ Jesus; the other with the story of how Jason got the Golden Fleece in the land of Colchis. . . .

When mass was over the duke led his imperial majesty by the hand into the hall where they were going to eat, which had been so superbly and expensively adorned and prepared that it seemed like King Ahasuerus's splendid feast. This room was hung with rich cloth of gold tapestries with the history of Gideon the regent of Israel and many precious and costly stones were sewn into them, which stood out and twinkled like stars.

At one end of the hall stood a treasury, ten stages high, on which stood firstly, thirty-three gold and silver vessels of many kinds. Item, seventy jugs, large and small. Item, a hundred dishes and cups decorated with pearls and precious stones. Item, six large silver ladles and twelve gold and silver basins for washing hands. Item, six unicorns' horns, two of which were the length of an arm. Item, six silver jugs, each of twelve quarts. Item, a large silver basket, to hold the reliquaries on the princes' table.

There were three tables, and everything on them, by way of jugs, cups, dishes and related things, was of gold and of silver. His imperial majesty sat in the middle of the first table and, on his right, the archbishop of Mainz, the archbishop of Trier, the bishop of Liège and the bishop of Utrecht. On the other side sat the high-born prince Duke Charles of Burgundy, Maximilian, archduke of Austria, the Emperor's son, Duke Stephen of Bavaria, Duke Albert of Bavaria–Munich and Duke Ludwig of Bavaria. On the second table sat, on the right, the bishop of Metz, the bishop of Eichstätt, Karl, margrave of Baden and Christoffel his son, the ambassadors and councillors of the margrave Albert of Brandenburg. . . . On the third table sat Count Eberhart of Sonnenberg, Albrecht von Baden, Jacob Craft knight, the ambassador and councillor of Duke Sigmund of Austria. . . .

In the first place thirteen dishes were presented and served, ushered in by sixteen trumpeters and twelve princes dressed in cloth of gold, that is to say, the young lord John, eldest son of the duke of Cleves, Philip, son of the lord of Ravenstein, Jehan, count of Marle, son of the count of St. Pol, Count Engelbert of Nassau, the marquis of Rötteln, the count of Salm, Guy, count of Meghen, lord of Humbercourt, Jan, eldest son of the lord of Egmond, the lord of Carency, Jaques, lord of la Hamaide, the lord of Roubaix, and Anthoine, Duke Philip's bastard son of Brabant. Besides these twelve princes were another hundred princes, lords, knights and noblemen, all clad in cloth of gold and silver, each according to his rank. Next time twelve dishes were brought, and the third time ten.

When the meal was over thirty bowls, cups and dishes of gold and silver were brought, decorated with precious pearls and costly stones, containing all kinds of confections and spices. One of them, standing before the Emperor, was valued at 60,000 gulden. After grace had been said all these lords went again into the church to hear vespers; after which the prince with all the lords accompanied the Emperor back to his palace by torchlight with much splendour and festivity.

In the intervals of feasting, courtesy calls and jousting, the Burgundian chancellor, Guillaume Hugonet, had ample opportunity from the first days of October onwards to indulge his talent for lengthy Latin speeches. But on Saturday 2 October, when Charles paid his first visit to Frederick, the chancellor had to act as a go-between while they wrangled over points of honour for an hour, for the duke refused to sit on the Emperor's right. Nor could they subsequently agree about the exact manner of the duke's departure for, while Frederick insisted on seeing Charles downstairs and out of the building, Charles would not hear of it. He did manage to get as far as the bottom of the stairs on his own, but had to remount them hurriedly when he noticed Frederick following him down. Next day the Emperor visited St. Maximin's and formal hearing was given to the archbishop of Mainz's plea for a general crusade against the Turk in 'a small room adorned with Dutch embroideries'. But in order to hear Guillaume Hugonet's reply, Charles the Bold had the assembled company moved into a larger room hung with tapestries of Alexander the Great. In essence, the Burgundian chancellor replied that the duke would willingly help with the crusade if only his enemy Louis XI could be deterred from attacking his lands in his absence; and Hugonet delivered an elaborate tirade against Louis XI and the wrongs he had done to the house of Burgundy.

What were Charles the Bold's exact aims in conferring with the Emperor at Trier? All the evidence points to the probability that he hoped, at any rate at first, to be crowned king of the Romans and be promised the succession to the imperial throne, in return for allowing Maximilian to marry his daughter Mary. Some claimed that he was so determined to become Emperor that he would try to take that throne by force of arms if he could not obtain it by negotiation. Even in the early stages of the Trier talks Charles must have realized that Frederick was still unwilling to crown him king of the Romans. Instead, he offered the duke an imperial vicariate and a territorial kingdom, dependent on the Empire, to be based on whichever lands Charles preferred. In mid-October the papal legate, Luca de' Tolenti, reported to Pope Sixtus IV that 'the duke would not agree to the marriage except in return for the kingdom of the Romans, but his imperial majesty would [only] agree to give him a vicariate and certain other things'.[1] Finding his principal ambition thwarted, Charles the Bold changed his tack. On 23 October Guillaume Hugonet, in another Latin oration which the Milanese ambassador thought 'poorly put together', made four specific demands on his duke's behalf: investment of the duke of Burgundy with the duchy of Savoy, on behalf of or as guardian of the young duke; the reconciliation of Frederick with the elector palatine; raising of the imperial ban on Holland and Zeeland; and investment with the duchy of Guelders. The Emperor, after a brief consultation with the imperial princes, promised a reply to these proposals, but the duke was evidently becoming impatient. 'Even he', commented the Milanese ambassador, 'was perhaps getting tired of these German "tomorrows".' On 30 October he gave orders for the departure of his people to Luxembourg, having sent his plate and tapestries on ahead; but he was persuaded at the last moment to stay. Soon after this he was granted two of his chancellor's requests of 23 October: on 3 November the imperial ban on Holland and Zeeland was raised, and on 6 November Charles was formally invested with the duchy of Guelders.[2]

Historians have debated the significance of the formal investment of 6 November. Was it a victory for Charles, or did it represent a concession, an admission by him that, whatever form his kingdom would take, he was an imperial vassal for the duchy of Guelders? The ceremony itself took place in the famous Hauptmarkt of Trier which the Emperor had cleared, for the occasion, of all the wooden butchers' and other shops which usually encumbered it. A throne was set up on a wooden structure in front of the church of St.

[1] Paquet, *BIHBR* xxv (1949), 124. The quotations below are from Cusin, *NRS* xx (1936), 36.
[2] Text in *Urkunden und Aktenstücke des Reichsarchivs Wien*, i. 2–4.

Gangolf, with seats below it for the imperial princes. Charles the Bold arrived on horseback, armed, with a crowd of attendants, and rode two or three times round the market place before he dismounted and ascended the steps to kneel before the Emperor, who was wearing his crown, and render 'the oath of homage and fealty' before receiving the solemn investiture of Guelders.

It was at about this time, in the first few days of November, that Charles the Bold at last lowered his sights from the kingdom of the Romans which Frederick had denied to him, to a kingdom made out of his own lands, the so-called territorial kingdom, which he had formerly refused. The evidence for this is incontrovertible though the duke of Burgundy's sincerity may be questioned: the following Latin report on the negotiations of 4 November was sent to Rudolf, margrave of Hochberg and lord of Rötteln. [1]

> The most serene lord Emperor has consented to restore and to create, and he will now restore and create, for the lord duke of Burgundy, the kingdom of Burgundy, in the person of the aforesaid lord duke, for himself and his heirs and successors male and female, with all the dignities, rights and prerogatives which in any way belong to the said kingdom of Burgundy. And into this kingdom he will incorporate each and every land, principality and lordship which the aforesaid lord duke holds and possesses at the moment or to which he has any kind of right within the Empire, with all their rights, dignities, prerogatives, pertinances and appendages as well as all fiefs, retrofiefs and lordships etc. enclaved or included in those principalities which are held from the Empire. He will also incorporate and add to the aforesaid kingdom the fiefs, retrofiefs, homages, rights and regalia of the duchies and lordships held within the Empire by the dukes of Cleves and of Lorraine, and those which the duke of Savoy holds both this side and beyond the mountains, as well as those of the principalities, lordships and lands of the bishoprics of Utrecht, Liège, Toul and Verdun. . . .
>
> For this kingdom the aforesaid lord duke and his successors in it shall do homage and fealty to the most serene lord Emperor and his successors and they shall receive from them the investiture of the kingdom. . . . And, to help [defend] Christianity, the said lord duke will provide at the Emperor's request, so long as he is at peace with the king of France, up to 10,000 men-at-arms.
>
> The above was agreed and concluded between the said most serene lord Emperor and the most illustrious lord duke in the city of Trier, on 4 November 1473, in the presence of Rudolf, count of Sulz.

---

[1] Stein, *BEC* xcviii (1937), 339–41.

This was only a report of a verbal agreement, not a diplomatic or definitive document, and the haggling continued, relieved from time to time by diversions such as those described by the Strasbourg town-runner Hans Wetzel in a letter of 20 November:[1]

Item on the Sunday next after St. Martin's day the duke rode into the woods with the Emperor's son, Margrave Karl of Baden and his two sons, a young duke from Cleves, etc. with many others, to shoot again at the popinjay, which was set high up in a tree with six poles fixed on end. It was knocked down by the first shot. Then a hat was set up on a pole: four shots went through the hat and two through the pole. After this, everyone went off and a king was chosen from among the archers, who was the person who had brought down the popinjay. This king was called the King of the Crows; he had a large retinue. There was another company of people from the kitchens, and the two groups opposed one another. The company of cooks made a defence of wood and manure round a cess-pool in the courtyard at St. Maximin's. They had many ways in and round about it and they put up a lively defence from these ways, using three serpentines which they had ready inside, with old cushions etc. Item the king had two serpentines got ready which fired at and stormed against the castle and they hurled manure and dirt at one another and struck each other. They had such a time that everyone had to watch, and they all got very wild. The duke, the Emperor's son, Margrave Karl, his two sons and many others lay there and watched.

Some days before these curious games or entertainments an agreement about the future of Europe, in the shape of a kingdom for Charles the Bold, had quite certainly been reached. Indeed the duke was within a hair's breadth of wearing a crown. But, as always, rumour ran ahead of fact. In a letter of 8 November from Toul the Italian mercenary captain in Charles's pay, Jacobo Galeoto, reported that the duke had been 'made and created king of the Romans and, after the death of the most serene [Emperor], the Empire will pass to the most illustrious duke of Burgundy, and thus he will become Emperor'.[2] At Basel the diarist cleric Johann Knebel recorded on 11 November that he did not know what Frederick and Charles were discussing at Trier 'unless it was that all the towns in the Empire should be subjected to them'. But on 14 November he refers to Charles as 'the lord king of Burgundy' and claims that the Emperor

---

[1] Heimpel, *ELJ* xxi (1943), 51. The people mentioned with Duke Charles are Maximilian, the Margrave Karl, his sons Christoffel and Albrecht, and John, eldest son of the duke of Cleves.
[2] Cusin, *NRS* xx (1936), 39.

had given him a kingdom comprising four duchies, of Zeeland, Holland, Brabant and Guelders, but the electors had rejected his request for four other duchies and four bishoprics. The marriage had been agreed to, even though Mary was 'scrofulous and, it is said, mad'.[1] More surprisingly perhaps, on 13 November Margrave Albert of Brandenburg wrote informing Duke William of Saxony that the Emperor had crowned Charles. Behind these rumours was a firm base of fact. Workmen had prepared the cathedral of Trier for the coronation before the original date fixed, which was 18 November, later deferred till 21 November, under the personal supervision of the Emperor himself. The crown, the sceptre, the standards, even the costumes of the new king, all are said to have been made ready. The bishop of Metz had even rehearsed the solemn mass and coronation office. But no coronation ever took place. On 24 November Frederick announced his intending departure and next morning he slipped unobtrusively down the Rhine in spite of Charles's efforts to detain him. The councillors of the margrave of Brandenburg described the manner of his departure as follows:[2]

> So the Emperor rose at daybreak on 25 November and hurriedly took ship. Peter von Hagenbach followed after his grace in a rowing boat and told the Emperor that the duke was distressed that he had got up so early. He had not expected this, and he asked him to go slowly, so that the duke could come and take friendly leave of him and talk further about all sorts of things. The Emperor agreed, if he was not too long. So the ships drifted without oars for half an hour. When the duke did not come, Peter von Hagenbach said he would hurry to the duke so that he would come soon but, as soon as he had rowed away and was out of sight, the Emperor had his oars put out and rowed off. So the duke did not come to see the Emperor off as arranged.

Two outstanding questions about the Trier conference remain to be answered in a convincing manner by historians. What was the actual title of the proposed kingdom? Why was there no coronation?

The kingdom which Charles the Bold so nearly accepted in November was to be within, and not independent of, the Empire. It has been argued persuasively that it was to be not a kingdom of Lotharingia, but of Burgundy, and Duke Charles's reference to the 'kingdom of Burgundy, usurped for a long time by the French and converted into a duchy' in a speech to the Estates of Burgundy at

[1] For this and the preceding sentence see Knebel, *Diarium*, ii. 20 and 22.
[2] *Urkundliche Nachträge zur österreichisch-deutschen Geschichte*, 237–8.

Dijon on 25 January 1474 has been cited to support this hypothesis. The chronicler and bishop of Lisieux, Thomas Basin, says that Charles wanted to be 'king of Burgundy' and, according to the Guelders ecclesiastic Willem van Berchen, he sought to have the imperial county of Burgundy, once a kingdom, restored to its former state. Others, for the most part less well-informed, insist that the proposed kingdom was essentially Frisian. Thus the Lübeck chronicle and Jacob Unrest both mention Charles's ambition to be king of Friesland, and so does Wilwolt von Schaumburg. A contemporary Burgundian document of doubtful significance, copied on 1 January 1474, also points to Frisia. It states that 'a new king of Frisia would have entirely new servants, new laws, new money, new seals and new arms', and explains that the twenty-four banners at his coronation would bear the arms of 'Frisia, Lotharingia, Brabant, Holland, Zeeland, Limbourg, Namur, Guelders, Hainault, Cleves, Malines, the marquisate of the Holy Empire, Antwerp, the churches of Liège, Cambrai and Utrecht, Upper Burgundy, Savoy, Lorraine, Vaudémont, Luxembourg and the churches of *Scheenem*, Toul and Verdun'.[1] Other reports complicate matters by stating that Charles wanted to be king of Frisia *and* Burgundy. Be this as it may, we may surmise that the Frisian alternative to Burgundy was seriously discussed as a possibility and that the Burgundian administration had Friesland in mind when they included land to which their duke has 'any kind of right within the Empire', in their document, quoted above, of 4 November.

The exact answer to the question, why was there no coronation? has yet to be found. Contemporaries speculated on inadequate evidence and modern historians have perforce followed suit. Some explanations may be summarily dismissed. Even though King Louis XI of France did write to the Emperor requesting him not to crown Charles the Bold, and even though he did offer his daughter, instead of Mary of Burgundy, to Maximilian in marriage, nonetheless the breakdown of the negotiations had nothing to do with him. Indeed,

---

[1] BN MS. fr. 1278, f. 277. For what precedes, see Bonenfant, *BARBL* xli (1955), 277–80, Chabeuf, *MSBGH* xviii (1902), 291–2, Basin, *Louis XI*, ii. 180, van Berchen, *Gelderse kroniek*, 138, *CDS*, xxxi. *Lübeck*, v. 122–3, Unrest, *Österreichische Chronik*, 54, and von Schaumburg, *Die Geschichten und Taten*, 16. For the next sentence, see for example, Aubrion, *Journal*, 65, *Hanserecesse*, vii. 192, Snoy, *De rebus batavicis*, 160–4, and the imperial secretary Balthasar's letter of 6 December 1473 in Heimpel, *ELJ* xxi (1943), 52–4. See too below, p. 185 and 186 n. 1.

Louis XI's diplomatic intrigues were a good deal less far-sighted and less successful, and his political influence less extensive, than his admirers have cared to admit. Nor was the failure of the Trier conference due to the activities of Carlo Visconti, the Milanese ambassador who had been sent to Trier by Galeazzo Maria Sforza with verbal instructions to wreck the negotiations, for we can surely discount his claim that, by persuading the Emperor's Portuguese doctor to tell Frederick that Mary of Burgundy 'was not sound of body, being on the way to becoming hunchbacked and consumptive', he had been instrumental in persuading the Emperor to postpone the marriage alliance and therefore break off the negotiations. Undoubtedly the duke of Milan feared that his interests would not be served by a successful outcome to the meeting, but his ambassador seems to have been unable to ascertain in what way his master's interests really were threatened, if at all. However, much of our knowledge of the reasons for the failure of the Trier negotiations is due to Carlo Visconti's intelligent speculation.

There were perhaps two fundamentally important difficulties in the way of the creation of Charles the Bold's kingdom. First, the duke himself was by no means happy with what to him was very much a second best. What he really wanted was the crown of the Romans, and he evidently found it hard to make up his mind about anything else. With some verisimilitude, Carlo Visconti makes Frederick complain, when he was leaving Trier, that Charles 'was always coming with some new proposal; what he promised one day, was nothing the next'.[1] Second, the electors were certainly opposed to the whole scheme, and the force of their opposition may have been greatly enhanced by Charles's insistence on their consent. A host of other explanations were advanced by Visconti and others, some of them important, others not. It is quite possible, for example, that Charles demanded the vote, or place in the college of electors, that belonged to the crown of Bohemia, if not that crown itself, and that this was too much for Frederick and his imperial colleagues. It is more than likely that Frederick was annoyed by Charles's references to 'our brother the count palatine' and by his determined refusal to abandon this ally in spite of repeated requests from Frederick. He may also have been annoyed by Charles's refusal to reinstate the count of Moers, who had tried to defend Guelders against him, in his lands and possessions. Besides these bones of

---

[1] Cusin, *NRS* xx (1936), 51.

contention between the two rulers another was mentioned by Visconti: Charles was the friend, Frederick the enemy, of Venice. Also of possible significance was the question of Upper Alsace or, as Wilwolt von Schaumburg rather more exactly put it, of the Breisgau and the Sundgau, but all we know for certain is that Sigmund had urged Frederick to demand the return of these territories at Trier and that Charles, who claimed that he feared they might pass to a third party, was unwilling to agree. Finally, in assessing the reasons for the failure of the Trier talks, one must take into account the character and attitudes of Frederick III. His diplomacy was habitually tortuous and evasive; politically, he invariably moved slowly and uncertainly. Moreover there are some grounds for supposing that he just could not bring himself to accept Charles the Bold as a king. He is on record as saying, in 1474, although admittedly in another connection, that there were only four crowns in the Empire, those of Aachen, Arles, Milan and Rome, and that they all belonged on his head.[1]

Charles left Trier empty-handed; *cum le trombe nel saccho*, as Carlo Visconti vividly put it.[2] He had failed to assure for himself succession to the Empire; he had failed to obtain the crown of the Romans; he had failed in his bid to become ruler of a territorial kingdom. Nonetheless, as he moved south in November 1473 through Luxembourg and Lorraine, to spend Christmas at Breisach, none could deny that his star was in the ascendent. His person and his court had been displayed at Trier as the most splendid in Europe; his circle of allies, his clientele of friends and supporters, was as widespread and all-embracing as ever; and he had completed the creation of a new army, led by some of the most expert captains of his day, *condottieri* from Italy. No wonder contemporaries speculated that autumn on the next moves of this powerful and evidently restless prince. Would he attack Metz, which had refused him entry? Would he turn once again against France in a bid to obliterate his royal enemy there? Or would his military attention be deflected by the rumblings of discontent and opposition now being heard along the Rhine and even in the Swiss mountains? All these possibilities were mentioned in a letter sent to Bern on 12 November 1473 by Jehan d'Aarberg, lord of Valangin,[3] but before we describe Burgundian

[1] Bachmann, *Deutsche Reichsgeschichte*, ii. 474.
[2] Cusin, *NRS* xx (1936), 50.
[3] Transcript from Fribourg, Archives municipales, Papiers de France, 1473–1551, in RTA material.

political events in 1474 and the years succeeding, some examination is called for of the three matters above-mentioned: Charles the Bold's court and person, his system of allies and partisans, and his military power.

CHAPTER FIVE

The Ruler and his Court

Among all the eye-witness descriptions of the person and physique of Duke Charles the Bold, by his own courtiers, by Italian ambassadors, and by chroniclers, one remains outstanding: the famous pen-portrait by that veteran courtier and official Burgundian historiographer, George Chastellain, inserted, probably not long after Charles succeeded his father as duke of Burgundy, into the author's *Declaration of all the noble deeds and glorious adventures of Duke Philip of Burgundy*.

> And although I am writing about his father . . . nonetheless I want to describe and portray him here and now for all time, present and future; and I shall refer to him in the past tense, which will serve for always.
>
> This Duke Charles was not so tall a prince as his father. He was stout, well-grown and well-knit; strong in the spine and the arms; he stooped forward somewhat, with rather heavy shoulders; he had strong legs and large thighs, long hands and elegant feet; neither too much flesh nor too little bone, but his body was light and brisk and well adapted for work and physical force. His face had a somewhat rounder appearance than his father's. His complexion was clear and dark; his eyes were laughing and expressive and angelically bright and, when he was pondering something in his mind, his father seemed to come alive in them. He had his father's rather full and well-coloured mouth; his nose was well-formed, his beard dark; his face was vividly coloured, with clear skin, fine forehead, thick black bushy hair and a white and well-proportioned neck. He looked downwards as he walked along. He was not quite so upright as his father but he was a handsome prince. . . .[1]

[1] Chastellain, *Oeuvres*, vii. 228–9. For what follows see, on the portraits, Chabeuf, *MAD* (4) viii (1901–2), 201–18, van den Gheyn, *AAAB* lvi (1904), 384–405 and lix (1907), 275–94, Rubbrecht, *ASEB* lx (1910), 15–64, Drouot, *MCACO* xix (1926–32), 12–14, and Keller, *Festgabe Paul Kirn*, 245–54 and references therein. On de Candida, see Tourneur, *RBN* lxx (1914), 381–411 and lxxi (1919), 7–48 and 251–97. For this chapter as a whole Fredericq, *Rôle politique* and Cartellieri, *The court of Burgundy*, are useful; see too Cazaux, *PCEEBM* x (1968), 85–91.

The surviving artistic representations of Charles the Bold confirm this description of his personal appearance. Apart from the famous illumination showing him as a boy among the courtiers watching the presentation of the *Chroniques de Hainault* to Philip the Good,[1] at least three important and probably more or less exact likenesses of him were executed during his lifetime. Pride of place goes to the superb portrait in the Museum Dahlem, Berlin, reproduced as the frontispiece of this book, and attributed by many to Roger van der Weyden himself. Here we see Charles as a young man, before he became duke, aged between twenty and thirty, with thick black hair, rounded face, full lips and greyish eyes. A second notable contemporary likeness of Charles was cut in gold between 1467 and 1471 by Gerard Loyet, for the famous reliquary, with figures of the duke and St. George, which the duke gave to the cathedral church of St. Lambert, at Liège, in 1471.[2] Unmistakably, this is the same person who figures in the Berlin portrait, with the same thick mop of hair, the same rather piercing eyes, the same somewhat protruding mouth and jaw. Thirdly, the Neapolitan medallist and ducal secretary, Johanne de Candida, engraved at least two medals some time after 1472 showing Charles the Bold's portrait in profile. Even though in one of them the duke is got up as a Roman Emperor, there is a distinct resemblance between their subject and that of the Berlin portrait, but it is just possible that Johanne de Candida used that painting, or its exemplar, for his engravings. There are many other representations of Charles the Bold, in manuscript illuminations, paintings or in some other form, but none has the same authority, none is so early and so authentic, as those just mentioned.

Although Charles the Bold's health was normally robust, contemporary sources reveal that he suffered, during his ten-year reign as duke, from at least three serious illnesses. On 4 January 1468 the provost of St. Andrew's, Cologne, reported from Brussels that the duke had been taken ill the day before. 'He had more than ten doctors with him; truly, he was very sick.'[3] But he seems to have recovered almost at once. More serious was an attack of feverish catarrh in the head which afflicted him in September 1475. It generated an abscess in his throat which probably caused his doctors some alarm, but he was reported out of danger by the Milanese ambassador on 27

[1] Vaughan, *Philip the Good*, plate 2, facing p. 62.
[2] Above, p. 36.
[3] *Hansisches Urkundenbuch*, ix. 277. For the next sentence, see ASM Pot. est. Borgogna 516–17/97. For what follows, see p. 384 below.

September. Most serious of all was the illness which laid him low in April 1476 after the defeat of Grandson. Its course is described in detail by Johanne Petro Panigarola, the Milanese ambassador at his camp, who obtained information both from the duke's doctors and from the sick man himself, and it will come to our notice in a later chapter. It affected him first on 15 April 1476 and, for a few days at the end of the month, he suffered intense stomach-aches and even lost consciousness for a time. But the duke was up and dressed on 1 May and by 3 May he seemed back to normal. At any rate he was well enough to harangue his councillors on Louis XI's bad faith and to swear by St. George that, if God gave him life, he would see to it that the king was suitably dealt with. Thereafter he recovered rapidly and no further ill-health seems to have troubled him during the last rigorous months of his life. He was only forty-three years old when he met his death on the field of Nancy on 5 January 1477.

Contemporaries, especially the Flemish legist Philippe Wielant, as well as subsequent historians, have amused themselves and misled others by elaborating on the contrasts between the chivalrous, elegant, courtly Duke Philip and his ambitious, austere and indefatigable son. This alleged antithesis was never more pronounced than in their respective treatment of women and here, at least, there is more than a grain of truth in Wielant's remarks:

> Duke Philip loved and very much honoured women and could not hear evil about them. He used to say that, by being nice to women he was inevitably making himself popular with their men-folk, because women were normally dominant and there was scarcely a single household in forty where the woman was not mistress. On the other hand Duke Charles did not bother about women and was ready to hear them slighted.
>
> Duke Philip always showed considerable affection for my lady Isabel of Portugal, his wife, and always took her with him everywhere and lodged her near him. But Duke Charles invariably lodged my lady away from him and his court, saying that he by no means wanted his household to be hampered by women. If he was at Ghent he sent her to stay at Drongen; if at Bruges, to Male; if at Louvain, to the abbey of Parc at Heverlee; if at Brussels, to St. Josse-ten-Noode; if at Lille, to Marquette; if at Arras, to La Motte; if at St. Omer, to Arques; if at Abbeville, to Le Crotoy; and he would go to visit her once or twice a week as he pleased. He turned the womens' lodgings in his household into a council chamber and an accounting office, saying that he would rather have the council and finances around him, than women.[1]

---

[1] Wielant, *Antiquités de Flandre*, 56. For what follows, Vander Linden, *Itinéraires*, may be supplemented by Wellens, *ABB* xxxviii (1967), 108–13.

How fanciful is Wielant's version of Charles the Bold's attitude to women and his relationship with his wife? He is certainly wide of the mark when he suggests that Charles visited his wife once or twice a week, and misleading if he gives the impression, as he seems to, that the duchess was invariably near at hand. Though it is true that when Charles was at St. Omer in the winter of 1471-2 Margaret was at Arques and that she was at the castle of Bellemotte, outside Arras, when Charles stayed in Arras in May–June 1472, nonetheless she was only once at Drongen while he was at Ghent; nor, apparently, was she ever at the abbey of Parc outside Louvain while he was in the town. In fact when Charles was at Louvain she was at Brussels or Hesdin. When she was at St. Josse-ten-Noode he was more often at Middelbourg, Antwerp or Brussels; and when he was at Lille she was at Hesdin or Brussels. But even if one concludes that the situation described by Wielant did arise from time to time, the normal relationship between Charles and Margaret was quite different. Usually she remained at Ghent, or for a time at Brussels, Hesdin or elsewhere, while he was far away. In the first six months of their married life, duke and duchess were together only for three weeks or so. On a generous estimate, they were together for one-quarter of the time in 1469 and 1470 and less than that in 1471. In the early months of 1472, it is true, Wielant's account is at its most accurate: in February and March they were at Bruges and Male; in May at Ghent and Drongen; in June at Arras and Bellemotte castle. But they were nowhere near each other during the rest of 1472 and Margaret only enjoyed her husband's company for a couple of weeks in 1473 and less than that in 1474. They were together for the last time at St. Omer, for a few days only, in July 1475.

If Charles did not normally live with his wife, did he do so with other women? Though he is traditionally supposed to have been chaste, if not puritanical, in contradistinction to his gallant and amorous father, yet he may have left illegitimate descendants in Lorraine.[1] There is some evidence, too, that he was homosexual. At any rate his illegitimate half-brother Baudouin and his associate Jehan de Chassa virtually accused him of buggery when they fled from his court at the end of 1470.

De la Marche, in a celebrated passage, says that Charles was not named *le Travaillant*, the hard-working or assiduous, for nothing, for

---

[1] Bergé, *IG* lx (1955), 395–6. For the next sentence, see below, p. 239.

no man drove himself as hard as he did.[1] How did he use his leisure? According to Wielant, 'the pastime of Duke Charles was to go in the morning from room to room to organize justice, war, finance and other affairs'. He certainly did become deeply interested in the routine minutiae of judicial administration, of military organization, of diplomacy and of his finances. 'All this week', wrote Panigarola on 31 December 1475, Duke Charles 'has been preoccupied with re-organizing the men-at-arms according to his new ordinances and making dispositions for, and drawing up the balance of, his receipts and expenses, so that he has scarcely eaten once a day'.[2] More remarkable is the description this same Milanese ambassador included in his despatch of 17 June 1476, of Duke Charles spending some hours signing letters with his own hand. It gave him much pleasure. He even paid himself a *scudo* for each letter, and earned over 200, which he kept in a little purse. Many hundreds of letters have survived, apparently signed by the duke himself, but some of these attestations may be the work of a secretary trained to imitate his signature, which he altered in 1471 to make it less easy to counterfeit.[3]

There is, with Charles the Bold, a quite unprecedented increase in the amount of autograph Burgundian governmental material; a product of his intense personal involvement in the administration of his territories. Who else would have written out a safe-conduct, for Louis XI to visit him at Péronne, in his own hand? Who else would have taken the trouble to send an *autograph* letter to the captain and garrison of Calais in the autumn of 1470 protesting his friendship for England, even if in most undiplomatic terms?[4] Characteristically, when a letter was sent in June 1476 to the bishop of Geneva to complain about the ill-treatment of some Burgundians, Charles added four lines in autograph, apparently in the hopes that the bishop would take more notice. Even in the ducal accounts we find mention of Duke Charles's autographs: on 12 June 1468 a messenger was paid for

---

[1] De la Marche, *Mémoires*, i. 147. The quotation which follows is from Wielant, *Antiquités de Flandre*, 57. See too below, pp. 172 and 173.

[2] *Dépêches des ambassadeurs milanais*, i. 262, and for what follows, ASM Pot. est. Borgogna 518–20/348.

[3] De Comines, *Mémoires*, ed. Lenglet du Fresnoy, iii. 18–20; compare Delisle, *BEC* xlv (1884), 201 and n.; the Péronne safe-conduct mentioned at the start of the next paragraph is printed in both places.

[4] Bittmann, *Ludwig XI. und Karl der Kühne*, i (2). 476, printed in Plancher, iv. no. 222. For the next sentence, see *Dépêches des ambassadeurs milanais*, ii. 249, and for what follows, ADN B2068, f. 118, ASM Pot. est. Borgogna 516–17/47 and *Briefe und Actenstücke von Mailand*, 110.

'carrying certain other letters close, at four o'clock after dinner, written by the hand of my said lord [the duke]' to the lord of Humbercourt. On one occasion Duke Galeazzo Maria Sforza of Milan sent an autograph letter to Charles, who was extremely gratified and promised to send an autograph reply, but when a few days later he wrote out the text of his alliance with Milan in his own hand with a view to sending it to Galeazzo, the Milanese ambassador found it necessary to copy it out

> because it was not very legible. He [Duke Charles] would rather arm himself six times over from head to foot than write one letter. He did it in my presence as willingly as possible and with a cheerful countenance, saying that your lordship would forgive him if he was not such a good scribe as you, but he wanted to demonstrate what little he knew how to do.

Although in the free use of his own handwriting in the work of government Charles the Bold might almost be regarded as an innovator, possibly subject to Italian influences, nonetheless the hand itself remained excruciatingly gothic: untidy, crabbed and, as Panigarola pointed out, by no means easy to read. It cuts a poor figure indeed beside Panigarola's superbly finished and impeccably legible italic script. The contrast could not be more striking or instructive.

Charles the Bold was deeply religious in the traditional sense and yielded to no other prince in piety and devotion. Thus the papal legate at his court, Luca de' Tolenti, reporting to the pope on 23 June 1472: 'He is very well resolved in our favour; steadfast, prudent, catholic and devout.'[1] Another papal legate, Onofrio de Santa Croce, describes how, during the night attack by the men of Liège on Charles the Bold's lodgings outside the city, the duke swore that if his life was saved he would walk thirty or fifty miles to the shrine of Our Lady at Boulogne in Picardy. The accounts of the *argentier* or treasurer include payments for the provision of candles. For example in June 1468 Charles sent knights with specified sums of money to burn candles for him in the churches of Notre-Dame at Liesse, St. Martin at Tours, St. Hubert in the Ardennes, St. Nicholas at Varangéville and the Holy Spirit at Rue.

Of Charles the Bold's intellectual interests music is one of the best attested. It is curious how exactly the most diverse contemporary witnesses agree with Chastellain: 'He had a fine clear voice, except

---

[1] Paquet, *BIHBR* xxv (1949), 84. For the next sentence, see Onofrio, *Mémoire*, 172–3, and for what follows, ADN B2068, f. 120.

for singing, and he was well-versed in music.' Thus Panigarola, describing Duke Charles at the siege of Neuss in May 1475: 'Even though he is in camp, every evening he has something new sung in his quarters and sometimes his lordship sings, though he does not have a good voice. But he is skilled in music (*perfecto musico*).' Wielant says, on the same subject and to the same effect: 'He also took pleasure in music and was himself a musician. He could compose and sing willingly though he by no means had a good voice.'[1] No wonder he took care that his chapel was staffed with the finest available musicians and composers, though some of the best musicians of the Low Countries, the Fleming Jan Okeghem for example and the Hainaulter Josquin des Prez, worked elsewhere, the former in Paris and the latter in Milan. But Charles the Bold, who had learned his music at least in part from the Englishman Robert Morton, retained the services of Anthoine Busnoys and Hayne van Ghijzeghem, to mention but two. His musical chapel helped to earn him a reputation among contemporaries by no means limited to battles and sieges. The author of the *Divisie-chronijk*, for example, records that, at Aachen in August 1473, Charles had with him 'his entire musical chapel and his master-singers, who performed a beautiful musical service and office all day long in honour of the Mother of God'.

Although all the Valois dukes of Burgundy had perforce to be linguists of a kind, Charles the Bold seems to have possessed a real aptitude for and interest in languages. Some of the earlier historians made him speak Latin and five other languages, but this is going too far. On his own admission, 'he was not very familiar with Latin, except soldiers' Latin', but he could certainly read it.[2] He knew Italian well enough to speak his mind in it at a public audience he gave to the papal legate, Alexander Nani, bishop of Forlì, in May 1475 in the presence of the Neapolitan and Milanese ambassadors and others, and to reply to the Venetian ambassador in it at the chapter of the Golden Fleece in May 1473. It is commonly supposed that he knew Flemish, or Netherlandish, well, and this seems likely, though exact

[1] Chastellain, *Oeuvres*, vii. 229, ASM Pot. est. Borgogna 516–17/44 and Wielant, *Antiquités de Flandre*, 57. The quotation at the end of the paragraph is from *Cronycke van Hollandt*, f. 337. See too, for this paragraph, Doutrepont, *Littérature française*, xxxi, Doorslaer, *RBAHA* iv (1934), 23–6, and van den Borren, *Geschiedenis van de muziek*, i. 75–229.

[2] *Briefe und Actenstücke von Mailand*, 82, and Doutrepont, *Littérature française*, xxxii. For the next sentence, see *Briefe und Actenstücke von Mailand*, 82 and AOGV Reg. 3, f. 43b.

and documentary proof that he ever spoke more than a few words of it is hard to come by.[1] Some scraps of English he must have known and on one occasion he quelled a mutiny of English troops after addressing them in their own language. Naturally, his mother tongue and habitual language was French and it was in French, and not Latin or Italian, that he read or had read to him in camp at Neuss 'Valerius [Maximus], Titus Livy or some book about Alexander the Great, or of battles'.

The chroniclers make much of Duke Charles's so-called 'classical' taste in literature. According to Wielant, he 'took pleasure in the deeds of Julius Caesar, of Pompey, of Hannibal, of Alexander the Great and of other great and famous men, whom he wished to follow and imitate'.[2] Books about these and others were already available in the ducal library but Charles the Bold commissioned some important translations of classical works into French which make it legitimate to classify him as a patron of humanism, though it must be borne in mind that his interest was in the great generals and conquerors themselves; it was in no sense literary. The Portuguese Vasco de Lucena was commissioned by Charles the Bold to replace the unsatisfactory medieval Romance of Alexander with a French version of what was the best available account of Alexander the Great, by Quintus Curtius. He also undertook for Charles the Bold a translation of Xenophon's *Cyropaedia* from Poggio's Latin version. In 1472 Charles commissioned a translation of Caesar's *De bello Gallico* from Jehan du Chesne. In their respective introductions, de Lucena and du Chesne compare Charles to Alexander and Caesar, but in each case the claim is made that the duke of Burgundy is superior. The ducal secretary, Charles Soillot, translated another work of Xenophon's for Duke Charles, and Jehan Miélot dedicated to the duke his translation of Cicero's letter to his brother Quintus. Charles the Bold's mother was of course a promoter of humanism in her own right and his third wife, Margaret of York, was a bibliophile: it was she who

---

[1] Armstrong, *Europe in the late middle ages*, 397–8, offers none. For the next sentence see below, p. 384; de Commynes, *Mémoires*, ed. Calmette and Durville, ii. 53 claims that Charles spoke in English to Edward IV in 1475. The quotation that follows is from ASM Pot. est. Borgogna 516–17/44.

[2] *Antiquités de Flandre*, 56. For what follows see Doutrepont, *Littérature française*, 177–86, Samaran, *BEP* (1938), 13–26, Bossuat, *BHR* iii (1943), 253–354 and viii (1946), 197–245, Willard, *SR* xiv (1967), 33–48 and the same in *Miscellanea sul quattrocento francese*, 517–44. Monfrin, *BSAF* (1967), 285–9 has little or nothing to add to these.

commissioned William Caxton, 'master and governor of the English merchants' at Bruges, to translate and print *The Recuyell of the Hystoryes of Troye*.[1]

In the provision of superb illustrated books for the ducal library Charles simply carried on or completed what his father had begun, employing the same artists. Thus in 1468–70 the accounts show the celebrated miniaturist Loyset Liédet at work on a manuscript of *Renaud de Montauban* which had been written under Philip the Good. At the same time he and Pol Fruit worked at Bruges on the second and third volumes of the *Histoire de Charles Martel* which David Aubert had taken three years to write in 1463–5. The most famous of all fifteenth-century Burgundian manuscripts, the *Chroniques de Hainault* in Jehan Wauquelin's translation, was only completed, by Loyset Liédet and Guillaume Vrelant, after Philip the Good's death. A few entirely new illuminated manuscripts were added by Charles to the ducal library. For example, a superb *Faiz du grant Alexandre* in the version of Vasco de Lucena, illuminated by Loyset Liédet, and George Chastellain's *L'instruction d'un jeune prince* illuminated by Jehan Hennecart of Brussels. One innovation of Charles the Bold was in the employment of the finest calligraphers and illuminators to produce de luxe versions of his ordinances. Clais Spierinc, for example, was paid in 1469 for illuminating the household ordinance of 1 January 1469, and British Museum Add. MS. 36,619 is a superbly illuminated military ordinance of Charles the Bold. Such manuscripts were produced in several copies which were distributed by the duke to his leading courtiers and captains.[2]

No doubt Charles the Bold added other books to his library by way of gifts. One such, which reflects one of his most characteristic interests, was a book about Charlemagne and other Frankish kings which Louis XI gave him in January 1474. It was written in Italian and the king explained to Charles that he gave it to him 'knowing that he was deeply devoted to the customs, ways of life and methods of government of the Italians, which could not possibly give him more

[1] Magnien, *ASRAB* (1912), 49–55, Jacquot, *La Renaissance dans les provinces du Nord*, 71–96, and Thielemans and others, *Marguerite d'York et son temps*.
[2] For this paragraph see Pinchart, *BCAA* iv (1865), 474–508, Durrieu, *Miniature flamande*, Delaissé, *Miniature flamande. Le mécénat de Philippe le Bon*, Dogaer and Debae, *La librairie de Philippe le Bon*, and Schryver, *Scriptorium* xxiii (1969), 434–58.

pleasure'.[1] Charles the Bold's knowledge of the Italian language bears out Louis's testimony, and his passion for things Italian is evident in all kinds of ways, even in his hats and clothes. He was brought up with Francesco d'Este, who remained his lifelong companion and, probably, friend. Other Italian princes visited the Burgundian court for protracted periods when Charles was duke: Rodolfo Gonzaga, for example, in 1469–70, and Federico, prince of Taranto, younger son of King Ferrante of Naples, who was a suitor for the hand of Mary of Burgundy,[2] in 1475–6. Throughout 1475 there was talk, enthusiastic at least on Charles's side, of a visit to the Burgundian court by Galeazzo's brother, Ludovico Sforza.[3] Besides these princes, Italian ambassadors and papal envoys flocked to, and remained for long periods at, the Burgundian court. With many of these Charles was on the most intimate terms. Bernado Bembo, official Venetian ambassador with Charles from 1470 to 1474, was probably closest to him of them all but, tragically, the despatches which he was under instruction to send home daily have not survived. Nor is his note-book of any historical value. Like so many of these Italians, he admired Charles the Bold, noting sadly in 1477: 'So did a cruel death carry away the most mighty duke of Burgundy.' Fewer than half the Burgundian despatches of the Milanese ambassador, who was also on very familiar terms with Charles the Bold, have so far been printed, and even these are incomplete. Johanne Petro Panigarola stuck to the duke of Burgundy like a leech from 13 March 1475 to 7 August 1476; before then he had represented Milan at the court of France. Like Bembo, he had Charles's private ear, enjoyed his confidences and even gave him advice. Others included Francesco Bertini, bishop of Capaccio, the Neapolitan ambassador, and papal

---

[1] Cartellieri, *Court of Burgundy*, 267, and Bittmann, *Ludwig XI und Karl der Kühne*, ii (1). 176–7. In what follows, I am particularly indebted to Professor Ralph Giesey of the University of Iowa, who kindly passed on to me a collection of manuscript notes and other material, much of it excerpted from the Burgundian archives and including drafts of a paper on *Charles the Bold and the Italian Renaissance in Flanders*, made by the late Professor Ernst H. Kantorowicz. The only part of this he published was a paper entitled 'The Este portrait by Roger van der Weyden', *JWI* iii (1939–40), 165–80. What follows must be regarded as tentative and provisional: 'Charles the Bold and Italy' is the subject of research now being undertaken for a Ph.D thesis by Richard Walsh at the University of Hull.
[2] Calmette, *BEC* lxxii (1911), 459–72, and Pontieri, *ASN* lxiii (1939), 78–112.
[3] *Dépêches des ambassadeurs milanais*, i. 77 and 254.

envoys like Onofrio de Santa Croce, bishop of Tricarico, and Petro Aliprandi, who stayed at the Burgundian court unofficially while waiting to execute his mission to England.

The list of Italians at the Burgundian court under Charles could be considerably extended because, besides the princes and ambassadors so far mentioned, there were secretaries like Salvatore de' Clarici and the famous medallist Johanne de Candida, doctors like Salvatore's brother Matteo and the Neapolitan Angelo Cato who later treated Louis XI for apoplexy, and businessmen like Tommaso Portinari the Florentine manager of the branch of the Medici bank at Bruges. Above all, after 1 October 1472, there were the Italian *condottieri*, so much admired by Charles, whom 'he had brought here to instruct his own people, who had become clumsy and blockheaded in the art of war because they had been maintained by his father in peace for twenty years'.[1] Admittedly, in spite of years of negotiation, he never managed to get hold of the most famous veteran of them all, Bartolomeo Colleoni, but he did retain the services of Troylo da Rossano and his two sons, Cola de Monforte, count of Campobasso, Jacobo Galeoto, the brothers Antonio and Petro de Lignana, and others. With these men too he was on more or less familiar terms and their influence on his policies and attitudes, their contribution to the general Italianate element at the Burgundian court, must be borne in mind alongside their military importance, the subject of a later chapter.

Besides the specific attributes and interests of Charles the Bold so far discussed, certain traits of character emerge prominently from the welter of contemporary evidence. He was violent and cruel. When he had some men hanged at the siege of Neuss the bishop of Capaccio remonstrated with him. ' "My lord, it is extremely cruel to cause these poor men to die." The duke made a strange reply: "The Italians say dead men cannot make war!" '[2] He was moody and temperamental. He nearly lost his temper when in conference with the papal legate, Onofrio de Santa Croce, in 1468. He was so annoyed when some of his people were robbed in Turin in 1476 that he tore up a letter of apology from the authorities there before even reading it, and when their spokesman explained that the trouble had been due to 'the fury of the

---

[1] ASM Pot. est. Borgogna 518–20/453.
[2] Croce, *Vite di avventure*, 128 n. 3. For the next sentence, see above, p. 27 and ASM Pot. est. Borgogna 518–20/432–3. For what follows, see *Dépêches des ambassadeurs milanais*, ii. 217, *IACB* i. 75 = Gazier, *MSED* (10) v (1935), 47 and ADN B2068, f. 31b.

populace', Charles replied that he would show them the fury of the prince in return. He was obstinate. When Panigarola, acting on instructions from Milan, did his best early in June 1476 to dissuade Charles from a direct attack on the Swiss, the duke was adamant. He was absolutely determined to avenge himself on them or die. But he was often indecisive, and given to changing his mind. Honoured with a formal farewell dinner at Besançon on 29 September 1476, Charles set off, unaccountably returned at 11.0 p.m., but left again at midnight. On New Year's Day 1468 a *chevaucheur* had to be sent to Aalst with a verbal message that the duke had changed his mind and would not be going there that day. The failure of the conference of Trier was in part surely due to Charles's indecision. At Namur, at the end of August 1475, after his ally King Edward of England had unexpectedly made peace with his enemy the king of France, Charles seemed for some days quite uncertain what to do. 'He could not even explain clearly', says Panigarola in his despatch, 'what he would do; the affair was so weighty and important.'[1] Perhaps it is as well to point out that Charles was by no means rash in the sense of reckless, in spite of his nineteenth-century French nickname Téméraire: he was much too sensible or cautious, in March 1471, to risk attacking or besieging Amiens with too few troops, and he told Panigarola on the eve of his campaign against the Swiss that he had 11,000 combatants 'because it would not do to advance against the Swiss with insufficient forces'. He did not, however, set much store by the advice of his councillors. According to Wielant, he often convoked his council which was 'well staffed with worthy people, and he willingly listened to their deliberations but, after hearing everything, he followed his own opinion, which was usually contrary to what had been advised'.

Perhaps the most immediately striking feature of Charles the Bold's personality was his immense vanity. He was egotistic and ostentatious in his personal appearance, his behaviour at court, his treatment of other princes and their envoys, and in his attitude towards his own territories and subjects. When we look at Charles the Bold as a ruler, these grandiose ideas of his own self-importance seem to motivate and dominate his policies. 'All his thoughts', wrote Panigarola on

---

[1] ASM Pot. est. Borgogna 516–17/87–8. For what follows, see Roux, *Histoire de l'abbaye de Saint-Acheul-lez-Amiens*, 61–75 (above, p. 69), *Dépêches des ambassadeurs milanais*, i. 266 and Wielant, *Antiquités de Flandre*, 54. Dufournet, *Destruction des Mythes*, 84–9 analyses the Burgundian chroniclers' attitudes to the duke's personality.

23 May 1475, 'are about the acquisition for himself of immortal glory, and he says that other things are all changing and perishable.'[1] The search for fame, the public expression and display of his own ego, the yearning to be great, to make a permanent mark on history: these were the mainsprings behind the activities and attitudes of Duke Charles the Bold. All this may not be entirely unconnected with the fact that he had no male heir. Might not this have helped to personalize Charles's political ambitions and experience? Unlike most of his contemporaries, he had no *Hausmacht* to consolidate, no dynasty to secure; his lands would inevitably pass elsewhere on his death. While others laboured for their posterity, Charles worked for himself.

Charles the Bold's egotism is evident in matters small and great. It ranges, so to speak, from shoe-buckles to world conquest. It permeates Burgundian government, but it is perhaps most apparent on ceremonial occasions such as a formal entry into a town, an audience given for ambassadors or a meeting of the Estates of one of the Burgundian territories. On these occasions the duke wore a splendid ceremonial hat, his robes or armour were studded with diamonds, rubies and pearls, and he invariably made a speech. The Italians at his court were extremely impressed.

The most famous of Duke Charles's ceremonial hats was left behind in his baggage after the battle of Grandson and fell into the hands of the Swiss, one of whom is said to have tried it on, then rejected it, saying he preferred a helmet. Its plumes and jewels were sold by Basel to Jacob Fugger, the Augsburg banker, at the beginning of the sixteenth century. A drawing of it has survived. It was an Italian-style hat in velvet, shaped like a rounded cone with a broad brim, and decorated with seven circles of pearls and precious stones, a large ruby at the top and two tall jewelled plumes at one side. Was this the 'wonderfully rich hat' which Charles wore at Dijon on 25 January 1474 when he took formal possession of the duchy?[2] An Italian observer described it as 'an extraordinarily splendid crown, with rubies and pearls, diamonds and saphires . . . to me it looked like the crown of a king'. One such hat is described in the accounts:

---

[1] ASM Pot. est. Borgogna 516–17/44.
[2] Chabeuf, *MSBGH* xviii (1902), 19 and Quarré, *BARBB* li (1969), 338 and n. 5. For the next sentence, see ASM Pot. est. Borgogna 515/152. The extract that follows is from *IADNB* iv. 240. For the hat lost at Grandson, see Grunzweig, *MA* lxii (1956), 158–65, and Deuchler, *Burgunderbeute*, 118–9. See too below p. 170 n. 2.

To Gerard Loyet, goldsmith and *valet de chambre*, the sum of £484 which was owing to him for certain pieces of workmanship, which by the duke's command he made and delivered last February, 1471, as follows: Firstly, for having made and lined a hat of steel and covered it with a ducal hat in gold garnished with eighteen large balas-rubies and forty great pearls, with large raised open-work leaves around the rubies and several other settings of leaves, to go round the said pearls, £105. Also for making for this hat an ornament of three great guns arranged in a triangle and adorned with three large balas-rubies in lieu of flints, with great flames of gold shooting outwards all round like a sun and, above the said ornament, a large flower enamelled in white with a very large balas set in it, £15. Also, for making gold buttons to go round the rim of the said hat and on the strap which does up under the neck, £3. . . .

Charles the Bold's sartorial extravagance and display of personal jewellery at Trier has already been mentioned. Even when wearing armour he appeared on state occasions encrusted with gems. The Neapolitan ambassador, Johanne Palomar, watched his entry into Dijon on 23 January 1474, apparently spellbound with admiration. Charles was mounted and fully armed, with the knee-caps, vambraces and other parts of his armour studded with pearls and gemstones. His gorget 'was all covered with balas-rubies, diamonds and huge pearls. He wore an Italian-style coat over his armour embroidered all over with the largest pearls'. Palomar remembered that King Darius was said to have worn similar armour. 'Truly it was a most splendid and magnificent spectacle.'[1] Towards the end of the prolonged siege of Neuss the publication of a treaty of alliance between Burgundy, Savoy and Milan was used as a pretext by the duke for another of those ceremonial court occasions he seems to have revelled in. In Panigarola's despatch of 3 April 1475 we meet again the hat, the jewels, and all the other rigmarole designed to inflate the duke's ego and project his image.

The lord duke, according to orders given yesterday morning, had the league published in the church in the following way. His lordship came to the church dressed in a long robe, of cloth of gold lined with sable, extremely sumptuous, in which silver was substituted for silk. On his head he had a black velvet hat with a plume of gold loaded with the largest balas-rubies and diamonds and with large pearls, some good ones pendent, and the pearls and gems were so closely packed that one could

---

[1] ASM Pot. est. Borgogna 515/152. The extract which follows is from ASM Pot. est. Borgogna 516–17/21–3, partly printed Colombo, *Iolanda, duchessa di Savoia*, 274–80.

not see the plume, though the first branch of it was as long as a finger. He stayed in his oratory, which was hung round as usual with curtains of black silk. After a time the curtains were drawn aside. His lordship was on a dais three steps high under a canopy, gold above and below, richly embroidered with the arms of Burgundy. On the dais was a quadriga similar to those used by your excellency, but all the wood, hafts and pommel were of solid gold. It had been sent as a gift to him this Christmas by his illustrious consort. Seating himself, he placed the bishop of Capaccio and myself next to him on the right side. I do not know where the Venetian ambassador was to be found; he was ill. On [the duke's] left hand was the son of the duke of Cleves; the lords of the Golden Fleece and the men-at-arms remained standing. In the centre, also standing, were the Kings-of-Arms and heralds with coats of arms, about twelve in number. All round, the entire church was full of people. Then the bishop of Auxerre began to speak, explaining the advantages and benefits accruing to the princes belonging to the League and union and how essential it was for the defence of their states and the advantage of their subjects. . . . When he had finished his lordship came down from the tribunal and spoke to me in the presence of all, congratulating me and felicitating with me on the League. . . . And at once the trumpets began to sound, eight of them; then the pipers, of which there were many. . . .

I particularly wanted to inform your lordship about this solemnity because every act of this prince is done with majesty and much ceremony.

A similar scene, likewise described in tones of admiration by Panigarola, was enacted at Nancy on 18 December 1475 to mark Charles the Bold's formal taking possession of the duchy of Lorraine. [1]

Having assembled yesterday evening the three Estates of this land of Lorraine, as is customary when a new ruler takes possession, this most excellent prince invited the ambassadors and lords who were at court to hear what was said. About two hours after dark—because the magnificent illuminations made for a greater show—they accompanied his highness, who was dressed in a long ducal robe of dark crimson velvet lined with ermine and beaver with a hat on his head more or less in the form of a crown richly adorned with the largest pearls, diamonds, balas-rubies and carbuncles,[2] from the room into the great hall, where the high tribunal was ready. His lordship went up a good six steps to the high seat, which was covered above and below down to the ground with brocade. On his right hand, on a lower seat, the papal legate was placed.

---

[1] ASM Pot. est. Borgogna 516–17/135–6, partly printed Colombo, *Iolanda, duchessa di Savoia*, 281–2.
[2] According to Wilwolt von Schaumburg, *Die Geschichten und Taten*, 30, this was an archducal hat; compare Grunzweig, *MA* lxii (1956), 158–60.

On the left, in another, Don Federico. Also on the right, to one side, on a raised bench, the king of France's ambassador was seated and I, on your lordship's behalf; for there is great regard here in the allotting of honourable positions to your people. There was no one else on the tribunal. On the left, one step below the tribunal, were seated the bishop of Metz, the duke of Cleves's son, Monsieur the bastard of Burgundy and the knights of the Order [of the Golden Fleece]; then, on the right, the captains, men-at-arms and other lords. His lordship being thus in majesty, his magnificence Messire Guillaume de Rochefort, on being requested, began in French to outline the great friendship there had been between this lord [duke] and the former dukes [of Lorraine] John and Nicolas his son and then with the present ex-duke René of Lorraine, who was established[1] and confirmed in this state by the agency of his lordship. . . .

The duke then added some[2] cordial words with his own mouth, saying that this land was in the middle of his own and could not have fallen[3] more appropriately to anyone else, nor be more secure than in his hands. He would hold it in the greatest affection, even more than his other territories, as commonly one prefers the works of one's own hands or things acquired by oneself. If they were loyal he would treat them extremely well.

According to Wielant, Duke Charles 'enjoyed making lengthy harangues'. He was apparently not unimpressive as an orator. Chastellain says:

He was fluent of speech. At times he found it difficult to express himself to start with, but when he got under way he was very eloquent. . . . His speeches were much more embellished and elaborate than his father's. He spoke with great intelligence and profundity and continued at length. Nonetheless he was passionate in his beliefs and impetuous in his expositions; obstinate in opinion, but wise and just.[4]

We have already had occasion to mention one of Charles's harangues, delivered at St. Omer on 15 July 1470 to the French ambassadors. Some of his best performances were recorded almost word for word in the minute book of the chapters of the Golden Fleece, but have not yet been printed. He was at his most loquacious and revealing when

---

[1] Colombo, unintelligibly, has *subito* for *stabilito* of the MS.
[2] For *alcune*, MS., Colombo, again unintelligibly, has *al. Cum.*
[3] Colombo omits the word *cadere*, MS.
[4] Wielant, *Antiquités de Flandre*, 55, and Chastellain, *Oeuvres*, vii. 229. For the next sentence, see above, pp. 65–6. The extract which follows is from AOGV Reg. 3, fos. 27–29b.

replying to the criticisms which tradition allowed, or even encouraged, the confrères of the Order to level at each other and even at their sovereign. At the 1473 chapter, held at Valenciennes, the complaints about Charles already politely submitted at the previous chapter in 1468 were repeated in a more elaborate form. Master Martin Steenberch, ducal secretary and clerk of the Order, writes as follows.

Afterwards, and lastly, this scrutiny was directed to the person of the most redoubted lord my lord the duke, chief and sovereign of the Order, who very kindly got up from his seat and left the chapter. When he had gone, all the lords of the said Order with one accord and voice praised, extolled and greatly and cordially recommended the most noble virtues, good sense, generosity, prudence, valour and prowess of his person, for which they scarcely knew how to praise or thank him sufficiently. Nor did they know how they could adequately give thanks to God for permitting them to live under so virtuous a prince and to have him for chief and sovereign in such noble company. For in him they knew of nothing but great virtues and deeds worthy of commendation and praise, and they earnestly prayed that our blessed creator would give grace to my lord the sovereign to persevere and continue without interruption, and to them, that is to each in his place, to bear themselves in such a way towards my lord and in this Order as would be to the glory and in the service of God and according to the honour, wishes and pleasure of my lord the sovereign, for the salvation of their souls and the welfare, honour, improvement and exaltation of the Order.

These congratulations and recommendations having been made in common by my lords of the Order, they proceeded, as they were bound to in the chapter, to the business of the scrutiny. Mention was made of the points, remonstrances and requests which, in all humility and obedience, had been made to my lord the sovereign at the last chapter-general of the Order, held in the town of Bruges in the year sixty-eight and included in the acts of the said chapter. These were, in effect:

1. That my lord sometimes speaks a little sharply to his servants.
2. That he becomes emotional sometimes when talking about [other] princes.
3. That he works too hard so that it is doubtful if he will live when he is older.
4. That, when he mobilizes his armies, he should make provision to ensure that his subjects are not oppressed as they have been.
5. That it please him to be benign and moderate and keep his lands in good justice.
6. That he be pleased to comply with what he has agreed to, and keep his word.

7. That he involves his people in war as late as possible and not without good and mature counsel.

These points were now elaborated as follows:

1. He calls his servants traitors which, subject to his amendment, is an evil-sounding and shameful word for his loyal servants. The good should not be blamed without cause but, against the culpable, evil and disloyal the said lords wish to help and serve him as much as they can.

3. That he be pleased to moderate and diminish his efforts and exertions.

4. Sometimes my lord is deceived by too easily accepting what he is told, especially with regard to his troops, for he is not aware of the great evils and damages they do, but thinks they are content with their wages. It is his noble wish that, through the agency of the subventions and *aides* they willingly pay, his people will be preserved from oppression by these troops. But the contrary has happened and happens frequently without his knowledge, for some of these troops do a great deal of damage to goods, and some of the said men-at-arms go through the country ransoming villages by threatening to lodge in them.

5. Concerning justice. Although my lord should above all be commended for his zeal for justice, yet sometimes there are errors because the minor posts are farmed out and their farmers considerably oppress the people, often making exactions in the guise of justice against innocent people, who lose thereby while the wicked are supported.

6. That it please my lord to observe the things agreed to by my late lord his father. Although it is necessary for him to satisfy a number of people, nevertheless a prince's word ought to be carefully weighed. May it please him henceforth to think about this and consider also his authority and good name.

7. Lastly, may it please my lord to have benign regard for the statutes and ordinances of the Order and give his mind to them, considering that all my lords of the Order are obliged to keep, observe and maintain them in their turn according to the contents of the book. May it please him for his part to do this also and maintain my lords in their prerogatives according to the said statutes, and for the love of God and the benefit of Christianity to devote himself as soon as possible to making peace for his own honour and for the benefit of himself and his loyal lands and subjects. But above all and in conclusion my lords of the Order thanked and praised my lord the sovereign for his very kind and gracious behaviour and for the very friendly relations which he has maintained and is maintaining among them in this present chapter. They deputed the reverend father in God my lord the bishop of Tournai, the chancellor of the Order, to express their thanks to him

and then to make the above-mentioned remonstrances and supplications to him in the most polite and moderate manner and terms and with the greatest humility he possibly could.

After these deliberations and scrutinies carried out in this way and the said commission made, my lord the sovereign returned to the chapter and took his seat. Then all my lords the confrères and knights together with the officers of the Order knelt down before him reverently. But my lord caused them to get up, and at once my lord the bishop of Tournai, the chancellor, according to the commission and instructions of my lords the confrères, first expressed in their name the congratulations and thanks above-mentioned and then expounded to him at length in the most humble terms and most politely the remonstrances and supplications in the points and matters set out above. My lord listened throughout most benignly and patiently and then he replied point by point as follows:

Firstly, concerning the said congratulations etc. My lord the sovereign explained that he was well pleased and content with what my lords had said concerning their love and affection for him but that the virtues, merits and perfections which the bishop of Tournai, chancellor of the Order, had attributed to him were not there at all and, if he did not know the fervour of the honour and true love they entertained and demonstrated towards him, which blinded and seduced them so that they attributed virtues and merits to him which were not there, he could impute to them the vice of adulation. But, because of the virtue and integrity he knows they possess, he excuses them, praying our Lord of his grace that he will make good and remove his faults because he has always truly and honestly wished to reach what perfection our Lord by his grace and goodness may give and grant him.

1. Concerning the first point, the remonstrance, declaration or addition touching his severity or rigour in reproving his servants and that, in speaking generally, he sometimes uses painful words concerning them, such as the word traitor or something similar etc. On the first part he said that he was fervent and ardent by nature for the welfare of his affairs and the public weal and he intends and desires that what he orders and commands be diligently and loyally carried out by his servants and by each in his place, and the thing he regrets more than anything else is when he has to severely correct and reprove his servants. The more fond he is of them, the more he fears to find them in fault or negligence needing reprimand and even punishment. It is his earnest wish that this is never necessary. And when he finds the occasional imperfection, he prefers to reprove, correct and instil fear into his servants with sharp words, to keep them and also those close to him fearful, so as to protect and preserve them from committing actual faults, rather than to dissimulate with them and leave them to fall into default, for which they would have to be punished.

Loyal servants and subjects ought to receive and interpret this in a good sense rather than otherwise when they appreciate his character and behaviour and the genuine affection he has for them, which he shows by the great advantages and services he tries to the best of his ability to provide for them.

As regards the general point concerning the said harsh words, my lord the sovereign distinguished between correction and punishment. Correction is the business of preachers, who preach it in their sermons, but punishment belongs to the parent, that is the prince or one of his subjects, servants or officials. Now he was nearly forty years old. During this time he had seen many things both in times of war and peace and had learnt of and found several of his servants who had not rendered to him the gratitude they owed him for the services and honours he had done them; for sometimes, indeed often, some of them had abandoned his interests and the service they owed him for their particular profit. . . . He has known that several of his servants have been suspected of faults or follies, some out of ignorance, others out of stupidity or fear for their persons or for other causes the discussion of which would require a great deal of time, for which reason my lord the sovereign, keeping in mind the end towards which he has striven to bring and conduct his affairs, to reprove them and make them realize their negligences, faults or despicable acts, has on occasion reprimanded them sharply with words in general somewhat poignant, by means of which he could make them see the error of their ways and fulfil the unpleasant duty, which was his, of having to punish for actual transgressions as late as was humanly possible. Although he has spoken in general terms nonetheless he did not mean to blame good people, and those who know themselves to be pure and innocent ought not to take such words to heart, but only those blameworthy and defaulting so that they can amend their ways. *Quia veritas vulneratur sed mori non potest.*

3. Concerning the troubles, work and labours undertaken by my lord the sovereign, he replied and said that, thanks be to God, he was in better health than he had been at Bruges five years ago and, when he considers the love he has for the welfare and security of his lands and subjects and for the honour and good estate of his house, he would not complain if, in caring for these things, he ended his days three or four years earlier than he would have done, to defend them and keep them from evil. But if he knew how to do this in some other way he would willingly do it, to spare himself. Nonetheless he warmly thanked my lords of the Order for their remonstrance and for the true love and affection which they had demonstrated for the preservation and health of his person.

4. On the fourth point, which he divided into two parts, one concerning

his armies and their mobilization and the other concerning the conduct of the troops: concerning the first part, my lord the sovereign explained, by way of reply, that his captains have been and are hard put to it to recruit the number of men they are supposed to, for many hold back from performing the service they owe. Because of this, he has his orders issued and published to make them turn out, so that each will do his duty. He has often considered how to find the best means and ways to obtain the aid and service which his vassals and subjects owe him at the least possible cost to the people, but so far he has made little progress. He well knows that what he has to do oppresses the country and this displeases him. He convokes his armies for the preservation and defence of his honour and of his lands and subjects and in this he spares neither body nor expense, so that his loyal vassals, appreciating the necessity and the justification he puts forward, ought also to excuse him and interpret the thing favourably. It is essential that his captains be helped and supported in mobilizing their troops and for this reason my lord has considered how to ascertain what service each [vassal] is bound to perform according to his quality, that is to say which fiefs and sub-fiefs owe him service and which do not and to whom he ought to and can turn in case of need when this arises. My lord would be glad if everyone would consider this and help and advise him how he can manage this affair most expeditiously and at the least cost to his lands and subjects.

As to the second point, on the discipline and conduct of his troops in the country, my lord has been and is sufficiently informed that they do not pay properly [for their purchases] when in the field. It is still not two years since he began to raise his ordinance. Before then, his captains allowed their people to behave badly, making evil extortions and disturbances. Their very lords had encouraged them in this way of life and this rut, so that it was difficult to reform them and they still are not [reformed]. But he trusts that his troops are not in such disarray and so undisciplined as they used to be and, if it please God, they will be even less so. To tell the truth, the fault is with the officers, for the complaints go from rank to rank, first to the *diseniers* then to their captains, and thence to those in command and even, if these officers default, to him personally. They ought not by any means to fail to obtain provision and reparation duly sealed, because my lord will very willingly provide a remedy. For this reason he has regulated the wages, both of the troops of his ordinance and of his guard, and he heartily desires by the best possible means to provide for this and to preserve his people from undue oppression and exactions. The security and defence of his lands and the peace of his people depend, after God, on his troops; otherwise this would mean the breakdown of his plans and intentions, which are entirely good and honest and tending towards the general well-being.

5. On the point concerning justice, my lord the sovereign replied that he has always desired and still desires above all that to each person be rendered his due and that each be rewarded according to his merits. When he succeeded to his seignory he found his lands deprived of justice. Without severity, rigour and hard work it could not have been reformed into its present state. To his knowledge he neither administers nor permits the administration of justice except in so far as he maintains and believes it is just to keep and maintain his servants and subjects in the fear and obedience of God the all-powerful.

As to the offices which are farmed out, my lord found at his accession that the officials were not keeping account at all, or to a very small extent, even of their judicial fines, still less of [the revenues of] the domain, for everything was disordered and chaotic and on one side and the other very little profit was coming in. When he took possession of his land of Artois and the lands on the River Somme he had intended to pay wages to his officials [instead], but he found that, from the time of St. Louis, the lesser provostships and similar offices had been farmed out. He convoked an assembly of good clerks and people experienced in that area together with some of his councillors to discuss this affair, and his councillors were of his opinion, mentioned above, but the local people argued against it, maintaining that justice would be better administered by officials who were farmers than otherwise, because farmers do not judge, but only issue summonses, while echevins or [jury]men make the judgements, sentences and judicial decisions. In the end my lord's councillors accepted the opinion of the local people. . . . And, in conclusion, my lord said that the farming out of the lesser offices was in accord with the advice of the officers and experienced people of the different territories, as mentioned above, and [it also] took into account the small inconvenience which might ensue. However, if some other way or means could be found which, without disadvantages, would make justice better administered and conducted, he should be informed and he would willingly undertake it.

6. On the sixth point, concerning things which my lord agrees to and promises, that he should accomplish them and keep his word, my lord replied that he has always wanted and tried to keep his word and he would be glad to know if anyone could show that he had done the contrary in whatever matter except when he had beforehand agreed to, promised and disposed something in one way which afterwards, through inadvertence, he had done or promised [in another way] and not kept [to]. For numerous people make requests to him at different times, and sometimes people ask or demand things which are not ready to be dealt with without inconvenience. Others ask him for estates or offices when at the time, for certain reasons, he is undecided

G

to whom to give or commit them. He suffers importunate requests to which he replies sometimes either that he will do what he can about it or that he will take advice about it or that he will see to it, reserving nonetheless to himself his freedom of conclusion and the interpretation of his words or replies. But the applicants choose to interpret or understand them to their advantage, blinded by their affection for their own ends. Nonetheless it will certainly not be found that my lord has agreed to or promised something affirmatively which he has not kept to except when he had already promised it beforehand to someone else and not been told or advised about this at the time of his second promise or agreement.[1]

7. Concerning making war etc. my lord the sovereign said and remonstrated by way of reply that he had never started a war because, as regards the war of Liège, it had already begun before his accession and even before he became involved in it. As to the war with France, God knows who started it. As regards the war of Péronne, the king was at that time making war on his allies whom he was obliged to succour and aid. He has only undertaken war to defend his said allies or to defend himself and his possessions. There is no man who desires and needs peace more than he. Up to now he has never started a war nor does he wish to, but he is content to defend what he has and what belongs to him.

This speech might be characterized as prolix, patronizing, authoritarian and self-centred, but it is restrained and moderate. It is when he is addressing a body like the deputies of the Estates of Flanders that Charles's oratory becomes forthright, vehement, even bullying, displaying his emotion in a much less sophisticated manner. Admittedly in May 1470 they asked for trouble by quibbling about the *aide* he requested. They were told that they had never granted anything, to Charles or his father, with a good grace. They were Flemish blockheads who insisted on persevering in their stupid and evil opinions. He was only asking for 120,000 crowns for three years

---

[1] In 1459 Philip the Good promised the next vacant post of *maître* in the Dijon *chambre des comptes* to Mongin Contault, but in 1466 Charles, then count of Charolais, persuaded him to promise the next vacancy to Jehan Gros the Elder and the one after to Jehan de Molesmes. On 29 May, 1467, therefore, Duke Philip issued new letters for Contault, promising him the next vacancy after Gros and de Molesmes. Thus, when Charles became duke, there was a queue of three applicants for the next vacancy and Contault was only appointed on 20 April 1470, after his two rivals. But the practice of promising posts in advance continued: on 1 October 1470 Charles appointed Jehan Guiot to the next vacancy. ACO B16, fos. 205b–209b, 215b–216 and 224b.

from all his lands, sufficient for 1,000 lances or 5,000 combatants, a mere one-third of his army. And this was not just for him, but for their own defence and security too, against attack by his enemy the king of France. They had always despised or hated their prince; despised him when he was weak and hated him when he was strong. He preferred their hatred but he would never permit them to infringe his prerogatives as their ruler. Five years later, on 12 July 1475, Charles was at it again, accusing the Flemings of causing his failure to conquer Neuss by withholding the reinforcements and pioneers he had needed, and of refusing to fight the French. He told them that 'since they had not cared to be ruled by him as children under their father' he would henceforth rule them as subjects under their lord. He had been requesting long enough; now he would start commanding. He pointed out to them that his authority came from God and that they could find the powers of princes set out in the Book of Kings. He swore by St. George before angrily leaving the room.[1]

Public speaking was only one of the many vehicles for Charles the Bold's prodigious vanity. He loved to surround himself, on court occasions, with swarms of foreign ambassadors. At the festivities of the Golden Fleece held in 1468 at Bruges, the second of those twelve public occasions or ceremonies which George Chastellain called 'the magnificences of Duke Charles', the splendour of the occasion was said to have been enhanced by the presence of ambassadors from the pope, Charles of France, the kings of Sicily, Aragon, Naples and Scotland, and the dukes of Calabria and Brittany.[2] Five years later, at Valenciennes, Charles invited Luca de' Tolenti, bishop of Šibenik and papal emissary, Francesco Bertini, bishop of Capaccio and ambassador from Naples, Bernado Bembo, the Venetian ambassador, and ambassadors from Bartolomeo Colleoni and England, to the festivities of the Golden Fleece, and some of them even to the chapter itself. Of course these invitations to court functions served the important purpose too, of impressing the ambassadors. 'We went to see my lord of Burgundy dining and we saw all the pageantry and pomp which is arranged at his dinners', reported one of the ambassadors of Metz admiringly in September 1473. Besides the physical presence of foreign ambassadors Charles the Bold loved to

---

[1] *Collection de documens inédits*, i. 219–24 and 249–59.
[2] Molinet, *Chroniques*, i. 171. For the next sentence, see AOGV Reg. 3, fos. 6b (where Colleoni is disguised as 'Messire Bertremy, conte de Couillon, ytalien') and 42b. For what follows thereafter, see Aubrion, *Journal*, 55. For another gathering of ambassadors, see above p. 8.

surround himself, on paper at least, with multitudes of allies. Indeed he liked to think that absolutely everyone was his ally, except of course the king of France. He raised no objection if some of these people, for example the kings of Denmark and Scotland in 1475, appeared in a treaty between himself and King Louis on his own list of allies and on the king of France's; and on one occasion he was said to have included the duke of Milan among his allies entirely on his own initiative and without the consent of that ruler, who found it necessary to dissociate himself formally from so dangerous a colleague with the assistance of notaries.[1] In 1471 Charles contrived to list nineteen allies. A year later he was able to enumerate twenty-four or twenty-five and in 1473 he mustered some twenty-six, including nine kings, six dukes and three archbishops, against Louis's fifteen or sixteen.

The excessive pride of Charles the Bold is apparent in many other ways. For example he loved to receive servile and flattering letters. His subjects knew of and exploited this failing. On 20 January 1475 Jehan Baugey wrote home to Dijon from the duke's camp at Neuss:

> Messieurs, because my lord the duke is extremely gratified when any of his towns recommend themselves to him and by no means forgets the fact, for I have heard him talk about it, when I saw that this messenger brought nothing from you, I got my master to explain to my lord [the duke] that you sent your recommendations and had sent him letters enquiring after his health and affairs, but these had been lost by the messenger. . . . On which, I promise you, upon my soul, my lord was very well contented with you and said that it was two months since he had received commendations from a town like yours, and he appreciated that you kept him in mind. . . . I did the same for Messieurs of the town of Auxonne, though they know nothing about it.[2]

[In the affairs of the Golden Fleece Charles the Bold's pride was displayed alongside an element of arbitrary authoritarianism. He bullied his confrères into agreeing to offer the collar, and membership of the Order, to Philip of Savoy and, at the same 1468 chapter, he insisted, undoubtedly against opposition, on sending an invitation to King Edward IV of England.]As to his pride, a recent hypothesis asserts that he flouted a well-established heraldic tradition in 1468 by

---

[1] De Comines, *Mémoires*, ed. Lenglet du Fresnoy, iii. 415, and *Lettres de Louis XI*, v. 140–2. For what follows, see pp. 73–6 above, de Comines, *Mémoires*, ed. Lenglet du Fresnoy, iii. 232, and *Foedera*, xi. 754.
[2] *Correspondance de la mairie de Dijon*, i. 160–1. For the next paragraph see Salet, *ASRAB* li (1966), 5–29, and *ASEB* cvi (1969), 5–16.

having his helm represented in full face above the ducal arms on his stall-plate in the church of Notre-Dame in Bruges. The front-facing helm was supposed to be reserved for kings alone, while the helms of dukes and others were usually placed in profile or three-quarters facing. On the Bruges stall-plates the ducal helm was the only one front-facing, all the others, including that of the king of Aragon, being placed sideways.

As a ruler, Charles the Bold is only explicable in terms of his egotism. If he was a tyrant, as Louis XI described him,[1] his tyranny was a product of this egotism. If his ideas about government, about administrative institutions and reform, were grandiose, this was a reflection of his own grandiose vision of his place in history. The same is true of his relations with his neighbours; it is true also of his attitude to justice.

Quite apart from his profound interest in things military and his love of camps, sieges and battles, which will find mention in a later chapter, it emerges over and over again that Charles the Bold fancied himself as a world conqueror. Victory was an end in itself. The remark was attributed to him that he would gladly die within three days of defeating in battle the two most powerful rulers of his day, the Emperor Frederick III and King Louis XI of France.[2] Everybody, including Charles himself, seems to have thought of him as, or compared him to, Alexander the Great, or Charlemagne, or Hannibal, or Caesar. These were the subjects of his tapestries, of his reading, perhaps of his dreams. He alluded to them in his speeches. Conrad Stolle, vicar of St. Severus's at Erfurt, who attributed to Charles the Bold the intention of conquering the entire River Rhine, wrote as follows in his vernacular memoirs:

It is said that the duke of Burgundy claimed there were only three lords in the world, one in Heaven, that is, God; one in Hell, that is the devil Lucifer, and one on earth, who will be he himself. Also, God had provided him with the means to bring the world under him as King

[1] Bittmann, *Ludwig XI. und Karl der Kühne*, ii (1). 128 n. 170.
[2] *Aktenstücke und Briefe zur Geschichte des Hauses Habsburg*, i. cxxxiv n. 1. For the next sentence see, for example, for Alexander, Pfettisheim, *Geschichte*, 22–3 and Nicolay, *Kalendrier des guerres*, 19, and for Alexander and Charlemagne, Boeren, *Twee Maaslandse dichters in dienst van Karel de Stoute*, 203, 215, 244, 248 etc. (Mulart). For Charles's speeches, see for example, Plancher, iv. p. cclxxxvi (Caesar and Hannibal). For tapestries see, for example, above pp. 50–1 and *IADNB* iv. 225 = de Laborde, *Ducs de Bourgogne*, i. 496 (Hannibal). For Charles as a world conqueror, see Febvre, *RB* xxiii (1913), 49–50.

Alexander had done. He said that Alexander had been a heathen and had conquered and brought the entire world under him in twelve years, nor did he have as much gold and silver and [as many] men as he had. He was a Christian and God had inspired him to conquer Christendom and the world. He would also be king of the Romans and defend everything that had been honoured in Christendom up to then and he would do that for the sake of justice. He also said that he would maintain peace and the Christian faith throughout the world, punishing the disloyalty and injustice of princes.[1]

Another German-speaking cleric who took the trouble to record his notions about this new all-powerful conqueror was the diarist of Basel, who wrote in Latin, Johann Knebel. He firmly believed that Charles planned to conquer Strasbourg, Basel and Cologne. 'Oh if God would free us from this tyrant!' he exclaimed in April 1476 when news came that the duke was dangerously ill, and when at last his death at Nancy was confirmed: 'I Johann Knebel celebrated solemn mass at the high altar of the church of Basel in a more joyful mood than ever before.'

What the Basel chaplain meant, when he called Charles the Bold a tyrant, was that he was an aggressive conqueror. But Louis XI's use of the word was probably more sophisticated. He was perhaps thinking more of the duke's authoritarianism; of that absolutist streak which comes out most clearly perhaps in Charles's attitude to the law. He simply takes it into his own hands. The story was told of how, when staying at Trier in 1473, he bought a nut tree in a poor man's garden for twelve pieces of gold and used it to hang malefactors from among his own servants and troops.[2] Even the faithful Chastellain, writing, it should be emphasized, early in 1469, cannot conceal his irritation at his duke's personal dispensation of justice, attendance at which he later compared to having to listen to a sermon.[3]

To help people whose cases had been pending before the judges without being brought to a conclusion, and to receive all sorts of complaints from poor people, he held audience three times a week, Monday, Wednesday and Friday after dinner, with all the courtiers seated on benches in order of rank, no one daring to absent himself. . . . He had the petitions read to him and then decided according to his pleasure. There he remained, for up to two or three hours according to the

---

[1] Stolle, *Thüringisch-Erfurtische Chronik*, 61–2. For what follows, see Knebel, *Diarium*, ii. 24–5 and 410–11 and iii. 94.
[2] *Aktenstücke und Briefe zur Geschichte des Hauses Habsburg*, i. p. lxvii.
[3] *Oeuvres*, v. 469.

number of petitions, often to the great annoyance of those present. . . .
In my time I have never seen, nor heard of, anything like this being done
by any prince or king.[1]

This taking of the law into his own hands is apparent in the way
Duke Charles ignored or infringed privileges or local jurisdictions
which he regarded as interfering with his own authority. In flagrant
violation of the promises made at his accession to the Estates of the
duchy of Brabant, which were enshrined in a formal document,
Charles the Bold undermined the powers of the council of Brabant by
appointing a lieutenant-general or seneschal over its head and
entirely abolished the office of chancellor of Brabant. He then proceeded to ignore completely the duchy's traditional judicial organization in a series of instructions of January 1469 which caused his
seneschal to raise a storm of protest. Privileged communities like
abbeys and universities were particularly vulnerable. In June 1473
Charles the Bold authorized a beer tax in Brabant which the 'doctors,
masters, students and scholars' of the University of Louvain refused
to pay. They had been exempted from all taxes on wine and beer by a
privilege granted by the town of Louvain in 1432, and they proceeded
not only to insult, but even to excommunicate, the duke's tax-
collectors. Charles the Bold reacted with characteristic warmth and
vigour: the University and the town of Louvain were ordered to send
representatives to appear before his council; meanwhile, the tax was
to be collected by force if necessary. Other examples of Charles the
Bold's disdain for local jurisdictions will be found scattered through
this book.[2]

Like his predecessors, Charles the Bold was prepared to go to
some lengths to support his own candidates for ecclesiastical benefices.
Perhaps he was more bullying and forceful than they had been. If so,
he may have been reflecting an increasing tendency of secular rulers
to resist, ignore, or attack the system of papal appointments. In any
event he was overriding the rights of others. In the spring of 1474 it
seemed that the dean of St. Peter's, Lille, Jehan de Carnin, was near
the end of his days. On 25 May Charles the Bold wrote to the canons
recommending them to fill the expected vacancy with Master Hue de
Lannoy, brother of his captain of ordnance, Baudouin de Lannoy,

[1] *Oeuvres*, v. 370 (compare BL Hatton MS. 13, fos. 27b–28). On the next
paragraph see Meynart, *BCRH* cxxvi (1960), 135–52, AGR CC134 fos.
76–8, van der Essen, *BCRH* xc (1926), 242–57, and above, pp. 7–9 and 24.
[2] See too van Hommerich, *Land van Herle*, xviii (1968), 94–5.

lord of Molenbaix. He wrote again on 16 November in the same year this time insisting that 'if anyone tries to obtain the said deanship by virtue of expectative bulls obtained from our Holy Father the pope or otherwise you shall proceed to the election notwithstanding and we shall stand by and support you against everyone'. [1]

Charles the Bold, then, was egocentric, and absolutist or at any rate authoritarian. We have glanced at the way these qualities were reflected in his attitudes to justice and the law; but how far was his practical political programme, if indeed such a thing existed, derived from them? His essential weakness as a ruler was in fact the complete absence of a single effective plan of political action. He was enormously ambitious, yet, as we have seen, curiously indecisive. The more far-fetched some scheme of conquest or expansion was, the more attractive it seemed. 'This duke's principal failing', the Neapolitan ambassador Francesco Bertini told Carlo Visconti in the autumn of 1473, 'is that he is too credulous and has faith in everyone, even superficial people who haven't three farthings and who make him believe in the greatest miracles in the world.' [2] No wonder his political schemes were far-reaching, even continental, in scope; but for him the perspectives of conquest were so constantly changing that one feels it was only the systematic determination of his enemies which gave some kind of theme and unity to his political programme. He hoped and planned for a crown: the imperial crown itself if possible. Failing that, the crown of Frisia or Burgundy or even both might have proved accept-able had he been able to make up his mind. But his imperial ambitions were hampered by grandiose schemes for the encirclement and obliter-ation of French royal power. He could not reject the temptation at least to stake claims to the kingdom of England; he seriously toyed with the idea of a military expedition to north Italy and the conquest of Milan. [3] At one time or another his attention was deflected to Savoy, and to Provence which he hoped to obtain from King René. As to the Rhine, he conquered Guelders and temporarily established a foothold in Alsace, and hopes of military success against towns like Cologne, Strasbourg and Basel may have crossed his mind. In any event, some other scheme invariably intervened to interrupt his original plan. Thus anti-French projects, in concert with Edward IV, thwarted his

[1] Hautcoeur, *Histoire de Saint-Pierre de Lille*, ii. 250–1.
[2] Cusin, *NRS* xx (1936), 41.
[3] See, for example, Janono Choyro's 12 January 1469 despatch, AGR MSS. divers 1173, f. 122. For this and what follows see especially the despatch on pp. 288–90 below.

original determination to take Neuss or die, while the expedition to Neuss itself thwarted his planned punishment and reconquest of Alsace after it had rebelled against him in the spring of 1474. Though his ideas were grandiose, his policies were thus capricious and erratic, wavering and irresolute; at least until Strasbourg, Basel and Bern and their friends began systematic attempts to throw him out of the ever-expanding area they regarded as their own sphere of influence.

So much then, for Charles the Bold as a continental ruler; but how did he govern his own territories? In particular, how far was he a reformer, a centralizer?[1] In succeeding chapters his reorganization of the Burgundian military machine and his system of regional or provincial governors or lieutenants will be examined. Both, and especially the former, bear witness to his undoubted administrative ability. But how successful was he in encouraging unity in his scattered territories?

Charles the Bold's most sweeping measures of reform were introduced at Thionville in Luxembourg in the first half of December 1473, in a justly famed group of ordinances. New central institutions for the administration of justice and finance were established permanently at Malines. A *Parlement* on the lines of the Paris *Parlement*, to be the new 'sovereign court' for all the Burgundian territories in the Low Countries, replaced, or absorbed the jurisdiction of, the *Parlement* of Paris and the imperial courts. The *chambres des comptes*, or accounting offices, at Lille and Brussels were closed and a new one, quite different in structure, was opened at Malines with two subordinate offices, the *chambres du trésor* and *des généraux*, with special responsibilities for the domains and the *aides* respectively. These far-reaching changes are not to be regarded as an attempt to provide the Burgundian state with really effective central institutions; after all, they did not include the two Burgundies. It is much more probable that they were connected with the scheme, mooted at Trier in autumn 1473, for creating a kingdom of Frisia for Charles the Bold. They were perhaps the new royal institutions designed to match the new royal title which, in the event, Charles never obtained. As the preamble of the ordinance establishing the *Parlement* makes clear, his thoughts and motives in setting them up were characteristically exalted. The special relationship

---

[1] See especially Lameere, *Grand conseil*, 178–95, Walther, *Die burgundischen Zentralbehörden*, 13–14 and 51–3, Heimpel, *Festschrift Gerhard Ritter*, 140–60, and Lambrecht, *BGN* xx (1965–6), 83–109.

G*

with God, claimed here as elsewhere, is particularly noteworthy.[1]

By divine bounty and providence, which directs and governs all terrestrial affairs, princes have been instituted and ordained to rule principalities and lordships, in particular so that the regions, provinces and peoples are joined together and organized in union, concord and loyal discipline by them, in the place of God our creator. This union and public order can only be maintained by justice, which is the soul and spirit of the public weal. Because of this we, desiring with all our heart and power in doing our duty to God the all powerful and to the lands, principalities and lordships which, by his esteemed bounty he has submitted to us, and following the example of our most noble progenitors, to fulfil, improve, maintain and defend the union, concord and public order of our said principalities and lordships, we have from our infancy taken, chosen and selected, as our principal shield and means to achieve this, true and thorough zeal for and observance of justice, without which the regions and provinces would more truthfully be described as assemblies of wicked men than as kingdoms or principalities. We believe that it is because of this zeal, care, solicitude and labour which we have undertaken, voluntarily and with a good heart, for the observance and maintenance of good justice in our lands and lordships, more than through any other power or merit in us, that we have enjoyed the victories which, in defending our said lands and lordships, in reducing to union with our holy mother church those who by prolonged obstinacy and contempt of her leaders and censures have been alienated from her and also in reducing to our obedience what justly has belonged and does belong to us, God our creator, who is the sole author of victories, has in a short time given us several times in the lands of France, Liège and Guelders, for which we render him most humble and infinite thanks.

Although in the new central financial institutions equal provision was made for French and Dutch speakers, the language of the *Parlement* was French and two-thirds of its personnel was Burgundian. No wonder it was described at Ghent as a *walsch Parlement*.[2] If it was,

---

[1] The ordinance is printed in *Placcaerten ende ordonnantien van Brabandt*, iv. 321–8; the quotation is from p. 321. The other Thionville ordinances are printed in *IAGRCC* i. 109–15. For the connection with Frisia: the notes about this kingdom excerpted on p. 152 above are mixed with some notes about the new *chambres* and bound in BN MS. fr. 1278 fos. 276–7 in the middle of the text of the ordinance establishing the *Parlement*. On the new *chambres* see too *IADNB* i (1). 24 and Kauch, *BSAB* (1945), 20–1.

[2] *Memorieboek der stad Gent*, i. 286. The extract which follows is from van Berchen, *Gelderse kroniek*, 129–30. On the Malines *Parlement* see too de la Marche, *Mémoires*, i. 132, Wielant, *Antiquités de Flandre*, 134–7, Lefèvre, *RGB* (1949), 407–9, Bartier, *Légistes et gens de finance*, 49–50, and *Listes chronologiques des procès et arrêts: Grand Conseil et Parlement de Malines*, i.

in a sense, a rival of Paris, an affront to France, it was equally an infringement of imperial rights. The remarks of the Guelders cleric Willem van Berchen are illuminating:

Exalting himself and extolling his name over all the Emperors, kings and princes who have existed in the Roman Empire since the incarnation of the Lord, having entered Malines in pompous state, he had the effrontery to institute and establish in the town hall, decorated with blue cloth, a certain supreme court, called a *Parlement*, after the example of the kings of France; like some strange and abominable idol to be worshipped by his subjects in all his lands. He appointed Jehan [Carondelet] president in his place, together with twelve French Doctors of both Laws, adorned with hoods lined with vair after the fashion of the auditors of the court of Rome, to sit on raised benches. He wanted the various other minor *Parlements* or law courts of his different lands and towns to be dependent on this *Parlement* as their head, to receive appeals from them. But from this supreme *Parlement*, in which, as indeed in the lesser *Parlements*, poor people are grievously persecuted by the execrable Picards after useless efforts and expenses, it was by no means permitted to appeal, on penalty of decapitation and confiscation of all goods. For a certain sworn messenger of the Emperor Frederick III, sent there to appeal to the Emperor in a certain case, died at Malines from the squalor of imprisonment and other tortures.

Willem van Berchen was not the only person to complain about the Malines *Parlement*. The Estates of the small but proud land of Hainault submitted an elaborate protest at this blatant infringement of the jurisdiction of the sovereign court of Mons, which alone had the right to hear appeals from the Hainault courts and from which appeals had never gone elsewhere.[1] In spite of the elevated motives of Duke Charles in setting them up, in spite of the galaxy of administrative talent he recruited to staff them, and in spite of the admirable vigour and clarity of the ordinances themselves, the only possible verdict on these institutions is that, like the same duke's schemes of conquest, they were too far-fetched, too radical, for effective implementation, let alone lasting success. Yet it must be conceded that the Malines *Parlement* was only a manifestation of that natural progress towards unification which had been continuing in the Low Countries since the thirteenth century; just as it was only a logical extension of the growth of the grand council as a law court: a feature of the preceding reign which Charles himself had already considerably furthered, for the judicial section of the great council had become

[1] *Coutumes de Hainaut*, i. 204–13.

increasingly sedentary from 1470 onwards and had been fixed at Malines since 28 June 1473. As to the new unique *chambre des comptes* for all the Low Countries, even this had been foreshadowed by the abolition of the *rekenkamer* at The Hague in 1463. Nevertheless, all these new institutions were abolished or transformed on Charles the Bold's death early in 1477.

Other sweeping reforms of the financial administration were promulgated by Charles the Bold, but none of them attempted in any way to unite the northern and southern territories; these remained quite distinct even in his most improbable schemes, unless we take seriously the claim of one of the most unreliable chroniclers of the age, that he proposed to set up at Nancy a single *chambre des comptes* for all his lands.[1] He began his financial reforming programme with the institution of an *argentier* or treasurer, the abolition of all receipts of the *épargne*, and the setting-up of a central five-man financial commission or office, all on 8 February 1468. Another series of changes was more in keeping with the administrative policies of Philip the Good, indeed in this respect as in so many others Charles only continued what his father had begun. The whole structure of receipts-general and local receipts was transformed in the decade 1463–72. The first receipt-general to be abolished had been that of Hainault, in 1463. In 1465 the receipt-general of Burgundy was abolished, only to be restored again soon afterwards. In 1468 the Flemish financial administration was restructured: three receivers, of the 'quarters' of Ghent, Bruges and Ypres, replaced the receiver-general and the various local receivers; and, in the same year, the multifarious local receivers in the two Burgundies were replaced by twelve only, while the receipt-general was again abolished. Brabant and Namur were similarly reformed in 1469; Luxembourg, the last, in 1472. This overall reduction in the number of separate receipts and standardization of the financial administration throughout the Burgundian lands may well have been logical and might even have promoted centralization, but it was premature, hurried and too far-reaching. In Burgundy it did not work at all, for the receiver-general, together with the traditional local receivers, were in office again by 1474. In the northern

---

[1] *Chronique de Lorraine*, ed. Marchal, 183–4. For the next sentence, see *IAGRCC* ii. 10–11, and Stein, *BEC* xcviii (1937), 293–4 and 324–32. For what follows, see Bruwier, *MA* liv (1948), 133–57 (Hainault), Cockshaw, *AB* xli (1969), 247–71 (Burgundy), *IAGRCC* ii. 32 n. 1 and *IADNB Rép. num.* i. 133 (Flanders), *IAGRCC* ii. 23 (Brabant), *IAGRCC* ii. 48 (Namur), and *IAGRCC* ii. 28 and *ICL* v. 29–30 (Luxembourg).

territories, reversion to the old system was general from 1477 onwards. Once again, Charles the Bold had overreached himself.

One of the more significant unifying forces in the fifteenth-century Low Countries was the States General, and its development was furthered by Charles the Bold simply because, like his father, he found it an essential, or at least valuable, instrument of government. But here again, as with the financial administration, no attempt was made to create a single Burgundian institution. No deputies from the southern territories were ever summoned to meetings of the States General of the Low Countries. However, during Charles's reign, there was an increasing tendency for the Estates of the duchy and county of Burgundy and their dependencies to meet together in a single assembly.

It was in the sphere of extraordinary taxation that Charles the Bold gave the largest single stimulus to the evolution of the States General and to the further unification of the Low Countries. From the start of his reign he displayed a novel attitude to *aides*. Relegating the two Burgundies to the background as being unimportant financially but instead productive of the best soldiers, [1] and abandoning his father's practice of treating each territory quite separately, in 1467–8 he is said to have sought the sum of one million guldens from his northern territories to pay for his accession, marriage, and campaigns in France and Liège, to be paid over a ten-year period. On that occasion the Estates of each territory were separately summoned and asked for their individual contributions. In 1470 an *aide* of 120,000 crowns was requested in the same way but when, in 1473, the duke wanted to replace existing *aides* with a new one, of 500,000 crowns *per annum*, he summoned the States General and put his request to it. Even then the sums actually voted were negotiated in detail with the Estates of the different territories. After 1473 no further global *aides* were demanded, but a significant step towards the unification and rationalization of extraordinary taxation had been taken.

Charles the Bold's centralizing ideas and his administrative radicalism found expression also in less obvious ways. He is said to

---

[1] *Collection de documens inédits*, i. 220. For what follows see *Hansisches Urkundenbuch*, ix. 277–8 (compare Chastellain, *Oeuvres*, v. 373–4, *Collection de documens inédits*, i. 190–1), *Collection de documens inédits*, i. 216–24, *Actes des États généraux*, 174–220 and *Handelingen van de Leden en Staten van Vlaanderen, 1467–1477*, 164–85. On the States General see too Heimpel, *Festschrift Gerhard Ritter*, 157–60 and van de Kieft, *500 Jaren Staten-Generaal in de Nederlanden*, 9–12, both with references.

have been negotiating for a diocesan reorganization so that he could have a sort of Burgundian church of his own.[1] Not that this was very novel: Duke John III had tried to have a diocese of Brabant created in 1332, to coincide with his duchy. The attitude of Charles the Bold or his officials to enclaves in his own territories is illuminating. A number of places in the eastern Netherlands and also in Artois, some of them belonging to the chapter of Cambrai, were requested to contribute to the 1473 *aide*, even though they were not Burgundian and did not in any sense belong to Charles the Bold. Their inclusion was justified on the grounds that the tax was for defence and, since they were surrounded by Burgundian territory, they would benefit as much as anyone else. Again, one cannot fail to notice the more radical aspects of the establishment in 1473 of a quite new judicial and administrative council at Maastricht which had far-reaching consequences. After all, Maastricht was only in part Burgundian, and no particular existing territory was attached to it. The competence and activities of the new council appear to have diminished and infringed the jurisdiction and rights of the councils of Brabant, Guelders and Namur, not to mention those of the bishop of Liège and the town councils of Maastricht itself, Liège and possibly Aachen. In a sense, Charles was creating a new territory along the Meuse; and he convoked the Estates of this area, as well as giving it a council, and a lieutenant in Guy de Brimeu, lord of Humbercourt.

Even in routine matters of economic policy, Charles the Bold can perhaps legitimately be described as 'ahead of his time'; for example in trying to consult the general interest against local pressures. In autumn 1473 he was loth to accept the proposals of the Flemish towns, supported by his officials in the *chambre des comptes* at Lille, for a ban on corn exports from Flanders to cope with the scarcity there until a conference of all interested parties had been called.[2] The general conclusion must surely be that, even in relatively humdrum matters arising out of the administration of territories and institutions, Charles the Bold was often too extreme, too progressive, or perhaps too idealistic, to make a thoroughly successful ruler.

So far in this chapter we have been mainly concerned with Charles the Bold's person and character and his qualities as a ruler. These are

---

[1] Jongkees, *Staat en kerk*, 39–40. For what follows see Gorissen, *Études dédiées à Ferdinand Courtoy*, 565–75 and the same, *De Raadkamer*, 79–102 and *BFPL* cciii (1972), 135–45, and van Hommerich, *PSAHL* ciii–iv (1967–8), 106–57 and *Liber Memorialis G. de Lagarde*, 89–110, and p. 254 below.
[2] Godard, *AHS* i (1939), 417–20.

naturally very apparent in the life of the court which, like the duke himself, became a legend in his own lifetime. One of Charles's German mercenaries, Wilwolt von Schaumburg, with some inaccuracies, and exaggeration especially of the officials' salaries, recollected it thus:[1]

First [the duke] had his chancellor, highest in rank after himself, who sat at the top of the table above all the other courtiers and who received 20,000 guldens per annum. He always, or at least usually, maintained four or five princes at his court, to whom, according to the exigencies of the moment, he paid 8 or 10,000 guldens, and four stewards, each paid 4,000 guldens per annum, twenty-four chamberlains, the lowest-ranking ones paid 1,200 guldens, fifty-two servers at table or carvers, the same number to serve his food at table, to serve his drink and to hold his stirrups when he rode, that is 208 persons in all, called 'of the four offices', all noblemen. Each of them had to maintain four horses and was paid 450 guldens. Now you must understand that not all the people 'of the four offices' had to stand by the table, bring food and drink or hold the stirrup at once, but whoever did so at the time replaced and represented the others. These 208, each of whom had to have four horses, received a gulden each day and were called the 'ordinance' or the 'court servants'. Then there was the guard, also nobles, [each of whom] had to keep at least three horses, and their numbers rose and fell daily; they were paid eighteen stivers each; also the paymaster who received and paid out all the sums of money, whose annual salary was 4,000 guldens, and all the other financial officials under him, also receiving large salaries. The chief huntsman received yearly, for his services, over 4,000 guldens. It is said that the huntsmen, falconers and greyhounds with their valets, hounds and lures cost a good 10,000 guldens. There was a provost to punish evildoers who got 2,000 guldens for his office and one can imagine that the waiters, cup-bearers, kitchen assistants, cooks, bakers, carvers, fish-masters and others with their valets and assistants cost no small amount. There were fifty lords with halberds organized as a bodyguard [for the duke]. Each had to have a horse, and got a gulden daily. He was always being sent children of foreign princes, counts and lords sent as lads, whom he maintained in costly and lordly style as befitted them, with beautiful cloth of gold and velvet clothes. Then there are his chaplains, choristers and other such people who had to stay with the court and follow him, who received, as he himself reckoned, 10,000 guldens.

Wilwolt von Schaumburg was evidently not particularly familiar with the court: he was a soldier and he wrote years after Duke Charles's death. An account of what it was like to serve as a courtier has survived from 1469, written by the tutor, or secretary, of the young

[1] *Die Geschichten und Taten*, 17–18.

Rodolfo Gonzaga, Enrico Suardo, in a letter sent from The Hague on 5 October to the marchioness of Mantua, Rodolfo's mother.

Most illustrious princess and my most excellent lady, in order that your ladyship may fully appreciate what form your most illustrious son's service for this most illustrious lord [duke] has to take, if he desires to do his duty according to courtly etiquette, I must tell you that, apart from being obliged, in order not to waste time, to accompany the duke to mass and vespers and attend at the audience, it is also necessary, not out of duty nor for fear of losing one's pay but to be of benefit and do pleasure to the duke, to be at supper every day about three hours after vespers and, about half an hour or sometimes an hour after his supper one has to be in the place where certain legends of the saints are read for a space of two hours. Afterwards, at the end, the collation is brought, that is, something to drink, and often he eats a mouthful of bread and, at this collation, the most worthy person present serves and brings him a drink and in this, nearly every time, Miser Redolfo has served him because he has been there every time, and it seems to me that [the duke] is very pleased with him. Collation over, [the duke] goes to his room to undress and get into bed. Miser Redolfo also enters there to help him undress and put him to bed, in such a way that the business lasts generally an hour, until nearly midnight. Throughout the day no other person who is charged with [attending to] his person goes there, except that between vespers, which are usually late, and supper, which is in the first hour of the night according to Italian reckoning—here at six o'clock or thereabouts—it is true that many people enter his chamber, and for the most part household people, that is, the lords 'of his ordinance', who are willing to take the trouble. And always when the duke leaves this place to hear mass about two leagues away from here anyone may go who wishes and, up to now, [Miser Redolfo] has always gone. Usually, this is at Our Lady of Seravesano on the Saturday and on Wednesday at San Giorgio.[1]

---

[1] ASMant Archivio Gonzaga, 567 (Fiandra). Professor E. H. Kossman has kindly informed me that 'Seravesano' is evidently a not unsuccessful phonetic rendering of 's Gravenzande, and San Giorgio is the St. Jorishof near the Vijver in The Hague. For the next paragraph see de la Marche, *Mémoires*, iii. 1–94 and, for the *escroes*, Brun-Lavainne, *BCHDN* viii (1865), 189–232 (*escroe* of 11 July 1470), Roux, *Histoire de l'abbaye de Saint-Acheul-lez-Amiens*, 522–34 (*escroes* of 4-7 March 1471) and David, *AB* xxxix (1967), 5–43 and 65–86 (detailed discussion and list of all ADN *escroes*, which are summarized in *IADNB* viii. 45–64). Other *escroes* of Duke Charles are in AGR Papiers de l'État et de l'Audience no. 9. On the organization of the Burgundian court under Charles, Vandeputte, *ASEB* xxviii (1876–7), 188–92 has been entirely replaced by the excellent thesis, sadly not yet printed, of Dr. U. Schwarzkopf, *Studien zur Hoforganisation der Herzöge von Burgund*, partly summarized in *PCEEBM* v (1963), 91–104.

It would be superfluous here to excerpt or summarize that most detailed and justly famous description of the Burgundian court under Charles the Bold written by Olivier de la Marche in November 1474, which goes under the title of *L'estat de la maison du duc Charles de Bourgogne*; nor does space permit analysis of the surviving *escroes*, the daily household rolls, many hundreds of which have survived for Duke Charles's reign. These last follow established patterns; but how far did Charles the Bold alter the character of the Burgundian court? In effect, he promoted still further its institutionalization: the evolution of the different groups of court personnel almost into separate institutions, even offices of state. This is particularly noticeable in the case of the secretaries, the heralds, the guard, the accounting office or *chambre aux deniers*, and above all the chapel. But he also introduced a novel element which meant more than the mere tightening of discipline or elaboration of rules and regulations. This new development can perhaps be described as militarization. It is first apparent in the remarkable household or court ordinance of 1 January 1469 which was preceded by, or perhaps announced and promulgated at, a grand assembly of courtiers apparently addressed by the duke in person, on 18 December 1468 at Brussels.[1] It was subsequently further developed in the ducal ordinance of 13 February 1474. Thereafter almost the entire court functioned as a select and personal section of the duke's army. By 1474, however, a period of continuous warfare was about to begin: everything was placed on a war footing. The 1469 ordinance shows how the duke's feeling for order and discipline found peacetime expression.[2]

A veritable college of heralds was established, comprising five Kings-of-Arms: Golden Fleece, Brabant, Flanders, Artois and Hainault; the marshal of arms of Brabant; seven heralds: Burgundy, Franche-Comté, Salins, Limbourg, Luxembourg, Charolais and 'Lotherich'; and four pursuivants: Fusil, Chasteau Belin, Gorinchem and Quesnoy. There were five *trompettes de guerre*, six *trompettes de menestrels* and three *joueurs des instrumens bas* permanently on the establishment of the court.

Apart from being greatly enlarged, the chapel was strictly disciplined in the 1469 ordinance: no longer was that 'dissolute festivity commonly called the feast of fools', in which one member of the chapel

---

[1] *Dagboek van Gent*, ii. 216–17.
[2] BL Hatton MS. 13, on which see Schryver, *Scriptorium* xxiii (1969), 437–40. The excerpts are from fos. 17b, 44a–b and 1a–b.

staff was elected 'abbot' and they exchanged clerical habits for 'illicit secular clothes', to be allowed. During services, the chaplains and clerks were now strictly enjoined to 'avoid all immoderate talking, chatting, conversation, mockeries, signs, derisions, games, laughing and other vain and frivolous things'. Any of them caught saying his own private hours during the service or when he should have been singing was to be fined two shillings, and the first chaplain was empowered to expel badly behaved ducal servants from the chapel. Once a week he was to preside over an assembly or chapter of chapel personnel to organize services for the coming week, to review those of the previous week, and to see 'if there is anything to reform and correct in anyone's behaviour'.

> At the end of each chapter or assembly the first chaplain is to give them some honest and salutary exhortations to encourage them to live virtuously in their estate and acquit themselves well before God. Also he is to pray to God for my lord [the duke] and his estate, asking him to give him grace to rule and govern his people and lands according to his holy will. After this they are all to process to the chapel . . . and kneel while the first chaplain devoutly says the psalm *Exaudiat te dominus in die tribulationis* etc. with some prayers, particularly this one: *Oremus pro principe nostro. Regem dominus conservet eum* etc. and, at the end of the collect, 'Oh lord, protect our duke' and such others as he pleases. And if anyone departs from the said assembly without leave of the first chaplain before the finish of all the above-mentioned things he is to lose his wages for that day.

The daily rations for the chamberlains and other courtiers were minutely laid down in the 1469 ordinance. They seem generous enough. On meat days the chamberlains were served for dinner with 'a piece of beef, two saddles of mutton, a leg of beef, a boiled capon or veal, chitterlings, sausages, tripe, small black puddings' and so on, with soup, salt and milk. For supper they had boiled hotch-potch, a larded joint or water-birds, two shoulders of mutton, four chickens, a piece of veal, two rabbits or partridges etc. All this was between ten. Just as the thirteen chaplains were firmly under the control of the first chaplain, so the hundred chamberlains had to obey the first chamberlain, Anthony, the bastard of Burgundy, half-brother of Charles the Bold, who was empowered to strike them off the day's roll or *escroe*, thus depriving them of their day's wages, if they misbehaved. Every day before supper a written return was to be submitted stating whether or not the chamberlains 'have served my lord [the duke] at all times according to his ordinances'. The courtiers were certainly kept on their toes: every Saturday evening the duke was to be given a list of all those who had been struck off the roll at any time during the week.

The councillors' duties were carefully defined. They were to meet twice a day, in the morning from 8.0 to 11.0 a.m. in winter and from 7.0 to 10.0 a.m. in summer, and in the afternoon from 3.0 to 5.0 p.m. except Sundays and feast days. Before meeting, they were to hear mass. After every morning meeting of the grand council, as it was called, its president the chancellor, together with certain councillors previously named to him by the duke, was to visit the duke in his oratory and report to him on that morning's proceedings and those of the evening before. An interesting attempt was made in this 1469 ordinance to limit and define the membership of the grand council:

Also my lord [the duke] orders that, from now on, no one of whatever rank may enter, come to or be at his council to attend it with his chancellor, the *maîtres des requêtes* of his household, his *procureur général* and his substitute named in this present ordinance, except for the eight chamberlains hereinafter named whom he has chosen to be ordinarily [members] of his council. That is to say, the lord of Arceys, Messire Symon de Lalaing lord of Montigny, Messire Jehan de Coppons, the lord of Humbercourt, the lord of Bièvres, Messire Michault de Chaugy, the lord of Eschanez and Messire Anthoine de Montjeu; and also Monsieur the bastard first chamberlain, the marshal of Burgundy, the first *maître d'hôtel* and the other ordinary *maîtres d'hôtel*. Except for the bishops and other prelates who are councillors of my lord [the duke], the president of the *Parlements* of Burgundy, the lieutenant-general of Holland, the governor of Luxembourg, the grand bailiff of Hainault, the bailiff of Amiens and the sovereign-bailiff of Flanders, who may attend and take part along with the above-mentioned when they come. Except however that my lord may bring or cause to be brought any other persons with him when it is his pleasure to attend in person.

The forty archers, or *archiers de corps*, under their two captains, had to be drawn up, mounted and wearing brigandines and sallets, outside the duke's lodgings or palace, whenever he was about to move from one place to another. They rode in front of him in close order without their pages and other attendants, who travelled in the rear. They were to practise with their bows at every opportunity.

This household ordinance of 1 January 1469 was prefaced with the customary propagandist preamble in which Charles the Bold once again set forth his elementary political philosophy and displayed his egocentricity, asserting that God had entrusted him with the business of justice, but that this, and seeing to his finances, made it impossible for him to ensure properly the good order of his court. Desiring 'to live as a just prince and not as a tyrant' he had drawn up this ordinance mainly in order to appoint subordinates—like the first chamberlain and the first chaplain—to exercise his authority at court and ensure its discipline when he was otherwise occupied. Of these occupations, neither the dispensation of justice nor the administration of his finances was to prove particularly significant in the future. Instead, it was, increasingly, military affairs which deflected the duke's attention. Having reorganized the Burgundian court at the beginning of 1469, he turned later that year to the reorganization of the Burgundian armies or, more accurately, to the creation of the new army 'of his ordinance'.

CHAPTER SIX

The Armies of Charles the Bold

When Charles the Bold fancied himself as a second Julius Caesar, or as a new Alexander the Great, when he revolved far-fetched schemes of conquest in his mind, he was not just idly dreaming. Contemporary evidence shows that he thoroughly enjoyed the life of the camp and the rigours of campaigning. Why else would he have remained 'fully-armed from head to foot for fourteen hours continuously' on one occasion at the siege of Neuss?[1] How else can one interpret the following passage in Panigarola's despatch of 11 July 1475?

> In the twelve days since we left Neuss to come here, the duke rode with his squadrons all the way to Maastricht, taking me with him, and showing me squadron after squadron and man after man. The trouble he takes is incredible. He always rides in his cuirass. All his pleasure, his every thought, is in men-at-arms: to make them look good and move in good order. He never dismounts until the whole camp is lodged and he has inspected all round the site and he makes it clear that he is master, for at the slightest disorder or insubordination in the ranks there is no lack of lunging points and slashing back-handers from his own sword. In short he is a man of strong will and much feared.

[1] ASM Pot. est. Borgogna 516–17/44. The extract that follows is from the same, 516–17/77. For this chapter as a whole Guillaume, *L'organisation militaire* and *Bandes d'ordonnance*, de la Chauvelays, *Diverses organisations des armées de Charles le Téméraire* and *Les armées de Charles le Téméraire dans les deux Bourgognes*, and the unpublished thesis of Schmidt-Sinns, *Heerwesen der Herzöge*, kindly lent me by Professor Heimpel, have been especially valuable. Less important are Brusten, *L'armée bourguignonne de 1465 à 1468*, the same author in *RIHM* xx (1959), 452–66, and in *PCEEBM* ii (1960), 55–67 and iii (1961), 42–9, Fredericq, *Rôle politique*, 160–4, Léderrey, *RMS* cvii (1962), 368–82, Lot, *L'art militaire*, ii. 102–36, Schneebeli, *ASMZ* cvi (1960), 125–35, and Verbruggen, *FN* v (1960), 224–34. For the French armies of this period see Contamine, *Guerre, état et société*.

Besides his evident enjoyment of the soldier's life, Charles the Bold evinced a deep personal interest in military affairs. An Italian correspondent observed as early as 21 January 1470 that 'scarcely a day passes during which he does not spend an hour or two alone writing and drawing up his [military] ordinances'.[1] Naturally this involvement increased when he was actually on campaign. On 12 May 1476 Panigarola reported that 'all day yesterday the duke stayed locked in his room writing certain ordinances' which included orders of battle against the Swiss, marching orders, and orders for the artillery. Every captain was to be given a copy of these instructions and Panigarola promised, if he could, to send one to the duke of Milan.

Nothing illustrates better Charles the Bold's attention to military detail and his handling of an army in the field than his own letter describing the famous but indecisive encounter between his army and the imperial forces outside Neuss on 23 May 1475. It was sent on 27 May to Claude de Neuchâtel, lord du Fay, the duke's lieutenant in Luxembourg.[2]

As to our news, last Tuesday 23 May[3] the Emperor struck camp in order to approach nearer our siege, but he only passed a wood which was very near him and pitched camp on this side of the wood. As soon as we were definitely informed of his move, which was at about 10.00 a.m., we at once caused the household troops and the companies of our ordinance to take the field, leaving our said siege defended and provided with sufficient forces to resist the sallies of the people in the town and to prevent those beyond the Rhine, who were in considerable force, from crossing to this side to help and revictual those in the town. After making these dispositions for the defence of our siege we took the field and marshalled all our troops on this side of a river which was between us and the Emperor, in the following way.

In the first battle [we posted] all the infantry, pikemen of our [companies of] ordinance, and the English archers both of Messire Jehan Middleton's company and of our household and guard, together with the infantry belonging to [the companies of] the lords of Fiennes, Roeux, Créquy, Haines, and Peene and other enfeoffed lords. [Among] all these pikemen were intermingled the archers in groups of four, so that there was a pikeman between every group of archers. On the right wing of these

---

[1] ASMant Archivio Gonzaga 567 (Fiandra), letter of Enrico Suardo. For what follows, see ASM Pot. est. Borgogna 518–20/278–9.
[2] Printed from a late copy in *Mémoires*, i. 360–4 and *Recueil du Fay*, 117–21. Both texts are corrupt.
[3] Both the printed texts have 24 May but 23 May was a Tuesday in 1475 and other sources show that this engagement was fought on 23 May.

infantrymen we posted Messire Jehan Middleton's mounted men-at-arms, as well as those of Jaques Galiot's company, all in a single squadron, with the count of Campebasse and all his men as the reserve for this wing. On the left wing of the infantry we posted the enfeoffed lords and their men-at-arms with the count of Celane and his company, all in one squadron and, for their reserve, the two companies of Messires Anthoine and Pierre de Lignanne, also in a single squadron. We appointed our cousin, councillor, and chamberlain the count of Chimay [commander-in-]chief of this battle.

CHARLES THE BOLD'S ARRANGEMENT OF HIS ARMY ON 23 MAY 1475

Men-at-arms of enfeoffed lords and the count of Celano	Infantry: pikemen and archers intermingled	Infantry: pikemen and archers intermingled	Men-at-arms of Sir John Middleton and Jacobo Galeoto
Reserve: Antonio and Petro de Lignana			Reserve: Colade Monforte, count of Campobasso

FIRST BATTLE: Philippe de Croy, count of Chimay

Men-at-arms of the companies of Berghes and Loyecte	Archers of the body-guard and archers of the companies of Berghes and Loyecte	Chamberlains and gentlemen of the chamber	Archers of the guard and archers of the companies of Brochuysen, Chanter-aine, Menton, Longueval and Vanperghe	Men-at-arms of the companies of Brochuysen and Chanter-aine
Reserve: gentlemen of the four estates of the household under St.-Seigne		Reserve: men-at-arms of the guard under Olivier de la Marche		Reserve: men-at-arms of the companies of Menton, Longueval and Vanperghe

SECOND BATTLE: Guy de Brimeu, lord of Humbercourt

In the centre of the second battle we placed the squadron of chamberlains and gentlemen of our chamber and, in reserve, the mounted guards
under the command of Messire Olivier de la Marche, our *maître d'hôtel*,
as their captain. In a squadron behind and some distance to the right of
the said chamberlains and gentlemen of our chamber [we placed] all the
archers of our ordinary guard and all the archers from the companies of
Messire Regnier de Brochuysen, the lord of Chanteraine, George de
Menton, Jehan de Longueval and Regnier de Vanperghe. The last three
of these were knighted that day. On the right wing of the said archers
we posted the men-at-arms of the companies of the said Messire Regnier
de Brochuysen and Chanteraine with, in reserve, the men-at-arms of the
companies of the said Messire George de Menton, Jehan de Longueval
and Regnier de Vanperghe, all in one squadron. On the left wing of the
said chamberlains and gentlemen of our chamber we posted the archers
of our bodyguard and those of the companies of Philippe de Berghes,
who was knighted then, and of Philippe Loyecte, and on the flank of
these archers all the men-at-arms of the companies of the said Messire
Philippe de Berghes and Loyecte in a single squadron with, as their
reserve, the gentlemen of the four estates of our household, in one
squadron, commanded by Messire Guillaume de St. Seigne, also our
maître d'hôtel, and, under him, by the chiefs of the said four estates. This
battle was commanded by the lord of Humbercourt, also our cousin,
councillor, and chamberlain, as commander-in-chief in the place of our
first chamberlain, [together with] the count of Joigny and the lord of
Bièvres.

After these battles had been organized in this way a certain amount of
time elapsed, more than was necessary, because the companies did not
arrive soon enough at their appointed places. Nevertheless, regardless of
the time, we crossed the said river at a ford which was not too deep, firm
with a good bottom and, because of the narrowness of the said ford, we
made the reserve of the right wing of the first battle march across it in
files, the men-at-arms with their swordsmen[1] and pages on their right
and likewise in file after them went the right wing and all the archers and
pikemen of this wing. Then followed the archers and pikemen of the left
wing and, after the wing, its reserve, and, in just the same way, the
second battle crossed, the reserve of the right wing followed by the
wing [itself], the archers of the said wing, and all the rest of the second
battle in similar order to the first. After the reserve of the left wing,
which consisted of the gentlemen of the four estates, our guard, which
constituted the reserve for the said squadron of chamberlains and gentlemen of our chamber, crossed over.

Because their camp, which backed on to the Rhine, extended towards
us, and we were nearest to this end of it, the enemy, thinking that we

---

[1] Both printed texts have *conseillers*, evidently for *coustilliers*.

would come this way, had placed most of their artillery there. They had even trained the artillery in the encampment on the far side of the Rhine to fire in front of this end of their said camp where they thought we would attack. But, in crossing the river, we made all the above-mentioned formations advance to the left of the said camp, that is to our right, and move towards the above-mentioned wood which they had passed through on the way to their camp, and we made all the formations and their reserves extend into the same order in which they had been on this side of the river. With regard to our artillery, we passed it over a bridge near the ford after the said battles, which, because they had been in order and crossed the ford as described above, were very quickly reorganized so that, when we crossed the said bridge after the artillery rather than passing through the ford after the said battles, we found they had all crossed over and were in excellent order. They were a very fine sight.

It is a fact that on our arrival we moved them further towards the said wood to dodge the fire from over the Rhine and from the side where most of the [enemy] artillery was placed, as well as to gain the sun and the wind which was causing a great deal of thick and stinging dust, and so that we could approach the left-hand side of the Emperor's camp, where it was fortified, but not so well as on the other side.

We gave the cry of Notre Dame! Monseigneur St. George! and our usual cry of Bourgogne! but, before we made any of our formations march, we moved up our artillery three or four bow-shots in front of us, together with the Italian infantry which had not been in any[1] of the above-mentioned formations, so that it fired at and shot into the Emperor's camp in such a way that no complete tents, pavilions or lodgings were left standing and people could only remain there with great difficulty. Then, in the name of God, of our Lady and of Monseigneur St. George we gave the signal for the troops to march. This done, the trumpets began to sound and everyone marched joyfully and with smiling faces, making the sign of the cross and recommending themselves to God; the English, according to their custom, making the sign of the cross on the ground and kissing it. Then they all shouted the above-mentioned cry.

Because the Germans held a [certain] hillock we caused Jaques Galiot to march there. He formed the right wing of the [first] battle with the count of Campebasse as his reserve. They captured it, and the Germans were forced to flee over the flat ground between the hillock and their camp. During the capture of this hillock several of the Emperor's people were killed. Realizing that they needed to defend and guard this flat ground to protect the security of their camp, a large number [of the enemy] sallied out both on foot and horseback and attacked the said

---

[1] Both printed texts have *milles*, evidently for *nulles*.

Jaques, who was forced to retreat towards the count, his reserve. He had gone some distance ahead of him at the first attack but now the count advanced with his reserve as Jaques fell back on him and they attacked again together and broke the enemy, putting them to flight back to the camp. Here too several of the enemy were killed.

Jaques and the count had no archers with them, for the count of Chimay had marched his men too far to the left, so it was not possible at this moment to attempt anything else against the enemy and, because of the artillery fire from the camp, Jaques and the count withdrew down a valley. After this retreat more troops than before, both infantry and cavalry, sallied out of the Emperor's camp to attack Jaques and the count, who let us know of this. So we had to send them the reserve of the right wing of the second battle, comprising Messires George de Menton, Jehan de Longueval and Regnier de Vanperghe and, immediately afterwards, we sent the reserve of the squadron of our chamberlains, that is, the guards under Messire Olivier de la Marche, and, because they needed archers, we ordered off the entire right wing of archers of the second battle. But the men of this wing, under the command of Messire Regnier de Brochuysen and the lord of Chanteraine, moved quicker than their archers who, because they were on foot, could not keep up with them, and these companies, of Messire Regnier, the lord of Chanteraine and our guard, united with Jaques and the count without waiting for the archers and attacked the [enemy] force which had sallied out, in which were the duke of Saxony and other princes, and drove them back into their camp but, because they did not have with them the archers of the right wing of the second battle, which we had sent them, they were forced by the artillery fire to withdraw to the above-mentioned valley. After this retreat, all the princes came out, deploying the imperial banner, which the duke of Saxony carried, accompanied by all their cavalry and a great number of infantrymen, to attack our people. They forced the right wing of the first battle and its reserve back onto the right wing of the second battle and its reserve, both wings and reserves falling back as far as our guard, which held firm. Seeing this, we took a squadron which had not yet been allocated and went with it towards the right, in order to charge the enemy. We advanced as far as our guard and the archers of the right wing of the [second] battle, in order to charge the enemy on our left, and we personally rallied and reorganized the squadrons which were dispirited and disordered. This done we attacked the said princes again, who were in considerable force of horse and foot, and they were broken and scattered. Many fled, about six or eight hundred horse towards Cologne. The rest stayed in great disorder in their camp. Our artillery continued to fire with such effect that it disrupted everything in their camp. Part of their infantry, up to two or three thousand of them, hoped to save themselves by boat, but a certain number were drowned. They threw their baggage into the boats in such a disorderly fashion that a good deal of it came floating down the Rhine, together with the dead and drowned, to the island where we had established part of our siege.

It was then reported to us that the left wing and the reserve of the first battle, commanded by the count of Chimay, had beaten back the enemy in much disorder to their camp, so we decided to make all the formations advance to attack the [enemy] transport and, with this intention, we moved our artillery to where it could be most effectively used against the defenders of the said transport. But before this could be accomplished the light failed and night made it impossible for us to see everything, so that we could advance no further. By the grace of God we returned in such a way as to bring back everything safe and sound and at our leisure, for it took us a good four hours to return to our siege. And, though their artillery fire was amazingly heavy and concentrated, nonetheless by the grace of God, our Lady and Monseigneur St. George, there were only three dead and six wounded among our people.

A more skilled reporter, though with a less meticulous military grasp, has left another eye-witness account of this series of skirmishes outside Neuss on 23 May 1475. The Milanese ambassador at the Burgundian court, Johanne Petro Panigarola, fully confirms the duke's own account just quoted, in his despatch of 4 June 1475.[1]

On 23 May[2] the Emperor with his army came and lodged nearer this lord [duke]'s camp, half a league from it, where he was below a hillock. At once the duke was as happy and full of good cheer as it is possible to say, hoping to give battle to the enemy. He gave orders to those who had to defend the camp, so that the town remained besieged and so that certain places were furnished with men-at-arms to stop the enemy sallying forth. He ordered some *conductieri* with their men-at-arms to advance to a plain near, or rather next to, the camp, from which there was a bridge convenient to cross over. His lordship armed himself from head to foot in my presence joking with me the whole time. Armed, he went to the church near his pavilion to pray to our glorious Lady, then straight away mounted on a fine courser, he had some sixty big artillery pieces, bombards, *spingarde* and *spingardelle*, set forward in the above-mentioned plain while organizing the squadrons, the battle and the wings.... Then he made his troops cross the bridge en masse, in all about 12,000 picked combatants turned out like St. George. Certainly I never saw people so resolved either to die or to return victorious and advancing with such spirit, as these.

---

[1] *Briefe und Actenstücke von Mailand*, 110–11.
[2] The text has 24 May, but see above, p. 198 n. 3.

The duke laughed and seemed to be jubilant. He presented himself with these squadrons in front of the Emperor's camp, which he found was already fortified with wagons and ditches with the [enemy] fully prepared behind the stockade, with much artillery. At about 20.00 hours the duke's artillery and large *spingarde* began to fire among the enemy and they replied in terrible fashion so that it seemed like hell, and as if the world would be destroyed by thunder and fire. Then they attacked the leading squadrons with some infantry composed of hand-gunners but these were driven back and numbers of them were killed by our infantry. Afterwards a squadron of about 2,000 horse with many hand-gunners came out and, by command of the duke, Jacobo Galeoto and the count of Campobasso with the Italians assaulted them and drove them ignominiously behind the barricades. Then they reinforced them-selves, so that 3,000 horse and about 6,000 hand-gunners on foot came out, their rear well protected by others. To bring them out further, Jacobo Galeoto and the count pretended to flee and, having gone some distance, they turned and pressed them so close that their horses passed over the bodies of many of their infantry, and again they drove them behind the barricades, killing a good many, with such impetus that many of our people penetrated inside. Here at the barriers the fight continued until dark night. . . .

I was in the field during this engagement and I saw the duke applying himself in person here and there admirably in organizing and command-ing. He has a mind like Caesar's . . . I have never seen anyone so assured as his lordship. The [shots from] *spingarde* and bombards flew furiously around his horse, yet he did not care. . . . It required no small spirit to have left the siege and the fortified camp to go and assault the Emperor and all the power of Germany, which has not been so united for 200 years, and to have returned with such honour.

There is much other evidence to confirm that Charles the Bold really was the effective commander of his own armies in the field and also the effective author of his own military ordinances. His very personal role in military affairs was typified by the way he interpreted his own rule, incorporated in the famous military ordinance of 1473, that the captains or *conducteurs* of the companies of ordinance were to be appointed at the beginning of each year, to take oath to the duke on assuming office, and to hand in at the end of the year their baton, their copy of the duke's ordinance, and their register containing the names and addresses of their men. At Nancy, shortly before Christmas 1475, on the eve of the campaign against the Swiss, Charles the Bold in-stalled himself on a tribunal and, surrounded by the inevitable ambassadors, conducted the ceremonial inauguration of the New

Year's captains in person, after his councillor Guillaume de Rochefort had delivered a lecture explaining how 'military skill (*l'arte militare*) and the virtue of loyal and obedient soldiers were necessary for the strength and stability of states.' Twenty captains were named for the coming year and mounted the tribunal one by one to kneel before the duke and swear their oath of fidelity, receiving from him a captain's baton covered with embroidered cramoisy and 'a paper book bound in cramoisy, with a silver-gilt clasp with the ducal arms on it, in which were written his orders for the war and what he had to know'. Then the duke himself addressed the new captains, assuring them that they would be properly paid and that the companies would never be disbanded while he lived, and entreating them to do their duty. [1]

Since he contrived to be defeated, often disastrously, in almost all his major battles, Charles the Bold's military reputation must principally depend on the remarkable series of ordinances which he issued regulating the organization and discipline of his armies in their minutest detail. Directly or indirectly, this legislation was applied to every sixteenth-century army and thus influenced the military history of the entire European continent in early modern times. In a succession of half-a-dozen remarkable documents issued between 1468 and 1476 and many less elaborate ones, several new ideas were worked out and applied, among them the first thorough attempt to impose rules of discipline and good conduct; the creation of permanent companies of ordinance divided into squadrons; compulsory drill and the first manoeuvres of modern times; and the transformation of the household troops and the guard into a *corps d'élite*.

The earliest of these military ordinances, of July 1468, was traditional in content and limited in scope, but it already displays

[1] ASM Pot. est. Borgogna 516–17/140 and see too de la Marche, *Mémoires*, iv. 84–6. Could BM Add. MS. 36,619, containing the text of the 1473 ordinance prefaced with an illumination evidently portraying the scene described here, be one of these books? They seem to be referred to in the following passage: 'To Philippe de Maseroles, illuminator of books, Jehan and Berthelemi Diers, suppliers of books, and Anthoine van der Haeghe, book-binder, all living at Bruges, what is owing to them for the following products of their craft. To the said Philippe for writing and illuminating twenty-one books containing the ordinances on the organisation and conduct of the troops of the ordinance of my lord [the duke], £86. Also, for the vellum, £30.' (*IADNB* iv. 248–9). But Panigarola specifically says the captains were each handed *uno libro in carta*. See too, on surviving copies of Charles's military ordinances, Schmidt-Sinns, *Heerwesen der Herzöge*, 130–41, and Deuchler, *Burgunderbeute*, 344–6.

Charles the Bold's characteristic authoritarianism and mastery of detail. It contains instructions for the marshal of Burgundy to review and pay the troops of the two Burgundies and bring them north to join in the campaign against Liège. They are to refrain from all acts of war en route unless attacked by the French. There is to be no 'pillaging, ransoming, rioting, mutilation of people or raping of women, whoever they may be, on Burgundian territory'. Offenders are to be executed. Nobody is to take lodgings without the marshal's permission and, every day, the captains must ascertain the password from the marshal. Each man-at-arms was to have three horses, one for himself, one for his swordsman or *coustillier*, armed also with a javelin, and the third for his valet. The marshal was to bring twelve serpentines, with 100 lead cannon-balls for each of them, and four cannoneers, each with an assistant. Nor was he to forget a dozen carpenters, a dozen masons and their tools, eighty pickaxes, eighty axes, lances, ropes and other equipment. Measures were prescribed too, for ensuring that all those owing military service on account of their fiefs either turned out or were punished.[1]

The next surviving military ordinance of Charles the Bold was issued at Abbeville on 31 July 1471. It was exclusively concerned with the organization of 1,250 lances of so-called troops 'of the ordinance' or permanent companies of mercenaries, which it called into being. Although each lance was said to be of six persons, in fact it comprised a man-at-arms with his mounted page and swordsman (*coustillier*); three mounted archers; and a crossbowman, a culverineer and a pikeman on foot: that is, nine men, at least eight of them combatants. The equipment and clothing of each man was laid down in detail. The man-at-arms was to have a complete suit of armour, three good horses, one worth thirty crowns, a combat saddle and a chamfrain, and blue and white plumes on his sallet and his horse's head. The *coustillier* was to arm himself with a good javelin, a medium length single-handed sword and a foot-long double-edged dagger, and the mounted archer must bring two and a half dozen good arrows as well as his bow, long two-handed sword, and dagger. Both mounted archer and *coustillier* would be issued with their uniform when reviewed for the first time. This was a paletot or coat in the ducal colours, half blue and half white, with a red St. Andrew's cross embroidered on it. The

---

[1] Printed in *Mémoires*, ii. 283–5, from ACO B16, fos. 187b–188b. The Abbeville ordinance, discussed in what follows, is printed in *Mémoires*, ii. 285–94 from ACO B16.

men-at-arms were issued with vermilion velvet St. Andrew's crosses to attach to their armour.

Organization and chain of command were also stipulated in detail. In each company of ordinance there were to be 100 men-at-arms, each the leader of a nine-man detachment or lance as described above. These men-at-arms were divided into tens, each commanded by a *disenier*. The commander of the company, called the *conducteur*, was himself also a *disenier*. Each group of ten men-at-arms was divided into two, five led by the *disenier* in one group or *chambre* as it was called, and three led by a *chief de chambre* or lieutenant of the *disenier* in the other group. It was explicitly laid down that the *chief de chambre* must obey the *disenier* and the *disenier* his *conducteur*, while the *conducteur* in turn had to obey the captain, or commander-in-chief. Leave of absence could be granted by the *conducteur* but the man-at-arms taking such leave must leave behind in camp, or at his lodgings, his best horse, his armour and his weapons. In each company a paymaster or *auditeur* was to be responsible for the troops' pay. All this and much else was stipulated in the ordinance issued at Abbeville in the summer of 1471.

The two famous Burgundian military ordinances of 1472 and 1473 were likewise concerned solely with the organization and discipline of the troops of Charles the Bold's ordinance.[1] In the ordinance issued on 13 November 1472 at Bohain-en-Vermandois after the close of that year's campaign against France, the number of these troops was somewhat reduced, the new figures being as follows:

TROOPS OF THE ORDINANCE AS LAID DOWN IN CHARLES THE BOLD'S ORDINANCE
OF 13 NOVEMBER 1472

Men-at-arms	1,200
Mounted archers	3,000
Crossbowmen	600
Archers on foot	1,000
Pikemen	2,000
Culverineers	600
TOTAL	8,400

---

[1] The ordinance of 13 November 1472 is printed in Gollut, *Mémoires historiques*, 846–52, and that of 1473 in the same, 853–63, as well as in *Lois militaires de Charles de Bourgogne*, SG ii (1817), 425–68, *Aktenstücke und Briefe zur Geschichte des Hauses Habsburg*, i. 62–82, and Guillaume, *Organisation militaire*, 191–202.

For the most part, the 1472 ordinance was an elaboration of its predecessor. The personal armament of the troops was stated in fuller detail, and more comprehensive instructions were given for setting out on march, an operation to be regulated by three separate soundings of trumpets. New in this ordinance was the roll call. A list of his men was to be submitted in writing by each man-at-arms to his *disenier* and by the *disenier* to the *conducteur*. One copy was to be kept by the *conducteur* 'so that he can check, whenever he takes the field with his ensign, that all the men-at-arms and other troops of his company are present'; and the other copy was to be sent to the duke. New too were the judicial powers now given to the officers and, notably, to the *conducteur*. In particular, disobedience was punishable summarily, on the spot, by the officer concerned, be he *conducteur* or *disenier*. Another innovation in the 1472 ordinance was the rule that all troops enrolled in the ordinance had to swear on oath 'to be true and loyal to my said lord [the duke] and that they would serve him against all'.

The remarkable ordinance issued by Charles the Bold while he was at the abbey of St. Maximin outside Trier in the autumn of 1473 marks the culmination of his military legislation. As the preamble makes clear, it too was limited to the troops of the ordinance:[1]

The most high, most excellent, most powerful and most redoubted sovereign lord, the duke of Burgundy, of Brabant, etc., having regard, especial zeal and desire for the safety, defence and improvement of the duchies, counties, principalities, lands, lordships and subjects which divine goodness and natural succession from his most noble progenitors have submitted to his authority, government and seigneury to protect them from enemies and those envious of his most noble house of Burgundy who, both by force of arms and by malice aforethought, have tried to undermine the dignity, preeminence, union and integrity of this most noble house and of his said principalities, lands and lordships, has, since a certain time ago, set forth and established the companies of his ordinance, of men-at-arms and archers and others, both foot and horse, who, like all other human societies, cannot be permanently in obedience, union and virtuous operation without law, both for the instruction of the various ranks in their duties, for the encouragement of loyal and virtuous deeds, and for the punishment and correction of their vices and faults. Therefore our most redoubted and sovereign lord, after careful, lengthy and mature consideration, has made and established the laws, statutes and ordinances which follow.

[1] Guillaume, *Organisation militaire*, 191.

Although much of the 1473 ordinance only repeats or elaborates the earlier ones, there are some new departures of prime importance. The organization of the companies was radically changed. The *diseniers*, or leaders of groups of ten men-at-arms, disappear altogether. Instead of being divided into tens, the men-at-arms of each company were now divided into four squadrons of equal size, each comprising a *chief d'escadre* or captain and four *chambres* each made up of a *chief de chambre* and five men-at-arms. Thus each squadron comprised twenty-five men-at-arms each of whom was still theoretically responsible for a nine-man detachment or lance comprising himself, his *coustillier*, his page, three mounted archers and the three infantry-men—a pikeman, culverineer and crossbowman. In each company, the *conducteur*, who was appointed annually by the duke in person, was allowed to appoint three of his *chiefs d'escadre*, but the fourth was to be appointed by the duke.

To help in keeping order on the march and in battle regulations were now drawn up to ensure the easy identification of officers by their men. The *conducteur* was to carry an ensign, distinctive in colour and design; the captains of squadrons were to have cornets of the same colour and design, a large gold-embroidered letter C on that of the first squadron, two C's on the cornet of the *chief d'escadre* of the second squadron, and so on. The *chiefs de chambre* were to have the same colours and design on the bannerols attached to their sallets and these were to be numbered C1, C2, C3, etc.

In the 1473 ordinance discipline was tightened up in all kinds of ways, particular attention being paid to deserters. The duke's soldiers were not allowed to swear or blaspheme, nor to play with dice. Nor was the private appropriation of individual women camp-followers to be permitted any longer. Instead, each company was allowed to have with it no more than thirty women, in common. The most remarkable section of the 1473 ordinance was that dealing with exercises and drill, which seems to have been wholly new.

Furthermore, my lord [the duke] ordains that, in order that the said troops may be better trained and exercised in the use of arms and better practised and instructed when something happens, when they are in garrison, or have time and leisure to do this, the captains of the squadrons and the *chambres* are from time to time to take some of their men-at-arms out into the fields, sometimes partly, sometimes fully armed, to practise charging with the lance, keeping in close formation while charging, [how] to charge briskly, to defend their ensigns, to with-

H

draw on command, and to rally, each helping the other, when so ordered, and how to withstand a charge. In like manner [they are to exercise] the archers with their horses, to get them used to dismounting and drawing their bows. They must learn how to attach their horses together by their bridles and make them walk forwards directly behind them, attaching the horses of three archers by their bridles to the saddle-bow of the page to whose man-at-arms they belong; also to march briskly forwards and to fire without breaking rank. The pikemen must be made to advance in close formation in front of the said archers, kneel at a sign from them, holding their pikes lowered to the level of a horse's back so that the archers can fire over the said pikemen as if over a wall. Thus, if the pikemen see that the enemy are breaking rank, they will be near enough to charge them in good order according to their instructions. [The archers must also learn to] place themselves back to back in double defence, or in a square or circle, always with the pikemen outside them to withstand the charge of the enemy horse and their horses with the pages enclosed in their midst. The *conducteurs* can begin by introducing this way of doing things to small groups and, when one of these groups is practised and instructed, they can take out others. While doing this, the *conducteurs* are to keep an eye on [all] their people every day so that none will dare absent themselves or be without horse and armour, because they will not be sure on which day the *conducteurs* will want to take them out on exercises. Thus each will be constrained to learn to do his duty.[1]

These carefully organized and apparently well-trained forces were among those put to flight by the Swiss and their allies at Grandson on 2 March 1476. The last of Charles the Bold's military ordinances was published after this defeat and before the second battle against the Swiss, on 22 June 1476, at Murten, when again the ducal army was routed. Though not dated, it was probably published at Lausanne early in May: the Milanese ambassador was able to send his duke an Italian translation of it on 13 May. Very different in character from the earlier ones, this ordinance applied to the entire ducal army in the field and not just to the companies of ordinance, which at this moment however must have comprised some two-thirds of Charles's forces. Moreover it was primarily concerned not with the organization of the constituent elements in the army, which remained unchanged, but with establishing the order of march, providing for the transport, and improving discipline.

[1] Guillaume, *Organisation militaire*, 200–1. For what follows, see *Dépêches des ambassadeurs milanais*, ii. 152–74, and de la Chauvelays, *Armées des trois premiers ducs*, 311–35.

The exact order in which the army was to march against the Swiss was set out in detail in the Lausanne ordinance. In place of the modest two battles with which Charles the Bold skirmished against the Emperor in May 1475 his much enlarged army now consisted of no fewer than eight battles, in six of which a contingent of infantry, or *enfants à pied* as they are called in the ordinance, in most cases 500 strong, was to march and fight between the cavalry contingents which made up the wings of each battle. As usual, care was taken in the ordinance to explain the chain of command. Discipline was tightened. The death penalty was now to be applied to anyone who disobeyed orders on the march or in battle. 'Even in enemy territory' the officers 'were not to allow any violation of churches or women, nor to spare the lives of any offenders'. Moreover, the austere and dedicated duke ordered them 'to see that all prostitutes and ribalds are expelled from their companies for this campaign and to make their people drink more water to keep them cool on the said campaign'.

In this brief review of some of the more outstanding of Charles the Bold's military ordinances a good deal of attention has inevitably been devoted to the companies of ordinance. In turning now to look at the main constituent elements of Charles the Bold's armies, we must again give them pride of place.

It seems to have been in the autumn of 1469 that Charles the Bold first resolved to create for himself what was virtually a new army of permanent mercenary companies of volunteers. The Italian prince Rodolfo Gonzaga wrote on 4 October 1469 to tell his mother that he might be entrusted with the command of some of the 1,200 five-horse lances which the duke was planning to raise. These troops, arranged in companies of ordinance, were to be paid and reviewed every month and they were to be organized, Rodolfo reported in another letter later that autumn, on the lines of those of the king of France and the signory of Venice. But nothing, it seems, was done. No ordinance establishing these forces has survived; probably none was issued. Nor indeed was much progress made in 1470 towards realizing the proposed military reforms. So far as is known, no detailed ordinances were published concerning the 1,000 lances 'of the ordinance' which were to be levied at the end of that year, apparently on a similar basis. It was partly because of these delays that Charles the Bold was caught unprepared when King Louis XI attacked him across the Somme in January 1471. No wonder he devoted his energies, as soon as the truce with France was signed on 4 April, to actually bringing into being the new army he had planned and dreamed of for so long. But now, instead of 1,000 lances, there were to be 1,250.[1]

A long succession of ducal *mandements*, issued between May and September 1471, illustrate the delays and difficulties which hindered the implementation of these plans. During May the ducal officials in Brabant received instructions to enrol volunteers to join the new standing army, which was to comprise 1,250 crossbowmen, 1,250 culverineers, 1,250 pikemen and 1,250 men-at-arms, and to send them to Arras by 15 June, but this assembly was subsequently deferred till 1 August, and as late as 31 August the duke ordered all those wishing to join his companies of ordinance to be at Brussels on 15 September. In spite of similar instructions issued at Abbeville on 29 June for the enrolment on 2 August of volunteers for these companies in the two Burgundies, delays occurred here too and it was only on 31 July 1471 that Charles the Bold's detailed ordinance concerning these troops, which has already been discussed above, was sent from Abbeville to the authorities at Dijon.[2]

The forces that were recruited so laboriously in 1471 were used to fight the French in 1472, for the account of the *trésorier des guerres* shows that the companies of ordinance formed an important element in the *armée générale* fielded by the duke that summer. The state of affairs just before this campaign, in the spring of 1472, was roughly as follows. A dozen companies of ordinance had been brought into being, as stipulated by the 1471 ordinance, under such captains as Olivier de la Marche and Peter von Hagenbach, and most of them were in garrison in Picardy, but none was at full strength. The situation in three of the largest was as follows:

STRENGTH OF CERTAIN COMPANIES OF ORDINANCE IN SPRING 1472[3]

	Men-at-arms	Mounted archers	Pike-men	Culveri-neers	Archers on foot	Total
Number laid down in summer 1471 ordinance	100	300	100	100	100	700
Company of O. de la Marche	99	300	100	48	67	614
Company of Jacques de Harchies	100	300	99	34	59	592
Company of Jehan de la Viefville	99	299	98	36	44	576

The relative importance of the companies of ordinance was demonstrated in 1473 by Guillaume Hugonet, Charles the Bold's chancellor, who told the States General that, not counting the artillery, the 'army of Burgundy' or the feudal levies of the two Burgundies, and the naval forces, the duke needed to fight the French, 1,200 lances of the ordinance, 1,000 lances of other troops to accompany the ordinance troops in the field, and a further 800 or 1,000 lances to garrison the frontiers. The proportion of ordinance companies increased still further after this, especially during the protracted siege of Neuss in 1474–5, when there were at least twenty. The account of the *trésorier des guerres* for 1476 shows that, by the end, with the exception of certain special or élite units, notably the household troops, some at least of the English archers, and the artillery and transport, almost the entire Burgundian field army had come to be 'of the ordinance'. These troops were organized for the campaigns against the Swiss in twelve separate heavy cavalry companies of 100 men-at-arms each, twenty-four or more light cavalry companies of 100 mounted archers each, and at least three contingents of infantry of the ordinance, each 1,000 strong. In addition, some of the mounted English archers and the household troops, which are entered in a separate section of the 1476 account, are described in it as 'of the ordinance'. Charles the Bold's field army, then, had been transformed from one composed of paid but conscripted feudal levies and civic militia, raised separately for each campaign among those obliged to perform military service, to an army of troops of the ordinance: that is, a standing army of mercenaries.

Although by no means all of them served in the ordinance, it is convenient to consider here the foreign mercenaries who were employed by Charles the Bold on an unprecedented scale. As a matter of fact, the creation of his new permanent army of ordinance

---

[1] For this paragraph, see ASMant Archivio Gonzaga 2100, letters of 4 October 1469 and 27 November 1469 (compare Bittmann, *Ludwig XI. und Karl der Kühne*, i (2). 423 n. 50), and BN MS. fr. 5041, f. 58a–b.

[2] For this paragraph, see AGR CC4181, fos. 157b, 159b, 162, 167b–168, 181, 183a–b, 189b etc. and above, pp. 206–7.

[3] From AGR CC25542, fos. 5a–10b. Mentioned neither in the account, nor in the description of the company's organization in the ordinance, nor in this table, are the mounted *coustilliers* and pages, for these were provided and paid for, privately as it were, by the man-at-arms. For what follows, see Bartier, *BCRH* cvii (1942), 152, and AGR CC25543, fos. 206–50.

troops had been severely hampered by the problem of recruitment and this was only solved, after 1472, by means of diplomatic negotiations and recruiting missions in Italy, land of those professional *condottieri* who were so much admired by Duke Charles. As early as 26 April 1471 he wrote to the signory of Venice asking if he could borrow the most famous and experienced *condottiere* of the age, Bartolomeo Colleoni. This seventy-year-old veteran, though living in semi-retirement in his castle of Malpaga, was still serving as captain-general of the Venetian army, and the Venetian authorities were unwilling to let him go, fearing that if they did Venice would be attacked by the duke of Milan. They explained to Charles the Bold that Colleoni simply could not be spared. Charles, however, was not easily deterred. On 15 September 1471 he sent two of his councillors, Antonio de Lignana and Guillaume de Rochefort, direct to Bartolomeo, and some time in 1472 Bartolomeo's secretary arrived at the Burgundian court to settle the terms of the contract.

Meanwhile the summer campaign of 1472 went badly for Charles. He failed to take Beauvais and he failed to engage and defeat the French forces. 'Because of this', wrote Bernhart von Ramstein to Peter von Hagenbach on 2 October 1472, 'my lord [the duke] wants to engage foreign troops in so far as he can,'[1] and the retention of Troylo da Rossano marks the beginning of a more determined and more successful effort by Charles to obtain the services of Italian captains which was in the first place partly dependent on Venetian assistance. It was, for example, the Venetian ambassador Bernardo Bembo who helped Troylo to recruit his men-at-arms.[2] Troylo had actually been appointed a captain in the Burgundian army on 29 September 1472, and he was paid the sum of £1,200 in advance on 1 October. He was to bring from Italy 150 lances, 200 infantry and 100 mounted crossbowmen. Fifty of the lances were to be commanded under him by his two sons Alexander and Johanne Francesco, and the entire company was to leave Italy by 1 March 1473 and reach

[1] Transcript of Innsbruck LRA Urk. I 8208 in RTA material. For what precedes, on Charles and Colleoni, see especially Plancher, iv. no. 248, Browning, *Bartolomeo Colleoni*, 39–40, Perret, *France et Venise*, i. 566 and 581 and ii. 9–11, Tourneur, *RBN* lxx (1914), 392–6, Belotti, *Bartolomeo Colleoni*, 461–74, Croce, *Vite di avventure*, 47–186, and Bittmann, *Ludwig XI. und Karl der Kühne*, ii (1). 40, 73, 86, 91, 424, 481 and 710.
[2] ASM Pot. est. Borgogna 515/79 (= *Cal. state papers. Milan*, i. 163). For what follows, see BN Coll. de Bourgogne MS. 59, fos. 27–8, and AGR CC25542, f. 74b.

Burgundy or Lorraine by 1 April. A similar contract was signed on 12 March 1473 with Jacobo de Vischi de' conti di San Martino, otherwise known as 'the count of St. Martin', a chamberlain-councillor of the duke whose force was likewise a family affair, his two sons Philippo and Baptista being empowered by Duke Charles to take over command of his 100-lance company whenever their father was absent.[1] Charles's instructions for a more important contract, that with Cola de Monforte, count of Campobasso, were drawn up on 10 November 1472. Cola was to bring from Italy what amounted to a small army: 400 four-horse lances, 400 mounted crossbowmen, and 300 infantry. They were to serve for three years for 82,800 crowns per annum and to travel via Savoy or Germany, leaving Italy by 1 March 1473. Cola de Monforte was accompanied by his two sons Angelo and Johanne and probably by another Neapolitan captain, who had served with him under John, duke of Calabria and Lorraine, in the War of the Public Weal against Louis XI in 1465, Jacobo Galeoto.[2]

The bustle and stir of this Burgundian recruitment resounded far and wide. Louis XI wrote to Galeazzo Maria Sforza, duke of Milan, asking him not to permit the count of Campobasso and others to pass through Milan on their way to Duke Charles, continuing 'and if you can manage to have them waylaid you will do me singular pleasure'.[3] Charles the Bold, on the other hand, wrote to Galeazzo on 10 November 1472 seeking free passage and assistance with lodgings for Cola and his men. Rumour spread that the duke had actually succeeded in signing on the great Colleoni;[4] a rumour that was not without a solid foundation in fact. In January 1473 Charles the Bold not only issued letters permitting the *condottiere* to bear the arms of Burgundy, he also drew up and issued a contract which Bartolomeo ratified at Malpaga on 25 February 1474, signing it with his own hand. This indeed seemed a brilliant coup for Charles the Bold. At a cost of 150,000 gold ducats per annum Bartolomeo Colleoni 'of Anjou and of Burgundy' as he now proudly described himself, having formerly been in the pay of the house of Anjou, promised to

[1] BN Coll. de Bourgogne MS. 59, fos. 38–40. For the next sentence, see ASM Pot. est. Borgogna 515/74–5.
[2] On Cola and Jacobo see respectively Croce, *Vite di avventure*, 47–186 (to which Calmette, *Études médiévales*, 208–14 adds little) and Perret, *BEC* lii (1891), 590–614.
[3] *Lettres de Louis XI*, v. 103–5, and for the next sentence, ASM Pot. est. Borgogna 515/57.
[4] See, for example, ASM Pot. est. Borgogna 515/80 and 83.

bring 1,000 Italian men-at-arms and 1,500 foot to serve the duke of Burgundy for three years.[1] But alas, Venice still obstinately refused to allow Bartolomeo to go, in spite of repeated requests, embassies and negotiations organized by Charles the Bold throughout the next two years. In spite of this setback, however, his recruiting campaign in Italy was a spectacular success. Already in April 1473, while Jacobo Galeoto was still enrolling captains around Reggio, including 'Olivero da Somo, Jacomo da Mantua, Antonello da Verona' and others, the Burgundian authorities in Dijon were arranging for the sum of 14,500 crowns to be paid over, at Geneva, to 200 lances from Lombardy under the command of the brothers Antonio and Petro de Lignana.[2] The former, Antonio, had already been for some time at the Burgundian court as a chamberlain and councillor; a third brother, Augosto de Lignana, abbot of Casanova, was one of the duke's most trusted and experienced diplomats.

The summer campaign of 1472, against France, was the last fought by Charles the Bold virtually without Italians.[3] Thereafter they formed an ever increasing proportion of the troops of the ordinance. Indeed on those fateful campaigns of 1476, against the Swiss and their allies, the Burgundian army can appropriately be described as predominantly Italian, certainly as far as its senior officers were concerned, and their numbers were maintained, or increased, by further recruiting drives, especially in the spring of 1476, in Piedmont and elsewhere in North Italy.

Yielding second place in Duke Charles's affections and respect only to the Italians, were the English, comprising mainly mounted archers. Early in the reign these valued mercenaries were in small numbers only. Some English troops arrived in time to take part in the 1467 campaign against Liège, others were countermanded. In 1468

---

[1] The original copy of the contract, with Bartolomeo's signature, is in BN MS. fr. 5040, f. 65a–b. Other documents concerning Charles and Colleoni are in this MS., fos. 67, 69, 117–121b and 125–9 and in BN MS. fr. 5041, no. 24; see de Barante, *Histoire des ducs*, ii. 422 n. 2.

[2] ASM Pot. est. Borgogna 515/86 and BN Coll. de Bourgogne MS. 59, f. 41.

[3] AGR CC25542, the account of the *trésorier des guerres* for 24 March to 31 August 1472, makes no mention of Italians except for two payments of 1 October 1472 to Troylo de Rossano and some payments to the count of St. Martin who, like Antonio de Lignana, had been a chamberlain-councillor of Charles before he became a captain. The troops with Nicolas, duke of Lorraine, were led by the 'German bailiff' of Lorraine, Jehan Wisse, lord of Gerbéviller, and were surely not Italians (fos. 72 and 74). For recruitment of Italians in 1476 see *Dépêches des ambassadeurs milanais*, ii. 139–40, etc.

English troops were said to be ready, but they were not called on. The English contingent in the 1472 army was small: only eleven men-at-arms, twenty-seven mounted archers and sixteen archers on foot are mentioned in the war treasurer's account,[1] but King Edward was supposed to have sent Charles two or three thousand more in the autumn of 1472. Others certainly followed in the spring of 1473, distinguishing themselves at the siege of Nijmegen in July 1473 by occupying the Nieuwstad gate and raising their banners on it. But they were not supported by Charles the Bold's other troops and were forced to withdraw with heavy losses. On this occasion King Edward was again said to have sent these troops himself, as he certainly did the 1,000 archers and thirteen men-at-arms ordered on 30 March 1474 to be mustered at Southwark by Sir John Parre and John Sturgeon Esq. At the siege of Neuss English archers distinguished themselves again, and from at least that time onwards Sir John Middleton was serving as captain of one of Charles's companies of ordinance, which was almost certainly entirely made up of Enhlishmen. In the autumn of 1475 over 2,000 Englishmen took service with Charles the Bold instead of returning home with their king and the rest of the English army after the signature of the treaty of Picquigny. It was on this occasion that Charles remarked that they might just as well stay with him and fight against the French as massacre each other in England.[2] Right to the bitter end at least ten 100-strong companies of mounted English archers formed part of the Burgundian army, their remnants straggling home in late January and February 1477 after the battle of Nancy with much depleted ranks. For instance John Turnbull, or Tourneboulle as the Burgundian accounting official rendered it, only contrived to bring back thirty-four men out of the ninety-six-strong company of which he was *centenier* or captain.

German mercenaries serving with Charles were much less important than English, but one cannot forbear to mention the author of one of the most vivid and entertaining contemporary German chronicles, Wilwolt von Schaumburg, who signed on with Charles at Trier in

[1] AGR CC25542, fos. 16, 18 and 74. For what precedes, see above p. 18 (1467) and de Haynin, *Mémoires*, ii. 71. For the rest of the sentence, see de Commynes, *Mémoires*, ed. Dupont, iii. 296 and transcript of Innsbruck LRA Urk. I. 8208 in RTA material. For the next sentence, see van Berchen, *Gelderse kroniek*, 133 and *Cronycke van Hollandt*, f. 336 and, for what follows, *Foedera*, xi. 791 = *Cal. patent rolls. Edward IV, Henry VI*, 440.
[2] ASM Pot. est. Borgogna 516–17/99 = *Cal. state papers. Venice*, i. 133–4. For what follows, see AGR CC25543, fos. 27–37 and 243–50.

October 1473 with the Emperor's permission. After serving with the duke, notably at Neuss and in Lorraine, 'summer and winter for two whole years in the field' Wilwolt and his German friends took four weeks' leave to buy new equipment and clothes: to refit, in fact. But while they were at Speyer doing this they received news of the Burgundian defeat at Grandson and resolved thereupon to quit the Burgundian army for good.[1]

Continuing to exist side by side with the companies of ordinance and the foreign mercenaries but called out for particular campaigns on a temporary basis only, were the lances of the ducal vassals or 'enfieffed lords' as they were frequently called. These troops did not, however, form a military entity entirely separate from the troops of the ordinance, for a number of vassals served as volunteers in the ordinance companies or were drafted into them. Nor were these so-called 'feudal' forces necessarily entirely feudal for, in the ducal ordinances convoking them, non-vassals were summoned as well. Thus in 1469 everyone 'accustomed to bear arms' was ordered to turn out with them, and on 30 April 1475 Charles the Bold ordered the immediate convoking 'of our loyal vassals and subjects of Luxembourg'.[2] As a matter of fact, the 'vassals and subjects' of Luxembourg were by no means excessively loyal, and their reluctance to serve the duke brought forth on 29 May 1475 a characteristically lucid and forthright declaration from him, addressed to Claude de Neuchâtel, lord du Fay, his lieutenant in Luxembourg:

> As regards the nobles, whom you found [have turned out] in small numbers, and who have [only] agreed to place themselves in the towns and frontier places for the defence of the country on condition that they are paid, we wish you to point out to them that, according to natural obligation and otherwise, all subjects are bound to defend their country, where they have their belongings, lands, lordships, wives and children. Since this defence is just as much, or even more, for their own benefit as for ours and since they are not leaving the country but staying in it in the towns and frontier places only, they ought not to demand or require any payment or allowance. Certainly it is true that, if we wanted to lead them on campaign outside their country or place them in garrison

---

[1] Von Schaumburg, *Die Geschichten und Taten*, especially 16 and 31. Wilwolt says that it was the news of Héricourt which caused him to leave Duke Charles's army, but this is quite inconsistent with the rest of his narrative: Grandson must have been meant.

[2] De Waurin, *Croniques*, ed. Hardy, v. 577 and *Recueil du Fay*, 115. The extract which follows is from *Recueil du Fay*, 121.

so that they could fight outside the country and in enemy territory, we would be bound to pay them their wages as is customary. But merely for the defence of the land, which is to their own advantage, it is certain that they ought to ask nothing. Nonetheless, if they will not accept this, negotiate with them for their pay at the lowest rate you can.

Charles the Bold's efforts to utilize the feudal, if not general, obligation of military service as effectively as possible included a survey and registration of fiefs and their values, undertaken in 1469–1470, and a system of financial contributions in lieu of service, that is to say, the levy of shield-money or scutage.[1] These efforts included too, an investigation into the condition of the available manpower which revealed, for example, a centenarian and another old man aged ninety, who, among others, were thought to be too weak and aged properly to perform military service. One gentleman of Luxembourg was excused by Duke Charles himself, on the unusual grounds that he was too fat. But, in spite of these efforts, the general levy of vassals and subjects was cumbersome and time-consuming. It took more than two months to bring together the army for the Liège campaign of 1467 and, even then, the troops from the southern territories failed to arrive in time. Later, in 1470, the device was tried of retaining these troops in a state of readiness, to be reviewed each month, on half pay. They, or elements of them, served to the end of Charles's reign, but they became more unwilling and more ineffective as time wore on, refusing to turn out in the first place, arguing about their pay and conditions of service, and going home without permission. They were excelled in these attitudes and activities only by the militia of the Flemish and other towns, which formed another distinct section of the duke of Burgundy's armies.

The pikemen of the Flemish towns and villages proved of no more value to Charles the Bold than they had been to his predecessors. As always, they were dilatory in the extreme in taking the field and inordinately hurried in returning home. When the duke was outside Amiens in March 1471 they arrived one afternoon after dinner and were drawn up and inspected by Charles himself, who demonstrated considerable pleasure in their arrival, addressing them with the

---

[1] But see p. 409 below and, besides the works cited on p. 197 n. 1 above, *IAGR CC* iv. 144–51. For what follows, see de la Chauvelays, *Les armées de Charles le Téméraire*, 13–18, Dumay, *MSE* xi (1882), 75–163, and *Recueil du Fay*, 130.

words; 'Mes enfants, vous êtes les bienvenus.'[1] The veteran cam-
paigner and chronicler, Jehan de Wavrin, described them on that
campaign as follows:

> The duke prohibited anyone from leaving camp without his per-
> mission. According to common report there were more than 100,000
> armed heads in it, without including four or five thousand fellows sent
> from Flanders, each having a sallet, jacket, sword and pike or a long
> lance with a slender shaft and a long sharp spear-head, cutting on three
> sides. They were on foot and are called pikemen because they know
> better than anyone how to handle pikes. The Flemings had recruited
> them in the villages of their country and paid them for a month. From
> each castellany [came] one or two men-at-arms to lead these pikemen,
> every ten of whom had a *disenier* whom they obeyed. These pikes make
> very convenient poles for placing a spike between two archers against
> the terrifying efforts of cavalry trying to break their ranks, for there is
> no horse which, if struck with a pike in the chest, will not unfailingly die.
> These pikemen can also approach and attack horsemen from the side and
> pierce them right through, nor is there any armour however good that
> they cannot pierce or break.

The ducal secretary, Jehan de Molesmes, writing to Dijon from
Amiens on 25 March 1471, echoed de Wavrin, claiming that the
French feared these pikemen because they killed their horses. The
sorry truth is that they were ignominiously put to flight by the French
on at least two occasions while the Burgundian army was near
Amiens.[2] From 1471 onwards the Flemings paid cash to their duke
instead of performing military service. Other foot-soldiers served in
Charles the Bold's armies and sometimes earned a better reputation
than the Flemings. Antwerp was asked to field thirty men-at-arms
and thirty crossbowmen for the campaign against France in summer
1472. Even 'the lands of Liège and of Looz', which were not Burgundian territory, were asked to contribute 400 pikemen in January
1476. Privileges were bartered for military service: Malines, providing
'thirty good fighting men, tough strong chaps, in good fettle', was
granted by the duke on 3 July 1476 freedom from tolls in Holland
and Zeeland for her citizens.

[1] De Barante, *Histoire des ducs*, ii. 371 n. 2. The extract following is from de
Waurin, *Croniques*, ed. Hardy, v. 625–6.
[2] Gachard, *Rapport sur les archives de Dijon*, 160 and de Haynin, *Mémoires*,
ii. 120 and 122. For the next sentence, see Blockmans, *Staten en Leden*,
161–70. For what follows, see Prims, *Geschiedenis van Antwerpen*, vi (1).
154, Gorissen, *De Raadkamer te Maastricht*, 203, *IAM* ii. 224, and *Boergoensche charters*, 150.

The forces attached to, or forming part of, the duke's court or household constituted a body of élite troops which was given pride of place in the Burgundian order of battle. The exact number and distribution of men in this category varied from time to time. In May 1476, on the eve of the campaign which led to the disastrous defeat at Murten, its main elements, totalling over 2,000 combatants, may have been as follows:[1]

HOUSEHOLD TROOPS IN MAY 1476

Description	Number of men
Forty mounted chamberlains and gentlemen of the duke's chamber with the ducal standard	40
Four cavalry squadrons of men-at-arms of the four estates or offices of the court	? 200
Four cavalry squadrons of men-at-arms of the guard under Olivier de la Marche, captain of the guard	? 250
Four 100-strong companies of mounted English archers of the guard also under Olivier de la Marche, called 'the squadrons of the guard'	404 (actually 392)
Four 100-strong companies of mounted English archers attached to the squadrons of the guard	404 (actually 388)
Four 100-strong companies of 'ordinary household infantry'	404 (up to strength)
Four companies of 'extraordinary household infantry'	404 (actually 332)

These household troops can be divided into several distinct groups. First, there were the courtiers and court officials, that is the chamberlains, the equerries of the four estates and so on, who were and always had been obliged to perform military service as part of their traditional courtly duty. Secondly, contingents of English archers and a body of men-at-arms formed the duke's life-guard or bodyguard and the guard. Thirdly, certain units were attached from time to time to the court by way of reinforcement for the household troops proper. Hence the additional companies detailed above.

[1] De la Chauvelays, *Armées des trois premiers ducs*, 315–18, and AGR CC25543, fos. 231a–232b etc.; compare the list of names, dating from winter 1474–5, in de Lannoy, *IG* xxi (1966), 120–6.

Much vaunted but in fact of limited value was the artillery of Charles the Bold. Towns which fell to him, like Liège and Nijmegen did not do so as a result of artillery bombardment; towns that successfully held out against him, Beauvais and Neuss above all, did so in spite of the utmost efforts of the Burgundian artillery. In almost all the field engagements involving Charles the Bold or his armies both sides used artillery as well as hand-guns, but the rate of fire of these weapons was far too slow for them to have any real effect. Indeed often there was time for a single artillery salvo only as battle was joined. The Burgundian artillery was kept in store in places like Lille and Dijon and brought out when needed, augmented by pieces borrowed or otherwise appropriated from towns and sometimes private individuals. When Charles the Bold conquered Nancy in autumn 1475 the fortifications were methodically stripped of their artillery, which was stored in the *hôtel de l'artillerie* there and subsequently used against the Swiss along with other artillery formerly belonging to the dukes of Lorraine. In 1475 the artillery required by the duke, apparently on the autumn campaign which led to the conquest of Lorraine and the above-mentioned fall of Nancy, comprised six bombards with twelve stones for them, six bombardells with twelve stones, six mortars with twelve stones, the serpentine called Lambillon with 100 balls, ten *courtaux* with 2,000 stones for them, and sixteen large serpentines and forty-eight small ones. A few years earlier a ducal official had set out the number of horses needed for the transport of the different types of cannon and their missiles in winter.[1]

Description	*Number of horses needed*
A bombard, in winter	24
A bombardell	14
A *courtaut*	8
The great serpentine	8
Fifty medium-sized serpentines	4
The hundred small serpentines	2
Stones for a bombard, weighing 163 lbs. each	4
Thirty stones for the *courtaux*	4
A mortar with its carriage	4
Powder casks	4

[1] For this paragraph and what follows see *IADNB* viii. 257–61 and, in general, besides the works cited on p. 197 n. 1 above, Garnier, *L'artillerie des ducs de Bourgogne*.

The capture by the Swiss at Grandson and Murten of a large part of Charles the Bold's artillery train caused a sensation, but contemporaries differ widely in their statements about the exact number of pieces involved. It may be safe to hazard a guess that Charles had over 100 cannon with him before the battle of Grandson and lost nearly all of them there. At Murten he may have had as many as 400. Today what remains of this artillery is preserved in seven museums, six of them in Switzerland, pride of place going to those at La Neuveville and Murten, each of which possesses several entire well-preserved Burgundian cannon.[1] It seems that Charles the Bold's artillery was thoroughly up to date, though several of the surviving pieces have certainly been modernized in the process of restoration. Some at least had trunnions and many, if not most, were wheeled. A proportion fired iron cannon-balls, and in nearly all of them the barrel was strengthened with iron rings fixed at intervals along its length.

Some mention has already been made, in connection with the famous ordinance of 1473, of the various banners and emblems employed by Charles the Bold in his armies.[2] The accounts show that in 1467 and 1468 the ducal standard which was carried into battle against Liège was of white taffeta painted in oils with 'a picture of St. George, mounted on a horse, fighting the dragon' which was breathing fire in all directions. Inevitably, it also bore the duke's motto *Je l'ay emprins*, 'I have undertaken it', together with St. Andrew's crosses and other Burgundian emblems. At the same time guidons and cornets were painted for the archers and others, but here St. George was represented fighting on foot.[3] Similar standards were employed on subsequent campaigns. In autumn 1474, for example, the duke had some 'large standards with pictures of St. George, guidons and cornets for the different estates of the household,

---

[1] See especially Deuchler, *Burgunderbeute*, 302–32, and Wyss and others, *Die Burgunderbeute*, 167–78, both with illustrations and references.
[2] Above, p. 209.
[3] ADN B2064, f. 263 (partly printed La Fons de Mélicocq, *BSHF* (2) i (1857–8), 299) and B2068, fos. 246b–249. For what follows see Deuchler, *Burgunderbeute*, 222–74 and 370–4, and Wyss and others, *Die Burgunderbeute*, 153–6. See too, in general, Brusten, *JBHM* xxxvii and xxxviii (1957–8), 118–32, and Martin, *BSAMD* (1949–51), 24–6.

archers of the bodyguard, and for his guard' made.[1] Each of the twenty companies of ordinance then in existence was provided with a distinctive standard of its own, with its own saint and colour: St. Sebastian on a gold ground, St. Adrian on azure, St. Christopher on silver, St. Anthony on red, and so forth. Naturally every standard had its sprinkling of flints, steels and flames, emblems of Philip the Good, with a St. Andrew's cross formed by two arrows or knobbly poles, not to mention Charles the Bold's motto. At Grandson and Murten the Swiss not only captured square heraldic banners, triangular decorated standards like those just mentioned, and guidons, pennons and cornets on the battlefield itself; they also found and appropriated whole chests of them. Few of these fragile but beautiful military emblems have remained intact to this day. What survives, in fragmentary form only, has been repeatedly patched and repaired. But fortunately many of them were exquisitely and accurately copied and inventoried by their proud possessers, the communal authorities of Luzern, Glarus, St. Gall and elsewhere, before their brilliant colours faded irretrievably and their silk material disintegrated and decayed.

Although there was a special 'governor of the duke's tents and pavilions',[2] these scarcely formed a separate branch of the Burgundian army, for they, and all kinds of other necessary equipment, tended to be included with the artillery. For the 1475 campaign in Lorraine it seems that Charles the Bold needed three pavilions and a tent for himself and 400 pavilions for his household troops and companies of ordinance, not to mention a portable wooden fortification made at Malines. He normally lodged when on campaign in one or more wooden buildings which could be taken apart and put together again. Thus in 1472 a Lille merchant supplied canvas to cover the roof of two *maisons* of *bois de Danemarche*, presumably pine, which the duke had taken with him on campaign against Liège and France. Such a structure seems to figure in early illustrations of the battle of Murten,

[1] De Comines, *Mémoires*, ed. Lenglet du Fresnoy, ii. 214. This passage, another part of which is paraphrased in the next sentence, is not from the text of de Commynes, as Deuchler would have us believe (*Burgunderbeute*, 373 repeated in Wyss and others, *Die Burgunderbeute*, 154), but from the annotated itinerary of Duke Charles compiled from documentary material by D. Godefroy and entitled *Extrait d'une ancienne chronique*.

[2] *Recueil du Fay*, 131. For what follows, see *IADNB* viii. 260; *IADNB* iv. 241 and Renet, *Beauvais et le Beauvaisis*, 153; Deuchler, *Burgunderbeute*, 365–8; and below, p. 387.

perched on the summit of the hillock now called Bois Domingue overlooking the town. After the battle of Grandson the Swiss found two silk tents belonging to Charles the Bold richly decorated with precious stones and gold flames. One was divided between Bern and Schwyz. The section taken to Bern was given to the cathedral of St. Vincent and made into vestments.

This brief survey of Charles the Bold's armies would be incomplete without some mention of the savage disciplinary measures awaiting defaulters of all kinds, especially towards the end of the reign. On 10 May 1475 the duke wrote from Neuss to his lieutenant in Luxembourg ordering him to arrest everyone who had been inside the castle of Pierrefort when it surrendered. Those who were found guilty of arranging the surrender were to be executed and quartered forthwith.[1] A similar fate awaited deserters, though early in the reign they may sometimes have escaped with imprisonment. After Grandson Charles ordered his lieutenant in Luxembourg to round up and execute all the deserters he could find. He added that the troops then on their way to his camp at Lausanne were to come to him as quickly as possible 'without staying anywhere en route, and if they delay in doing this our pleasure is that you proceed against them in the manner described above'. On 14 October 1476 the duke appointed a special officer to arrest criminals and deserters, Jehan de Dadizele, then lieutenant of the sovereign-bailiff of Flanders. He was empowered, everywhere in the duke's lands, to arrest 'all soldiers, of whatever condition or estate' who have returned home 'after receiving wages or pay from us, without leave and permission from us or our chiefs and captains'. Those found guilty of inciting others to desert were to be put to death at once, 'as an example to the rest'. Those found guilty of deserting only were to be sent back to rejoin the army after being held for a few days. If necessary, Jehan de Dadizele was to secure the extradition of malefactors and deserters from 'places outside our jurisdiction' and territory. Finally on 4 December 1476, only a month before his death, Charles the Bold issued fresh instructions for dealing with deserters which the nineteenth-century Belgian historian Kervyn de Lettenhove suggested might be taken as

---

[1] *Recueil du Fay*, 116. For the next sentence, see for example ADN B2068, fos. 286a–b and 311. What follows is from *Recueil du Fay*, 134 and de Dadizele, *Mémoires*, 50–4 (compare Kervyn de Lettenhove, *Histoire de Flandre*, v. 206 n. 1).

evidence that the duke was going out of his mind. This curious and somewhat frenzied document reads in part as follows:

Charles, by the grace of God duke of Burgundy, of Lothier, of Brabant, of Limbourg, of Luxembourg and of Guelders, count of Flanders, of Artois, of Burgundy palatine, of Hainault, of Holland, of Zeeland, of Namur and of Zutphen, marquis of the Holy Empire, lord of Frisia, of Salins and of Malines. To our sovereign-bailiff of Flanders or his lieutenant, greetings. We recently commanded expressly enough in other letters patent and close of ours that all foot-soldiers and other troops sent [from the Low Countries] to serve with us who had since then stopped on the way without coming to us or who, after they had come, had returned without leave to their homes or wherever they thought fit, thus scorning our service and proving themselves false and disloyal towards us, were to be constrained to return to us and come back into our service or, in default of this, were to be arrested and then executed as an example to others. Since, however, no result or obedience has been achieved by this and also because from such people, who are false and disloyal to us and who have not only stolen the pay they received from us but also left our army and person in danger . . . no useful service can ever result, we have no desire or need to retain them. Therefore we order, command and expressly enjoin you . . . to take bodily and arrest all that you can find of the said soldiers, horse or foot, who have deserted from our army, wherever they can be caught and apprehended outside holy places, without sparing any . . . and promptly carry out criminal execution on them, inflicting the extreme penalty on them as traitors and disloyal to us, without in any way receiving them or exhorting them to return to us. If they cannot be taken and apprehended you are to summon and adjure them . . . to appear at a fixed and suitable date before our well loved and loyal [councillors] the president and members of our *chambre de conseil* in Flanders, on penalty of exile and seizure of body and goods, and you are to certify the said president and members of our said *chambre de conseil* in Flanders of the said summonses. We order them to carry out the said criminal punishment on all those of this condition appearing before them, putting them to death without any dissimulation, and in the case of the default and contumacy of those summoned, they are to banish them for ever outside all our lands and lordships . . . in such a way that no relative or friend of the banished person can ever succeed to their belongings.

Moreover because we have heard that some of the said deserters have been secretly advised to desert by people in our army . . . we want them to be interrogated by all methods before execution as to how and by whom they were encouraged and persuaded to desert, and for what reason.

Moreover we wish and command you to send a statement of every

action you take in this affair to us, or to our chancellor and the members
of our grand council to send to us, without any fault or fraud.
Given in our siege before Nancy, 4 December 1476.

While historians have vied with each other in acclaiming Charles
the Bold's military genius, and a good deal, though by no means
enough, scholarly attention has been devoted to his armies, the
Burgundian navy in his reign has been largely neglected. Not that
there was any maritime equivalent of the companies of ordinance,
for warships were not manned on a permanent basis. Instead, they
were hired or commandeered as required. Thus in 1468 Charles the
Bold retained some Breton warships at Sluis for use in his navy,[1]
and in 1469 ships were chartered from the Spanish, Portuguese and
Genoese merchants in Flanders. Although Burgundian warships put
to sea, mainly to protect Flemish and Dutch fishing vessels against
French warships and pirates, in 1472 and 1475 and in other years, the
most important naval expedition of Duke Charles's reign was seen
off from the neighbourhood of Flushing (Vlissingen) in early June
1470 by the duke in person, with orders to stop Richard Neville, earl
of Warwick, from doing any further damage to Burgundian shipping
and also to hinder his return from France to England.[2] In fact,
Warwick's return was effected without any opposition from the
Burgundian fleet, and its captain, Henrik van Borselen, was accused
by Charles at the chapter of the Golden Fleece in 1473 of neglecting
his duty. The old man died in March 1474 after a distinguished
career. He had been a knight of the Order of the Golden Fleece since
1445 and, as lord of Veere, or Ter Vere as it was then called, he was
a major maritime power in fifteenth-century Holland and Zeeland.
He was often described as an admiral, but his official title seems in
fact to have been 'stadholder-general and captain of the duke of
Burgundy at sea'. His sailing orders, which bear comparison with the
marching orders and other ordinances for Duke Charles's armies,
may have been issued in the early summer of 1470. They are rightly
renowned in the annals of naval warfare as among the earliest known
instructions of their kind to have come down to us.[3]

[1] ADN B2068, f. 117. For what follows, see Degryse, *MAMB* xvii (1965),
163–72, de la Roncière, *Histoire de la marine française*, ii. 325–68, and pp.
61–4 above.
[2] For this and the next sentence, see AOGV Reg. 3, f. 23b.
[3] Printed in French and Dutch in de Jonge, *Nederlandsche zeewezen*, i.
736–40. My translation is taken from the Dutch text, which is evidently the
original.

Hereafter follow the ordinances made by my lord the count of Grandpré, lord of Ter Vere, appointed by my lord the duke of Burgundy stadholder-general and captain of the fleet which he is now fitting out, in order to make known the way things should be done, how to recognize each other's ships at sea, and how they should sail; [ordinances] which each of them must take care to obey and bear in mind so that no difficulties arise through their neglect.[1]

First my aforesaid lord of Ter Vere will give and allot to all ships of the above-mentioned fleet, until otherwise ordered by him and his captains, a cry or password for each night, as follows. On Sunday he will give the word Jesus Christ, on Monday, our Lady, on Tuesday St. Mark, on Wednesday St. John the Baptist, on Thursday St. James, on Friday the Holy Cross, on Saturday, St. Nicholas. And in order to receive and know this cry or password, every evening each ship is to approach as near as possible, as best it can, either down-wind or against the wind, to the captain's ship, taking care to cause no damage or hindrance to the other ships, and solely for the purpose of ascertaining the cry of the night or password.

None of the above-mentioned ships may go or sail up-wind of the captain's ship on pain of his indignation and such further penalty as he shall see fit to ordain.

If at night the captain wants to put up a bonnet he will place a lighted lantern on the poop [of his ship], and there the lantern will remain until each of the other ships has made him a similar signal. When the captain decides to take down the bonnet he will light a lantern in the same place on the poop and move it up and down until the other ships make a similar signal to him. If the force of the wind makes it necessary to strike or reduce sail, the captain will set two lighted lanterns amidships, side by side, until the other ships make a similar signal to him. If he wants to make sail by night he will light three lanterns side by side amidships as above-mentioned. If he wants to go about or alter course at night he will light two lanterns in the poop, moving one up and the other down, until the other ships make a similar signal to him.

If by night any ship is seen or discovered at sea, whoever finds or sees it is to light a lantern on his top and leave it there until the other ships have made him a similar signal. And if there is more than one ship he is to move the above-mentioned lantern up and down as many times as there are ships. But if the ships are so close to him that he cannot place

---

[1] In place of most of the above, the French text has the following, which reads like one of Charles the Bold's preambles: 'Because discipline and good government is the beginning and end of all the good in the world, and on the contrary disorder without rule is the cause of evil, great damage and perdition, the said captain commands that the ordinances written below shall be firmly obeyed.'

the lantern on his top he is to fire as many shots of a veuglaire as he has seen ships. Then all the other ships are to approach him to arrange themselves in order and do whatever is commanded by their captain.

If it happens, which God forbid, that one or more of the ships of the fleet lose their way or get so far from the others that they are out of sight of each other and then by chance they meet together again, the westernmost ship is to display a banner on his right-hand yard and keep it there until the other ships make him a similar signal. After this the ship or ships which first made this signal are to take down the banner and display it on the other side of the yard, on the left.

The first of the ships to see or find any sail or foreign ship at sea is to display a banner on its top and keep it there until the other ships have made similar signals. The same shall be done by those first sighting or discovering land.

If it happens that the captain finds it necessary for the fleet to arm itself, by day he will fly a pennon on the front of his poop, by night he will light four lanterns, two above the other two. When this is done, the other ships are to approach the captain's ship. At the first sound of trumpets everyone is to arm himself; at the next sound of trumpets, everyone is to take up his position and station as ordered by his captain; and at the third sound of trumpets another pennon or signal, [the one] used for going into battle, is to be substituted for the above-mentioned pennon. And then everyone is to do the best he can to harm the enemy.[1] No one is to be so bold as to hold back or do the contrary of what his captain has ordered and commanded, on pain of losing his life. And likewise the mates, councillors and other officers of the ships shall be subject to the aforesaid obedience and penalty.

Anyone who starts to pillage the enemy, or otherwise takes to the water or [boards] another ship before the entire [enemy fleet] has been completely defeated and conquered, shall likewise suffer the death penalty.

When the captain wishes to speak with any of the other ships by day, he shall display a banner on the poop, down-wind and, if it is by night, he shall light three lanterns in the middle of the poop, one above the other. When that is done, all the other ships are to approach him in such a way that it is possible to speak without the ships doing any damage to one another.

---

[1] For this sentence the French version has: 'And then, in the name of the Holy Spirit, they must fight and attack the enemy heartily and with good courage for the honour of our most redoubted prince Monsieur the duke, in such a way as vigorously to obtain the victory.'

CHAPTER SEVEN

Clients and Partisans of Burgundy

It is the purpose of this chapter to say something of Charles the Bold's principal agents or auxiliaries. Who were the people on whom he chiefly relied to realize his projects and ambitions, to assist him in the government of his state, to support him in case of need? Of course his officials, his councillors and his captains were of supreme importance in this respect. His military activities depended for their success on men like Cola de Monforte, count of Campobasso, and Jacobo Galeoto.[1] His diplomacy was entirely dependent on the skill and experience of clerics like the abbot of Casanova, Augusto de Lignana, and noblemen like Guillaume de Rochefort, expert on the affairs of Savoy and Venice. His finances and financial administration were efficiently organized by men like his old tutor Anthoine Haneron, and Guilbert de Ruple who successively held the three highest financial offices of *argentier* or treasurer, receiver-general of all finances, and *trésorier des guerres*. Legists like the Fleming Philippe Wielant and the Burgundian Jehan Carondelet saw to it that justice was done. These two and others were promoted in 1473 to the staff of the highest court in the land, the *Parlement* of Malines. Above all, the head of the Burgundian civil service, the chancellor, who supervised the entire administrative machinery, played a crucial role in aiding and abetting the duke's plans and projects. From 22 May 1471 this vital post was filled with distinction by Guillaume Hugonet, lord of Saillant.[2] All these men were salaried officers of the duke: captains and bureaucrats who worked entirely within the framework of the ducal service and employment. The subject of this chapter is in the main a different category of person, those who served or supported

---

[1] See p. 215 n. 2 above and, for many of those mentioned in what follows, above pp. 4–5.
[2] On him, see Paravicini, in *Festschrift für H. Heimpel*, ii. 443–81.

the duke either because they were members of his family, or because they were clients or allied princes, or because he chose to employ them as governors with extended powers in one or other of his territories or, lastly, because it was in their financial interests to do so. In general terms, these people were princes or nobles from the Burgundian geographical sphere of influence, that is from the Franco–German borderlands between Holland and Piedmont. It is the identity and role of these for the most part aristocratic satellites of Burgundian power that is the subject of this chapter.

It must be said at once that these Burgundian satellites did not form any kind of system; nor was their loyalty retained in any particular manner other than by straightforward financial remuneration, though some of them, especially members of the duke's family, seem to have received no payments of any kind. Others, the governors or lieutenants of the duke, were paid substantial salaries, or pensions as the accounting officers called them. None, so far as may be ascertained, became fief-rentiers of the duke. That is to say, they did not do homage in return for their pensions.

In view of the somewhat sinister reputation which has been given to Charles the Bold, of being the victim of treachery on a more or less systematic scale, it would seem appropriate to emphasize here that the clientele under discussion was on the whole firmly loyal to the duke. The defectors, or traitors, such as they were, were inspired by widely differing motives and were by no means simply a product of Louis XI's allegedly diabolical enticements. In fact defection, from Burgundy to France or vice versa, had always been commonplace. Numerous too were the cases of loyalties divided between the two in a single family or wavering from one to another in a single individual. Moreover, in considering the phenomenon of treachery at this time, we must bear in mind that de Commynes was by no means the only contemporary to have had a complex about it. Louis XI was extremely suspicious by nature, and Charles the Bold himself seemed to see a traitor round every corner, most of them as he supposed encouraged by the arch-traitor Louis XI. The duke's favourite forum for exposing and condemning his courtiers for dubious relations with France was the chapter of the Golden Fleece. In 1468, apart from an elaborate and vituperative tirade against the Croys, Charles had Henrik van Borselen, lord of Veere, accused of accepting an office and a pension from the king of France and ordered him to surrender these royal favours. In 1473 Henrik was in trouble again and was apparently suspected of French sympathies; Philip of Savoy, lord of

Bresse, was accused of going over to France, rightly in point of fact; and no less a person than Anthony, bastard of Burgundy, was accused by Charles, even though he felt sure of his loyalty, of accepting monetary gifts from Louis XI, again quite rightly.[1]

In the 1430s Burgundian nobles had deserted Philip the Good for Charles VII. In or before 1467 some French captains defected to Burgundy from Louis XI. Families like the Croys, the la Trémoilles, the Chalons and the Luxembourgs, with interests and lands in both France and Burgundy, had long divided their allegiances between the two. Two of these families will come under notice in what follows: a third, the Chalons, is particularly instructive. When Louis III de Chalon, prince of Orange, died in 1463 his succession was disputed between his three sons by two different wives. The eldest, Guillaume de Chalon, prince of Orange, refused to accept his virtual disinheritance by his father in favour of the elder of his half-brothers, Louis de Chalon, lord of Châteauguyon. In applying to King Louis XI for 'advice, comfort and help' Guillaume complained that, three days before his father's death, his younger step-brother Hugues had made off with his father's *trésor*, comprising title-deeds, jewels and other valuables. Three weeks later the other step-brother, Louis, went to Charles, then count of Charolais, took service at the Burgundian court, and began litigating against him in the duke's court, or grand council. Moreover, continued Guillaume, when his son Jehan de Chalon, lord of Arguel, complained to Charles the Bold, he was expelled from the court and even exiled from Burgundian territory altogether while he, Guillaume, received orders from Duke Charles to quit his principality of Orange and come and live in Burgundy and perform his obligation of military service to the duke.[2] In these circumstances, we can hardly speak of treachery. Naturally, while Guillaume, who died in 1475, and his son Jehan de Chalon, successive princes of Orange, gravitated to Louis XI, the brothers Louis and Hugues, successively lords of Châteauguyon, served Charles the Bold. Louis died gallantly fighting at Grandson, of which he was lord; Hugues, who was another of Charles the Bold's leading

[1] AOGV Reg. 2, fos. 7b and 49b–50 and Reg. 3, fos. 19b–20 and 20b–21b and 23b. For the next paragraph, see Vaughan, *Philip the Good*, 66 and Maupoint, *Journal*, 105–6; and, for the Chalons, Blondeau, *MSED* (8) iii (1908), 295 ff.
[2] BN MS. fr. 5040, fos. 41–43b.

captains, was sent off to Piedmont in April 1476 to recruit Italian mercenaries.[1]

Most of the treachery surrounding Charles the Bold was like that of Jehan de Chalon, in no sense personal to Charles. Some of the traitors defected before he became duke. His relative Jehan de Bourgogne, count of Nevers, for example, went over to Louis XI early in that king's reign. He and Charles were personal enemies, rivals at court and territorially.[2] Another early defector was the ecclesiastic Jehan Jouffroy, bishop of Arras and cardinal, who started working for Louis XI in or about 1461. A whole group of defectors emerged, in the two Burgundies especially, immediately after Charles the Bold's death, and some prominent Burgundian civil servants, most notably Guillaume de Rochefort who became chancellor of France, took service thereafter with Louis XI. But these men were neither commonplace turncoats nor were they motivated by bitterness or opposition against Charles the Bold. Men like Philippe Pot, Jehan de Neuchâtel, lord of Montagu, Philippe de Crèvecoeur, lord of Esquerdes, all of them knights of the Golden Fleece, and others, went over to France after 1477 because no other reasonable alternatives were open to them now that Louis XI had control of the duchy of Burgundy.

The treachery of some others is either of a dubious nature, as in the case of Guillaume Hugonet and Guillaume de Clugny,[3] or else venal, as in the case of Philippe de Commynes, one of the few who allowed his loyalties to be purchased. He was a minor figure at the Burgundian court until he deserted to Louis XI in the night of 7–8 August 1472. Later he won historical renown as the author of the most brilliant memoir of the age; a renown however which has always, in the minds of exact scholars, from Jacob de Meyere who percipiently but bluntly dubbed him a *falsus historicus*, down to Karl Bittmann, who has exposed his lies in detail, been tarnished by his

[1] *Dépêches des ambassadeurs milanais*, ii. 94–5.
[2] See above, pp. 9–10 and 14 and de Mandrot, *RH* xcii (1907), 1–45. For the next sentence, see Fierville, *Jean Jouffroy*, 9. For the rest of this paragraph, see Mangin, *PTSEC* (1936), 117–23 (de Rochefort), Chabeuf, *MSBGH* xviii (1902), 339–49 and Bouchard, *PTSEC* (1949), 23–7 (Pot), below p. 256 (de Neuchâtel), and Dufournet, *Destruction des mythes*, 46–9 (de Crèvecoeur).
[3] Paillard, *Procès du Chancelier Hugonet*, 57–69.

unparalleled mendacity.[1] A traitor himself, de Commynes goes out of his way to present another traitor to Charles the Bold, Cola de Monforte, count of Campobasso, in an unfavourable light, for he transforms this experienced and prudent captain, whom a distinguished modern compatriot, Benedetto Croce, thought only withdrew from and betrayed Charles at the last moment to save the lives of himself and his men, into a traitor and murderer of the worst kind who had long premeditated his inhuman crimes.

In the pages that follow a few other so-called traitors will be considered, but even if every scrap of evidence is taken into account, and magnified, the essential truth of the matter is that Charles the Bold was well and loyally served by a substantial group of friends, relatives, nobles, princes and supporters. Among the members of his immediate family two women were of some political significance: his mother the dowager-duchess of Burgundy, Isabel of Portugal, and his third wife, King Edward IV's sister Margaret of York. It has been suggested that Charles's mother may have exercised a moderating influence on her son during the early years of his reign, but no evidence for this has been adduced.[2] She did, however, come out of semi-retirement in 1467 to conduct important negotiations with England while Charles was on campaign against Liège and he certainly kept in touch with her in the years that followed, writing to her, for example, on 25 October 1468 with news of his second Liège campaign, and visiting her at Aire in Artois in 1469 and 1470. He was with her when she died there on 17 December 1471.

In the government of the Burgundian state under Charles the Bold the role of Margaret of York increased in importance towards the end when, along with her step-daughter Mary of Burgundy, she became established in the palace of Ten Walle at Ghent. From the spring of 1473 she was there almost continuously, apart from a visit to Bruges in January 1474 and a stay at Brussels through the second half of that

---

[1] Meyer, *Commentarii sive annales rerum flandricarum*, 364 and Bittmann, *Ludwig XI. und Karl der Kühne*. For what follows besides Bittmann see especially, *Lettres et négotiations de Philippe de Commines*, de Mandrot, *RH* lxxiii (1900), 241–57 and lxxiv (1900), 1–38, Croce, *Vite di avventure*, and Dufournet, *Destruction des mythes* (especially 54–64), and *La vie de Philippe de Commynes*. Charlier, *RUB* iv (1951–2), 324–8 and Cerioni, *NH* xiv (1962), 80–122 add little.

[2] Willard, *Miscellanea di studi e ricerche sul quattrocento francese*, 540–1. For what follows see Calmette, *AB* i (1929), 209–10 and ADN B2068, f. 337b and, in general, Lagrange, *ACFF* xlii (1938), 171–5.

year. In and after 1475 she was away from Ghent significantly only in July 1475 when she went off to Calais to see her brother, and in October 1476 when she went to The Hague. She seems to have taken governmental initiatives of her own at least from 1472, when we find her writing to Dijon asking for her nominee to be appointed *procureur* there. In 1473 the palace of Ten Walle, in Ghent, was being altered for her use and convenience. In the crisis of May 1475, caused by the French invasion of Artois and Hainault while the duke was away at Neuss, she emerged as an energetic and effective figure, welcoming the Portuguese ambassadors at Ghent while helping to organize the movement of troops for the defence of the land. On 13 May, for example, Jehan, lord of Dadizele, the sovereign-bailiff of Flanders, received orders from her to march out with all the troops he could muster to defend Artois against the invading French. During the whole of 1476 Margaret of York appears to have been closely and actively engaged, together with the chancellor Guillaume Hugonet, the bishop of Tournai Ferry de Clugny and Adolf of Cleves, lord of Ravenstein, lieutenant-general of Duke Charles in the Burgundian Low Countries, in raising finance, assembling troops, convoking the Estates of different territories as well as the States General and carrying out other governmental activities, in an atmosphere of crisis and turmoil.[1]

A family supporter and associate of Charles the Bold in the very first rank was Anthony, senior surviving bastard son of Philip the Good, lord of Beveren and count of La Roche-en-Ardenne. His supposed title or appellation of *le grand bastard* seems to be yet another fabrication derived from de Commynes.[2] In fact he was known to contemporaries as 'the bastard of Burgundy'. His private life followed more closely the example of his father than his half-brother's austere habits. At the chapter of the Golden Fleece held at Bruges in 1468, though his 'valour, prowess and prudence and several other good habits and virtues' were recognized, he was reproved for his open

---

[1] For this paragraph, see Vander Linden, *Itinéraires* and Wellens, *ABB* xxxviii (1967), 108–13, *Correspondance de la mairie de Dijon*, i. 124–5, AGR CC2706, fos. 78–100b, ASM Pot. est. Borgogna 516–17/50 and 51, de Dadizele, *Mémoires*, 47–8 and, for 1476, see for example ADN B10440, fos. 15, 16b etc. and BN Coll. de Bourgogne MS. 99, p. 746 and Hommel, *Marguerite d' York*, 88–92.

[2] De Commynes, *Mémoires*, ed. Calmette and Durville, i. 179, uses the phrase 'le grand bastard' once, apparently only to distinguish Anthony from Baudouin. The quotation that follows is from AOGV Reg. 2, f. 45b.

fornication and adultery. He was invaluable to Charles the Bold in several capacities. As first chamberlain from 1468 on he was in charge of the court.[1] As a military man he played a prominent part in almost every one of Charles the Bold's campaigns. At the siege of Beauvais in 1472 he lost his best jewels.[2] In the late summer of 1475 he organized the defence of the two Burgundies, and he was said by the Milanese ambassador Panigarola to have made an unsuccessful bid to have himself appointed Charles's governor there. He fought in all three great battles against the Swiss and their allies and filled the vitally important post, in 1476, of 'general commissaire' or 'maressal general de lost et armee'.

It was perhaps as a diplomat that the bastard of Burgundy was of most value to Charles the Bold. Instead of accompanying the duke to the siege of Neuss he set off on 13 July 1475 from Malines, according to the account of the ducal *argentier*, on embassy to the king of England, the duke of Brittany, the kings of Sicily (Ferdinand of Aragon), Portugal, Aragon and Naples, as well as to the pope and Venice.[3] But this grand tour may have been modified and divided. Probably, the bastard visited England, but omitted the rulers of the Iberian peninsula, for he called in at the siege of Neuss early in November and gave advice about the siting of some artillery before continuing on his travels.[4] The purpose of his visit to England had been the signing of an alliance between Charles the Bold and Edward IV, aimed against Louis XI. In Italy his principal business was to take the insignia of the Order of the Golden Fleece to King Ferrante of Naples.[5] Wherever he may have gone in the meantime, he passed through Geneva with a fellow bastard, Francesco d'Este, illegitimate son of the marquis of Ferrara Lionello d'Este, and others forming a cavalcade of 110 persons in all, on 18 February 1475. They reached

---

[1] *Dagboek van Gent*, ii. 216–17, compare *IAM* iii. 192.
[2] *Précis analytique* (2) ii. 128. For the next sentence, see Leguai, *AB* xvii (1945), 111, *Correspondance de la mairie de Dijon*, i. 172–7 and ASM Pot. est. Borgogna 516–17/129. For his military post in 1476, see AGR CC25543, fos. 206 and 256b.
[3] ADN B2105, fos. 115b and 127.
[4] Molinet, *Chroniques*, i. 63 and Stolle, *Thüringisch-Erfurtische Chronik*, 81.
*[5] De Reiffenberg, *Toison d'Or*, 86 and Ruwet, *Archives et bibliothèques de Vienne*, 773. For this and what follows, see *Briefe und Actenstücke von Mailand*, 81, *Chroniques de Yolande de France*, 132, and *Dépêches des ambassadeurs milanais*, i. 65. The extract is from *Cronycke van Hollandt*, fos. 356b–7 (compare *Codex indulgentiarum neerlandicarum*, 260–1).

Moncalieri in Piedmont on 4 March and were at Milan ten days later. In Rome the bastard of Burgundy concluded some important personal business, as a Dutch chronicler explained:

Pope Sixtus IV, hearing of his arrival, sent many of his cardinals and others of his nobles and household people to meet him, and they accompanied him with great honour into the city of Rome on the eve of Whit Sunday [13 May]. On the Tuesday after Whit Sunday our father the pope invited Count Anthony to eat with him in the castle of Engelburch.[1] In this he greatly honoured and exalted him, for it seldom or never happened that a secular prince or lord went to eat in the aforesaid castle. As the feast of the venerable Holy Sacrament was approaching, the pope got ready for the procession. When all was prepared, Lord Anthony was placed on the pope's right side. He was dressed in cloth of gold and carried in his hands certain insignia and ornaments or jewels which are usually carried before the pope on such occasions. On the left side [of the pope] went the cardinal of St. Peter ad Vincula. They arrived with the procession at St. John Lateran and, when they were inside the church, the noble lord Anthony went and knelt before the pope and the cardinal aforesaid pronounced many benedictions and blessings over him. This done, our holy father aforesaid removed from him all illegitimacy and spuriousness, and legitimized and ennobled him, making him an acceptable nobleman because he was noble in morals, behaviour and deeds. And he constituted and made him successor and heir of his brother Duke Charles of Burgundy if the duke left no nearer heir or successor after him. This done, and the business for which he had come being expedited and accomplished, he rode out of Rome on the Saturday following.

On his way back towards Burgundy Anthony probably collected more Italian troops for his half-brother's army. He lodged in the papal apartments at Santa Maria Novella, Florence, between 3 and 9 June and arrived in Venice on 19 June.[2] In the autumn of 1475 he played an important part in the conquest of Lorraine and continued to serve Charles in a military capacity until he was taken prisoner on the battlefield of Nancy. He lived on thereafter into the first years of the sixteenth century. During Charles the Bold's ducal reign he had received a salary or pension of 5,000, then 6,000, francs per annum,

---

[1] Castel Sant Angelo. The feast below-mentioned is that of Corpus Christi, 25 May 1475.
[2] Morelli, *Cronaca*, 191 and BN MS. fr. 5041, f. 72. For his pension, see ADN B2068, f. 16 and B2079, f. 5.

which made him one of the best paid of Burgundian allies, courtiers and civil servants.

Anthony's younger brother Baudouin was far from being a useful, still less loyal, supporter of Charles the Bold, but the truth about his defection to Louis XI towards the end of 1470 at the age of twenty-four[1] is by no means easily ascertainable. Were he and Louis XI really parties to a conspiracy to murder Charles the Bold? First news of this affair was reported in the last letter sent by Rodolfo Gonzaga to his mother from the Burgundian court, dated Ghent, 29 November 1470:

> News has come how a bastard brother of the duke called Miser Balduino, in a conspiracy with twenty-two gentlemen of the duke's household, intended to betray him and put him in the hands of the king, in this way. When the duke was going to a place called Le Crotoy not far from the frontiers of France, a bastard of Holland who had on another occasion fled from this duke to the king would be in a certain pre-determined wood and, as he passed there with these other companions, they would [seize him and] take him to the king. This plot is said to have been discovered through the tailor of a certain Miser Giohana de Chiasa who had fled from the duke a few days before and was the leader in this affair. In short, all have fled except for the tailor who is said to have been taken.[2]

A rather more credible explanation for Baudouin's hurried departure from the Burgundian court was given by the Milanese ambassador at Louis XI's court, then at Amboise, in a despatch which he sent to Galeazzo Maria Sforza on 5 December. He reported that Duke Charles's bastard brother Baudouin, who had been received by Louis at Amboise with much kindness, had fled because he feared Charles the Bold's anger. He had been placed in command of the fleet mounted to blockade the earl of Warwick in France, and Charles had accused him of negligence when he utterly failed to stop Warwick sailing to England.

On 13 December 1470 Charles the Bold published a manifesto giving his own version of Baudouin's conspiracy and treachery. This document took the form of propaganda against Louis XI even

---

[1] He was about thirty-one in May 1478 when he submitted evidence concerning Duke Charles's autograph, BN MS. fr. 5042, f. 9b. This document is only partly printed in de Comines, *Mémoires*, ed. Lenglet du Fresnoy, iii. 18–20.

[2] ASMant Archivio Gonzaga 2100. For what follows, see AGR MSS. divers 1173, f. 175 = *Cal. state papers. Milan*, i. 144.

though, according to Charles, it was not Louis but Baudouin and Jehan de Chassa, an insignificant nobleman from the Franche-Comté, who had taken the initiative in the plot 'to kill us and cause us to die by the sword or by poison'.[1] The duke had this manifesto proclaimed and pinned up throughout his territories and beyond them. At Liège it was read out during a sermon on treachery delivered on 4 January 1471 and followed by prayers for the duke's welfare. Naturally, the chroniclers' accounts of the affair are derived from this ducal document.

A different explanation of the defection of Baudouin and de Chassa was prepared for and possibly signed by the culprits themselves. Draft statements supposedly by each of them but couched in part in similar words and in the same handwriting, both texts much corrected, have survived in a Paris manuscript. Both statements refer to Duke Charles's letters of 13 December and utterly reject the accusations set out in them. They describe the letters as 'false, evil, disloyal and mendacious'. Neither Baudouin nor Jehan de Chassa ever conspired to take the life of the duke. Both had quitted his service mainly because of the 'most vile, detestable and dishonest things he indulges in against God our creator, against our law and against all rules of nature'. Baudouin neither wished nor felt able to mention these things 'without causing offence to God' and danger to his conscience and honour. De Chassa accused Charles, who is referred to repeatedly in both documents as 'soi-disant duke of Burgundy', of trying to persuade him to join him in these malpractices. Baudouin's document adds another reason for his flight from the Burgundian court. The duke had conceived a 'most unjust and unreasonable hatred and fury' against him ever since he, Baudouin, had refused to support Charles in his quarrels with his father, so that Baudouin feared for his life.[2]

Baudouin's flight is thus surrounded by a web of lies, accusations, dark hints, rumours and speculations, but it seems improbable that he was associated in a plot to kill Charles, especially as the only favour he received afterwards from Louis XI was the vice-county of

---

[1] Plancher, iv. no. 228 and *Analectes belgiques*, i. 66–9. For what follows, see d'Oudenbosch, *Chronique*, 231–2. For the chroniclers' accounts of this affair see Chastellain, *Oeuvres*, v. 469–83, Basin, *Louis XI*, ii. 32–48, *Cronycke van Hollandt*, f. 331, and de Haynin, *Mémoires*, ii. 94–5.

[2] BN MS. fr. 5041, fos. 180–1b and 184–5b. For the next paragraph, see *Lettres de Louis XI*, iv. 221–4 and nn., *Cronycke van Hollandt*, fos. 359b–360, Molinet, *Chroniques*, i. 119 (text of treaty of Soleuvre), de Haynin, *Mémoires*, ii. 216, *IAM* iii. 222, ASM Pot. est. Borgogna 516–17/142, and *Dépêches des ambassadeurs milanais*, i. 267.

Orbec, near Lisieux in Normandy, of which the royal officials were in any case loth to put him in possession. Some years later, soon after the signing on 13 September 1475 of the truce of Soleuvre between Louis and Charles, in which he and Jehan de Chassa were explicitly excluded from amnesty, Baudouin made his way back to Charles the Bold's territories. He turned up at Malines in November, was held for a time at Vilvorde, then taken to Charles the Bold at Nancy and interrogated by the duke for three hours, apparently at the end of December. Finally in January 1476 he made public apology to Charles and was forgiven.

The close connections between the houses of Cleves and Burgundy have been discussed in earlier volumes of this history.[1] At least three members of the house of Cleves were of special service to Charles the Bold, two of them, the brothers Duke John I and Adolf, lord of Ravenstein, were his first cousins. Duke John of Cleves became a knight of the Golden Fleece in 1451. Although at the 1468 chapter he was criticized for withholding the military assistance which the sovereign of the Order, Charles the Bold, had asked him to furnish against Liège in 1467, he welcomed the opportunity, in the summer of 1473, of leading an army to help the duke of Burgundy conquer Guelders. After all, he was substantially rewarded with a sizeable slice of that duchy and a quarter of the sum of 80,000 Rhenish florins paid by Nijmegen when it surrendered. In 1469, when he sent his son John to the Burgundian court, he had been granted an annual pension by Charles of 6,000 francs, 2,000 for the upkeep of his son, who served in the Burgundian army at the siege of Neuss.

Adolf of Cleves, lord of Ravenstein, was even more useful to Charles the Bold than his elder brother the duke of Cleves. His annual pension of 5,000 francs was increased to 6,000 in 1470, when he was permitted or persuaded to take as his second wife one of Philip the Good's *bastardes*, Anne de Bourgogne. He served prominently in the ducal army on the campaign against Liège in 1467 and he was one of those thought likely, in autumn 1469, to become a captain of ordinance. By

---

[1] See especially Vaughan, *Philip the Good*, 289–92. For what follows, see de Reiffenberg, *Toison d'Or*, 52, above, pp. 113-15, *Urkundenbuch für die Geschichte des Niederrheins*, iv. nos. 351, 369 and 370, Gachard, *BCRH* (4) ix (1881), 295–360, van Berchen, *Gelderse kroniek*, 137, Molinet, *Chroniques*, i. 36, de Fouw, *Philips van Kleef*, 7–18, above pp. 17 and 33, ASMant Archivio Gonzaga 2100, letter of Rodolfo Gonzaga of 4 October 1469, *Cal. state papers. Milan*, i. 169–70, *Cronycke van Hollandt*, f. 345b, *Analectes historiques*, xii. 276–8, and for example ADN B10440, fos. 14b, 15, 16b etc.

1472 'my lord of Ravenstein' was reckoned by the Milanese agent Petro Aliprandi among Duke Charles's leading captains. Only a serious illness in Brussels prevented him from commanding a contingent of the ducal army at the siege of Neuss. Soon afterwards his military career was somewhat modified when, on 22 August 1475, the duke appointed him his 'lieutenant-general in all his lands and lordships' in the Low Countries. He was 'to employ himself in our absence in looking after the security and defence of these lands against our said enemies and all those who try to undertake anything in them to our damage or theirs'. He was specifically empowered to summon Estates, inspect and fortify towns, convoke and distribute troops, carry out acts of war against the enemy 'and generally to do and cause to be done each and every thing appertaining to the office of lieutenant-general which we ourselves would and could do if we were present in person'. Thereafter, as the accounts show, he was kept busy in conjunction with the chancellor Guillaume Hugonet and the duchess Margaret of York supervising the administration of these territories and, in particular, supplying the duke with the men and money he needed to fight the Swiss. Adolf of Cleves stayed at his post after Charles's death, becoming Mary of Burgundy's 'lieutenant and governor-general' at the end of January 1477.

There were other potential clients or supporters of Burgundy among the princes of north-west Germany besides members of the house of Cleves, but none of them were in point of fact of any significance to Charles the Bold. In Guelders, Burgundian influence had been pushed so far that after 1473 the conquered duchy was incorporated into the Burgundian state while its rightful ruler Duke Adolf languished in a Burgundian prison. In Jülich-Berg sympathy for Burgundy seems to have remained lukewarm in spite of the alliance with Charles the Bold of 8 December 1470. During the siege of Neuss the two dukes, Gerhard and William, were under pressure from both sides. They could scarcely avoid helping Charles the Bold with supplies and communications but did not repeat the only serious assistance they ever gave him. This was in March 1471, when the young duke William was reported to be bringing 300 lances, 1,000 mounted crossbowmen and 200 culverineers on foot to reinforce Charles outside Amiens. A truce was arranged before these troops could have been brought into action.[1]

---

[1] For this paragraph see above pp. 112–22 (Guelders), below p. 320 and, for example, Gachard, *BCRH* (4) ix (1881), 297 and 300, *Analectes historiques*, xvii. 12–23, and de Commynes, *Mémoires*, ed. Dupont, iii. 279.

Among Charles the Bold's princely blood relatives two of the most important and powerful were brothers of Duke Amadeus IX of Savoy.[1] One of them, Philip, count of Bagé and lord of Bresse, later duke of Savoy, abandoned his service for Louis XI, while the other, Jaques, count of Romont, remained a loyal Burgundian to the end.

Philip of Savoy was one of the first new allies of Charles the Bold after that duke's accession. On 21 July 1467 at Pinerolo in Piedmont he announced that 'from this day forward we shall be his true and loyal friend and we shall to the best of our power protect and defend his person, his honour, his lands, lordships and subjects and help him to defend them'.[2] The connection evolved further in May of the following year, when Charles the Bold insisted quite unconstitutionally on having Philip elected a member of the Order of the Golden Fleece at the Bruges chapter. It was a political appointment. Philip was not only 'well qualified to be received and accepted into the said Order. It will also be very convenient for the well-being and security of my said lord the sovereign [of the Order] and of his lands and subjects, especially in these days, troubled and anxious because of the quarrels in the kingdom of France.' On 24 June 1468 Philip was appointed Duke Charles's 'lieutenant-general and governor' in the two Burgundies. His duties were mainly, if not entirely, military, and he brought a larger force to the Liège campaign in the autumn of 1468 than the marshal of Burgundy, Thibaud, lord of Neuchâtel. His salary was the princely one of 6,000 francs per annum.[3]

It is by no means clear for how long exactly Philip of Savoy remained a loyal Burgundian, nor for how long he acted as governor of the two Burgundies. He was still in office in November 1470 but had certainly quitted Charles's service a year later; he signed a treaty with Louis XI on 6 October 1471. His Burgundian sympathies were

---

[1] See the genealogical table below, p. 301.

[2] De Comines, *Mémoires*, ed. Lenglet du Fresnoy, ii. 630–1 and Guichenon, *Histoire de Savoie*, iv. 437. See, in general, Guichenon, *Histoire de Bresse*, especially 91–2. For what follows, see AOGV Reg. 2, f. 66, Chastellain, *Oeuvres*, v. 379, and Salet, *ASRAB* li (1966), 25. See too Daviso, *Filippo II il Senzaterra*, 58–90.

[3] For the last three sentences see respectively Richard, *MSHDB* xix (1957), 109, ADN B2068, fos. 263b ff., and ADN B2079, f. 16b. For the next paragraph, see *Chroniques de Yolande de France*, 293–4, Bittmann, *Ludwig XI. und Karl der Kühne*, i (2). 519–20 and ii (1). 399 ff. etc., AGR MSS. divers 1173, fos. 122–5, 132, 161a–b, etc. (transcripts of Milanese despatches), and ASM Pot. est. Borgogna 515/15 and 27–9.

probably never very profound. Indeed he seems to have become dissatisfied with Charles the Bold at an early date and this dissatisfaction was reinforced, through 1469 and 1470, by the efforts of Louis XI and the bribes of the duke of Milan, both of whom did their best to detach him from Burgundy. A Milanese observer reported in January 1469 that Philip of Savoy was extremely annoyed with Charles because when, at Liège, Philip had asked him to try to persuade Louis XI to pay him 200,000 crowns in reparation for damages done by royal troops in Bresse in September 1468, 100,000 crowns in compensation for his imprisonment by Louis in 1464–6, as well as a further 70,000 crowns, Charles had virtually refused to help him, telling him to ask the king himself. Another reason for Philip's growing coolness towards Burgundy was probably Charles's failure to assist him, in spite of promises to do so, in his projected attack on Milan early in 1469. Louis on the other hand was generous in his favours, and early in 1471 he found Philip a wife in the shape of Marguerite de Bourbon.

When the chapter of the Golden Fleece was convened at Valenciennes in May 1473 Philip of Savoy, the Order's new recruit, had been campaigning in Roussillon, against Charles the Bold's ally king John II of Aragon, as Louis XI's commander-in-chief. Charles had an opportunity of expressing his displeasure when the customary examination was held into the morals and behaviour of the knights, and this was followed up by a letter, sent to Philip by 'The knights of the Order of the Golden Fleece, your brothers and companions', setting out the complaints against him in detail. Not only had he exhibited the basest ingratitude and treachery by abandoning his post in Burgundy without even troubling to send back his letters of appointment to the duke; he had also gone over to the king of France and fought against Charles's ally the duke of Brittany. To these political misdeeds were added more domestic ones. He had refused to acknowledge his invitation to the present chapter and he had failed to send a proctor. Moreover it was common knowledge that, instead of wearing the fleece on its collar, he had attached it to a silk thread round his neck and even allowed anyone who wished to remove a piece of it.[1] Needless to say, he does not appear in Burgundian service again: in July 1476 he became royal lieutenant-general in Piedmont.

Jaques, count of Romont and baron of Vaud, was only about eighteen years old when he set out on 7 August 1468 with his elder

[1] AOGV Reg. 3, fos. 19b–20 and 49b–50b.

244 CHARLES THE BOLD

brothers Philip of Savoy and Jehan Louis, bishop of Geneva, to join the army of Charles the Bold, then poised on the frontier of Picardy ready for war against France, though in the event it was used against Liège.[1] In 1472 Jaques appeared again in the military service of Burgundy, this time among the captains of the forces raised for the defence of the duchy of Burgundy rather than in the main army campaigning against the French in Picardy. In May 1473 he emerged as a central figure in the government of Charles the Bold's territories. The duke was about to set off on the campaign to conquer Guelders and, suspicious as ever of the designs of Louis XI, took care to leave behind him in the Burgundian Low Countries a military, or at any rate emergency, government comprising a single supreme commander or lieutenant-general for all these lands with a subordinate lieutenant-general under his orders in each territory. Thus Messire Jehan de Halewin was 'lieutenant-general of Flanders and the bailiwick of Lille under Monsieur de Romont' and Engelbert, count of Vianen and of Nassau, was to be lieutenant-general in Brabant and Limbourg 'under our most dear and well loved cousin the count of Romont, our lieutenant-general in all our lands round here (*pays de par deça*)'.[2]

Jaques de Savoie was installed at Arras from May 1473, with 600 lances and a group of Golden Fleece knights, among them the newly-elected Philippe de Croy, count of Chimay, and Philippe de Crèvecoeur, lord of Esquerdes, the duke's lieutenant and captain-general in Ponthieu, to assist and advise him. He seems to have remained there, on a salary of £3,000 per annum, more or less continuously thereafter until he was relieved by Adolf of Cleves in August 1475, having found himself in the front line during the crisis of May 1475 when the French invaded Artois and Hainault and he was defeated by them outside Arras. At the end of the summer of 1475 he was transferred to an equivalent post in the two Burgundies, being referred to as the duke's 'governor and lieutenant-general'

[1] For this and what follows see the biography of Jaques, count of Romont, in Gingins-La Sarraz, *Épisodes*, 417–63. For the next sentence, see *Lettres de Louis XI*, v. 60–2, de la Chauvelays, *Les armées de Charles le Téméraire dans les deux Bourgognes*, 103–4, and de Chevanne, *Les guerres en Bourgogne*, 124–6, 146, etc.

[2] AGR CC21842, f. 12b and Meynart, *BCRH* cxxvi (1960), 149. For the next sentence see AGR MSS. divers 1173, fos. 200–2 (letter to Duchess Yolande of Savoy of 20 May 1473) and de Haynin, *Mémoires*, ii. 154. For the count of Romont at Arras as lieutenant-general see, for example, Robert, *Journal*, 2 and 5, ADN B10438, f. 37 and B10439, 22b, 41a and 41b, etc.; ADN B2105, 121b; and *IAGRCC* iii. 6–7. For his pension, see ADN B2100.

there in the minute-book of the Dijon town council; described probably erroneously in an Italian translation of a ducal letter of 28 November 1475 as 'my governor of Burgundy'; and said by the Milanese ambassador to have been appointed 'lieutenant in Burgundy'.[1] According to the last-mentioned person, Johanne Petro Panigarola, Charles only appointed Jaques de Savoie to this post because his bastard half-brother Anthony had applied for it for himself. Jaques was a singularly unsuitable choice for, after his barony of Vaud was invaded by the Swiss in October 1475 he became increasingly involved in that area, playing a crucial part in the military events of 1476, above all the siege and battle of Murten. He lived to take service with Charles's daughter, Mary of Burgundy, once again defending Flanders and Artois against the French.

The other brother of Duke Amadeus IX who served in the Liège campaign of 1468 beside Philip, lord of Bresse, and Jaques, count of Romont, was the bishop of Geneva, Jehan Louis de Savoie. Although his actual service in Burgundian employment seems to have been limited to that occasion, his Burgundian loyalty and support for his brother Jaques rather than Philip, was made clear on numerous occasions. His zeal for the Burgundian cause was however hampered by the lack of enthusiasm of the citizens of Geneva. When he sought 1,500 men-at-arms from the city council to help Jaques defend the Vaud in autumn 1475 he obtained only 600. When, on the eve of the battle of Grandson, he asked them for 300 men-at-arms to help the duke of Burgundy, the council resolved 'that rather than raise troops for the bishop they would give him money—but as little as possible'.[2]

While in the case of the house of Savoy, allegiance tended to be divided between Burgundy and France, in other families it was their situation between Burgundy and the Swiss and their allies which gave rise to divided loyalties. Thus Jehan d'Aarberg, lord of Valangin, remained loyal to Bern though his two sons continued to serve in the Burgundian army. Outstanding in this category was Rudolf, margrave of Hochberg or Hachberg, near Freiburg im Breisgau, count of Neuchâtel in modern Switzerland, and lord of Rothelin or Rötteln in

---

[1] *IACD* i. 43, Colombo, *Iolanda, duchessa di Savoia*, 281 and ASM Pot. est. Borgogna 516–17/102. For what follows, see the same, 102 and 129.
[2] On this paragraph, see Roget, *Les Suisses et Genève*, i. 19 and 29. For what follows on the Hochbergs, see Bauer, *Négociations et campagnes de Rodolphe de Hochberg* and Reutter, *Le rôle joué par le comté de Neuchâtel*.

the Breisgau. He was brought up at the home of his uncle Jehan, count of Fribourg and of Neuchâtel, marshal of Burgundy and Philip the Good's governor and captain-general there between 1435 and 1440. He married a member of a Burgundian noble family, Marguerite de Vienne, daughter of Guillaume de Vienne, from whom he acquired the lordship of St. Georges and other Burgundian fiefs, and these important Burgundian connections were strengthened in 1458 when his uncle, who had made Rudolf his sole heir, died childless. On the other hand, in becoming count of Neuchâtel he also became a co-burgess of Bern. His career in the Burgundian service began when he was appointed chamberlain-councillor of Philip the Good in 1458. He fought at Montlhéry. He was the principal Burgundian negotiator of the treaty with Bern and other Swiss communities which Philip the Good signed on 22 May 1467. On 8 March 1468 Charles the Bold appointed him governor and captain-general of the duchy of Luxembourg with a salary of 1,000 Rhenish florins per annum.[1] But other duties soon intervened. In 1469 he was occupied for several months, as one of the ducal commissioners for Alsace, negotiating with Duke Sigmund of Austria, with Mulhouse, and with the Swiss. After 1473, when he accompanied Charles the Bold to Trier, he more or less withdrew from Burgundian service, though he still played a part as a go-between between Charles the Bold and the Swiss, presiding, for example, over an abortive peace conference at Neuchâtel at the end of 1475, and he was still described as governor of Luxembourg, for instance in the treaty of Soleuvre of 13 September 1475 and in a document of June 1476.[2]

Meanwhile, Rudolf's son Philipp von Hochberg, lord of Baudeville or Badenweiler, had enrolled in Duke Charles's army. At Neuss the young Hochberg was knighted by the duke whose father, Philip the Good, had held him at the font and given him his name at Neuchâtel in 1454. Charles the Bold's campaign against the Swiss in 1476 caused considerable embarrassment to the Hochbergs, especially as the duke had decided that the best route to attack Bern was through the county of Neuchâtel. Even though Rudolf temporarily abandoned all his territories to the Swiss and went to live in Bern, they were distrustful. His son Philipp was accused of complicity in the execution by Charles

---

[1] AGR CC2631, account for year ending 30 September 1468, f. 18, and van Werveke, PSHIL xl (1889), 261.
[2] Molinet, *Chroniques*, i. 120, and *Chartes de la famille de Reinach*, no. 1995.

the Bold of the Swiss garrison in Grandson. Then, at Murten, the Swiss suspected treachery when they captured a cannon which was engraved with what they thought were the arms of Hochberg. Fortunately for the marquis it was claimed by the men of Strasbourg, whose arms were said to be similar to his. Philipp von Hochberg was no longer serving with Charles on his last campaign in Lorraine. He married a princess of the house of Savoy in 1478 and transferred his allegiance to France.

Another princely house with significant Burgundian connections was that of Nassau. Count John IV of Nassau-Dillenberg, lord of Breda and count of Vianen, had been seneschal or *drossard* of Brabant since 1436 and a councillor of Duke Philip the Good. His son Engelbert who, according to the practice of the time, confusingly used exactly the same titles as his father, accompanied Charles the Bold against Liège in 1468, became Charles's castellan of Turnhout on 1 January 1470, and was elected a knight of the Golden Fleece in May 1473. It was the father who, as seneschal of Brabant, objected in a detailed written protest to the instructions for the government of Brabant issued by Charles the Bold on 1 January 1469. Count John remained seneschal of Brabant until his death on 3 February 1475, when he was succeeded by his son Engelbert. In 1470 Charles the Bold appointed one of them, probably Count John, his lieutenant-general in Brabant, but in 1471 Engelbert seems to have taken his place as the duke's stadholder or lieutenant there. Later, in 1473 and again in 1475, Engelbert was appointed or reappointed ducal lieutenant in Brabant, on the first occasion 'in the absence of the count of Nassau his father'. Thus the government and the defence of Brabant, and of Limbourg, were assured throughout Charles the Bold's reign by two members of the house of Nassau.[1]

A noble Picard family that continued to furnish Charles the Bold with loyal supporters in spite of their quarrel with him at the end of his father's reign were the Croys. They were in disgrace when Charles the Bold succeeded to his father on 15 June 1467 but hastened to write to him on 23 June to assure him of their loyalty and desire to serve him, though without actually apologizing for their

---

[1] For this paragraph see *IAGRCC* ii. 258, *Table chronologique de Luxembourg*, no. 120 (= AGR CC134, f. 121), AGR CC134, fos. 76–8 and Chartes de Brabant, carton 226, Meynart, *BCRH* cxxvi (1960), 135–52, *IADNB* iv. 234, and AGR CC4181, fos. 159b, 161, 170b, 173b etc. (references to 'myn Jonchere' of Nassau).

alleged misdeeds.[1] The two senior members of the family, the brothers
Anthoine, lord of Croy, and Jehan, lord of Chimay, claimed to be and
perhaps really were dismayed to discover when they arrived at Bruges
at the end of April 1468 for the chapter of the Golden Fleece, of
which they were both members, that the duke had neither forgiven
nor forgotten his earlier quarrels with them. The same went for their
nephew, Jehan, lord of Lannoy. At a meeting of the knights of the
Golden Fleece on 29 April detailed accusations were made against
the three of them by Charles the Bold. The lord of Croy had said
that Duke Charles 'was ill-conditioned, malevolent and that . . . if he
lived he was cut out to cause a great deal of evil some day'. He had got
the provost of Warneton to cast a false horoscope of Charles, then
count of Charolais, to persuade his father Duke Philip of his son's
wickedness. They had promised the king that they would not try to
conciliate Charles with his father. They had tried to obtain possession
of Boulogne, Namur and Luxembourg after Duke Philip's death with
the king's help, and they had made an alliance with the count of
Nevers, promising to help him acquire Brabant. Asked to choose
between the duke's mercy and a fair trial, the three accused opted for
the latter on the grounds that the former would entail their confessing
to faults they had not committed. On the whole, the knights of the
Golden Fleece were sympathetic to them, but the duke refused to
permit the Order, which he insisted was a court of honour only, to
exercise jurisdiction in a criminal matter such as this. The accused
had no option but to withdraw from Bruges to await a further ducal
summons or eventual pardon. As a matter of fact, Jehan de Croy and
his son Philippe were forgiven in August 1468, but Anthoine was not
finally pardoned until 1473, when he was well over seventy years old.

Meanwhile Jehan de Croy's son, Philippe, lord of Quiévrain, had
not only regained Charles the Bold's confidence and favour but
quickly became prominent as a Burgundian captain and courtier. In
September 1471 he was chosen to lead an important embassy to
King Ferrante of Naples and Pope Sixtus IV.[2] By 1472 he was

[1] *Collection de documens inédits*, i. 152–4, and de Haynin, *Mémoires*, i. 203–5.
On the Croys, see Vaughan, *Philip the Good*, 336–8 (genealogical table on
p. 337), 345–6 and 377–8, and especially Grunzweig, *Études F. Courtoy*,
531–64, *Les Cröy, conseillers des ducs de Bourgogne*, and Gachard, *BCRH* xi
(1846), 113–20 and 191–5. For what follows, see AOGV Reg. 2, fos. 6–17.
[2] Above p. 75 and de Haynin, *Mémoires*, ii. 131. For the next sentence, see
Cal. state papers. Milan, i. 169–70 (where he is described as 'lord of Chiverem'
for Quiévrain) and de Barante, *Histoire des ducs*, ii. 402 n. 1.

numbered among the duke's principal captains, and early in 1473 he was permitted to take over Chimay, which was now converted by Charles the Bold into a county, from his dying father. The esteem in which he was held at the Burgundian court was demonstrated at Valenciennes in May 1473, when he was one of five persons elected knights of the Golden Fleece out of the forty-six non-royal candidates whose names were put forward.[1] He accompanied the duke to the siege of Neuss in 1474, was appointed captain of Rupelmonde on 28 August of that year, and on 23 May 1475 he had the distinction of being commander-in-chief of one of the two battles or divisions into which the ducal army was divided as it advanced to attack the imperial forces outside Neuss. Some time before this, on 22 November 1474, Charles the Bold had appointed Philippe de Croy his stadholder or lieutenant in Guelders, though he did not take up the post until some time later, with sweeping powers which were by no means confined to military matters. They are stated as follows in the letters of appointment.[2]

We have given and granted and we do give and grant to our said cousin of Chimay full power, authority and particular command from henceforth to well and duly exercise and serve in the said office of lieutenant in and throughout our said land of Guelders and its appurtenances; to guard, maintain and defend our rights, dignity, lordship and domain; to provide or cause to be provided watch and ward in all the towns, places and fortresses of the said land in the event of imminent peril or otherwise and in default of the captains or others defending them, and we want all the said towns, places and fortresses to be open to him as to ourselves; to have them repaired and fortified as necessary and constrain those who ought to contribute to do so; to see that the numbers of soldiers fixed for the defence of the said places are maintained by the said captains; to assemble whenever necessary or when it seems to him desirable the Estates of our said land of Guelders for the conduct and expedition of our affairs there; to renew annually the magistratures (loix) of our good towns of the said land with the commissioners we shall appoint for this purpose; to audit the accounts of their officials; together with our well loved and loyal friends the members of the council set up and established in our land of Guelders to offer and administer law and justice under the jurisdiction of our sovereign court of Parlement to all

---

[1] AOGV Reg. 3, f. 33a–b. For the next sentence, see Molinet, Chroniques, i. 36, ADN B4166, fos. 48b–49, and above, p. 199.
[2] Les Cröy, conseillers des ducs de Bourgogne, 124; see Maris, GBM lx (1961), 157–62, and above p. 121.

J*

our subjects in our said lands and to others requesting it . . . , and especially and in general to do and cause to be done each and every thing for the good, honour, profit and utility of us and of our said land and of our subjects there which a good and loyal lieutenant can and ought to do and which we personally would do if we were present there.

The remarkable loyalty of the Croys to Charles the Bold was probably partly due to the fact that nearly all their lands were in Burgundian territory and Louis XI had failed to provide for them effectively during their exile in France after 1465. Even the stubborn and proud Anthoine, lord of Croy, whose pardon may have been delayed because he could not bring himself to promise, as he was required to do, to serve Duke Charles against everyone, returned eventually in 1473 to his lands and possessions on the Burgundian side of the frontier. The situation, and attitude, of his son Philippe, lord of Renty, remains in doubt. He was at court in July 1470, but at least one chronicler makes him desert to Louis XI in 1471 or thereabouts.[1] Although Charles the Bold made him a chamberlain on 18 March 1475 he was among those excluded from the amnesty established by the truce of Soleuvre on 13 September that year. Had he abandoned Duke Charles in the meanwhile? If so his defection must have been very short-lived, for in letters of 18 December 1475 the duke formally restored him to favour, stating that he had withdrawn to France at the instigation of some young courtiers and to please his father-in-law the count of St. Pol. On 6 October 1477 he was reappointed chamberlain by Maximilian.

The branch of the house of Luxembourg which had established itself in Picardy and Artois suffered just like the Croys from the clash of interests and loyalties occasioned by the confrontation of France and Burgundy in the fifteenth century. The most prominent member of this family in Charles the Bold's reign was Louis de Luxembourg, count of St. Pol, who for years contrived to augment his wealth and maintain his importance by consulting and abetting alternately the interests of France and Burgundy and even by promising at one and the same time to serve the king of France and the duke of Burgundy against all comers. Under Philip the Good he had already suffered the confiscation of his estates and towns in Burgundian territory, but these had been restored to him in 1461 and in 1465 he rendered

---

[1] Brun-Lavainne, *BCHDN* viii (1865), 204 and de But, *Chronique*, 514. For what follows see *Les Cröy, conseillers des ducs de Bourgogne*, 130, and Molinet, *Chroniques*, i. 119.

important services to the Burgundian cause in the war of the Public
Weal, commanding the van of Charles the Bold's army and displaying
great valour on the field of Montlhéry. It was immediately after this
campaign that he accepted from Louis XI the post of constable of
France, that is, titular head of the French army. In the succeeding
years he appears more and more as a French partisan; on
embassy to Charles the Bold, for example, in July 1467, trying on
Louis's behalf to deter him from attacking Liège, and during the late
summer of 1468.[1] For a time it suited both sides to use him as a spy,
an intriguer, a go-between. Early in 1471, however, when the count
of St. Pol secured the surrender to France of St. Quentin, one of the
so-called Somme towns, Charles took action against him by confiscating his Burgundian lands, which were extensive and valuable.
Some of them, Gravelines and Warneton, were granted to one of his
sons in Burgundian service. The others, mostly in Artois and
Hainault, were kept by Duke Charles, and their revenues, totalling
some £14,000 in the calendar year 1474, contributed to his receipt-
general.[2]

The recovery of St. Quentin now became an ambition or obsession
of Charles the Bold, and it may have been with the intention of
offering it to him in return for regaining his favour that the constable
took the bold step, in December 1473, of seizing the town from its
French garrison. Louis was furious and tried every means to regain
this strategic place, though he had had it fortified too well to think
seriously of trying to take it by assault. After this incident the king's
suspicions and dislike of his constable became more and more
manifest. Even so it was not until the summer of 1475 that the
constable's delicately balanced situation on the fence between
Burgundy and France became disastrously uncomfortable for him.
It was Edward IV's arrival on the scene which caused his undoing.
Apparently the constable managed to offend Charles the Bold by
defending St. Quentin against the English instead of permitting them
entry, and to extinguish Louis XI's last spark of trust in him by giving
him false information about Edward's intentions and then secretly

[1] Above, pp. 16 and 53-4, and, for the fall of St. Quentin mentioned in what
follows, above p. 68.
[2] De Barante, *Histoire des ducs*, ii. 494 n. 2 (= AGR CC134, fos. 127-8)
and *Table chronologique de Luxembourg*, no. 262; ADN B2099, fos. 24-8.
For what follows see Bittmann, *Ludwig XI. und Karl der Kühne*, ii (1).
167-78.

negotiating with him. Not surprisingly, Louis and Charles came to terms. Having at last regained St. Quentin on 14 September, Louis offered it, among other things, to Charles in return for the constable. Thus Louis de Luxembourg was excluded from the truce of Soleuvre signed on 13 September 1475 and on the very same day Charles the Bold issued a manifesto against him. He was apprehended in Hainault; his pathetic letter to Charles imploring mercy was ignored; and he was handed over to royal officials to be tried for high treason by the *Parlement* of Paris and executed in the Place de Grève on 19 December 1475 before a large crowd of onlookers, which included two Dominican brothers who had found it worthwhile to rent a couple of windows overlooking the square for four shillings each.[1]

Louis de Luxembourg himself was in royal not Burgundian service in Charles the Bold's reign. Not so his brother Jaques and two of his sons, Jehan and Anthoine, all of whom served Charles the Bold at some time and in some capacity. It was Jehan de Luxembourg, count of Marle, who was given some of his father's confiscated estates by Charles the Bold in April 1471. In May 1473 he became a knight of the Golden Fleece, and he lost his life in June 1476 on the disastrous field of Murten. Another son of Louis de Luxembourg, Anthoine, count of Roussy and Charny, was a councillor-chamberlain of Charles the Bold. On 18 February 1472 he was appointed 'lieutenant-general and governor' of the duke in the duchy and county of Burgundy and the other territories in that area as well as marshal of Burgundy, this appointment not however to affect the position of Jehan de Damas, lord of Clessy, lieutenant and governor in the Mâconnais, nor that of Tristan de Toulongeon, the governor of Auxerre.[2] He too suffered military disaster. Defeated at the battle of Montreuillon or Guipy on 20 June 1475 by the French, he was taken prisoner and remained in French hands until after Charles's death. A similar fate overtook a

---

[1] The main chronicle sources for the events leading to the constable's execution in 1475 are Basin, *Louis XI*, ii. 246–50 and 266–72, de Commynes, *Mémoires*, ed. Calmette and Durville, ii. 33–7, 56–7, 73 and 83–8, Molinet, *Chroniques*, i. 130–7, Nicolay, *Kalendrier des guerres*, 13–16, and de Roye, *Chronique scandaleuse*, i. 349–66; documents are printed in de Comines, *Mémoires*, ed. Lenglet du Fresnoy, iii. 422–4 (=Plancher, iv. no. 258), 424–6 and 452–7, Devillers, *BCRH* (4) xvii (1890), 302–28, and Poncelet, *BCRH* xci (1927), 181–98; see too ASM Pot. est. Borgogna 516–17/87 and 99–100.

[2] Richard, *MSHDB* xix (1957), 110–11, and ACO B16, fos. 238b–240. For what follows, see de Chevanne, *Les guerres en Bourgogne*, 203 and de Haynin, *Mémoires*, ii. 200–02.

third member of the family at almost exactly the same time. Jaques de Luxembourg, lord of Richebourg, brother of the count of St. Pol, was taken prisoner by the French in a skirmish outside Arras on 27 June 1475, wounded it was said in ten places. He had been a councillor-chamberlain of Charles the Bold but he passed into French service, apparently in return for his release.

Another Picard family provided Charles with one of his most powerful and effective lieutenants, Guy de Brimeu, lord of Humbercourt. His activities in the duke's service were centred along the River Meuse between Namur and Maastricht and he managed to combine them nicely with his own advancement. He was count of Megen, on the Meuse not far from Nijmegen, and was granted a toll there in 1473.[1] In Brabant he was hereditary marshal after 1473 and a landowner. He became captain of the castles of Herzogenrath and Wassenberg on the borders of Jülich. He contrived to buttress his own private authority along the Meuse by acquiring an astonishing number of ducal posts. His connection with Liège began in 1466 when he was appointed one of the duke's commissioners to receive the city's oath of recognition of the duke of Burgundy as its guardian. On 28 November 1467 he became ducal lieutenant-general in Liège; on 17 September 1468 he was appointed lieutenant and captain-general and placed in command of the campaign against Liège. He remained ducal lieutenant-general in Liège during the rest of Charles's reign, becoming in addition, in October 1469, governor of the new town or fortress Charles the Bold planned to construct on an island in the Meuse in the heart of the city. Later he was appointed captain of Huy. His sphere of influence on the Meuse was greatly enhanced when he was appointed in or before 1469 governor of Limbourg, Maastricht and Namur and when, after Charles the Bold's conquest of Guelders, he became governor of the towns, fortresses and lands of Montfoort, Buren, Kessel and Venlo and, later, 'governor and captain-general of the town, castle, land and lordship of Grave and the land of Cuyk'. These places were all in the duchy of Guelders.

---

[1] For this and what follows see the map on p. 114 above and see especially AGR CC134, fos. 112a–b, 135b–136, 142a–b, 144–5 and 149a etc., de Barante, *Histoire des ducs*, ii. 725–9, Maris, *GBM* lvi (1957), 53–8, 106–12, etc., Gorissen, *De Raadkamer te Maastricht*, Düsseldorf StA Jülich-Berg I. 255, fos. 45, 70, 76, etc., transcribed in RTA material, and Paillard, *Procès du Chancelier Hugonet*. I have not been able to see the forthcoming book on Guy de Brimeu by Dr. Paravicini, but see the same, *BFPL* cciii (1972), 147–56.

The local chroniclers, some of whom disliked Guy de Brimeu just because he was a Picard foreigner, misunderstood his true position and status. The Liège monk Adrian d'Oudenbosch describes him correctly in 1472 as governor of Namur, but erroneously makes him, two years later, 'governor of Guelders, Limbourg, Luxembourg, Namur and all the duke's lands beyond the Meuse'. [1] He relates how the lord of Humbercourt, when he travelled from Maastricht to Liège, was escorted by a boatload of armed men from Maastricht. At the Porte de St. Léonard, Liège, he would be met by eighty archers from Namur to escort him there; and so on. No wonder the Guelders chronicler Willem van Berchen thought Charles had appointed him governor of the whole of Guelders. In fact he never was stadholder of Guelders, and his appointment on 2 August 1473 as ducal lieutenant-general in Luxembourg seems to have been only temporary; an *ad hoc* response to the potentially critical situation in Lorraine. The same is probably true of his appointment in the following month as a military lieutenant-general, to supervise the troops of the ordinance and their captains, as well as the artillery, and to receive complaints about damages done by the troops. In 1475 Humbercourt's territorial lieutenancy was defined in a ducal document as including the duke's 'duchies, counties, lands, lordships, protectorates and *advoueries* beyond the River Meuse; my land and county of Namur; my town of Maastricht on the Meuse and the lands of Liège and Looz'. [2]

In the last few years of Charles the Bold's reign Humbercourt proceeded to establish for himself what can only be described as a state within a state. His 'capital' was Maastricht and it was here that he instituted, at the end of September 1473, no doubt with ducal permission, a council or *raadkamer* which, though in theory ducal, was in a sense also his own private organ of government. Too busy to administer all his ducal offices in person, Humbercourt appointed lieutenants to act for him. By 1476 he was negotiating on equal terms and possibly even on his own behalf as well as the duke's, with Cologne, Duke William of Jülich-Berg, and other neighbouring powers. He had been a chamberlain of the duke of Burgundy since 1456; he became a knight of the Golden Fleece in 1473. But his career was cut short soon after the death of his duke. On 3 April 1477 he was decapitated at Ghent after such severe torture that he had to be placed on the scaffold slumped in a chair.

[1] D'Oudenbosch, *Chronique*, 238, and for the next sentence, p. 235. Compare van Berchen, *Gelderse kroniek*, 136–7.
[2] *Analectes historiques*, xii. 274–5 = *Acten zum Neusser Krieg*, 138.

Passing from Humbercourt to Hagenbach is in some sense moving from the sublime to the ridiculous. Yet both men were powerful, both were on intimate terms with Charles the Bold, and both met their death by decapitation. In most respects Peter von Hagenbach was a much lesser figure than the Picard nobleman from a famous line of aristocratic Burgundian captains. Humbercourt was invested by his duke, for example in the commission of 2 August 1473 appointing him lieutenant-general in Luxembourg and elsewhere, with wider powers than any other ducal officer, and he was permitted or encouraged by Charles to wield his own personal authority on an unprecedented scale. Humbercourt was a prince, Hagenbach was a servant, an instrument, a mere official. Never for one moment was he given in Alsace the support he deserved nor the funds he repeatedly asked for. Instead, the bailiff of Upper Alsace was virtually abandoned to his fate when it did not suit Charles the Bold to go to his aid. Yet the course of events and with it the entire destiny of Charles the Bold and of Burgundy was decisively affected by the attitudes and antics of Peter von Hagenbach. He was indeed a lesser man than Humbercourt, but he made a greater impact on history.

Peter von Hagenbach belonged to the lesser nobility of the Sundgau. The ancestral castle of Hagenbach was in the village of that name a few kilometres north-east of Dammekirch or Dannemarie and 22 km south-west of Mulhouse. His mother was from French-speaking Sundgau, and Hagenbach was brought up with her at her deceased husband's lordship and castle of Belmont in the Franche-Comté, so that he spoke and wrote fluent French. The date and means of his taking up service with Burgundy are unknown, but he was present at the Feast of the Pheasant early in 1454 and, by about 1460, he was a *maître d'hôtel*. Soon after then he took sides with Charles, then count of Charolais, in the quarrels between him and his father Philip the Good, and he was able to earn Charles's undying gratitude in the summer of 1462 when he exposed Jehan Coustain's alleged plot to murder him,[1] a plot which he himself may have contrived on Charles's behalf in order to eliminate Coustain and discredit his patrons the Croys. It was probably soon after this that Charles wrote to Hagenbach addressing him as 'my very good friend' and assuring him that he would neither abandon nor fail him whatever might happen.

[1] See Vaughan, *Philip the Good*, 344 and 343 n. 3. For Hagenbach I have relied on Brauer-Gramm, *Peter von Hagenbach*.

Hagenbach won military renown in the war of the League of the Public Weal and in the campaigns against Dinant and Liège. His most brilliant exploit was the seizure of the town of Péronne on 3 October 1465 from the count of Nevers, Jehan de Bourgogne. Because of his knowledge of German he was employed on diplomatic missions: the alliance between Burgundy and the count palatine of the Rhine in 1465 was his doing. In the summer of 1469 he was an obvious choice for the post of ducal bailiff in Upper Alsace. There he remained until the uprising against him in the spring of 1474 and his subsequent execution but, throughout these last few years, he still played a part in Charles's imperial and German diplomacy, negotiating with Duke Sigmund of Austria and with the Emperor Frederick III on Charles's behalf, and figuring prominently at Trier in the autumn of 1473.

Of the many noble Franche-Comté families whose members served the dukes of Burgundy with loyalty and distinction the most powerful in Charles the Bold's time were the Neuchâtels, whose ancestral seat was the fortress of Neuchâtel-Urtières 15 km south of Montbéliard. When Charles became duke in 1467 the head of the family was Thibaud IX. He had been marshal of Burgundy since 1443 and had acquired important lordships, notably Châtel-sur-Moselle, in Lorraine.[1] Thibaud IX died in 1469. Two of his relatives were placed, with Burgundian help, in bishoprics of vital importance for the promotion of Burgundian power. His son Anthoine was given the bishopric of Toul in 1460 though he was only twelve years old at the time, and his nephew Charles de Neuchâtel was archbishop of Besançon from 1463 to 1498.

No fewer than three Neuchâtels became lieutenants of Charles the Bold. Thibaud's brother, Jehan de Neuchâtel, lord of Montagu, was lieutenant or lieutenant-general in the Franche-Comté and commanded the duke's forces in Burgundy in 1471 and again in 1475. Thibaud's eldest son Henry, who became lord of Neuchâtel and Châtel-sur-Moselle on his father's death in 1469, was also lord of Blamont and Héricourt. In 1474 he was Charles the Bold's 'lieutenant-general on the frontiers of Germany', apparently with instructions to recover the duke's rights in Upper Alsace;[2] but his main task was

---

[1] On this and what follows see, besides Loye, *Histoire de Neuchâtel-Bourgogne*, above pp. 101-3, Marot, *AE* xliv (1930), 21-36, and Piquard, *BHPTH* (1932-3), 35-46.
[2] See for example *Dépêches des ambassadeurs milanais*, i. 168-9, BN Coll. de Bourgogne MS. 29, p. 334, and *Mémoires*, ii. 259 n. *d* and 272.

probably the defence of the county of Burgundy against the Swiss and their allies. His younger brother, Claude de Neuchâtel, lord du Fay, was appointed in 1474 the duke's 'lieutenant on the frontiers of Luxembourg' or 'in our duchy of Luxembourg', or 'our lieutenant-general in our land of Luxembourg', as he was variously described in the remarkable series of letters sent to him by Charles the Bold in 1474–6 which happen to have survived.[1] Other people addressed him as governor of Luxembourg, but we may allow that Duke Charles was better informed than they. His strategic position at Luxembourg, midway between the northern and southern Burgundian territories, as it were, and between France and Germany, made him of supreme importance to Charles the Bold throughout 1475 and 1476 and, especially, in the last few months of 1476, when the duke was struggling desperately to win control of neighbouring Lorraine.

Representatives of one more family may be added to this by no means exhaustive list of lieutenants and partisans of Charles the Bold. Nicolas Rolin of Autun had spent his long life in the service of Philip the Good, much of it as chancellor, and in amassing lands and wealth for himself and his sons. One of these, Jehan Rolin, became bishop of Autun. Another, Anthoine, lord of Aymeries, Autun and Lens, served throughout Charles the Bold's reign as the principal ducal officer in Hainault with the title, after 22 December 1467, of grand bailiff and captain-general and, after 1473, of ducal lieutenant in addition. The accounts which he rendered to the *chambre des comptes* at Lille show that he was under the orders of the count of Romont, Charles's lieutenant-general in all the northern lands, as well as the chancellor Guillaume Hugonet. The publication and implementation of the duke's letters and ordinances, particularly those relating to the convocation of the three Estates of Hainault and the recruitment and mobilization of troops, formed the main part of his duties.[2] While he continued loyally to serve Charles's successors, his brother Guillaume Rolin, lord of Beauchamp, had apparently gone over to Louis XI in or before 1470, though only, according to Chastellain, after Charles had confiscated all his goods and lands because he had appealed, in

---

[1] Printed *Recueil du Fay* and partly in *Mémoires*, i. 355–72. For his title of lieutenant and the designation of him as governor see *Recueil du Fay*, 98, 108, 116, 155, etc.

[2] ADN B10433–10441. See too Gondry, *Grands baillis de Hainaut*, 110–11. For what follows see Chastellain, *Oeuvres*, v. 469–70 and de Chevanne, *Les geurres en Bourgogne*, 90 n. 1 and 91, and *Correspondance de la mairie de Dijon*, i. 167–9, 171–2, etc.

a case that went against him, to the *Parlement* of Paris. This defection can only have been temporary, for he was serving with the ducal army in Burgundy in 1471, and in 1475 he was captain of Dijon.

Although he was a very different kind of person from the other Burgundian clients and supporters so far discussed, Tommaso Portinari can scarcely be omitted from any attempt to enumerate the leading instruments of Charles the Bold's power.[1] A Florentine citizen and merchant, he was a descendant of Folco Portinari, the father of Dante's Beatrice. He arrived at Bruges as an office boy in 1439 and lived there for more than fifty years, becoming in 1464 manager of the Bruges branch of the Medici bank on the retirement of Agnolo Tani. He was one of Charles the Bold's devoted Italian admirers who, as a ducal councillor, could be summoned at any time to visit the duke on business; as he was, for example, in February and March 1468.[2] From 1465 onwards he farmed the ducal toll at Gravelines paying, after 1470, £16,200 p.a. for it and doubtless making a handsome profit. For a time he was the official agent for the import of papal alum into the Burgundian Low Countries.[3]

Tommaso Portinari's services to Charles the Bold were many and various, but the idea that he broke the Medici bank at Bruges by irresponsibly lending enormous sums to Charles to finance his campaigns scarcely corresponds with reality. It is, however, clear that he did exceed the £6,000 credit he was permitted to give Charles under the terms of his 1471 contract with Lorenzo il Magnifico, and Louis XI did have a letter written to Piero de' Medici on 10 September 1468 complaining that the Medici branches in London and Bruges had been lending money to his enemies.[4] This must surely have been with reference to the financial arrangements accompanying the marriage in the summer of that year of Charles the Bold and Margaret of York, for Portinari advanced to Edward at least the first 50,000 crown instalment of Margaret's dowry of 200,000 crowns. The total sum owed to Portinari by Charles the Bold at the time of the duke's death is said to have been £57,000 of Artois, but this probably

[1] On Portinari see in general *Correspondance de la filiale de Bruges des Medici*, de Roover, *Money, banking and credit in medieval Bruges*, 87 etc., the same, *MKVAL* xv (1953), and the same, *The Medici Bank*, 341–8 etc. In what follows I have found the unpublished thesis of Maeght, *Les emprunts de Charles le Téméraire*, 78–87, useful.
[2] ADN B2068, fos. 41b and 50a–b.
[3] Delumeau, *L'alun de Rome*, 32–6, 85–6 and 91–2.
[4] Buser, *Beziehungen der Mediceer zu Frankreich*, 437.

comprised mainly payments due for services rendered and goods, such as cloth and plate, supplied, rather than loans.

What were the services rendered to Duke Charles by Tommaso Portinari? It was he who had the ducal seal made at Bruges at the start of the new duke's reign. In 1467 he arranged for the payment of ducal messengers going to England and Rome. He must often have acted as a financial adviser and as a supplier. He furnished a large part of the de luxe materials and other things required for the duke's extravagant wedding festivities in 1468. On occasion he was offered an honoured place at court, for example at Trier in 1473. His name occurs time and again in the ducal accounts, and this chapter may perhaps fittingly close with a characteristic entry which demonstrates his real value to Duke Charles not as a money-lender but as a financial agent.[1]

To Sire Thomas de Portunary, Florentine merchant residing in the town of Bruges, the sum of £2,000 of the said price of forty groats the pound, which is owing him and which by order of Mademoiselle the duchess of Burgundy and by her letters patent given in her town of Malines on the penultimate day of June 1477, has been delivered to him in cash by the *trésorier des guerres* for this reason. In June 1476 the late Monsieur the duke Charles of Burgundy, may God pardon him, ordered the *généraux sur le fait de ses aides* to send to him in Savoy with all diligence the moneys from the instalment of his aid of 500,000 crowns falling due at the end of April 1476, to be used for the payment and expenses of the army which he had and was maintaining in Germany. The said *généraux* remonstrated with the late duke's councillors concerning the perils and dangers of the roads along which the said moneys would have to be sent to him, explaining that it would be better to have them placed safely in the hands of the said Sire Thomas so that by his means the duke could recover them at the exchanges of Geneva, Besançon, Dijon or elsewhere. So it was decided to deliver these moneys, to a total of £72,000 of forty groats, into the hands of the said Sire Thomas to be sent with all diligence to the late lord duke at the peril and risk of the said Sire Thomas and that, for his pains, expenses and costs which he had to undertake in this matter, he would have £2,000 of the said £72,000. The said Sire Thomas agreed and consented to do this, as appears more fully in a certain act of the said council etc.

To accomplish this the said Sire Thomas received the said sum of £72,000 from the *trésorier des guerres*, for which he delivered his receipts

---

[1] AGR CC25543, fos. 190a–191a. For this paragraph see ADN B2064, fos. 233 and 334 and 2068, f. 375 etc., and above, p. 142.

etc. Of this sum of £72,000 he delivered into the hands of the late duke
in Burgundy the sum of £51,000 by two of his quittances, one of 6
August 1476 for £20,000 and the other of 7 September in the same year
for £31,000, which comes to £51,000. And the rest, totalling £21,000,
was sent back here by the agents and factors of the said Sire Thomas
because the late duke did not want to receive it. Of this, the sum of
£19,000 was paid by Sire Thomas into the hands of Pierre Lanchals,
councillor and receiver-general of all finances of my said Demoiselle, by
three letters of receipt made out to the said *trésorier des guerres* as
follows: on 12 February 1477 for £2,898.10s, on 29 June 1477 for
£3,810, and the third on 3 July in the same year for £12,261.10s. These
three letters total £19,000 (*sic*) so that there only remains, to make up
the sum of £72,000, the £2,000 which were allotted to Sire Thomas for
his pains, expenses and costs. . . .

CHAPTER EIGHT

The Revolt of Alsace and the League of Constance

The mortgage to Charles the Bold of the Habsburg lands and rights in Upper Alsace by Duke Sigmund of Austria-Tirol, which was formally effected by means of the treaty of St. Omer of 9 May 1469, has been discussed in an earlier chapter.[1] This transference of power, which brought the landgraviate of Alsace, the county of Ferrette, the Black Forest towns of Rheinfelden, Säckingen, Laufenburg and Waldshut, as well as Breisach, into the Burgundian sphere of influence and partly under Burgundian control, was of the utmost significance for the future relationship of Charles the Bold with his new neighbours, most of whom resented or feared this intrusion. Unlike the Austrians, the Burgundians were *welsch*, or French-speaking foreigners, in a thoroughly Germanic area. Their arrival, and the administrative activities which accompanied it, aroused the suspicions and distrust of Charles's ally the imperial *Landvogt* of Alsace, Frederick the Victorious, elector palatine of the Rhine, as well as of two of the most powerful and populous cities on the Rhine, Strasbourg and Basel. Strasbourg in particular was a force to be reckoned with. She exercised a sort of commercial protectorate over the trade routes her economy depended on, especially down-river to the fairs of Frankfurt and to Cologne, and up-river to Basel and

---

[1] Above, pp. 84–100. Inevitably, this chapter is based on the masterly analysis of Bittmann in *Ludwig XI. und Karl der Kühne*, ii (1). The following have also been useful: Ammann, *RHB* iv (1927), 57–8, Bernoulli, *BVG* xiii (1893), 313–80, Brauer-Gramm, *Peter von Hagenbach*, Dändliker, *Ursachen und Vorspiel der Burgunderkriege*, Dierauer, *Geschichte der schweizerische Eidgenossenschaft*, ii, Durr, *ZGA* x (1911), 259–414, and *La politique des Confédérés au xive et au xve siècle*, Fischer, *Campagnes des Confédérés*, Gagliardi, *Geschichte der Schweiz*, i, Gingins-La Sarraz, *Épisodes* and *Lettres sur la guerre*

thence over the mountains to Geneva, and her trading connections extended to Avignon and Italy. She exercised a political protectorate over a wide area by means of her castles and vassals. Her town-councillors kept a wary eye on all those whose interests and activities might impinge on their own. They expressed their feelings about Charles the Bold's acquisitions in and near Upper Alsace by tearing up the letter Rudolf von Hochberg sent announcing them. Thereafter they and their community remained more consistently and radically anti-Burgundian, perhaps, than any other town or indeed any ruler, not excluding Louis XI.

In important respects the treaty of St. Omer was also a more or less direct provocation of the Swiss and, especially, of Bern. After all, territorially speaking, Burgundy now took the place of the Habsburgs, hitherto the traditional enemies and victims of Swiss expansion. The imperial decrees against the Swiss published in the summer of 1469 were a direct result of the treaty of St. Omer,[1] and Sigmund's only motive in signing it was to obtain Burgundian military aid against

---

des Suisses contre le duc Charles-le-Hardi, Janeschitz-Kriegl, ZGO cv (1957), 150–224 and 409–55, de Mandrot, JSG v (1880), 130–82 and vi (1881), 203–16, Mantel, Die Burgunderkriege, Matzenauer, Studien zur Politik Karls des Kühnen bis zum Jahre 1474, Matzinger, Zur Geschichte der niederen Vereinigung, Mieg, BMM, especially lxxvi (1968), 47–154, Ochsenbein, Kriegsgründe und Kriegsbilder, Oechsli, PJSE v (1890), 302–616, von Rodt, Feldzüge Karls des Kühnen, Stenzel, RHB iv (1927), 50–7, Toutey, Charles le Téméraire et la Ligue de Constance, Witte, ZGO (N.F.) i (1886), 129–69, the same, ZGO (N.F.) ii (1887), 1–58 and 201–35, the same, ZGO (N.F.) vi (1891), 1–81 and 361–414, the same, ZGO (N.F.) vii (1892), 414–77, viii (1893), 197–255 and x (1895), 78–112 and 202–66, the same, Herzog Sigmunds von Oestreich Beziehungen zu den Eidgenossen, and Zellweger, ASG v (1847), 3–149 (with documents). On particular towns, see Feller, Geschichte Berns, i and Zesiger, BBG xxii (1926), 169–78, Bernoulli, BNB lxxvi-lxxviii (1898–1900) and Wackernagel, Geschichte der Stadt Basel, i and Stenzel, Politik der Stadt Strassburg. Some important documents are calendared or printed in Aktenstücke und Briefe zur Geschichte des Hauses Habsburg, i, Basler Chroniken, iii. 364–583, Büchi, FG xiii (1906), 1–60, Cartulaire de Mulhouse, iii and iv, Dépêches des ambassadeurs milanais, i, Eidgenössischen Abschiede, ii, Rechtsquellen des Kantons Bern, iv (1), Urkunden, Briefe und Actenstücke, and Urkundenbuch der Stadt Basel, viii. The main chronicles are Knebel, Diarium, ii, Schilling, Die Berner-Chronik and Trausch Strassburgische Chronick, representing Basel, Bern and Strasbourg respectively, and Reimchronik über Hagenbach; see too Historischen Volkslieder, ii. I have also made use of Dr. Grüneisen's manuscript RTA material for parts of this chapter.

[1] Grüneisen, Aus Reichstagen des 15. und 16. Jahrhunderts, 154–212.

them. Bern's interests and aspirations were most directly thwarted by the treaty, for she had hoped to implement the clause in the treaty of Waldshut which permitted her to take possession of that place if Sigmund failed to pay her a stipulated 10,000 Rhenish florins in reparations by 24 June 1469. Now Charles the Bold took over this obligation at St. Omer, and the money was paid over by his emissaries at Bern on 23 June, thus disappointing Bern of her projected conquest of Waldshut, which was one of the four Black Forest towns ceded to Charles by Sigmund. The treaty of St. Omer also conferred a Burgundian protectorate over Duke Sigmund and made him a Burgundian ally. Since he had proved himself an inveterate enemy of the Swiss, this action on Charles the Bold's part could well have been interpreted as an infringement of his treaty with Bern, Zürich, Solothurn and Fribourg of two years before. Thus a Swiss–Burgundian war was by no means a distant possibility, or unlikely result, of the treaty of St. Omer. It was made quite probable.

Who exactly were 'the Swiss'? The word itself, in the form *Switzeri*, *Switzer*, or *Zwitsois*, was only just coming into use in the fifteenth century, among people of other areas, as a loose synonym for the confederates or *Eidgenossen*, literally oath companions, and their allies.[1] The word is of course derived from the name of one of the three original communities, the so-called Forest Cantons or *Waldstätten*, that joined to form the nucleus of the Swiss federation at the end of the thirteenth century: Uri, Schwyz and Unterwalden. Properly speaking, the word *Eidgenossen* can only be applied, in the fifteenth century, to the eight *alte Orte*, literally old places, that is, the old and established members of the federation. Besides the three above-mentioned, they comprised two other rural communities, Zug and Glarus, and the three towns of Luzern, Zürich and Bern. The word Swiss, however, conveniently comprises also the allies and dependencies of the *Orte* or *Eidgenossen*. Officially, the federation referred to itself as 'the great league of Upper Germany': in Latin, *magna liga Alamanie superioris*; in German, *der grosse Bund ober-deutschen Lands*. If these people thought of themselves as belonging anywhere in particular, they were imperial and German. No geographical name existed for the area they occupied; it was referred to by themselves and others as Germany. Their affairs were regulated by

---

[1] Schilling, *Die Berner-Chronik*, i. 93, complains that Charles the Bold referred to 'the *Switzer*' in a letter instead of to 'the *Eidgenossen*'.

the one and only federal institution, the *Tag* or diet, which met irregularly and in different places, but most often at Luzern.

This fifteenth-century Swiss federation, or at any rate a large part of it, was dynamic, expansionist and aggressive. Neighbours were terrorized by raids, forced into dependent alliances, if necessary conquered outright. The town of Bern, most westerly and therefore nearest to Burgundy of the *Orte*, was also a brilliantly successful empire builder on her own account, though she had found it convenient, since 1353, to operate her entirely self-interested and thoroughly aggressive policies within the framework of the federation. Inside her ever-expanding sphere of influence Bern constructed a sort of *Eidgenossenschaft* of her own which necessarily extended westwards, since her expansion in the area of the Rhine, above Basel, was hampered or even blocked by Zürich and the other *Orte*. Solothurn had been an ally and virtual satellite of Bern since the late thirteenth century. By the time of Charles the Bold other places, among them Biel, Fribourg and Murten, stood in a similar relationship to her. In Fribourg, the influence of Bern extended to the borders of the French-speaking world, for part of that town was and still is German-speaking and the other part French; and the minutes of the town council in the fifteenth century were entered in a curious mixture of the two languages, with Latin used to help out.

Other places and regions that were wholly French-speaking had become dependencies of Bern, notably Valangin and Neuchâtel, the second comprising the town and the county of the same name. Her influence, too, extended through the Vaud or Waadt which formed part of Savoy. It was in this area that Bern first found herself in direct territorial contact with Burgundy. The count of Neuchâtel at this time was Charles the Bold's trusted councillor and governor of Luxembourg, Rudolf von Hochberg; moreover the Burgundian house of Chalon possessed the lordships of Orbe, Grandson and other places along Bern's western frontier, while the baron of Vaud was none other than Jaques de Savoie, count of Romont, soon to become one of Charles the Bold's most active and loyal captains and supporters.

The treaty of St. Omer opened, as we have seen, a second frontier between Burgundy and Bern besides that existing already in the Vaud. The hub of this new frontier was Mulhouse, and some mention has already been made in an earlier chapter of the way this imperial town was surrounded, threatened and repeatedly damaged in one way or another by the restless and ambitious rural aristocrats outside her walls. Up to 1469 these vassals were Austrian, and in 1466 Mulhouse signed a treaty with Bern and Solothurn in order to protect herself against their depredations. In 1468 this treaty was invoked and Bern and her associates went to war against Duke Sigmund on behalf of beleaguered Mulhouse. Now, after 1469, it was Burgundian vassals that threatened Mulhouse and Burgundian, instead of Austrian, authorities were held responsible for her troubles. It is not without significance that the official Bern chronicler of the Burgundian wars, Diebold Schilling, begins his narrative with an account of Bern's alliance with Mulhouse, though he erroneously postdates it by two years.

Peter von Hagenbach lost no time, after his appointment as Burgundian bailiff in Upper Alsace on 20 September 1469, in demonstrating his intense dislike of the townspeople and of the Swiss. He is supposed to have written to Strasbourg in 1470 ordering them not to proceed to the election of the new *Ammeister*. Instead, 'we will come in person to give you one, who will be neither a butcher nor a baker nor a ribbon merchant; you will have the honour of having for chief the noblest of princes, the duke of Burgundy himself'.[1] Charles the Bold certainly seems to have condoned his bailiff's hostile sentiments and provocative actions. On 10 May 1470 Bern's ambassador at the Burgundian court, Adrian von Bubenberg, who was a Burgundian pensionary, reported in Basel that

he himself had heard and seen the duke of Burgundy's secretary Besançon [Philibert] telling the duke of the practices, carryings on and conduct of Herr Peter von Hagenbach in these lands against us, the nobility and people etc. and, after everything Besançon had said, our lord of Burgundy publicly replied that he did not want Herr Peter von Hagenbach to do what his neighbours, subjects and the people wanted him to do, but he wanted to have a bailiff who did what he wanted him to do.[2]

Hagenbach's attitude to the Swiss was by no means a purely personal one. It is paralleled, for example, in a memorandum sent by the Burgundian councillors at Ensisheim to Charles the Bold in July 1469, which claims that the *Eidgenossen* 'have for a long time grievously oppressed, ravaged and damaged the nobility, land and people [of Alsace] with excessive force, arrogance and injustice'. It was, in essence, an Austrian and an aristocratic attitude; but it was not wholly shared by Charles the Bold. Thus, while Hagenbach would have been

---

[1] Trausch, *Strassburgische Chronick*, 11. For what follows, see *Cartulaire de Mulhouse*, iii. 351.
[2] *Eidgenössischen Abschiede*, ii. 409. On von Bubenberg, see Ziegler, *AHKB* xii (1899), 1–130, and, on his Burgundian rent, *IACOB* iv. 256. For the next paragraph, see de Comines, *Mémoires*, ed. Lenglet du Fresnoy, iii. 238–45.

only too glad to join with Sigmund in making war on the Swiss, Charles was quite unwilling to accede to Duke Sigmund's repeated requests for a joint campaign against them. He instructed his ambassador to Sigmund in the spring of 1470 to tell him firmly that their duke was militarily committed to his ally the duke of Brittany, who was about to be attacked by the king of France. He was also bound to keep forces ready to go to the aid of his ally the king of England, who was threatened by his enemies. The ambassadors were to go further, and warn Sigmund of the danger of provoking the Swiss, which he should be careful not to do, at the same time pointing out that the duke of Burgundy was only bound to make war on the Swiss if they actually attacked Sigmund, which they had not done. The duke planned to organize a conference which he hoped would settle all differences between Sigmund and the Swiss, as well as certain points at issue between himself and them.

Just over a year after Charles the Bold's acquisition of Alsace his bailiff's behaviour provoked interested neighbours into conferring together for the first time on the best means of dealing with the situation. The meeting, attended by representatives of the imperial *Landvogt*, Frederick the Victorious, of Strasbourg, Colmar and Sélestat, and of Basel and the *Eidgenossen*, was held in Basel at the end of June 1470. Hagenbach's threats to take Mulhouse into the 'protection' of the duke of Burgundy were reported and deplored and it is perhaps permissible to discern at this meeting the birth of a new political idea, that of an alliance to expel the Burgundians from Alsace. The initiative in these first moves against Burgundian power there was taken by the elector palatine of the Rhine, though he was careful not to endanger thereby his alliance with Charles the Bold. These anti-Burgundian moves coincided with Louis XI's first treaty with the Swiss, of 13 August 1470, but this was a purely negative affair, for each signatory only promised to remain neutral in the event of the other becoming involved in a war with Charles the Bold,[1] and it is noteworthy that Louis attacked Charles in January 1471 without making any attempt whatsoever to persuade the Swiss to do so at the same time.

Early in 1471 Sigmund received a letter from Charles the Bold renouncing, or purporting to renounce, his plan for a crown for himself and for a closer alliance with the Habsburgs.[2] By this time

[1] Printed Thommen, *ZGA* xv (1916), 138–42.
[2] Above pp. 131–2.

Sigmund's hopes of recovering his ancestral possessions from the Swiss by means of a combined attack with Charles the Bold must have worn thin indeed. The treaty of St. Omer had by no means fulfilled his expectations, and he now turned from plans of attacking the Swiss to possibilities of arbitration. The bishop of Constance, Hermann von Breitenlandenberg, was entrusted in January with the task of making conciliatory initiatives, but it was not until October 1471 that a peace conference was actually convened, at Einsiedeln. The aim was the time-honoured one, of achieving a lasting settlement or *ewige Richtung* between the Austrians and the Swiss. A clause of the treaty of Waldshut of 27 August 1468 had called on Duke Ludwig of Bavaria-Landshut to negotiate such a peace and Ulrich, count of Württemberg, had tried to achieve one as recently as December 1470.[1] Now it was to be negotiated afresh but with the novel proviso, laid down by the Swiss as a result of pressure from Strasbourg, that Sigmund was to regain possession of the lands and rights in and near Alsace which he had mortgaged to Charles the Bold. In point of fact the conference of Einsiedeln achieved nothing; nonetheless it was a further significant step towards the formation of a grand alliance against Burgundy, again without any encouragement from Louis XI.

Charles the Bold can scarcely have been unaware of these negotiations for an alliance against him. In January 1471 he sent one of his most experienced diplomats, Guillaume de Rochefort, to Bern and her allies to assure them of his continuing friendship and good intentions, and to propose a peace conference under Burgundian auspices at Besançon, Basel or Montbéliard at which their differences with Duke Sigmund could be ironed out. They were not impressed. Another Burgundian ambassador, Jehan de Bauffremont, arrived at Bern on 29 June 1471 with similar instructions and was likewise disregarded. He offered the Swiss an investigation into allegations against Burgundian officials in Alsace, an alliance with Burgundy, supplies of Salins salt, and other unspecified economic benefits in return for facilities for recruiting Swiss mercenaries for Charles the Bold's armies and the abandonment by the Swiss of any alliances they might have with Louis XI. But the Swiss remained distrustful and suspicious of Charles and more or less favourable to Sigmund, who persisted in his pacificatory initiatives. At their diet in Luzern on 10 April 1472 the *Eidgenossen* resolved to assure the bishop of Constance

---

[1] Liebenau, *AnzSG* (N.F.) iii (1878–81), 84–7.

that a majority were in favour of a peace settlement with Sigmund, and they sent him a new set of conditions.

Sigmund at this time was playing a double game. He told the Swiss he wanted peace with them, but his ambassador at Bruges early in the year insisted that his duke planned to attack the Swiss if he could get Burgundian help. Charles the Bold too, was playing a double game. At the end of May 1472 he sent Peter von Hagenbach on embassy to Sigmund to discuss the possibility of joint military action against the Swiss but warning him of the likely outbreak in the near future of war between himself and Louis XI. Earlier in the same spring he had despatched yet another pacificatory embassy to the Swiss, whom his ambassadors took the trouble to approach individually. Jaques de Savoie, count of Romont, Bern's territorial next-door neighbour and, at that time, friend, who organized this embassy on Charles the Bold's behalf, sent him a report which opens with the ambassadors' instructions:[1]

> What Messire Henry de Colombier and Jehan Alard are to say to the allied powers on the part of my most redoubted lord Monsieur the duke of Burgundy and of Brabant, and also on the part of my most redoubted lord Monsieur the count of Romont.
>
> First, our most redoubted lord the count of Romont has charged us to tell you on behalf of Monsieur the duke of Burgundy of the great and long-standing friendship and good neighbourliness which has always existed between the house and lands of Burgundy and you, Messieurs the allies. Never has he nor have his predecessors done anything to you or caused anything to be done to you which could have resulted in grief or damage, but you have been well and benignly received in the duke's lands and treated favourably there like his own subjects, and his subjects have been treated likewise in your lands, so that you and he have not had occasion to be discontented one with another.
>
> Item, nonetheless the duke has been told that, through the means and activities of certain people trying to introduce discord between him and you, untrue things have been attributed to him, among others that he did not by any means have you excepted from the treaty he made with the duke of Austria, and that he has taken the duke of Austria into his protection against you and has acquired the lands of Ferrette and Alsace against you. The ambassadors shall say and remonstrate on the duke's behalf that what was negotiated by him with the duke of Austria was not at his instigation or request, for the duke of Austria came to him in

---

[1] De Comines, *Mémoires*, ed. Lenglet du Fresnoy, iii. 347–56, wrongly placed here and elsewhere under the year 1474.

person in his lands over there[1] and asked and requested him to come to an agreement concerning the said lands of Alsace and Ferrette which he transferred to him in mortgage. My said lord [the duke of Burgundy] agreed, and he was forced to do so because he was definitely informed that if he had not taken them the said duke of Austria would have transferred them elsewhere, which could have caused [the duke of Burgundy] great prejudice and harm, and not just him, but you too and others. In this affair the duke never meant to do anything which is or could be to your prejudice but rather for your better defence and security. As for the protection into which my said lord has taken the duke of Austria, you must realize that he has not done this against you, nor to damage you in any way, but to help appease any differences there might be between the duke of Austria and you, in aid of which appeasement my said lord has often sent to you and made certain approaches to you through which you could have seen and appreciated that my said lord wanted to please you, as he still does, and offers to employ himself, if you wish it, in [making] a good and lasting appeasement and settlement between you [and the duke of Austria].

Item, as to what is alleged about the deeds and words of Messire Pierre de Hagenbach, they are to say that my said lord [the duke] was quite unaware that the said Hagenbach had undertaken anything against you or harmed any of your people, and if he was informed of such a thing he would not suffer it, but he would reprimand him and make him do reparation for his misdeeds as was proper. Indeed he has appointed officials to hear and receive all the complaints people want to make, and if he finds that [Hagenbach] or any other of his officers has wronged them in any way he will put the matter right and correct and punish those of his said officers, of whatever estate they may be, who have offended or misbehaved under cover of their office and estate or otherwise, without any dissimulation, in such a way that you will appreciate that he is a just prince and that he wants to render to each person his due, which is one of his great and particular desires.

Item, [they are to explain] that my said lord has heard, whatever report or statement may have been made to you, that since the said lands of Alsace and of Ferrette have been in his hands you have been in much greater peace, tranquillity and security there than you have ever been, which was quite the reverse before, when you could only traverse the said lands in great danger even with safe-conducts and sureties. Now they are open to you and everyone to go and seek corn, wine, provisions

---

[1] In documents drawn up in the duke's southern territories, that is the two Burgundies, the Burgundian Low Countries are referred to as the lands 'de par de la': 'the lands over there'. See p. 412 below.

and all other merchandize, to your great profit, and the lands are as safe and sure for all those passing through as are my said lord's other lands.[1]

And the said Messire Henry and Jehan Alard shall assure all the said allies that the duke wants to live in all gentleness, friendship and good neighbourliness with them in so far and for as long as they feel the same towards him, and they will not find him in any respect otherwise, whatever opinions or imagined words may be expressed to them.

Jaques de Savoie

Here follow the replies made by the allies to Messire Henry de Colombier, knight, and to Jehan Alard, concerning the instructions which my most redoubted lord Monsieur the duke of Burgundy sent to Monsieur the president and the council at Dijon to send to Monsieur the count of Romont. . . .

The reply of Fribourg

Having arrived in the town of Fribourg the said ambassadors were most honourably received, and while they were in the town they were waited on by the most important people there and they gave them some of their wine. In the morning all the most notable members of their council assembled, and Messire Roul de Vulpens, *advoyer* of the place, said to them in the presence of the council:

'Messieurs, you are very welcome. We ask you to thank most humbly their graces our most redoubted lord Monsieur the duke of Burgundy and our redoubted lord Monsieur the count of Romont for the honour, attention and declaration of goodwill which you have made to us on behalf of our said most redoubted lord. . . . Damage has never been done to us by our lords the predecessors of our most redoubted lord the duke of Burgundy nor by their people, but only profit and honour, and their lands have always been open to us for all our needs, wars and other affairs. [From them] have come to us provisions and other commodities, such as salt, iron, corn and all other goods, and we have communicated and traded, gone and come in all ways as we pleased through their lands without suffering any damage or disturbance. In the time of our most redoubted lord Monsieur the last-deceased duke Philip, may God pardon him, one of our burgesses called Vuilly Preez was taken prisoner by the late Messire Jehan Loys in our said most redoubted lord's lands and taken to Montjoye and to Hardemon, so that we appealed to the mercy of our late most redoubted lord, seeing that he had been arrested in his lands. Without making a lengthy reply he found the means to get our said burgess out of Messire Jehan Loys's hands and he was returned to us without ransom or any other expense. Considering the goodwill and good deeds they have always done to us, we are resolved to do him all the

---

[1] On this paragraph see Ammann, *ELB* vii (1928), 36–61.

good deeds and pleasure that we can, as we are bound to do, especially considering the understanding we have with our said most redoubted lord which, with God's pleasure, we shall maintain with all our power. As regards the counties of Ferrette and Alsace, no damage has occurred there to us, but we go there safely and surely, without safe-conduct or security, which we did not dare do before they were in the hands of our said most redoubted lord. And, as regards Messire Pierre de Hagenbach and the [duke's] officers, we know of nothing to complain about, but only good. . . .'

With the exception of the story of Vuilly Preez the Fribourg reply is reflected in the others, sometimes almost word for word. Indeed one cannot help suspecting that the astonishing unanimity and the exceptional friendliness and politeness exhibited on this occasion by the Swiss to the duke of Burgundy is due to the fact that his ambassadors took round a nearly identical statement for each of them to approve or sign. But the antics of Peter von Hagenbach were by no means entirely masked by this diplomatic smoke-screen of artificial goodwill. At Solothurn the Burgundian ambassadors were requested to persuade the duke to 'order and command' Hagenbach 'to live and communicate more graciously in future with the people of Mulhouse'. At Bern more detailed and specific complaints were made about him by Adrian von Bubenberg and his colleagues. They complained in particular of Hagenbach's rude remarks about the good citizens of Basel and Strasbourg. When their deputies came to confer with him on business he would exclaim mockingly: 'Ha! Ha! Have you come here to oppose my lord of Burgundy? By Christ you villains! you've got it coming to you!' He 'boasted that he would be bailiff of the allies and lord of better houses than the Bernese had, and that they would yet be the duke of Burgundy's [subjects]'. They complained, too, of his hostility towards their ally Mulhouse whose provisions he had confiscated, whose fairs and markets he had interfered with, and whose citizens he had molested.

Some at least of the Swiss felt strongly enough about Hagenbach and Burgundian expansionism in general to continue their so far abortive negotiations with Sigmund for a *Richtung* to be based, among other things, on the return of Upper Alsace to Austrian control. But the conference held at Constance in August 1472 followed the pattern of Einsiedeln. It was a failure. This time the hopes for a *Richtung* were dashed by Burgundian diplomacy, aided perhaps by Adrian von Bubenberg and other Swiss opponents of a peace with Austria at Burgundian expense. Charles the Bold's ambassador was Peter von

Hagenbach, who reached Sigmund at Bregenz at the end of July before the conference opened with instructions to explain why, because of the war with France, his duke was unable just then to attack the Swiss on Sigmund's behalf. Negotiations must continue for the time being, and the impulsive and forceful Hagenbach was told somewhat hypocritically by Charles to explain to Sigmund, misquoting Terence, that 'the wise man ought to try everything first before resorting to arms'.[1] Nonetheless, Hagenbach was to question Sigmund closely about the military prospects and possibilities: exactly what numbers of horse and foot could Sigmund field? What would be the best route to attack the Swiss? How would supplies be assured?

All this was well calculated to raise once more Sigmund's expectations of Burgundian help in a war against the Swiss. His talks with Hagenbach at Bregenz delayed his arrival at Constance until after the appointed time, so that the Swiss deputies threatened to go home there and then. But in the end Sigmund did assist them in the preparation of a draft treaty or *Richtung* which was dated 12 August 1472. Thereafter, however, he abandoned the distasteful idea of a rapprochement with the traditional enemies of his house and placed his trust once more in warfare against them with the aid of his dubious ally Charles the Bold. The new arrangement, or expectation, of Sigmund, was set out in a document of 10 August optimistically described as an 'alliance between Austria and Burgundy against the Swiss'. On the Burgundian side it was agreed that Hagenbach would hold himself ready to bring immediate military aid from Alsace if Sigmund was attacked, that Charles would provide a force of 4,000 horse and 2,000 foot to attack the Swiss or be available to garrison Duke Sigmund's towns, and that, when war broke out, he would prohibit all traffic with the Swiss throughout his lands on pain of decapitation.[2]

How far was Charles the Bold sincere in his encouragement of Sigmund's warlike expectations? His military involvement with Louis XI in 1472 made it quite impossible for him to contemplate immediate action: that year's campaign only came to an end on 3 November, with a truce for five months. But Charles does seem to have seriously considered at this time a joint Austro–Burgundian attack on the Swiss, and such a move was made more likely, and more

---

[1] Terence, *Eunuchus*, iv. 1.789. These instructions are printed in *Akten-stücke und Briefe zur Geschichte des Hauses Habsburg*, i. 14–16.
[2] Printed *Urkunden, Briefe und Actenstücke*, 417–19.

attractive, by the reopening in summer 1472 of the negotiations for a marriage alliance between the houses of Habsburg and Burgundy and for a crown for Charles the Bold. The leading Burgundian exponents of a military alliance with Sigmund were the bailiff of Alsace, Peter von Hagenbach, and his second-in-command, as it were, in Alsace, Bernhart von Ramstein, lord of Gilgenberg, both of whom were as enthusiastic in their support for Sigmund as they were in their hatred of the Swiss. But their influence with Charles the Bold was counteracted and eventually nullified by a strong anti-Austrian party at court led by two councillors who were infinitely better placed than they were to impinge on ducal decisions and policies: Guillaume de Rochefort and the chancellor Guillaume Hugonet.

Although Peter von Hagenbach's authority at the Burgundian court was thus restricted, in Alsace he could do as he pleased, and it was here, at the beginning of 1473, that his blustering, aggressive activities once again significantly affected the course of events by provoking further important moves towards an anti-Burgundian alliance. In particular, on 22 January 1473 he badgered the imperial city of Mulhouse for the third time to open her gates to Duke Charles.[1] A month later, at Luzern on 24 February 1473, the Swiss diet resolved in principle, after every deputy had been furnished with a copy of Hagenbach's threatening letter to Mulhouse and details of his acts of hostility, to work for an alliance with the imperial towns on the Upper Rhine in common defence against Burgundy. Two days before this, on 22 February, deputies from Strasbourg, Colmar, Basel and Sélestat had conferred together at Colmar and concluded that Burgundian rule in the Sundgau must be brought to an end, if necessary by force of arms, and without reference to Sigmund who was rightly thought at that time to be hoping for Charles the Bold's help in a military solution to his problems with the Swiss.

The climax came at a conference in Basel on 14 March 1473. A project for a ten-year alliance was drawn up between the bishops of Strasbourg and Basel, the margrave of Baden, and the towns of Strasbourg, Basel, Colmar and Sélestat on one side and the Swiss with Mulhouse on the other. If any 'foreign *welsch* people', that is French, 'try unjustly by force to take away the liberties of or detach from the Holy Empire one or more members of this alliance, we others shall help and advise them truly in whatever way we and they

---

[1] Above, p. 96.

consider necessary'.[1] The contracting parties agreed to solve Mulhouse's problems by paying her debts and, more important, the four
imperial towns promised, if necessary, to find the funds needed for
the redemption of mortgaged Alsace from Charles the Bold. All the
main elements of a grand alliance against Charles the Bold had thus
emerged by the spring of 1473, but the pieces had not been put
together, nor had anything been implemented.

This progress towards ejecting Burgundy from Alsace had been
made without any initiative whatsoever from Louis XI. When he did
begin to concern himself more or less seriously with Swiss affairs in
May 1473, it was by no means because of his own positive interest in
them, but simply in response to requests from them and their allies.
On 19 May 1473 the Swiss diet at Luzern resolved to write to Louis
to complain of the passage of Charles the Bold's Italian mercenaries
through the Alpine passes 'against him or against us, we do not know'.
Earlier in May, the Milanese ambassador at the French court reported
from Tours, 'the community of Strasbourg has sent an ambassador
here to seek help from His Majesty against the duke of Burgundy'.[2]
Finally, in the same month, Duke Sigmund of Austria, finding himself on the brink of a war with the Swiss but deprived still of any
effective military assistance from his supposed ally the duke of
Burgundy, applied to King Louis XI for help, protection and an
alliance. Naturally, Louis turned down this request, writing to inform
his Swiss allies of it from Amboise on 31 May.[3] But he made no
attempt to exploit the opportunities now offered, almost thrust at,
him of stirring up trouble for his enemy Charles the Bold. He sent
no help of any kind to Strasbourg or to the Swiss nor did he encourage
them to make war on Burgundy. All Louis XI did, in the summer of
1473, was to suggest something which had already been discussed:
the redemption of the Alsace mortgages from Charles the Bold, for
which however Louis categorically refused to pay, and a reconciliation
or *Richtung* between Sigmund and the Swiss. The king of France,
that much-vaunted and allegedly far-sighted diplomat, had no far-
reaching plans, no subtle intentions, no special mastery or monopoly
of diplomatic initiatives. He fumbled along in a series of rather

---

[1] *Cartulaire de Mulhouse*, iv. 103–4.
[2] Bittmann, *Ludwig XI. und Karl der Kühne*, ii (1). 472 n. 291; the quotation
in the preceding sentence is from the same, p. 461 n. 272.
[3] *Lettres de Louis XI*, iii. 336–7, wrongly placed in 1469; see Bittmann,
Ludwig XI. und Karl der Kühne, ii (1). 284–6 and 468.

negative reactions to the impact of Charles the Bold's projects and Hagenbach's provocations.

It was in the summer of 1473 that Augusto de Lignana, the abbot of Casanova, a Piedmontese monastery which a Swiss document confusingly renders *Causa nefa*, undertook his famous embassy to the Swiss on Charles the Bold's behalf. He was empowered at Maastricht on 1 June 1473 just as the duke set out on his Guelders campaign, and his mission was to propose an alliance between Burgundy and the *Eidgenossen*. In fact, he sought an extension of the existing alliance of May 1467 between the duke of Burgundy and Bern, Solothurn, Zürich and Fribourg which would embrace all the other *Orte*. In exchange for this alliance, which the abbot maintained was aimed against the duke of Milan, Charles the Bold was ready to offer the Swiss the four Black Forest towns of Waldshut, Säckingen, Laufenburg and Rheinfelden which he currently held in mortgage from Sigmund. It was perhaps typical of Charles the Bold to attempt to swing the hostile Swiss over to him with a visionary or theoretical scheme of this kind, while ignoring the practical irritations and provocations to which Hagenbach was constantly subjecting them in and around Alsace. Once again, the Swiss were unimpressed. They ignored these blandishments. They felt themselves threatened by Burgundian power, and they were indeed.

In the autumn of 1473 another interested party, the Emperor Frederick III, was invited by the Swiss to help them achieve a settlement with Duke Sigmund, but his discussions with the Swiss deputies at Basel early in September 1473 came to nothing. Frederick was personally in favour of a *Richtung* and also of the return of Alsace to the house of Austria; so were the Swiss; and Sigmund, becoming at last utterly disillusioned with Charles the Bold, took up these ideas again himself towards the end of the year. The breakdown of the Trier talks between Frederick and Charles, which some attributed to Charles's refusal to hand back Alsace,[1] was crucial in all this, because the prospects of any kind of an arrangement between the houses of Burgundy and Austria receded rapidly thereafter. On the very last day of the Trier conference, 25 November 1473, Sigmund's ambassadors were told by the Burgundian chancellor that their duke was convinced that Sigmund was planning to transfer Alsace to a third party, and they were invited to seek from Sigmund a definite promise that Charles the Bold would be left in possession of Alsace during his

---

[1] For example von Schaumburg, *Die Geschichten und Taten*, 16–17.

lifetime. Sigmund was in fact in touch with Louis XI; so were the Swiss. Both now hoped that, since all else had failed, the *Richtung* between them, and the redemption of Alsace, could be achieved with the help of French diplomacy.

Charles the Bold's determination to hold on to Alsace was reinforced and publicly displayed by his visit there at Christmas 1473 on his way to Dijon for the interment of his parents' remains in the Charterhouse of Champmol. Some accounts credit him with bringing an army. The Basel authorities were so afraid of a possible siege that they extracted a promise from the *Eidgenossen* that they would send them an 800-strong garrison in case of need. But in fact Charles probably had only a few cavalry detachments with him, apart from the household personnel who alone may have numbered 500 persons. Coming from Lorraine, he arrived at Bergheim on 22 December, but the civic authorities of Colmar refused his request for leave to enter their town with 2,000 men. They would, however, gladly welcome him with up to 200 persons. He did not take up their offer. At Breisach there was no such trouble, and it was here that Charles the Bold spent Christmas week and left a substantial garrison before going on to Ensisheim and Thann. Wherever he went, he insisted on the inhabitants swearing oaths of fealty to him. [1]

In January 1474 two embassies of the utmost importance for the future were sent to the duke of Burgundy. The first, led by two well-known citizens of Bern, Niclaus von Scharnachtal and Peterman von Wabern, was received by Charles at Ensisheim on 8 January. The chronicler of Bern, Diebold Schilling, maintains that the duke kept these Swiss ambassadors waiting on their knees a good half hour and that their embassy achieved nothing; but the opposite was the case. The Swiss deputies were impressed by the generous way they were treated by the duke, who sent food and drink round to them at their hotel on silver dishes and entertained them with trumpeters. Moreover they achieved a notable success in arranging for a conference to settle the difficult problem of Mulhouse and her unpaid debts. They did not, however, omit to make their discontent on a number of important points abundantly clear. In particular, they complained of the protection extended by Charles the Bold and Hagenbach to their enemy Bilgri von Heudorf, who had seized and robbed some Swiss merchants travelling down the Rhine to the Frankfurt fair in the

---

[1] On this paragraph, besides the works cited above, p. 89 n. 1, see Megkynch. *Bericht*, and Pfettisheim, *Geschichte*, 19.

spring of 1473, and of Peter von Hagenbach's threat 'that he would shortly conquer many of the *Eidgenossen*'s lordships and would soon be lord of Bern'.[1]

The second embassy to Charles was from Duke Sigmund of Austria. It reached him at Dijon at the end of January 1474 with excuses for Sigmund's failure to visit Charles at Breisach and an explanation of his negotiations with the king of France which quite untruthfully made Louis take the initiative. The Burgundian reply shows that Charles was angry and that the Austro–Burgundian alliance was now a thing of the past. Sigmund was accused of going behind Charles's back. Why did he need to seek French help in a rapprochement with the Swiss unless this move was specifically anti-Burgundian? Was it not true that the duke of Burgundy had given him such excellent protection against the Swiss that he had not had 'the smallest house burnt or the smallest chicken stolen'?[2]

As usual the initiative, in the further round of negotiations for an alliance against Burgundy which now ensued, was urban. It was Strasbourg which raised the matter with Bern at the end of 1473, and at Basel on 13 January 1474 the Swiss ambassadors returning from Ensisheim agreed to what amounted to a revival of the scheme discussed there in March 1473. At this stage there was no suggestion of redeeming the Alsace mortgage from Charles the Bold, but in the talks which followed, in February and March 1474, the redemption was once more proposed as an essential element in the settlement, partly because Louis XI insisted, in return for his good offices in helping to mediate between the parties, that Sigmund terminate his alliance with Charles and regain possession of Alsace. But Louis's role was a limited one. Instead of employing his own French diplomats in these negotiations, he allowed the Swiss and the Austrians to undertake them themselves, by accrediting two recently appointed titular councillors of his, the Swiss Jost von Silenen, provost of Beromünster,[3] and the Austrian Hans, count of Eberstein.

The insignificance of Louis's part in what followed is reflected in the statement of the chronicler Gerold Edlibach, that the settlement between Austria and the Swiss was brought about by Jost von Silenen, who had been sent to make peace by God. He does not mention Louis XI. In fact, Louis took no action until requested by

---

[1] Schilling, *Die Berner-Chronik*, i. 128.
[2] *Aktenstücke und Briefe zur Geschichte des Hauses Habsburg*, i. 88.
[3] See on him Müller, *Innerschweiz Essays*, 59–83. For the next sentence, see Edlibach, *Chronik*, 139–40.

Sigmund, nor had he any new plans or ideas. Instead, he fell back once more on the conditions for the *Richtung* which had been drawn up at Constance in August 1472. Moreover, as before, he was by no means prepared to make a financial contribution towards the redemption of the Alsace mortgage. This crucial step had to be undertaken by the towns: Basel, Colmar, and Sélestat agreed to pay half and Strasbourg undertook to find the other half, of the 80,000 Rhenish florins which was thought necessary. Far from being ahead of events, Louis XI had been trailing behind them. His embassy to the Swiss in mid-March, with its belated suggestion that Charles the Bold might try to take Mulhouse by siege more than a month after that town's problems had been settled at the conference table, arrived when the general alliance against Charles the Bold had already virtually been created. All that was still necessary at this late stage was for Bern and Zürich to persuade the other *Eidgenossen* to agree to it. This tricky task was undertaken by Bern. She sent ambassadors to put pressure on Schwyz after the following state of affairs had been revealed at the Luzern diet of 14 March 1474:

> Zürich, Bern and Luzern agreed unreservedly to an alliance with the Alsace towns and to the *Richtung* with Sigmund.
> Uri would agree if either Schwyz or Unterwalden agreed.
> Schwyz would agree if Uri and Unterwalden agreed.
> Zug would agree to whatever was agreed by all the *Eidgenossen* or a majority of them.

It was on 27 March 1474 at Constance that these various negotiations reached a definitive stage with the opening of a conference, as the Basel cleric Johann Knebel put it, 'to consider the peace of the land and how to extricate it from the tyranny of the duke of Burgundy and his wicked bailiff Peter von Hagenbach'. The documents sealed on 31 March and 4 April enshrined four separate elements which lay behind the creation of the League of Constance. First, the *ewige Richtung* or everlasting peace between Austria and the Swiss, was accepted and proclaimed in principle, but the detailed and final arrangements were left for subsequent settlement under the aegis of Louis XI's arbitration. Second, a ten-year defensive alliance of Upper Rhine powers was created which acquired the name of Lower Union in contradistinction to the *Eidgenossen*, who described themselves as the alliance or league of Upper Germany. The original members of the Lower Union were Duke Sigmund of Austria, Ruprecht bishop of Strasbourg, Johann von Venningen bishop of Basel, and the four imperial towns of Strasbourg, Basel, Sélestat and Colmar. But it willingly accepted new recruits. On 27 July 1474 a group of Alsace towns joined: Kaysersberg, Oberhergheim, Munster, Rosheim and Turckheim, and they were followed on 1 October by the town of Montbéliard and Count Henry of Württemberg's officers there, Marquart and Jacob von Stein. Last to join, on 18 April 1475, was René, duke of Lorraine.

A third element in the League of Constance was the redemption by Duke Sigmund of his lands and rights in Upper Alsace mortgaged to Charles the Bold. While Sigmund promised to take these back from Charles by force if necessary and at the same time renounced all his agreements with and obligations to Charles the Bold, the money was to be paid over by the towns and deposited at Basel. Finally, on 4 April 1474 a ten-year defensive alliance was signed between the bishop and towns of Basel and Strasbourg, with Colmar and Sélestat, on the one side, that is the members of the Lower Union with the exception of Sigmund, and, on the other side, the *Eidgenossen* with Solothurn.

Thus, in a somewhat roundabout way, was brought into being the League of Constance, the grand alliance against Charles the Bold. It was defensive in character: the only element of it that might be construed as aggressive, though it was certainly not illegal, was the return of Upper Alsace to Sigmund. It was urban in nature: its creators and leading members were Basel and Strasbourg, Zürich and Bern. And it was so loosely organized and geographically scattered that it was almost incapable of concerted offensive activities. Its formation by no means in itself represented a serious threat to Burgundian power, except perhaps in Alsace, where however Burgundian rule was toppled at this very time by internal mutiny and revolt, followed up, only, by decisive action from the League.

In the spring of 1474 it was becoming increasingly clear that the future plans and prospects of Charles the Bold depended on the course of events in Alsace which in their turn were contingent on the behaviour of his bailiff there, Peter von Hagenbach. Though the problems of Mulhouse had virtually been settled in February, all interested parties had agreed at Constance that Hagenbach must go, and some of those most interested had agreed to meet the cost. Typical in this respect was the attitude of Basel. Charles the Bold sent an embassy there at the end of March protesting his friendship, but complaining of the city's supposed plan to join an alliance with the *Eidgenossen* and his enemy the king of France. The Burgundian

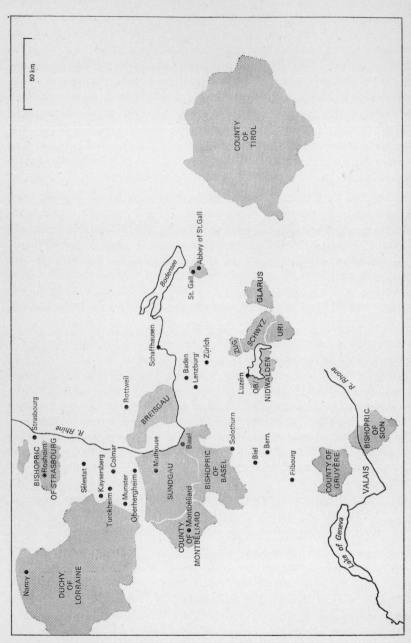

6. The grand alliance against Charles the Bold

ambassadors, Christoph von Rechberg and Anthoine de Palant, arrived on 1 April but received Basel's reply only on 6 April after the treaties of Constance had been signed. The charge of entering an alliance with Louis XI was easily brushed aside; they had made no such alliance. But the goodwill with which they had originally accepted the extension of Burgundian power into Alsace and along the Rhine in the immediate environs of their city had been entirely nullified by the insulting and intolerable proceedings of Hagenbach. They found it absolutely impossible to continue to accept him as bailiff of this area and they submitted to the Burgundian ambassadors one of the longest and most comprehensive lists of complaints against him ever compiled. Some of them were as follows:[1]

The bailiff Herr Peter von Hagenbach's behaviour towards the town of Basel.

When he came into our town for the first time he came to discuss [a delay in] the instalment of money owed for the lordship of Rheinfelden,[2] but this did not fall out according to his wishes. So he gave voice to many grossly unreasonable insults both inside and outside the council, in particular that he would prohibit the town from buying goods and do it harm, and if he caught any of our people in his territories he would hang them on the branches.

Item, he then prohibited in general the purchase of goods for the town, afterwards again allowing purchases apart from corn, all against the agreement [made at] Breisach etc.

Item, without any right and against the laws he completely over-powered and captured a person from Strasbourg and held him prisoner in the Crown Hotel. He held him by the ear and he and his servants nearly killed him with naked swords. All this in our town, forcefully, before he was rescued from their hands. He and his people also broke a garland of pearls belonging to the same man from Strasbourg, and took by force a costly silver pipe and returned nothing. All this [was done] by night and in the fog. . . .

Item, he has maintained untruthfully before princes, counts, lords, knights and servants that we have made a present [to him] of the out-standing payments he owes us for the use of the lordship of Rheinfelden, to which we have never agreed and are still not agreeing. In clarification of this, we sent for Herrn Bernhart von Gilgenberg, Peter Rich and Marquart von Schonemberg, who were present when the agreement was

---

[1] *Basler Chroniken*, iii. 373–80.
[2] For this and the reference below to Rheinfelden, see Wackernagel, *Geschichte der Stadt Basel*, ii. 57–9.

K*

made, but he refused and rejected this. He was offered justice on this before the councillors of our gracious lord of Burgundy, but he refused this too and thereupon directed many threatening remarks at the town, and mischievously employed his words and deeds so that he brought us a great deal of harm. . . .

Item, he also told our servant Stǔmpf at Augsburg that the town must pay him some money or he would do so much to it that Herr Peter Rot [the burgomaster] would be stabbed and this would be done when he was in bed.

Item, he also spoke with the said Stǔmpf here on our Rhine bridge and asked him if he had told us this. [He added] much more; that we kissed calves under the tail, with many suchlike flippant insults.

Item, through such violence, wickedness and wilfulness, which he has shown against us in the prohibition of trading and other evil deeds, he has forced us to make him rebates and gifts.

Item, we wrote to him on behalf of our burgesses who had presented themselves for justice before him and our gracious lord of Burgundy's councillors, concerning Anshelm von Maszmunster, and on that account requested his reply. And as our messenger waited for the answer he tore up the letter and said 'that is my reply to Basel'. . . .

Item, on Good Friday 1473 the bailiff wrote to us requesting a safe conduct. We had our messenger with him on Easter Day with a statement that it was not usual nor was it the practice for the bailiff to ask for or need a safe conduct. Still, since he had asked, so should he have from us free passage and safe conduct according to his request. Thereupon he answered us that neither we nor our people should wander without his safe conduct in the lands he administered, for one day, if he could get hold of them, he would pickle twenty or thirty of our people in gaol and cut off their hands and feet. He attached no value to our seal, for it was not legal, and he snapped his fingers.

Item, he has often sent word to our people and announced to us that he would bring it about that our town would be flattened, so that the same would happen to it as happened to Dinant. . . .

Item, in front of the chancellor of our gracious lord [the bishop] of Basel he attacked Herr Peter Rot's good name, with remarks such as that he was not upright and that he was an evil fellow.

Item, at the time when the *Eidgenossen* were here in our town at a conference, and he was also here, he gave his people long knives to wear and they went mischievously and defiantly against [the *Eidgenossen*] on the Rhine bridge. At the same time, also before and afterwards, he many times called them scullions. . . .

Item, at the time when our most glorious lord the Roman Emperor was with us in our town, the bailiff was also here, and he untruthfully gave out that we had at that time tried to murder him.

Item, the bailiff has said many times, in front of strangers and inhabitants, that when he wants to he will conquer our town in three days
and he will not desist. One day in this town he will lay some people's
heads before their feet and cut off the scalps of some and fix them on their
houses.

In the months between Charles the Bold's departure from Alsace
on 11 January and the presentation of these complaints against him
at Basel on 6 April, Peter von Hagenbach's behaviour had become
increasingly arbitrary, offensive and indecorous. Fearful perhaps for
his safety in a place like Thann, which had already plotted against
him in the summer of 1473, he installed himself in Breisach with a
numerous garrison, partly of Picard and partly of German mercenaries.
He had hurt a good many people's feelings, according to the Basel
chaplain Johann Knebel, by enclosing with the invitations to his
wedding in January requests for specific gifts, such as beef, veal,
chicken or wine, so as to enjoy himself at the expense of others. On
Hagenbach's alleged sexual offences against nuns and others the
contemporary sources are especially loquacious, and none is more
informative or extravagant than the above-mentioned cleric. Some
of his anecdotes of Hagenbach's crudities might be dismissed as
preposterous if other sources did not bear them out. He makes the
bailiff boast in public that, before a banquet organized by himself at
Breisach on 20 February 1474, he had the pubic hair of his wife and
three noblewomen shaved off and given to his cook to pulverize and
then sprinkle on the dishes served to the ladies. He claims that on one
occasion Hagenbach made his wife publicly exhibit her pudenda and
tell the assembled company how many times he had intercourse with
her on their wedding night.

Whatever his crimes and obscenities, Hagenbach's biggest mistake
was attributable to Charles the Bold: he failed to pay his troops.
When these began to mutiny against him at Breisach on Easter
Sunday, 10 April 1474, the citizens of the place, who had suffered at
Hagenbach's hands the total abrogation of their civic institutions and
liberties, encouraged and supported them. The Picard, or *welsch*,
troops of the garrison were expelled forthwith, lucky to be spared
their lives, but Hagenbach was arrested and held prisoner.

Following within a few days only of the formation of the League of
Constance, the detention of Hagenbach was a more serious and more
immediate setback to Burgundian power. Charles had been confident
that his bailiff could hold out in well fortified, well garrisoned Breisach
against any immediate attack. His messenger assuring Hagenbach

that he would by no means be abandoned had reached Breisach on the day of his arrest. But Sigmund of Austria had already taken an important initiative on 6 April, when, while still at Constance, he formally renounced his alliance with Charles the Bold in the presence of four imperial notaries and sent his herald off to Charles at Luxembourg to announce the resumption of his rule in Alsace; he had deposited the money for the redemption of the mortgage in Basel, though he claimed that he was not legally bound to repay it. The Austrian herald also returned to Charles the safe conduct or letters of protection against the Swiss which he had given to Sigmund at St. Omer on 9 May 1469. Sigmund certainly meant business. He appointed a bailiff of his own to replace Hagenbach in Alsace, the Sundgau nobleman Hermann von Eptingen, and on 20 April he arrived in Basel to the great delight of the inhabitants, with an escort of troops.

An equally aggressive spirit was demonstrated by the urban elements of the League of Constance. In mid-April Strasbourg initiated military activities on her own behalf against the remnants of Burgundian rule in Alsace, by taking possession of various places in the Val-de-Villé (Weilerthal). The services of her civic artillery were not however needed, for even the powerful and strategically placed castle of Ortenberg, which Hagenbach had seized in 1470, surrendered without a blow. Sigmund had not exactly or explicitly declared war on Charles the Bold. Nor did Basel and Strasbourg, but on 22 April they sent him a polite though curt declaration announcing that they were bound, as allies, to help Sigmund to recover his Alsace territories. Some of the Swiss too were in hostile mood. Throughout the second half of April and into May Bern was actively preparing for a war against Burgundy and there was much talk, about the middle of the month, of sending a Swiss military contingent into Alsace. In the event, however, Bern only managed to persuade her fellow-*Eidgenossen* to agree that, if necessary, they would be prepared to help defend Alsace against the duke of Burgundy by force of arms.

Meanwhile the fate of Hagenbach hung in the balance, but not for long. At first the Breisach authorities, with their autonomy newly restored, wrote informing Charles almost apologetically of their action in arresting his bailiff, and they might perhaps have acceded to his request for Hagenbach to be handed over to him for justice had not Bern and others insisted on his trial and execution. The execution was resolved on first; the trial was a mere formality. The justice meted out to Hagenbach, if justice one can call it, was imperial, but the court was set up and the sentence carried out by the League of Constance. As the Strasbourg chronicler put it, he was judged 'on behalf of all the members of the alliance',[1] and among the twenty-eight judges were representatives of the four towns of the Lower Union, four Austrian towns, Bern, Solothurn and Breisach. The new Austrian bailiff of Alsace, Hermann von Eptingen, acted as public prosecutor. The accused had been held for several weeks in chains and maimed by the most savage tortures when he was finally brought to court. The day chosen for the beastly ritual was 9 May 1474: five years exactly since Charles the Bold had first taken over Alsace. Hagenbach was charged with the following crimes:

1. Against imperial law, he had beheaded three or four Thann burgesses. The occasion was the suppression on 3 July 1473 of a revolt in Thann.
2. In Breisach, in breach of his own oath to introduce no reforms, or taxes, or *welsch* troops there, he had abolished the guilds, dismissed judges and councillors, demanded new taxes, and brought in Picard troops.
3. He had planned to order his Picard troops to murder their Breisach hosts, and was going to sink their bodies and drown the women and children in specially prepared leaky boats.
4. Both in Breisach and elsewhere he had outraged married women, virgins and even nuns.

Against these charges Peter von Hagenbach's principal defence was that he was acting under orders. The fourth charge he denied outright: he had never used force and had only done what many others in the courtroom had done, paying good money for it. Predictably, the judges refused to accept his request to allow the duke of Burgundy to confirm that his bailiff had only been carrying out his orders. He was taken out and beheaded before a large crowd which had flocked to Breisach from far and near; several hundred onlookers having come from Basel alone. He died in all appearance a devout Christian. He had been a bully, a braggart, a man of violence, but scarcely a criminal. His end was brought about by the proud and obstinate townspeople he despised so much, his enemies and Duke

---

[1] *Straszburgische Archiv-Chronik*, 187. For the trial of Hagenbach, besides the works cited above p. 261 n. 1, see Heimpel, *ZGO* (N.F.) lv (1942), 321–57 (with references) and the same, *Festschrift für E.E. Stengel*, 443–52. De Ring's work on the revolt of Alsace, *MSHB* (1841), 351–87, is of limited value.

Charles's; but it was due also in large measure to his own follies, as well as to Charles the Bold's failure to give him the support he needed in money and troops. In legend and in literature Hagenbach lived on and lives on still, as the archetypal tyrant, the Burgundian bogey man, the iniquitous immoral official of a detested foreign regime. A shrivelled mummified head, supposed to be his, was for a long time exhibited in the museum at Colmar, together with his executioner's sword: grisly testimony to the popular appeal of this imagined nefarious monster.

For Charles the Bold the execution of Hagenbach and the loss of Alsace were grave and critical events. They were his first serious reverses and they probably made a powerful and lasting impression on him, arousing perhaps an irrational desire for revenge and provoking the obstinate, emotional, violent and aggressive side of his character which was to become increasingly apparent in the months and years that followed. Admittedly he wrote to Sigmund in moderate terms on 22 April pointing out that the money for the redemption of the mortgages should be paid, according to the treaty of St. Omer, at Besançon, not at Basel. If Sigmund would care to send his money, and deputies, to Besançon, Charles would appoint councillors to confer there with them. Meanwhile his officers in Alsace would forcefully oppose any Austrian incursions there. But a week later, still some time before the execution of Hagenbach, Charles expressed his feelings on the subject of Alsace a good deal more bluntly, at the same time entertaining characteristically grandiose ideas about punishing Sigmund for his aggression. He swore to the Neapolitan ambassador at his court, Johanne Palomar, on 27 April at Luxembourg, that he would revenge himself on the duke of Austria or lose his life and his state. He suggested a joint Burgundo–Venetian campaign against Sigmund. While the Venetians attacked his lands south of the Alps he would attack north of the Alps, and he requested the ambassador to ask the king of Naples to write to Venice urging this. He himself was considering sending his Portuguese doctor, Messer Lupo, on embassy to Venice and to his captain Bartolomeo 'da Bergamo' to make the necessary arrangements. According to Johanne Palomar Charles had ordered all the men-at-arms of his guard to Alsace and was preparing to send artillery there, as well as the Burgundian vassals and Italian mercenaries stationed in Burgundy.[1]

[1] ASM Pot. est. Borgogna 515/149–50. For Bartolomeo Colleoni, of Bergamo, see above pp. 214 and 215–16.

Other things and other aspirations kept interfering with Duke Charles's undoubted intention in the summer of 1474 to restore his authority in Alsace and revenge himself at least on Sigmund and on Strasbourg and Basel. One place of exceptional strategic importance in the military implementation of any such plans was Montbéliard, 15 km south of Belfort, which commanded the approach from the valley of the Doubs into Alsace, the Upper Rhine region in general and the town and bishopric of Basel in particular. The town and county of Montbéliard constituted an imperial fief in the possession of the comital house of Württemberg, and the three counts had signed a partition treaty in 1473 which allotted Montbéliard to seventeen-year-old Count Henry, while the other family possessions went to his relatives Counts Ulrich and Eberhard. Although Count Henry, like other members of his house, had been on perfectly good terms with Charles the Bold, receiving in 1473 an allowance of 120 florins per month while he was at the Burgundian court,[1] difficulties arose over his taking possession of the Burgundian fiefs which formed dependencies of his county of Montbéliard. In mid-April 1474, in circumstances which so far remain mysterious, Henry fell into Charles the Bold's hands, apparently while he was travelling near Metz or Thionville, either to visit Charles, or on a pilgrimage, or on his way to see the Emperor. He was held prisoner first at Luxembourg, where he read and annotated a copy of Conrad von Megenberg's *Book of Nature* to help while away the time, and then at Boulogne. He suffered indeed the same unfortunate fate that had overtaken another prince, Duke Adolf of Guelders: detention in a Burgundian prison during the rest of Duke Charles's lifetime.

As to Montbéliard, in May Olivier de la Marche and Claude de Neuchâtel were sent to seize it after Count Henry had been forced to sign a document transferring it to Charles. But the count's promise could not be implemented because his captain in Montbéliard refused to surrender the place, even though the Burgundians, who had brought

---

[1] *IADNB* iv. 242. Among chroniclers mentioning the arrest of Count Henry and the Montbéliard affair are de Haynin, *Mémoires*, ii. 175, Knebel, *Diarium*, ii. 82, de la Marche, *Mémoires*, iii. 207–8, Schilling, *Die Berner-Chronik*, i. 170–1 and 194–5 and Trausch, *Strassburgische Chronick*, 14. See too *Politische Correspondenz*, i. 663 (letter of Count Ulrich of 13 May 1474) and *Recueil du Fay*, 98 (letter of Duke Charles of 22 June 1474) and von Rodt, *Feldzüge Karls des Kühnen*, i. 229–42, von Stälin, *Wirtembergische Geschichte*, iii. 575–7, Witte, *ZGO* (N.F.) vi (1891), 24–8, Liebenau, *AnzSG* (N.F.) v (1886–9), 29–36, and Bittmann, *Ludwig XI. und Karl der Kühne*, ii (1). 667–9 etc.

the count with them, threatened to behead him there and then outside the walls if Montbéliard did not surrender. The disappointed de la Marche records in his chronicle that 'the attitude of Montbéliard is such, that they would sooner see soldiers cut off the head of their lord than surrender their place'. The fact is that Montbéliard, though French-speaking, had a distinct preference for neutrality and non-involvement, and was not at all prepared to become Burgundian. Indeed, after the German garrison had been reinforced by Count Henry's relatives, the place entered into negotiations with Bern and other elements of the League of Constance, eventually joining the Lower Union on 1 October 1474.

The Burgundian attempt on Montbéliard was by no means part of a preconceived plan; it was merely an effort to exploit a chance opportunity. In fact, in the summer of 1474 Charles the Bold does seem to have been planning to invade and recover Alsace, but only after he had restored the authority of his ally Ruprecht of Bavaria in the archbishopric of Cologne. In an important despatch sent from Luxembourg by Francesco Bertini to the court of Naples on 24 June 1474, Charles described his prospects and intentions to the ambassador just after the prolongation on 13 June of the truce with France for a further year.[1]

Yesterday around midday I found the French herald with news of the reaffirmed truce. I did not fancy going to the duke immediately for fear of seeming too curious, but I went to my friend to hear his news. Straight away he told me about these one-year truces, though he did not seem very happy about it for he would have preferred a French campaign to leaving these territories in their present state and concentrating on a German campaign. He fears that the king of France, seeing his chance, may attempt something against the duke's lands. Furthermore he told me, very confidentially, that the king of France was trying, by means of the herald Charolais who has now arrived from His Majesty, to arrange for a meeting with the lord duke in one of two ways, either [for both] to come to some frontier place, such as near Namur, or for one to stay in one place and the other in another and to arrange, through mediators, for them to talk together on horseback in the country; the said king being very desirous of achieving a settlement with the lord duke. I asked my friend what he thought of it; he replied, not at all, because our lord [the duke] would in no circumstances go. He seems to me to have the right idea, for to arrange such a thing is nothing less than to divert himself from the German undertaking, for it is already after mid-June. . . .

---

[1] ASM Pot. est. Borgogna 515/159–63.

This morning I was at court and, while I was in the lord duke's chamber, he called me and told me how the truces had been arranged till 1 May of the following year on the same terms as those expiring and how he had included all his allies in general and especially, among others, the king of Aragon. The king of France had not included anyone apart from the usual ones; neither Cologne, nor Strasbourg, nor Speyer, nor Basel, nor Ferrette[1] nor any others who are not his allies. This is a good point for the lord duke. The Swiss indeed are included, but only they themselves, not their supporters, nor do I think they will attack on behalf of those against whom the duke plans to move. The king of France was content to promise to allow through and to escort the messengers the duke is sending to notify the king of Aragon of these truces and [he agreed] that if he molested the king of Aragon within the three months allowed for the king of Aragon to ratify the truces, they would be considered broken.[2]

[The duke] says that for this reason he will soon be sending his ambassadors to the king of England and the duke of Brittany with instructions to say that he has made the truce in the above-mentioned way. He agreed to this for their benefit. It would have been better for him to have made war in France now rather than wait, even if he had been all alone in the said war and without the help of the English and the said duke of Brittany, for this reason: he had secret intelligence in France that certain lords and nobles were ready to declare themselves [for him] whenever he attacked. Furthermore he had been informed that the king's people were in disorder, badly paid and in a bad way; that the country was discontented because of dearth and taxation; and the whole populace starving; there were few troops in Amiens and St. Quentin and much hunger; the king was in difficulties; so that if the duke had begun the war he would have come out of it with honour. He appeared to have missed a great opportunity, but he had been happy to negotiate in order to please the king of England and the duke of Brittany. He firmly declared and protested that from now on he had no intention of continuing the truces, long or short. Even if they wanted him to he would in no way assent, but next year he was determined to make war in France with or without them. . . .

[The duke] said he wanted to go to Lille or to Malines to deal urgently with some financial matters. He was determined that everyone in his household should know what his task was, both during the war and outside his lands towards Cologne. From Cologne [he would march] to Strasbourg; thence to Ferrette to revenge himself for the rebellion of

[1] A usual Burgundian name for all the rights and possessions in and near Upper Alsace mortgaged to Charles the Bold in 1469 by Sigmund.
[2] But see Calmette, *RB* xviii (1908), 161 and 191–3.

those people. He said that the king of France must be considered its
cause. He spoke to me about some people nearer at hand. I do not know
if he meant the duke of Milan or the duke of Lorraine against whom,
when he has finished in Germany, he has something in mind. He told me
furthermore that he had cause to do this for many reasons. I said that his
lordship had had more opportunity [in Lorraine] at the time of the death
of Duke Nicolas than now, because of the commotions there were at that
time, but he replied that he had a better opportunity than ever at the
moment because the present duke [René] is a man of little worth, his
mother is completely crazy, and [he mentioned] other things through
which something could be tried against this present duke more easily
and with more justification. He himself has included him in the truce
[among his allies] because he wants to make war there. The king of
France does not know [this] and cannot get mad about it.

The war which he is now undertaking in Germany he says is
justified on three grounds. The first is that they rebelled before they paid
the money. Second, they had killed his officer. Thirdly, the land [of
Alsace] belonged to him by inheritance, through a woman he said.

Charles the Bold was referring to the dubious Burgundian claim
on Alsace through Catherine, Philip the Bold's daughter, who
married Leopold IV of Austria in 1387. Although at this moment he
evidently hoped to deal with the problems of Cologne expeditiously
and without serious difficulty in order to continue his German
campaign southwards against Duke Sigmund and his allies, Charles
also envisaged immediate measures against Alsace. On 8 July he
ordered artillery to be moved from Burgundy to the neighbourhood
of Montbéliard under the command of Henry de Neuchâtel, who was
commissioned as his 'lieutenant to bring back to obedience his rebel
subjects of Ferrette and to make war on their allies, that is the people
of Basel, Strasbourg, Sélestat and Colmar'.[1] But it was not until 18
August, three weeks after Charles had begun the siege of Neuss, that
an authentic act of revenge was carried out against Alsace. Led by the
murdered bailiff's brother, Stefan von Hagenbach, Burgundian
troops spent four days destroying, burning or removing everything
they could lay their hands on around Belfort, Dannemarie and
Altkirch. They were much too quick for any defensive or even
retaliatory moves to be made against them; indeed it was several
weeks before letters of protest, with an inventory of damage done and
atrocities committed, were circulated to Cologne, the Emperor and

---

[1] BN Coll. de Bourgogne MS. 29, f. 334b.

elsewhere by 'the princes and towns who formed themselves into the League at Constance'.[1] Though it soon became apparent that the siege of Neuss would be protracted and difficult, Charles the Bold was still astonishingly optimistic as late as mid-September. On 18 September he wrote to his lieutenant in Luxembourg, Claude de Neuchâtel, instructing him to hold some troops he had mobilized 'ready in their homes until we come through our duchy of Luxembourg to advance towards Ferrette which, with God's help, will be shortly' and on 19 September he informed the civic authorities at Dijon that he would be on his way to punish his rebellious subjects of Ferrette just as soon as he had dealt with the archbishop of Cologne's rebellious subjects of Neuss. This is the last we hear of the plan to restore Burgundian rule in Alsace. The siege of Neuss dragged on till the summer of 1475, by which time new projects had intervened. Charles the Bold never did revenge himself on Strasbourg, Basel and Sigmund; Burgundian rule in Alsace never was restored.

The treaties of Constance of April 1474 had proclaimed the *ewige Richtung*, or everlasting settlement between the Swiss and the Habsburgs, but the many outstanding difficulties between the two had been set aside for subsequent French mediation. Louis XI was involved with the Swiss in the summer of 1474 in another respect because Bern, determined on war with Charles the Bold or convinced that it was inevitable, naturally turned to the king of France as a possible ally. But, while Bern was dynamically anti-Burgundian, Louis was intent on a settlement with Charles the Bold. It was in June 1474, as Francesco Bertini reported to the king of Naples, that the Franco–Burgundian truce was extended for a further year and that Louis sought a personal meeting with Charles. Indeed he had absolutely nothing to gain in the summer of 1474 from an offensive against Charles; he rejected Frederick III's proposals at that time for a Franco-imperial alliance aimed at Burgundy and he disappointed Bern by refusing to make war on Charles the Bold. He was primarily interested in the reconquest of Roussillon from Aragon, an enterprise which however he deferred until late in 1474. Then, during the winter of 1474–5, while Neuss was besieged in vain by Charles the Bold, Perpignan was invested by Louis XI and eventually forced to surrender to the French on 10 March 1475.

[1] Printed *Acten zum Neusser Kriege*, 25–9, *Basler Chroniken*, iii. 392–404, *Speierische Chronik*, 512–14, and see Toutey, *Charles le Téméraire et la Ligue de Constance*, 441–9 with references. For what follows, see *Recueil du Fay*, 99, and *Correspondance de la mairie de Dijon*, i. 149–50.

Although it was Bern and some of the Lower Union powers, not France, which hoped to inaugurate an assault on Burgundian power in 1474, Louis XI was by no means willing to lose credit with his Swiss and Austrian allies, or abandon the potentially valuable diplomatic situation now enjoyed by France in the Upper Rhine region. On 11 June 1474 he announced his arbitral decision on the *ewige Richtung*, which was wholly favourable to the Swiss, and at Feldkirch on 12 October, after pressure had been applied by the French ambassador, Sigmund at last signed a treaty with France which comprised his acceptance of the *ewige Richtung*, of French protection and of a French pension.

Louis XI now offered the Swiss what Bern had been clamouring for: an offensive alliance against Charles the Bold; though this did not take its definitive form until 2 January 1475, more than two months after the *Eidgenossen* had declared war on Charles and the League of Constance had mounted its first attack on Burgundian territory. According to the terms drawn up on 26 October 1474 Louis was to pay the Swiss 20,000 francs per annum at Lyons for the rest of his life and help them if required with money and men in their wars, especially those against the duke of Burgundy. If he was unable to give the Swiss military assistance when asked, the king of France would pay them an additional 80,000 francs per annum while they were involved in a war without his help. In return, the Swiss promised to send troops to Louis wherever he required them, at his expense. In a private arrangement which Bern originally accepted on 2 October it was agreed that Louis would only be obliged under the treaty to help the Swiss if they were hard 'pressed and in urgent need' and 'could not otherwise resist their enemy'. Moreover Bern guaranteed that, if the king ever asked the Swiss for troops, 6,000 men at least would be made available, if necessary by herself alone.

In spite of their subsequent historiographical impact, these French diplomatic successes were of rather limited significance. It is a gross misrepresentation to claim that Louis XI persuaded the Swiss into a war against Charles the Bold. This was the work, above all, of Strasbourg and of Bern. But French diplomacy had brow-beaten Sigmund into accepting the *ewige Richtung* on terms somewhat unfavourable to Austria, and French cash had helped to bring the less aggressive *Eidgenossen* into line with Bern. Pressures for a campaign against Charles the Bold had been building up among the League of Constance powers ever since Strasbourg and Basel had sent Charles what amounted to declarations of war on 22 April 1474. In May

Johann von Venningen, bishop of Basel, had 1,000 men mobilized, all in red tunics with the colours of the bishopric on their left arms, and towards the end of June a raiding force from Alsace had penetrated Burgundian territory in the Franche-Comté. At the end of July the Lower Union planned a large-scale raid into Burgundian territory; but they decided that such an action could never succeed without Swiss participation. On this climate of opinion the Burgundian raid into Alsace on 18 August had a dramatic impact, and Bern in particular went as far as ordering her troops on 22 August to be ready to leave at once, while the Lower Union assembled its forces at Altkirch and appealed to the Swiss to join them in an immediate campaign. By September 1474 others had joined the Lower Union powers in pressing for aggressive action against Charles the Bold, notably the Emperor Frederick III, who hoped that a determined attack on the Franche-Comté by the League of Constance might cause Charles to abandon his siege of Neuss. An imperial ambassador attended the diet of Feldkirch in October to encourage them in their aggressive intentions.

The Swiss declaration of war on Charles the Bold, which was carried aloft on a cleft stick by a mounted messenger dressed in the town livery of Bern, was delivered on 29 October to Henry de Neuchâtel at his castle of Blamont in the Franche-Comté. Frederick, not Louis, was named as the immediate instigator of this hostile challenge.[1]

To the most illustrious prince and lord, Lord Charles, duke of Burgundy, or to his lieutenants and officers whatever their names, wherever they reside, we the burgomasters, *Schultheisse*, *Ammanner*, councillors and communities of the great league of Upper Germany, namely Zürich, Bern, Luzern, Uri, Schwyz, Unterwalden, Zug and Glarus and the two towns of Fribourg and Solothurn, at this moment assembled in the town of Luzern, give notice, at the pressing and most vehement exhortation and command of the most invincible, most serene and most illustrious lord, Lord Frederick, Roman Emperor, our most gracious lord whom, as members of the Holy Empire, we are bound to obey, also of the most illustrious prince and lord, Lord Sigmund, duke of Austria, and of the other princes, lords and communities joined in alliance with us, on whom numerous injuries, deeds of violence and

---

[1] Latin text in *Eidgenössischen Abschiede*, ii. 515, and Knebel, *Diarium*, ii. 119–20; German text in Schilling, *Die Berner-Chronik*, i. 174–5, and see Wyss and others, *Die Burgunderbeute*, 49–50, and the illustration reproduced in Stettler, *Schodoler*, 12.

atrocious oppressions have been and are daily perpetrated by your people, we now declare and announce our public defiance on behalf of us, our people and those who are allied to us, to your illustrious lordship and to each and every one of your subjects and allies, of whatever name. From now henceforth whatever happens as a result of this defiance to your lordship, your people, your supporters and your allies by way of rapine, homicide, arson, plunder, invasion and other such afflictions by day or by night, carried out by us and our allies in this affair, we wish our honour and that of our allies and supporters by virtue of these present letters to be untarnished and secure. We have publicly attached the seal of the city of Bern to these our letters on behalf of all. Given on the Tuesday before the feast of SS. Simon and Jude the Apostles, 1474.

In a famous scene, the Bern chronicler Diebold Schilling, whose sparklingly vigorous narrative style is accompanied by an almost systematic mendacity rivalling that of Philippe de Commynes, makes Charles the Bold read the Swiss declaration of war at the siege of Neuss in a blazing temper, and cry out 'Oh Berna! Berna!' in his indignation. In point of fact the document, if indeed he ever saw it, would probably not have troubled him much. His officials in the southern territories had been expecting an attack for some time and the ducal accounts show that, just as Louis XI promised to pay the Swiss to make war on the duke of Burgundy, so the duke of Burgundy distributed sums of money to them and others in order to persuade them not to attack him. On 11 September 1474, for example, Symon de Cleron received the second of two sums of 600 Rhenish florins to distribute among 'certain lords and knights of Germany' because 'German and Swiss forces were assembled in large numbers with the intention of entering the lands of my said lord [the duke of Burgundy] in the county of Burgundy in the neighbourhood of Joux and Pontarlier in order to invade and damage it as much as possible'.[1]

When it eventually came, at the end of October, the target of the allied attack was not Pontarlier but the strategically placed castle of Héricourt, on the frontier of the Franche-Comté between Belfort and Montbéliard, belonging to Henry de Neuchâtel, lord of Blamont. Nor was this frontier raid against Burgundy in any real sense the work of the Swiss. It was due, as the declaration of war implied, primarily to the initiative of Sigmund of Austria and the Lower Union, and they provided the bulk of the forces and the so-called commander-in-chief, Wilhelm Herter. It was their war, and in part Bern's, which

---

[1] ACO B1773, fos. 309b–310, partly excerpted in *Mémoires*, ii. 262 n. *b*.

the *Eidgenossen* as a whole had reluctantly agreed to support. On the other hand, the Héricourt campaign was the only major act of aggression against Burgundy, apart from the execution of Hagenbach, which by any stretch of the imagination could be said to be the work of the League of Constance as a whole. The men of Bern set out on 28 October 'in the name of God and the heavenly queen, maid Mary', with banners unfurled.[1] They marched over the Jura passes between Biel and Porrentruy, accompanied by contingents from Nidau, Fribourg, Solothurn, Biel and Neuchâtel. At Montbéliard they were joined by the forces of Luzern. The other allied contingents, from the town and bishop of Strasbourg, Colmar, Sélestat, Breisach, Basel, Duke Sigmund, Zürich and the other *Eidgenossen* and their associates assembled at Basel and set out thence in the first few days of November.

By contemporary standards it was a big army which encamped from the evening of 5 November onwards in cold wet weather around the remote, isolated, forest-surrounded castle of Héricourt. There could have been 18,000 troops assembled in all; there were surely at least 15,000. From Strasbourg alone 2,000 men marched on foot, with 250 horse and 140 wagons. Nor was heavy artillery lacking. The great gun of Strasbourg, *der Strauss*, the ostrich, was dragged to Héricourt by eighteen horses. Conrad Pfettisheim, himself of Strasbourg, tells us that it buzzed and did a wild dance; 'when it had a crop full of powder, then it laid hard eggs'.[2] It achieved a rate of fire of fourteen shots per day and a hole was made in one of the towers. But the siege of Héricourt did not progress well. The weather continued cold and wet and some of the Swiss troops were soon near mutiny: they wanted to try to take the castle by assault rather than be slowly frozen to death in their camp. But an enemy initiative altered their predicament. Henry de Neuchâtel, Duke Charles's 'lieutenant on the German frontier',[3] was by no means ill-prepared. He was determined, too, to take what action he could to reinforce or relieve his own people and help defend his own castle. Assembling what mounted troops he had available, he advanced on Héricourt on the morning

---

[1] Schilling, *Die Berner-Chronik*, i. 177. For what follows on the Héricourt campaign, besides the works cited on p. 261 n. 1 above, see Gagliardi, *AnzSG* (N.F.) xiii (1915), 268–9, Bell and Schneller, *Geschichtsfreund* xxiii (1868), 64–6, Rüsch, *Beschreibung der Burgunderkriege*, 303–5 and 308–9, and Colombo, *Iolanda, duchessa di Savoia*, 120.

[2] Pfettisheim, *Geschichte*, 21.

[3] *Dépêches des ambassadeurs milanais*, i. 166, compare above p. 256.

of Sunday 13 November 1474 southwards down the valley of the
River Lisaine, which, since Montbéliard was hostile, was the only
practicable route for his cavalry. The allies were caught more or less
unawares but lost no time in forming into battle order and advancing
against the Burgundians.

The events that followed have by no means been satisfactorily
established by historical research, but Henry de Neuchâtel withdrew
his forces, perhaps on discovering that the Swiss were ready to fight
and easily outnumbered him. They pursued him northwards, some
of them advancing through the thick deciduous forest which bordered
and still borders the river and narrow winding road, through what
amounts to a defile. Somewhere along the lane between Chenebier
and Châtebier where the valley broadens into what is now open
undulating grassy terrain about 10 km north of Héricourt, Henry de
Neuchâtel's troops tried to make a stand in defence of their encampment. But the allies attacked them fiercely from two different directions
and put them to flight. Three or four days later the castle of Héricourt
capitulated, and its garrison, several hundred strong, was replaced by
a detachment of Austrian cavalry. The castle, which had been
Austrian before 1377, became Austrian again. On the battlefield
1,617 Burgundians, mostly infantry, were left dead. The allied
casualties were exceptionally light. The Strasbourgers returned home
triumphantly, 'fresh and joyful with all their folk and equipment',[1]
on 25 November, with five captured enemy flags to hang in their
cathedral. Against the wishes of the Swiss, whose rule it was never to
take prisoners, some fifty Burgundians were captured. The lucky ones
were ransomed, but eighteen unfortunate 'Lombards' from among
Charles the Bold's Italian mercenaries, after being accused of sodomy,
rape, sacrilege and other unspeakable crimes, were burnt alive as
heretics at Basel on Christmas Eve 'in honour of God Almighty, of
our Christian faith, and of all Germans'.[2]

The Héricourt campaign was a successful raid on an isolated
frontier outpost, a pinprick which Charles the Bold could well afford
to ignore. Frederick, who had hoped for a large-scale invasion and
perhaps the conquest of the Franche-Comté, which might have
persuaded Charles to withdraw from Neuss, was disappointed. In
spite of the absurd optimism of the Basel chaplain, Johann Knebel,
who recorded the 'crazy' duke of Burgundy as fleeing 'in great

[1] Von Königshoven, *Chronicke*, 374.
[2] Schilling, *Die Berner-Chronik*, i. 187.

confusion' from Neuss in autumn 1474 when he found 'all Germany against him',[1] a minor raid such as that on Héricourt could surely not have diverted Charles from a major undertaking like the siege of Neuss. Frederick wrote to the allies complaining of their withdrawal and even ordering them out on another campaign. But there was no instant enthusiasm for further military adventures, though Basel and Strasbourg made it clear in January and February 1475 that they favoured further action on similar lines to the Héricourt campaign. Bern also favoured hostilities against Burgundy but she was becoming increasingly involved with Savoy, and when one of a series of 'unofficial' or 'free-lance' Swiss raiding parties was caught in Pontarlier on the frontier of the Franche-Comté on 7 April 1475 and she had to send a detachment to extricate it, this force was employed not in the Franche-Comté but against Savoy in the *pays de Vaud*. As to Louis XI's much-vaunted diplomacy, he had accused his Swiss allies of attacking prematurely at Héricourt; now, in the spring of 1475 when he was desperately trying to organize a combined attack on all the Burgundian territories by all Charles the Bold's enemies simultaneously, they resisted his bribes and blandishments and refused to move.

When hostile incursions into the Franche-Comté were officially resumed in July 1475 it was not at the instigation of Louis XI, nor as a result of Swiss initiatives. Once again, as in October 1474, it was the Lower Union, above all the towns of Strasbourg and Basel, which insisted on, organized, and largely carried out the attack. Strasbourg indeed had maintained a detachment of cavalry at Montbéliard throughout the first half of 1475 and used it to raid Burgundian territory. At the diet of the Lower Union held at Ensisheim on 17 June 1475 it was decided that the Union's forces would assemble at Dannemarie, between Mulhouse and Belfort, on 8 July, and invade the Franche-Comté the next day, even though the Swiss had refused to participate in the campaign. In the event, when Strasbourg asked Bern to supply her with 400 mercenaries, she agreed, and decided on 2 July to send an additional 1,000 men on her own account under a diplomat and captain from one of the foremost noble families of Bern, Niclaus von Diesbach,[2] who however lost his life on the campaign. None of the other *Eidgenossen* participated, though Basel

---

[1] Knebel, *Diarium*, ii. 119 and 112.
[2] For von Diesbach and his role in the events related here see Stettler, *Niklaus von Diesbach*.

was permitted to recruit 500 Swiss mercenaries to reinforce her own contingent. The allied army was perhaps not much more than 5,000 strong, and the largest single contingent was probably that brought on behalf of the house of Austria by Duke Sigmund's newly appointed bailiff in Alsace, Oswald von Thierstein.

In spite of disputes about the purpose of this campaign, which led, among other things, to the departure of the bailiff and his Austrians, who preferred to fight against Charles the Bold in defence of Lorraine, the plan of action demanded by Basel, Strasbourg and the bishop of Basel in particular was effectively carried out. This was the elimination of a group of frontier places from which Burgundian garrisons had been menacing and raiding the Sundgau and especially the territories of the bishopric of Basel. For example a Burgundian detachment had assaulted and taken the episcopal castle of Kallenberg in spite of the resistance of its six defenders. In all, between 12 July when the fortified bridge over the River Doubs at Pont-de-Roide was captured, and the dispersal homewards on 24 August, the allied forces conquered some dozen castles in the extreme north-east of the Franche-Comté. The most redoubtable was Henry de Neuchâtel's castle of Blamont, between Pont-de-Roide and Porrentruy, which resisted a four-hour assault in hot weather on 4 August. This failed partly because the allied scaling ladders were too short, but the defenders also employed an unusual weapon against their assailants to good effect: they threw down onto them hives full of bees. However Blamont capitulated on 9 August and was thereafter systematically dismantled and demolished. Earlier, after the capture of Granges, the allies had planned to demolish its fortifications, but could not summon sufficient energy to carry out this wearisome task. At Grammont, which was successfully assaulted on 21 August, the Bernese and others smashed their way through the walls and gates with axes and pikes and were able to refresh themselves at the end of three hours of these exertions with a cellar full of wine.

The Blamont campaign was indecisive and insignificant. Sordid disputes over the distribution of booty, the death of Niclaus von Diesbach, and constant bickering among the commanders all cast a shadow over the proceedings. It certainly failed to arouse the interest of the usually alert diarist of Basel, the chaplain Johann Knebel. He took his summer holiday during it:[1]

---

[1] Knebel, *Diarium*, ii. 278.

In those days I, Johann Knebel, wanted to have a good time, so I took myself to Upper Baden in the Aargau and there, with congenial companions, both men and women, noble and ignoble, at the house of Schindler, which was presided over at that time by a certain Clingelfusz, I lived admirably, with my maid Enilina Baders and my servant Ulrich Muller. I stayed there for four weeks, during which time I spent more than ten Rhenish florins, and I returned on 5 August.

So far in this chapter we have been concerned to trace the growing confrontation in the region of the Upper Rhine and the northern Jura, between Charles the Bold and the powers which became loosely and defensively associated in April 1474 in the League of Constance. This confrontation had been effectively initiated when Charles the Bold acquired rights in Upper Alsace from Duke Sigmund in May 1469. It was perpetuated after the enforced withdrawal of Burgundian power and the death of Hagenbach in April and May 1474, by Charles's persistent refusal to abandon his Alsace claims, by the counterstroke he organized in August 1474, and perhaps even more by the suspicions, fears and, it must be admitted, outrightly aggressive attitudes and policies of those proud and powerful urban communities: Strasbourg, Basel and Bern. These developments were a product of Charles the Bold's interest in Alsace, but there were other parallel and simultaneous events, of equal importance for his future political prospects, which tended to involve him with the same potential enemies. They relate to two distinct areas, Savoy and Lorraine.

Long before Amadeus VIII was promoted to the ducal dignity in 1416, the forceful and ambitious counts of Savoy, based at Chambéry, had extended their powers, not only in the region of high mountains immediately south of the Lake of Geneva, but also north-westwards to the Saône and southwards to Turin and even to the shores of the Mediterranean at Nice. From the Saône to the Lake of Neuchâtel they were neighbours of Burgundy, and the first Valois duke, Philip the Bold, had made the first serious move towards Burgundian intervention in Savoy when he married his daughter Mary to Amadeus VIII in 1393; just as in 1387 he had staked a shadowy Burgundian claim in Alsace by the marriage of his daughter Catherine to Leopold of Austria. Under Mary of Burgundy's husband, Amadeus VIII, Savoy had been influential and prosperous, but his death in 1451 was followed by years of crisis and decline in which, especially after 1460, Savoy's aggressive neighbours exploited her internal difficulties to their own advantage.

The dukes of Milan had their eyes on Piedmont. The king of France, Louis XI, hoped to bring Savoy into the orbit of the French crown and perhaps to acquire it outright for France; he was married to Charlotte de Savoie and his sister Yolande was married to Amadeus IX, who succeeded his father Louis as duke in 1465. The duke of Burgundy's interest in Savoy was transformed, around 1467, by the personal ambitions of Charles the Bold and by the growing Burgundian, as opposed to French, sympathies of many of the princes of Savoy. Thus in 1467 Amadeus IX and Yolande signed treaties with Duke Charles and with his ally, Yolande's brother, Charles of France and, in 1468, three of Amadeus IX's brothers joined Charles the Bold's expedition against Liège. The most powerful of them, Philip, lord of Bresse, had already signed a treaty with Charles in the preceding year and earlier in 1468 had taken service with him as his lieutenant in the two Burgundies.

The most dangerous and powerful of all Savoy's neighbours at this time was Bern. After the treaty of Waldshut in 1468 had blocked her expansion north-eastwards, and further limitations had been set to her freedom of action in this direction by the intervention of Charles the Bold in Alsace, it was only natural that Bern should turn her political ambitions westwards, towards her now weak neighbour Savoy. From about 1460 onwards she had displayed an increasing and somewhat sinister interest in Savoy's internal affairs; by the end of the decade this amounted to outright intervention or interference.

Duke Amadeus IX was an epileptic weakling, and his wife Yolande was recognized as regent of Savoy in 1469 by the Estates. But a struggle for power intervened, in 1470–1, between Yolande and two at least of her brothers-in-law, one of whom, Philip, lord of Bresse, was being actively encouraged by her brother Louis XI. In spite of this opposition, Yolande contrived to maintain her status and authority through this crisis, and her regency was confirmed in 1472 after her husband's death. The delicate internal equilibrium of Savoy had been preserved, though only with difficulty, because the ambitions there of Galeazzo Maria Sforza, of Louis XI, of Charles the Bold and of Bern had tended to cancel or counterbalance each other. But it was upset completely in 1472–5 when in a series of diplomatic initiatives, which almost certainly included proposals for the marriage of Duke Philibert of Savoy to Mary of Burgundy, Charles the Bold managed not only to win Yolande firmly over to a Burgundian alliance, but also to establish what amounted to a Burgundian protectorate over Savoy. In this, Charles the Bold's motives or aims may have been to

THE HOUSE OF SAVOY IN THE FIFTEENTH CENTURY

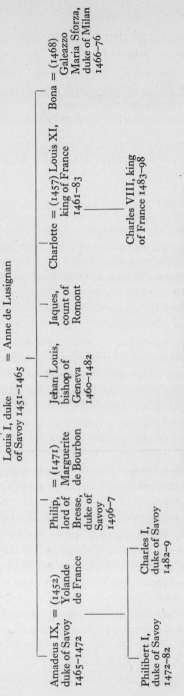

Amadeus VIII, count and duke of Savoy 1391–1451 = Mary of Burgundy

Louis I, duke of Savoy 1451–1465 = Anne de Lusignan

Amadeus IX, duke of Savoy 1465–1472 = (1452) Yolande de France

Philip, lord of Bresse, duke of Savoy 1496–7 = (1471) Marguerite de Bourbon

Jehan Louis, bishop of Geneva 1460–1482

Jaques, count of Romont

Charlotte = (1457) Louis XI, king of France 1461–83

Bona = (1468) Galeazzo Maria Sforza, duke of Milan 1466–76

Philibert I, duke of Savoy 1472–82

Charles I, duke of Savoy 1482–9

Charles VIII, king of France 1483–98

A selection only of the numerous children of Louis I are included here.

protect his frontier and to repel French influence decisively from the area. But, even if he was not already entertaining hopes that Savoy might one day fall to him, he was now directly threatening the interests of Bern and directly intervening in Bern's sphere of influence. In a letter sent to Yolande on 2 August 1473 Charles the Bold expressed himself on this subject as follows: [1]

> Dearest and honoured lady and cousin, I recommend myself most warmly to you. Messire Guillaume de Rochefort, my councillor and *maître des requêtes* of my household has informed me of the understandings and secret undertakings which the Swiss have made to your prejudice with the king's approbation. I well realize that these understandings are not designed to trouble and damage you only, but also me, and for this reason I am determined to resist them and deal with them in whatever way may become necessary. I am sending some of my people to make my intentions abundantly clear to them, so that they fully understand my good will towards you. Rest assured that in these affairs and in all others concerning yourself, my nephews your children, and your lands and lordships, I shall never abandon you whatever happens to me.

If Bern was merely awaiting a suitable pretext to initiate a series of acts of aggression against Savoy, the alliance of Charles the Bold and Yolande would perhaps alone have been sufficient. But Charles went much further than this. In 1472 he took into his service and pay Jaques, count of Romont, also baron of Vaud, which was an apanage or fief of the duchy of Savoy. Its possession made him virtual ruler of the entire *pays de Vaud* for his barony included, after he had taken them over in 1471, Payerne, Cudefrin, Grandson and Murten. Thus the Vaud, corresponding roughly to the present canton, passed, in a sense, into Burgundian hands, and Jaques de Savoie was added, in the suspicious eyes of Bern, to the Burgundian vassals and potential enemies already in this area: members of the house of Chalon, owners of the Vaud lordships of Erlach, Grandson, Echallens, Jougne and Orbe; Guillaume de la Baume-Montrevel, lord of Illens and other places along the River Saane; and the family of Vergy, lords of Champvent and La Motte. The Vaud was not only important to Bern as a field

---

[1] ASM Pot. est. Borgogna 515/145. For this and what follows on Savoy see especially, besides the works cited above, p. 261 n. 1, Guichenon, *Histoire de Savoie*, Gabotto, *Lo stato sabaudo*, ii, Colombo, *Iolanda, duchessa di Savoia*, Daviso, *La duchessa Iolanda*, Grand, *Der Anteil des Wallis*, Despond, *Les comtes de Gruyère*, Thomas, *PTSEC* (1931), 187–92, and *Chroniques de Yolande de France*.

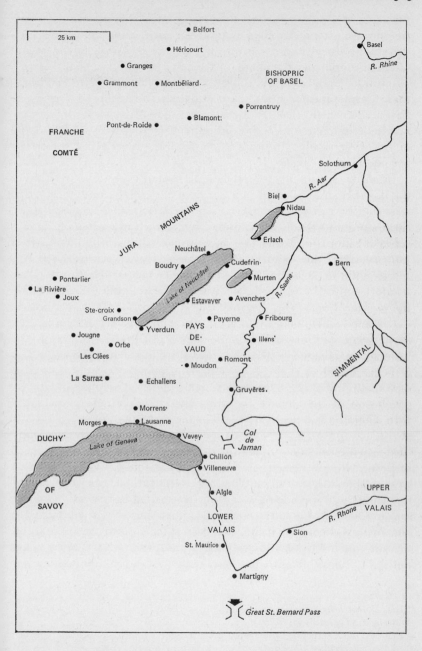

7. The *pays de Vaud* and neighbouring territories

for expansion and a frontier area; it was also of immense economic significance. It produced in abundance corn, wine and other agricultural products, and it was one of the main highways for Swiss and German merchants travelling to the fairs of Geneva and Lyons.[1] No wonder Bern reacted in a hostile and not just defensive manner to these developments. From 1473 onwards she regarded Jaques de Savoie as an enemy; from then on she began to plan a series of countermoves designed to undermine Burgundian influence in the Vaud and in Savoy generally. She was certainly not prepared to see Savoy become another Alsace.

From the spring of 1473 Italian mercenaries recruited by Charles the Bold began to pass through Savoy in increasing numbers and this was angrily resented by Bern, who felt that she and her allies, Strasbourg and Basel for example, were directly threatened. After a series of bitter complaints, she presented an ultimatum to Yolande in January 1475: the count of Romont must leave Charles the Bold's service and the passage of Charles the Bold's mercenaries through her territories must be stopped forthwith. Otherwise Bern would invade the *pays de Vaud*. The hostility and suspicion of Bern was greatly exacerbated when, on 30 January 1475, at Moncalieri in Piedmont, a masterpiece of Burgundian diplomacy was brought about in the form of an alliance between Savoy, Burgundy and Milan.[2] The principal architect of the League of Moncalieri was the Burgundian diplomat Guillaume de Rochefort, who expressed his pleasure on the conclusion of the alliance by embracing the Milanese ambassador with whom he had negotiated it. The treaty was not only a deft blow at French prestige in the Italian peninsula, for Galeazzo Maria Sforza had been Louis XI's principal ally there, but it was a menace to Bern, who felt herself encircled and threatened. On 14 February 1475, responding to rumour, her civic authorities wrote to Fribourg reporting the formation of a vast alliance against the Swiss. 'And it is said in Geneva', the letter continued, 'that these lords will make for our town, will conquer it first and then utterly destoy it, placing [on the site] an inscription saying "Here once there was a town called Bern".'[3] These fears were probably not even authentic, for

[1] See Borel, *Foires de Genève*, Ammann, *Freiburg und Bern und die Genfer Messen*, and Gandilhon, *Politique économique de Louis XI*, 223–9.
[2] Printed de Comines, *Mémoires*, ed. Lenglet du Fresnoy, iii. 356–62, Guichenon, *Histoire de Savoie*, iv. 425–8, and Plancher, iv. no. 239.
[3] Büchi, *FG* xiii (1906), 31–2.

Bern commonly roused her allies with such tales. But it was certainly true that Savoy had by this time become little more than a Burgundian annexe. An Italian observer reported on 17 January 1475 that the duchess of Savoy was 'entirely Burgundian' and that 'she conducted her affairs as the duke of Burgundy wished and not otherwise. She has with her a certain Monsignore di Rozeforte acting for the said duke, who makes her act as he pleases. He has posted about eighty mercenaries with her, all Burgundians, to guard her person.'[1]

It was in these circumstances that Bern, aided by her close associate Fribourg, began a private, undeclared war on Savoy which was carefully slanted against the Burgundian elements there. It was begun, and continued, at just the same time as the war of raids into the Franche-Comté organized by the Lower Union and already described above. But it was somewhat different in character. It never had the support of the other *Eidgenossen*, and it was a war of conquest, the object of which was to put certain strategic places and castles firmly into the hands of Bern. On 27 October 1474, the day after the Swiss declaration of war against Burgundy, a force from Bern conquered and occupied the village of Erlach on the Bieler See, which belonged to the Burgundian house of Chalon. The next target was Guillaume de la Baume's castle at Illens, on the River Saane south of Fribourg, which fell to a joint Bern–Fribourg expedition on 2 January 1475. Finally, at the end of April 1475, soon after authentic details of the League of Moncalieri had become known in Bern, the remaining Chalon lordships in the Vaud were conquered by her troops, helped by contingents from Fribourg, Solothurn, Basel and Luzern. The town of Grandson fell on 30 April; the castle surrendered the next day. Echallens and Jougne fell easily, but a three-hour assault was required for the conquest of the castle of Orbe. As usual, after the Swiss had fought and smashed their way in, both living and dead defenders were thrown over the battlements. Thus, within a matter of days, the ring of castles which had limited the power of Bern at the southern end of the Lake of Neuchâtel was broken and she had gained control of the most important pass leading over the Jura into Burgundy. Two of the chief victims of this act of aggression, Charles the Bold and Louis de Chalon, the owner of Grandson, were far off at the siege of Neuss when the blow was struck. Naturally Duchess

---

[1] Gabotto, *Lo stato sabaudo*, ii. 125 n. 2. 'Monsignore di Rozeforte' is Guillaume de Rochefort.

Yolande protested, but nothing by way of retaliation could be done for the time being. Bern had triumphed.

In the summer and early autumn of 1475 there was a marked lull in Bern's activities against Savoy in the Vaud, though the garrison of Jougne carried out a series of raids into Burgundian territory which culminated on 11 September. But important anti-Burgundian steps were being taken further south, in the Lower Valais, along the route from the Great St. Bernard Pass through Martigny and Lausanne which many of Charles the Bold's mercenaries had followed on their way from Lombardy. Between this French-speaking part of Savoy and the German-speaking Bern area there was no love lost. A letter written in 1475, admittedly on 1 April, claimed that a hairdresser of Vevey, on the shores of the Lake of Geneva, had exhibited a cartoon showing a man in the livery of Bern, wearing the badge of Fribourg, riding on a cow. In August a force from Bern carried out a midnight attack on Aigle, through which a contingent of Charles's Italian mercenaries was passing at the time, and burnt down the castle. In September Bern signed an alliance with the bishop of Sion, Walter Supersax, and the people of the Upper Valais, which was specifically aimed at Savoy. After all, it was well known that the bishop had for some time been planning to reconquer those parts of the patrimony of St. Theodul in the Lower Valais which had in the past been forcibly annexed by Savoy. Thus in September 1475 the scene was set for a major offensive against Savoy which would at the same time constitute a blatant attack on Charles the Bold. Even if in 1475 he might conceivably have extricated himself from the commitments resulting from his penetration into Alsace, Charles could scarcely have withdrawn from the clash with Bern towards which his Savoy policies had almost inexorably led him.

No attempt to explain the origins of those fateful campaigns of 1476, which brought about the end of Charles the Bold and the disintegration of the Burgundian state, would be complete without some mention of Lorraine for here too, as in Alsace and Savoy, Charles the Bold's policies led to a confrontation with his powerful urban enemies which could scarcely have ended otherwise than in war.

Although the duchy of Lorraine formed part of the Empire, Frederick III had no vestige of authority there, and René II of Vaudémont, when he became duke in the first days of August 1473, was faced with the need to protect himself and his duchy by means of an alliance either with King Louis XI of France or with Charles the

Bold.[1] He applied first, on 11 September 1473, to Louis XI, but the demands he made were so exorbitant that one can only assume they were insincere. Surely he and his advisers did not really expect Louis solemnly to swear to hand over the entire Angevin inheritance, including Provence, to him; to cede Champagne to him for his lifetime; and to pay him a pension for life of £50,000 per annum? Perhaps he had planned from the start to make the arrangement with Charles the Bold which was finalized in the treaty of Nancy on 15 October and which represented a diplomatic defeat for Louis XI. By this treaty, Charles obtained all he needed in Lorraine: the assurance of free passage for his troops going to and fro, and the friendship of the duke.

These friendly relations seem still to have obtained in December 1473 when Charles visited René on his way through Nancy to Alsace, but they were upset during the first half of 1474 apparently as a result of the depredations of Burgundian troops in Lorraine which Charles was powerless or possibly unwilling to stop. Other things may have weighed with René in persuading him to change his allegiance from Burgundy to France: the earnest diplomatic representations and promises of Louis XI; the requests and threats of the League of Constance powers, notably in May 1474; and, perhaps most important, growing distrust of Charles the Bold who, at any rate by the end of June, had probably formulated quite definite plans for the outright incorporation of Lorraine into the Burgundian state.[2] But all these pressures came to bear on René in May and June 1474, whereas it seems probable that he had already approached Louis for an alliance in March or April, though it was not until July–August that he signed a firm alliance with the king in which he formally but secretly renounced his treaty with Burgundy. Nevertheless, he still continued thereafter to allow the passage of Burgundian troops through his duchy and continued too, to resist representations from the Lower Union to take sides openly with it against Charles the Bold.

What was it that prompted René, in the spring of 1475, to throw caution to the winds and send a formal declaration of war to the duke of Burgundy? He must by this time have suffered long enough the damages and acts of hostility of the Burgundian troops passing through Lorraine. He must have felt more secure, in his increasing

[1] For what follows on Lorraine, besides pp. 100–107 above, see the works referred to on pp. 101 n. 1 above and p. 417 n. 2 below.
[2] Above, p. 290.

hostility to Charles, because of his alliance with France, reinforced as it seemed to be by Louis's promises to come to his aid in person if necessary. On 18 April 1475, yielding to the pressing invitations of the ambassadors of Sigmund and the bishop of Basel who arrived at Baccarat on 6 April, he at last joined the Lower Union. He was also encouraged at this same time to take active military measures against Charles by the Emperor Frederick III, with whom he signed a treaty on 17 May in which each promised not to make a separate peace with the duke of Burgundy. It was therefore on the strength of assurances of support from Louis XI, Frederick III and the Lower Union that René sent his herald Lorraine to Charles the Bold at the siege of Neuss. The official record of the terse challenge, which was dated 9 May, together with its frothy prolegomena and Charles's reply, runs as follows:

> *First, the entry and respects [of the herald] in the form of a supplication, as follows:*
> Most high, most excellent and most illustrious prince, greetings, honour and most humble reverence to your magnificent highness on the part of the most high, most powerful and my sovereign lord the duke of Lorraine, Regnier, second of this name. I have been sent as his most humble and most obedient herald of arms in order to tell you and explain what I have been commanded and enjoined to do. And because I would not dare nor do I wish to presume to begin to declare my said commission without first requesting you to give me audience and permission to do what I have been ordered, I shall proceed no further without your consent to this, if you are prepared to accord it.
> *The reply of the said Duke Charles:*
> Herald, declare what you have been charged with by your master, and remember what you say so that you can certify it, as is incumbent on a person in your office.
> *The exposition of the herald's commission, dressed in his coat of arms and wearing his cap and speaking on behalf of his master:*
> I announce to you Charles, duke of Burgundy, on behalf of the most high, most powerful and most redoubted prince my lord the duke of Lorraine, my most redoubted and sovereign lord, defiance with fire and blood against you, your lands, subjects and allies. I have no other commission to proceed further.
> *The reply of the said Duke Charles to the herald, speaking as if to his master:*
> Herald, I have heard and understood the exposition of your commission, which has given me matter for joy and, to show you that such is the case, you shall clothe yourself in my robe and [have] this gift. Tell your

master that I shall soon be in his lands and the greatest fear I have is not to find him there. So that you may have no fears for your return I am ordering the marshal of my army and the King-of-Arms of my Order, Golden Fleece, to escort you securely, for I should be sorry if you were not to make your report to your master as a good and loyal officer of arms ought to do.

The gift which the Duke Charles made to the herald of arms:
When the said officer left he was given the robe of cloth of gold in which [the duke] was then dressed and, with it, a silver-gilt cup in which there were 500 gold lions.[1]

At the time he received this dramatic challenge Charles the Bold had at least three pressing matters in hand: the siege of Neuss, his planned joint assault with Edward IV against France, and the punishment of Sigmund and the Lower Union for their part in the expulsion of Burgundy from Alsace. Nonetheless, he evidently decided that the Burgundian conquest of Lorraine, for which he now possessed an admirable pretext, must be given every possible priority. Perhaps his political acumen was blunted by feelings of anger and desires for revenge against René; but perhaps his attack on Lorraine at this juncture was the result of cool deliberation. After all, with some help from Louis XI, René was mustering his forces on the Luxembourg frontier and that duchy seemed in imminent danger. Moreover, Lorraine itself was just as important to Charles the Bold as was Savoy, and for the same reason: as an essential route for the troops he was still recruiting in Italy, as well as for his diplomatic communications with that country. Thus on 19 May 1475 Charles had to send his lieutenant in Luxembourg instructions for the difficult task of arranging to meet and escort the prince of Taranto, Federico, through Lorraine. He wrote again to the same officer on 8 June advising him that, as soon as his affairs at Neuss were completed, he would be moving his entire army against Lorraine.[2] Meanwhile, he was sending the count of Campobasso, Cola de Monforte, to help defend Luxembourg with his 300 lances.

In the event, Duke René was treacherously abandoned by his princely allies, Frederick III and Louis XI, each of whom made his separate peace with Charles the Bold in the second half of 1475. Louis, who had promised Duke René's ambassadors at the end of August that if necessary he would come in person at the head of

---

[1] Printed in *Lettres de rois et autres personnages*, ii. 495–6, and partly in Kervyn de Lettenhove, *BARB* lvii (1887), 147–8.
[2] *Recueil du Fay*, 117 and 122.

10,000 troops to help defend Lorraine,[1] took care to see that René got no French help at all. He had in fact made a secret bargain with Charles the Bold, in which Charles was given a free hand in Lorraine in return for the surrender to the king of Louis de Luxembourg, constable of France and count of St. Pol. But Duke René's other allies made what efforts they could to help him defend his lands against the might of Burgundy. Nor was it mere coincidence that, a few weeks after the invasion of Lorraine by Charles the Bold on 23 September 1475, Bern and her more aggressive associates invaded the *pays de Vaud*. For these two events, Charles's invasion of Lorraine and Bern's invasion of the Vaud, in September–October 1475, though geographically separated, were in fact part of one and the same phenomenon. They comprised together yet another phase in the struggle between Burgundy and the League of Constance.

The events and developments outlined in this chapter occurred in the absence of Duke Charles the Bold. Many of them were far removed, in a corner of his territories which was more or less peripheral and remote from the duke and his court. The battle of Héricourt could be dismissed as a frontier skirmish; the conquest of Blamont and other places as mere raids; the loss of Alsace as an insignificant trifle. The eyes of Europe and the attention of Duke Charles were riveted on Neuss, and the duke's camp there became the diplomatic centre of Europe. After the siege he was involved in negotiations at Calais and elsewhere with Edward IV, which he had hoped would lead to a triumphant Anglo–Burgundian invasion of France. In a sense, however, it was the expedition to Neuss and these plans for the conquest of France which turned out to have been, at least as far as Charles the Bold was concerned, remote, obscure and unimportant. For, while the duke was mesmerized by such extravaganzas as these, the destiny of Burgundy was being settled by the humdrum and sometimes sordid events on his south-eastern frontiers, which have been the subject of this chapter. It was in connection with these events that the grand alliance against Charles the Bold, the League of Constance, comprising the Lower Union and the *Eidgenossen*, was brought into being and held together. The influence of the king of France on its formation has been shown by Dr. Bittmann to have been minimal. Louis XI did not even take such a direct initiative

---

[1] Knebel, *Diarium*, ii. 290–2 (letter of René's ambassadors with Louis at Amiens to René, 31 August 1475).

as his father Charles VII had done in 1430, when he sent ambassadors to the duke of Austria, to Strasbourg, Bern, Basel and Zürich, inviting them directly to join France in an alliance against Philip the Good.[1] It was not Louis XI, but the towns, notably Strasbourg, Basel and Bern, which brought the League of Constance into existence. The first initiatives were urban; the finances were urban; and the armies fielded by the League were primarily recruited in or by the towns. It was the towns, rather than princes like Sigmund or René, still less the rural peasantry of Switzerland, which formed the backbone of the opposition to Charles the Bold. In this connection it is as well to remember that the very earliest league of German-speaking towns, formed in 1250, comprised among others Bern, Zürich, Rheinfelden, Breisach, Sélestat, Colmar and Mulhouse. Without the long tradition of urban cooperation in this area the League of Constance is incomprehensible. But Charles the Bold's confrontation and eventual defeat by the League was by no means the result of opposition to Burgundian expansion in the one area of the Upper Rhine. It was equally a product of his policies and ambitions in Savoy and Lorraine: policies of safeguarding his lines of communication with Italy; ambitions for the eventual annexation or conquest of both duchies. Indeed, all the way from Cologne and Frankfurt to Lyons and Geneva and over the Alps to Italy, Charles the Bold's activities, besides menacing the independence of princes, threatened the very existence of the towns and, more important, interrupted what is the life blood of any urban system, the free movement of goods and commodities.

[1] Vaughan, *Philip the Good*, 64.

CHAPTER NINE

The Siege of Neuss and the Conquest of Lorraine

The events and pressures which led to the appearance of Charles the Bold's army outside the walls of the town of Neuss on the Rhine opposite Düsseldorf on 29 July 1474 are by no means easy to disentangle and describe.[1] Even if Conrad Stolle, the vicar of St. Severus's in Erfurt, is correct in claiming that Charles the Bold planned to conquer the entire River Rhine, this would not necessarily have brought him to Neuss. Moreover, any realistic assessment of Charles's plans of conquest along the great river must take into account the fact that one of the most persistent and successful territorial rulers of the day, Frederick the Victorious, elector palatine of the Rhine, who was firmly ensconced along the middle reaches of the Rhine between Strasbourg and Koblenz, was Charles's indispensable friend and ally. True, the acquisition of Upper Alsace in 1469 had brought

---

[1] For what follows on Charles the Bold's Neuss expedition and the imperial counter-attack the main chronicles are Basin, *Louis XI*, ii, van Berchen, *Gelderse kroniek*, *CDS*, *Lübeck*, v and *Cöln*, iii, *Cronycke van Hollandt*, fos. 342–56, de Haynin, *Mémoires*, ii. 176–99, Knebel, *Diarium*, ii, de la Marche, *Mémoires*, iii. 88–100, *Magnum chronicon Belgicum*, 441–56, de Margny, *L'Aventurier*, 57–61, 83–5 and 99–100, Molinet, *Chroniques*, i, von Schaumburg, *Die Geschichten und Taten*, 18–27, Stolle, *Thüringisch-Erfurtische Chronik*, Unrest, *Österreichische Chronik*, 53–61, and Wierstrait, *Beleegs van Nuys*; see too *Historischen Volkslieder*, ii. 42–58. Documents are printed or calendared in *Acten zum Neusser Kriege*, *Correspondance de la mairie de Dijon*, i. 143–61, *Dépêches des ambassadeurs milanais*, i, *Frankfurt's Reichscorrespondenz*, ii, *Politische Correspondenz*, *Regesten zur Geschichte der Belagerung von Neuss*, *Reichstags-Theatrum unter K. Friedrichs V*, ii. 646–718, *Urkunden und Acten betreffend die Belagerung der Stadt Neuss* and *Urkundliche Nachträge zur österreichisch-deutschen Geschichte*. Among modern authorities the following have proved useful: Ennen, *Geschichte*

about a measure of Burgundian control over the river above and below Basel, but this was lost in April 1474. In the north, the conquest of Guelders in the late summer of 1473 had placed Burgundian power firmly astride the Lower Rhine at Nijmegen and brought it at least temporarily to Moers opposite Duisburg. But Charles the Bold was a long way indeed from planning, still less realizing, the grandiose project attributed to him by Stolle which included the outright conquest of the towns of Neuss, Bonn and Cologne, the archbishoprics of Trier, Mainz and Cologne, and the Rhine Palatinate as well. Better evidence suggests that in 1474 Charles the Bold's Rhine plans were limited, even at their most extensive in the weeks before he laid siege to Neuss, to the conquest of Cologne and Strasbourg and the restoration of Burgundian power in Upper Alsace.[1]

It was Philip the Good, not Charles the Bold, who began the policy of Burgundian interest in the archbishopric of Cologne. On 7 March 1463, only three weeks after the death of Archbishop Dietrich von Moers, his ambassadors Count John of Nassau and Anthoine Haneron were given audience in the 'Gilded Chamber of the town hall' at Cologne. They pleaded that the new archbishop should be chosen from one of Duke Philip's Bourbon nephews: either Charles, archbishop of Lyons, or better, because he knew German as well as Latin and French, Louis, bishop of Liège. Either was wealthy enough to pay off the debts with which the archiepiscopal see had been encumbered by the extravagant policies of Dietrich von Moers. There would be no question of any infiltration of French officials; after all, the administration of Brabant had not

---

der Stadt Köln, iii, Löhrer, Geschichte der Stadt Neuss, Tücking, Geschichte der Stadt Neuss, Diemar, Entstehung des deutschen Reichskriegs, Markgraf, De bello burgundico a Carolo Audace contra archiepiscopatum Coloniensem suscepto, Schmitz, RG ii (1895–6), 1–10 etc., Kallen, Die Belagerung von Neuss and Zimmermann, RHB iv (1927), 66–72. The general histories of Bachmann, Deutsche Reichsgeschichte, ii and von Kraus, Deutsche Geschichte zur Zeit Albrechts II und Friedrichs III are valuable, as are the recent discussions of Grüneisen, RV xxvi (1961), 66–70, Helbig, RV xxix (1964), 43–5, Petri, Gemeinsame Probleme, 115–16 and 193–8 and Steinbach, Festschrift Neuss, 37–46. I have been fortunate in being allowed to consult Dr. Grüneisen's MS. material on the Neuss expedition assembled for vol. xxiii of the Deutsche Reichstagsakten (RTA material); unfortunate in writing before the publication of Dr. Bittmann's next volume which will cover the subject matter of this chapter.
[1] Above, p. 289. What follows is from Ennen, Geschichte der Stadt Köln, iii. 431–4.

L*

been taken over by French speakers, nor had that of the bishopric of Utrecht. But the Burgundian ambassadors were rebuffed. They were told that in any case the election had nothing to do with the town of Cologne, which was one of the four free imperial towns; it was a matter for the chapter and the see or *Stift* of Cologne. Instead of a Burgundian candidate the chapter proceeded shortly after this incident to the election of Ruprecht, brother of the elector palatine of the Rhine, who was confirmed as archbishop of Cologne a year later by the pope, though not until 1 August 1471 by the Emperor. Philip the Good lost no time in making the new archbishop a Burgundian client and ally: the treaty was signed on 26 September 1465 and in it the duke of Burgundy promised to be Ruprecht's 'true, faithful and perfect friend'.[1] Just before his death Philip the Good received a gift of a lion from the grateful archbishop.

With the city of Cologne the dukes of Burgundy had always had commercial relations, and Charles the Bold was a natural person for the king of Denmark to turn to when in 1468 he wanted pressure to be put on Cologne in order to effect the return of some valuables seized there from a Danish ambassador returning from Rome.[2] Throughout his reign Charles was in touch with Cologne over the tolls on wine and other commodities passing along the Rhine and he did his best to persuade the city to lower her tariffs. One of the ducal councillors used on embassies to Cologne was the dean of Heinsberg, Symon Mulart, ex-student of the University of Cologne. On 15 March 1470, acting apparently on behalf of Charles the Bold, he presented a copy of his eulogy of the duke to the city council. At this time and for years before the duke of Burgundy had been involved with Cologne because of the *Schossstreit*, a long-drawn-out dispute between her and the *Kontor* of the Hanse at Bruges over certain dues charged by the *Kontor*. In April 1467, before he became duke, Charles was approached about this by Johann Zeuwelgin, the provost of St. Andrew's, Cologne, who asked him to transfer the case then pending between Cologne and the Bruges Hansards before the Burgundian grand council to the diet of the Hanse. Although he was sympathetic, the grand council was still trying to settle the

---

[1] De Comines, *Mémoires*, ed. Lenglet du Fresnoy, ii. 496–9, and for the next sentence, ADN B2064, f. 174 = de Laborde, *Ducs de Bourgogne*, i. 497.
[2] *Epistolae regis Christiani*, 442–3. For Philip the Good and Cologne, see Vaughan, *Philip the Good*, 295. For what follows see above, p. 125 and Boeren, *Twee Maaslandse dichters in dienst van Karel de Stoute*, 71–82 and above p. 131.

dispute when Charles became duke, and he was again involved in discussions about it during the winter of 1467–8. Judgement in Cologne's favour on part of the dispute only was eventually given by the grand council in March 1470, after Cologne had submitted complaints in Latin in 88 articles, and the Bruges Hansards had countered with 145 points against Cologne in German.[1]

It was in the autumn and winter of 1467–8, when Duke Charles was particularly concerned that no fugitives from Liège were given refuge in Cologne,[2] that he first appears in what seems to be the guise of mediator in a quite different series of disputes, those between Archbishop Ruprecht of Cologne on the one hand, and the city, Estates and cathedral chapter of Cologne on the other. On 3 October 1467 the provost of St. Andrew's wrote reporting that, at the duke's request, he had explained to him all about the judicial dispute between city and archbishop, and in a subsequent letter, dated 17 January 1468, the provost reported from Brussels that the archbishop's chancellor, Georg Hesler, was waiting to see the duke.[3]

Whatever the outcome of this particular initiative, internal disputes at Cologne continued and worsened in the years that followed. The nature of these quarrels was complex, but in many respects the dispute was a traditional one of ruler versus Estates, for Ruprecht not unnaturally did his best to ignore and undermine the powers the Estates had arrogated to themselves and imposed over their future archbishop in a characteristic document issued during the vacancy immediately before his election, called the *Erblandesvereinigung*. Not unnaturally, too, Ruprecht clashed with the Estates when he attempted to restore the crippled archiepiscopal finances by levying taxes and, even more so, when his policy of mortgage-redemption by force of arms brought about a state of civil war in the *Stift*. To these elements in the troubles at Cologne must be added the traditional, almost commonplace, hostility of archbishop and chapter, exacerbated at Cologne by the immense power of the chapter, which by itself comprised the senior, or ecclesiastical Estate of the *Stift*. There was, too, a rival candidate for the archiepiscopal throne of Cologne who injected a powerful undercurrent of personal ambition into the troubles there. This was one of three brothers, landgraves of Hesse,

---

[1] Daenell, *Blütezeit der Hanse*, ii. 54–145 and *Hansisches Urkundenbuch*, ix. nos. 319, 340, 343, etc.
[2] See above, p. 37.
[3] *Hansisches Urkundenbuch*, ix. nos. 405 and 425.

Hermann, who had made an unsuccessful bid for the bishopric of Hildesheim in 1471. A year later a document shows that he hoped to become archbishop of Mainz, Trier or Cologne.[1]

Important as they were, all these elements in the struggle were overshadowed by the relentless antagonism between the prince and the towns or, in this case in particular, between Archbishop Ruprecht and Neuss, which was the most important of the five main towns of the *Stift*, the others being Bonn, Ahrweiler, Linz and Andernach. Neuss had demonstrated her opposition to the archbishop in 1468 by taking up arms for the duke of Cleves, while Ruprecht sent troops to help Cleves's enemy Guelders. When in 1472 Ruprecht tried to seize Neuss by treachery, two of his alleged supporters in the town, convicted of taking part in the conspiracy, were beheaded and their quartered remains exhibited on poles at the street corners. Neuss was the heart and soul of the opposition to Ruprecht and her overruling ambition in this was to throw off the last vestiges of the archbishop's authority over her. This was why the city council of Neuss symbolically placed the town under the highest authorities by setting up the papal and imperial arms on the gates.

Finally, and in the event perhaps most decisively, the situation in the *Stift* of Cologne was affected at every point and on every side by the territorial ambitions of the neighbouring princes. Nor was Charles the Bold necessarily the most dangerous in this respect. The territories of the elector palatine of the Rhine might have been considerably augmented as a result of his brother's activities in the *Stift*, and he sent troops to Ruprecht's assistance long before Charles the Bold did. More threatening still, perhaps, were the landgraves of Hesse, whose territorial ambitions might be expected to extend to the conquest of the duchy of Westphalia from the archbishop of Cologne. One wonders if the citizens of Neuss may have felt a tingle of apprehension, along with relief at the additional security provided, when on 26 July 1474 Landgrave Hermann of Hesse marched into their town at the head of his troops to garrison it against the duke of Burgundy. The landgraves of Hesse still maintained their dubious claims to Brabant, and Landgrave Ludwig, brother of Hermann and Henry, had even visited that duchy, on the pretext of a pilgrimage, in 1468.[2]

---

[1] *Urkundenbuch für die Geschichte des Niederrheins*, iv. no. 358.
[2] Knetsch, *Des Hauses Hessen Ansprüche auf Brabant*, 10–11 and Vaughan, *Philip the Good*, 73.

It was in the winter of 1471-2 that deadlock was reached in the negotiations between the archbishop and the towns of the *Stift* over the archiepiscopal revenues, after the towns had refused to permit Ruprecht to levy a tax and Ruprecht had riposted by seizing the toll at Zons, on the Rhine between Cologne and Neuss. The chapter supported the towns and publicly circulated twenty-seven articles of accusation against the archbishop, who was said to have broken his oath by continuing to create mortgages, seizing and levying tolls illegally, misappropriating wine, wasting the archiepiscopal forests and so on. During 1472 and 1473 would-be mediators stepped in from all directions. Charles the Bold warned the chapter in March 1472 to desist from acts of violence against Ruprecht; instead they should arrange a conference to which he would gladly send deputies. Ruprecht's brother, Frederick, elector palatine of the Rhine, intervened and tried to effect a settlement. The papal legate, Alexander Nani, bishop of Forlì, attempted in 1473 to achieve what a predecessor of his, Onofrio de Santa Croce, bishop of Tricarico, had failed to do in 1468 on his way to Liège, and both Hermann of Hesse and the Emperor Frederick III offered their mediatory offices in 1473-4, though to no avail.

In 1473 the situation at Cologne rapidly developed beyond the influence of any ordinary mediation. On 29 March 1473 most of the cathedral chapter, some of the nobles, and the four towns of Neuss, Bonn, Andernach and Ahrweiler formally withdrew their obedience from Ruprecht and appointed Hermann, landgrave of Hesse, 'captain and protector' of the *Stift*. The city of Cologne threw in its lot with these rebels on 6 June 1473, when it signed an alliance with them for 100 years. Then on 24 July Cologne signed a military alliance with Hermann's brother, Landgrave Henry of Hesse. This intensification of the internal confrontation in Cologne coincided exactly with the onset of a new and threatening intervention by Charles the Bold. His interest in the affair was completely transformed in the second half of 1473 by his successful conquest of Guelders, which made him a territorial neighbour of the city and *Stift* of Cologne. It also underlined his position as an ally of Ruprecht and an enemy of Cologne, for he now stepped into the shoes of Duke Adolf of Guelders, who had not only been at war with Cologne but was also a military ally of Ruprecht. Charles's interest in Cologne was intensified towards the end of 1473 by the failure of his negotiations with Frederick III at Trier for a marriage alliance between the houses of Habsburg and Burgundy and for his own promotion to the imperial, or at least royal, dignity. It is no coincidence that the document in which Charles announced that he was taking over the guardianship of the *Stift* on Ruprecht's behalf and ordered his arms to be set up in public places in Cologne was dated 11 December 1473, less than three weeks after Frederick's withdrawal from Trier. Just as Ruprecht had been to see Charles at Zutphen during the conquest of Guelders in August 1473, so he was with him again at Thionville early in December. Now no longer interested in maintaining friendly relations with Frederick III, since he had gained Guelders and lost his hoped-for crown, Charles committed himself in the winter of 1473–4 to assisting Ruprecht, if need be by force of arms.

The date and exact terms of the treaty between Charles and Ruprecht have so far eluded historical research, but it was signed before the end of March 1474.[1] Charles agreed to act as protector of the *Stift* for life, to help Ruprecht regain control of Andernach, Neuss and other rebellious places and to help him recover his rights over the city of Cologne. In return, Ruprecht was to guarantee to Charles the sum of 200,000 Rhenish florins, to be paid in the form of half the annual taxes from the *Stift*, Charles in the meanwhile to enjoy right of entry into all the archbishop's places and to take possession of Uerdingen and two other towns. How far Burgundian intervention at Cologne was made inevitable by this treaty remains open to doubt, for attempts to achieve a peaceful settlement continued at least until the failure of the conference organized by Charles the Bold at Maastricht on 20 May 1474. Meanwhile, though he committed some troops to the assistance of Ruprecht, ostensibly in the defence of Westphalia against Henry of Hesse,[2] Charles tried to persuade Neuss to place itself under his protection and to frighten Cologne into cooperating with himself and Ruprecht. Thus in March a Burgundian herald contrived to display the Burgundian arms in public places in Cologne, though they were plastered with mud and torn down almost at once; and in May a secretary of Charles the Bold invited the city authorities to purchase the duke's favour with a gift of 100,000 gold lions. The effect of these more or less pacific initiatives was somewhat lessened by the activities of Charles

---

[1] Compare the text printed in *Urkundenbuch für die Geschichte des Niederrheins,* iv. no. 375 with the summary of a draft treaty in *Analectes historiques,* xvi. 152 n. 1.

[2] See the duke's letters to Ruprecht of 16 and 23 April 1474 printed in *Analectes historiques,* xvi. 148–54.

the Bold's captain Bernhart von Ramstein, who arrived in Cologne at the end of March 1474 as an ambassador, but was operating thereabouts a month later as one of Ruprecht's captains. He vied with his colleague Hagenbach in diplomatic indiscretions. He was credited, for example, with saying that he would rather anger God his creator than his lord the duke, and that Charles would soon be as powerful at Cologne as he already was at Nijmegen.

The final decision to embark on a large-scale military expedition against the rebels in the *Stift* of Cologne was delayed by Charles the Bold until the delicate and difficult question of his relations with Louis XI had been settled for the time being by the truce of Compiègne, which was to run from 13 June 1474 until 1 May 1475. Then, on and after 22 June, Charles's letters-patent given at Luxembourg announcing an expedition 'to bring the rebellious subjects of the archbishop of Cologne back to his obedience' were circulated far and wide.[1] The fact that the same document ordered a general prohibition of commerce with all members of the Lower Union and the inhabitants of Upper Alsace bears out what the Neapolitan ambassador claimed on 24 June, to the effect that Charles hoped to punish Cologne, Strasbourg and the rebels of Alsace in a single victorious campaign in Germany. But, as usual with Charles, the grandiose political vision was carefully trimmed to the practical military prospects. When it came to the point, he actually laid siege, not to the powerful city of Cologne, which had been busy laying in provisions and making other preparations to withstand him, but to the smaller town of Neuss, which most contemporary observers seem to have thought would easily fall to him. Both strategically and politically this was a sensible move. Neuss lay between Guelders and Cologne so that it was almost a military necessity for Charles to conquer it before he could hope to lay siege to Cologne, and at the same time it seemed possible that a political settlement might follow its fall. In the event, Neuss held, and the siege which was started on 29 and 30 July 1474 continued until 13 June 1475. Even in the third week of September Charles still firmly believed Neuss would soon be his. But by mid-November, when contemporaries were crediting him with a stubborn determination to take it or die, he must have resigned himself to a lengthy siege.

[1] Gorissen, *De Raadkamer te Maastricht*, 145. For what follows, see pp. 289–90 above.

The siege of Neuss was of course much more than a straight-forward Burgundian military operation against a single town. Hermann, landgrave of Hesse, the commander of Neuss's garrison and chief architect of its heroic defence, was naturally aided and supported by his brother Landgrave Henry, and on 1 August 1474 the city of Cologne had taken sides firmly with Neuss and the house of Hesse by officially declaring war on Archbishop Ruprecht. Beside Neuss and Cologne stood Bonn and Andernach, both on the Rhine south of Cologne, and Cologne soon established garrisons at Zons, on the left bank of the Rhine 13 km south-east of Neuss as the crow flies, and at Hülchrath, 9 km south-south-west of Neuss and commanding the route thence to Jülich. On the other hand, a group of places in the south of the archbishopric, the so-called *Oberstift*, held firmly for Ruprecht. Chief among these were Linz with its Burgundian garrison, Remagen, Erpel, Unkel and Königswinter. Apart from Hesse, none of the principalities bordering on the *Stift* of Cologne took up arms against Charles or even interfered with his siege of Neuss, until they found it necessary to join the army which the Emperor eventually led northwards down the Rhine from Koblenz via Cologne to Neuss in May 1475. As Cologne put it in a letter to Frederick III on 27 September 1474, nobody has helped Neuss so far save God, the landgrave Hermann, and ourselves with soldiers.

But, while nobody assisted Neuss, Charles the Bold's lines of communication north down the Rhine to Holland and westwards to his nearest territories of Limbourg and Guelders were thoroughly secured by the rulers of the territories through which they passed: respectively John, duke of Cleves, and Gerhard and William, the older and younger dukes of Jülich-Berg. The house of Cleves was a staunch ally; Jülich-Berg was bullied into toeing the Burgundian line. In April 1475, when the two dukes of Jülich-Berg were subjected to a great deal of imperial pressure against Burgundy, they received a veritable barrage of propaganda from Charles in the form of a series of Latin letters justifying his intervention in the affairs of Cologne. But it was the Burgundian military presence which decided their attitude and ensured that supplies and provisions of all kinds for Charles the Bold's siege could not only pass through their territories of Jülich on the left Rhine bank and Berg on the right, but also be procured in them. The general political situation in and around the *Stift* of Cologne as Charles stabilized himself firmly in it at Neuss was thus extraordinarily favourable to him. But then he

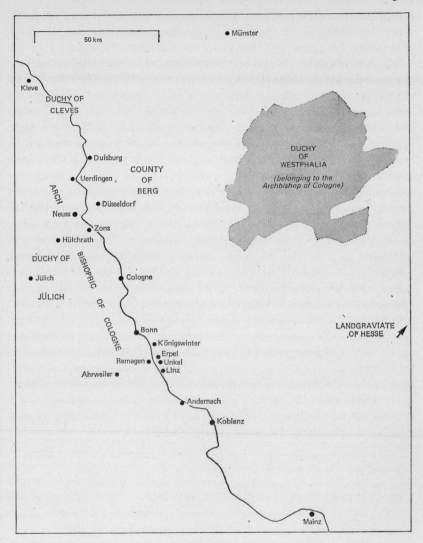

8. The River Rhine and the archbishopric or *Stift* of Cologne

never did embark on a major campaign without first securing every possible advantage in terms of geography, of strategy, and of diplomacy.

The topography of Neuss was not greatly dissimilar in the fifteenth century from what it is today. The town, of course, which was surrounded by excellent walls and moats, was much smaller. A contemporary Burgundian observer, Jehan Baugey, thought it was about the same size as Beaune. The main stream of the Rhine, which was not then spanned by a bridge, was no nearer to Neuss than it is now: three bow-shots, according to Baugey; or perhaps a little less than 2 km. But a branch of the river which has now disappeared, swollen by the waters of the Rivers Erft and Krur, flowed at that time past the walls on the eastern side of Neuss and fed its moats. The flat land between Neuss and the Rhine was divided into a large islet called the Waidt or Weide, a smaller one called the Wert, and a peninsula to the south of them, between the Erft and the Rhine, called the Hamfeld. Charles the Bold's first task was to capture and occupy the two islands in order to gain control of Neuss's communications by water. After an unsuccessful attack on 6 August, undertaken by an over-enthusiastic contingent of Italian infantry without the duke's knowledge or permission,[1] the Rhine islands were seized on 11 August and bridges built thereafter, one of them on wine barrels, to enable the troops on them to communicate freely with the rest of the army and to blockade the branch of the Rhine north and south of Neuss. These and other early operations were described in some detail by Jehan Baugey in a letter he sent to the mayor and echevins of Dijon on 16 September.

It is a fact, most honoured and redoubted lords, that six weeks ago last Saturday my most redoubted and sovereign lord, Monseigneur the duke of Burgundy, arrived and established his camp of honour before the town of Neuss. Since he began his siege in this way he has fired against the said town with about ten bombards, six mortars and a large number of culverins, serpentines and other pieces of artillery, so that the town has been badly damaged in places. My lord has established six sieges around the town; that is to say, my lord and his household people on one side; the Lombards[2] on another; Jaques Galyot on another; Lancelot de Bellemont; Messire Baudouin de Lannoy; and Messire Josse de Lalaing with 300 lances on an island in a branch of the Rhine which my

[1] *IAM* iii. 208–9.
[2] Charles's Italian troops were invariably referred to as 'Lombards'. This letter is translated from *Correspondance de la mairie de Dijon*, i. 143–8.

lord has taken since the siege and which has never been conquered in all the thirteen sieges which have been laid to this place by King Charlemagne and others. Near it are about 2,000 English. Now these sieges are so placed that one of them can go to the assistance of another.

Nothing remarkable has occurred since my said lord began the siege except that, in winning the above-mentioned island, about 120 Lombards were killed because of the failure of the bridge which the duke had had made to connect his quarters with the island, and because of a sally made by the people in the town. My lord has lost no other people, except for about 200 foragers. Since then the town has been bombarded as well as possible and the duke has enclosed his entire army [with fortifications].

Since then, that is to say on Saturday last, the tenth day of this present month and the last day of the six weeks the duke had been before Neuss, the duke had all his men armed at about 9.0 a.m. and sent them to the Lombards' quarters to try to capture a fortification which the Neussers had constructed in front of one of their gates where the Lombards were, which the said Lombards had claimed could be captured. During the attempt on the said fortification the duke and his household people were decked out in fine array in the fields, a good 3,000 men waiting to see if anyone came.... Count Campobasso, Jaques Galyot, the vicomte of Soissons, the lord of La Ferté, son of my lord of Arcies, and the English contingent, were committed in four companies to attack the said fortification, one company at a time. It was pitiful how culverins were fired at them thicker than rain, and hot water, great stones and other things [thrown at them], so that in the four hours our people were in front of the fortification they achieved nothing, and they were forced to withdraw. About eight of our people remained dead, not more, and a good sixty were wounded. Some may claim that this was an assault, but it was not, because the attack was in one place only and without ladders.[1]

The night after this attempt the Cologners sent a few people in boats down the Rhine, bringing with them a large boat loaded with wood, grease, oil and gunpowder and, when they were near the duke's army, they set fire to this boat and let it go with the water, intending that it should run up against and burn the bridge which the duke had made to cross into the above-mentioned island. As soon as the said bridge was burnt the Cologners planned to attack the 300 lances on the island, the duke being unable to help them since the bridge would have been burnt. But, thanks be to God, and because of the good watch kept by the people in boats and ships (about 50 of them) which the duke had brought up the Rhine from Holland, whose duty it was to prevent the Neussers leaving by water and see that no help or provisions could reach them, the said

---

[1] This attack on 10 September was described by some of the German sources, and has been accepted since, as a major assault on Neuss.

boat was anchored in the Rhine and it burned there without doing any harm to the bridge.

At that time, which was at daybreak on Sunday, the day after the above-described attack, a great alarm was raised. The Cologners, to the number of about 4,000, came along the Rhine and made a strong showing on the bank opposite my lord the duke. But, in spite of their demeanour, that day our foragers, accompanied by about 300 lances under the lord of Beauvoir, went foraging near the said Cologners without danger. But at that time we had a great alarm.

On the following Monday my lord [the duke] heard that a company of about 300 English wanted to leave the army, saying that the duke was not paying them at all, though they would not be owed anything so long as they were amply paid. At once the duke, himself in person armed, made everyone mount and take the field, intending to attack the English, whom he thought were about to leave. But they calmed down, and the duke took two of their captains prisoner. He was in battle order almost the whole day on the Rhine, to show himself to the Germans on the other bank.

That Monday after supper the English quarrelled over a wench and wanted to kill each other. As soon as the duke heard of this he went to them with a few people to appease them but they, not recognizing the duke, as they claimed, fired two or three times directly at him with their bows. [The arrows went] very near his head and it was extraordinarily lucky that he was not killed, for he had no armour on at all. Soon afterwards rumour spread everywhere that the duke had been wounded, and everyone rushed to the place and began to attack any English that could be found. The duke was worried by this and he did not manage to avoid some being killed. On the Tuesday following the duke caused it to be proclaimed that anyone who had anything belonging to the English was to return it; there was to be no debate or argument with them, for he regarded them as his friends and subjects, and he pardoned them for having offended him.

As for other news, my said lord has proclaimed that no one is to speak to the Neussers, who had wanted to parley. But, in spite of the pro-hibition, someone has dared to speak to them. The Neussers have allowed those of our people who were killed in front of their fortification on the day of the above-described attack to be taken and buried in a cemetery in the presence of some people from Neuss who invited [our people] to come and take them [away] in safety. The Cologners sent a man to Neuss swimming in the Rhine to take letters to the town in a wooden bottle, stating that the Emperor and his son were at Cologne and instructing the Neussers to hold firm as the Emperor was coming to attack the duke. But our night watch caught the man carrying these letters and he was taken to the duke and interrogated by him. And my lord discovered several things concerning the Emperor's plans and his enterprise, against which, with God's help, the duke will defend himself well. The duke wants to bombard the town again more thoroughly than it has been, and it is planned to throw fire into it with some engines which are in the army. Some people claim it as true that the Emperor has written to the duke [to say] that he will attack him next Monday. . . .

Written in the camp of honour, before the town of Neuss, Friday 16 September [1474].

A good many contemporary texts describe Charles the Bold's military dispositions round Neuss; it is a pity that the plan which Charles himself had made, showing his forces encamped outside the town, no longer survives. It was found on a Venetian ambassador who was intercepted on his way home by Duke Sigmund of Austria. Very possibly the information it contained was similar to that shown on the plan printed here. It is taken from an account of the siege brought away from it on 10 October 1474,[1] which is closely paralleled by the famous description of the chronicler Jehan Molinet. The Austin canon of the Oberkloster outside Neuss, who was evacuated with his colleagues when Charles the Bold requisitioned his monastery and who subsequently supplied information which was incorporated into the *Magnum chronicon Belgicum* or *Great Belgian Chronicle*, described the Burgundian army at Neuss from a different viewpoint. According to him it was composed of Frenchmen, who served as obedient subjects; of Lombards and Englishmen who served as mercenaries; and of Germans, mostly from Liège and Guelders, who were compelled to serve. Evidently he did not know about the German volunteer Wilwolt von Schaumburg, whose chronicle gives a soldier's view of the siege, with information about the trench warfare; about the already-mentioned pontoon bridge Charles built on wine barrels over the branch of the Rhine from near the Oberkloster to the Wert; about the duke's unsuccessful attempts to block off this branch of the Rhine completely by sinking earth-laden barges in it. Wilwolt describes how some of the 4,000 women in the Burgundian camp were organized to help with this work. 'These women were given a banner by the duke with a woman painted on it and, in going to or from their work, they went with the banner, preceded by trumpets and pipes.'[2]

---

[1] BN fr. MS. 1278, fos. 281–282b, printed corruptly with wrong date in Chastellain, *Oeuvres*, viii. 262–4, and in Guillaume, *Bandes d'ordonnance*, 31–4.
[2] Von Schaumburg, *Die Geschichten und Taten*, 19–20.

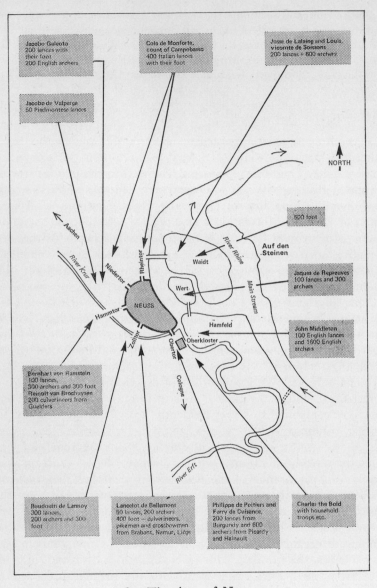

9. The siege of Neuss.
Dispositions and numbers of Burgundian troops in September–
October 1474

Before the Burgundians arrived the Oberkloster of Neuss had had its finest trees felled and taken into Neuss and the lead stripped off its roofs to make cannon balls. The cannons were dispersed elsewhere. Charles had his portable wooden pavilion, which had two separate rooms in it, set up in the abbey garden. There he lived throughout the siege and was said to have slept not in a bed, but reclining in an easy chair and wearing his armour. The ardent Molinet goes further and pretends that, 'following the noble and exalted characteristic of the lion', he slept most of the time with his eyes open. The same Molinet gives a rosy description of the siege with its tents, pavilions, markets, shops and houses. More buildings, according to Knebel, were put up by Duke Charles outside Neuss than there were inside it. But one of the duke's captains, Philippe de Croy, count of Chimay, in a letter he sent from Neuss towards the end of the year to George Chastellain, called Monsieur *l'Indiciaire*, or historiographer, describes life in the camp rather more realistically, though at times in the same words as Molinet, who evidently made use of this source in his chronicle.

It is a long time and many days, Monsieur *l'Indiciaire*, since I was refreshed with your affection either by memory, by recommendation, or by letter. And you are ungrateful in your ease and repose to forget my suffering; this will not be to your honour. The works we are engaged in are more like those which Hannibal endured crossing the Alps than he experienced in Capua. The thunder of the two bombards and their fumes in which we are cured are not musical instruments nor do they make a cordial syrup. Shot from hackbuts and culverins flies at us thicker than arrows in an English battle. Imagine that our icy and snow-covered pavilions are German baths; that the feathers of our beds are Dutch down; or that the pavements of our roads where we are in mud to our knees, are the market at Valenciennes! Where is the dinner ushered in with the sound of a bell? Alas! Where are women to entertain us, to inspire us to do well, to provide us with undertakings, devices, desires and wimples? The chemists' and jewellers' shops and banks of Bruges are far away from us.

We have a flying duke who moves about more than a swallow. One moment he is in the Italians' quarters; another moment in those of the English. He visits the Hollanders, the Hainaulters and the Picards. He commands the troops of the ordinance. He gives orders to the feudal forces; and I can assure you that he doesn't keep his household troops and those of his guard in idleness. He is always on his feet, never rests, and manages to be everywhere. One day he pierces the ground with mines and trenches. On another, he climbs up on piles and causeways.

CHARLES THE BOLD

He alters watercourses and has dried up a river more than 800 feet wide and deeper than a pike or lance could measure, which had such an impetuous current that no boat could ascend it. He has altered a river which was formerly a small stream so that it is now so deep and wide that it is without a bank or ford and seems to the judgement of men to have been navigable for all time. . . .

I am lodged in an abbey, in its dormitory, where there are small rooms and lodgings for religious people of other profession than those who used to converse there. In this place I can daily experience a great many of the abuses of this world, because in some [rooms] here through excess of money games and gambling go on all day long and in others, in default [of money], there is only dinner. Some sing and play flutes and other instruments, others weep and regret their dead relatives or even their own infirmity. On one side I hear the cheery cry 'A right royal drink!'; on the other 'Jesus', to encourage those who are in the last agony of death. There are whores in some rooms; in others the cross which leads the lifeless body to the grave. To God alone who knows the cause of these diversities these and other things must be referred.

Do not imagine, Monsieur *l'Indiciaire*, that good cheer is not made among us who can use it, and that the majesty of kings and their envoys does not make the doings of this army esteemed. The king of Denmark has been received here in greater state than he would have been in Bruges or Ghent. The English have been more watched and admired in our army and better esteemed than were our robes of cloth of gold and costly adornments at the last feast of the Golden Fleece. Admiration of our honour has encouraged the king of Naples's son to come to see what is going on. The king of Hungary has sent here his venerable ambassador for the arbitration, which he and the king of Poland awarded to the duke, of their quarrel over the kingdom of Bohemia. . . .[1]

The astonishing fact of the successful resistance of Neuss was partly due to the preparations that had been carefully made in advance, as well as to the numerous garrison of soldiers from Hesse. Enough cattle had been taken into the town to yield fresh meat until Christmas. Even after then three cows were still providing milk for small and sick children. Before the end of the siege all the local horses and all those belonging to the soldiers from Hesse had been eaten. As to powder, supplies for a very long time were assured on a murky night in November when five or six hundred men from Cologne contrived to slip through the Italians' lines each carrying a 40 lb bag of gunpowder and wearing a St. Andrew's cross. The

---

[1] The text in de Haynin, *Mémoires*, ii. 182–4 is on the whole better than that in Chastellain, *Oeuvres*, viii. 266–8.

defenders were credited with almost super-human powers of organization. They had established a strict rationing system, 'as with boys at school', and all available provisions had been stored in two houses which were permanently under armed guard. They had divided themselves into three groups. While one slept, another ate, and the third manned the walls, sometimes taunting the Burgundians by advising them to go and hang themselves or telling them that, while they were away from home, the priests would be with their wives. Naturally it was not long before the patron saint of Neuss, St. Quirinus, appeared in person to encourage the citizens. Johann Knebel says they were full of confidence in the captains under whom they had placed themselves: Jesus Christ, St. Quirinus, St. Michael, and the Three Kings whose relics were supposed to have been brought to Cologne in the twelfth century.

The main events of the siege of Neuss were recounted in detail in several eyewitness descriptions, the most important being Christian Wierstrait's verse *History of the siege of Neuss*, which was printed in 1476. We have seen how, by the middle of August 1474, the Rhine islands had been captured, connected by makeshift bridges with the rest of the camp, and their fortification begun. It was in the early autumn that Charles diverted the River Erft in an attempt to dry out the moats of Neuss, and tried to seal off the Rhine branch that flowed past the town. From 10 September onwards a succession of Burgundian attacks was made on different gates, and successful sorties in retaliation were undertaken by the defenders. Charles tried in vain to persuade the Neussers to surrender. King Christian of Denmark arrived in November on a fruitless peace-making mission. By January 1475 several of Neuss's gates lay in ruins and the attackers had even obtained a temporary foothold on at least two occasions inside the fortifications. But Burgundian military pressure on the town was eased when the Rhine rose and flooded its banks on 20 January, for Charles's troops were forced to evacuate the islands. At this time, too, a sortie from Neuss was successful in obtaining much-needed supplies of powder, wine, bread and other provisions from Charles's camp.

Throughout the spring of 1475 the principal gates of Neuss were continually bombarded and repeatedly attacked. In February-March the Rheintor fortifications were captured or demolished and the gate reduced to rubble. To encourage the defenders it was officially renamed the Quirinustor, but Wierstrait tells us that it continued to be known by its original name. In April, when the

Obertor too lay in ruins, it was given similar treatment, being renamed the Marientor. Meanwhile a body of troops mostly from Cologne arrived on 17 February and camped *auf den Steinen*, literally 'at the stones', opposite Neuss on the far side of the main stream of the Rhine. Their presence certainly cheered the Neussers, and they did manage to intercept some Burgundian shipping on the river, but they were on the wrong side of it to be of any real value to the defenders of Neuss.

Communication of a kind between Neuss and the outside world was now made possible. At first the men *auf den Steinen* made signal fires which the Neussers acknowledged with flags from the towers of St. Quirinus's. Then the Cologners at the stones were seen to fire three large cannon-balls towards Neuss, apparently with long streamers of ribbon attached to them. All of them fell short, two landing in the water and one on the enemy-occupied Wert. One of those which had splashed into the river was recovered and the letter it contained, bringing news of the imminent approach of a relieving army, was publicly read out in Neuss. Further messages to and fro followed, including at least one from the soldiers of the garrison which was successfully fired out of Neuss to the stones, though generally the defenders preferred to keep their powder for more pressing affairs. Their historic cannon-ball letter, written in German, still survives in the Cologne archives. It reads as follows:[1]

> To the high-born prince Herr Heinrich, landgrave of Hesse, count of Ziegenhain and of Nidda, our dear friendly brother and gracious lord, and to the honourable learned burgomaster and councillors of the town of Cologne, our special good friends and dear lords. Also to the captains at the stones.
>
> High-born prince, dear friendly brother and gracious lord, honourable and learned lords and especial good friends. You may well have been made aware, through the verbal and written messages of ourselves and of the councillors of Neuss, of the wretched and considerable distress which oppresses us daily more and more. On this matter sweet words have been sent to us to the effect that without any doubt we shall be joyfully relieved by force within a short time, but unfortunately, since then manifold disasters have overtaken us so that we have lost one fortification after another, with moats too, at the Quirinustor, and we can turn no way without regretting it and wishing that no relief had been promised us while we have to remain in this wretched situation and that God would deign to intervene. Writing to you about this seems to be of no avail.

---

[1] Printed Kuphal, *Festschrift G. Kallen*, 155–7.

Now it saddens us that the honourable and noble burgomaster, council and entire community here at Neuss, who have so manfully and whole-heartedly borne such great damages by way of fire, expense and other things should thus, together with us, be left in the lurch so wretchedly and in such difficulty through your optimistic messages, which is some-thing we never expected or believed could have happened. Unless we are relieved soon and powerfully and with the utmost expedition we are bound to report to you that we shall suffer a complete disaster. We know no one to appeal to except the Almighty God. We request you, through your love and honour, in affection and obedience, not to allow our misery to become worse than we have described to you. And, if no relief comes in the above-mentioned time, then we want to undertake discussions [concerning surrender], in order to avoid losing our lives and goods. But we still wish to serve you in a friendly and dutiful way.

Dated at Neuss on the eve of holy Palm Sunday, 18 March 1475. . . .

From Hermann, by God's grace landgrave of Hesse, count of Ziegen-hain and Nidda, and from all the soldiers now inside Neuss.

The day after this letter was shot out of Neuss the Milanese ambassador at the Burgundian court, Johanne Petro Panigarola, included in his third despatch—he only arrived on 13 March—a description of the siege as seen by the besiegers. He surely exaggerates the numbers in the Burgundian army, but otherwise gives his duke a balanced view of the situation and prospects. [1]

To tell the truth, my lord, this undertaking at Neuss is a difficult thing and, according to people expert in the art of war, it will take a long time to have it by force. The place is strong in its site and because of the river. It is well defended, with perhaps over 3,000 stout defenders within it, with good artillery—one person exhibits a hat that has been shot off. It is necessary to work underground in tunnels which, as they are made, so likewise the [enemy] makes theirs, assembling inside to defend them, and they defend themselves so valiantly that anyone wishing to do battle with them will send a whole crowd of men to the butcher's shop.

This is a very fine camp, in which there are more than 30,000 com-batants and a mass of artillery. There have been even more people here than there are now, but there is no need [for them]. This lord [duke] could have the place on terms but he doesn't want this; he wants it at discretion. He is in close touch with the Emperor and the lords of Germany concerning an agreement. In any case, whether by honourable agreement in his own way or otherwise he says he is resolved not to leave until he achieves his aim. His lordship is most diligent, by day and by

---

[1] ASM Pot. est. Borgogna 516–17/12–13, repeated from 10–11 with vari-ations.

night he inspects the bombards and excavations as if he were the least person in the camp, and he takes the utmost trouble.

What will happen I am unable to tell yet though I would have liked to have advised your lordship of the limits [of endurance] of this place. . . .

From the camp by Neuss, at four hours after dusk, 19 March 1475.

At this time, more than seven months after the start of the siege, contemporary observers were everywhere in agreement concerning its significance. 'It seems to many, and I agree', wrote an Italian at Geneva on 19 March, 'that the affair of Neuss is of great importance. If the duke doesn't take it, the Germans will become more enthusiastic to attack him.'[1] Early in March Frederick III's ambassador to the *Eidgenossen*, Count Hug of Montfort, had insisted at Zürich that 'should Neuss be lost, such destruction would result to all German lands that nobody can conceive of it'. However, though the siege of Neuss was fully maintained through the spring and early summer of 1475, and further assaults were made, notably on 27–8 April, the attention and the energies of all the participants and most European princes as well were now directed towards the imperial campaign to relieve the beleagured town.

The idea of armed opposition to Charles the Bold by the Emperor was as old as the siege of Neuss; indeed Henry of Hesse had been appointed imperial captain and protector of the *Stift* before the siege began and, on the day before the Burgundian army arrived outside Neuss, Frederick III had written to Cologne promising his support in the war against Charles. This was followed up, with the usual delays brought about by Frederick's habitual procrastination, by an imperial summons to the electoral princes, sent out on 26 and 27 August, ordering them to assemble troops at Koblenz on 21 September in order to resist the duke of Burgundy.

The princes seem to have been more interested, in the autumn of 1474, in dreaming up and even describing in detail the most extravagant alliances and the most enormous armies that might possibly be brought to bear against Charles, than in actually doing anything to help Neuss in its predicament. On 16 November 1474, for example, Albert, elector of Brandenburg, sent a confidential memorandum to Duke Albert of Bavaria which listed in detail some 70,000 men promised before Christmas by the imperial princes and towns. It went on to state that an army 30,000 strong, comprising

---

[1] *Dépêches des ambassadeurs milanais*, i. 79. The quotation that follows is from *Eidgenössischen Abschiede*, ii. 528.

16,000 Swiss, 10,000 men from other League of Constance powers, and 4,000 French troops, would invade Upper Burgundy and lay siege to Besançon. The king of France, besides providing this small force, would send 40,000 men into Luxembourg while he invaded Picardy in person with 60 or 80,000 men. Charles's ally England was not forgotten: she was to be assailed by the kings of Scotland and Denmark and their allies, making 100,000 men in all.[1] Another document, said to have been drawn up by the electors of Mainz and Brandenburg, takes into account those other imperial enemies the Turks and the Hungarians, as well as the Burgundians, contrives an imperial army 130,000 strong, and even suggests means of paying this freak military assembly.

Some modern German historians have described in glowing terms the German patriotism, the imperial ardour, and the fraternal sentiments which they allege were brought into being in the German-speaking world by Charles's attack on Neuss, which is supposed to have been universally resented as a *welsch* invasion of German territory.[2] In point of fact, parts of the Empire flatly refused to assist Frederick III in the relief of Neuss: the *Eidgenossen*, for example, the elector palatine of the Rhine, the dukes of Jülich-Berg and Cleves. Frederick himself can scarcely be said to have demonstrated any real enthusiasm for the task, though one must make allowances for the fact that his movements, if that be not too grand a word to describe his intermittent ambling pace, were hampered by his desperate financial situation. He fell deeply in debt with the local tradesmen at Augsburg; at Würzburg some of his horses and carts were impounded by the guildsmen against payment of his debts. An embassy from Cologne had to bail him out of his difficulties. The nearer he approached to Neuss, in the spring of 1475, the more protracted were his delays and the shorter his days' marches. He managed to stay in Bonn for ten days in March before even entering Cologne. The moment everyone had been awaiting so eagerly came at last on 6 May 1475, when he set out from Cologne at the head of his troops. But he camped that day on the heath of Mülheim just outside the walls to the north of the town and, crawling thence to Zons, he dallied several days there.

[1] *Politische Correspondenz*, i. 751–2. For the next sentence see *Aktenstücke und Briefe zur Geschichte des Hauses Habsburg*, i. 418–27.
[2] Compare Franz, *JSFB* v (1942), 161–74 and Fritzsche, *Deutscher Grenzlandkampf*, with Kallen's more judicious analysis in *Die Verteidigung von Freiheit und Recht*.

If anyone demonstrated genuine enthusiasm for the imperial campaign against Charles the Bold it was surely the towns. Naturally the co-operation of places like Strasbourg and Frankfurt was above all due to their awareness of the threat of Burgundian power to their own interests. Their enthusiasm was neither imperial nor German, it was urban and self-interested. No German sentiment, only an intensely civic one, is evinced by the care and pride which they lavished on their military contingents and by the vivid and informative letters which were sent home by their commanders in the field. Every town too had its chronicler. The Lübeck chronicle describes in glowing terms the 600-man contingent sent by that town to the imperial army. The men wore red and white uniforms, and the twenty-seven wagons which comprised their transport were painted white and red. They bore the imperial arms on one side and those of Lübeck on the other and each wagon was decorated with a different device.[1] Immense trouble was taken by Frankfurt to ensure that her men looked their best when they marched into Cologne on 24 or 25 April. They were instructed to cross the Rhine in their old uniforms and not change into the new ones the city authorities had specially sent them, until the last possible moment. They were given the entire weekend before this important parade to clean and prepare their gear.

The spirit which produced such spit and polish caused petty rivalries which occasionally broke out into serious quarrels among the imperial troops. Substantial casualties on both sides were occasioned during a nocturnal fight between the bishop of Münster's men and the civic troops of Strasbourg on 19 May.[2] The Westphalians, it was said, had started the quarrel after getting drunk according to their usual custom. It may have been after this that imperial orders were issued prohibiting the use of cannon, crossbow or other weapon except against the enemy and ordering that no one was to sit by the wine or beer to drink it. It was to be taken away and consumed in the tents. There were quarrels too, over who should carry the banner of St. George, which had to be settled by imperial decree: the Swabians and Franconians were the only people admitted to this privilege, which they were to exercise on alternate days. There was further trouble between the towns over the carrying of

[1] CDS, xxxi. Lübeck, v. 142–3.
[2] On this and what follows, the letter printed in Weiss, ZGO (N.F.) ix (1894), 718–21, adds significantly to what is printed in the sources referred to p. 312 n. 1 above. The letter of 15 May in von Königshoven, Chronicke, ed. J. Schiltern, 1105–7 is also in Reichstags-Theatrum unter K. Friedrichs V, ii. 709–10.

the large imperial banner. In nearly all these incidents urban pride played a part. The towns gave life and soul to the ponderous military machine marshalled so gradually by Emperor Frederick against Charles the Bold.

The war between Burgundy and the Empire was not only fought with armies. Manifestos, declarations of war, letters, bribes, rumours and falsifications of all kinds played their part, as they have done in every war. Charles the Bold carefully justified his intervention in imperial affairs in an elegant Latin letter sent to Adolf, archbishop of Mainz, and probably other imperial princes.

Most reverend father in Christ and illustrious prince, our dearest relative. We have been informed that His imperial Majesty has asserted in writing and by word of mouth to many of the princes and cities of Germany that we are waging war by sequestering one of the best parts of the Empire so that we can appropriate it, thus derogating from the rights of the electoral princes. This indeed, unworthy as it is, is far from our mind and purpose. May so much evil be remote from us! However, even though we believe that you, because of your humanity and through mutual goodwill and consanguinity, will judge otherwise, still we are unwilling that your Grace should remain ignorant of this contumely falsely heaped on us. Because if the Emperor, as a result of our steadfast skill and his inactivity, is envious of our fortune, he ought not to accuse us of a fault we are far removed from, nor allure princes whom we love as brothers or relatives into our hatred and enmity with false suggestions. It certainly seems to be an unworthy thing to contrive enmity in someone who habitually has abundant goodwill towards us, especially as we are working, not to harm, but for the splendour and glory of, the Empire. The destruction in preparation for princes if subjects are permitted to rise up with impunity against their lords is hidden from no one. Even if some people long to inflame such a fire, we shall hasten to extinguish it. Who does not know what has happened in the three finest churches in the whole extent of German territory? Once at Trier, then at Mainz and now, the latest, at Cologne. . . .

We indeed, moved by the unworthiness of the thing, would have thought it shameful and dishonourable to abandon the said archbishop, who was requesting our help, in such a great calamity for himself and his church and in such legal right, especially as we are linked to him by blood, by old friendship, and by the most stringent alliance. Moreover in his letters the pope has warmly commended him and his church to us and, in addition, before doing anything else, the chapter made an alliance with pernicious terms against us with our enemy the king of France. Because of this we are utterly amazed if anyone should think we are doing an injury when we are only repelling one.

The Emperor has recently written to us ordering us to lay down our arms and to permit him to judge the case. He knows from our reply the reasons why it is not open to us to lay down our arms, nor could we do so without disaster, especially as nothing is offered in satisfaction. It is not fair for the same person to be at the same time judge and party, for who cannot see how hostile he is towards the archbishop and all his supporters, and how he favours his enemies? Surely this Landgrave Hermann, as a usurper, can be seen to have no standing in this affair by right or equity, yet the Emperor appoints his brother Landgrave Henry in his name and place to lead his cause and does him as many favours as he can. Any schoolboy knows whether these actions are more likely to settle differences or inflame things further. And indeed in letters and promises he has tried to persuade our subjects to rebel against us. He was not being a just judge in calling before his own jurisdiction someone whose ruin he was trying so hard to contrive, and in attributing what was his own fault to someone else's crime. Indeed, we have never deserved such severe proceedings against us; and we think we ought not to be accused of something in which we are far from blame. We have always cherished him as a lord and an honoured relative and recently at Trier, as you know, we offered him obedience and an alliance and did him what honour we could. For all of which we now discover he is ungrateful. Although this is so, we are in no way hostile to him but, as before, we earnestly desire his glory and renown, just as your Grace should know that it is on behalf of an afflicted church, a prince elector endangered by force of arms, the repudiation of force, the renown and glory of the Empire and, lastly, on behalf of justice and equity, that we have taken up arms, so that we can make way for peace, ready, supported by the best rights, to repel injury, insult and all force. In the pursuit of this we shall continue, as we began, with unswerving intent, being in no doubt of obtaining the well deserved victory which the Almighty offers us. Most reverend father and illustrious prince, our dearest relative, we ask you to let us know if there is anything we can do for your glory and renown so that we can fulfil it according to your wishes and with the help of God; may he keep watch on us always.

In the camp against Neuss, 1 November 1474.[1]

Frederick III certainly did circulate letters in the Burgundian Low Countries inciting Charles the Bold's subjects to revolt against him. At Dordrecht his messenger was taken into custody and handed

---

[1] This letter is printed in Pius II, *Historia rerum Frederici, Diplomata*, 57–8, *Reichstags-Theatrum unter K. Friedricks V*, ii. 663–4, *Aktenstücke und Briefe zur Geschichte des Hauses Habsburg*, i. 120–2 and Knebel, *Diarium*, ii. 170–2. For the beginning of the next paragraph, see *Cronycke van Hollandt*, f. 349.

over, with his letters, to the council of Holland. He also wrote inviting Groningen, Deventer and other places outside the ducal territories to come to the aid of Neuss and Cologne, and, to encourage the bishop of Münster's hostility to Charles, he gave him the county of Zutphen which the duke of Burgundy had recently conquered with Guelders.[1] The climax of the imperial war of words against Charles the Bold came in Frederick's manifesto of 3 December 1474 which was evidently meant in part as a reply to the ducal letters above quoted.

Frederick by the grace of God Emperor of the Romans etc. to Charles, prince and duke of Burgundy, greetings—if you deserve any.

The obligation of the burden we have undertaken compels us to seek you out in arms by freeing from the jaws of doom the city which you are besieging, unless you undertake to withdraw from arms of your own accord. From your earliest years, indeed, because of your fecklessness and vanity of character you have had an inordinate desire to conquer Germany, to lay claim to the Roman Empire, and to break the bonds of human society, never being content with your own territories. You lead armies, ravage the lands of others, and either massacre or subjugate free peoples. In augmenting your own strength and diminishing that of other princes you have relied upon your power and arms. You have engaged in many wars although provoked by no injury. There has been much effusion of blood; indeed you are eager to commit aggression on the borrowed blood of the people and in the slaughter of others. Many towns have been destroyed by your agency, many lands occupied by force, and you unjustly possess certain lands as though they are your own; many noble princes and dukes have been cast into chains; many churches consecrated to God have fallen—things well known to the minds of men, and space forbids the recital of them all.

You think it no difficult matter for those who are at variance among themselves, who enjoy peace and are not trained in warfare, to be conquered by you, but in fact things will turn out very differently from what you think. We believe that you are not so ignorant of our affairs as to be unaware of the power of the Germans and of the whole Roman Empire, nor of the ardour, martial character and fierceness of Germany, its spirit and aggressiveness, its boldness and energy, courage and experience in military matters. In every nation one can find brave men and cowards as soldiers, but in the same way nation rises superior to nation. One single tiny town in Germany has weakened you and your power, as you have learned by experience, and your treasury, and it has laid low your innumerable host. For the nature of the Germans is different, their strength is different, their character is different. They, used to command,

---

[1] *Gedenkwaardigheden*, v. 57–8.

M

do not know how to be subjects. Do not underestimate this nation: it does not quake with idle fear nor is it frightened by any mortal danger and it finds its salvation not in flight but in arms. He who seeks to subjugate it and expel it from its place must needs be braver, more aggressive, and superior in courage. Nor indeed should you think that the dissensions and quarrels of the princes of Germany favour your designs for, when they know that public quarrels threaten, they will cease their own internal quarrels, they will unite and be reconciled, and take up arms with all their forces against you, as against the common foe. If you wish to extend your rule among the Germans and make your name glorious you have no need of arms and armies, but the courtesy and good faith by which friends are made who can become the defence of one's kingdom, not treasures or armies.

We have now learned that, under the guise of honour and justice, your pretence is that you have taken up arms on behalf of the afflicted church of Cologne, of the prince elector the bishop in his distress, of resistance to force, and of the renown and glory of the Roman Empire, not in order to inflict but to repel injury and insult, for the attainment of which end you wish to conduct yourself with the unswerving resolve with which you began. Nor is this surprising, for no man is such a rascal as not to draw a veil of honour over his own crimes, and it will be discovered in actual fact how fictitious and far from the truth these statements are. Your are aware of the rich revenues of the church of Cologne and to them you direct your attention, not in defending the bishop from his enemies, if he suffers any injury, but in depriving him of what is his. And even if his holiness our apostolic lord, at an earlier time in consequence of false advice, did commend the church of Cologne to you, yet, better schooled by the clear light of truth, in the course of the summer he despatched to you from his side his legate Mark, the cardinal of St. Mark, to whom you refused to grant audience, fearing that you would have to relinquish your arms at the bidding of his holiness and that he would show you an apostolic letter aimed against you and the bishop of Cologne who is involved in the severest sentence of anathema.

Since, after taking up arms, with fixed resolve you do not intend to relinquish them, you should at the present time know that almost the whole of Germany has been summoned to campaign against you with a stout host of valorous horse and foot. And since we find you proud, arrogant and rebellious against us and the king of France, and claiming to be free of the law of the fief you hold from us, behaviour which least befits a vassal, we proclaim our intention of wiping you out with might and main, both in Upper Germany and in the coastal areas of the Channel, and of there wreaking your ruin and downfall, and your disgrace too, since you strive to scale the steps to the peak of supreme power and disregard the stages thereto. A universal peace must thereby be established, so that the golden age may be reborn, so that leopard may lie down with lamb and the calf with the lion, so that swords may be turned into sickles and all iron return to ploughshares and mattocks; so that cities which you have destroyed may rise again and churches consecrated to God may reemerge; so that ruined monasteries may ring with the sound of divine praises; so that princes and dukes, nobles of every estate and eminence, who have been cast into chains, may regain their freedom, and so that the lands which you wrongly possess may be restored to their rightful heirs. All this will come upon you by justice and divine punishment, for the lord on high, looking down from heaven, can no longer contemplate your tyranny with equanimity. And if you wish to escape the jaws of doom, in which you lie, you should be zealous to obey us and the Roman Empire as the law demands. This will be of profit and advantage to you, as you will in fact shortly discover. Farewell, if you choose to say farewell to us.

Frankfurt, 3 December 1474[1]

In the spring of 1475 Charles the Bold continued to issue a stream of letters justifying the siege of Neuss, addressed particularly to doubtful Burgundian allies like the dukes of Jülich-Berg. But his propaganda also took on a somewhat more positive tone: he tried to persuade some of the German princes to withdraw from the coalition against him. He caused a hint to be dropped to the most dynamic and belligerent of all the princes, Albert, elector and margrave of Brandenburg, to the effect that he was an obvious choice to replace Frederick as Emperor and that he could, in certain circumstances, count on the votes of the archbishop of Cologne and the elector palatine. Albert ignored these advances. His namesake of Saxony seemed a more hopeful possibility. After all, Duke Albert of Saxony had been for some time on the brink of packing up. He found the campaign much too expensive for his limited financial resources. On 20 March Charles wrote congratulating him on going home with his men after telling Frederick that he did not think the duke of Burgundy would aggress against the Empire. Charles the Bold offered him a close alliance between Burgundy and Saxony. If there was anything to the advantage of himself or his lands that Charles could do for him, he had only to let him know, and he would treat the affair as if it was his own.

Besides this warfare of letters and manifestos, both Charles and Frederick made use of diplomacy, during the siege of Neuss, to widen their circle of alliances. Frederick naturally did his best to

[1] Professor Frank Norman has kindly translated this letter for me from Pius II, *Historia rerum Friderici, Diplomata*, 58–60.

secure the co-operation against Charles the Bold of every part of the Empire and on the whole he was not unsuccessful, even obtaining contingents from many individual Hanseatic towns, though the maritime power of that organization was by no means brought into play against Burgundy.[1] But Frederick's main hope was King Louis XI of France. Right through the early months of 1475 he believed, or pretended he believed, that an army of 30,000 Frenchmen promised by Louis XI would be invading Luxembourg at any moment. Frederick was perhaps not too worried by Louis's delays in implementing the treaty of Andernach, signed on 31 December 1474, since he himself had promised to lead 30,000 men against Charles at the same time. Eventually both parties renewed the agreement on 17 April and both did in fact lead their forces out against Charles in the first week of May. At the same time René, duke of Lorraine, was enlisted as a third member of this anti-Burgundian alliance. His dramatic declaration of war against Charles, delivered at Neuss soon after 9 May, has already been described.[2]

Charles the Bold for his part was also diplomatically active. Indeed, he more than held his own in this sphere for, during the Neuss campaign, he scored three notable successes: with England, Milan and Hungary. The treaty of London, which was negotiated on Charles's behalf by his bastard half-brother Anthony and dated 25 July 1474, actually four days before the start of the siege of Neuss, included a quite explicit promise by Edward IV to invade France in the following summer, 1475, to claim his rightful kingdom from the usurping Louis XI. This was something which Charles had probably been hoping for ever since his wedding in 1468; he promised to provide 10,000 men to help Edward. The treaty was accompanied by the usual extravagances. Edward, as king of France, ceded Bar, Champagne, Nevers, Rethel, Eu, Guise, Donzy, Tournai and other places to Charles, who was excused from doing homage for any of his lands. In a separate document, since he had been given Champagne, Charles graciously gave Edward IV permission to be crowned king of France at Rheims![3] The treaty of Moncalieri, of 30 January 1475, which detached Milan from its French connection and brought it into close alliance with Savoy and Burgundy has already been

---

[1] See von Ropp, *HG* xxvi (1899), 43–55.
[2] Above, pp. 308–9. Documents concerning the alliance of Louis and Frederick are printed in *Aktenstücke und Briefe zur Geschichte des Hauses Habsburg*, i. 271–9 and 282–96.
[3] Documents in *Foedera*, xi. 804–14.

mentioned.[1] With Hungary Charles was less successful, yet his close diplomatic connections with Matthias Corvinus constituted a standing threat to Frederick. A treaty was drawn up between them in November 1474 and the chronicler-parson of Erfurt reports in January that Charles and Matthias had agreed to partition the Empire between them. Charles was to conquer and keep the towns and bishoprics along the Rhine and become king of the Romans, while Matthias was to have Breslau and Bohemia. In May Hungarian ambassadors arrived at Neuss seeking an alliance against Frederick, and a full-scale Burgundian embassy set out for Hungary on 1 August 1475.

The military task which confronted Frederick and the German princes at the beginning of 1475 was twofold: the relief of Neuss and the conquest of those parts of the *Stift* of Cologne which held out for Archbishop Ruprecht and were garrisoned by Burgundian troops. Since the imperial army was assembling at Koblenz and on the fertile plain between there and Andernach and all these archiepiscopal places were between Andernach and Bonn, it was strategically sensible for the Emperor to attack and conquer them first before advancing to Neuss. On the other hand, since, with the notable exception of Linz, these places, Remagen, Erpel, Unkel, Königswinter, Sinzig and the rest, fell to Margrave Albert of Brandenburg like a pack of cards in mid-January, an immediate march to Neuss would then have been easy, safe and desirable. But there was no spirit of urgency and aggression among the imperial military leaders. Margrave Albert, who was supposed to be ardently anti-Burgundian, wrote coolly to his wife on 15 January reporting that Neuss had been so well strengthened and reinforced that she could well hold out till Easter. They had 30,000 men with them and were awaiting the promised French onslaught on Luxembourg of a further 30,000 men. They expected too, an additional 20,000 men from Cologne, Jülich, Berg, Cleves and other princes.

Halfway between Bonn and Koblenz, on the steep right bank of the Rhine, Linz was an important place which had been thoroughly fortified in the fourteenth century. A first attempt against it was made in November 1474, but when troops from Cologne arrived at Koblenz to join forces for an attack on Linz with the archbishops of Trier and Mainz, they found that neither prelate had arrived. One had gone to

---

[1] Above, p. 304. For what follows, besides Fraknoi, *Matthias Corvinus*, see Bachmann, *Deutsche Reichsgeschichte*, ii. 507 and 531–2, Stolle, *Thüringisch-Erfurtische Chronik*, 91 and ASM Pot. est. Borgogna 516–17/52.

Frankfurt to fetch the Emperor; the other had not found it possible
to take the field until the Emperor did. In the event the first assault
on Linz was not undertaken until 17 January 1475. A regular siege
followed under the direction of Albert, margrave of Brandenburg.
He built a redoubt opposite Linz but this was stormed and taken on
16 February by a relieving expedition sent by Charles the Bold under
Olivier de la Marche, who contrived also to send ample provisions
across the Rhine into Linz and to find and fight his way safely back
to the Burgundian camp at Neuss. Naturally the account of this
little escapade takes up more space in his chronicle than his description of the entire siege of Neuss, but it did not save Linz, which was
forced to surrender on 7 March after its walls had been breached
and some of its towers brought down. The way down the Rhine to
Neuss was now entirely clear of the enemy. Still, it took the imperial
army two months to advance along a mere 60 km of river. Charles had
done his best to slow down the imperial advance by holding on to
Linz; then, in the night of 12–13 May, he sent an expedition to seize
Bonn which, however, was unsuccessful.

The military events of May 1475 seem to demonstrate that
Frederick after all had no serious intention of attacking Charles
the Bold's camp outside Neuss. Leaving Cologne on 6 May, he
contrived to advance so slowly that it was not until 23 May that he
eventually arrived at the River Erft. After some skirmishes that
afternoon with Charles the Bold's forces,[1] he established himself and
his men in a fortified defensive position not far from the Burgundian
camp. Some Burgundian observers give the impression that the indecisive engagement of 23 May was sufficient to cause the Emperor to sue
for peace. Panigarola says that 'having seen and experienced the spirit
of this prince, the enemy sent the legate on the following day to say
that they were ready to treat'.[2] De Commynes claims that Charles
the Bold was in a crazily obstinate mood at Neuss and simply could
not bring himself to leave the place. In fact he had been trying to
extricate himself for some time. His efforts took the form of peace
proposals which were submitted to Frederick in March, long before
the arrival of the papal legate. On 2 April Frederick held a conference
to discuss the Burgundian terms. Charles had offered to abandon the
protectorship of the church of Cologne; each side was to retain

---

[1] Above, pp. 198–204.
[2] *Briefe und Actenstücke von Mailand*, 111. For the next sentence, see de
Commynes, *Mémoires*, ed. Calmette and Durville, ii. 14–15.

what it currently held; Neuss was to be placed in neutral hands until a final settlement; and the Emperor was to arbitrate a peace between Charles and Louis. Almost everyone was favourable to this plan, but it was rejected because of the opposition of Cologne.

In the middle of May Alexander, bishop of Forlì, the papal legate, who had arrived at Cologne on 26 April, was busily travelling between Frederick at Zons and Charles outside Neuss. Charles stuck to his proposals. 'We are content' he wrote on 18 May to the dukes of Jülich-Berg,[1] as he had already informed the legate, 'to relinquish and entirely renounce the protectorate (*advocacia*) and to have no authority in the diocese of Cologne.' He agreed that Neuss should be handed over to the pope and that the commercial privileges and peace of Cologne and the rest of Germany should be restored; he agreed 'to do every obedience to His imperial Majesty as an imperial prince' and to permit Frederick to arbitrate amicably his differences with Duke Sigmund over Alsace. But Frederick now found a new excuse for procrastination: the terms of his treaty with Louis XI did not permit him to make a separate peace with Charles the Bold. But negotiations continued and on 29 May a truce was agreed and the provisional terms of a peace treaty accepted by both sides. Charles informed his lieutenant in Luxembourg that day that 'affairs between us and the Emperor have gone so far that we hope shortly to make a settlement and bring them to an end'.[2]

The events which followed this truce, which was to last till sunset on 29 or 30 May, were partly comic and partly tragic. At first all went well, but neither Charles nor Frederick wished to be the first to retreat. Charles agreed to withdraw provided Frederick did so simultaneously, but Frederick insisted that Charles must first withdraw three miles towards his own territories; then, after a wait of three days, Frederick would withdraw. The Burgundians did begin packing up on 31 May and they evacuated the Wert. There was fraternization, visits to each other's camp and, above all, people flocked into Neuss. Charles even sent two barrels of wine into the town for Hermann of Hesse. But something went wrong; the soldiers were ordered back to their posts, and it was not until 5 or 6 June that the gates of Neuss were once more open to visitors. On 6 June the Emperor attended a thanksgiving service in St. Quirinus's

---

[1] *Analectes historiques*, xvii. 20–3 (see too pp. 16–19) = *Acten zum Neusser Kriege*, no. 157.
[2] *Recueil du Fay*, 122.

church, the peace was formally published, and on 8–9 June a tremendous smoke was caused by the Burgundians burning their tents and rubbish. But a conference on 11 June showed that there were still difficulties over the exact timing of the withdrawals; a fight broke out between some of Charles's troops and the Westphalians, and at about this time the Cologners at the stones on the opposite bank of the Rhine slipped across the river and stole five boats which Charles had loaded with his heavy artillery. On 16 June Charles offered to withdraw four miles the very next day if these boats and their contents were restored to him, but that evening an enemy force sallied forth from the imperial camp and attacked his guards. He had posted them in person too near the camp for the enemy's liking. He went to their rescue with a body of élite troops and a regular butchery of Germans followed. 'Their throats were cut, they were shot at like St. Sebastian, and they were drowned in large numbers, 100 or 200 at a time, yelling for mercy, for an hour-and-a-half. It was a harsh and most cruel affair.'[1] Thus reported Panigarola, who met Charles immediately afterwards and found him in excellent spirits. The next day the duke sent off letters to Luxembourg, Flanders and doubtless elsewhere, describing 'this victory', as he called it, in detail.[2] In the end the stolen boats and bombards were returned on 26 June; Charles left on 27 June but hovered near the German frontier until the legate notified him that the Emperor too was striking camp.

In his despatch of 12 June 1475 to Galeazzo Maria, duke of Milan, Panigarola explained that the honour of both sides had been saved by the papal legate, who had commanded both Frederick and Charles to lay down their arms on pain of excommunication. He also reported to his duke a long conversation he had had with the duke of Burgundy in which Charles expounded his plans and hopes as he prepared at last to raise the siege of Neuss. He had made peace because his allies of England and Brittany were pressing him to leave Neuss; because Louis was already making war on him; and because he had successfully protected the rights of Archbishop Ruprecht of Cologne. He was convinced that the archbishop's enemies would not attack him again and that Frederick would not try to use his army against his ally the count palatine of the Rhine. His plan now was to go to meet Edward IV at St. Omer with his household

---

[1] *Briefe und Actenstücke von Mailand*, 130.
[2] *Recueil du Fay*, 123–4 = *Collection de documens inédits*, i. 243–6.

people only and thereafter move to Lorraine to join the troops already there. Then, while Edward invaded France through Picardy, Charles himself would do so through Champagne.[1] These plans were not substantially altered in an autograph postscript Charles added on 7 July to a letter to his lieutenant in Luxembourg: he was off to see King Edward with a small company while his main army would remain at Namur under the count of Campobasso.

The damages and disadvantages suffered by Charles the Bold at the siege of Neuss were grossly exaggerated by contemporaries. According to Johann Knebel, by the end of the siege the Neussers had brought the cuirasses of 15,000 dead Burgundians into the church of St. Quirinus. They planned to sell them and use the money to decorate the church in honour of the Virgin Mary and St. Quirinus. A German report on the raising of the siege, dated 16 June, records statements that the duke of Burgundy lost over 3,000 men and 12,000 horses and that he was supposed to have shot 100,000 florins worth of powder.[2] Whatever his losses and expenses at Neuss may have been, it is a fact that, having succeeded in keeping a substantial army in the field for close on a year, Charles was in a position to tell Panigarola, as the epic siege drew to its close, that he proposed to spend the next six months in the field. And he kept his word. The siege of Neuss indeed made little difference to Charles the Bold's military potential and probably even less to his political standing. He had been checked but by no means decisively defeated.

It is scarcely surprising that Charles the Bold's enemies attacked his territories during his absence at the siege of Neuss. We have seen in a previous chapter how the powers of the Lower Union, aided by the Swiss, descended on the county of Burgundy in November 1474 and in April and July 1475, and how Bern seized the territories of Burgundian vassals in the Vaud. The activities of Guillaume de la Marck, lord of Aremberg, against Charles the Bold remain somewhat obscure. He seems to have been encouraged, if not bribed, by Louis XI. He was a vassal of the bishop of Liège who was involved in a dispute with the bishop in May 1474 which led to deeds of violence

---

[1] ASM Pot. est. Borgogna 516–17/62–9, incompletely printed in *Briefe und Actenstücke von Mailand*, 86–8 and 109–10 and less fully in *Dépêches des ambassadeurs milanais*, i. 154–62, and *Cal. state papers. Milan*, i. 196–7. For the next sentence see *Recueil du Fay*, 127.
[2] *Eidgenössischen Abschiede*, ii. 546. For the next sentence, see *Briefe und Actenstücke von Mailand*, 112.

M*

that August. 'An audacious and bellicose man, terrible to all, wearing
a prolific beard, tall in stature',[1] he later became known as the Wild
Boar of the Ardennes. He sought refuge at Cologne in the winter of
1474–5 and in April 1475 set out thence with Raes de Lyntre and other
exiles from Liège to raid parts of the duchy of Luxembourg and
Stavelot in the bishopric of Liège. His hostilities against Charles
seem, however, to have been completely ineffective. Duke René of
Lorraine, too, must be numbered among those whose tried to exploit
Charles's situation at the siege of Neuss to their own military advantage, but his efforts to invade Luxembourg in June, with French
assistance, were by no means pressed home.

None of these attacks on Charles the Bold's territories could
compare with the onslaught delivered by Louis XI when his truces
with Charles expired on 1 May 1475.[2] The attack was delivered on
three fronts simultaneously. Some time in April or early May, French
warships, or pirates, captured some fishermen from Amsterdam off
the coast of Zeeland and appeared at Scheveningen and Katwijk.
Later one of these ships sailed to the waters off Amsterdam, looking
for prizes, and thence made for Texel. A fleet was equipped in Amsterdam to deal with these French naval incursions, probably in
May or June. Meanwhile Louis himself with the bulk of his forces
attacked the Somme towns, Artois and Hainault. His assault was
launched on the very day of the expiry of the truces, 1 May, and was
swift and successful. Montdidier surrendered on 5 May and was
destroyed by fire on 10 May. Roye and Corbie fell in early May too
and, during the weeks that followed, French troops penetrated as far
as St. Riquier, Hesdin, Doullens, Arras, and Bavay, Avesnes and

[1] De Los, *Chronique*, 71. See too for this paragraph d'Oudenbosch, *Chronique*, 238–9, Gorissen, *De Raadkamer te Maastricht*, 174, 178 and 180–2,
and *Recueil du Fay*, 115–16.
[2] See the truces of 13 June 1474 printed Plancher, iv. no. 253 and de
Comines, *Mémoires*, ed. Lenglet du Fresnoy, iii. 315–18. For this paragraph,
the main chronicles are Basin, *Louis XI*, ii. 210–20, de Commynes, *Mémoires*,
ed. Calmette and Durville, ii. 17–19, *Cronycke van Hollandt*, fos. 357–9,
de Haynin, *Mémoires*, ii. 190–203, *Histoire de Charles, duc de Bourgogne*,
307–11, Knebel, *Diarium*, ii. 246–8 and 294–7, de Roye, *Chronique scandaleuse*, i. 328–38 and *Speierische Chronik*, 516–17 and 518. Some documents
are printed in de Commynes, *Mémoires*, ed. Dupont, iii. 299–301 and *Lettres
de Louis XI*, v. 363–70. Among modern accounts of these campaigns von
Rodt, *Feldzüge Karls des Kuhnen*, i. 410–15, de Beauvillé, *Histoire de la
ville de Montdidier*, 172–6, de Gingins-La Sarraz, *Lettres sur la guerre des
Suisses contre le duc Charles-le-Hardi*, 69–71, and de Chevanne, *Les guerres
en Bourgogne*, 166–217 are useful.

Valenciennes in Hainault.[1] Wherever they went, villages were burnt down and crops ruined, but no important places were besieged and there was only one significant pitched battle when, on 27 June, a group of Burgundian captains rode out of Arras straight into a French ambush. There were a number of casualties, and some notable prisoners were taken by the French. Charles's lieutenant-general in the Low Countries, Jaques de Savoie, count of Romont, narrowly escaped, losing his horse. The French campaign in the two Burgundies, which also began on 1 May, was similar in character. In the north of the Franche-Comté, Jonvelle and Jussey fell early in May; other French forces attacked the Mâconnais and the Charolais, and the duchy itself was raided in June. Again, there were no great sieges; it was a war of devastation rather than conquest. There was one pitched battle, at Guipy near Château-Chinon on 20 June, when a Burgundian force was routed and the governor-marshal of Burgundy, Anthoine de Luxembourg, count of Roussy, and several other captains, were taken prisoner by the French. Although lengthy lists of places captured by the French, both in Picardy and Burgundy, were circulated far and wide, the French attack on Charles the Bold seems to have made little permanent impression in either area and still less in Luxembourg. The French forces were much too dispersed to achieve a major conquest, and Louis XI's military attention was centred on the projected invasion of France by Edward IV, which he rightly feared much more than an attack by Charles the Bold. His invasion of Artois in particular was severely hampered, if not completely ruined, by his preoccupation with the defence of Normandy against the English; a preoccupation which many observers attributed to the sinister and treacherous influence of Louis de Luxembourg, constable of France.

Had the enemies of France contrived in summer 1475 to combine together and launch three or more simultaneous attacks on Louis, French royal power might have suffered a crushing setback. They did not. It may have been apparent to Louis that he had little to fear from Charles who, though he had earlier refused the French offer to extend the Franco-Burgundian truce after 1 May, was evidently being distracted from France by the possibility of conquering Lorraine. The Aragonese threat to France had been effectively met by the siege and conquest of Perpignan. Its surrender to the French on 10 March 1475 was followed by a six-month truce

---

[1] See the map on p. 78 above.

published on 2 April,[1] though an Aragonese embassy was at Neuss in May, trying to persuade Charles to make war on France. Only Edward IV, allied to a potential enemy of Louis, Francis II, duke of Brittany, seriously threatened to inflict military disasters on the French crown by reviving the dying embers of the Hundred Years War, especially if Charles the Bold collaborated effectively with him.

No one can have been in doubt as to the seriousness of Edward's aggressive intentions in 1474–5. He had promised in the treaty of London of 25 July 1474 to invade France jointly with Charles by 1 July 1475 and he seemed to mean his word. Intending 'to take his Journey in his propre Persone, toward his Realme of Fraunce, his Old and Due Enheritance', Edward had proclaimed, to ensure a sufficient supply of arrows for his campaign, that no fletcher was to make 'any maner of Taccle for shoting but only Shefe Arrows', and all bowyers were to make their bowstaves into bows. On 1 February 1475 the captains and noblemen were ordered to be ready 'at Portes Downe in the Counte of Suthampton' by 26 May 'in their best and most defensible Arraye'.[2] Charles agreed to provide additional shipping for Edward from Holland and on 23 April 1475 the ducal secretary Ghijsbrecht van der Mye left The Hague in company with Edward's commissioner William Caxton, to requisition ships at Delft, Rotterdam, Gouda, Dordrecht and elsewhere. The army crossed in June. De Haynin records the disembarkation of the English contingents in detail, beginning with Geoffrey Gate's arrival at Boulogne on 1 June with eight men-at-arms and sixty or eighty archers.[3] It was a month later, after virtually the entire army had crossed over, that Edward himself arrived in Calais, to be greeted there on 6 July by his sister Margaret of York, and a week later by her husband Charles the Bold, who had come direct from Neuss with only a few days' halt at Malines en route, and only a handful of troops.

[1] Vicens Vives, *Juan II*, 355–6. For the next sentence see ASM Pot. est. Borgogna 516–17/43. For this and what follows in general, see Scofield, *Edward IV*, ii. 113–51, Calmette and Périnelle, *Louis XI et l'Angleterre*, 176–215 and Calmette and Déprez, *Les premières grandes puissances*, 78–88. The most important chroniclers are Basin, *Louis XI*, ii. 232–44, de Commynes, *Mémoires*, ed. Calmette and Durville, ii. 27–82, and Molinet, *Chroniques*, i. 105–11. Some of the relevant despatches are partly printed in *Dépêches des ambassadeurs milanais*, i. and *Cal. state papers. Milan*, i.
[2] *Foedera*, xi. 804–14 and 837–41. For the next sentence, see *Bronnen van den handel met Engeland*, ii. 1109–10.
[3] De Haynin, *Mémoires*, ii. 206–9.

There seem to have been differences of opinion between Edward and Charles at least from May onwards. Panigarola reported from Neuss on 23 May that Lord Scales, Anthony Woodville, earl of Rivers, had been trying to persuade Charles 'to break up altogether from here and move into France, because His Majesty will cross over and is ready, otherwise he will not do so at all'.[1] Was Edward's protracted crossing, and in particular his personal delay, due to the fact that he was not prepared to attack Louis while Charles was still at Neuss? Louis XI himself seems to have been surprised at the inactivity of the English. Writing to his chancellor on 15 July, he claimed that 'they have done nothing so far except dance at St. Omer'.[2] Was Edward even more annoyed with Charles when he arrived at Calais without his army? On the other hand Charles the Bold had some grounds for being disgruntled with his English ally. After all Edward had flatly rejected the advice Charles had sent him in a letter which has unfortunately lost its date:

> Most honoured lord and brother, I commend myself to you. . . . I understand that some of your councillors are of the opinion that you should land in Guienne; others advise Normandy, others Calais. If you landed in Guienne you would be far from my assistance, though my brother of Brittany might help you. But you would be too far away for us to meet outside Paris. As regards Calais, you would not find sufficient provisions for your people nor I for mine, so that the two armies could not remain peaceably together. Also, my said brother of Brittany would be too far from us both. It seems to me that you should disembark in Normandy, either in the River Seine or at La Hogue, and I have no doubt that you will soon conquer towns and places. In this way you will be at my brother of Brittany's right hand and at mine. Let me know how many ships you need and where you want me to have them taken, and I will do it.[3]

It seems probable that, right from the start, Edward IV had planned to play things his own way. He may indeed all along have provided for the possibility of negotiation, rather than battle, with the king of France. If he felt that his principal ally, Charles the Bold, had let him down, he must have been even more dissatisfied with his other ally the duke of Brittany, who not only failed to provide him

---

[1] ASM Pot. est. Borgogna 516–17/44 = *Cal. state papers. Milan*, i. 195–6.
[2] *Lettres de Louis XI*, v. 366.
[3] De Commynes, *Mémoires*, ed. Dupont, i. 336 n. and Toutey, *Charles le Téméraire et la Ligue de Constance*, 257 n. Incompletely printed Plancher, iv. no. 260.

with the troops he had promised, but even hesitated to receive a contingent of English archers in his duchy.[1] But at first, all seemed well to Charles the Bold. At Calais Edward accepted his plan for two simultaneous campaigns: an English invasion of Champagne and a Burgundian invasion of Lorraine. Edward would march first to Guise and thence advance into Champagne towards Rheims, where he had to be crowned king of France, and where the citizens were frantically improving their fortifications.

The first news of Edward's negotiations with Louis, which had initially been slow and secret, reached Charles when he was at Valenciennes, probably on 17 August after he had set out for Namur to join his army in the invasion of Lorraine. He turned back at once and saw Edward in the English camp near Péronne on 19 and 20 August. Edward promised not to negotiate any further with Louis without his participation and consent, and Charles thereupon resumed his journey to Namur. It was while he was at Namur that Charles received a Latin document from Edward which was brought him on 26 August by the royal messenger Thomas Danet.[2] Evidently Edward was being careful to keep his promise of a few days before to inform Charles of what was going on between himself and Louis. His ambassador now told Charles that Louis's ambassadors had offered King Edward a marriage alliance, 75,000 crowns for his war expenses, and an annual pension of 50,000 crowns, in return for a truce in which Edward had taken care to see that the duke of Burgundy could be included provided he applied within three months. Edward sought Charles's advice, emphasizing that his people were in favour of a settlement with Louis: winter was almost upon them, they were very short of cash, and not one of their supposed allies— the dukes of Burgundy and Brittany and the count of St. Pol—had offered the help he had promised. Charles immediately sent the bishop of Tournai, the count of Chimay and other leading councillors to Edward with instructions to try to deter him from his peace plan or, failing this, to encourage him to get better terms. They left Namur on 27 August, but they were too late. The game was up.

---

[1] Pocquet du Haut Jussé, *François II duc de Bretagne et l'Angleterre*, 193.
[2] Printed Calmette and Périnelle, *Louis XI et l'Angleterre*, 356–8; there is a French version in de Haynin, *Mémoires*, ii. 209–12. For this paragraph Panigarola's despatches in ASM Pot. est. Borgogna 516–17/87–91 partly printed in *Cal. state papers. Milan*, i. 206–9 are important. On the embassy of 27 August 1475 see too *IADNB* vii. 366.

While Charles the Bold had annoyed King Edward by refusing his army entry to any of his places, including Péronne, Louis opened Amiens to the English on or soon after 25 August and even ordered the taverns there not to charge them for their drinks. The famous meeting between the two kings took place at Picquigny on 29 August, on a specially made wooden bridge over the Somme across the centre of which a trellis was erected so that the parties could not come to blows. There was no door through this barrier and Louis XI told de Commynes that this would ensure that there could be no repetition of the incident on the bridge of Montereau-Faut-Yonne in 1419 when John the Fearless was assassinated. But the Picquigny meeting was held in an atmosphere of meretricious friendliness, and resulted in the ratification of a seven-year truce and other amicable arrangements between England and France.[1] In spite of his annoyance, which he did not conceal from the Milanese ambassador Panigarola, Charles had to accept the situation. He resolved on 28 August to set out from Namur for Lorraine as soon as possible.

Within a week of the meeting at Picquigny Burgundian ambassadors were negotiating a settlement with Louis XI.[2] This settlement was comprised in the treaty of Soleuvre itself, dated 13 September 1475, which was made public, and in a group of related documents, some of that date, some later, which were kept secret. In important respects it was identical to the projected settlement of April–May 1474, which would have been known as the treaty of Bouvignes. Drawn up between two rulers who profoundly distrusted one another and who were both utterly unscrupulous, one can sympathize with contemporaries like the clerical chronicler Thomas Basin who roundly condemned the settlement as shameful and iniquitous. It was nonetheless of the utmost importance, for it was respected and maintained by both sides during the rest of Charles the Bold's lifetime.

---

[1] De Comines, *Mémoires*, ed. Lenglet du Fresnoy, iii. 397–405. On the Picquigny meeting, besides the works cited on p. 348 n. 1 above, see *Aktenstücke und Briefe zur Geschichte des Hauses Habsburg*, i. 213–14, de Commynes, *Mémoires*, ed. Dupont, iii. 307–8, Knebel, *Diarium*, ii. 291 and de Roye, *Chronique scandaleuse*, i. 341–6.

[2] *Dépêches des ambassadeurs milanais*, i. 225. For what follows, see the text of the truce itself in de la Marche, *Mémoires*, iii. 214–34, Molinet, *Chroniques*, i. 115–27, *Table chronologique de Luxembourg*, 151–8, and, with other supporting documents, in de Comines, *Mémoires*, ed. Lenglet du Fresnoy, iii. 409–49. See too Basin, *Louis XI*, ii. 252–8, and de Haynin, *Mémoires*, ii. 213–14.

A truce between France and Burgundy on land and sea was to last for nine years, from 13 September 1475 until 13 September 1484. There were to be no more confiscations or acts of aggression on either side. Four persons regarded by Charles the Bold as traitors were explicitly excluded: his bastard half-brother Baudouin and his alleged accomplice Jehan de Chassa, Philippe de Commynes and Philippe de Croy, lord of Renty. A fifth person, regarded by both Louis and Charles as a traitor, was likewise excluded: Louis de Luxembourg, count of St. Pol and constable of France. Some of his places, St. Quentin, Ham, Bohain and Beaurevoir, were to be given to Charles the Bold, who promised never to pardon him and to hand him over to the king if he could lay hands on him. The allies of both signatories were given until 1 January 1476 to decide whether or not to accept the truce, but they were only to be included if they had not made war on either signatory since such time as 'the truce could reasonably have come to their knowledge'. Bern and the Swiss and the duke of Lorraine were included among Louis's allies, but not the Lower Union. If either signatory was attacked by the allies of the other he was free to defend himself, by attacking if necessary, without infringing the truce. Specifically, Louis was permitted to conquer Roussillon and Cerdagne from Charles's ally the king of Aragon, provided he first ceded St. Quentin to Charles, and Charles was permitted, without any infringement of the truce, to recover Upper Alsace. Moreover, if the Swiss in any way helped the people of Upper Alsace, then Charles the Bold was free to attack them, even though they were Louis's allies, without infringing the truce. Finally, Charles was permitted to move troops to and fro between his northern and southern territories by the most convenient route, provided his men were peaceable and paid their expenses. This last clause was subsequently particularized: provided Charles really did hand over Louis de Luxembourg to the king, he could proceed with the conquest of Lorraine without infringing the truce.

By the settlement of Soleuvre Louis secured the elimination of his treacherous constable, who was executed in Paris on 19 December after Charles the Bold had reluctantly turned him over to the French. As a result of it, too, he was able to lay his hands firmly on the duchy of Bar, which had been claimed and even occupied by the ally he had so perfidiously abandoned, Duke René of Lorraine. Some of Louis's more fervent admirers have attributed other royal advantages to the treaty of Soleuvre and the related secret agreements, even suggesting that they were brilliantly and deliberately conceived in order to encompass the downfall of Charles and the destruction of Burgundian power by permitting the duke to destroy himself fighting his German enemies while the French remained inactive and unharmed. In actual fact the settlement of Soleuvre represented an appallingly dangerous gamble for the French monarchy. It may have permitted and even encouraged Charles to stake everything on success in his campaigns and victory in a handful of battles, but it meant also that Louis was gambling everything on Charles's defeat in those battles. If Charles was playing the dangerous game of relying on military power, Louis was doing the same.

Charles the Bold certainly seems to have toyed with the idea of conquering Lorraine as early as the summer of 1474, if not before.[1] René's declaration of war against him early in May 1475 gave him a pretext and encouraged his resolve. On 3 July he sent an ultimatum to René warning him to desist from acts of war or take the consequences, and he issued a manifesto calling on the nobles of Lorraine, who had guaranteed the treaty of alliance of 15 October 1473 in which René had granted Burgundian troops free passage through Lorraine, to support him against René, whom he accused of breakinh the terms of that treaty, not least by his declaration of war.[2] In his letters dated Valenciennes, 22 August, Charles the Bold appointed Adolf of Cleves, lord of Ravenstein his lieutenant-general in the northern territories,

> because, since our return from our recent campaign in Germany we have resolved and concluded to move and personally lead our camp and army into the land of Lorraine, to open the passage so that we can go or come from our lands round here into our land of Burgundy and from our lands of Burgundy to our lands round here . . . and so that we can make war more effectively against the French and our other enemies.

---

[1] Above, pp. 290 and 307 and see in general pp. 306–10.
[2] Calmet, *Histoire de Lorraine*, vii. cols. cliii-clvii and Plancher, iv. no. 257. See too above, pp. 105–6. For the next sentence see *Analectes historiques*, xii. 276. For what follows on the conquest of Lorraine the most important documentary sources are *Dépêches des ambassadeurs milanais*, i. 217–63 and ASM Pot. est. Borgogna 516–17/95–136. Among chronicles, Basin, *Louis XI*, ii. 260–4, the largely fanciful *Chronique de Lorraine*, ed. Marchal, 160–85, Molinet, *Chroniques*, i. 111–14 and 127–30, and von Schaumburg, *Die Geschichten und Taten*, 27–30 are important. Berlet, *MSBGH* viii (1892), 331–60 adds little or nothing to the admirable account of Witte, *JGLG* ii (1890), 56–100; see too Pfister, *Histoire de Nancy*, i. 397–409.

Like Charles the Bold's other campaigns, the conquest of Lorraine was a carefully planned military operation. No chances were taken. Before the invasion began Duke René had been stripped, partly by Burgundian diplomacy, of his principal allies, Frederick III and Louis XI. The attack was on two fronts, for the count of Campobasso and later Charles himself advanced into Lorraine from the north, while the bastard of Burgundy, Anthony, with the troops available from the two Burgundies, invaded from the south in the first days of September. By 17 September, having counter-attacked in the very same area in the extreme north of the county of Burgundy, where the French had made some of their most dangerous incursions at the beginning of this same summer, the bastard had advanced some 30 km into Lorraine and conquered Bulgnéville, Châtillon-sur-Saône, Lamarche, Darney, Monthureux-sur-Saône and Passavant-la-Rochère. Thereafter the threat of a Swiss attack on the Franche-Comté apparently caused him to halt or even withdraw.[1] Charles himself, having crossed the northern frontier of the duchy on 23 September, occupied the strong place of Pont-à-Mousson, commanding the valley of the Moselle, on 25 September. The next day he was joined by Federico of Aragon, prince of Taranto, who had somehow contrived to travel through Lorraine unscathed. No organized or large-scale resistance was offered to Charles in the weeks that followed. Duke René wasted time visiting Louis and trying to secure French help; the few troops he did manage to muster were distributed among the larger towns of his duchy as garrisons, and he was quite incapable of taking the field against Charles. René's allies and colleagues of the Lower Union also failed to muster sufficient forces at the right time. From Strasbourg, for example, 500 foot and 300 horse set out on 21 August to help defend Lorraine, but they returned on 13 September having achieved nothing except that some of them had remained behind to reinforce the garrison of Nancy.[2]

The conquest of Lorraine really consisted only in the reduction of the few places which offered resistance to Charles the Bold. His strategy was impeccable. Marching past Nancy, he was at Laneuveville, just south-east of it, by 30 September. Then he divided his forces and, while he himself took Bayon and then laid siege to Charmes on the Moselle, other contingents attacked and captured

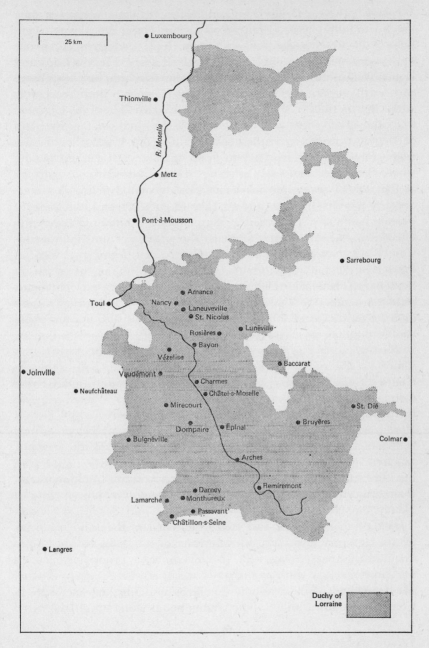

25 km

Luxembourg

Thionville

R. Moselle

Metz

Pont-à-Mousson

Sarrebourg

Amance

Nancy

Laneuveville

St. Nicolas

Toul

Lunéville

Rosières

Bayon

Vézelise

Baccarat

Joinville

Vaudémont

Neufchâteau

Charmes

Châtel-s-Moselle

Mirecourt

St. Dié

Dompaire

Épinal

Bruyères

Bulgnéville

Colmar

Arches

Remiremont

Darney

Monthureux

Lamarche

Passavant

Châtillon-s-Seine

Langres

Duchy of
Lorraine

10. The duchy of Lorraine

Vézelise, Mirecourt and Dompaire. These military successes were accompanied by deeds of savagery on Charles the Bold's part which were evidently designed to strike fear into the hearts of anyone attempting to oppose him and probably did so. The German mercenary Wilwolt von Schaumburg has a horrific account in his chronicle of the experiences of himself and his German colleagues, serving with Charles the Bold, after the fall of Charmes. The three Germans had pitched their tent under a tree on which thirty-seven members of the garrison were afterwards hanged. The work went on until midnight, by which time they had to stoop down as they entered the tent to avoid the feet dangling just above. Then a branch broke with the weight of the seven persons hanged on it, and dangling feet were actually pressing against the tent. But no one dared ask the duke for permission to move elsewhere. On 19 October Épinal surrendered to Charles and he turned back towards Nancy, taking Vaudémont on his way. By 24 October, when the siege of Nancy began, the whole of the rest of the duchy of Lorraine, with the exception of the outpost of Sarrebourg, had surrendered to or been conquered by Charles the Bold. In spite of considerable privations due to lack of provisions and the hardships of forced marches, sometimes through the night, the Burgundian army had been brilliantly successful.

The capital of Lorraine, Nancy, strongly garrisoned with Lower Union troops and Lorrainers, still held firmly for Duke René. As Charles's men began digging trenches round the town they must have wondered whether Nancy would prove another Neuss. But its fortifications were less elaborate and it was not protected by a river. It had, too, evidently been caught unawares, possibly because it had relied on its inclusion, along with Duke René, in the treaty of Soleuvre. The count of Campobasso had captured the entire civic herd of cattle a few days before the duke arrived and began the siege. Furthermore Duke René, instead of encouraging resistance, wrote on 25 November permitting the garrison and citizens to surrender. This they did a day or two later, and Charles the Bold made his triumphal entry into the town after one of the gates had been dismantled for the purpose,[1] on 30 November, appropriately enough St. Andrew's Day. Lorraine, abandoned by its duke, betrayed by its allies the king of France and the Emperor, and only very ineffectively aided by the forces of the Lower Union, had become Burgundian.

---

[1] *IADNB* viii. 260.

December 1475 perhaps marks the high peak of Charles the Bold's political fortunes; the zenith of Burgundian power in Europe. It was then that the great city of Strasbourg, seized with near panic, made her costly and crippling preparations for a Burgundian siege. A committee of eight leading citizens reported early in November that only the systematic demolition of buildings outside the walls could enable Strasbourg to withstand Charles the Bold.[1] The work continued through the winter until five monasteries and 620 houses had been destroyed and a two-mile wide belt of open flat ground surrounded the walls. An enormous moat was dug, in which up to 800 men worked at once, to bring the waters of the Rhine round the city. Powder and artillery were bought in Nürnberg and elsewhere, and the committee laid in enough corn to last the inhabitants for ten years and a three-year supply of wine and salt. All this is an accurate pointer to the military credit of Charles the Bold. Never did his reputation as a successful and ambitious conqueror stand higher than at this time. Politically, too, his position seemed more assured than ever. He had made an advantageous settlement with Louis XI, and, on 17 November, as a result of an imperial embassy to him at the siege of Nancy, he had made peace with the Emperor.[2]

We have already had occasion to cite the Milanese ambassador's description of the ceremonial inauguration of Charles the Bold as duke of Lorraine on 18 December, when he addressed the assembled Estates in person and received their oaths of fealty.[3] It must have been with reference to this occasion that the Strasbourg chronicler remarked that Charles assembled the nobles of Lorraine at Nancy 'and preached to them as if he had become God'. Nancy, perhaps, would become the new capital of an enlarged, unified and geographically more integrated Burgundian state or even kingdom. But, though some such scheme or vision may have crossed Charles the Bold's mind and even been expounded to the assembled Estates on

---

[1] On this and what follows see Specklin, Les collectanées, 462–3, Strasz-burgische Archiv-Chronik, 195–8, Trausch, Strassburgische Chronick, 17–18, Dépêches des ambassadeurs milanais, i. 257–9, de Bussière, Histoire de la Ligue formée contre Charles le Téméraire, 249, and Witte, ZGO (N.F.) x (1895), 238–9.
[2] Printed Plancher, iv. no. 259, and Aktenstücke und Briefe zur Geschichte des Hauses Habsburg, i. 125–30.
[3] Above, pp. 170–1. For the next sentence, see Straszburgische Archiv-Chronik, 198.

18 December,[1] he could not stop to begin implementing it now. Appointing Jehan de Rubembré, lord of Bièvres, his lieutenant or governor in Lorraine, and leaving some of his troops to garrison the principal towns of the duchy, he set off on 11 January 1476 on his ill-starred expedition in support of Savoy against Bern and her allies. For it was Bern, not Strasbourg, against which Charles the Bold now hoped to lead his victorious army.

[1] The versions of Charles's speech in the *Chronique de Lorraine*, ed. Marchal, 183–5 and Cayon, *Souvenirs et monumens de la bataille de Nancy*, fos. 6–7, in which he promises to make Nancy his residence or capital are interesting but suspect; compare Panigarola's report, above, pp. 170–1.

CHAPTER TEN

Savoy, Grandson and Murten

During the summer of 1475, while Charles the Bold was personally occupied in winding up the Neuss campaign and with the affairs of France and England, he was attacked by the Lower Union, whose forces conquered and destroyed Blamont and some other castles in the north-eastern extremity of the Franche-Comté in July and August, and indirectly also by Bern and her associates, who seized the castles and lands of the Burgundian vassals in the Vaud early in May and who tried unsuccessfully to intercept a contingent of Charles's Italian recruits at Aigle on 16 August.[1] Charles the Bold's attack on Lorraine diverted the attention, and the troops, of the Lower Union, some of whom even abandoned the Blamont campaign in favour of opposing the Burgundians in Lorraine. But if, for this reason, Duke Charles's own territories had little to fear in the autumn

---

[1] See above, pp. 297–8 and 305–6. Most of the works cited in the notes on pp. 261 and 302 above are important also for this chapter; in addition the following have been used here. Documents: Bell and Schneller, *Geschichtsfreund* xxiii (1868), 54–106, *Frankfurts Reichscorrespondenz*, ii. 368–78, and von Mülinen, *SG* vi (1826), 145–60. Chronicles: besides Knebel, Schilling and Trausch already cited above n. 1 p. 261, *Die Anonyme Chronik der Burgunderkriege*, Anshelm, *Berner Chronik*, von Bonstetten, *Beschreibung der Burgunderkriege*, Brennwald, *Schweizerchronik*, *Chronik der Stadt Zürich*, Edlibach, *Chronik*, *Entreprises*, Etterlin, *Kronica von der loblichen Eydtgnoschaft*, Fries, *Chronik*, von Molsheim, *Freiburger Chronik*, Nicolaus, *De preliis et occasu ducis Burgundie historia*, Rüsch, *Beschreibung*, Tschudi, *Chronicon helveticum*, and Tüsch, *Burgundische hystorie*. On the Burgundian side Basin, *Louis XI*, ii. 278–96, de Commynes, *Mémoires*, ed. Calmette and Durville, ii. 98–129, de Margny, *L'Aventurier*, 63–8, and Molinet, *Chroniques*, i. 138–47 are important. On military affairs von Elgger, *Kriegswesen*, and Schaufelberger, *Der alte Schweizer und sein Krieg*, and the same, *SAV* lvi (1960), 48–87 are of more value than Delbrück, *Perserkriege*, 148–259, and the same, *Kriegskunst*, iii. 629–67, Lot, *L'art militaire*, ii. 118–25, and Kurz,

of 1475 from the Lower Union, the Franche-Comté and the lands of his ally Savoy remained exposed to further acts of aggression from Bern as well as from the Valais, whose bishop Walter Supersax had on 7 September signed a treaty with Bern which was implicitly aimed against Savoy.

The motives behind Bern's mounting aggression towards Charles the Bold were complex and were not necessarily shared by all her citizens. She continued to resent the growing Burgundian influence in Savoy. She was anxious to stop the movement of Italian troops through the Alps on their way to join Charles's army, rightly fearing that they might be used against herself or her allies. She resented the fact that Jaques de Savoie, count of Romont and baron of Vaud, had taken service with Charles the Bold. She probably felt some obligation to do what she could to assist her allies of the Lower Union. Most important of all, she was determined to do her utmost to extend her power and enlarge her sphere of influence south-westwards towards the Lake of Geneva and westwards towards the frontiers of Burgundy.

The Burgundian authorities were well aware of Bern's hostility and of her expansionist ambitions, but Charles the Bold was for a long time unwilling to divert his forces and postpone the realization of his ambitions by mounting a special campaign against her. Instead, he stalled and tried to make peace. In the autumn of 1475 attempts were again made, this time under the auspices of Anthony, bastard of Burgundy and the councillors and *gens des comptes* at Dijon, to bribe some of the citizens of Bern to use their influence in the cause of peace: Adrian von Bubenberg received 100 florins, and so did 'the astrologer of Bern, by whose advice more than by anyone else's the Bernese conducted themselves in this war'.[1] Duchess Yolande of Savoy tried to mediate between Charles and the *Eidgenossen* early in September, and in the same month Burgundian ambassadors were empowered to negotiate at Neuchâtel with deputies from Bern, who however referred the matter to the federal diet. It was in September

---

Schweizerschlachten, 83–128. Deuchler, *Burgunderbeute* and Wyss and others, *Die Burgunderbeute*, are invaluable. Among the more or less popular accounts of Grandson and Murten I have found Hoch and de Mandrot, *Morat et Charles le Téméraire*, Perrier, *Guerre de Bourgogne* and Frédérix, *Mort de Charles le Téméraire* useful. For its detailed narrative, based on a knowledge of the sources perhaps unsurpassed since, Kirk, *Charles the Bold*, iii. remains invaluable.

[1] *Mémoires*, ii. 262 n. *b*.

too that the archbishop of Besançon approached the bishop of Basel with a view to making peace between Charles the Bold and the Swiss.

As earlier in 1475, so in the autumn, the attention of Bern's more aggressive statesmen, whose leader since Niclaus von Diesbach's death had been Niclaus von Scharnachtal, was increasingly turned not to Burgundy but to Charles's ally Savoy. A simple, stark act of aggression was now planned and perpetrated by these determined men: an invasion of the *pays de Vaud*. Although it would be a direct military and political affront to both Savoy and Burgundy, such a move could nonetheless be construed merely as an attack on Jaques de Savoie, count of Romont, though he, as baron of Vaud, was a vassal of the duchess of Savoy. Indeed, Bern persuaded Fribourg to join with her in this enterprise on the implausible pretext that Savoy itself was not to be attacked. The conquest of the Vaud could also be viewed in a different light, as a war between French and German speaking populations. The chronicler Knebel naively and quite unacceptably attributed the campaign to a proposed nocturnal massacre, at the count of Romont's command, of all Germans in his lands. This fantasy does underline the antithesis in this area between German and *welsch* populations, just as Philippe de Commynes's famous remark, that the war started because of 'a cart of lambskins which my lord of Romont took from a Swiss who was passing through his territories',[1] does point to the underlying economic problem of Swiss trade through the Vaud. Among a whole series of incidents of a similar kind, on 9 October 1475 two cartfuls of skins were arrested between Morges and Lausanne by the count of Romont's officials. They were being smuggled through Savoy on their way to the fairs of Lyons by some German merchants, in direct contravention of Amadeus IX's ruling that such goods, brought into Savoy, must first be offered for sale at Geneva. Although goods from Bern and Fribourg merchants were exempt from this regulation, merchandise from other German towns was not, and since the other possible route to Lyons through the Franche-Comté had been closed since autumn 1474, an economic grievance against Savoy was widely felt among the south German towns and was certainly shared by Bern and Fribourg.[2]

These commercial difficulties were, however, pretexts for, rather than causes of, the invasion of the Vaud by Bern on 14 October 1475.

---

[1] Cited from de Commynes, *Mémoires*, translated by Kinser and Cazeaux, i. 302 = de Commynes, *Mémoires*, ed. Calmette and Durville, ii. 105.
[2] Gingins-La Sarraz, *Épisodes*, 176–82 and see the works referred to in n. 1 p. 304 above.

The real reason for the campaign, apart from Bern's aggressive ambitions and her wish to put pressure on Savoy, was probably the urgent need to protect or extricate honourably the garrisons she had established at the beginning of the summer in Jougne, Orbe and Grandson, especially that of Jougne, which was actually in the Franche-Comté, remote and threatened, yet of considerable strategic importance since it controlled one of the main routes into the *pays de Vaud* from Burgundy. Significant, too, as a cause of Bern's aggression was perhaps the count of Romont's arrival at Lausanne early in October. Although he had not, as Bern alleged, brought any quantity of troops with him, nor it seems had he any aggressive intentions, yet he probably was under instructions from Charles the Bold to organize defences against a possible Swiss attack.

As always, it was in the name of God and 'his beloved mother maid Mary queen of heaven' that the Bernese set out 'with banner unfurled and all their power' on Saturday 14 October 1475.[1] Outside the walls of Murten, their first objective, they met with their friends and allies of Fribourg. The inhabitants of Murten, divided in language and sympathy between German and *welsch*, were summoned to surrender at once as it was getting dark and raining hard, or else be taken by assault. They surrendered, and accepted a garrison from Fribourg, while the allied army marched against Payerne on Sunday morning 15 October, receiving en route the surrender of Avenches. In the event, Payerne also submitted without a blow and it was not until they reached Estavayer on the shores of the Lake of Neuchâtel, on 17 October, that the allies met with serious resistance. But, in spite of a garrison placed there by the count of Romont, Estavayer quickly succumbed. While some assailants hacked their way through a small gate, others clambered up ropes left dangling from the walls by people who had resolved at the last minute to escape the rigours of siege or assault. A savage massacre followed; the small town was systematically pillaged and its castle of Chenaux burnt down. People came over the lake from Neuchâtel and elsewhere to share the loot; the Fribourgeois are said to have dismantled and removed to their own town in 100 carts the entire equipment of Estavayer's cloth manufacturing industry. Although the chroniclers have probably exaggerated the atrocities perpetrated during the sack of Estavayer, they were savage enough for the authorities at Bern to write on 21

---

[1] Schilling, *Die Berner-Chronik*, ii. 290. For what follows, see the map on p. 303 above.

October severely reprimanding their captains in the field for permitting such inhuman cruelties, 'which might move God and the
saints against us in vengeance'.[1] In spite of orders, or intentions,
to demolish entirely the walls and castle of Estavayer, these were
left standing, and the men of Bern and Fribourg, joined now by a
contingent from Solothurn, moved on towards Yverdun, receiving
the surrender of Moudon, Romont and other places on the way.
The surrender of Yverdun was negotiated by Guillaume d'Aarberg,
son of Jehan d'Aarberg, lord of Valangin, to the annoyance of some
of the Bernese, who thought the place deserved to be conquered and
sacked.

By the end of October the entire Vaud had submitted to the
victorious troops of Bern and Fribourg, who had been joined towards
the close of their brief campaign by contingents from Luzern and
Zürich as well as from Solothurn. The castles of Ste. Croix, Les
Clées and La Sarraz were assaulted, conquered, burnt down and their
garrisons butchered. On the instructions of the federal diet, the
Bernese garrisons were withdrawn from Orbe and Jougne and these
castles too were left in flames, but a strong garrison was placed in
Yverdun, and the garrison of Grandson was reinforced. The allied
advance penetrated as far as Morges on the shore of the Lake of
Geneva but, in spite of the hopes of some, of attacking and doubtless
looting the imperial city of Lausanne, and of the Bern authorities of
advancing on and perhaps conquering Geneva, the Swiss were
content with ransoms of 2,000 and 26,000 Rhenish florins respectively
from these two places. It was on 2 November that they returned home,
laden with booty, having perhaps been credited with more bloodshed
and destruction than they had really inflicted. The military advantage
they gained was restricted to the destruction of several castles,
especially Jougne and Orbe, which might be of value to Charles the
Bold in the event of a Burgundian invasion of the Vaud; the strength-
ening of their hold on the southern end of the Lake of Neuchâtel;
and the outright conquest only of Murten, which Bern and Fribourg
declared to be theirs on 1 November.

The invasion of the Vaud in October 1475 could scarcely be ignored
by Charles the Bold: Duchess Yolande of Savoy was his ally and the
count of Romont was one of his leading captains who had recently

[1] Von Rodt, *Feldzüge Karls des Kühnen*, i. 531. For the sack of Estavayer
see de Vevey, *AF* xxxiv–v (1946–7), 18–26, 34–50 and 113–16. For events at
Yverdun, see Gilliard, *ZSG* xxiv (1944), 313–51.

been transferred from the post of ducal governor and lieutenant in the Burgundian Low Countries to its equivalent at Dijon.[1] But other Swiss acts of aggression in the autumn of 1475 were equally provocative and dangerous to the duke of Burgundy. Geography dictated that his military lifeline, the stream of Italian recruits for his companies of ordinance, must lie over the Great St. Bernard Pass and along the Rhône to the Lake of Geneva. This lifeline had been interfered with by the occupation of Jougne and Orbe in May 1475; it was temporarily cut when Bern attacked Aigle in August and again in October when the Swiss momentarily occupied Morges. At that very time, in the second half of October, the men of the Simmental and other Bern dependencies made their way over the Col de Jaman to thank the people of Vevey, as Schilling puts it, for the insults[2] they had hurled at and the damages they had done to Bern. The conquest and sack of Vevey was followed in early November by Bishop Walter Supersax of Sion's long awaited campaign in the Lower Valais. A Savoy counter-attack was defeated outside Sion on 13 November by the chance intervention of some troops from Bern, and thereafter the bishop and his men overran and conquered a large part of the Lower Valais, including the strategically vital places of Martigny and St. Maurice. Conthey, near Sion, and St. Maurice were now garrisoned jointly by Bern and Fribourg. The route from Italy was effectively blocked, and Savoy had suffered a further serious loss of territory.

The peace negotiations which had been interrupted in October by Bern's invasion of the Vaud were taken up again in November, but the talks between the Burgundian deputies Guillaume de Rochefort, Symon de Cleron and others and representatives of some of the League of Constance powers, which were held at Neuchâtel under the presidency of the more or less neutral count of Neuchâtel, Rudolf von Hochberg, only resulted in a truce from the end of November until 1 January 1476, for the parties to it, on the one side Charles the Bold, Savoy and their allies, on the other Duke Sigmund of Austria and the powers of the League of Constance as well as the bishop of Sion and the Valaisans, could not agree on its proposed extension until 1 April 1476.[3]

---

[1] Above, pp. 244-5.
[2] Above, p. 306; for the Valais see especially Grand, *Der Anteildes Wallis*.
[3] Besides the works already cited on p. 359 n. 1 above, see on the Neuchâtel peace talks Bauer, *Négociations et campagnes de Rodolphe de Hochberg*, 80-6, and Reutter, *Le rôle joué par le comté de Neuchâtel*, 181-3.

The day after the signing of the truce of Neuchâtel Charles the
Bold made his triumphant entry into Nancy, capital city of the duchy
of Lorraine. It was 30 November 1475. The Lower Union troops who
had been defending it against him were allowed to go home un-
molested. It was scarcely likely, however, that the dispossessed Duke
René of Lorraine, who was a member of the Lower Union, would
accept the loss of his duchy, nor that the other Lower Union powers,
especially Strasbourg and Basel, would tolerate for long a Burgundian
occupation of Lorraine. On the Burgundian side, Charles the Bold
had by no means abandoned his hopes of regaining Upper Alsace,
while Jaques de Savoie was certainly planning the recovery of his
barony of Vaud. Indeed he and Yolande of Savoy hoped above all to
enlist Charles the Bold's aid in a retaliatory campaign against Bern
and her allies. Thus, in spite of the truce and in spite of the efforts of
mediators like Frederick the Victorious, count palatine of the Rhine,
the hostile confrontation continued. In the night of 12–13 January
1476 the count of Romont and his men entered Yverdun with shouts
of 'Long live Burgundy!' and tried but failed to drive out the Swiss
garrison, which escaped by taking refuge in the castle. At the same
time the captain of the Swiss garrison of Grandson castle, Brandolf
von Stein, was tricked into being taken prisoner, but again the castle
itself held firm. After this the Swiss grip on these two places was
considerably tightened; but already, on 11 January, Charles the Bold
had set out from Nancy to go to the rescue of the house of Savoy. The
following letter, though its text has only survived in a somewhat
corrupt Italian translation, shows that he had resolved on this course
of action even before the surrender of Nancy.[1]

Charles by the grace of God duke of Burgundy, of Lotharingia, of
Brabant, of Limbourg, of Luxembourg and of Guelders, count of
Flanders, of Artois, of Burgundy palatine, of Hainault, of Holland,
of Namur and of Zutphen, marquis of the Holy Empire, lord of Frisia, of
Salins and of Malines, to our dearest and well loved cousin the count
of Romont, my governor of Burgundy, greetings and affection. Because of
the news we have had both of the enterprise which the Germans are
endeavouring to undertake in our land of Burgundy and of the defeat
which the troops of our most beloved and honourable lady and cousin
the duchess of Savoy have suffered against the Valaisans, we have decided
to go in person to our land of Burgundy, with the help of God and

[1] Partly printed Colombo, *Iolanda, duchessa di Savoia*, 281, whence my
translation.

Monsieur St. George, to make the Germans and Valaisans who are attacking the said land see reason. Therefore we want you to have it proclaimed and published at once with all possible diligence throughout our said lands of Burgundy, Charolais and Mâconnais, by those who customarily make such proclamations, that all our faithful vassals, sub-vassals and others owing military service are to place themselves immediately under arms with such diligence that we shall find them all ready to join our army on our arrival in our said lands; on pain not only of confiscation to us of their belongings but also of losing their heads. . . .

> In our camp outside Nancy,
> 28 November 1475

Charles the Bold expressed exactly similar intentions in letters he sent to Jehan de Dadizele a month later and in remarks he made to the Milanese ambassador which Panigarola passed on to the duke of Milan in his despatch of 31 December 1475.[1] The enemy too was perfectly well informed about his plans. For example on 26 December Bern wrote to Basel stating that the duke planned to leave Nancy and stay with the archbishop of Besançon. Sure enough, after leaving Nancy on 11 January, Charles was at Besançon from 22 January to 6 February, making his final preparations for the campaign. It was thence that letters were sent to Dijon and Geneva, and perhaps elsewhere, requesting a supply of provisions.[2] Dijon was told that it would be considered rebellious and disobedient if it did not send ample supplies of bread, wine, meat, fish and oats; Geneva was politely informed that everything would be paid for. To Dijon, Charles explained that he hoped, 'with the help of God and Monsieur St. George, to deliver our lands and subjects of Burgundy and those of the house of Savoy from the Swiss, Valaisans and other Germans who, up to now, have interfered in order to cause them various injuries, oppressions and damages'. To Geneva, he claimed that he was about to attack 'the Bernese, Zürichers and their allies, your enemies and ours' for the 'glory and solace of the land of Savoy'; and they were advised not to pay the 26,000 Rhenish florins of ransom money recently demanded from them by the Swiss.

The Milanese ambassador's despatch of 26 January shows that Charles the Bold was supremely confident as he assembled his forces

---

[1] De Dadizeele, *Mémoires*, 48 and *Dépêches des ambassadeurs milanais*, i. 261–3. For what follows see Knebel, *Diarium*, ii. 332 n. 2.
[2] *Correspondance de la mairie de Dijon*, i. 181–2, and *Registres du conseil de Genève*, ii. 481–2.

at Besançon. The Swiss were said to have boasted that they would fight the Emperor, the duke of Milan, the king of France and the duke of Burgundy all at once; Charles swore 'by St. George, he would go there and find them, and they would see what happened and if they were so terrible'. After dinner one day, when one of the Burgundian captains suggested that the mountains of Savoy could present them with difficulties, Charles referred to Hasdrubal and concluded that 'nothing was so harsh and difficult that it could not be conquered by the courage of men and military discipline, and he would certainly attempt it'.[1] Diplomatically speaking at least the duke's optimism was surely well-founded for, as usual before he embarked on a campaign, he had deprived his enemies of almost all their allies. Even though the *Eidgenossen* were part of the Empire and might have hoped for military assistance from Frederick III, that ruler had instead negotiated an alliance with Charles the Bold on 17 November. Even though the *Eidgenossen* were the allies of King Louis XI of France, that ruler too had made a bargain with Charles the Bold in the autumn of 1475. Thus Burgundian diplomacy had ensured that the Swiss would get no help from the Empire or France. Louis XI's only intervention was to do his best to dissuade Charles from setting out on campaign and to try to arrange a personal meeting with him instead: Louis feared—justifiably—that Savoy was about to pass into Burgundian hands; he was not in the least concerned about the defence and safety of his allies. While the Swiss were thus isolated, Charles could count among his own allies the duke of Milan and the republic of Venice and a host of others, and his already powerful army was reinforced for this campaign by the forces of Savoy many of whom were, like his own, highly skilled Italian professionals.

The phrase 'the Swiss' is both misleading and inaccurate, though not so much so as the ridiculous designation 'the mountaineers' beloved of American biographers.[2] Against Charles the Bold in the early months of 1476 was ranged a motley and apparently ill-assorted collection of small powers, a mixture of towns like Strasbourg, Basel and Bern, rural communities like Uri, Schwyz and Unterwalden, prelates like the bishops of Strasbourg, Basel and Sion, and two substantial secular rulers, the dukes of Lorraine and Austria–Tirol,

[1] ASM Pot. est. Borgogna 518–20/8–9.
[2] Putnam, *Charles the Bold*, 417, and Kendall, *Louis XI*, 302.

René and Sigmund.[1] In essence, this alliance was an enlarged League of Constance. Although it had ignored Bern's appeals to take part in her attack on the *pays de Vaud* in autumn 1475, it now showed itself fully prepared to rally to her defence against this threatened Burgundian attack on one of its members, especially when stimulated by the eloquent and urgent summonses for assistance sent out almost daily by that member from early February onwards. For Bern now became the natural leader of the alliance and its moving spirit. Next in importance, perhaps, to Bern was Luzern, for she acted as a link between Bern and Zürich and the other *Eidgenossen*.

The letters sent by Bern to Luzern at this time are illuminating in this and many other respects. On 10 February when Panigarola reported from Jougne that Charles planned to set out thence on 13 February to reduce Yverdun and Grandson, Bern wrote imploring Luzern 'from the bottom of our hearts, on the strength of your brotherly love, to set out at once with all your power for our town, to save our land, people, lives and belongings';[2] they themselves planned to set out against Charles early next Friday, 15 February. On 11 February another pressing letter reported that the whole of the *pays de Vaud* was in enemy hands except for Yverdun, Grandson, Payerne and Murten. The Bern councillors feared next Friday would be too late and that they might have to take the field earlier. Meanwhile they had ordered the garrison of Yverdun to burn the place down and withdraw to neighbouring Grandson. On Tuesday 12 February appeals went out from Bern to Luzern once more, but also to Strasbourg and to Nürnberg and other imperial towns in south Germany. Luzern was told that Bern still proposed to take the field on Friday and that Charles was at Jougne. Yet another letter to Luzern, dated 13 February, when Panigarola was with Charles at Orbe, claimed that he had laid siege to Payerne with 60,000 men and threatened Murten, but this report was corrected on the next day,

[1] The following works discuss the role of some individual members of the alliance: Ammann, *Der Aargau*, Mittler, *Geschichte der Stadt Baden*, i. 237–9, Bernoulli, *BNB* lxxvi–lxxviii (1898–1900) (Basel), Zesiger, *BBG* xxii (1926), 169–78 (Bern), Büchi, *Freiburgs Bruch mit Oesterreich*, 119–42, Despond, *Les comtes de Gruyère et les guerres de Bourgogne*, Châtelain, *MN* xxxiv (1897), 285–94 (Neuchâtel), Anon, *St. Gallens Antheil*, Schmid, *Staat und Volk im alten Solothurn*, 35 ff., Dändliker, *JSG* v (1880), 183–307 (Zürich).
[2] Bell and Schneller, *Geschichtsfreund* xxiii (1868), 66, and for what follows, 66–70.

14 February, when Charles was rightly reported to be at Orbe, 'intending to move against us all to our eternal subjection and destruction, which God forbid'.

Day after day, week after week, a never-ending stream of correspondence, requests, appeals, warnings, reports and commands, issued from Bern to her allies in all directions. Without this enthusiastic and efficient headquarters organization the resistance to the advancing Burgundians would have been piecemeal and probably ineffective. Indeed the assumption by Bern of the leadership of the powers of the League, and with it the emergence of the *Eidgenossen* in a primary role, transformed the prospects and policies of the entire organization. Hitherto, the allied campaigns had been aggressive raids on the territories of Burgundy or Savoy but, with the possible exception of Héricourt, each of these had only evoked the interest and participation of one or other part of the alliance. In the course of these raids the allies had contrived to garrison remote places in enemy territory, like Héricourt and Jougne, for protracted periods, and they had been savagely successful in besieging and assaulting castles and strong places. They had even, at Héricourt, marched out and fought a pitched battle with brilliant success against the Burgundian cavalry. Now, in response to an impending and large-scale Burgundian attack, the entire alliance became united and unanimous in its resolve and directed its energies to the concentration of all its military resources in order to engage the enemy in a single decisive combat. Charles the Bold, though his immediate military target was the reconquest of Grandson from the Bernese, who had seized it from the count of Romont on 1 May 1475, entertained, as we have seen, exactly similar hopes. Thus as he left Jougne and crossed the frontier of Savoy on 12 February a direct and massive military confrontation between his army and that of the allies became virtually inevitable. Each side fully intended to stake everything on one big battle.

The first Burgundian assault on the town of Grandson, which even now is little more than a village, was on 18 February. Charles himself arrived the next day in the worst possible weather and on 21 February conquered the town but not the imposing rectangular castle with its round corner towers which rose and still rises above the shore of the lake and the roofs at the eastern end of Grandson. This castle, garrisoned by several hundred Bernese, was so closely invested by land and water that a boat-load of men sent by night over the lake on 23–24 February could not get within earshot. They attracted the garrison's attention by waving spears and dancing happily to the

N

music of their piper, but it is doubtful if the garrison correctly interpreted these signals to mean that help was coming soon, and the same
seems to be true of the fires which were lit at night along the shores of
the lake. All kinds of explanations have been given for the surrender
of the castle on 28 February. Diebold Schilling of Bern and other
Swiss chroniclers claimed that the captain and garrison were tricked
by Germans in Charles's army who told them that Charles had
already conquered Fribourg and massacred all the inhabitants; that
he would shortly do the same to Bern and Solothurn; and that he
would willingly take them into his service if they surrendered. More
probably the surrender was due to their impossibly precarious
situation, already reported to Bern by two men who managed to
escape from Grandson on 24 February. The battlements had been
shot away by the Burgundian artillery; they had nothing to eat but
damp unmilled corn and only enough of that to last until 27 February;
they had lost three barrels of powder by fire and their artillery master
had been killed. Though the Swiss sources unanimously claim that
Charles promised the garrison their lives in order to help persuade
them to surrender, other contemporaries state that the surrender was
definitely unconditional. Be this as it may, it is certain that most of the
several hundred men who had been inside the castle were hanged on
walnut trees outside it or drowned in the lake. This sort of atrocity
seems characteristic of Charles; the same thing had been done at
Charmes in Lorraine a few months before. Both appear to have been
acts of calculated terrorism. Later on the pretext was found that the
horrible deed at Grandson was carried out at the behest of others in
revenge for Swiss atrocities in the Vaud or, more plausibly, that it was
a reprisal for the savage massacre on 2–3 May 1475 by the Bernese of
the Burgundian garrison at Orbe. [1]

The surrender of Grandson and the elimination of its garrison had
all but completed the Burgundian reconquest of the Vaud, the rest of
which had fallen to other Burgundian detachments under the command of Jaques de Savoie, count of Romont, between 9 and 24
February. Only Murten remained in Bernese hands. Because of the
urgent need to relieve the garrison of Grandson, which could not in
any case have held out against Charles's entire army and heavy
artillery for more than a very short time, Bern had summoned her
allies to assemble at Neuchâtel, and this they began to do on 28
February. It was in that area, probably actually at Boudry, that on

---

[1] Duronzier, *Mémoires historiques*, 151.

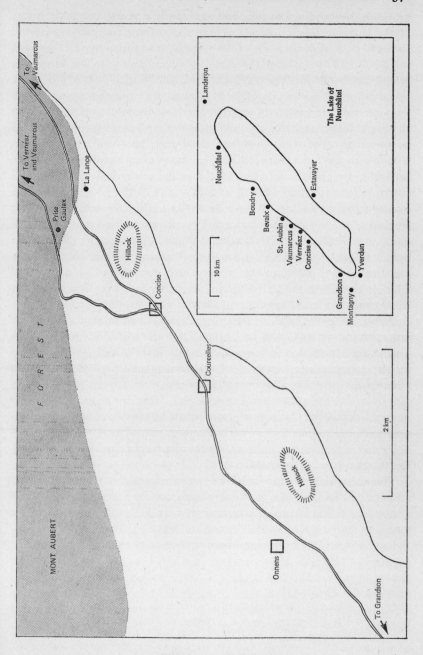

11. The battle of Grandson

1 March they had news of the fall of Grandson castle and the murder of the garrison. Bern had already expressed the fear, in a letter to Luzern of 22 February, that Charles might advance from Grandson along the north shore of the Lake of Neuchâtel in order to attack Neuchâtel itself and then Erlach, Biel and Nidau, comprising the outer defences, as it were, of Bern herself. In fact, it seems probable that Charles's decision to march north-eastwards from Grandson along the north shore of the lake rather than round its southern tip and past Yverdun into the *pays de Vaud*, was a straightforward response to the news he may have had on or before 28 February, that the allies were making for Neuchâtel on their way to relieve Grandson. On 29 February (1476 was a leap year) he personally reconnoitred in strength along the shore of the lake and made some contact, visual or otherwise, with the allies, beyond Vaumarcus. At the same time he seized and garrisoned with some élite household troops the dilapidated but strategically important and well sited castle of Vaumarcus, which dominated and more or less controlled the narrowest and most difficult part of the route along the north shore of the lake, where a wooded spur of Mont Aubert and a steep-sided wooded ravine abutted onto the shore. On 1 March, Friday, Charles was so busy consulting his captains on the plan of action and perhaps drawing up and inspecting troops against a possible Swiss attack, that he kept three Milanese ambassadors waiting till late for an audience in his camp at Grandson.[1] That very evening, only about 20 km away along the shore of the lake, the allies encamped and still arriving around Bevaix and Boudry resolved to storm the castle of Vaumarcus the very next morning. After that, as the Luzerners in the field explained in a letter they sent to the *Schultheiss* and council of Luzern from 'a village half a mile from Vaumarcus on Friday at night', they would 'take further council in the field with the members of the federation, as to whether or not we should attack the duke of Burgundy, to his advantage, in his laager or whether we should attack some place he has taken in order to make him come and relieve it'.[2]

---

[1] See their letter in Colombo, *Iolanda, duchessa di Savoia*, 288–9 and compare Panigarola's unpublished despatch of 2 March, sent from Orbe, in ASM Pot. est. Borgogna 518–20/57.
[2] Bell and Schneller, *Geschichtsfreund* xxiii (1868), 73–4. For what follows on the battle of Grandson, besides the more general works already cited on p. 359 n. 1 above, see Chabloz, *Bataille de Grandson*, du Bois, *MAGZ* ii (2) (1844), 33–53 and Feldmann, *SMOW* xiv (1902), 225–50; see too references in Dierauer, *Geschichte der schweizerischen Eidgenossenschaft*, ii. 246–52,

The allies were active at an early hour on the morning of Saturday 2 March, hearing mass and eating a frugal breakfast before the attack on Vaumarcus castle, which was led by the men of Bern. If some of their leaders thought Charles might be enticed to leave his well-defended Grandson encampment by this attack on Vaumarcus, subsequent developments showed that they were extraordinarily ill-prepared to meet such an eventuality. More probably, it was only after the event that the claim was made that the attack on Vaumarcus had tempted Charles out of his fortified lines. The statements in the letter from the Bielers to the bishop of Basel, that Charles set out to relieve Vaumarcus, and, in Jorg Hochmut's report, that Charles only left his laager when the guns of the defenders of Vaumarcus signalled to him their need of support and help, are both surely based on deduction after the event rather than on real knowledge. On the whole it seems that, while they assaulted Vaumarcus castle unsuccessfully through the first half of the morning of 2 March, the allies had no further moves planned out, and in particular, by no means expected Charles to march out of his Grandson camp.

The Burgundians must have been on the move on 2 March almost as early as their enemy. Their advance from the environs of Grandson has been variously explained, and one tradition claims that Charles ordered it directly against the advice of his most experienced captains.[1] Olivier de la Marche, who was sick at Salins at the time, pretends that Charles had garrisoned Vaumarcus on purpose to tempt the allies to attack him, implying against all verisimilitude and the other evidence that the Burgundians moved out of Grandson to be ready for battle. In fact Charles's intention was to advance his entire army some five miles at least and to establish it in a new laager nearer Vaumarcus and nearer the end of the gently undulating plain between the steep wooded slopes of Mont Aubert on his left and the shore of the lake on

---

nn. Besides those in *Dépêches des ambassadeurs milanais* I have used the despatch of 2 March 1476 in ASM Pot. est. Borgogna 518–20/57 and that of 4 March 1476 printed in Colombo, *Iolanda, duchessa di Savoia*, 288–9. I have also used a transcript of an unpublished letter of Jorg Hochmut of Nordlingen dated 18 March 1476 kindly supplied to me by Dr. H. Grüneisen (Nordlingen SA Missiven 1476, fos. 171–4).

[1] D'Oudenbosch, *Chronique*, 240–1, and de Haynin, *Mémoires*, ii. 218. For the next sentence, see de la Marche, *Mémoires*, iii. 209–10.

the right.[1] This plain is some 2 km wide at first but narrows beyond Concise and comes to an end at La Lance, beyond which the forest-clad mountain slopes end abruptly with the lake shore. Only two quite difficult tracks led from Concise to Vaumarcus, one through the trees on the mountain slope, the other along the lake shore. While the main Burgundian army moved in three divisions, one along the lake shore, one along the centre of the plain, and the third on the left wing and lowest slopes of Mont Aubert, it seems that Burgundian pioneers and quartermasters began erecting tents and wooden huts, and setting up artillery, as a start towards making the new laager, probably on and around the hillock between Concise and La Lance, possibly on the very prominent one near Onnens. Unaware of the enemy's moves, Charles may have hoped that this advance would facilitate his reinforcement of Vaumarcus and firm occupation of the wooded defile between Concise and St. Aubin so that he would there-after be able to march his army through it and on to Neuchâtel and beyond.

How many men were engaged at Grandson on either side? In a fit of pique, Charles the Bold complained shortly after the battle that 20,000 of his men had fled from 10,000 Swiss, but he was probably exaggerating the size of his own army and certainly underestimating that of the allies. No exact information about the numbers in the Burgundian army is available but, on the allied side, lists have survived giving the numbers from each town and region so that it can be ascertained with reasonable certainty that their army comprised some 20,000 men, the largest single contingent being that of Bern.

While the castle of Vaumarcus was being unsuccessfully attacked by one section of the allied army, another contingent, comprising men from Schwyz and Thun and probably Bern and Zürich, made its way forwards through the woods towards Vernéaz, apparently without the permission or knowledge of some of the allied leaders and perhaps intending only to find better quarters. That there was an element of disorganization on the allied side appears from the fact that some at least of the Basel troops were ignorant, on the morning of 2 March, even of the plan to attack Vaumarcus. The men of this unofficial

---

[1] The only Burgundian eyewitness of the battle, de Margny, *L'Aventurier*, 63–4, states that Charles sent baggage and quartermasters on ahead, while Jorg Hochmut mentions that a second Burgundian laager had been started and that, in the Grandson laager, much of the gear was already packed. See too the despatch in Colombo, *Iolanda, duchessa di Savoia*, 288: 'vogliando questo signore duca andare col campo piu ultra'.

COMPOSITION OF THE ALLIED ARMY AT GRANDSON[1]

The eight 'alte Orte'		Dependencies and allies of the 'alte Orte'		Lower Union	
Zürich	1,701	Fribourg	828	Basel	1,200
Bern	7,343	Biel	213	Strasbourg	259
Luzern	1,861	Solothurn	928	Colmar	35
*Uri	458	St. Gall, town	131	*Sélestat	26
Schwyz	1,181	St. Gall, abbey	151	?Rottweil	100
Obwald		Baden and		?Sundgau, Breisgau	
and Nidwald	455	Freiamt	286	and Black Forest	1,500
Glarus and		Schaffhausen	106		
Thurgau	780	?Appenzell	200		
Zug	434				
	14,213		2,843		3,120

GRAND TOTAL 20,376

vanguard clashed, along their road, which was the upper of the two rough tracks already mentioned leading through the wooded lower slopes of Mont Aubert, with some Burgundian troops and brushed them aside. They were either scouts sent ahead of the main army or defensive forces posted there the day before. Some time probably in the late morning this allied van emerged from the woods in the neighbourhood of the modern farmhouse called Prise Gaulax, to see the entire Burgundian army advancing in the plain below, its formations reaching back beyond the village of Concise towards Grandson, five miles away.

The Burgundians were marching in the three contingents already mentioned; they were not drawn up ready for battle, but Charles's reaction to the appearance of what was soon seen to be a sizeable phalanx of infantry on the heights above him was to redeploy his forces into a single body or battle. Although this unofficial allied vanguard, which must have been over a thousand strong, sent back messages to explain the situation to their colleagues, they were unable or perhaps unwilling to avoid engaging the Burgundian forces. Their massed pikes and halberds moved downhill, and Charles partly withdrew his men in the hopes of encircling them. When this was almost accomplished he delivered a series of attacks against them which

[1] See *Eidgenössischen Abschiede*, ii. 593 n. 1, and Deuchler, *Burgunderbeute*, 43. My figures are from Wyss and others, *Die Burgunderbeute*, 277–8, supplemented by von Elgger, *Kriegswesen*, 67–8 (marked with an asterisk) and Jorg Hochmut's letter referred to in n. 2 p. 372 above (marked with queries). See the map on p. 371 above.

included at least one vigorous cavalry charge. This was effectively repelled by the pikemen. Even so, this allied force, which had by now moved down into lower ground from Prise Gaulax towards Concise, where it came under heavy fire, was in a most dangerous predicament.

It was at this juncture that two things happened, possibly at the same time, which had the almost instant effect of giving victory to the allies. A panic began in the Burgundian ranks as a result of a further withdrawal of troops from in front of the allied vanguard. Charles the Bold had apparently ordered this withdrawal either to tempt the enemy to advance still further so that they could more easily be encircled or in order to train his artillery on them, but the movement was misinterpreted as a retreat. Other troops followed suit, and soon the partial withdrawal became a general flight. The Zürich chronicler sized the situation up accurately enough when he wrote, laconically, 'God gave us luck so that they fled'.[1] The other event which decided the day against Charles was the arrival on the scene of the rest of the allied army, which had abandoned the attack on Vaumarcus and made its way as fast as possible through the woods to come to the help of the advance party. The emergence of these troops from the forest, some high up at Prise Gaulax, others, perhaps the main body, from low down by the lake shore near La Lance, making blood-curdling noises with their horns and other instruments, further terrorized the Burgundians, who never stopped to offer them battle. 'Our people chased and killed them from Vaumarcus to Montagny, which is as far as from Porrentruy to Blamont', wrote Biel to Basel with some exaggeration.[2] In fact, there was more chasing than killing, Burgundian casualties probably amounting to a few hundred only. Charles tried desperately to rally his men, but to no avail. 'The thing was so sudden that we were only just able to escape, though we were about two leagues from the camp', wrote the Milanese ambassador on 4 March.[3] One ambassador expressed the hope to Galeazzo Maria Sforza that 'God would not put it into your lordship's head to give me ever again such an unfortunate and dangerous legation as this one'.

While Charles withdrew precipitately as far as Nozeroy, returning cautiously to Jougne and then Orbe when he found, a week after the battle, that his enemy had no intention of following up their success, the allies remained on the battlefield for the traditional three days.

[1] *Chronik der Stadt Zürich*, 204.
[2] Knebel, *Diarium*, ii. 363.
[3] Colombo, *Iolanda, duchessa di Savoia*, 289. For the next sentence, see Dürr, *ZGA* x (1911), 343 n. 1.

At Grandson, they cut down and buried the bodies of their comrades, which were still hanging on the walnut trees, and broke into the castle and threw the thirty-odd Burgundians they found inside it to their deaths from the battlements. Only with great difficulty was one nobleman saved from this slaughter so that he could be exchanged for Brandolf von Stein, the former Bernese captain of Grandson castle who had been captured by the Burgundians in January. At Vaumarcus the allies were cheated of their prey, for the Burgundian household troops who had been posted in the castle there by Charles under the command of George de Rosimbos contrived to slip silently away over the mountains in the dead of night, leaving their horses and all their belongings behind.

The allies could congratulate themselves on the fabulous booty which they gained as a result of their victory, for the fleeing Burgundians left nearly all their baggage and heavy equipment behind, much of it stowed in chests ready to be moved to the new camp Charles was planning. There was a great deal of private plundering and appropriation, in spite of the time-honoured federal ruling that all booty was to be made in common and then shared out. The captured artillery was taken to Nidau and there divided among the cantons. The provisions found in Vaumarcus were taken by boat to Landeron and auctioned. Immense numbers of pennons and banners were found, many of them among the baggage; but the white, brown and blue banner, with a gold St. Andrew's cross on it, belonging to Louis de Chalon, lord of Châteauguyon, was taken in battle by a Luzerner. Its owner had been killed while leading a cavalry attack on the allied vanguard. Tapestries, tents, plate, books, reliquaries and their contents, diamonds and other jewels, weapons of every kind, clothing, gold and silver coins, the privy seal of Charles the Bold, the seal of Anthony, bastard of Burgundy which the Basel captain Peter Rot jokingly used to seal a letter of his to Basel, Charles the Bold's throne, his jewelled hat; all this and more was among the priceless treasure abandoned by the retreating Burgundians. Much of it was dismantled, cut into pieces, sold, lost, even burnt by the victorious allies; much has been subsequently lost; but a great deal has survived to be superbly described and illustrated in recent years by scholars, who have also minutely traced the history of the transmission of individual pieces from generation to generation like some aristocratic family tree.[1] Among the *Eidgenossen*, wrangles over the distribution

---

[1] Deuchler, *Burgunderbeute* and Wyss and others, *Die Burgunderbeute.*

N*

of this booty or the proceeds of it continued to occupy the federal diet until the end of the fifteenth century.

Some imaginative contemporaries made Charles the Bold so shattered by his defeat at Grandson that he went for two, or even three, days thereafter without food and drink. In fact he was far too conceited to permit a single piece of ill luck or, more probably as he supposed, treachery, to interfere with his self-confidence. Four days after the battle he was consoling himself with the thought that, if the two armies had fought the thing out properly, victory would certainly have been his. Panigarola reported on 4 March that the duke was by no means downhearted: he was already taking steps to collect new artillery and round up fugitives and hoped to take the field again in a fortnight. On 5 March he sent to Lorraine for reinforcements and on 6 March, reporting his defeat at the hands of the 'Swiss, Bernese, Valaisans and their allies' to Guy de Brimeu, lord of Humbercourt, he ordered the recruitment on pain of death of 'all those fit to bear arms' in the lands of Overmaas, Namur, Liège and Looz, 'because his intention was and he had decided with God's and his subjects' help to withstand the pride of the said Swiss and see that they did not enter his lands again'.[1] On 8 March he wrote to Dijon asking if he might borrow the civic artillery and promising to return it on the word of a prince. On 14 March he established himself and his forces outside Lausanne and henceforth devoted all his energies to the prosecution of the war.

Although Bern's allies refused outright her request to exploit their Grandson victory by advancing into Savoy or occupying the *pays de Vaud*, the war against Burgundy was by no means confined to this one defensive expedition. On the very next day after the battle of Grandson the garrison of Héricourt went off on a marauding raid into the Franche-Comté, and in April and May a succession of raids into Burgundian territory was organized and carried out by the Lower Union powers, especially Basel. The situation in Savoy was not dissimilar. On 18 March the bishop of Sion was able to report that the 'militia of the holy Theodul' had been active again against Savoy in the Lower Valais. Villeneuve had been conquered on 10 March, according to Schilling by a 400-strong force which contrived to butcher the entire garrison of 500 men. Chillon, however, held firm. On 5 April Charles sent a joint expedition with Savoy from Lausanne to lay

---

[1] Gorissen, *De Raadkamer te Maastricht*, 209–10. For the next sentence, see *Correspondance de la mairie de Dijon*, i. 183–4.

waste and if possible reconquer the Lower Valais and reopen the
Great St. Bernard Pass, but it was an abject failure. Later in the month
a simultaneous attack on this Alpine route was staged in another
attempt to regain control of it and thus facilitate the passage of
Italian recruits to Charles's army. While a force from Piedmont
advanced northwards on 13 April from Aosta, other troops from
Savoy and Burgundy advanced southwards towards Martigny, but
again to no avail.

The warfare in the Franche-Comté and the Valais was somewhat
peripheral. Charles's removal to Lausanne after the battle of Grandson
showed that future hostilities would be centred on the *pays de Vaud*,
most of which had been occupied since January by the Burgundians.
Advancing against Bern from Lausanne, Charles would inevitably
have to conquer either Murten or Fribourg, for these were the two
great outer bastions of Bern against attack from the south-west. The
federal diet had agreed to garrison Fribourg which was regarded as
one of their number, but not Murten, which they rightly considered
as a conquest of Bern from Savoy. The responsibility for garrisoning,
provisioning and improving the defences of Murten, all of which was
actively undertaken in March with the help of Fribourg and of
artillery masters from Basel and Strasbourg, thus lay with Bern alone,
and the occasional attacks on Burgundian-held places in the Vaud
which were carried out at this time were not supported by Bern's
fellow-*Eidgenossen*. On 18 March an attack was launched on Payerne
from Fribourg; it was unsuccessful. On 28 March, at 3.0 a.m., a force
from Bern, Fribourg, Solothurn and some of the Lower Union powers
marched out of Fribourg to attack the main Burgundian stronghold
and advanced post in the Vaud, Romont, perched seemingly impreg-
nable on the flat summit of the perfectly round hill which has given it
its name. But the attackers could make no impression on its defences
and were forced to retire.

Charles the Bold was encamped with his army at or near Lausanne
from 14 March until 27 May 1476. Just as, in 1474–5, the eyes of
Europe were riveted on Neuss, so now they were on the imperial city
of Lausanne. Contrary to the allegation of de Commynes, the battle
of Grandson had by no means undermined Charles's international
credit, nor did his preoccupation with revenge interfere with the
maintenance of his system of alliances and treaties. Crucial to his
whole situation, which the rout at Grandson might easily have
rendered precarious, was the attitude and behaviour of Louis XI,

who was at Lyons throughout the spring of 1476 with troops readily available in Dauphiny. But the moves he did make, or was accused of making, against Charles, were not made until some time after the battle. It was only on 11 April 1476, after a summons of the Paris *Parlement* of 6 April, that he persuaded or forced King René of Sicily to swear on the four gospels and the 'true cross of St. Lau' that he would have no 'understanding, league or federation with the duke of Burgundy or any other enemy or rebellious subject'[1] and that he would not put his land of Provence in their hands. This action of Louis's had nothing to do with the battle of Grandson; it was a natural response to the negotiations which had been in progress in March between René and Charles for the transference of Provence into Burgundian control. Indeed, on 4 April Charles had actually sent the bailiff of Mâcon, Jehan Damas, lord of Clessy, to Provence to try to prevent it from falling into the hands of Louis XI, and if possible to secure it for himself.

Another move against Charles the Bold, which took place on 14 April 1476, was the rebellion of Vaudémont in Lorraine against Burgundian rule. But there is little evidence that Louis was involved in this: it was the result of an act of war by Duke René of Lorraine; the first step in the recovery of his duchy of Lorraine, which Charles had seized the previous autumn. Louis XI was in fact hovering at Lyons, not with the intention of pouncing on Charles the Bold with all his available forces, as Bern and her allies hoped, but to safeguard the future of Savoy, which he hoped to preserve from the clutches of both Burgundy and Bern and even obtain for himself. His involvement with Bern was limited to writing to congratulate her on the victory of Grandson 'about which he is so joyful that he could not be more so, and he could have had no better news in all his life',[2] and he made no response to Bern's urgent appeal on 11 April for a French military intervention to prevent Savoy falling into Charles's hands. Was there a hint of sarcasm in Bern's remark, in this letter, that they were glad to know the king would live and die for them?

Louis XI remained equally unresponsive to the secret anti-Burgundian overtures made to him by Charles's supposed ally

---

[1] Lecoy de la Marche, *René*, ii. 359, and see the same, i. 400–11, Dürr, *ZGA* x (1911), 362–4 and ASM Pot. est. Borgogna 518–20/87, 105, etc., besides works already referred to in n. 1 p. 359 above.
[2] Knebel, *Diarium*, ii. 402–3 = *Urkunden der Belagerung und Schlacht von Murten*, 179–80.

Galeazzo Maria Sforza, which may have been initiated before the battle of Grandson. 'Johanne, we want you to transfer yourself with all speed to Lyons dressed in conformity with the people of that country' wrote Galeazzo to his ambassador Johanne Bianco on 14 March.[1] He offered Louis 200,000 crowns payable by the Medici bank at Lyons, if he would attack Charles, and suggested that they might partition Savoy between them, Galeazzo taking Piedmont and Louis the rest. In point of fact, instead of organizing hostilities against Charles the Bold, in the weeks after Grandson, Louis negotiated with him. At Noyon in April it was the Burgundians who brought the talks to a standstill[2] and it was Louis, not Charles, who pressed at this time for a personal meeting of the two rulers to settle the affairs of Bern and Savoy as well as their own differences.

In spite of Galeazzo Maria Sforza's approach to Louis XI he did not forsake Charles the Bold's alliance in the spring of 1476, though he ignored Charles's repeated requests to send troops to his aid and even secretly encouraged the *Eidgenossen* to attack Piedmont. The other member of the League of Moncalieri, Savoy, not only held firm for Charles but was virtually taken over by him after the battle of Grandson while the other interested parties and neighbours of Savoy —the king of France, the duke of Milan and Bern—looked on and did nothing. In spite of a reminder, from her brother King Louis, of what had happened at Charles's hands to the dukes of Guelders and Lorraine and the bishop of Liège, Yolande joined Charles at Lausanne on 22 March, placing all her trust in him. A few weeks later she handed over a number of strategic places in Savoy to Burgundian garrisons. Before the end of April Charles was already considering the possibility of taking custody of her person and removing her to Burgundy on the pretext of protecting her from her brother, while he organized recruitment for his army in Turin as if Piedmont was already his own.

More significant, perhaps, than this further extension of Burgundian power over Savoy was the development of Charles's relationship with the Empire and the Habsburgs which also took place while he was at Lausanne. In spite of the fact that he had with him there Federico of Aragon, prince of Taranto, younger son of King Ferrante of Naples, who had been an aspirant for the hand of Mary of Burgundy, Charles had his peace treaty of 17 November 1475 with Frederick III formally published in Lausanne cathedral on Easter Day, 14 April,

---

[1] Colombo, *Iolanda, duchessa di Savoia*, 292.
[2] Plancher, iv. nos. 264–5.

and he signed the treaty of engagement of Mary and Maximilian on 6 May.[1] The Swiss and their allies, all of whom formed part of the Empire, were now left to their fate by the Emperor himself, whose Habsburg dynasticism had taken priority over the welfare of his Empire. Further evidence that the defeat at Grandson had by no means undermined Charles's standing in Europe was afforded by the friendly and reassuring letters he now received from King Edward IV of England, although to the Milanese ambassador Charles confided that he still hoped to obtain that kingdom for himself some time, and had many friends and supporters there.[2] The king of Hungary, too, sent Charles a friendly letter on 7 May, in which he advised him not to risk his fortunes again in battle against the Swiss, but it only reached him after his second defeat, at Murten.

The Milanese ambassador's despatches confirm that Charles the Bold's intention to attack the Swiss again was not seriously affected by the advice not to do this which was given him by his allies. Thus in May Yolande of Savoy asked the duke of Milan to try to persuade Charles not to risk his fine army against the Swiss, who threatened to overthrow and ruin all princes and nobles. In any event, what use would a victory be to him? Even if he succeeded in conquering and pacifying all their lands, these would only yield him 5,000 ducats per annum.[3] Nor was Charles's resolve to revenge himself weakened by the efforts of the duke of Milan and the count palatine of the Rhine,[4] and others, to arbitrate between himself and his enemies. The only element of weakness in his determination was his fear and dislike of Louis XI, which found repeated expression in his talks with Panigarola. On 1 February Panigarola reported that Charles had told him that the king 'was of evil behaviour, so that as long as he lived he would never cease troubling the world. They ought to think of some

---

[1] For Federico see Pontieri, *ASN* lxiii (1939), 78–112. The treaty of engagement is in *Aktenstücke und Briefe zur Geschichte des Hauses Habsburg*, i. 134–5.

[2] ASM Pot. est. Borgogna 518–20/21, and see the same, 160 and 242. The letter referred to in the next sentence is printed in *Dépêches des ambassadeurs milanais*, ii. 126–8, and *Briefe und Actenstücke von Mailand*, 158–9; and translated into German in *Urkunden der Belagerung und Schlacht von Murten*, 184–5, and into English in Kirk, *Charles the Bold*, iii. 350–1.

[3] *Dépêches des ambassadeurs milanais*, ii. 202–3.

[4] Tourneur, *RBN* lxxi (1919), 11–12 and nn. = ASM Pot. est. Borgogna 518–20/304 etc.

way of confining him so that he could not move.'[1] Charles's hatred of
Louis flared up in mid-April when he suspected him of organizing
the defection of Vaudémont in Lorraine. On 19 April Panigarola
reported a faltering in the duke's resolve against the Swiss now Louis
had broken the truces with him: he 'would finish with them quickly
either by battle or through an agreement'. If necessary he would leave
200–300 lances to garrison the passes while he himself went off to deal
with Louis. He delivered another tirade against Louis on 2 May, but
the Swiss and their allies remained his prime target. On 23 May
Panigarola described his feelings and his plans as follows:

> His lordship was for many reasons not inclined to make this peace
> [with the Swiss], nor did he want it in any form, because it would affect
> his honour too much. Their attack had come against all reason. He had
> embarked on this campaign with the utmost justice; it was provoked,
> not premeditated as they claim, by the insults, murders, damages and
> incursions they had made in Burgundy, persuaded by the king of France.
> Also, it was to defend the lands of his allies, which they want to swallow
> up. . . . He was resolved now to set out from here with his camp and to
> enter their territory. He would neither halt anywhere nor establish him-
> self in any town until he had found the enemy, with whom he would
> fight, and he vowed to God that he would either die with his men or
> conquer. . . . His route hence would be to Fribourg and then to Bern
> and wherever he heard the enemy were assembling, unless they came
> against him first. And this is the settlement he intends to make, with
> justice, and with sword in hand.

The preparations in Charles the Bold's camp outside Lausanne for
the coming campaign against the Swiss and their allies were interrupted
on several occasions by serious quarrels between different sections of
his army. One such clash, between English and Italians, in which
many casualties occurred on both sides, was reported by Panigarola
in his despatch of 25 March. Another, between the same people,
which required Charles's personal intervention, occurred on 21 April.
'The English are proud people without respect [for others] and they
claim superiority over every other nation', commented Panigarola.[2]

---

[1] ASM Pot. est. Borgogna 518–20/15 and, for what follows, the same,
197–8, 243 and 306–7 whence the extract.
[2] *Cal. state papers. Milan*, i. 225 = ASM Pot. est. Borgogna 518–20/205,
and compare the same, 208–10 and de Margny, *L'Aventurier*, 86–7. See too
Dépêches des ambassadeurs milanais, ii. 83–7, 90, etc. and *Cal. state papers.
Milan*, i. 223–6 etc. For the next sentence see ASM Pot. est. Borgogna

On 16 May a serious mutiny broke out among the English, who left camp and made for the duke's quarters brandishing their bows and demanding their pay. The duke harangued them in English from a window and persuaded them to lay down their arms and kneel to ask his pardon.

More serious perhaps than these disturbances, in delaying Charles's departure on campaign, was an illness, which affected him on 15 April and kept him in his room all day on 19 April.[1] A week later he was taking medicine and on 27–29 April he was suffering from a serious and painful disorder of the stomach. Some attributed this condition to the medicine he had been taking for his melancholy; others thought his stomach had been weakened by the water he had been drinking. Crisis came early on 29 April when he almost lost consciousness, the doctors despaired of him, and they, the household servants and the bastard Anthony were all in tears. Moved during a blizzard which left six inches of snow on the ground from the cold camp into a house in Lausanne, Charles had recovered sufficiently on 30 April to eat some chicken, and drink some undiluted wine which the doctors forced on him. By 2 May he was well enough to recount his sick-bed experiences to Panigarola. His stomach trouble, he thought, had been brought on by melancholy. He was much better, though pale and gaunt. But the doctors were still persecuting him: they made him shave off the long beard he had vowed to grow after the battle of Grandson until he had revenged himself for that defeat. Even as late as 12 May Charles was still taking medicine.

In a famous despatch of 10 May the Milanese ambassador at the court of Savoy, Antonio de Aplano, gave a remarkable though somewhat disparaging account of Charles the Bold's army, which he began to have reviewed on 9 May 'in the name of God and St. George'. The reviews continued on 12 and 13 May, as described by Panigarola, and a new military ordinance was published which organized the army in eight divisions or battles, each including horse and foot. What was the size of this army? According to de Aplano Charles had about 18,000

518–20/291; for the preceding sentence, the same, 105–6. In 1841 a corpse was disinterred in a Lausanne cemetery with a rose noble between its teeth, perhaps a victim of one of these clashes, Reymond, *RHV* xxiii (1915), 193–4.

[1] Besides the extracts printed in *Dépêches des ambassadeurs milanais*, ii. 60, 105, etc. I have used for what follows: ASM Pot. est. Borgogna 518–20/201, 205, 226, 232, 234–6 etc. etc. See too, on Charles's illness and beard, Armstrong's note in Mancini, *Usurpation of Richard III*, 35 n. 5.

men, equally divided between horse and foot; but he had been told there were not more than 16,000 in all. The troops actually reviewed and paid at Lausanne in May 1476 are set out in detail in the account of the *trésorier des guerres* and the information recorded in this source is summarized in the accompanying table.

SIZE AND COMPOSITION OF THE BURGUNDIAN ARMY AT LAUSANNE IN MAY 1476
ACCORDING TO THE ACCOUNT OF THE TRÉSORIER DES GUERRES [1]

	Men-at-arms	Mounted archers	Infantry	Total
Mounted troops from the twelve 100-lance companies of ordinance	1,241	2,685		3,926
Infantry in four contingents, each, at full strength, of 1,000 men			3,709	3,709
Eight companies of ordinary and extraordinary household infantry, each of 100 men			736	736
Mounted English archers, including the household squadrons, in companies of 100		1,377		1,377
	1,241	4,062	4,445	9,748

On the whole, the units were at full strength. For example a company of ordinance should theoretically have comprised 101 men-at-arms and a mounted trumpet and 202 mounted archers: 304 mounted men in all, always excluding pages and other auxiliary attendants. The twelve ordinance companies thus actually yielded more troops than their theoretical full strength of 3,648 men, mainly because three of them included three, instead of the usual two, contingents of 100 mounted archers with a captain. The companies of ordinance were all reviewed again, at Morrens or at Murten, in June, and losses had been minimal: they still mustered 3,854 mounted men Among the infantry, assembled at Lausanne in May, 367 men from

[1] AGR CC25543, fos. 206–46. In a few individual cases where figures are missing in the account an approximate average figure has been supplied.

Flanders, Guelders and Overmaas are specifically mentioned, as well as 100 'Swiss' (*Suichois*). Three important contingents must be added to those recorded in the table: the men-at-arms of the household, numbering about 500 combatants,[1] the troops from the two Burgundies, and those from Savoy. Even so, the grand total engaged at Murten may not have exceeded 12,000 combatants. The figures given in the table are borne out by the war treasurer's statement on the eve of the battle of Murten that the duke's infantry and mounted archers together numbered about 8,000 men, and by Panigarola's claim that there were 1,600 men-at-arms in the Burgundian army at Murten.[2]

On 27 May 1476 Charles the Bold set out from Lausanne. Just as in February he had attacked and conquered one of the Vaud places belonging to Jaques de Savoie, count of Romont, so now his immediate target was another of these places, Murten. It was in any case an essential military objective, since this small well-fortified town on the shores of its lake effectively barred the approaches to Bern, which Charles rightly considered his principal enemy. The general alliance which had confronted him at Grandson had soon fallen into disarray. The *Eidgenossen* had refused to help or even permit Bern to occupy any places or conquer any territory after Grandson. They had ignored or rejected her repeated appeals, made in March and April, for help in an attack on Charles before he was ready to attack her, and in April they made it perfectly clear to Bern that they would prefer her to evacuate Murten and that, though they were glad to help garrison Fribourg, which they regarded almost as a member of their federation, they would by no means consider a Burgundian attack on Murten as a *casus belli* against Charles the Bold. Thus even when Bern reported on 9 June to the other *Eidgenossen* that Charles had arrived that very day at Murten and begun to lay siege to it, and that he was about to attack her and intended to 'subject the entire German nation and all of us', her appeal to them to turn out at once and march to her aid fell on deaf ears.[3]

---

[1] That is, the first three contingents mentioned on p. 221 above.
[2] Below, p. 392 and p. 394 n. 1.
[3] *Urkunden der Belagerung und Schlacht von Murten*, 246. This monumental work is of course of prime importance for the Murten campaign. Besides the more general works already referred to, I have also used Blösch, *BT* (1877), 171–227, Brusten, *PCEEBM* x (1968), 79–83, Meister, *NFZ* lxxii (1877), de Vallière, *Morat*, Wattelet, *FG* i (1894), 11–94, Wirz, *RHB* iv (1927), 59–66, and Zesiger, *BBG* xxii (1926), 153–69 for what follows. See too Dierauer, *Geschichte der schweizerischen Eidgenossenschaft*, ii. 264–74 with references.

On 4 June, the day he left Morrens to begin his advance to Estavayer and Murten, Charles the Bold explained in detail to the Milanese ambassador why he was so determined to attack the Swiss. It was not just a point of honour, though it was true that 'he could not live with the disgrace of having been defeated by these bestial people'.[1] It was essential also in order to prevent the Swiss from continuing their raids on his territory, in order to regain possession of Upper Alsace and, above all perhaps, so that he might seize complete control of Savoy from under Louis XI's nose. He was utterly resolved: even if he could be certain of becoming Emperor peacefully he would renounce that dignity in favour of a battle, though he well knew he was risking 'his state, his life, and everything'. The duke's strategy on this crucial campaign was characterized initially by the utmost caution. With his flanks protected by a screen of Burgundian garrisons, notably at Romont and Yverdun, Charles sent reconnoitring parties on ahead in early June to Payerne and Estavayer and even beyond along the strip of land between Lakes Neuchâtel and Murten as far as the Broye, a waterway linking the northern ends of the two lakes. On 11 June he settled down to besiege Murten.

Charles the Bold's headquarters were established, and his wooden tent set up, on an isolated hillock 1·25 km due south of Murten, called Bois Domingue, from which he enjoyed a splendid view of Murten with the lake beyond and, beyond that, the partly wooded heights of Mont Vully. On the open cultivated slopes around him and on other hillocks and knolls not far from the Bois Domingue the main part of the Burgundian army set up its tents and quarters, north of Münchenweiler and not south as many of the older historians affirmed. While these contingents, comprising two of the four Burgundian army corps, blocked the roads leading from Murten to Fribourg and elsewhere 'inland' from the lake, the other two army corps were stationed by the lake at either end of Murten. At the northern end of the town, Jaques de Savoie, count of Romont, commanding the Burgundian and Savoyard troops, was posted at Muntelier and occupied also the hillock between there and Burg. At the opposite end of Murten, towards Avenches, the bastard Anthony held Meyriez and Greng and protected the Burgundian lines of communication. Working mostly at night because of the artillery fire from the town, the besiegers dug trenches nearer and nearer the walls until, after two large bombards had begun firing with considerable

---

[1] *Dépêches des ambassadeurs milanais*, ii. 216.

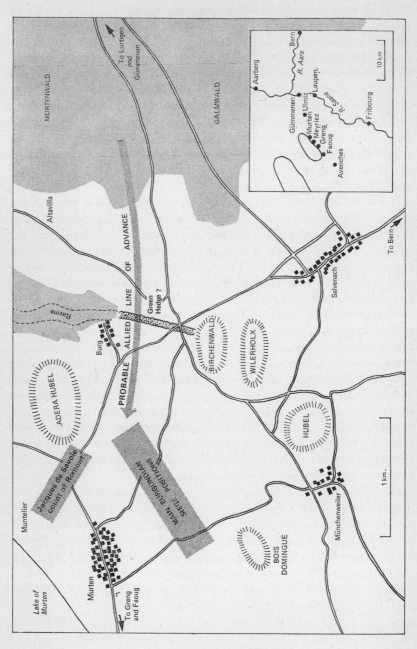

12.   The battle of Murten

effect from the count of Romont's quarters on 17 June, the first
assault was made on the evening of 18 June by the count of Romont's
men. It was unsuccessful.

Murten was in fact well garrisoned and ably captained by the
Bernese soldier-statesman Adrian von Bubenberg.[1] There had been
ample time before the arrival of the Burgundian army to strengthen
its fortifications, and the garrison may have been encouraged in its
resistance by memory of the fate of the garrison of Grandson. In any
case they ignored the notes fired into Murten on Burgundian
crossbow-bolts telling them they would never be relieved and that
'we shall shortly enter the town and take you and kill you and hang
you by your throats'.[2]

'I do not know if [Murten] will be succoured by the enemy, but
you will do well to continue the processions more and more', wrote
Guillaume de Rochefort to Dijon from the Burgundian camp on
18 June. Charles the Bold was in fact reasonably well informed about
the movements and plans of his enemies. He had ascertained by 10
June that Bern's allies would not help her defend or relieve Murten,
but would assemble as soon as she herself was attacked. It may have
been because he aimed at a decisive battle that he made no effort to
exploit this situation by confining his attentions in the first place to
Murten alone. Instead, on 12 June his men pushed on directly
towards Bern. Three substantial detachments assaulted and tried to
seize the river crossings defending Bern, at Aarberg over the Aare,
and at Gümmenen and Laupen over the Saane. These attacks were
all repulsed, but their effect on Bern's allies was electric: the general
mobilization began at once. Now, Charles could expect Murten to be
relieved, or avenged, not just by the 10,000-strong army of Bern,
Fribourg and their allies, but by the 20,000 or more men which the
League of Constance powers could field.

It was widely believed in the Burgundian camp on Thursday 20
June that the enemy would attack on Saturday. They had indeed
entertained such an intention for a time; then put the proposed attack
forward because of the dire straits of the defenders of Murten. But at
the last moment they decided to await the one substantial contingent
still outstanding, that of Zürich. It was this that delayed their advance

[1] On him see Ziegler, *AHKB* xii (1889), 1–130, which is useful also on the
siege and battle of Murten, pp. 41–70 and 107–9.
[2] Schilling, *Die Berner-Chronik*, ii. 34. The quotation that follows is from
Correspondance de la mairie de Dijon, i. 186.

until Saturday 22 June. Charles the Bold expected an attack on 21 June, and the bulk of his army was drawn up throughout that day in battle order 'on elevated ground where there was a fine plain above the camp'.[1] He and the Milanese ambassador Panigarola accompanied a scouting party and actually saw part of the Swiss camp, apparently in the neighbourhood of Ulmiz. But, when no attack came, the duke changed his mind and made a fatal error of judgement. Under the impression, which was perhaps well founded, that Louis XI had asked the Swiss not to attack, Charles, who invariably over-estimated the hostility, abilities and influence of the king he regarded as his arch-enemy, now decided that they must have accepted this supposed royal advice and would conduct a defensive war only. A heavy downpour of rain which continued throughout that night and much of the following morning, 22 June, confirmed his view, which was not shared by his captains and advisers nor by the Milanese ambassador, that no enemy attack was forthcoming.

In point of fact the *Eidgenossen* and their allies were quite incapable of fighting a defensive war. They found it extraordinarily difficult to keep an army in the field for any length of time. Their forces lacked provisions and supplies of all kinds. Once it was mustered in strength the army of the League of Constance had only two choices open to it: to advance and attack the enemy or to disband and return home. On this occasion it was only with great difficulty that the forces already assembled at and around Ulmiz had been persuaded to await the men of Zürich. Urged on by the captain of the Zürichers in garrison at Fribourg, Hans Waldmann,[2] these several thousand men performed the extraordinary feat of marching 140 km in three days, though they left hundreds of exhausted stragglers by the roadside. They arrived at Bern on the Friday afternoon, set out thence at 10.0 p.m., and heard mass and rested for an hour or two in the middle of the night, in pouring rain, at the Gümmenen bridge. But there was no question of allowing these men any additional time to restore or refresh themselves: they had to form up and go into battle that Saturday morning with the rest of the allied army. Another contingent that arrived only in the nick of time was a small mounted

---

[1] Ghinzoni, *ASL* (2) ix (1892), 104. This despatch of Panigarola dated St. Claude, 25 June 1476, first printed by Ghinzoni, has been translated into German (Dierauer, *SMOW* iv (1892), 1–16), French (Frédérix, *La mort de Charles le Téméraire*, 235–46, with Italian text), and English (Kendall, *Louis XI*, 436–9).

[2] See Dändliker, *JSG* v (1880), 183–307.

force from Lorraine, led by Duke René in person. They had ridden almost non-stop via Basel, Solothurn and Bern since they set out from Strasbourg on the Wednesday: René himself having reached Solothurn at 11.0 a.m. on Friday 21 June. Even with the delay until Saturday, by no means all the allied contingents could arrive on time. The 440 men, whose names have come down to us in a roll, recruited on the abbot of St. Gall's behalf in the Upper Thurgau assembled at Wil on 19 June with two five-horse carts. One was piled high with eight sides of bacon, two sacks of salt, dried beef, barley, oatmeal with butter to cook it in, and other provisions. The other contained scythes, sickles, shovels, axes, mattocks, kettles with hooks and tripods, copper and tin ladles and fifty-two dishes. They set out with a cook, a chaplain and a coffer containing 300 gulden on 20 June with no prospect at all of reaching Ulmiz in time.[1]

Saturday morning, 22 June 1476, was dull and wet. Many of the allied troops had not slept at all that night; many had no breakfast that morning. The task of sorting out the various contingents and placing them in order of march was given to Wilhelm Herter, captain of the Strasbourgers.[2] This difficult process, which was probably carried out in the neighbourhood of Ulmiz, was accompanied by a certain amount of confusion and even hilarity. When a voice cried 'Where is Lenzburg placed?' the answering shout was said to have been heard: 'Gone ahead with their banner and 100 men to wake up the duke, so that he knows we are here.' The van was commanded by Hans von Hallwil of the Aargau, a burgess of Bern; the centre by the Züricher Hans Waldmann; and the rearguard by Caspar von Hertenstein, *Schultheiss* of Luzern. A cavalry contingent from the Lower Union powers led by Duke René of Lorraine and the Austrian bailiff of Upper Alsace, Oswald, lord of Thierstein, advanced separately, ready to protect the flanks of the van. A mounted reconnaissance party had already been sent forward to view the Burgundian positions, and the entire allied army now advanced through the thick deciduous woodland of the Murtenwald or Galmwald directly towards these positions and Murten itself, halting on the way for the traditional ceremony of knighting some of the more prominent young noblemen in the army, among them the duke of Lorraine. No exact figures concerning the size of this army have survived, but it was substantially larger than that of Grandson. Perhaps it approached 25,000 men in all.

[1] Anon, *St. Gallens Antheil.*
[2] See on him, for example, Ristelhuber, *L'Alsace à Morat*, 7–9.

In spite of reports, which reached Charles the Bold during the morning, of enemy troop movements in the woods, and then of a definite advance, he persisted in his belief that no attack was coming, and the Burgundian army was in consequence taken completely by surprise[1] when the allied van emerged from the forest in battle order just over a kilometre away from the nearest Burgundian positions. These were occupied by a skeleton force which Charles had stationed along a hedge or palisade which ran approximately north–south across the plateau south of Burg, the famous 'green hedge'. Thomas Basin, who had no first-hand information about the battle, has been followed by many, if not most, modern historians in stating that Charles the Bold had his army drawn up in battle order for six hours on the morning of Saturday, 22 June, and had just dismissed it for dinner when the Swiss attacked. In fact, as Panigarola's despatch, confirmed by Molinet, shows, it was on the day before that the Burgundian army was drawn up ready for battle.[2] What was actually happening in the Burgundian camp on the Saturday morning is described in the account of Charles the Bold's war treasurer.[3]

> Other expense in cash lost on 22 June 1476, day of the battle of Morat. While my said lord the duke was at the siege of Morat on 22 June 1476, at about 10.0 a.m. in the presence of Lyonnel Donguieres his *maître d'hôtel* and of Maître Thibault Barradot his secretary he ordered the said *trésorier des guerres* to pay immediately to his troops, and in particular to each infantryman 12 shillings, to each mounted archer 16s., and to each English archer 20s.; which three contingents could amount to about 8,000 men. To this the treasurer replied that it would be impossible to do this in detail. Nonetheless my lord the duke said that he must do it and that he would assign some people to help him and proclaim at the sound of the trumpet in all parts of the camp that everyone should report to his captain, *conduictier* or *centenier*. This he did, and at once the said treasurer assembled as many clerks as he could to help him. To begin with, he gave to Jaques de la Frette, clerk appointed in Pierre Maillart's place in Dommarien's company, the sum of 500 florins of Burgundy of 24s. each, as appears from his letter dated on the

---

[1] De Margny, *L'Aventurier*, 65–8, the only Burgundian eyewitness apart from Panigarola, emphasises the element of surprise.

[2] But the writer of a letter to Johanne Scarampo states that Charles's army was drawn up on 22 June because an attack was expected; no attack came and Charles began to think there would be none; then, when no longer expected, the Swiss attacked, ASMant Archivio Gonzaga, letter of 4 July 1476.

[3] AGR CC25543, f. 196a–b.

said day, to start making the above-mentioned payments to the 800 foot of my lord's household and to the said Dommarien's archers, who were in the trenches. The said Jaquet could not make these payments because the battle came an hour after the money had been given him, and the said Jaquet said that he put the money in Maître Guillaume de Chaumont's coffers and these coffers were loaded onto a horse which left hastily with the others, and there has been no news of it since, so that the said sum has been lost.

Battle was joined late on the Saturday morning, just as the rain cleared and the sun came out. There was no time for the entire Burgundian army to form up on the plateau south of Burg during the twenty minutes it may have taken the allied van to advance from the forest edge. The allies were in fact temporarily halted along the line of the hedge by English archers and artillery fire, but they soon turned this position and subsequently continued their advance, cutting their way without serious difficulty through the hastily mustered cavalry contingents which were rushing towards them in a piecemeal and haphazard fashion. From the plateau south of Burg, soon after they had fought their way through the hedge, they could see the Bois Domingue, covered with Burgundian tents, and beleaguered Murten. They continued to advance, meeting and overcoming resistance here and there and probably separating now into several contingents, at least one of which may have swung left to pass south of the Bois Domingue, while others continued straight towards Murten. Charles himself was slow in getting his armour on though he had the assistance of two Italians, Johanne Petro Panigarola and Matteo de' Clarici. By the time he reached the plateau there was no longer any hope of forming a line of battle against the enemy advance and many of his troops were already dead or dispersed. The flight became general; the attack so precipitate that some Burgundians were even killed in their tents. The only effective escape route along the lake shore through Greng and Faoug soon became hopelessly blocked, and hundreds of Burgundians were driven into the shallow water and killed or drowned there. A few stragglers were credited with the feat of swimming across to safety on the far shore, a distance of some three kilometres. The allies, in conformity with the battle orders laid down by the federal diet on 18 March 1476, killed all the enemy they could lay their hands on and took no prisoners, and the carnage was extensive and prolonged. Several thousand of Charles the Bold's men, mainly infantry, were killed, among them Johanne Francesco, one of Troylo de Rossano's sons, and Antonio de Lignana, George de

Rosimbos, who had escaped from Vaumarcus, and Jehan de Luxembourg, count of Marle. Fugitives were searched out in cellars and barns; they were shot as they swam in the water like ducks; they were shot like birds as they hid in the foliage of trees. The lives at least of the camp women were spared, though they were compelled or found it necessary to demonstrate their sex by exhibiting their breasts or genitals. The count of Romont managed to extricate himself and most of his men later that same day while the allies were occupied cutting the throats of the men in the camp, seizing and collecting booty, and pursuing and killing the fugitives along the shore of the lake. The booty captured at Murten was nothing to that of Grandson, but the Burgundian defeat was incomparably greater. Adding the numerous deserters to the dead, Charles had lost one-third of his army, perhaps more.[1] He was the victim of one of the most destructive and decisive battles in the military history of the middle ages.

The effects of the battle at Murten were much more far-reaching than those of Grandson. The duke himself arrived at Gex in Savoy, 17 km north-west of Geneva, on the evening of 23 June, having stopped briefly en route at Morges. He spent most of July at Salins, and was thereafter at La Rivière, also in the Franche-Comté, until 25 September.[2] Panigarola's despatches show that he was not drastically dispirited by his defeat. On 3 July the ambassador reported to Galeazzo Maria Sforza that Charles had garrisoned the Jura passes against a possible Swiss incursion and was busy with military preparations for a third campaign against the Swiss. 'He laughs, jokes and makes good cheer', quite unlike someone who has been defeated. He claimed that God had given him such power that it would take many defeats to shake him: he could still field 150,000 men when he seemed finished.[3] In an eloquent speech to the Estates of the two Burgundies, assembled at Salins on 8–12 July, the duke urged them to contribute money and men for further military operations and detailed many examples, from Roman and modern history, of rulers who had been helped by their subjects to recover from defeats and

[1] At the end of July Troylo de Rossano still had 800 of his 1,000-strong infantry company, ASM Pot. est. Borgogna 518–20/438. According to Panigarola, of the 1,600 lances at Murten, 1,000 were saved, *Dépêches des ambassadeurs milanais*, ii. 360–1.

[2] See the rather slight accounts of the duke at La Rivière in Suchet, *MAB* (1899), 129–40, and Gros, *MAB* clxxi (1956), 59–73.

[3] *Dépêches des ambassadeurs milanais*, ii. 342. For what follows, see Billioud, *États de Bourgogne*, 146–53 with references.

setbacks. He was indeed his old self, if anything more self-confident, more arrogant, more obsessed with revenging his defeats and restoring his military reputation, than ever before.

The duke's own letters tell the same tale, of military determination and activity; they also reveal his exact plans. Thus, when he wrote to Dijon on 21 July asking them 'on pain of being considered rebels, disobedient, traitors and enemies of us and of our lands' to send their contingent of the 3,000 men for frontier defence the Estates had recently voted him, he pointed out that, in spite of the growing need for troops in Lorraine, he himself intended to march as soon as possible against the Germans.[1] But soon afterwards the situation in Lorraine had so far deteriorated that on 11 August Charles informed Claude de Neuchâtel, his lieutenant in Luxembourg, that he would shortly be marching to Lorraine in person with all his power. Thus he was perfectly capable of realistically assessing military priorities, though this switching of the principal theatre of war from Savoy to Lorraine, which does mark a new and as it proved final stage in the duke's military and political career, did not of course entail facing a new enemy.

It was not the health and personal well-being of Charles the Bold which was at stake at Murten; nor was the entire Burgundian military power at risk. The former was not affected; the latter could be restored. But the fate of Savoy was in the balance. Had Murten been a Burgundian victory, Savoy would have been Charles's. He had already taken steps to seize Piedmont but, in spite of the forceful arrest of Duchess Yolande in the night of 26–27 June, which was undertaken on Charles's orders but with misgivings by Olivier de la Marche, chronicler and captain of the Burgundian guard, Savoy slipped from his grasp. In Geneva the news of the arrest of Yolande was greeted with riots against the Burgundian and Italian troops then lodged there, many of whom were killed. Moreover, Charles's coup was unsuccessful as well as unpopular, for Olivier de la Marche had failed to apprehend the young Duke Philibert along with his mother. More important was the intervention of Louis XI who, while offering the palm of friendship to Charles with one hand, even inviting him to a personal conference, grabbed Savoy with the other. He appointed his partisan Philip of Savoy, lord of Bresse, his lieutenant in Piedmont, and French officials arrived at Chambéry. But he managed even better

---

[1] *Correspondance de la mairie de Dijon*, i. 189–90. For what follows, see *Recueil du Fay*, 137.

than this. On 2 October he contrived the dramatic rescue of his sister
Yolande from Rouvres castle, brought her to Tours, and persuaded
her on 2 November 1476 to formally renounce all her Burgundian
connections.[1] Meanwhile, between 25 July and 12 August the Congress of Fribourg, attended by almost everyone except the defeated
Burgundians, had settled the fate of the Vaud. Rejecting Louis
XI's invitation to them to take up arms once more against Charles the
Bold, the *Eidgenossen* and their allies persuaded Bern to be content
with the eventual return of this territory to Savoy; but Murten and
one or two other places she was to keep. Thus the battle of Murten,
though, like Grandson, it was not followed by any further military
moves against Charles on the part of the allies, resulted indirectly in
his decisive exclusion from the affairs of Savoy as well as, more
directly, from the Vaud.

Of less significance than events in Savoy, which Charles the Bold
had hoped to appropriate, was the response of his Italian allies to his
defeat at Murten. Galeazzo Maria Sforza, duke of Milan, who had
been in touch with Louis after Grandson, now completely abandoned
his Burgundian ally and signed a treaty of friendship with Louis XI
on 29 August. Even the faithfully Burgundian Venetians sent an
emissary to France, though they insisted that they did not propose to
break with Charles the Bold. But, if Charles's Italian connections
were thus weakened, if his hopes for the acquisition of Savoy, perhaps
of Provence, even of Lombardy itself, were thus shattered, still Louis
XI showed no signs of open hostility to him and he was still buttressed

---

[1] Plancher, iv. no. 267 = *Chroniques de Yolande de France*, 302–4. For this
paragraph and the next, see in general Colombo, *Iolanda, duchessa di Savoia*,
157–69 and 189–99, Daviso, *La duchessa Iolanda*, 245–7 etc., Dürr, *ZGA* x
(1911), 411–13, Gabotto, *Lo stato Sabaudo*, ii. 185–213, Gingins-La Sarraz,
Épisodes, 333–67, and Perret, *France et Venise*, ii. 80–9. In spite of the (mainly
Milanese) documents printed in *Briefe und Actenstücke von Mailand*, 181–4
and 193–9, Buser, *Beziehungen der Mediceer zu Frankreich*, 459–65, Colombo,
Iolanda, duchessa di Savoia, 295–9, and *Dépêches des ambassadeurs milanais*,
ii. 302–70, others still unprinted are in ASM Pot. est. Borgogna 518–20/
383–471. There is an account of Yolande's arrest in ASMant Archivio
Gonzaga, letter of 4 July 1476 to Johanne Scarampo. Among the chroniclers
mentioning Yolande's capture and subsequent escape de Aquino, *Chronica*,
cols. 681–4, de Commynes, *Mémoires*, ed. Calmette and Durville, ii. 123–8,
de Haynin, *Mémoires*, ii. 220–1, and de la Marche, *Mémoires*, iii. 234–6 are
the most important. See too the material printed in *Chroniques de Yolande
de France*, 141–56 and 175. For the next sentence, see Büchi, *FG* xxiv
(1917), 24–74.

by his alliances with the Empire and with England. His defeats at the hands of the League of Constance had not led to complete diplomatic isolation, but only to the dissolution of the League of Moncalieri.

What, apart from Charles the Bold's errors of judgement, excessive self-confidence, and failure to take advice, is the explanation for the Burgundian military disasters at Grandson and Murten? First and foremost, though more or less exact figures are only available for the allied army at Grandson and the Burgundian at Murten, it is clear that the Burgundians were grossly outnumbered on both occasions. At Murten, for example, it seems quite incredible, on the basis of the known evidence, that Charles the Bold had more than 12 or 15,000 combatants at the very most, and possible that he only had some 10,000. Moreover these troops were spread out in the lines besieging Murten and in the camp itself, as well as on the battlefield, where they arrived, or were surprised, piecemeal. On the other hand the allies had probably mustered some 25,000 men, who advanced in concentrated columns or masses in such a way that, at any point of particular contact, they must have enjoyed a numerical superiority much greater than that which they had overall. Secondly, in spite of Charles the Bold's careful reconnoitring beforehand, the Burgundians were taken completely by surprise in both battles. At Grandson the allied attack was launched from behind a spur of Mont Aubert; at Murten it broke from the near impenetrable thickets of the Murten-wald. In both cases the attackers emerged suddenly in close proximity to the unprepared Burgundians. A third explanation for the Burgundian defeats lay in the heterogeneous nature of the ducal army, comprised as it was of French-speaking Burgundians and Picards, some Flemish or Dutch-speaking soldiers from Flanders or Holland, English archers, and Italians. At first glance, perhaps, the allied army looked equally heterogeneous, with its contingents of mounted noblemen from the Austrian Vorlande and French-speaking troops from Neuchâtel and Fribourg. But it was not. Two long-standing and closely linked traditions gave it a unity, a common purpose, an esprit de corps, an aggressive urge, a religious self-confidence which Charles the Bold's army lacked. These two traditions were supplied on the one hand by the great trading and manufacturing communities of south Germany and the Rhine—Bern and Zürich, Basel and Strasbourg, especially—and on the other by the *Eidgenossen* or Swiss federation. The one was urban, the other had once been predominantly rural, but the two had merged so that the urban element now predominated even among the *Eidgenossen* themselves. It was indeed an army of townsmen which defeated the Burgundians at Grandson and Murten; an army of townsmen opposed by a prince, a territorial ruler whose entire political career was dominated, from Dinant to Nancy, by his opposition to the towns and their opposition to him.

CHAPTER ELEVEN

The Collapse of Burgundian Power

The sudden collapse of Burgundian power and the swift extinction of the Burgundian state which, created and enlarged by successive Valois dukes, had been an important element in the European political scene for almost a hundred years, was to all intents and purposes a direct result of the personal follies and failures of Charles the Bold. After suffering severe defeats at the hands of the League of Constance at Grandson and Murten he led himself and his army into battle at Nancy in the most unfavourable circumstances imaginable and against the same determined enemies. The fact that he failed to provide himself with a legitimate male heir in spite of three marriages cannot be held against him, but he could justifiably be blamed for his failure or refusal to provide his daughter Mary with a husband who might have been able and willing to act as his lieutenant and thus be prepared and trained to succeed him; and he has been rightly blamed, too, for his extravagant and unpopular policies. Of course, the government of nearly every fifteenth-century state was fundamentally personal, and no analysis of the downfall of Burgundy can possibly avoid centring on the person of Charles the Bold. But to what extent did the collapse consist merely of his military defeat and death, and how far was it a process of internal disintegration? This chapter may go part of the way towards answering these large questions.

Of fundamental importance in any assessment of Burgundian internal disintegration at the end of Duke Charles's reign is the question of his personal standing. It is easy to claim that he was becoming increasingly unpopular and that his policies were arousing increasing opposition but difficult to find positive proof of this, for the evidence of hostility and unpopularity occurs here and there throughout his reign, rather than being accumulated towards the end of it. As early as 1468 Panigarola, then at the French court, was told that the new duke was unpopular and was not loved as his father had been[1] and it was in that same year that criticisms were first levelled at him by his confrères in the Order of the Golden Fleece. They were elaborated in 1473. There was, as we have seen in an earlier chapter, no significant increase in the number of so-called traitors towards the end of the ducal reign; it was only in the very altered situation after Duke Charles's death that large-scale changes of loyalty, from Burgundy to France, took place. Furthermore, although the chronicler Basin implies that it was in 1476 that Charles the Bold's subjects criticized and even disobeyed him,[2] the most notable piece of evidence for popular dislike of ducal policies dates from 1470. The document is remarkable for the duke's very characteristic defence of his actions, which takes a propagandist form. It was probably sent to local authorities throughout Flanders and Hainault and perhaps elsewhere.

Dearest and well loved, it has come to our notice that there are murmurings and rumours against us in our lands concerning three matters. First, concerning the *aides* which we maintain and take in our said lands, which are [said to be] larger than they ever were in the time of our late and most dear lord and father, whom God pardon. Second, concerning the bailiffs, provosts and others who hold the offices of our said lands at farm, offices which they [are said to] have taken at such a high and excessive price that they have to exploit and devour the wretched populace in order to recover their expenses. Third, concerning the contributions which are levied on fiefs and sub-fiefs in our lands for the service that they owe us.

Concerning which, in regard to the said *aides*, we are utterly amazed at what is being said and even more at those who are saying these things, especially as all the *aides* that we take in our said lands by no means total more than 200,000 good *livres* per annum, which is not much considering the estate and the great expenses and charges which we have to maintain, support and undertake. And, as you know, those *aides* which were granted to our said late lord and father which have fallen to us through his decease were only to run for a further two or three years at the most and, when they expire, the sum total of our said *aides*, ordinary and

---

[1] AGR MSS. divers 1173, f. 94b.
[2] Basin, *Louis XI*, ii. 312–20. The letter which follows is translated from *Coutumes du Franc de Bruges*, ii. 574–9; see too *Collection de documens inédits*, i. 131, de Barante, *Histoire des ducs*, ii. 361 n. 2, and *IAEH* i. xciii. For the criticisms of the knights of the Golden Fleece, see above, pp. 172–3.

extraordinary, will not amount to more than 150,000 good *livres* per annum, which is very little considering the great riches and wealth of the said lands in which, apart from the said *aides*, we have not levied a single penny to our profit, nor charged or taxed our subjects in any way for whatever affair we have been involved in, whether it be the armies we have raised, led and paid at our own expense both in France and in Liège, or anything else.

Indeed we have always, quite apart from our expenses, which have been of such magnitude that everyone knows about them, been prepared to expose our own person to adventure and danger for the security and peace of our said lands and subjects and to guard, preserve and defend them from the power and ferocity of enemies, and although for the three following reasons, that is to say because of the above-mentioned great expenses undertaken by us, because of the war and the armies fielded by us as has been said, and because of our newly acquired lordship and our marriage, we would have had good cause and justification to require and obtain in our said lands three *aides* of considerable value, nonetheless to relieve them more and oppress them less we have been content to demand and have a single *aide* for the said three causes which is a very small charge on them considering the power and wealth of our said lands and considering that the subjects of the lands and duchies of Brittany and Savoy, as we are told, never grant less to the princes and lords of the said lands when they ask them for an *aide*, than 300 or 400,000 crowns in each of those lands at one time, and as you know we have lands that are much more rich and powerful than any of the said lands of Brittany and Savoy. Certainly, if everyone acquitted himself and did his duty loyally in remonstrating and explaining the truth of all these things wherever necessary, the wilful and untrue statements on this matter which are spoken and spread round daily in our lands without cause or reasonable pretext would cease.

As to the said offices farmed out to the said bailiffs, provosts and others we believe that it is not unknown to you that the king St. Louis, for the general good and justice of the kingdom of France, which he ruled so virtuously and in such justice and order that it has always powerfully prospered since his time up to the present, ordained and established in his lifetime that the offices of the said kingdom should be farmed out so that the officers, bailiffs, provosts, and other farmers would be more careful, attentive and diligent in furthering the criminal punishment of malefactors and delinquents, in collecting the forfeitures and fines incurred by them, and in risking making a loss for the well-being and advancement of justice; but officers paid normal wages do not do [these things]. . . .

As far as the business of fiefs and sub-fiefs is concerned, the effort to abolish the military service of the said fiefs and sub-fiefs is nothing else than to want to weaken our power by [removing] the most just, useful, rightful and reasonable authority it has; certainly more necessary to the general good than the authority of justice. . . . [This authority] has been enjoyed by all princes and lords up to the present and by those living now. It would be a piteous and detestable thing if princes had to risk their goods and lives for the defence of the common weal without the military service of their subjects, apart from those who volunteered to do it, and without being able to compel them. Because of the inordinate love which many people have for their particular profit, the public welfare would never survive if it were not entrusted to princes, who are public persons. Where is the prince or lord who does not have the authority to constrain his subjects to follow him in war, especially for the defence of the land . . . ?

Certainly for the relief both of the nobles and of the people, and so that they will not be worked on our behalf beyond their capabilities and power, we have enquired and tried to ascertain the value of all fiefs and sub-fiefs which are held from or under us by nobles and others, so that a light and easily bearable charge, according to their powers, may be fixed for them and so that everyone will know what he has to do and thenceforth, whatever happens, will not be worked beyond [what is laid down in] our ordinance. . . .

Thus it evidently appears that this [military service] carefully organized and established will be useful and profitable to all estates, for the general alleviation of all and for the maintenance of the public welfare of our lands, because in all quarters by this means people will be ready to defend themselves if necessary, which will very much deter enemies from trying anything against us and our lands so that, with God's help, we shall have peace, for which one cannot pay too much. For these reasons we have decided and concluded that, whatever happens, we shall not abandon this [military service] but by all means maintain it. There is no need for the discontent of our people to menace us, for although God our Creator has given us power and means to remedy their follies in such a way as to provide an example for them, nonetheless, we know for certain that we have not done wrong to them but rather in our sins towards God, to punish which he could send them this unjust desire. Since we do not wish to resist his pleasure and we want to obey his decisions, there is no need for our people to move against us, nor for this reason to acquire the reputation of being rebels, disobedient and traitors, as some of their neighbours maintain. For any time they seriously wish, in agreement, to send to us asking us to abdicate the government of our seignory, declaring us not to be agreeable to them, we shall gladly abdicate. . . .

We are writing to you at length about this to reply to the false assertions which the detractors of our honour have spread around and do daily spread around among our good people against the truth, and so that you will be fully notified and assured of the complete good will which we, as the person whom the thing mainly and more than any other concerns, have for the safety, honour and maintenance of our said lands and subjects. And we wish and order you expressly to notify, declare and proclaim the content of these present letters in our justification in all the places and to all the persons you think necessary, so that our good and loyal subjects know and understand for certain that we have not wished and do not wish to do anything in our said lands to trouble, molest or harm them, but only to guard, defend and preserve them from the power and damnable desires of our and their enemies and evil-wishers, without wishing to spare our person, nor all the belongings we possess in this world, for the sake of the public welfare of our lands.

Dearest and well loved, may our Lord have you in his holy care. Written in our castle of Hesdin, 19 December 1470.

No doubt the rumblings of discontent so hypocritically rebutted by the duke in this document continued, but little evidence of them has survived. In 1474 there were complaints about the newly established *Parlement* of Malines, and in the same year a German report suggested that the inhabitants of Luxembourg would welcome another ruler.[1] The discontent in Guelders in 1475–6 is only feebly attested; in any case there was every likelihood that Charles would remain unpopular in this conquered duchy. As to Johann Knebel's reports of a state of near rebellion both in Burgundy and in Holland, in 1476, these, like so much else in his colourful chronicle, cannot be taken at face value. When the authorities, especially of the county of Burgundy, tried to arrange local truces with the Swiss, they were not verging on rebellion; nor did the opposition of the Dutch clergy to ducal taxation amount to the revolt of that province. In fact the only authentic armed revolt against Charles the Bold was that of Alsace in April 1474, which was in so many respects a special case that it would be unwise to regard it as evidence of the duke's unpopularity, still less of the weakness of his authority in his patrimonial lands. Of course, Charles was faced with the inevitable urban riots and commotions: at Ghent in 1467 and again, very nearly, in

---

[1] Above, p. 187 and *Politische Correspondenz*, i. 744–5. For the next sentence, see *Dépêches des ambassadeurs milanais*, ii. 94, and, for what follows, Knebel, *Diarium*, iii. 29–30 and 66. Basin, *Louis XI*, ii. 312–28 also seems to exaggerate the opposition to Charles.

1476, and at Zierikzee, where there was an isolated anti-tax riot in August 1472 made serious by the murder of two officials.[1]

If there is no substantial evidence of a crisis of confidence in Charles the Bold himself at the end of his reign, exactly the same is true of the governmental machinery of his territories. Far from disintegrating, the administrative framework remained intact and for the most part in working order, in spite of the immense strains imposed on it through 1476. The only hint of breakdown seems to have been an episode in November 1476 when the Estates of Hainault were assembled at the duke's command to hear a ducal official expound the duke's wishes, but no official arrived. The hard-worked chancellor, then at Malines, had forgotten to send someone, and the Estates had to be recalled later in the month.[2]

The material well-being and general economy of the Burgundian lands must surely have suffered severely from the wars and policies of Charles the Bold and the inevitable financial demands that went with them. But detailed evidence of economic troubles in 1475–6 has yet to be assembled. The burden of taxation is extremely hard to assess. It has been calculated that Malines paid something like one-fifth of its annual income to the duke, but half of this represented payment of the fine imposed for its rebellious behaviour in 1467.[3] Naturally, every town tried to persuade the duke to reduce the level of taxation. Much material damage was caused not by taxation but by the recruiting, movement and general behaviour of large numbers of troops. In Burgundy there was large-scale pillaging in 1476, and as early as April 1475 the civic authorities of Dijon had complained to Charles the Bold that some of his Italian mercenaries had broken into the town gaol to rescue one of their number.[4] The *Chronijk van Overmaas* is full of complaints about the misdeeds and damage caused by the ducal troops and their horses which were operating in that

[1] For Ghent, see above, pp. 6–9 and AGR CC21845, f. 29b. For Zierikzee, which has not yet caught the attention of historians, see especially *Cronycke van Hollandt*, 333a–b, *Collection de documens inédits*, i. 270–1, Bittmann, *Ludwig XI. und Karl der Kühne*, ii (1). 50, Innsbruck LRA Sigmund IVa no. 182 (transcribed in RTA material) and, for example, ADN B2104 f. 30b.

[2] ADN B10441, fos. 17a, 18–20 and 161.

[3] Trouvé, *HKOM* lvi (1952), 63–7. For the next sentence see for example de Boer, *HB* lxiv (1957), 403–12, on Haarlem.

[4] De la Marche, *Mémoires*, i. 140–1, and *Correspondance de la mairie de Dijon*, i. 161–2. For the next sentence, see *Chronijk van Overmaas*, 39–40, 45, 46–7, etc.

area in the summers of 1473 and 1474 on the campaigns of Guelders and Neuss, and it takes due note, also, of the widespread economic effects of the siege of Neuss.

Also significant, but hard to assess, was the effect of the economic warfare waged by Charles the Bold. Here the damage must surely have increased considerably at the end of the reign as the ducal bans proliferated. On 20 June 1474 all safe-conducts issued to French merchants during the truce were cancelled and the goods of all French merchants in Burgundian territories were declared forfeit, the proceeds to be shared equally between the duke and whoever contrived to seize the goods.[1] On the same day all trade with the rebellious subjects of the archbishop of Cologne, with the duke of Austria's subjects, and with Strasbourg and Basel was prohibited. Imports of Rhenish wines into the Burgundian Low Countries were banned in January 1476 and, later that year, prohibitions were imposed on the circulation in the duke's territories of certain French coins, of gold and silver coins of Liège, and of certain coins minted at Cologne. It would be interesting to be able to confirm that these and other similar prohibitions caused widespread economic disruption in Charles the Bold's territories, but for the time being this must remain a mere hypothesis.

Just as the administration of Charles the Bold's territories seems to have continued working quite effectively right to the end of his reign, so the military organization remained in being even though pressures were put on it. In spite of desertions, in spite of recruiting difficulties, in spite of delays in performing military service or even outright refusals, Charles the Bold was able to field a powerful army in March 1476, reconstitute and even enlarge it in June 1476, and retain or reassemble sufficient forces to fight a successful campaign in October 1476 against the duke of Lorraine. Right at the end, on the eve of the battle of Nancy, a large body of reinforcements was successfully though with difficulty recruited in the Low Countries. There is every reason to believe that, had Charles the Bold taken the advice of his captains and withdrawn from Lorraine at the end of 1476, he would have been able to raise another substantial army in the spring of 1477.

Outright refusals to serve in the Burgundian army seem to have

---

[1] For this and what follows see Gorissen, *De Raadkamer te Maastricht*, 144–5, 208, 215, 222 and 268 and ADN B10439, f. 41b, B10440, fos. 26a, 30b–31, 33b and 34a–b, and B10441, f. 21b.

been exceptional. Asked by the bastard Anthony to send a contingent for the defence of the duchy in September 1475, the civic authorities at Dijon resolved to make 'the best and fullest explanations and excuses'; on account of the poverty of the inhabitants they could not perform this military duty. But they willingly mustered a contingent to serve with the forces promised by the Estates at Salins in mid-July 1476.[1] In 1475 Charles the Bold accused the vassals of Brabant and Flanders of ignoring his instructions to turn out and help defend Artois and Hainault from the French, and he ordered the cost of the damages done by the French, assessed at £14,000, to be paid by them. Vassals invariably resisted requests for military service outside their own lands, even for pay. Thus from November 1475 at the latest the Flemish forces in garrison at Abbeville were in a state of near-mutiny and some nobles were prosecuted at the end of 1476 for refusing to serve there.[2] At the end of 1475 Charles the Bold found it necessary to order the immediate arrest and execution of those members of the garrison of St. Quentin who had gone home without their captain's permission and, likewise, on 12 January 1476 he sent his officers in Hainault a list of deserters from the Nijmegen garrison who were to be apprehended and executed.[3] The accounts of the bailiff of Hainault vividly demonstrate the lack of enthusiasm for military service among the duke's vassals and their men there in 1476:

> Because few of the nobles of the said land of Hainault did their duty in sending the requisite number of men to Thuin on 21 August the bailiff wrote to them again telling them to send them to Thuin at once because, in their default, he would quickly place their lands and lordships in the hands of my lord the duke.

On 30 September the bailiff ordered the arrest of those troops who had been reviewed at Thuin, received their pay, and then returned into Hainault instead of accompanying Philippe de Croy, count of Chimay, to Lorraine. But such difficulties certainly did not

---

[1] *Correspondance de la mairie de Dijon*, i. 176–7 and 189–90. For the next sentence, see *Collection de documens inédits*, i. 249–59 and AGR CC4183, account for the year ending 30 September 1476, fos. 1a–2b. On the damage itself, see Bocquet, *Recherches sur la population rurale de l'Artois et du Boulonnais*, 64–5 and 134–8.

[2] AGR CC21844, f. 21 and CC21845, fos. 9b, 16b, 18b, 25b, 26b, etc.

[3] ADN B10440, fos. 21a–22 and 25a and, for what follows, fos. 41b (whence the quotation), 42b, 43 and 45.

amount to the breakdown of the Burgundian military machine which, after all, was by this time largely based on English and Italian mercenaries. The foundation of Charles the Bold's military power was cash, not loyalty.

Charles the Bold's finances, once he had used up the treasure said to have been left him by his father in the castle of Lille, are supposed to have been overstrained in a manner little short of disastrous. But the detailed evidence for this financial exhaustion has yet to be produced. The ducal accounts, for example, which might be expected to provide valuable information on this point, have yet to be scrutinized in a systematic and scholarly manner. It really is not good enough to consult one series of accounts only, those of the receiver-general of all finances, and pretend that an accurate picture of the ducal finances as a whole may be obtained from them. When a historian points out that the annual average expenses of the receiver-general of all finances rose from £366,000 in the last ten years of Philip the Good's reign to £693,000 under Charles, he is by no means providing information about the ducal income as a whole. But in that supposedly authoritative work, *The Cambridge Economic History of Europe*, we find this historian cited as authority for the following quite erroneous statement: 'Charles's average annual revenue was nearly twice as large as the average income of his father during the last ten years of his rule (a yearly average of 366,000 *li. tur.* for Philip and of 693,000 *li. tur.* for Charles)'.[1] In spite of his misleading title the receiver-general of all finances did not receive all the duke's finances, nor did he pay all the duke's expenses. The turnover on his account increased under Duke Charles partly because that duke reorganized the accounting system and made it more centralized than it had been under his father. An exact notion of his global financial resources and expenditure will only be obtained by examining the various regional and local accounts of all his territories, a task (beyond the scope of this work) made more difficult and complex because of his abolition of the provincial receipts-general. Instead, we may glance at some other aspects of the duke's finances which perhaps reflect their strength and weakness almost as sensitively as the accounts themselves.

[1] Professor J. Bartier in *Algemene geschiedenis der Nederlanden*, iii. 293, and Dr. E. B. Fryde in *The Cambridge Economic History*, iii. 506. An analysis of the accounts of the receipt-general is given by Mollat, *RH* ccxix (1958), 285–321.

A great deal of information has survived about loans raised by Charles the Bold. The same sources of credit were open to him as had been exploited by his predecessors and were being exploited in France by Louis XI. Civil servants had their wages and salaries withheld or temporarily diminished;[1] the towns were laid under contribution. In 1471 and 1472 Duke Charles raised loans to the value of nearly £400,000 by compelling his towns to create and sell annuities and lend him the capital sums thus realized. In 1473 he ordered the closing of Italian pawnshops in his territories, but their owners were subsequently permitted to recommence trading in return for a substantial loan. As in earlier years, so under Charles the Bold, the loan was a device for obtaining short-term finance, and the individual sums were often very small. Thus when, early in 1474, Charles's officials contrived to borrow some 14,000 francs in Burgundy, a great majority of creditors provided less than 10 francs each, and loans of as little as $2\frac{1}{2}$ francs were solemnly collected and entered up in the ducal books.[2] As early as 1471 Charles appointed special officials to take charge of the business of raising loans. In 1476 officials sent to Dijon to borrow money there were instructed to

... summon before them or their deputies the duke's *procureurs* and receivers in each country and region, together with others who might be of assistance to them, and insist on interrogating them secretly under oath as to what wealthy ecclesiastics there are in their country, what laymen, officials, clerks at law, advocates, notaries and others in a position to lend, stating the value of their belongings and how much it seems to him they might lend to the duke. From this the said commissioners are to compile a book or register in which are to be entered the names and surnames of all those whom they know to be able to lend and the sum which the said *procureur* or receiver suggested might be imposed on them. This done, the register is to be brought or sent by the said commissioners to my lord the duke, so that he can see to what total the said loans amount.[3]

---

[1] See, for example, for France, Tardif, *Monuments historiques*, p. 489 no. 2504, and for Charles the Bold, Stein, *BEC* xcviii (1937), 347–8 and the heading *Autre recepte des parties extraordinaires* of the receiver-general's accounts, for example ADN B2099, fos. 31a–45a. For what follows, see Bigwood, *Régime juridique et économique du commerce de l'argent*, i. 28–9, 386–7 etc. and the unpublished Lille dissertation, Maeght, *Les emprunts de Charles le Téméraire*.
[2] ACO B1773, fos. 52b–78b, compare Clerc, *États Généraux*, i. 146 n. 1. For the next sentence, see AGR CC4181, f. 161b.
[3] ACO B17, fos. 21–2, transcribed in BN Coll. de Bourgogne, 99, pp. 742–3.

In general, it does seem that Charles the Bold was a more success-ful borrower than his father had been. His continuing ability to raise credit lends no credence to the idea that he was on the verge of financial ruin. Right up to his death he was obtaining goods on credit from the Florentine banker Tommaso Portinari. He was also active and enterprising in devising and levying new taxes. One of these, the 'sixth penny' or 16½ per cent on the annual income of fiefs, was levied in 1470 and 1475 but with limited success. Although the vassals evidently regarded this tax as an alternative to military service in person, and the duke conceded this point in 1475, yet his officials in Flanders were soon afterwards insisting that payment of the sixth penny was unacceptable as an alternative to turning out to help garrison Abbeville.[1] Unlike the sixth penny on fiefs, the yield of which was unimportant, Charles's other fiscal novelty produced over £100,000, partly through the tax itself, partly in payments to be quit of it. This was the imposition in all his northern terri-tories of a tax on feudal lands newly acquired by clerics and religious institutions. Such a tax was well-known in France but virtually unknown in the Burgundian Low Countries, though the obligation on religious houses to obtain a licence from the prince to acquire land in mortmain was widely accepted and had been the subject of legislation by earlier Valois dukes in Flanders, Brabant and elsewhere. Charles the Bold's ordinance of 10 July 1474 ordering the immediate return by religious houses of a detailed statement of all lands acquired by them in the last sixty years, with a view to levying a tax on them equivalent to three years' income, fell like a bombshell on the unsuspecting clergy and caused an immediate chorus of protest. Nobody could have been more rebellious and defiant than the Sister Agnes, who wrote as follows, in Dutch, from a convent in Antwerp in September 1474.[2]

---

[1] AGR CC21844, f. 21. On this and what follows see *IAGRCC* iv. 144–51 and 154–61, Bartier, *Le sixième denier et l'amortissement sous Charles le Téméraire* and the same in *Algemene geschiedenis der Nederlanden*, iii. 295–6. In addition, on what follows, see Jongkees, *Staat en Kerk in Holland en Zeeland*, 214–40, de Moreau, *Église en Belgique*, iv. 92–106 and Bartier, *Charles le Téméraire*, 247–52.
[2] The Falkonsklooster, destroyed in 1793. The letter is printed by van Gelder in *BGBH* xxvi (1901), 451–3.

Reverend father, may it please you to know that we received and spoke to your messenger on the eve of St. Matthew,[1] who told us that you had requested to know from us how we were getting on in our land with these unjust ordinances and commands of the prince. You should know that more than a month has elapsed since we were ordered to set down all our earthly possessions in writing within eight days, on pain of 100 silver marks. But we have not yet done this, nor are we willing to do it, and we have always put the decision off with sweet words to the commissioners, saying that we stand under our superiors, without whose advice and consent we can do nothing, who are also far away from us. Meanwhile the three Estates of Brabant, that is the clergy, the knights and the commons, together decided to prevent this if they could. The clergy, who had been assembled at Antwerp, sent a messenger to us asking us to let the convents of our Order know that deputies from every house should be sent to the *Parlement* of Malines to empower there a proctor to claim justice for all the regular clergy of Brabant. And the day fixed for this is the Monday before [St. Michael] the archangel's Day,[2] ... and we are hopeful of obtaining justice. On this matter a doctor of Louvain, called Master Raymond,[3] has written up a good thirteen pages of relevant material from the canon law. And in this affair we have also engaged Willem Storm, the prior of Bethlehem,[4] who is also one of those principally involved. Once again, dearly beloved father, do not give in but ask for a delay until you have heard how we get on. Some people have given in, which is a pity, because their possessions have been served at the prince's table. We would rather follow St. Ambrose's example and give up our lives in this cause than hand over the church's possessions, which do not belong to us, to the prince. And we would rather pay the price of obtaining an equitable judgement than give things unjustly to our mortal enemies. If we cannot obtain justice this will be due to force and power and we would rather let our things be taken away thus than willingly hand them over. Nor will we agree to make any compromise settlement, because if one is made, others will follow. We have been permitted by the councillors to show all our privileges in ecclesiastical law at the above-mentioned meeting, and the [execution of the duke's] ordinances is deferred until Michaelmas.[5] So we hope for the best.

---

[1] 20 September.
[2] 26 September.
[3] Raymondo da Marliano, who was subsequently appointed to defend the Dutch clergy in their appeal against the tax.
[4] At Herent, near Louvain.
[5] 29 September.

This rumpus among the clerics was echoed by the clerical chronicler Jehan Molinet when he claimed that 'nothing so tarnished the reputation of Duke Charles as his giving credence to certain evil spirits, inflamed with burning greed, who whispered in his ear the advice to levy three years' revenues from benefices, chapels, and chantries [which were] without licences of mortmain in order to help finance his affairs'.[1] But, though the Dutch clergy held out until well into 1476 and some hardy spirits were even taken into custody, the duke had his way and his money in the end. Nor were the proceeds of this activity slow in coming in: already in the year 1474 some £63,000 was entered in the books of the duke's receiver-general as having been paid over by a special receiver of these moneys.[2] Nor was Burgundy proper ignored, for an ordinance of 17 March 1474 had ordered the verification of all licences of mortmain and other ducal privileges issued in the two Burgundies during the previous sixty years. In all this the duke must not be envisaged as risking unpopularity, opposition, even open rebellion, in the pursuit of desperate expedients to stave off financial ruin. On the contrary, he was successfully exploiting a valuable source of revenue. He was milking the ecclesiastical cow which had long been avariciously eyed by princely and municipal governments throughout Europe. Taxation of one wealthy sector of the community does not necessarily provoke general revolution. Nor can the clergy of Charles the Bold's territories as a whole be described as seething with discontent; for the most part they merely grumbled and gave way.

A good deal of information about the duke's finances is to be found in Charles the Bold's correspondence with his senior financial officers. This source of information reveals a series of short-term crises rather than continuous or complete financial exhaustion. Thus on 8 June 1475 they wrote to the duke explaining the dire need for instant cash to pay garrisons and meet other immediate expenses; until more money came in from the tax on newly acquired ecclesiastical lands in Brabant and Holland they would have to have recourse to the somewhat dangerous expedient of selling domanial

[1] Molinet, *Chroniques*, i. 169; compare *Chronijk van Overmaas*, 50–1 and see too *Cronycke van Hollandt*, fos. 360a–363b.
[2] ADN B2099, fos. 29b–30a. For the next sentence, see BN Coll. de Bourgogne 59, f. 49.

rents.[1] Even after Charles the Bold's two crushing defeats at Grandson and Murten the impression one gets, for example from the letter the duke sent in July 1476 from Burgundy to his chancellor and lieutenant-general in the Low Countries, is one of immediate but surmountable financial difficulties rather than of a complete collapse.[2]

From the duke of Burgundy.

Fair cousin and most dear and loyal chancellor, we have received your letters written in our town of Ghent on the first day of this present month in which you let us know, as you, chancellor, have recently informed us, that you were in our said town of Ghent, where the lords of Chimay, Esquerdes, Humbercourt, Aymeries and Clary had assembled with the first president of our *Parlement*, the *président des comptes*, the protonotary of Clugny, the treasurers and *généraux*, and our sovereign bailiff of Flanders, in order to get ready to make arrangements for our frontier garrisons according to what had been agreed beforehand and ordered you in our letters, and so that our said treasurers and *généraux* could regularize the payment of the said garrisons. [You also let us know] that, before your departure [thence], you had news about [our defeat on] the vigil of St. John. Considering this and the rumours which were spreading round the countries bordering on our lands over there you, on the advice of the above-named and with the knowledge of our dearest and well loved companion the duchess, decided to reinforce all our garrisons immediately and, over and above this, to raise as many troops as possible. To prevent their excuses and expedite their turn-out you have also decided to pay them with moneys from our *aides* and other available sources. . . .

Concerning which, fair cousin and most dear and loyal chancellor, we have been and are well content with the good work done by you and the above-named in suggesting and deciding on the organizing and reinforcing of our garrisons and the raising of others of our troops. But, as regards the payment of our garrisons, which you have decided to do with moneys from our *aides*, we are not, nor can we be, content, since you, chancellor, know well enough and cannot ignore that we have never meant the proceeds from our *aides* to be used or employed in any other way than for the payment of our army established for the security and defence of our person and not otherwise. Furthermore, you also know and realize that, if we establish and maintain any garrisons, wherever they are, our said lands are bound to maintain and support them

---

[1] Stein, *BEC* xcviii (1937), 300–01. Compare the other letters printed by Stein, *BEC* xcviii (1937), 341–8, and see too the ducal letters of 27 April 1475 in *Analectes historiques*, vii. 391–4.

[2] This letter to Guillaume Hugonet and Adolf, lord of Ravenstein, is printed in *Analectes historiques*, iii. 59–63.

financially at their expense and not from the proceeds of our *aides*. In accordance with this, on the request and remonstrance which we have made in this our town of Salins to the people of the three Estates of our lands round here, assembled for this purpose, they have generously, freely and without any limitations agreed to furnish and maintain all the garrisons in these lands of ours round here at their expense, in time of war, truce and peace. And these lands are neither so rich in population in towns and places, nor in money, as our lands over there, but on the contrary they have been more devastated and troubled because of the war.

So, arrange things in such a way that, if any money, at the time you receive this, has been taken and used from our said *aides* for the payment of the said garrisons over there, you replace and repay it at once and without delay from where it was taken, and this at the expense and charge of our said lands over there. And we let you know that, if you do not do this, we will have such moneys taken and recovered from you, chancellor, and from our said treasurers and *généraux*; and we want you to tell them this. Besides this, following what we recently explained and commanded to you through the chaplain, we order you yet again to see to the pay ment of the said garrisons with such moneys as the said chaplain has informed or will inform you about.

Furthermore, you are to recruit and send to us, in such a way and by such a route as the chaplain will explain or has explained, and as diligently and quickly as possible, the 10,000 combatants we need to replenish our companies of ordinance and put us in the field. And, besides this number, you are to raise all the fief and sub-fief holders in our lands over there, and send with the utmost diligence to our land of Lorraine, if you haven't done this already, the 400 lances of our ordinance which we have stationed in our northern territories, in order to defend and preserve that land until we can provide for it more amply. Besides this, you are to send us the proceeds of the instalment of our said *aide* which fell due last April and has already been received, amounting to £200,000, together with all the moneys from our domain, likewise levied and received, and indeed everything that can be levied and obtained both from our said domain and *aides* and otherwise, together with the moneys from the constable ['s lands], already received, amounting to about £60,000,[1] as well as those yet to be received, so that we can pay our troops with this money and use it for our current needs.

---

[1] Since 1471 Charles had been enjoying the revenues of the constable's confiscated estates in Burgundian territory. By the treaty of Soleuvre other important places owned by the constable, including St. Quentin and Ham, were ceded to Charles. See above, pp. 251 and 352.

Furthermore, concerning our artillery, you are to send us up to four bombards with their attendants, and as many serpentines, bows, arrows, pikes, lances, *vouges*, spears and other weapons, and as much powder, as you can find. . . .

Fair cousin and most dear and loyal chancellor, may our Lord be your guard. Written in our town of Salins, 13 July 1476.

P.S. Fair cousin and most dear and loyal chancellor, we could not be more amazed that you and our said treasurers and *généraux* have dared to or wanted to touch our said *aide*, as mentioned above, and that you did it, or wanted to do it, because you held us for lost, and our army likewise. However, this is not the case, but on the contrary, thanks be to God, we have our army around us and, next week, we plan to hold reviews of those who are newly-arrived so that thereafter, with God's help, we can take the field against our enemies. So be sure, treasurers and *généraux*, that you do not touch our *aide*, either for our garrisons or otherwise than for our said army.

Charles

The financial status of fifteenth-century rulers is reflected with some accuracy in the amount of extraordinary taxes or *aides* which their subjects were persuaded to vote them. Is it true, as some dissatisfied ducal subjects complained in 1470, that Charles the Bold was receiving more than his father had from this source of taxation?[1] Certainly the 120,000 crowns of 48 groats he was granted in 1470 in each of the next three years significantly exceeded the 97,700 riders his father had been receiving annually in the last ten years of his reign from the northern territories excluding Artois.[2] But Duke Charles managed even better in 1473, when he obtained 500,000 crowns per annum for six years from the northern lands and, to set against the mere £6,200 of Tours per annum his father had been receiving from the two Burgundies, an annual £100,000 *estevenants* for six years from these southern lands.[3] Thus, in terms of *aides* granted and levied, Duke Charles was astonishingly successful. Not only did he obtain a great deal more money than his father, but he extended to all territories the system of obtaining *aides* in advance

---

[1] Above, p. 400.

[2] See the table in Vaughan, *Philip the Good*, 262. For Charles's global *aides*, see *Actes des États Généraux*, 165, 202–3, etc., and on the *aides* in general, see p. 189 above.

[3] A *livre estevenant* = 22s. of Tours, Billioud, *États de Bourgogne*, 147 n. 2. On the *aides* from the two Burgundies see the same work, pp. 405–11.

for a number of years, and at the same time he successfully introduced a single centralized northern *aide* voted by the States General of the Burgundian Netherlands. In view of these much increased, and regularized, financial impositions it is scarcely surprising that, towards the end of the reign especially, the duke was confronted here and there with an occasional refusal to accept some additional burden, such as money to pay for carts for his army, for troops to garrison the frontier, or for ships to defend the coast.[1] These refusals culminated in the refusal of the States General, in April and May 1476, to accept what amounted to universal military conscription and to vote any further sums of money. They rightly insisted that the 1473 six-year *aide* had been voted on the express condition that no further demands would be made during this period. Yet time and time again Charles successfully persuaded the Estates of individual countries to ignore that condition. The Estates of the two Burgundies agreed in July 1476 to pay for the defence of their frontiers in addition to the annual *aide*; the Flemish voted additional moneys in 1474 and 1475, though they turned down a further request in 1476; even the obstinate and probably impoverished people of Artois eventually agreed to an additional *aide*, in the winter of 1476–7; and in Hainault additional *aides* were granted in 1475 and 1476.[2]

On the whole Charles the Bold was supremely successful, even at the end of the reign, in obtaining money from his subjects—whether in the form of loans, *aides*, or otherwise. He seems neither to have been facing financial ruin nor large-scale rebellion, and one can only conclude that, in spite of the very evident pressures placed upon it by his activities and policies, the framework of the Burgundian state remained firm until his defeat and death. It is fitting therefore that this history of Burgundy under the Valois dukes should conclude with some account of Charles the Bold's last, and most catastrophic, military disaster, for it was this, rather than internal disintegration, that brought its history to a sudden and dramatic close in January 1477.

---

[1] See for example Bartier, *Charles le Téméraire*, 259, Hirschauer, *États d'Artois*, ii. 39 and i. 211–12, *Correspondance de la mairie de Dijon*, i. 177, and Blok, *Eene hollandsche stad*, 59–60. For what follows see *Actes des États Généraux*, 225–66, and Gachard, *Études et notices historiques*, i. 1–19.

[2] Billioud, *États de Bourgogne*, 146–53 = *MA* xxvi (1913), 352–9; Blockmans, *Staten en Leden*, 163–4, etc. and *Handelingen van de Staten en Leden*, nos. 152, 162, etc.; Hirschauer, *États d'Artois*, ii. 40; and *IAEH*, i. xciv.

It must have been indecision, as much as the need to reorganize and reinforce his army, which kept Charles the Bold camped at La Rivière, 10 km west of Pontarlier on the frontier of the Franche-Comté and the Vaud, for two months in the late summer of 1476. He arrived there on 22 July, a month after his defeat at Murten, and remained until 25 September. His first thoughts, his overriding emotions, were of revenge against the allies of the League of Constance who had just defeated him; 'these boorish Swiss', as one of his Italian captains loosely described them.[1] But several more pressing affairs intervened to protect the Swiss from yet another Burgundian invasion of their homelands. Firstly, the project of a personal meeting with Louis XI, which was seriously entertained by Charles and Louis intermittently throughout 1476, became an urgent priority for Charles in July.[2] The Milanese ambassador was able to report from La Rivière on 31 July that the meeting between the two rulers had been fixed for 20 August, on a bridge over the River Yonne at Auxerre. It was evidently Charles who took the initiative on this occasion. Louis was far from enthusiastic. He was at Plessis-les-Tours suffering from a bout of hypochondria. He told the Milanese ambassador at the French court one morning that he was suffering from a heart tremor, a headache, and piles which he attributed to his not having had sexual intercourse for some time. The duke of Burgundy, the ambassador reported to Duke Galeazzo Maria, was King Louis's 'Turk, the Devil he loathes most in this world'.[3] No wonder the meeting he had been persuaded to agree to never took place.

Other projects and possibilities were revolving in the duke of Burgundy's restless mind at this time. His influence in Savoy had been almost totally undermined by his defeat at Murten, but he still held Duchess Yolande in custody at Rouvres. She might have been used as a key to open the door to Savoy and bring it again under Burgundian control. Indeed, on 7 August, in his last surviving despatch from the Burgundian court, Panigarola reported Duke Charles's plan to lead an army into Savoy to reinstate Yolande and

---

[1] 'Questi vilani Siviceri': Croce, *Vite di avventure*, 117. For Charles at La Rivière, see too above, p. 394.
[2] See for example *Dépêches des ambassadeurs milanais*, i. 282–4; *Briefe und Actenstücke von Mailand*, 182 and 195 and ASM Pot. est. Borgogna, 518–20/14, 129, 209, 389, etc., and, for the next sentence, 447.
[3] *Briefe und Actenstücke von Mailand*, 181.

restore his own position there.[1] But this project, too, was shelved and Charles was rid of the embarrassment of keeping Yolande any longer in prison by her escape to her brother Louis on 2 October.

The abandonment or postponement by Charles the Bold of these hopes of revenge against the Swiss, of a final settlement with Louis XI, and of the recovery of Savoy, were probably due to the state of affairs in Lorraine.[2] He had conquered that duchy at the end of 1475, expelled its ruler the youthful Duke René, installed Burgundian garrisons in the principal places, had himself accepted and proclaimed duke of Lorraine by the three Estates in Nancy, and entrusted the country to a veteran soldier, Jehan de Rubempré, lord of Bièvres, to administer it as his governor and lieutenant-general. But this apparently secure possession had been slipping from his grasp ever since Duke René's partisans, encouraged by Charles's defeat at Grandson, and possibly helped by the French, had seized Vaudémont, both castle and county, in April 1476. The efforts of these supporters of René were uncoordinated, and René himself was absent at this time, either at Strasbourg, seeking that city's military assistance, or in Normandy, collecting a legacy of £200,000 of Tours from his dying grandmother, or fighting with his other allies on the field of Murten. His absences doubtless delayed the reconquest of his duchy, but they bore valuable fruit in the shape of troops from Strasbourg, money to hire mercenaries, and, above all, the practical demonstration on the battlefield of Murten of his hostility to Charles the Bold and of his profound commitment to the League of Constance which he had joined when he was accepted as a member of the Lower Union on 18 April 1475. After Murten, especially in the second half of July, the reconquest of Lorraine from the Burgundians proceeded apace until, at the end of the month, after René had

---

[1] ASM Pot. est. Borgogna 518–20/458.

[2] For what follows on Lorraine I have relied on the narratives of Witte in *JGLG* iii (1891), 232–92 and iv (1892), 74–137, Pfister, *Histoire de Nancy*, i. 412–512, and Toutey, *Charles le Téméraire et la Ligue de Constance*, 250–302. Much less valuable are Berlet, *MSBGH* viii (1892), 297–393 and ix (1893), 1–120, Calmet, *Histoire de Lorraine*, v. cols. 330–87, Digot, *Histoire de Lorraine*, iii, Gain, *Histoire de Lorraine*, Huguenin, *Guerre de Lorraine*, Parisot, *Histoire de Lorraine*, i and Rolland, *Guerre de René II*. The main chronicles are Basin, *Louis XI*, ii. 305–40, de Blarru, *Nanceis, Chronique de Lorraine*, ed. Marchal, 186–311, de Commynes, *Mémoires*, ii. 128–53, Knebel, *Diarium*, ii. 430 and iii. 1–107, Lud, *Dialogue*, ed. Lepage, and Molinet, *Chroniques*, i. 148–69. The only published documentary material of importance is in *Eidgenössischen Abschiede*, ii. 600–640.

put in a brief personal appearance to receive the surrender of Épinal, his supporters pitched camp round Nancy, by that time practically the only important place still remaining in Burgundian hands.

This first attempt to besiege the capital of Lorraine was badly organized and unsuccessful. Duke René was absent at the Congress of Fribourg, where his requests for immediate help in the reconquest of his duchy were met by his allies with promises only of agreement to help in principle at some unspecified date in the future. Duke Charles was known to be reassembling his forces at La Rivière and they insisted first on awaiting his next move. Louis XI was of even less use to René as an ally: he promised to help him *after* he had recovered his duchy. Meanwhile the siege of Nancy was easily raised by a time-honoured ruse. The Burgundians contrived to have a messenger, carrying letters announcing that Duke Charles was at Neufchâteau on his way to relieve Nancy, apprehended by the besiegers. They fled that very night on 10–11 August, so hurriedly that the delighted Burgundians found six cart-loads of Alsace wine in their deserted quarters next morning. A week later the situation was restored by the arrival of Duke René, who immediately restarted the siege and organized a close investment of the town.

Charles the Bold could scarcely have stood aside and done nothing while the duchy of Lorraine was snatched from him by a ragged collection of local volunteers intermittently led by a boy who had failed to obtain help from any of his allies. In April he talked about sending a body of English archers to defend Lorraine; in June and July he tried, but failed, to persuade the nobles of Luxembourg to fight for him there; but it was apparently only in August that he finally decided to march into Lorraine in person at the head of his troops.[1] Why then did he tarry till late September at La Rivière? Evidently because of the other schemes mentioned above and perhaps also because he did not take the activities of René and his friends very seriously. He was probably encouraged to defer his march by the news of their temporary abandonment of the siege of Nancy in mid-August and he may also have reckoned that René himself, after he had re-established the siege in person, was unlikely to risk the destruction of his own capital by bombardment or assault. Perhaps too, Charles was relying on Cola de Monforte, count of Campobasso, who was under orders to assist Jehan de Rubempré in the defence of Nancy and to look after the duke's interests in Lorraine. The

[1] *Cal. state papers. Milan,* i. 223 and *Recueil du Fay,* 136 and 137.

curious delays of this Italian captain, his complete failure to advance against the Lorrainers at this time, have been attributed to the probable fact that he was already a traitor.[1] In any event, when Charles the Bold eventually did take the field, on 25 September, he was too late. The English contingent in the garrison of Nancy mutinied at the end of September and Jehan de Rubempré was forced to capitulate on 6 October. It was certainly this mutiny, not starvation, which caused the surrender, though the famous account, by one of the most imaginative chroniclers of the age, of how de Rubempré sent Duke René a large horse-meat pie and received in exchange capons, venison and three sorts of wine, may possibly mean that the garrison had been short of provisions.[2] It was only on 11 October that Charles the Bold arrived on the scene and united his forces with those of Campobasso in the neighbourhood of Toul.

The army which Charles now had at his disposal for the reconquest of Lorraine comprised four separate elements. The forces he had brought with him from La Rivière, which the abbot of Lure disparagingly reckoned at 10,000 men, 5,000 of them worth nothing and the other 5,000 of moderate value only; the count of Campobasso and his men, who had stood by inactive while Nancy was besieged and taken; the troops who had been garrisoning Nancy under Jehan de Rubempré; and, finally, a body of reinforcements from the Netherlands under Philippe de Croy, count of Chimay, comprising over 8,000 combatants on foot who had set out for Lorraine in September and October in the blue and white ducal uniforms issued to them and with two months' pay in their pockets.[3]

Duke René, with his ill-disciplined and exiguous army of French-speaking Lorrainers and German-speaking contingents from Strasbourg, Basel and elsewhere, failed to attack these Burgundian forces piecemeal and he also failed to prevent them from uniting. Indeed, after being marched and counter-marched fruitlessly up and down the Moselle valley in October his troops melted away altogether. Leaving garrisons in most of the principal places of his duchy, René once more went off to seek help from his fellow-members of the League of Constance, while Charles the Bold, apparently acting

---

[1] Croce, *Vite di avventure*, 121–3 and 148–9 etc., by no means critically refutes Witte, *JGLG* iii (1891), 281 etc.
[2] *Chronique de Lorraine*, ed. Marchal, 234.
[3] AGR CC25543, fos. 46–59b. Of these troops, Brabant and Flanders provided approximately 2,000 each, Artois some 1,300 and Hainault, 1,000.

against the advice of his leading captains, who are said to have suggested a general withdrawal northwards to Luxembourg for the winter, marched south on 19 October from Pont-à-Mousson, and established his siege round Nancy on 22 October. Strategically his situation here was exposed and dangerous. Admittedly there was no prospect of Duke René being able to bring a relieving army to the scene for several weeks, but the citizens and garrison of Nancy hoped, and may have promised, to hold out for two months. Meanwhile Charles the Bold's main line of communication, which was down the Moselle valley through the friendly bishopric of Metz to Thionville and Luxembourg, was tenuous and insecure, and his army was exposed to attack from all directions by Duke René's garrisons. For Charles had this time invested Nancy without troubling to conquer the rest of the duchy of Lorraine, and René's men were installed at Épinal, Vaudémont, Lunéville, Mirecourt, Arches, St. Dié, Bruyères, Remiremont, Rosières-aux-Salines, Gondreville and elsewhere. As the siege continued through November and into December these garrisons became bolder and more aggressive while Charles the Bold's forces were weakened or depleted by hunger and disease.

Charles the Bold's austere resolve to take Nancy whatever the cost can only have been increased by that city's successful and protracted resistance, which itself was perhaps stimulated by the conviction of its defenders that they would all be hanged if they surrendered.[1] His obstinacy was by no means crazy, or even wholly irrational; it was based on the reasonable hope that Nancy would fall before René could obtain the assistance he had been refused so often before. After all, even at this late date, when Savoy, Milan, Hungary, even the count palatine of the Rhine, had abandoned his alliance,[2] Charles could still follow his habitual policy of attacking an enemy who was virtually isolated diplomatically. He had nothing to fear from Louis XI, who had consistently refused to lend serious assistance to René in the past and who seemed to have every intention of continuing to honour his truce with Charles. Louis was perhaps too closely involved at this time with the affairs of his sister Yolande and the fate of her duchy of Savoy to give much attention to Lorraine: it was in November and early December that Yolande was reinstated there as duchess under a French protectorate. Nor had Charles

---

[1] Von Königshoven, *Chronicke*, 379.
[2] See, for example, Bachmann, *Deutsche Reichsgeschichte*, ii. 566–8.

the Bold omitted in the autumn of 1476 to revitalize his alliance with the Emperor by inviting him on 4 November to go ahead with arrangements for the wedding of Maximilian and Mary at Cologne or Aachen. A few weeks later Mary and Maximilian became engaged and on 1 December a dispensation for their marriage was issued at Antwerp by Luca de' Tolenti, bishop of Šibenik and papal nuncio in the Burgundian Low Countries.[1]

As to the Swiss, they were under pressure to make peace with Charles at the end of 1476 from Alexander Nani, bishop of Forlì, on behalf of Pope Sixtus IV, who optimistically hoped to transform Charles the Bold into a crusader,[2] and from Dr. Georg Hesler on behalf of Frederick III. Though they rejected the proposals made to them locally, and apparently without Charles the Bold's knowledge, by the authorities of the Franche-Comté, they were prepared to make peace with Burgundy provided Charles withdrew from Lorraine. They had countered Louis XI's suggestion in September, that they should continue the war against Charles, by pointing out that it was high time Louis himself declared war on Burgundy; and they continued, even after their treaty with him of 7 October, to refuse Duke René any direct military assistance, though they did agree to permit him to raise mercenaries in the cantons. Even when René arrived at Luzern in person and harangued the Swiss diet on 23 November, he failed to persuade the *Eidgenossen* to turn out on campaign for the relief of Nancy. On 4 December Schwyz, Unterwalden and Glarus reported that it was too cold for campaigning; Bern and Fribourg pretended that they feared an attack from the county of Burgundy; Zürich, Luzern and Solothurn agreed to turn out, but only if all the other *Eidgenossen* did so too. René had to be content with an 'unofficial' army of Swiss volunteers, who were to assemble at Basel by 15 December, and the various contingents provided by the members of the Lower Union, who were considerably more willing and helpful than the Swiss. Modern scholarship has not yet satisfactorily elucidated the origin of the funds used by René to pay his Swiss mercenaries but it seems likely that Louis XI was among those who helped to provide the necessary cash.

---

[1] Printed in *Urkundliche Nachträge zur österreichisch-deutschen Geschichte*, 392. See too Rausch, *Die burgundische Heirat Maximilians I*, 157–8.
[2] See, for example, Paquet, *BIHBR* xxv (1949), 128–31. On Nani's missions to Charles in 1476 see Combet, *Louis XI et le Saint-Siège*, 135–40.

René had certainly for some time been in receipt of a pension from the king.

Meanwhile the siege of Nancy dragged on, but we are sadly ill-informed about it. No journal has survived from inside the town; no Burgundian chronicler recorded his experiences; no ambassadors' despatches written at the siege have been unearthed. Those who have described the events of that sombre winter [1] obtained their information at secondhand and disagree with each other, though all agree in emphasizing Duke Charles's increasingly obstinate resolve to hold on come what may. Just as he had refused to believe, on that fateful morning at Murten, that the Swiss would attack him, so now, these writers claim, he refused to believe that the Swiss would come to Duke René's assistance. He refused to believe that the count of Campobasso was contemplating treachery. He refused to believe that a detachment of French troops had been posted near Toul to be ready to help the Lorrainers against him, claiming that this was a story put about by people who wanted him to raise the siege. In Strasbourg it was reported that the defenders were reduced to eating dogs, cats, rats and even mice; that Christmas Eve was so cold that 400 Burgundians froze to death; and that a Burgundian knight who suggested that the duke should be fired into Nancy from a bombard was hanged for his impudence. [2]

Burgundian documentary sources do, however, provide some hard facts about Charles the Bold's prospects and situation during the siege of Nancy in November and December 1476. In spite of attacks on his men by troops from the garrisons of Gondreville and Rosières, the war treasurer's account shows that the duke had contrived to keep open his lines of communication throughout November and even to obtain substantial reinforcements, especially from his northern territories. Thus in mid-November 123 men-at-arms, five 100-strong companies of mounted archers and twenty-seven 100-strong companies of infantry arrived from Artois, Hainault and elsewhere. There was even sufficient cash for these men, as well as 250 workmen and pioneers, to receive eight days' pay on or about 20 November. To these 3,000 men others were subsequently added, at least up till 8 December, when several contingents, including a company of ninety-nine men-at-arms from Burgundy,

[1] Most important are Molinet, Knebel and the author of the Chronique de Lorraine.
[2] Von Königshoven, Chronicke, 379–80 and Straszburgische Archiv-Chronik, 202. For what follows, see AGR CC25543, fos. 70–84, 190–195b, etc.

were described as 'newly arrived'. In December, however, it seems that enemy activity between Thionville and Nancy virtually cut Charles the Bold off from further reinforcements, as well as from cash to pay the troops, for we read in the same account of the transport of cash and artillery in December from Namur and elsewhere through Luxembourg to Thionville, but no further. Three remarkable letters sent at this time by Charles the Bold to Claude de Neuchâtel, lord du Fay, his lieutenant in Luxembourg, illustrate these difficulties, as well as the duke's awareness of the growing danger of his situation:[1]

> From the duke of Burgundy, etc.
> Dearest and loyal cousin and dearest and well loved, because we have been informed of the approach of our enemies and are awaiting a battle hour by hour and also in order to pay our men, we are ordering the people at Thionville who have our cash in their hands to bring it to us. We wish and we expressly command you, immediately you read this, putting aside all excuses, and on [the strength of] all the services that you would ever like to perform for us, to raise in our land of Luxembourg with the utmost possible diligence as many mounted troops and infantry, nobles and others whoever they may be, as can be found in that country and, with them and yourselves in person, accompany and provide an escort for the above-mentioned cash, together with such gunpowder and artillery as is at Thionville, in order to bring them safely to us in the manner we shall be describing to those responsible. Make no fault whatever, for such is our pleasure. Dearest and loyal cousin and dearest and well loved, may our Lord keep you.
> Written in our siege before Nancy, 3 December 1476.
>   Charles.
>   Coulon
> To the lord du Fay our cousin and to Messire Evrard d'Aremberg, lord of Roulers, and to each one of them.

> From the duke of Burgundy, etc.
> Dearest and loyal cousin and dearest and well loved, you know that in other letters of ours we wrote some time ago and very expressly commanded that, immediately on reading them, in accordance with the instructions we verbally gave you, lord of Aremberg, when you left us, you should bring to us all the cash, gunpowder and artillery now in our town of Luxembourg, with as many troops, mounted and on foot, as could be found and raised promptly in our land of Luxembourg. Nonetheless we have heard nothing from you about this and we still cannot ascertain that in this affair you have applied any despatch, duty or diligence. Considering the instructions on this we have given you, we

---

[1] *Recueil du Fay*, 138–9.

are astounded, and we have no reason to be content with you since, because of the lack of the said money, powder and artillery, we have been and are daily in danger of receiving irreparable damage. Because, dearest and loyal cousin and dearest and well loved, it is necessary for us to have the said money, powder and artillery immediately and without delay, we are writing again to you and we order and command you very expressly, and on [the strength of] your desire to obey and serve us, that as soon as you read this, all excuses ceasing, you two together, with the best and the largest number of troops that can be found, bring and escort to us our said money and artillery, especially, so far as the artillery is concerned, all available gunpowder, bows, arrows, pikes and lances (*vouges*), all with the best possible security and diligence and so that we have news of this from you shortly. Dearest and loyal cousin and dearest and well loved, may our Lord keep you.

Written in our siege before Nancy, 14 December 1476.

Charles
Kesele

To our well loved and loyal the lord du Fay, knight, our cousin and lieutenant-general in our land of Luxembourg, and Messire Evrard de la Marck, lord of Aremberg, also knight, our councillors and chamberlains, and to each of them.

From the duke of Burgundy, etc.

Dearest and loyal cousin, since we have now been truthfully informed of the approach of our enemies, we wish and we expressly command you that, as soon as you read this you come to us and in our service, and bring with you all the nobles with fiefs and sub-fiefs and all other troops both mounted and on foot that you can find in our land and duchy of Luxembourg. If you cannot come in person, send us with the greatest possible diligence those nobles and others both mounted and on foot. Do not fail in this in any way. Dearest and loyal cousin, may our Lord keep you. Written in our siege before Nancy, 31 December 1476.

Charles
Coulon

To the lord du Fay, our cousin, lieutenant-general in our duchy of Luxembourg.

The approach of Charles the Bold's enemies was indeed imminent on 31 December. One contingent of the allied army had left Basel by boat as early as 19 December but suffered casualties after a drunkard fell into the Rhine and the rush of his friends to one side of the boat to help him caused it to capsize. The main body of Swiss, comprising for the most part well-disciplined veteran contingents under experienced captains like Hans Waldmann of Zürich and Brandolf von

Stein of Bern, set out from Basel on Boxing Day. Their progress through Ensisheim, Colmar and other places in Alsace was interrupted by displays of savagery against the local Jews, whose valuables were everywhere looted and sent back to Bern for subsequent distribution. Orders had been sent by René from Basel, by the mouth of the author of the *Chronique de Lorraine*, to the captains of his garrisons in Lorraine, at Bruyères, Épinal, Mirecourt, Vaudémont and Gondreville, to march out with all their men and rendezvous with the rest of the allied army on 4 January at St. Nicolas-du-Port. This union was successfully effected and the bridge over the River Meurthe, as well as St. Nicolas itself, was occupied by the allies after a Burgundian force had been driven out. It must have been at St. Nicolas that the count of Campobasso, Cola de Monforte, arrived with his two sons and some 300 men-at-arms to offer to fight alongside Duke René, after his services had been refused by the French forces near Toul, who were under instructions not to infringe the truce. It is said that the Swiss would not trust such a traitor on the field of battle; instead, René posted him in the Burgundian rear to hold the bridge over the Meurthe at Bouxières-aux-Dames. His defection did not affect the main issue. No one else in Charles's army followed suit, except for a handful of Swiss soldiers who preferred to fight with, rather than against, their compatriots.

Nancy in the fifteenth century was a smallish walled town in a broad hollow or shallow valley through which flowed the River Meurthe, fordable only in places. Wooded hills rose on all sides, intersected here and there by streams. The walls of Nancy were pierced by only two gates, the still-standing Porte de la Craffe in the north and the Porte St. Nicolas, through which a main route led southwards up the Meurthe valley to Lunéville, Baccarat and over the Vosges to Alsace. This was the road along which Charles's enemies had advanced, and on which they set out from St. Nicolas early in the morning of Sunday 5 January, heading directly towards Nancy. Charles was likewise on the move early that morning, for he evacuated the bulk of his army from the trenches round Nancy and drew it up ready for battle in a fortified defensive position astride or very near the main road from St. Nicolas between two streams which crossed that road at right angles. The Jarville stream in front of him flowed in a ravine with thickets growing along it, thus constituting an admirable first line of defence. Along his left flank was the River Meurthe, with a ford leading to the village of Tomblaine; on his right was the forest. Now, the town of Nancy has spread over

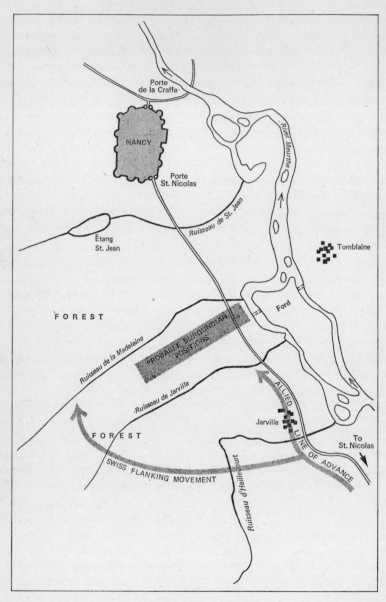

13. The battle of Nancy

the entire area of the battlefield, obliterating the woods, streams and ponds which dominated the scene in those days.

All sources of information agree that Charles the Bold was hopelessly outnumbered at Nancy.[1] The Burgundian chroniclers vied with each other in minimizing the size of the duke's army: Basin made it 8,000 strong; de Commynes reduced that figure to 4,000; de la Marche insisted that Charles had only 2,000 combatants. The last date on which his men were reviewed and paid was 8 December and he must have suffered heavy losses through desertion and enemy action between then and the battle. However, the entries in the war treasurer's account refer to only a proportion, though certainly a substantial one, of the duke's forces. Thus while the three leading Burgundian commanders in the battle of Nancy, Jehan de Rubempré, Josse de Lalaing and Jacobo Galeoto figure here with their men, others who fought with Charles at Nancy, like Jaques de Savoie, count of Romont, and Olivier de la Marche, do not. Nor is there any

---

[1] The most important contemporary accounts of the battle are *Chronique de Lorraine*, ed. Marchal, 291–310, *Desconfiture de Monseigneur de Bourgogne*, Edlibach, *Chronik*, 163–6, Etterlin, *Kronica von der loblichen Eydtgnoschaft*, 96–7, Knebel, *Diarium*, iii. 90–104 and 106–7, von Liebenau, *AnzSG* (N.F.) viii (1898–1901), 66–9, Lud, *Dialogue*, 180–5, Molinet, *Chronique*, i. 165–7, Schilling, *Die Berner-Chronik*, ii. 111–23 and *Vraye déclaration*. Less important are Aubrion, *Journal*, 88, Basin, *Louis XI*, ii. 336–46, de Blarru, *Nanceis*, von Bonstetten, *Beschreibung der Burgunderkriege*, 295–6, de Commynes, *Mémoires*, ed. Calmette and Durville, ii. 148–53, Gollut, *Mémoires historiques*, 883, *Historischen Volkslieder*, ii. 107–9, de la Marche, *Mémoires*, iii. 239–41, de Margny, *L'Aventurier*, 69–70, Meyer, *Chronique strasbourgeoise*, 107, Motta, *BSSI* x (1888), 191–2, Schilling, *Luzerner Chronik*, 87–8, *Straszburgische Archiv-Chronik*, 202–3, Trausch, *Strassburgische Chronick*, 25–6, Tschudi, *Chronicon helveticum*, 476, Tüsch, *Burgundische Hystorie*, ed. Wendling and Stöber, 440–6 and Wintersulger, *Chronik*, 122–3. The accounts of the battle by Marchal, *Mémoire sur la bataille de Nancy* (1851), de Lacombe, *Le siège et la bataille de Nancy* (1860), Schoeber, *Die Schlacht bei Nancy* (1891) and Laux, *Über die Schlacht bei Nancy* (1895) are greatly inferior to those of Witte, *JGLG* iv (1892), 116–37, Bernoulli, *BNB* lxxviii (1900), 29–37, and above all Pfister, *Histoire de Nancy*, i. 464–525. Since then no critical study has appeared, but Lot, *L'art militaire*, ii. 127–9, Dumontier, *LPL* xxxix (1958), 41–51 and Frédérix, *Mort de Charles le Téméraire*, 200–12, are noteworthy. On the booty, see Boyé, *Le butin de Nancy*, Deuchler, *Burgunderbeute* and Wyss, *Die Burgunderbeute*. On monuments, traditions, etc., see Collignon, *MSAL* xliv (1894), 291–338, and the same, *AE* (1897), 497–528, Dumontier, *LPL* xxxix (1958), 151–9, and Garreta, *La bataille de Nancy*.

mention of Campobasso and his two sons. Few of the 100-strong companies into which the army was divided at this time were anywhere near full strength, and many comprised a mere fifty or sixty men. The numbers entered in the accounts in each of the three main categories on 8 December were as follows: mounted men-at-arms, 1,136; mounted archers, 1,788; infantry, 2,463, giving a grand total of 5,387 combatants. On 5 January, when the battle of Nancy was fought, Charles still had to maintain his siege of the town and it thus seems most unlikely, whatever proportion of his men were not reviewed and paid on 8 December, that he had anything like 10,000 men with him on the battlefield; 5,000 was probably nearer the mark.

The army which was advancing to attack Charles the Bold and relieve the hard-pressed city of Nancy had no single commander-in-chief. It was an army of allies, of contingents from the enemies of Burgundy and their supporters, which had been assembled from far and wide though its nucleus had marched from Basel. Alongside Duke René's Lorrainers and the mercenaries he had raised in Bern, Zürich, Luzern, Schwyz, Glarus, Zofingen and elsewhere among the *Eidgenossen*, were the men of the Sundgau, of Basel, of Colmar, of Sélestat and of Strasbourg. Among the banners and pennons which fluttered over the allied army were those of Duke Sigmund of Austria and of the bishops of Basel and Strasbourg. In the description of this army which Duke René apparently dictated to one of his secretaries he claimed to have with him some 19–20,000 men: 2,000 horse and 7,000 foot in the vanguard, and the whole of the rest of the army, apart from a reserve of 800 culverineers, in the main battle, which included a further 2,000 horse. Detailed statements elsewhere leave no doubt that there were at least 6,000 Swiss in the army, and there seems no reason to dispute Duke René's figures. Thus Charles was probably outnumbered by something like three or four to one. Furthermore, his cold, exhausted, demoralized and unpaid troops were attacked by an army of volunteers, many of them the victorious veterans of Grandson and of Murten, fresh, eager, united and determined. The resultant Burgundian military catastrophe was not due merely to the betrayal of Campobasso and Charles's tactical errors in positioning his men near an unreconnoitred forest. It was a foregone conclusion once he had rejected the advice to withdraw which had apparently been repeatedly proffered by his captains. This rejection was the result of a flaw in his character, an inability to admit and rectify his own errors. It was this above all which led him to the disaster of Nancy.

Though many of the details remain confused, the main events of the battle of Nancy can be soundly established on the basis of the surviving eyewitness accounts. On the Burgundian side, two participants afterwards wrote chronicles, Olivier de la Marche who was taken prisoner, and Jehan de Margny; but both are extremely laconic. On the side of the allies we are fortunate in having the ebullient narrative of the Luzerner Peterman Etterlin and that of Diebold Schilling also of Luzern, both of whom fought in the battle, as well as a colourful and detailed description by another participant in the *Chronique de Lorraine*, and several other contemporary reports or letters all emanating from the side of the allies.

The weather at Christmas 1476 had been bitterly cold, then wet. Now, on the morning of Sunday 5 January 1477, heavy snow was falling as the allies moved forward, and visibility remained extremely poor throughout the morning. The only sign of the enemy was a Burgundian scout whom they came across installed in the church tower at Laneuveville. He was hurled to his death in the cemetery below. They halted just short of Jarville and held council of war. A flanking movement in strength was resolved on since the direct line of advance on Charles the Bold's position was covered by his artillery. Turning to their left and advancing with difficulty over rough and wooded ground, which also entailed wading through ice-cold streams, the van of the allied army, with perhaps part of the battle, worked its way round until it could attack Duke Charles's right flank. This manoeuvre was unseen by the Burgundians, either because of the snow and mist, or because of the forest, or, more likely, because most of it was carried out in dead ground, behind the low ridge which runs parallel to the Meurthe at this point. In any case Charles the Bold had apparently not troubled to patrol or reconnoitre this area. Soon after mid-day the allied van emerged in view and, after three mournful blasts, each as long as the air in a man's lungs would allow, had been blown by the Swiss on the horn or horns which had supposedly struck terror into the Burgundians at Grandson, the attack began. It was not long before the cavalry on Charles's right wing began to give way under the onslaught, nor was there time for the Burgundian artillery to be trained on the attackers. While the allied van continued its advance, the rest of the army now delivered a frontal assault on the Burgundian positions across the Jarville stream. Jacobo Galeoto and his cavalry were forced back and were soon in flight over the Tomblaine ford. The Burgundian artillery positions were overrun and Charles's infantry was either cut down or thrown back in confusion. His entire army was converted into a ragged collection of desperate fugitives, himself among them. Escape was by no means easy. The direct route north down the Meurthe valley was blocked at Bouxières-aux-Dames by the traitor Campobasso and his men. They took the wealthier fugitives prisoner for their ransoms and killed those others who did not drown themselves trying to cross the half-frozen Meurthe. It was over 50 km to more or less friendly Metz, where the fugitives might expect to find refuge. Here, the terrible rout was graphically described by a contemporary:[1]

After the battle, in the evening at about midnight, my lord of Romont, of the house of Savoy, and several other great lords passed by the Pont des Morts at the city of Metz in great disorder. And the next day, which was Epiphany, and even eight days afterwards, Burgundians returning to their own country were continually passing through and near the said city. Among the first [arrivals] there was not a man who could say where my lord of Burgundy was.

On the next day and three days afterwards the peasants were still killing the fugitives along the roads as far as Metz so that, for five or six leagues on the way towards Metz, one found nothing but people killed and stripped by the roads. At that time it was freezing and it was more horribly cold than ever, so that many of those who hid died of hunger, of cold, and of discomfort.

Several there were who came as far as Metz from that battle, arriving more than two or three hours after midnight. They threw themselves right into the moat, between the Camoufle Tower and the Porte St. Thiebault; though the place was all full of snow. They were so distraught that they kept thinking they were still being pursued, but their limbs were so paralysed with cold that they would have been powerless to defend themselves. Large numbers of these fugitives entreated the watchmen on the wall in the name of God's Holy Passion to let them in, and they cried out so much that it was piteous to hear them. The watch on the walls went to notify the guards at the Porte St. Thiebault. At that time Lord Andrieu de Rineck, knight, was in charge there. Though he did not believe what they said, nonetheless he got up and, taking with him the merchant Mathieu Bay who was on guard with him, they went along the wall with the watchmen to a point near Ste. Glocine's, and from there the said Lord Andrieu interrogated them. But because they were quite unable to reply properly to his request, he left them and, although with their hands joined [in prayer] they most piteously begged

---

[1] *Chroniques de Metz*, 424–5. For the last paragraph see Viaene, *Biekorf* lix (1958), 353–7.

to be allowed in, he returned to his bed, unwilling to believe their words. He said they were only a group of rogues who had been in some fight, got scared, and fled away from it.

Not long afterwards the said watchmen came to the gate again and reported that the whole moat was full of people newly arrived who were lamenting in an astonishing way, entreating, for God's sake, that they be allowed to enter. So the said Lord Andrieu returned there and addressed his words to a noble gentleman from a great family. He replied so well to everything Lord Andrieu asked him that it seemed as though he had seen everything with his own eyes and been in the thick of the fight. Lord Andrieu was quite amazed to hear the news and asked the gentleman who he was, since he could not see him at all because of the darkness of the night. The man named himself, Christian name and surname, and Lord Andrieu realized that he was indeed a friend of his, and explained this to him. As soon as the said Lord Andrieu had heard this man name himself, he had gladly descended to greet and embrace him while he, noticing this show of friendship, asked Lord Andrieu his name. So he named himself. Then the said Burgundian stretched his hands up high as if weeping and said:

'Ah! Lord Andrieu! Loyal knight! Save the life of this poor miserable knight, your friend!' 'Alas! This is piteous news,' exclaimed Lord Andrieu, 'I will do my duty and go where necessary to have you let in, and first I must go to the Council to ask them if you may enter.' 'For God's sake hurry,' he cried.

After a few more words the said Lord Andrieu went to the Council and the whole city was roused, and they were ordered to be let in. When it came to opening the gates, with due ceremony as is required in such a case, the Burgundians, as soon as they passed the first gate, thinking they were already inside the city, rushed so impetuously between the first gate and the barrier that they almost caused one another to fall into the moat. A good 140 or 160 of them died in the great hospital of St. Nicolas at Le Neufbourg, [either] because they were all chilled and frostbitten, or from hunger or from their wounds; and there were innumerable panic-stricken and wounded people in the city.

The battle was indeed a woeful catastrophe for the said [ruler] of Burgundy, who was then the most feared and redoubtable prince one could think of and also the best loved by his subjects. This was well shown by the fact that they would not believe in his death, especially the people of Artois and several others of these Burgundians; for they stupidly and obstinately asserted that he had escaped from the battle into Germany and had there vowed to undertake a seven-year penance, after which he would return in great power and avenge all his injuries and insults. His subjects were so convinced that this was so that I knew several who, extremely obstinate in this credulity, put up for sale clothes and armour, horses, precious stones and other goods and, if anyone bought them, they sold them on credit at two or three times the right price, with payment deferred until their prince Charles returned after completing his penance. I know that this is true because I, the writer and author of this, helped to write several contracts and agreements concerning such sales, being then a young man staying at Metz with the *Amman* Jennat de Hainonville. And there was a citizen of that city called Jehan le Tambourin, living in Vieseneuf, who sold nearly everything he had, and several others did the same, so that eventually they became poor and beggars. The thing that deceived them most and increased their foolish belief was that a man was found at that time in the town of Bruchsal, leading an austere life and doing great penance and resembling the said Charles in voice and stature, who hardly ever showed himself, as if he were melancholic, so that the populace readily took him for Charles until the truth was ascertained from the clearest evidence.

As a matter of fact it took two days of careful searching through the frozen and dismembered corpses littering the field of battle before the body of the forty-four year old duke was found. It had been stripped of clothes and jewels and the face was mangled, cut open and partly eaten by dogs or wolves, but it was identified by its long nails and battle scars. Apparently Charles the Bold's horse had failed to clear a stream in the general flight. He had fallen, perhaps already wounded, and was then despatched with a blow which cut open his head. With him fell the Burgundian state which his great-grandfather Philip the Bold had founded, the history of which has been traced in this and the foregoing volumes. For what survived after 1477 was in many respects a different political entity, bereft as it was of the duchy of Burgundy. The death of Charles the Bold was indeed a decisive event. As the senate of Venice wisely put it, 'the fate of the duke of Burgundy cannot be otherwise than of the utmost importance and gravity, because so much depended on him. It certainly ought to exercise for many a year the mind of every intelligent man intent on considering the future.'[1]

[1] *Dépêches des ambassadeurs milanais*, ii. 397.

Bibliography

Full titles of works consulted and referred to in the notes. For abbreviations used see pp. ix-xiii.

Aachener Chronik. Ed. A. Loersch. *AHVN* xvii (1866), 1–29.

Abel, A. and M. Martens. 'Le rôle de Jean de Vésale, médecin de la ville de Bruxelles, dans la propagande de Charles le Téméraire.' *CB* i (1956), 41–86.

Acten zum Neusser Kriege, 1472–5. Ed. A. Ulrich. *AHVN* xlix (1889), 1–191.

Actes concernant les rapports entre les Pays-Bas et la Grande Bretagne de 1293 à 1468 conservés au château de Mariemont. Ed. P. Bonenfant. *BCRH* cix (1944), 53–125.

Actes des États Généraux des anciens Pays-Bas, i. Ed. J. Cuvelier and others. CRH. Brussels, 1948.

Additions et corrections à la notice sur les archives de la ville de Malines, iii (1 and 2). Ed. D.J.F.C. Gyseleers-Thys. Malines, 1838.

Aktenstücke und Briefe zur Geschichte des Hauses Habsburg. Ed. J. Chmel. 3 vols. Vienna, 1854–8.

Alberts, W. Jappe. *De Staten van Gelre en Zutphen.* 2 vols. BIMGU xxii and xxix. Groningen, 1950, 1956.

——. *De eerste Bourgondische bezetting van Gelre, 1473–7.* BIMGU xxvii (1954), 49–82.

Algemene geschiedenis der Nederlanden. Ed. J. A. van Houtte and others. 13 vols. Utrecht, 1949–58.

Algra, N. E. *Een Spionagerapport van omstreeks 1468.* Ljouwert, 1967.

Ammann, H. *Freiburg und Bern und die Genfer Messen.* Aarau, 1921.

——. *Der Aargau in den Burgunderkriegen.* Aarau, 1927.

P

Ammann, H. 'Die Bedeutung der Burgunderkriege für die Schweiz.' *RHB* iv (1927), 57–8.

——. 'Elsässisch-schweizerische Wirtschaftsbeziehungen im Mittelalter.' *ELJ* vii (1928), 36–61.

Analectes belgiques, i. Ed. L. P. Gachard. Brussels, 1830.

Analectes historiques, iii. Ed. L. P. Gachard. *BCRH* (2) vii (1855), 25–220.

——, iv. Ed. L. P. Gachard. *BCRH* (2) viii (1856), 67–268.

——, v. Ed. L. P. Gachard. *BCRH* (2) ix (1857), 103–256.

——, vii. Ed. L. P. Gachard. *BCRH* (2) xii (1859), 359–516.

——, ix. Ed. L. P. Gachard. *BCRH* (3) iii (1862), 345–554.

——, xi. Ed. L. P. Gachard. *BCRH* (3) vii (1865), 15–208.

——, xii. Ed. L. P. Gachard. *BCRH* (3) viii (1866), 273–506.

——, xvi. Ed. L. P. Gachard. *BCRH* (3) xii (1871), 141–316.

——, xvii. Ed. L. P. Gachard. *BCRH* (3) xiii (1872), 9–176.

Angelo de Curribis Sabinis or of Viterbo. *De excidio civitatis Leodiensis.* Ed. E. Martène and U. Durand. *Veterum scriptorum . . . amplissima collectio* iv. cols. 1379–1500. Paris, 1729.

Ankringa, J. D. 'Wat heeft Karel de Stoute gedaan, om Friesland onder zijn beheer te krijgen.' *DVF* vi (1852), 186–94.

Anonyme Chronik der Burgunderkriege, Die. Ed. A. Bernoulli, *Basler Chroniken*, v. 501–27. Leipzig, 1895.

Anon. *St. Gallens Antheil an den Burgunderkriegen. Neujahrschrift des historisches Vereins St. Gallen.* St. Gall, 1876.

Anshelm, V. *Berner-Chronik.* Ed. E. Stierlin and J. R. Wyss. 6 vols. Bern, 1825–33.

——. ——. Ed. E. Bloesch. 6 vols. Bern, 1884–1901.

Aquino, J. de. *Chronica, 1475–1515. Monumenta historiae patriae, Scriptores*, i. cols. 679–700. Turin, 1840.

Armstrong, C. A. J. 'A letter of James III to the duke of Burgundy.' *MSHS* viii (1951), 19–32.

——. 'The language question in the Low Countries.' *Europe in the late middle ages*, 386–409. Ed. J. R. Hale. London, 1965.

——. 'La politique matrimoniale des ducs de Bourgogne de la Maison de Valois.' *AB* xl (1968), 5–58 and 89–139.

Aubrion, J. *Journal.* Ed. L. Larchey. Metz, 1857.

Baader, J. 'Die Zusammenkunft Kaiser Friedrichs III mit Herzog Karl dem Kühnen von Burgund zu Trier im Jahre 1473.' *AKV* (N.F.) xi (1864), cols. 202–7 and 233–42.

Bachmann, A. *Deutsche Reichsgeschichte im Zeitalter Friedrich III und Max I.* 2 vols. Leipzig, 1884, 1894. Reprinted, Hildesheim, 1970.

Barante, A. de. *Histoire des ducs de Bourgogne de la maison de Valois.* Ed. L. P. Gachard. 2 vols. Brussels, 1838.

Bartier, J. *Le sixième denier et l'amortissement sous Charles le Téméraire.* Unpublished thesis, Université Libre, Brussels, 1938.

——. 'Un discours du chancelier Hugonet aux États Généraux de 1473.' *BCRH* cvii (1942), 127–56.

——. *Charles le Téméraire.* Brussels, 1944. New edition, Brussels, 1970.

——. *Légistes et gens de finances au xve siècle. Les conseillers des ducs de Bourgogne.* MARBL 1 (2). Brussels, 1952.

Basin, T. *Histoire de Louis XI.* Ed. C. Samaran. 2 vols. CHF. Paris, 1963, 1966.

Basler Chroniken. Ed. W. Vischer and others. 7 vols. Leipzig, 1872–1915.

Bauer, E. *Négociations et campagnes de Rodolphe de Hochberg, 1427–87.* Neuchâtel, 1928.

Beauvillé, V. de. *Histoire de la ville de Montdidier.* 2nd edn. 3 vols. Paris, 1857.

Bell, F. and J. Schneller. 'Zur Geschichte der Burgunderkriege.' *Geschichtsfreund* xxiii (1868), 54–106.

Belotti, B. *La vita de Bartolomeo Colleoni.* 1st edn. Bergamo, 1923.

Berchen, W. van. *Gelderse kroniek.* Ed. A. J. de Mooy. Arnhem, 1950.

Bergé, M. 'Les bâtards de la maison de Bourgogne, leur descendance.' *IG* lx (1955), 316–408.

Berlet, A. 'Charles le Téméraire et René de Lorraine.' *MSBGH* viii (1892), 297–393 and ix (1893), 1–120.

Bernoulli, A. 'Basels Antheil am Burgunderkriege.' *BNB* lxxvi, lxxvii and lxxviii (1898, 1899 and 1900).

Bernoulli, C. C. 'Der Landvogt Peter von Hagenbach.' *BVG* xiii (1893), 313–80.

Bertalot, L. 'Ein neuer Bericht über die Zusammenkunft Friedrichs III und Karls des Kühnen zu Trier, 1473.' *WZ* xxx (1911), 419–30.

Bigwood, G. *Le régime juridique et économique du commerce de l'argent dans la Belgique au moyen âge.* 2 vols. MARBL xiv (1921 and 1922).

Billioud, J. 'L'attitude des États des deux Bourgognes à l'égard de Charles le Téméraire après la bataille de Morat, 1476.' *MA* xxvi (1913), 352–9.

——. *Les États de Bourgogne aux xive et xve siècles. MAD* (5) iv (1922), extra number.

Bittmann, K. 'Zwei Briefe zur Geschichte Lüttichs und der Auseinandersetzung zwischen Frankreich und Burgund von 1467.' *SBAG* vii (1949), 140–52.

——. 'Der Kardinal Balue und die Zusammenkunft von Péronne.' *WG* xvi (1956), 98–123.

——. 'Die Zusammenkunft von Péronne. Ein Beitrag zur Kritik an den Memoiren des Philippe de Commynes.' *HZ* clxxxiv (1957), 19–64.

——. *Ludwig XI und Karl der Kühne. Die Memoiren des Philippe de Commynes als historische Quelle*, i (1 and 2) and ii (1). Göttingen, 1964, 1970. In course of publication.

Blarru, P. de Nanceis. *La Nancéide ou la guerre de Nancy, poème latin de Pierre de Blarru avec la traduction française.* Ed. F. Schütz. 2 vols. Nancy, 1840.

Blockmans, W. *De Staten en de Leden van Vlaanderen en hun rol in de Staten-Generaal der Nederlanden, 1467–1477.* Unpublished thesis, University of Ghent, 1966.

Blok, P. J. *Eene Hollandsche stad onder de Bourgondisch-Oostenrijksche heerschappij.* The Hague, 1884.

——. 'De financiën van het graafschap Holland.' *BVGO* (3) iii (1886), 36–130.

Blondeau, G. 'Jean Jouard, seigneur d'Échevannes et de Gatey, président des Parlements des comté et duché de Bourgogne.' *MSED* (8) iii (1908), 247–358.

Blösch, E. 'Die Schlacht bei Murten im Rathsaale zu Bern.' *BT* (1877), 171–227.

Bocquet, A. *Recherches sur la population rurale de l'Artois et du Boulonnais, 1384–1477. MCMP* xiii. Arras, 1969.

Boer, B. de 'Karel de Stoute in de Haarlemse stadsekeningen.' *HB* lxiv (1957), 403–12.

Boeren, P. C. *Twee Maaslandse dichters in dienst van Karel de Stoute.* The Hague, 1968.

Boergoensche Charters, 1428–82. Ed. P. A. S. van Limburg Brouwer. Amsterdam, 1869.

Bonenfant, P. 'État bourguignon et Lotharingie.' *BARBL* xli (1955), 266–282.

Bonenfant, P. and J. Stengers. 'Le rôle de Charles le Téméraire dans le gouvernement de l'État bourguignon en 1465-1567.' *AB* xxv (1953), 7-29 and 118-33.

Bonstetten, A. von. *Beschreibung der Burgunderkreige.* *ASG* xiii (1862), 283-324.

Borel, F. *Les foires de Genève au quinzième siècle.* Geneva and Paris, 1892.

Bormans, S. 'Liste d'objects enlevées de Liège en 1468 par les soldats de Charles le Téméraire.' *BIAL* viii (1866), 181-207.

——. *Liégeois et Bourguignons en 1468.* PSBL. Liège, 1881.

Bossuat, R. 'Traductions françaises des Commentaires de César à la fin du xvᵉ siècle.' *BHR* iii (1943), 253-411.

——. 'Vasque de Lucene, traducteur de Quinte-Curce, 1468.' *BHR* viii (1946), 197-245.

Bouchard, H. 'Philippe Pot, grand sénéchal de Bourgogne (1428-93).' *PTSEC* (1949), 23-7.

Boyé, P. *Le butin de Nancy, 5 janvier 1477. Étude d'histoire et d'archéologie.* Paris, 1905.

Brauer-Gramm, H. *Der Landvogt Peter von Hagenbach. Die burgundische Herrschaft am Oberrhein, 1469-74.* Göttingen, 1957.

Brennwald, H. *Schweizerchronik.* Ed. R. Luginbühl. QSG. 2 vols. Basel, 1908, 1910.

Bricard, G. *Un serviteur et compère de Louis XI, Jean Bourré, seigneur du Plessis.* Paris, 1893.

Briefe und Acten zur österreichisch-deutschen Geschichte im Zeitalter Kaiser Friedrich III. Ed. A. Bachmann. FRADA xliv. Vienna, 1885.

Briefe und Actenstücke zur Geschichte der Herzoge von Mailand von 1452 bis 1513. Ed. J. Chmel. *NBAG* vi (1856).

Broeckx, J. L. and others. *Flandria nostra.* 5 vols. Antwerp and Brussels, 1957-60.

Bronnen tot de geschiedenis van den handel met Engeland, Schotland en Ierland, 1150-1485. Ed. H. J. Smit. 2 vols. RGP lxv and lxvi. The Hague, 1928.

Browning, O. *The life of Bartolomeo Colleoni.* London, 1891.

Brun-Lavainne. 'Analyse d'un compte de dépenses de la maison du duc Charles de Bourgogne.' *BCHDN* viii (1865), 189-232.

Brüning, W. 'Herzog Karl der Kühne von Burgund und die Reichsstadt Aachen.' *Aus Aachens Vorzeit* xiii (1900), 34-52.

Brusten, C. *L'armée bourguignonne de 1465 à 1468.* Brussels, no date.

Brusten, C. 'Les emblèmes de l'armée bourguignonne sous Charles le Téméraire. Essai de classification.' *JBHM* xxxvii and xxxviii (1957 and 1958), 118–132.

——. 'L'armée bourguignonne de 1465 à 1477.' *RIHM* xx (1959), 452–66.

——. 'Les itinéraires de l'armée bourguignonne de 1465 à 1478.' *PCEEBM* ii (1960), 55–67.

——. 'Le ravitaillement en vivres dans l'armée bourguignonne, 1450–77.' *PCEEBM* iii (1961), 42–9.

——. 'À propos de la bataille de Morat.' *PCEEBM* x (1968), 79–83.

Bruwier, M. 'Notes sur les finances hennuyères à l'époque bourguignonne. Le domaine de Mons de 1438 à 1477.' *MA* liv (1948), 133–59.

Büchi, A. *Freiburgs Bruch mit Oesterreich. Collectanea Freiburgensia* vii. Fribourg, 1897.

——. 'Freiburger Missiven zur Geschichte des Burgunderkrieges.' *FG* xiii (1906), 1–102.

——. 'Der Friedenskongress von Freiburg, 1476.' *FG* xxiv (1917), 24–74.

Buser, B. *Die Beziehungen der Mediceer zu Frankreich, 1434–1494.* Leipzig, 1879.

Bussierre, M. T. de. *Histoire de la Ligue formée contre Charles le Téméraire.* Paris, 1849.

But, A. de. *Chronique.* Ed. Kervyn de Lettenhove. *Chroniques relatives à l'histoire de la Belgique sous la domination des ducs de Bourgogne. Textes latins. Chroniques des religieux des Dunes,* 211–717. CRH. Brussels, 1870.

Cabinet du roy Louis XI, Le. Ed. L. Cimber. *AC—F* i. 1–76. Paris, 1834.

Calendar of the patent rolls. Edward IV, Henry VI. 1467–1477. London, 1901.

Calendar of state papers. Milan, i. Ed. A. B. Hinds. London, 1912.

Calendar of state papers. Venice, i. *1202–1509.* Ed. R. Brown. London, 1864.

Calmet, A. *Histoire de Lorraine.* 7 vols. Nancy, 1745–57.

Calmette, J. *Louis XI, Jean II et la révolution catalane, 1461–1473.* Toulouse, 1903.

——. 'L'origine bourguignonne de l'alliance austro-espagnole.' *Études médiévales,* 215–39. Toulouse, 1946. Reprinted from *Bulletin de la Société des amis de l'Université de Dijon* viii (1905), 59–84.

——. 'Contribution à l'histoire des relations de la cour de Bourgogne avec la cour d'Aragon au xvᵉ siècle.' *RB* xviii (1908), 138–96.

Calmette, J. 'Le projet de mariage bourguignon-napolitain en 1474.' *BEC* lxxii (1911), 459–72.

——. 'Le mariage de Charles le Téméraire et de Marguerite d'York.' *AB* i (1929), 193–214.

——. 'Campobasso et Commynes.' *Etudes médiévales*, 208–14. Toulouse, 1946. Reprinted from *AB* vii (1935), 172–6.

—— and G. Périnelle. *Louis XI et l'Angleterre, 1461–1483*. Paris, 1930.

—— and E. Déprez. *Les premières grandes puissances. Histoire générale. Moyen âge*, vii (2). Ed. G. Glotz. Paris, 1939.

Cambridge Economic History, The, iii. Ed. M. M. Postan and others. Cambridge, 1963.

Cartellieri, O. 'Theaterspiele am Hofe Karls des Kühnen von Burgund.' *GRM* ix (1921), 168–79.

——. 'Ritterspiele am Hofe Karls des Kühnen von Burgund (1468).' *TG* xxxvi (1921), 14–30.

——. *The court of Burgundy*. London, 1929. Translated from *Am Hofe der Herzöge von Burgund*. Basel, 1926.

——. 'Zum Vertrage von St. Omer, die Schweiz und der Oberrhein.' *ZGO* xlii (1928), 629–36.

Cartulaire de l'ancienne Estaple de Bruges. Ed. L. Gilliodts van Severen. 4 vols. Bruges, 1904–6.

Cartulaire de l'église St. Lambert de Liège. Ed. S. Bormans and E. Schoolmeesters. CRH. 6 vols. Brussels, 1893–1913.

Cartulaire de Mulhouse. Ed. X. Mossmann. 6 vols. Strasbourg and Colmar, 1883–90.

Cayon, J. *Souvenirs et monumens de la bataille de Nancy*. Nancy, 1837.

Cazaux, Y. *Marie de Bourgogne*. Paris, 1967.

Cerioni, L. 'Per la storia della storiografia francese del quattrocento: Carlo il Temerario, Luigi XI, Carlo VIII ed i "Mémoires" di Filippo di Commynes.' *NH* xiv (1962), 80–122.

Chabannes, H. de, ed. *Preuves pour servir à l'histoire de la maison de Chabannes*. 4 vols. Dijon, 1892–7.

Chabeuf, H. 'Un portrait de Charles le Téméraire.' *MAD* (4) viii (1901–2), 201–18.

——. 'Charles le Téméraire à Dijon en janvier 1474.' *MSBGH* xviii (1902), 79–349.

Chabloz, F. *La bataille de Grandson d'après vingt-sept auteurs*. Lausanne, 1897.

Charlier, G. 'Philippe de Commynes et la cour de Bourgogne.' *RUB* iv (1951–2), 324–8.

Chartes de la famille de Reinach. PSHIL xxxiii (1879).

Chastellain, G. *Oeuvres.* Ed. Kervyn de Lettenhove. Académie royale de Belgique. 8 vols. Brussels, 1863–6.

Châtelain, C. 'Les Neuchâtelois et les guerres de Bourgogne.' *MN* xxxiv (1897), 285–94.

Chevanne, J. R. de. *Les guerres en Bourgogne de 1470 à 1475.* Paris, 1934.

——. 'Épisodes des dernières luttes au duché de Bourgogne, 1470–75.' *Douzième Congrès de l'Association bourguignonne des Sociétés savantes,* 45. Dijon, 1937.

Chronijk der landen van Overmaas en der aangrenzende gewesten. Ed. J. Habets. *PSAHL* vii (1870), 1–231.

Chronijk van Maastricht en omstreken van Maastricht. Ed. J. Habets. *PSAHL* i (1864), 70–93.

Chronik der Stadt Zürich. Ed. J. Dierauer. QSG xviii. Basel, 1900.

Chroniken der deutschen Städte, Die, xxii. *Augsburg,* iii. HKBAW. 2nd edn. Göttingen, 1965.

——, xiii and xiv. *Cöln,* ii and iii. HKBAW. 2nd edn. Göttingen, 1968.

——, xxxi. *Lübeck,* v. HKBAW. 2nd edn. Göttingen, 1968.

Chronique de Lorraine. Ed. A. Calmet. *Histoire de Lorraine,* vii. cols. v–cl. Nancy, 1757.

——. Ed. L. Marchal. *Recueil de documents sur l'histoire de Lorraine,* v. Nancy, 1859.

Chroniques de la ville de Metz, Les. Ed. J. F. Huguenin. Metz, 1837.

Chroniques de Yolande de France, duchesse de Savoie, soeur de Louis XI. Ed. L. Ménabréa. Chambéry, 1859.

Chronique ou dialogue entre Joannes Lud et Chrétien. See Lud, J. *Dialogue.*

Clerc, E. *Histoire des États Généraux et des libertés publiques en Franche-Comté.* 2 vols. Besançon, 1882.

Cockshaw, P. 'Heurs et malheurs de la recette générale de Bourgogne.' *AB* xli (1969), 247–71.

Codex documentorum sacratissimarum indulgentiarum neerlandicarum. Ed. P. Fredericq. RGP xxi. The Hague, 1922.

Cohn, J. H. *The government of the Rhine Palatinate in the fifteenth century.* Oxford, 1965.

Collection de documens inédits concernant l'histoire de la Belgique. Ed. L. P. Gachard. 3 vols. Brussels, 1833–5.

Collignon, A. 'Souvenirs artistiques et littéraires de la bataille de Nancy.' *MSAL* xliv (1894), 291–338.

——. 'Note sur les monuments, l'iconographie et les légendes de la bataille de Nancy.' *AE* (1897), 497–528.

Colombo, E. *Iolanda, duchessa di Savoia, 1465–78. Miscellanea di storia italiana* xxxi (1894), 1–306.

Combet, J. *Louis XI et le Saint-Siège, 1461–1483.* Paris, 1903.

Comines, P. de. *Mémoires.* Ed. D. Godefroy and Lenglet du Fresnoy. 4 vols. Paris, 1747.

Commynes, P. de. *Mémoires.* Ed. Dupont. SHF. 3 vols. Paris, 1840–7.

——. ——. Ed. J. Calmette and G. Durville. CHF. 3 vols. Paris, 1924–5.

——. ——. English translation by S. Kinser and I. Cazeaux. Vol. i only so far published. Columbia, South Carolina, 1969.

Coninckx, H. 'Une émeute à Malines en 1467.' *BCAM* ii (1892), 300–24.

Contamine, P. *Guerre, état et société à la fin du moyen âge. Ëtude sur les armées des rois de France, 1337–1494.* Paris, 1972.

Coremans, P. and others. *Flanders in the fifteenth century: art and civilization. Catalogue of the exhibition Masterpieces of Flemish Art: Van Eyck to Bosch.* Institute of Arts, Detroit, 1960.

Correspondance de la filiale de Bruges des Medici, i. Ed. A. Grunzweig. CRH. Brussels, 1931.

Correspondance de la mairie de Dijon. Ed. J. Garnier. 3 vols. Dijon, 1868–1870.

Coutumes des pays et comté de Flandre. Coutume du Franc de Bruges. Ed. L. Gilliodts van Severen. 3 vols. Brussels, 1879–80.

Coutumes du pays et comté de Hainaut. Ed. C. Faider. 3 vols. Brussels, 1873–83.

Croce, B. 'Il conte de Campobasso, Cola di Monforte.' *Vite di avventure, di fede e di passione,* 47–186. Bari, 1953. Reprinted from *La Critica* xxxi and xxxii (1933 and 1934).

Cronycke van Hollandt, Zeelandt ende Vrieslant, Die. Leiden, 1517.

Cröy, Les, conseillers des ducs de Bourgogne. Documents extraits de leurs archives familiales, 1357–1487. Ed. M. R. Thielemans. *BCRH* cxxiv (1959), 1–141.

Cusin, F. 'Impero, Borgogna e politica italiana.' *NRS* xix (1935), 137–72 and xx (1936), 34–57.

Dabin, J. 'La politique française à Liège au xve siècle.' *BIAL* xliii (1913), 99–190.

Dadizeele, J. de. *Mémoires*. Ed. Kervyn de Lettenhove. Bruges, 1850.

Daenell, E. *Die Blütezeit der deutschen Hanse*. 2 vols. Berlin, 1905, 1906.

Dagboek van Gent van 1447 tot 1470. Ed. V. Fris. MVP. 2 vols. Ghent, 1901, 1904.

Dändliker, K. *Ursachen und Vorspiel der Burgunderkriege*. Zürich, 1876.

——. 'Bausteine zur politischen Geschichte Hans Waldmann's und seiner Zeit.' *JSG* v (1880), 183–307.

Daris, J. *Histoire du diocèse et de la principauté de Liège pendant le xve siècle*. Liège, 1887.

Daumet, G. 'Étude sur l'alliance de la France et de la Castille au xive et xve siècles.' *Bibliothèque de l'École des Hautes Études* cxviii. Paris, 1898.

David, H. 'Charles "le Travaillant", quatrième et dernier duc Valois de Bourgogne.' *AB* xxxix (1967), 5–43 and 65–86.

Daviso di Charvensod, M. C. *La duchessa Iolanda*. Turin, 1935.

——. *Filippo II il Senzaterra*. Turin, 1941.

Degryse, R. 'De admiraals en de eigen marine van de Bourgondische hertogen, 1384–1488.' *MAMB* xvii (1965), 139–225.

Delaissé, L. M. J. *La miniature flamande. Le mécénat de Philippe le Bon*. Brussels, 1959.

Delbrück, H. *Die Perserkriege und die Burgunderkriege*. Berlin, 1887.

——. *Geschichte der Kriegskunst im Rahmen der politischen Geschichte*, iii. Berlin, 1923. Reprinted, Berlin, 1964.

Delisle, L. 'Catalogue of the collection of autograph letters formed by Alfred Morrison.' *BEC* xlv (1884), 196–202.

Delumeau, J. *L'alun de Rome, xve–xixe siècle*. Paris, 1962.

Dépêches des ambassadeurs milanais en France sous Louis XI et François Sforza. Ed. B. de Mandrot and C. Samaran. SHF. 4 vols. Paris, 1916–23.

Dépêches des ambassadeurs milanais sur les campagnes de Charles le Hardi, 1474–77. Ed. F. de Gingins-La Sarraz. 2 vols. Paris and Geneva, 1858.

Desconfiture de Monseigneur de Bourgogne, La. Ed. Lenglet du Fresnoy in de Comines, *Mémoires*, iii. 493–6; J. Meyer, 'Bericht eines Zeitgenossen über die Schlacht bei Nanzig und den Tod Karls des Kühnen,' in *Alemannia. Zeitschrift für Sprache, Litteratur und Volkskunde Elsasses, Oberrheins und Schwabens* x (1882), 137–42; and by F. Mugnier in *Mémoires et documents publiés par la Société savoisienne d'histoire et d'archéologie* xl (1901), 145–69.

Despond, M. *Les comtes de Gruyère et les guerres de Bourgogne*. Fribourg, 1925.

Deuchler, F. *Die Burgunderbeute*. Bern, 1963.

Devillers, L. 'Documents relatifs à l'arrestation de Louis de Luxembourg, comte de Saint-Pol, connétable de France, à Mons, en août, 1475.' *BCRH* (4) xvii (1890), 302–28.

Diemar, H. *Die Entstehung des deutschen Reichskriegs gegen Herzog Karl den Kühnen*. Marburg, 1896, reprinted from *WZ* xv (1896), 60–106 and 274–328.

Dierauer, J. *Geschichte der schweizerischen Eidgenossenschaft*, ii. 3rd edn. Gotha, 1920. Reprinted Bern, 1967.

——. 'Panigarolas Bericht über die Schlacht bei Murten.' *SMOW Extrabeilage* iv (1892), 1–16.

Diesbach, L. von. *Chronik und Selbstbiographie. SG* viii (1830), 161–215.

Digot, A. *Histoire de Lorraine*, iii. 1st edn. Nancy, 1856.

Discours du siège de Beauvais en 1472. Ed. Lenglet du Fresnoy in de Comines, *Mémoires*, iii. 203–18; L. Cimber in *ACHF* i. 111–35, Paris, 1834; and in *Album historique et paléographique beauvaisien*, Beauvais, 1913.

Dispatches with related documents of Milanese ambassadors in France and Burgundy, 1450–1483. Ed. P. M. Kendall and V. Ilardi. Vols. i and ii, Ohio, 1970.

Documents concernant la bataille de Brusthem et la reddition des villes de St-Trond, de Tongres et de Liège, 1467. Ed. J. Diegerick. *BSSLL* v (1856), 357–71.

Documents pour servir à l'histoire des relations entre l'Angleterre et la Flandre. Ed. E. Scott and L. Gilliodts van Severen. CRH. Brussels, 1896.

Documents relatifs aux troubles du pays de Liège sous les princes-évêques Louis de Bourbon et Jean de Horne (1455–1505). Ed. P. de Ram. CRH. Brussels, 1844.

Dogaer, G. and M. Debae. *La Librairie de Philippe le Bon*. Brussels, 1967.

Doorslaer, G. van. 'La chapelle musicale de Philippe le Beau.' *RBAHA* iv (1934), 21–58 and 139–66.

Doutrepont, G. *La littérature française à la cour des ducs de Bourgogne*. Paris, 1909.

Drouot, H. 'Portraits de Charles le Téméraire.' *MCACO* xix (1926–32), 12–14.

Du Bois, F. 'La bataille de Granson.' *MAGZ* ii (2) (1844), 33–53.

Duclercq, J. *Mémoires*. Ed. J. A. C. Buchon. *Choix de chroniques et mémoires relatifs à l'histoire de France. Jacques du Clercq, Mémoires*, etc., 1–318. Paris, 1875.

Dufournet, J. *La destruction des mythes dans les Mémoires de Ph. de Commynes.* Geneva, 1966.

——. *La vie de Philippe de Commynes.* Paris, 1969.

Dumay, G. 'État militaire et féodal des baillages d'Autun, Montcenis, Bourbon-Lancy et Semur-en-Brionnais en 1474.' *MSE* xi (1882), 75–163.

Dumontier, M. 'Les trois sièges de Nancy en 1475–6. La bataille de Nancy du 5 janvier 1477.' *LPL* xxxix (1958), 33–51.

——. 'Traditions et souvenirs de la bataille de Nancy, 5 janvier 1477.' *LPL* xxxix (1958), 151–9.

Dupuy, A. *Histoire de la réunion de la Bretagne à la France.* 2 vols. Paris, 1880.

Duronzier. *Mémoires historiques sur la Franche-Comté.* Besançon, 1833.

Dürr, E. 'Galeazzo Maria Sforza und seine Stellung zu den Burgunderkriegen. Eine Untersuchung über die südfranzösisch-italienische Politik Karls des Kühnen.' *ZGA* x (1911), 259–414.

——. 'Ludwig XI, die aragonesisch-castilianische Heirat und Karl der Kühne.' *MIOG* xxxv (1913), 297–332.

——. 'Karl der Kühne und der Ursprung des habsburgisch-spanischen Imperiums.' *HZ* cxiii (1914), 22–55.

——. 'Das mailändische Kapitulat, Savoyen und der burgundisch-schweizerische Vertrag von Jahre 1467.' *ZGA* xiv (1915), 203–73.

——. *La politique des Confédérés au xive et au xve siècle. HMS* iv. 1–483. Bern, 1935.

Durrieu, P. *La miniature flamande au temps de la cour de Bourgogne.* Paris and Brussels, 1931.

Duverger, J. 'Wilde Karel de Stoute een burcht tegen Gent oprichten in het domein van de St. Baafsabdij.' *Miscellanea historica in honorem Alberti de Meyer,* ii. 748–51. Louvain and Brussels, 1946.

Edlibach, G. *Chronik.* Ed. J. M. Usteri. *MAGZ* iv (1846).

Eidgenössischen Abschiede aus dem Zeitraume von 1421 bis 1477, Die. Amtliche Sammlung der älteren Eidgenössischen Abschiede, ii. Ed. A. P. Segesser. Luzern, 1863.

Elgger, C. von. *Kriegswesen und Kriegskunst der schweizerischen Eidgenossen im xiv, xv und xvi Jahrhundert.* Luzern, 1873.

Ennen, L. *Geschichte der Stadt Köln.* 5 vols. Cologne and Neuss, 1863–1880.

Enschedé, A. J. 'Huwelijksplechtigheden van Karel van Bourgondië en Margaretha van York.' *KHGU* (5) ii (1866), 17–71.

Entreprises du duc de Bourgogne contre les Suisses, Les. Ed. A. Schnegg. QSG. Basel, 1948.

Epistolae regis Christiani I vel ad eum scriptae. Ed. J. Langebek. *Scriptores rerum danicarum medii aevi,* viii. 360–446. Copenhagen, 1834.

Etterlin, P. *Kronica von der loblichen Eydtgnoschaft.* Basel, 1507.

Evans, J. 'The garter of Charles the Bold, duke of Burgundy.' *Antiquaries' Journal* xxxii (1952), 70–71.

Excerpta historica. Ed. S. Bentley. London, 1831.

Extraits analytiques des registres des consaux de la ville de Tournai, 1431–1476. Ed. A. de la Grange. Tournai, 1893.

Fairon, E. 'Notes sur la domination bourguignonne dans la principauté de Liège, 1468 à 1476.' *BIAL* xlii (1912), 1–89.

——. 'Les six cents Franchimontois.' *Wallonia* xxii (1914), 136–55.

Febvre, L. 'Les ducs Valois de Bourgogne et les idées politiques de leur temps.' *RB* xxiii (1913), 27–50.

Feldmann, M. 'Die Schlacht bei Grandson.' *SMOW* xiv (1902), 225–50.

Feldmann, R. M. and H. G. Wirz. *Histoire militaire de la Suisse.* Published also in German and Italian editions. 12 vols. Bern, 1915–36.

Feller, R. *Geschichte Berns,* i. Bern, 1946.

Fierville, C. *Le cardinal Jean Jouffroy et son temps, 1412–1473.* Paris, 1874.

Fischer, R. *Les campagnes des Confédérés au nord des Alpes de la guerre de Laupen à la guerre de Souabe. HMS* ii. 1–292. Bern, 1936.

Foedera, conventiones, etc. Ed. T. Rymer. 20 vols. London, 1704–35.

Fouw, A. de. *Philips van Kleef. Een bijdrage tot de kennis van zijn leven en karakter.* Groningen, 1937.

Fraknoi, W. *Matthias Corvinus, König von Ungarn, 1458 bis 1490.* Freiburg im Breisgau, 1891.

Frankfurts Reichscorrespondenz. Ed. J. Janssen. 2 vols. Freiburg im Breisgau, 1863.

Franz, G. 'Die Bedeutung der Burgunderkriege für die Entwicklung des deutschen Nationalgefühls.' *JSFB* v (1942), 161–74.

Fredericq, P. *Essai sur le rôle politique et social des ducs de Bourgogne dans les Pays-Bas.* Ghent, 1875.

Frederiks, J. G. *De intocht van Hertog Karel den Stoute te Zutfen, 4 Augustus 1473.* Utrecht, 1876.

Frédérix, P. *La mort de Charles le Téméraire.* Paris, 1966.

Freeman, E. A. 'Charles the Bold.' *Historical Essays,* i. 314–72. London, 1871.

Fries, H. *Chronik*. Ed. A. Büchi in Schilling, D. *Die Berner-Chronik*, ii. 391–441. Bern, 1901.

Fris, V. *Histoire de Gand*. Brussels, 1913.

——. 'La Restriction de Gand, 13 juillet, 1468.' *BSHAG* xxx (1922), 57–142.

Fritzsche, H. *Ein deutscher Grenzlandkampf im ausgehenden Mittelalter*. Berlin, 1937.

Gabotto, F. *Lo stato sabaudo da Amedeo VIII ad Emanuele Filiberto*. 3 vols. Turin and Rome, 1892–5.

Gachard, L. P. 'Rapport sur la bibliothèque du roi etc.' *BCRH* iii (1840), 20–39.

——. [L'instrument du 3 novembre 1471]. *Trésor national* ii (1842), 122–7.

——. *Rapport sur les archives de Dijon*. Brussels, 1843.

——. 'Notice des archives de M. le duc de Caraman, précédée de recherches historiques sur les princes de Chimay et les comtes de Beaumont.' *BCRH* xi (1846), 109–256.

——. 'Les archives royales de Düsseldorf; notice des documents qui concernent l'histoire de Belgique.' *BCRH* (4) ix (1881), 267–366.

——. 'Les États de Gand en 1476.' *Études et notices historiques concernant l'histoire des Pays-Bas*. 3 vols. Brussels, 1890.

Gagliardi, E. 'Ein freiburgischer Bericht über die Schlacht von Héricourt, 13 November 1474.' *AnzSG* (N.F.) xiii (1915), 268–9.

——. *Geschichte der Schweiz*, i. Zürich, 1934.

Gain, A. and others. *Histoire de Lorraine*. Nancy, 1939.

Galesloot, L. 'Confiscation et donation par le duc de Bourgogne de l'hôtel de Nevers, à Bruxelles, 1467.' *BCRH* (4) iii (1876), 41–52.

Gandilhon, R. *Politique économique de Louis XI*. Paris, 1941.

Garnier, J. *L'artillerie des ducs de Bourgogne*. Paris, 1895.

Garreta, J. C. and others. *La bataille de Nancy, 5 janvier 1477. Exposition du 20 septembre au 6 octobre 1968*. Dijon, 1968.

Gasser, A. 'Les relations historiques de la Bourgogne et de l'Alsace.' *RB* vi (1916–17), 277–95 and 321–36.

Gazier, G. 'Charles le Téméraire et la ville de Besançon.' *MSED* (10) v (1935), 37–47.

Gedenkwaardigheden uit de geschiedenis van Gelderland. Ed. J. A. Nijhoff. 6 vols. Arnhem and The Hague, 1830–75.

Gelder, H. E. van. 'Karel de Stoute en de geestelijke goederen.' *BGBH* xxvi (1901), 449–65.

Geldersche kronieken, ii. Ed. P. N. van Doorninck. WG v. Arnhem, 1908.

Ghinzoni, P. 'La battaglia di Morat.' *ASL* (2) ix (1892), 102–9.

Gilliard, C. 'Yverdon et les guerres de Bourgogne.' *ZSG* xxiv (1944), 313–51.

Gingins-La Sarraz, F. de. *Lettres sur la guerre des Suisses contre le duc Charles-le-Hardi.* Dijon, 1839.

——. *Épisodes des guerres de Bourgogne, 1474 à 1476.* Lausanne, 1850. Reprinted from *Mémoires et documents publiés par la Société d'histoire de la Suisse romande* viii (1849), 114–510.

Godard, J. 'Dans les Pays-Bas bourguignons: Un conflit de politique commerciale.' *AHS* i (1939), 417–20.

Goechner, E. 'Les relations des ducs de Lorraine avec Louis XI de 1461 à 1473.' *AE* xii (1898), 412–20.

Gollut, L. *Les mémoires historiques de la république séquanoise.* Dole, 1592.

Gondry, G. H. *Mémoire historique sur les grands baillis de Hainaut. MPSALH* (4) x (1888), 1–247.

Gorissen, P. 'Caractères originaux de l'aide namuroise de 1473.' *Études dédiées à Ferdinand Courtoy*, ii 565–75. Namur, 1952.

——. *De Raadkamer van de hertog van Bourgondië te Maastricht, 1473–77.* Louvain and Paris, 1959.

——. 'La politique liègeoise de Charles le Téméraire.' *Liège et Bourgogne, BFPL* cciii (1972), 129–45.

Grand, A. *Der Anteil des Wallis an den Burgunderkriegen.* Brig, 1913.

Griveaud, M. 'Un conflit entre Charles le Téméraire et l'abbé de Lure au sujet des mines d'argent de Plancher-les-Mines, 1470–1472.' *BHPTH* (1932–3), 143–65.

Groot Placaat en Charter-Boek van Vriesland. Ed. G. F. Baron thoe Schwartzenberg. 7 vols. Leeuwarden, 1768–1880.

Gros, G. 'Charles le Téméraire en Franche-Comté après Morat.' *MAB* clxxi (1956), 59–73.

Grüneisen, H. 'Herzog Sigmund von Tirol, der Kaiser und die Ächtung der Eidgenossen, 1469.' *Aus Reichstagen des 15. und 16. Jahrhunderts. HKBAW* v. 154–212. Göttingen, 1958.

——. 'Die westliche Reichstände in der Auseinandersetzung zwischen dem Reich, Burgund und Frankreich bis 1473.' *RV* xxvi (1961), 22–77.

——. 'Friedrich I der Siegreiche, Pfalzgraf bei Rhein, Herzog von Bayern, Kurfürst von der Pfalz.' *NDB* v (1961), 526–8.

Grunzweig, A. 'Namur et le début de la Guerre du Bien Public.' *Études dédiées à Ferdinand Courtoy*, ii. 531–64. Namur, 1952.

Grundzweig, A. 'Le Grand Duc du Ponant.' *MA* lxii (1956), 119–65.

Guichenon, S. *Histoire de Bresse.* Lyons, 1650.

——. *Histoire généalogique de la royale maison de Savoie.* 4 vols. Turin, 1778–80.

Guillaume, H. L. G. *Histoire de l'organisation militaire sous les ducs de Bourgogne.* MARB xxii. Brussels, 1848.

——. *Histoire des bandes d'ordonnance des Pays-Bas.* MARB xl. Brussels, 1873.

Handelingen van de Staten en van de Leden van Vlaanderen, 1467–1477. Ed. W. P. Blockmans. CRH. Brussels, 1971.

Hanserecesse von 1431 bis 1476. Ed. G. von der Rupp. 7 vols. Leipzig 1876–92.

Hansisches Urkundenbuch. Ed. K. Hohlbaum and others. 11 vols. Halle, Leipzig, etc., 1876–1939.

Harsin, P. 'Liège entre France et Bourgogne au xve siècle.' *Liège et Bourgogne, BFPL* cciii (1972), 234–53.

Hasselt, G. van. *Oorsprong van het Hof van Gelderland.* Arnhem, 1793.

Hautcoeur, E. *Histoire de l'église collégiale et du chapitre de Saint-Pierre de Lille.* 3 vols. Lille, 1896–9.

Haynin, J. de. *Mémoires, 1465–77.* Ed. D. D. Brouwers. Liège, 1905–6.

Heimpel, H. 'Das Verfahren gegen Peter von Hagenbach zu Breisach, 1474.' *ZGO* (N.F.) lv (1942), 321–57.

——. 'Peter von Hagenbach und die Herrschaft Burgunds am Oberrhein, 1469–74.' *JSFB* v (1942), 139–54.

——. 'Karl der Kühne und Deutschland.' *ELJ* xxi (1943), 1–54.

——. 'Burgund am Rhein und auf dem Schwarzwald.' *Genius* ii (1) (1948), 19–44.

——. 'Karl der Kühne und der burgundische Staat.' *Festschrift Gerhard Ritter,* 140–60. Tübingen, 1950.

——. 'Mittelalter und Nürnberger Prozess.' *Festschrift Edmund E. Stengel,* 443–52. Münster, 1952.

——. 'Burgund—Macht und Kultur.' *GWU* iv (1953), 257–72.

Helbig, H. 'Fürsten und Landstände im Westen des Reiches im Übergang vom Mittelalter zur Neuzeit.' *RV* xxix (1964), 32–72.

Henrard, P. 'Les campagnes de Charles-le-Téméraire contre les Liègeois, 1465–8.' *AAAB* xxiii (1867), 581–678.

——. 'Appréciation du règne de Charles le Téméraire.' MARB xxiv, 8vo. Brussels, 1875.

Heuterus, P. *Rerum burgundicarum libri sex.* Antwerp, 1584.

Hirschauer, C. *Les États d'Artois de leur origines à l'occupation française, 1340–1640.* 2 vols. Paris, 1923.

Histoire de Charles, dernier duc de Bourgogne. Ed. Dupont in J. de Wavrin, *Chroniques,* iii. 219–334. SHF. Paris, 1863.

Historie of the arrivall of Edward IV in England. Ed. J. Bruce. Camden Society, old series. London, 1838.

Historischen Volkslieder der Deutschen, Die. Ed. R. von Liliencron. 4 vols. Leipzig, 1865–9.

Hoch, C. and A. de Mandrot. *Morat et Charles le Téméraire.* Neuchâtel, 1876.

Hommel, L. *Le grand héritage.* 4th edn. Brussels, 1951.

——. *Marguerite d'York.* Paris, 1959.

Hommerich, L. E. M. A. van. 'La politique centralisatrice de Charles le Téméraire à l'égard des assemblées d'États dans la vallée de la Meuse, 1469–1477.' *PSAHL* ciii–iv (1967–8), 106–57.

——. 'Karel de Stoute en het land van's Hertogenrade,' *Het Land van Herle* xviii (1968), 87–100.

——. 'La politique centralisatrice de Charles le Téméraire à l'égard des assemblées d'États du duché de Limbourg et des autres pays d'Outre-Meuse, 1469–1477.' *Liber Memorialis Georges de Lagarde,* 89–110. Studies presented to the International Commission for the history of representative and parliamentary institutions, xxxviii. Louvain, 1970.

Huguenin, A. *Histoire de la guerre de Lorraine et du siège de Nancy.* Metz, 1837.

Huizinga, J. 'Koning Eduard IV van Engeland in ballingschap.' *Verzamelde werken,* iv. 183–94. Haarlem, 1949. Reprinted from *Mélanges Henri Pirenne,* i. 245–56. Brussels, 1926.

——. 'Burgund. Eine Krise der romanisch-germanischen Verhältnisses.' *Verzamelde werken,* ii. 238–65. Haarlem, 1948. Reprinted from *HZ* cxlviii (1933), 1–28.

IAB. L. Gilliodts van Severen. *Inventaire des archives de la ville de Bruges, 13ᵉ–16ᵉ siècle.* 7 vols. Bruges, 1871–8.

IACB. M. Prinet and others. *Inventaire sommaire des archives. Série BB. Ville de Besançon,* i. Besançon, 1912.

IACOB. C. Rossignol and others. *Inventaire sommaire des archives départementales de la Côte d'Or. Série B.* 6 vols. Dijon, 1863–94.

IADNB. A. le Glay and others. *Inventaire sommaire des archives départementales du Nord. Série B.* 10 vols. Lille, 1863–1906.

IADNB. M. Bruchet, *Répertoire numérique. Série B.* 2 vols. Lille, 1921.

IAEG. C. Wyffels. *Inventaris van de Oorkonden der graven van Vlaanderen.* Ghent, no date.

IAEH. L. Devillers. *Inventaire analytique des archives des États de Hainaut.* 3 vols. Mons, 1884–1906.

IAG. P. van Duyse. *Inventaire analytique des chartes et documents de la ville de Gand.* 3 vols. Ghent, 1849–57.

IAGRCC. L. P. Gachard and others. *Inventaire des archives des chambres des comptes.* 6 vols. Brussels, 1837–1931.

IAM. P. J. van Doren. *Inventaire des archives de la ville de Malines.* 8 vols. Malines, 1859–94.

ICL. A. Verkooren. *Inventaire des chartes et cartulaires du Luxembourg.* 5 vols. Brussels, 1914–21.

Jacob, E. F. *The fifteenth century, 1399–1485.* Oxford, 1961.

Jacquot, J. 'Les lettres françaises en Angleterre à la fin du xve siècle.' *La Renaissance dans les provinces du Nord,* 71–96. Ed. F. Lesure. Paris, 1956.

Janeschitz-Kriegl, R. 'Geschichte der ewigen Richtung von 1474.' *ZGO* cv (1957), 150–224 and 409–55.

Janvier, A. *Les Clabault, famille municipale amiénoise, 1349–1539.* Amiens, 1889.

Johnsen, A. O. 'Kong Christian I's forbundspakt med Karl den Dristige av Burgund og hans allierte, 1467.' *HT* (2) ii (1947), 111–31.

Jonge, J. C. de. *Geschiedenis van het Nederlandsche zeewezen,* i. 2nd edn. Haarlem, 1858.

Jongkees, A. G. *Staat en Kerk in Holland en Zeeland onder de Bourgondische Hertogen, 1425–1477.* BIMGU xxi. Groningen, 1942.

——. 'Bourgondië en de Friese vrijheid.' *DVF* xli (1953), 63–78.

Kallen, G. *Die Belagerung von Neuss durch Karl den Kühnen.* Neuss, 1925.

——. *Die Verteidigung von Freiheit und Recht in den Burgunderkriegen.* Cologne, 1950.

Kantorowicz, E. H. 'The Este portrait by Roger van der Weyden.' *JWI* iii (1939–40), 165–80. Reprinted in E. H. Kantorowicz, *Selected studies,* 366–80. New York, 1965.

Kauch, P. 'Note sur l'organisation matérielle de la chambre des comptes de Bruxelles, 1404–73.' *BSAB* (1945), 15–22.

Keller, H. 'Ein neues Bildnis Karls des Kühnen?' *Festgabe Paul Kirn,* 245–54. Berlin, 1961.

Kendall, P. M. *Warwick the kingmaker*. London, 1957.

——. *Louis XI*. New York, 1971.

Kervyn de Lettenhove. *Histoire de Flandre*. 6 vols. Brussels, 1847–50.

——. 'Relation du mariage du duc Charles de Bourgogne et de Marguerite d'York.' *BCRH* (3) x (1869), 245–66.

——. 'Défi adressé par le duc de Lorraine au duc Charles de Bourgogne.' *BARB* lvii (1887), 147–8.

Kingsford, C. L. *English historical literature in the fifteenth century*. Oxford, 1913.

Kirk, J. Foster. *History of Charles the Bold*. 3 vols. London, 1863–8.

Knebel, J. *Diarium*. Ed. W. Vischer and H. Boos. *Basler Chroniken* ii and iii. Leipzig, 1880, 1887.

Knetsch, K. *Des Hauses Hessen Ansprüche auf Brabant*. Marburg, 1915.

Königshoven, J. von. *Chronicke*. Ed. J. Schiltern. Strasbourg, 1698.

Kraus, V. von. *Deutsche Geschichte zur Zeit Albrechts II und Friedrichs III, 1438–1486*. Stuttgart and Berlin, 1905.

Krause, G. *Beziehungen zwischen Habsburg und Burgund bis zum Ausgang der Trierer Zusammenkunft im Jahre 1473*. Göttingen, 1876.

Krebs, M. *Die Politik von Bern, Solothurn und Basel in den Jahren 1466–1468*. Zürich, 1902.

Kremer, C. J. *Geschichte des Kurfürsten Friedrichs des Ersten, von der Pfalz*. Frankfurt and Leipzig, 1765.

Kronyk van Vlaenderen van 580 tot 1467. Ed. P. Blommaert and C. P. Serrure. MVP. 2 vols. Ghent, 1839, 1840.

Kuphal, E. 'Der Neusser Kugelbrief von 1475.' *Aus Mittelalter und Neuzeit. Festschrift Gerhard Kallen*. Bonn, 1957.

Kurth, G. *La cité de Liège au Moyen Age*. 3 vols. Brussels, 1910.

Kurz, H. R. *Schweizerschlachten*. Bern, 1962.

Laborde, L. de. *Les ducs de Bourgogne. Études sur les lettres etc.* 3 vols. Paris, 1849–52.

La Chauvelays, J. de. *Les armées de Charles le Téméraire dans les deux Bourgognes*. Paris, 1879. Reprinted from *MAD* (3) v (1879), 139–369.

——. *Les armées des trois premiers ducs de Bourgogne de la maison de Valois*. *MAD* (3) vi (1880), 19–335.

——. 'Les diverses organisations des armées de Charles le Téméraire, leurs exercises, et le grand règlement militaire du duc pour sa seconde campagne de Suisse.' *Spectateur militaire*, 15 June, 1 and 15 July, 1894.

Lacombe, F. de. *Le siège et la bataille de Nancy, 1476–1477.* Nancy, 1860.

Laenen, J. *Geschiedenis van Mechelen tot op het einde der middeleeuwen.* 2nd edn. Malines, 1934.

La Fons de Mélicocq, A. de. 'Documents sur l'histoire des xive, xve et xvie siècles.' *BSHF* (2) i (1857–8), 5–15 and 294–9.

Lagrange, A. de. 'Itinéraire d'Isabelle de Portugal.' *ACFF* xlii (1938).

Lalaing, A. de. *De congressu Friderici III imp. et Caroli ducis Burgundiorum.* Ed. M. Freher and B. G. Struve, *Rerum germanicarum scriptores,* ii. 302–5. Strasbourg, 1717.

Lallemand, A. *La lutte des États de Liège contre la maison de Bourgogne, 1390–1492.* Brussels, 1910.

La Marche, O. de. *Mémoires.* Ed. H. Beaune and J. d'Arbaumont. SHF. 4 vols. Paris, 1883–8.

——. *L'estat de la maison du duc Charles de Bourgoigne.* Ed. H. Beaune and J. d'Arbaumont, O. de la Marche, *Mémoires,* iv. 1–94. Paris, 1888.

Lambrecht, D. 'Centralisatie onder de Bourgondiërs. Van audiëntie naar Parlement van Mechelen.' *BGN* xx (1965–6), 83–109.

Lameere, E. *Le grand conseil des ducs de Bourgogne de la maison de Valois.* Brussels, 1900.

Langlois, E. 'Notices des manuscrits français et provençaux de Rome antérieurs au xvie siècle.' *NEBN* xxxiii (2) (1889).

Lannoy, A. de. 'La garde de Charles le Téméraire à Nancy en 1477.' *IG* xxi (1966), 120–6.

La Roncière, C. de. *Histoire de la marine française.* 6 vols. Paris, 1899–1932.

Laux, M. *Über die Schlacht bei Nancy.* Berlin, 1895.

Leblond, V. 'L'Hôtel-Dieu de Beauvais et le siège de cette ville par les Bourguignons en 1472.' *MSO* xxiii (1922), 385–422.

Lecoy de la Marche. A. *Le roi René.* 2 vols. Paris, 1875.

Léderrey, E. 'Les armées de Charles le Téméraire durant les guerres de Bourgogne.' *RMS* cvii (1962), 368–82.

Lefèvre, J. 'Le grand conseil de Malines.' *RGB* xlv (1949), 407–20.

Legros, E. 'Liège contre Bourgogne et spécialement les 600 Franchimontois chez les littérateurs et les historiens.' *La Vie Wallonne* xliii (1969), 113–21.

Leguai, A. 'Dijon et Louis XI, 1461–1483.' *AB* xvii (1945), 16–37, 103–15, 145–69 and 239–63.

Lejeune, J. *Liège. De la principauté à la métropole.* Antwerp, 1967.

——. *Exposition. Liège et Bourgogne.* Musée de l'Art Wallon, Liège, 1968.

Lettres de rois et autres personnages. Ed. J. Champollion-Figeac. CDIHF. 2 vols. Paris, 1839, 1847.

Lettres de Louis XI roi de France. Ed. J. Vaesen and E. Charavay. SHF. 12 vols. Paris, 1883–1909.

Lettres et négotiations de Philippe de Commines. Ed. Kervyn de Lettenhove. 2 vols. Brussels, 1867, 1868.

Lettres missives originales du chartrier de Thouars, série du quinzième siècle. Ed. P. Marchegay. *BSAN* x (1870–1), 149–87 and xi (1872), 47–66, 107–30 and 183–225.

Libellus de magnificentia ducis Burgundiae in Treveris visa conscriptus. Ed. C. C. Bernoulli. *Basler Chroniken,* iii. 332–64. Leipzig, 1887.

Liebenau, T. von. 'Versuch einer ewigen Richtung zwischen der Schweiz, dem Kaiser und dem Hause Oesterreich durch Graf Ulrich von Württemberg.' *AnzSG* (N.F.) iii (1878–81), 84–7.

——. 'Mümpelgard und die Schweiz, 1474–1476.' *AnzSG* (N.F.) v (1886–1889), 29–36.

——. 'Ein Zürcher-Schlachtbericht über Nancy.' *AnzSG* (N.F.) viii (1898–1901), 66–9.

Lindner, F. *Die Zusammenkunft Kaisers Friedrich III mit Karl dem Kühnen von Burgund.* Köslin, 1876.

Listes chronologiques des procès et arrêts des anciens Conseils de justice de la Belgique. 1re série. Grand Conseil et Parlement de Malines, i. *1465–1504.* Ed. J. T. de Smidt and E. I. Strubbe. Brussels, 1966.

Lists and Indexes, xlix. Public Record Office, London, 1923.

Löhrer, F. J. *Geschichte der Stadt Neuss.* Neuss, 1840.

Lois militaires de Charles de Bourgogne de l'an 1473. Ed. N.F. von Mülinen. *SG* ii (1817), 425–68.

Lory, E. L. 'Les obsèques de Philippe le Bon.' *MCACO* vii (1869), 215–46.

Los, J. de. *Chronique.* Ed. P. de Ram. *Documents relatifs aux troubles du pays de Liège sous les princes-évêques Louis de Bourbon et Jean de Horne, 1455–1505,* 1–132. CRH. Brussels, 1844.

Lot, F. *L'art militaire et les armées au moyen-âge en Europe et dans le Proche Orient.* 2 vols. Paris, 1946.

Loye, L. *Histoire de la seigneurie de Neuchâtel-Bourgogne.* Montbéliard, 1890.

Lud, J. *Dialogue.* Ed. J. Cayon. Nancy, 1844, and H. Lepage, *Journal de la Société d'archéologie et du Comité du Musée Lorrain* iii (1854), 149–94.

Maeght, X. *Les emprunts de Charles le Téméraire.* Unpublished dissertation, University of Lille, 1956.

Magnien, C. 'Une page de l'histoire Anglo-Belge: Caxton à la cour de Charles-le-Téméraire, à Bruges.' *ASRAB* (1912), 49–55.

Magnum chronicon Belgicum, 54–1474. Ed. B.G. Struve, *Rerum germanicarum scriptores,* iii. 1–456. Regensburg, 1726.

Mancini, D. *The usurpation of Richard III.* Ed. C. A. J. Armstrong. 2nd edn. Oxford, 1969.

Mandrot, B. de. 'Étude sur les relations de Charles VII et de Louis XI rois de France avec les cantons suisses.' *JSG* v (1880), 59–182 and vi (1881), 203–77. Reprinted separately, Zürich, 1881.

——. 'L'autorité historique de Philippe de Commynes.' *RH* lxxiii (1900), 241–57 and lxxiv (1900), 1–38.

——. 'Jean de Bourgogne, duc de Brabant, comte de Nevers, et le procès de sa succession.' *RH* xciii (1907), 1–45.

Mangin, J. 'Guillaume de Rochefort, conseilleur de Charles le Téméraire et chancelier de France.' *PTSEC* (1936), 117–23.

Mantel, A. *Die Burgunderkriege.* Zürich, 1914.

Marchal, L. *Mémoire sur la bataille de Nancy, gagnée par René II, duc de Lorraine, sur Charles de Bourgogne.* Nancy, 1851.

Margny, J. de. *L'Aventurier.* Ed. J. R. de Chevanne. Paris, 1938.

Maris, A. J. 'De raadkamers of hoven van Karel den Stoute in Gelre en Zutphen, 1473–7.' *GBM* lvi (1957), 45–123.

——. 'De aanstelling van Philips van Croy, graaf van Chimay, tot stadhouder van Gelderland in 1474.' *GBM* lx (1961), 157–62.

Markgraf, K. A. H. *De bello Burgundico a Carolo Audace contra archiepiscopatum Coloniensem suscepto a. 1474.* Berlin, 1861.

Marot, P. 'Notes sur l'intrusion bourguignonne en Lorraine au xvᵉ siècle. Les Neufchâtel et la maison d'Anjou.' *AE* xliv (1930), 21–36.

Martin, P. 'Les étendards de l'armée de Charles le Téméraire.' *BSAMD* (1949–51), 24–6.

Matzenauer, M. *Studien zur Politik Karls des Kühnen bis zum Jahre 1474.* SSG (N.F.) xi. Zürich, 1946.

Matzinger, A. W. *Zur Geschichte der niederen Vereinigung.* SSG ii. 255–846. Basel, 1910.

Maupoint, J. *Journal parisien.* Ed. G. Fagniez. *MSHP* iv (1877), 1–114.

Megkynch, G. *Bericht über Herzog Karls von Burgund Besuch im Elsass.* Ed. A. Bernoulli. *Basler Chroniken,* vii. Leipzig, 1915.

Meier, M. A. *Die Waldshuterkreig von 1468. Eine Gesamtdarstellung.* Basel, 1937.

Meier, M. A. 'Der Friede von Waldshut und die Politik am Oberrhein bis zum Vertrag von Saint-Omer.' *ZGO* (N.F.) li (1937–8), 321–84.

Meister, U. 'Betrachtungen über das Entstehen der Burgunderkriege und den Verlauf des Tages von Murten den 22 Juni 1476.' *NFZ* lxxii. Zürich, 1877.

Mémoires pour servir à l'histoire de France et de Bourgogne. 2 vols. Paris 1729.

Memorieboek der stad Ghent. Ed. P. J. van der Meersch. 4 vols. Ghent, 1852–64.

Merica, H. de. *De cladibus Leodensium.* Ed. S. Balau, *Chroniques liégeoises,* i. 221–308. CRH. Brussels, 1913.

Meyer, J. *Commentarii sive annales rerum Flandricarum.* Antwerp, 1561.

Meyer, J. J. *Chronique strasbourgeoise.* Ed. R. Reuss. Strasbourg, 1873.

Meynart, A. 'Un gouverneur de Brabant sous le règne de Charles le Téméraire.' *BCRH* cxxvi (1960), 135–52.

Michelet, J. *Histoire de France,* viii. new edn. Paris, 1879.

Mieg, P. 'Les difficultés de Mulhouse à l'époque de son alliance avec Berne et Soleure.' *BMM* lxxiii (1965), 31–84, lxxiv (1966), 5–109, lxxv (1967), 39–118, lxxvi (1968), 47–154 and lxxvii (1969), 39–148.

Mittler, O. *Geschichte der Stadt Baden,* i. *Von der frühesten Zeit bis um 1650.* Aarau, 1962.

Molinet, J. *Chroniques.* Ed. G. Doutrepont and O. Jodogne. 3 vols. Brussels, 1935–7.

Mollat, M. 'Recherches sur les finances des ducs Valois de Bourgogne.' *RH* ccxix (1958), 285–321.

Molsheim, P. von. *Freiburger Chronik.* Ed. A. Büchi. Bern, 1914.

Moltzer, H. E. *Frederik III en Karel de Stoute te Trier, 1473. Bibliotheek van Middelnederlandsche Letterkunde,* xliv. 1–35. Leiden, 1890.

Monfrin, J. 'Le goût des lettres antiques à la cour de Bourgogne au xve siècle.' *BSAF* (1967), 285–9.

Monumenta Habsburgica. See *Aktenstücke . . .*

Moreau, R. E. de. *Histoire de l'église en Belgique.* 5 vols. Brussels, 1940–52.

Morelli, L. *Cronaca.* Ed. I. di San Luigi, *Croniche di Giovanni di Jacopo e di Lionardo di Lorenzo Morelli. Delizie degli eruditi toscani,* xix. 165–212. Florence, 1785.

Motta, E. 'Un documento per la battaglia di Nancy.' *BSSI* x (1888), 191–2.

Mulart, S. *See* Boeren.

Mülinen, N. F. von. 'Einiges aus dem Burgunderkriege.' *SG* vi (1826), 145–60.

Müller, K. *Innerschweiz Essays*. Luzern, 1960.

Müller, K. E. H. *Die deutschfeindliche Politik Karls des Kühnen von Burgund; ein Vorspiel der Annexionsbestrebungen der französischen Regenten*. Prenzlau, 1874.

Myers, A. R. 'The outbreak of war between England and Burgundy in February, 1471.' *BIHR* xxxiii (1960), 114–15.

Nerlinger, C. *Pierre de Hagenbach et la domination bourguignonne en Alsace, 1469–74*. Nancy, 1890.

——. 'Thann à la fin du xve siècle.' *AE* vi (1892), 582–610. Reprinted separately, Paris, 1893.

——. 'La seigneurie et le château d'Ortenberg sous la domination bourguignonne.' *AE* viii (1894), 32–65.

——. 'Les revenues des ducs de Bourgogne à Thann à la fin du xve siècle.' *RA* (1896), 87–101.

——. 'État du château de Thann en Alsace au xve siècle.' *BEC* lix (1898), 304–21.

Nicolas, D. *De preliis et occasu ducis Burgundie historia*. Ed. R. Luginbühl, Basel, 1911, and K. Ohly, *ZGO* cvi (1958), 53–93 and 277–363.

Nicolay, J. *Kalendrier des guerres de Tournay, 1447–1479*. Ed. J. B. J. F. Hennebert. Brussels, 1854.

Niessen, J. 'Karl der Kühne und die niederrheinischen Herzogtümer.' *RHB* iv (1927), 80–3.

Ochsenbein, F. *Die Kriegsgründe und Kriegsbilder des Burgunderkrieges*. Bern, 1876.

Odlozilik, O. *The Hussite king. Bohemia in European affairs, 1440–1471*. New Brunswick, 1965.

Oechsli, W. 'Die Beziehungen der schweizerischen Eidgenossenschaft zum Reiche bis zum Schwabenkrieg.' *PJSE* v (1890), 302–616.

Onofrio de Santa Croce, *Mémoire*. Ed. S. Bormans. CRH. Brussels, 1885.

Ordonnances des ducs de Bourgogne sur l'administration de la justice du duché. Ed. E. Champeaux. *RB* xvii (2, 3). Dijon, 1907.

Ordonnances des rois de France de la troisième race. Ed. D. F. Secousse and others. 21 vols. Paris, 1723–1849.

Ostfriesisches Urkundenbuch. Ed. E. Friedländer. 2 vols. Emden, 1874, 1880–1.

Oudenbosch, A. d'. *Chronique.* Ed. C. de Borman. Liège, 1902.

Paillard, C. '*Le procès du chancelier Hugonet et du seigneur d'Humbercourt.*' MARB xxxi, 8vo. Brussels, 1881.

Paquet, J. 'Une ébauche de la nonciature de Flandre au xvᵉ siècle: les missions dans les Pays-Bas de Luc de Tolentis, évêque de Sebenico, 1462–1484.' *BIHBR* xxv (1949), 27–144.

Paravicini, W. 'Zur Biographie von Guillaume Hugonet, Kanzler Herzog Karls des Kühnen.' *Festschrift Hermann Heimpel,* ii. 443–81. Göttingen, 1972.

——. *Guy de Brimeu,* seigneur de Humbercourt, lieutenant de Charles le Téméraire au pays de Liège'. *Liège et Bourgogne, BFPL* cciii (1972) 147–56.

——. *Guy de Brimeu. Der burgundische Staat und seine adlige Führungsschicht unter Karl dem Kühnen.* Bonn, 1973.

Parisot, R. *Histoire de Lorraine.* 3 vols. Paris, 1919–24.

Paston letters and papers of the fifteenth century, i. Ed. N. Davis. Oxford, 1971.

Pauwels, T. *Alia narratio de ducibus Burgundiae.* Ed. Kervyn de Lettenhove. *Chroniques relatives à l'histoire de la Belgique sous la domination des ducs de Bourgogne. Textes latins,* 264–328. CRH. Brussels, 1876.

——. *Historia de cladibus Leodensium.* Ed. P. de Ram. *Documents relatifs aux troubles du pays de Liège sous les princes-évêques Louis de Bourbon et Jean de Horne, 1455–1505,* 185–232. CRH. Brussels, 1844.

Perret, P. M. 'Jaques Galéot et la République de Venise.' *BEC* lii (1891), 590–614.

——. *Histoire des relations de la France avec Venise.* 2 vols. Paris, 1896.

Perrier, F. *Guerre de Bourgogne. Batailles de Grandson et de Morat.* 2nd edn. Fribourg, 1876.

Petit–Dutaillis, C. *Charles VII, Louis XI et les premières années de Charles VIII, 1422–1492.* E. Lavisse, *Histoire de France* iv (2). Paris, 1902.

Petri, F. 'Nordwestdeutschland in der Politik der Burgunderherzöge.' *Gemeinsame Probleme deutsch-niederländischer Landes- und Volksforschung,* 92–126. BIMGU xxxii. Groningen, 1962. Reprinted from *WF* vii (1953–4), 80–100.

——. 'Niederlande, Rheinland und Reich.' *Gemeinsame Probleme ...,* 172–202. BIMGU xxxii. Groningen, 1962.

Petri, S. *Gesta pontificum Leodiensium a Joanne de Bavaria usque ad Erardum a Marcka.* Ed. J. Chapeaville. *Gesta pontificum Leodiensium,* iii. Liège, 1616.

458   BIBLIOGRAPHY

Pfeiffer, G. 'Die Bündniss- und Landfriedenspolitik der Territorien zwischen Weser und Rhein im späteren Mittelalter.' *Der Raum Westfalen*, ii (1). Ed. H. Aubin. Münster, 1955.

Pfettisheim, C. *Geschichte Peter Hagenbachs und der Burgunderkriege*. Ed. E. Picot and H. Stein, *Recueil de pièces historiques imprimées sous le règne de Louis XI*, no. 4, Paris, 1923, and L. Fischel and E. Müller, Plochingen, 1966.

Pfister, C. *Histoire de Nancy*, i. 2nd edn. Paris, 1902.

Phillipps, T. 'Account of the marriage of Margaret, sister of King Edward IV, to Charles, duke of Burgundy, in 1468.' *Archaeologia* xxxi (1846), 326–38.

Pinchart, A. *Miniaturistes, enlumineurs et calligraphes employés par Philippe le Bon et Charles le Téméraire et leurs oeuvres. BCAA* iv. 474–508. Brussels, 1866.

Piquard, M. 'Charles de Neufchâtel, archevêque de Besançon de 1463 à 1498.' *BHPTH* (1932–3), 35–46.

Pius II, Pope. *Historia rerum Friderici tertii*, i. Ed. J. G. von Kulpis. Strasbourg, 1685.

Placcaerten ende ordonnantien van de hertoghen van Brabandt. Ed. A. Anselmo and others. 10 vols. Antwerp and Brussels, 1648–1774.

Plancher, U. *Histoire générale et particulière de Bourgogne*. 4 vols. Dijon, 1739–81.

Pocquet du Haut Jussé, B. A. *François II duc de Bretagne et l'Angleterre 1458–1488*. Paris, 1929.

——. 'Deux féodaux: Bourgogne et Bretagne, 1363–1491, vii. Charles le Téméraire et François II, 1461–73.' *RCC* xxxvi (2) (1934–5), 177–86 and 363–75.

Politische Correspondenz des Kurfürsten Albrecht Achilles. Ed. F. Priebatsch. 2 vols. Leipzig, 1894, 1897.

Poncelet, E. 'L'execution de Louis de Luxembourg, comte de Saint-Pol, en 1475.' *BCRH* xci (1927), 181–98.

——. 'Le combat du faubourg Saint-Léonard à Liège, 27 octobre 1468.' *ACCAL* viii (1940), 268–95.

Pons, J. 'L'Ortenberg et le Ramstein.' *Annuaire de Sélestat* (1967), 77–107.

Pontieri, E. 'Su le manccate nozze tra Federico d'Aragona e Maria di Borgogna.' *ASN* lxiii (1939), 78–112.

Prarond, E. *Abbeville au temps de Charles VII, des ducs de Bourgogne, maîtres de Ponthieu, et de Louis XI, 1426–83*. Paris, 1899.

Précis analytique des documents que renferme le dépôt des archives de la Flandre-Occidentale à Bruges. Ed. O. Delepierre and F. Priem. 2ᵉ série. 9 vols. Bruges, 1845–58.

Prims, F. *Geschiedenis van Antwerpen.* 11 vols. Brussels etc., 1927–1949.

Procès-verbal du massacre de Nesle. Ed. *BSHF* i (2) (1834), 11–17 and *BCLF* ii (1853–5). 231–5.

Prunelle, F. [Documents relatifs aux guerres entre Louis XI et Charles le Téméraire.] *BAD* ii (1849), 639–56.

Putnam, R. *Charles the Bold.* London, 1908.

Quarré, P. 'La "joyeuse entrée" de Charles le Téméraire à Dijon en 1474.' *BARBB* li (1969), 326–40.

Ram, P. de. 'Détails concernant le mariage de Charles le Téméraire avec Marguerite d'York en 1468.' *BCRH* (1) (1842), 168–74.

Rausch, K. *Die burgundische Heirat Maximilians I.* Vienna, 1880.

Rechtsquellen des Kantons Bern, Die. Ed. H. Rennefahrt. First part, iv (1). Aarau, 1955.

Recueil de choses advenues du temps et gouvernement de très haulte mémoire feu Charles, duc de Bourgogne, estant le seigneur du Fay gouverneur au pays de Luxembourg. Publications de la Société pour la recherche et la conservation des monuments historiques dans le Grand-Duché de Luxembourg=PSHIL iii (1847), 85–153.

Recueil de documents relatifs aux conflits soutenus pas les Liégeois contre Louis de Bourbon et Charles le Téméraire, 1458–1469. BCRH xciv (1930), 245–353.

Recueil des ordonnances de la principauté de Liège, 1ᵉ série, 974–1506. Ed. S. Bormans. Brussels, 1878.

Regesten zur Geschichte der Belagerung von Neuss, 1474–5. Ed. K. Höhlbaum, *Mitteilungen aus dem Stadtarchiv von Köln* viii (1885), 1–36.

Régestes de la cité de Liège. Ed. E. Fairon. 4 vols. Liège, 1933–40.

Registres du conseil de Genève. Ed. E. Rivoire and others. 13 vols. Geneva, 1900–40.

Reichstags–Theatrum unter K. Friedrichs V. Ed. J. J. Müller. 3 parts. Jena, 1713.

Reiffenberg, F. A. F. T. de. *Histoire de l'Ordre de la Toison d'Or.* Brussels, 1830.

Reilhac, A. de. *Jean de Reilhac.* 3 vols. Paris, 1886–8.

Reimchronik über Peter von Hagenbach. Ed. F. Mone. QBL iii. 183–434. Karlsruhe, 1863.

Renet, M. *Beauvais et le Beauvaisis dans le temps modernes. Époque de Louis XI et Charles le Téméraire.* Beauvais, 1898.

Rettig, G. 'Die Beziehungen Mülhausens zur schweizerischen Eidgenossenschaft bis zu den Burgunderkriegen.' *AHKB* xii (2) (1889), 163–215.

Reutter, G. *Le rôle joué par le comté de Neuchâtel dans la politique suisse et dans la politique française à la fin du xvᵉ siècle et au début du xviᵉ, 1474–1530.* Geneva, 1942.

Reymond, M. 'La guerre de Bourgogne et Lausanne.' *Revue historique vaudoise* xxiii (1915), 161–72 and 193–205.

Richard, J. 'Le gouverneur de Bourgogne au temps des ducs Valois.' *MSHDB* xix (1957), 101–12.

Ring, M. de. 'Révolte des provinces autrichiennes du Rhin contre Charles le Téméraire, 1474.' *MSHB* (1841), 351–87.

Ristelhuber, P. *L'Alsace à Morat.* Paris, 1876.

Robert, G. *Journal.* Ed. Académie d'Arras. Arras, 1852.

Rodt, E. von. *Die Feldzüge Karls des Kühnen, Herzogs von Burgund, und seiner Erben.* 2 vols. Schaffhausen, 1843, 1844.

Roget, A. *Les Suisses et Genève.* 2 vols. Genève, 1864.

[Rolland, A.] *La guerre de René II, duc de Lorraine, contre Charles Hardy, duc de Bourgogne.* Luxembourg, 1742.

Roover, R. de. *Money, banking and credit in medieval Bruges.* Cambridge, Mass., 1948.

——. 'Oprichtung en liquidatie van het Brugse filiaal van het bankiershuis der Medici.' *MKVAL* xv. Brussels, 1953.

——. *The rise and decline of the Medici bank, 1397–1494.* Cambridge, Mass., 1963.

Ropp, G. von. 'Die Hansa und der Reichskrieg gegen Burgund, 1474–1475.' *HG* xxvi (1899), 43–55.

Rotuli Parliamentorum, 1278–1503. 7 vols. London, 1832.

Roux, J. *Histoire de l'abbaye de Saint-Acheul-lez-Amiens.* Amiens, 1890.

Roye, J. de. *Chronique scandaleuse.* Ed. B. de Mandrot. SHF. 2 vols. Paris, 1894, 1896.

Rubbrecht, O. 'Trois portraits de la maison de Bourgogne par Memlinc.' *ASEB* lx (1910), 15–64.

Rüsch, N. *Die Beschreibung der Burgunderkriege.* Ed. C. C. Bernoulli. *Basler Chroniken*, iii. Leipzig, 1887.

Ruwet, J. *Les archives et bibliothèques de Vienne et l'histoire de Belgique.* CRH. Brussels, 1956.

Salet, F. 'La fête de la Toison d'Or de 1468.' *ASRAB* li (1966), 5–29.

——. 'La fête de la Toison d'Or et la mariage de Charles le Téméraire, Bruges, mai-juillet, 1468.' *ASEB* cvi (1969), 5–16.

Samaran, C. *La maison d'Armagnac au xvᵉ siècle.* Paris, 1907.

——. 'Vasco de Lucena à la cour de Bourgogne.' *Bulletin des études portugaises* (1938), 13–26.

Sanuto, M. *Vitae ducum Venetorum.* Ed. L. A. Muratori, *Rerum italicarum scriptores*, xxii. cols. 399–1252. Milan, 1733.

Schaufelberger, W. *Der alte Schweizer und sein Krieg. Studien zur Kriegführung vornehmlich im 15. Jahrhundert.* Zürich, 1952.

——. 'Zu einer Charakterologie des altschweizerischen Kriegertums'. *SAV* lvi (1960), 48–87.

Schaumburg, W. von. *Die Geschichten und Taten.* Ed. A. von Keller, BLVS l. Stuttgart, 1859.

Schilling, D. *Die Berner-Chronik, 1468–1484.* Ed. G. Tobler. 2 vols. Bern, 1897, 1901.

——. ——. Facsimile of the superbly illustrated Bern, Burgerbibliothek, MS. Hist. Helv. I. 3, ed. H. Bloesch and P. Hilber. 4 vols. Bern, 1943–5.

Schilling, D., of Luzern. *Chronik.* Ed. R. Durrer and P. Hilber. Geneva, 1932.

Schmid, M. *Staat und Volk im alten Solothurn.* Basler Beiträge zur Geschichtswissenschaft, xcv. Basel and Stuttgart, 1964.

Schmidt-Sinns, D. *Studien zum Heerwesen der Herzöge von Burgund, 1465–1477.* Unpublished thesis, University of Göttingen, 1966.

Schmitz, F. 'Der Neusser Krieg.' *RG* ii (1895–6), 1–10, 33–60, 65–80, 97–113, 129–45, 161–77, 193–209, 225–41 and 257–63.

Schneebeli, M. 'Das Heer Karls des kühnen.' *ASMZ* cvi (1960), 125–35.

Schoeber, R. *Die Schlacht bei Nancy.* Erlangen, 1891.

Schryver, A. de. 'Nicolas Spierinc, calligraphe et enlumineur des ordonnances des états de l'hôtel de Charles le Téméraire.' *Scriptorium* xxiii (1969), 434–58.

Schwarzkopf, U. *Studien zur Hoforganisation der Herzöge von Burgund aus dem Hause Valois.* Unpublished thesis, University of Göttingen, 1955.

——. 'La cour de Bourgogne et la Toison d'Or.' *PCEEBM* v (1963), 91–104.

Scofield, C. L. *The life and reign of Edward IV.* 2 vols. London, 1923. Reprinted 1967.

Sittler, L. *La Decapole alsacienne des origines à la fin du moyen-âge.* Strasbourg and Paris, 1955.

Snoy, R. *De rebus batavicis libri xiii.* Frankfurt, 1620.

Specklin, D. *Les collectanées.* Ed. R. Reuss. FACA ii. Strasbourg, 1890.

Speierische Chronik, 1406–1476. Ed. F. J. Mone. QBL i. 367–520. Karlsruhe, 1848.

Stälin, C. F. von. *Wirtembergische Geschichte.* 4 vols. Stuttgart, 1841–70.

Stein, H. *Charles de France, frère de Louis XI.* Paris, 1921.

——. 'Un diplomate bourguignon du xve siècle, Antoine Haneron.' *BEC* xcviii (1937), 283–348.

Steinbach, F. 'Die Rheinlande in der Burgunderzeit.' *Festschrift Neuss,* 37–46. Ed. G. Kallen. Cologne, 1950. Reprinted in *Collectanea Franz Steinbach,* 91–5, ed. F. Petri and G. Droege, Bonn, 1967.

Stenzel, K. 'Das Reich, Karls des Kühnen und die Lande am Oberrhein.' *RHB* iv (1927), 50–7.

Stettler, K. *Ritter Niklaus von Diesbach, Schultheiss von Bern, 1430–1475.* Bern, 1924.

——. *Schodoler, Bilder aus seiner Chronik.* Aarau, 1943.

Stintzi, P. 'Die "vier Waldstädte" und der Cartulaire des seigneuries-gageries vom Jahre 1469.' *AJ* vii (1959), 147–58.

Stolle, K. *Thüringisch-Erfurtische Chronik.* Ed. L. F. Hesse. BLVS xxxii. Stuttgart, 1854.

Stouff, L. *Les origines de l'annexion de la Haute-Alsace à la Bourgogne en 1469. RB* x (3–4) (1900) and separately, Paris, 1901.

——. *La déscription de plusieurs forteresses et seigneuries de Charles le Téméraire en Alsace et dans la haute vallée du Rhin, par Maître Mongin Contault, maître des comptes à Dijon, 1473.* Paris, 1902.

——. *Les possessions bourguignonnes dans la vallée du Rhin sous Charles le Téméraire d'après l'information de Poinsot et de Pillet, 1471. AE* xviii (1904), 1–86 and separately, Paris, 1904.

——. *Catherine de Bourgogne et la féodalité de l'Alsace autrichienne. RB* xxiii (2, 3, 4) (1913) and separately, Paris, 1913.

Stracke, J. 'Ein Spionagebericht von 1468 aus Friesland für Karl den Kühnen van Burgund.' *JGKA* xlviii (1968), 25–33.

Straszburgische Archiv-Chronik. Ed. L. Schneegans and A. Strobel. *Code historique et diplomatique de la ville de Strasbourg,* i (2). 131–220. Strasbourg, 1843.

Stuart, D. M. 'The marriage of Margaret of York and Charles, duke of Burgundy, July 1468.' *History Today,* viii (1958), 256–63.

Suchet. 'La fin de Charles le Téméraire.' *MAB* (1899), 129–40.

Sulzer, P. *Die Burgunderkriege in der schweizerischen Geschichtschreibung von Johannes von Müller bis Emanuel von Rodt.* SSG. Zürich, 1945.

Table chronologique des chartes et diplômes relatifs à l'histoire de l'ancien pays de Luxembourg. Charles le Téméraire, 1467–1477. PSHIL xxxiv (1880), 1–191.

Tardif, J. *Monuments historiques. Inventaires et documents publiés par ordre de l'Empereur.* Paris, 1866.

Thielemans, M. R. and others. *Marguerite d'York et son temps.* British week in Brussels, 29 September–7 October 1967. Exposition organisée par la banque de Bruxelles. Catalogue illustré. Brussels, 1967.

Thomas, E. 'Étude sur les relations de Louis XI avec la Savoie.' *PTSEC* (1931), 187–92.

Thommen, R. 'Friedensverträge und Bünde der Eidgenossenschaft mit Frankreich, 1444–1777.' *ZGA* xv (1916), 117–214.

Thomson, J. A. F. 'The arrival of Edward IV. The development of the text.' *Speculum* xlvi (1971), 84–93.

Tourneur, V. 'Jehan de Candida, diplomate et médailleur au service de la maison de Bourgogne, 1472–80.' *RBN* lxx (1914), 381–411 and lxxi (1919), 7–48 and 251–300.

Toutey, E. *Charles le Téméraire et la Ligue de Constance.* Paris, 1902.

Trausch, J. *Strassburgische Chronick.* Ed. L. Dacheux. FACA iii. 1–74. Strasbourg, 1892.

Trouvé, R. 'Enkele bijzonderheden over de Mechelse stadsfinanciën in de xv⁵ eeuw.' *HKOM* lvi (1952), 46–67.

Tschudi, G. *Chronicon helveticum, Fortsetzung. Helvetia* (N.F.) ii (1828), 463–620.

Tücking, K. *Geschichte der Stadt Neuss.* Düsseldorf, 1891.

Tüsch, H. E. *Die Burgundische hystorie.* Ed. E. Wendling and A. Stöber. *Alsatia* (1875–6) and separately Colmar, 1876, and by E. Picot and H. Stein, *Recueil de pièces historiques imprimées sous le règne de Louis XI,* no. 5, Paris, 1923.

Unrest, J. *Oesterreichische Chronik.* Ed. K. Grossmann. *Monumenta Germaniae Historica Scriptores* (N.F.) xi. Weimar, 1957.

Urkunden, Briefe und Actenstücke zur Geschichte der habsburgischen Fürsten, 1443–1473. Ed. J. Chmel. FRADA ii. Vienna, 1850.

Urkunden der Belagerung und Schlacht von Murten, Die. Ed. G. F. Ochsenbein. Fribourg, 1876.

Urkunden und Actenstücke zur österreichischen Geschichte im Zeitalter Kaiser Friedrichs III und König Georgs von Böhmen, 1440–1471. Ed. A. Bachmann. FRADA xlii. Vienna, 1879.

Urkunden und Acten betreffend die Belagerung der Stadt Neuss am Rheine, 1474–75. Ed. E. Wülcker. Neujahrs-Blatt des Vereins für Geschichte. Frankfurt, 1877.

Urkunden und Aktenstücke des Reichsarchivs Wien zur reichsrechtlichen Stellung des burgundischen Kreises. Ed. L. Gross and others. 3 vols. Vienna, 1944–5.

Urkundenbuch der Stadt Basel, viii. Ed. R. Thommen. Basel, 1901.

Urkundenbuch für die Geschichte des Niederrheins. Ed. T. J. Lacomblet. 4 vols. Düsseldorf, 1840–58.

Urkundliche Beleuchtung der Verpfaendung einiger Landschaften des Herzogs Siegmund von Östrich an Herzog Karl von Burgund. Ed. J. C. Zellweger. *SMHW* ii (1838), 103–23 and 299–333.

Urkundliche Nachträge zur österreichisch-deutschen Geschichte im Zeitalter Kaiser Friedrich III. Ed. A. Bachmann. FRADA xlvi. Vienna, 1892.

Ussel, P. van. *Maria van Bourgondië.* Bruges, 1944.

Vallière, P. E. de. *Morat. Le siège et la bataille, 1476.* Lausanne, 1926.

Van de Kieft, C. 'De Staten-Generaal in het Bourgondisch-Oostenrijkse tijdvak, 1464–1555.' *500 jaren Staten-Generaal in de Nederlanden.* Assen, 1964.

Van den Borren, C. *Geschiedenis van de muziek in de Nederlanden,* i. Antwerp, 1948.

Van den Gheyn, J. 'Contributions à l'iconographie de Charles le Téméraire et de Marguerite d'York.' *AAAB* lvi (1904), 384–405.

——. 'Encore l'iconographie de Charles le Téméraire et de Marguerite d'York.' *AAAB* lix (1907), 275–94.

Vandeputte, F. 'Dignitaires et employés à la cour de Charles le Téméraire.' *ASEB* xxviii (1876–7), 188–92.

Van der Essen, L. 'Un conflit entre le duc Charles le Téméraire et l'Université de Louvain à propos du paiement des impôts en 1473.' *BCRH* xc (1926), 242–57.

Vander Linden, H. *Intinéraires de Charles, duc de Bourgogne, Marguerite d'York et Marie de Bourgogne.* CRH. Brussels, 1936.

Varenbergh, E. *Histoire des relations diplomatiques entre le comté de Flandre et l'Angleterre au moyen âge.* Brussels, 1874. Reprinted from *MSHB* (1869–73).

Vaughan, R. *John the Fearless*. London, 1966.

———. *Philip the Good*. London, 1970.

Vayssière, A. 'Instructions données par Charles le Téméraire, duc de Bourgogne, à des émissaires auprès du duc et de la duchesse de Savoye.' *RSS* (6) vii (1878), 363–7.

Veen, J. S. van. 'Bijdragen tot de geschiedenis der jaren 1467 en 1468.' *GBM* xxxii (1929), 45–127.

——— and A. P. van Schilfgaarde. 'De raden of hoven van Karel den Stoute in Gelderland.' *GBM* xxxvi (1933), 23–36.

Ven, A. J. van de. 'Het hof van justitie te Zutfen.' *GBM* xlvi (1943), 46–8.

Verbruggen, J. 'De militairen. De krijgers van de hertogen van Bourgondië.' *FN* v (1960), 224–34.

Vernunft, W. 'Karl der Kühne, Herzog von Burgund.' *JSFB* v (1942), 115–129.

Vevey, B. de. 'Estavayer et les guerres de Bourgogne.' *AF* xxxiv–xxxv (1946–7), 18–26, 34–50 and 113–16.

Viaene, A. 'Weddenschappen op de vermiste hertog na de slag bij Nancy, 1477.' *Biekorf* lix (1958), 353–7.

Vicens Vives, J. *Juan II de Aragon, 1398–1479*. Barcelona, 1953.

Vraye déclaration du fait et conduite de la bataille de Nancy, La. Ed. Lenglet du Fresnoy in de Comines, *Mémoires*, iii. 491–3; Calmet in *Histoire de Lorraine*, vii. cols. cli–cliii; Cayon in *Chronique ou dialogue entre Joannes Lud et Chrétien*, 60–4; and (uncritically) in Frédérix, *Mort de Charles le Téméraire*, 249–51.

Vrancken–Pirson, G. 'La destruction de la cité de Liège en 1468 par Charles le Téméraire.' *CAPL* xxxix (1948), 35–6.

Wackernagel, R. *Geschichte der Stadt Basel*. 3 vols. Basel, 1907–24.

Walther, J. E. A. *Die burgundischen Zentralbehörden unter Maximilian und Karl V*. Leipzig, 1909.

Wattelet, H. 'Die Schlacht bei Murten'. *FG* i (1894), 11–94.

Waurin, J. de. *Cronicques*. Ed. Dupont. 3 vols. SHF. Paris, 1863.

———. *Recueil des croniques*. Ed. W. Hardy. RS. 5 vols. London, 1864.

Weiss, J. 'Ein Brief aus dem Feldlager vor Neuss, 1475.' *ZGO* (N.F. (1894), 718–21.

Wellens, R. 'Un fragment d'itinéraire des ducs de Bourgogne, 1469–? *ABB* xxxviii (1967), 108–13.

Q

Werveke, N. van. 'Notice sur le conseil provincial de Luxembourg, avant sa réorganisation par Charles-Quint, c. 1200–1531.' *PSHIL* xl (1889), 253–382.

Wickersheimer, E. '*De custodia principum*, oeuvre d'un médecin de Charles le Téméraire.' *RN* xxiv (1938), 46–9.

Wielant, P. *Recueil des antiquités de Flandre*. Ed. J. J. de Smet. *Recueil des chroniques de Flandre*, iv. 1–442. CRH. Brussels, 1865.

Wierstrait, C. *Historij des belegs van Nuys*. Ed. K. Meisen. Bonn, 1926.

Willard, C. C. 'The concept of true nobility at the Burgundian court.' *SR* xiv (1967), 33–48.

——. 'Isabel of Portugal, patroness of humanism.' *Miscellanea di studi e ricerche sul quattrocento francese*, 517–44. Turin, 1967.

Wintersulger, L. [*Chronik*]. Ed. P. Ruppert, *Konstanzer Beiträge zur badischen Geschichte*, 96–132. Constance, 1888.

Wirz, H. G. 'Die Entschiedung von Murten.' *RHB* iv (1927), 59–66.

Witte, H. *Zur Geschichte der Entstehung der Burgunderkriege. Herzog Sigmunds von Oestreich Beziehungen zu den Eidgenossen und zu Karl dem Kühnen von Burgund, 1469–1474*. Haguenau, 1885.

——. 'Der Mülhauser Krieg, 1467–1468.' *JSG* xi (1886), 261–332.

——. 'Zur Geschichte der burgundischen Herrschaft am Oberrhein'. *ZGO* (N.F.) i (1886), 129–69.

——. 'Der Zusammenbruch der burgundischen Herrschaft am Oberrhein.' *ZGO* (N.F.) ii (1887), 1–58 and 201–35.

——. 'Zur Geschichte der Burgunderkriege. Die Konstanzer Richtung und das Kriegsjahr 1474.' *ZGO* (N.F.) vi (1891), 1–81 and 361–414.

——. 'Lothringen und Burgund.' *JGLG* ii (1890), 1–100, iii (1891), 232–292 and iv (1892), 74–137.

——. 'Zur Geschichte der Burgunderkriege. Das Kriegsjahr 1475.' *ZGO* (N.F.) vii (1892), 414–77, viii (1893), 197–255 and x (1895), 78–112 and 202–66.

Wyss, R. L. and others. *Bernisches Historisches Museum. Die Burgunderbeute und Werke burgundischer Hofkunst*. Bern, 1969.

Zellweger, J. C. 'Versuch die wahren Gründe des burgundischen Krieges aus den Quellen darzustellen.' *ASG* v (1847), 3–149.

Zesiger, A. 'Der Burgunderkrieg im bernischen Rathaus.' *BBG* xxii (1926), 169–78.

——. 'Murten.' *BBG* xxii (1926), 153–69.

Ziegler, A. 'Adrian von Bubenberg und sein Eingreifen in die wichtigsten Verhältnisse der damaligen Zeit.' *AHKB* xii (1889), 1–130.

Zilverberg, S. *David van Bourgondië, bisschop van Terwaan en van Utrecht.* BIMGU xxiv. Gronigen, 1951.

Zimmermann, K. 'Die Belagerung von Linz durch das Reichsheer im Winter 1474/5.' *RHB* iv (1927), 66–72.

Zumthor, P. and W. Noomen. *Un prêtre montheysan et le sac de Liège en 1468: La complainte de la cité de Liège.* St. Maurice, 1963. Reprinted from *Annales Valaisannes* (1963).

Zuylen van Nyevelt, A. van. *Épisodes de la vie des ducs de Bourgogne à Bruges.* Bruges, 1937.

Index